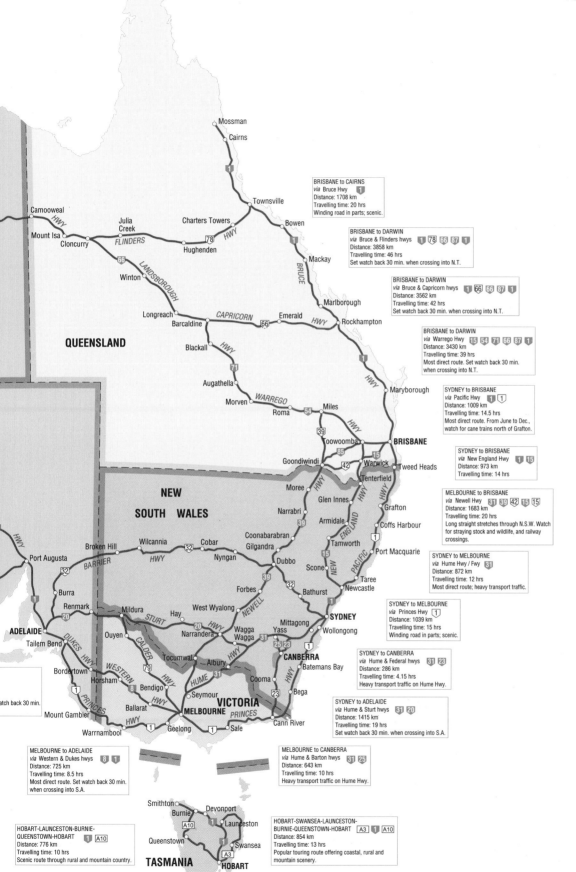

Mossman
Cairns
Townsville
Camooweal
Julia Creek
Charters Towers
Bowen
Mount Isa
Cloncurry
FLINDERS HWY
Hughenden
Mackay
Winton
LANDSBOROUGH
BRUCE
Longreach
Barcaldine
Emerald
Marlborough
QUEENSLAND
CAPRICORN
Rockhampton
Blackall
HWY
Augathella
Maryborough
Morven
WARREGO
Miles
Roma
Toowoomba
Goondiwindi
Warwick
Tweed Heads
BRISBANE
NEW
SOUTH WALES
Moree
Tenterfield
Glen Innes
Grafton
Narrabri
Armidale
Coffs Harbour
Coonabarabran
Tamworth
Port Macquarie
Broken Hill
Wilcannia
Cobar
Gilgandra
Port Augusta
HWY
Nyngan
Dubbo
Taree
BARRIER
Scone
Burra
Forbes
Bathurst
Newcastle
Renmark
West Wyalong
NEWELL
Mildura
Hay
SYDNEY
ADELAIDE
Ouyen
Narrandera
Wagga Wagga
Yass
Wollongong
Tailem Bend
Tocumwal
Albury
CANBERRA
Bordertown
Horsham
Bendigo
Seymour
Cooma
Bega
Mount Gambier
Ballarat
VICTORIA
MELBOURNE
PRINCES
Warrnambool
Geelong
Sale
Cann River

BRISBANE to CAIRNS
via Bruce Hwy 1
Distance: 1708 km
Travelling time: 20 hrs
Winding road in parts; scenic.

BRISBANE to DARWIN
via Bruce & Flinders hwys 1 78 66 87 1
Distance: 3858 km
Travelling time: 46 hrs
Set watch back 30 min. when crossing into N.T.

BRISBANE to DARWIN
via Bruce & Capricorn hwys 1 66 66 87 1
Distance: 3562 km
Travelling time: 42 hrs
Set watch back 30 min. when crossing into N.T.

BRISBANE to DARWIN
via Warrego Hwy 15 54 71 66 87 1
Distance: 3430 km
Travelling time: 39 hrs
Most direct route. Set watch back 30 min.
when crossing into N.T.

SYDNEY to BRISBANE
via Pacific Hwy 1 1
Distance: 1009 km
Travelling time: 14.5 hrs
Most direct route. From June to Dec.,
watch for cane trains north of Grafton.

SYDNEY to BRISBANE
via New England Hwy 1 15
Distance: 973 km
Travelling time: 14 hrs

MELBOURNE to BRISBANE
via Newell Hwy 31 39 42 15 15
Distance: 1683 km
Travelling time: 20 hrs
Long straight stretches through N.S.W. Watch
for straying stock and wildlife, and railway
crossings.

SYDNEY to MELBOURNE
via Hume Hwy / Fwy 31
Distance: 872 km
Travelling time: 12 hrs
Most direct route; heavy transport traffic.

SYDNEY to MELBOURNE
via Princes Hwy 1
Distance: 1039 km
Travelling time: 15 hrs
Winding road in parts; scenic.

SYDNEY to CANBERRA
via Hume & Federal hwys 31 23
Distance: 286 km
Travelling time: 4.15 hrs
Heavy transport traffic on Hume Hwy.

SYDNEY to ADELAIDE
via Hume & Sturt hwys 31 20
Distance: 1415 km
Travelling time: 19 hrs
Set watch back 30 min. when crossing into S.A.

MELBOURNE to CANBERRA
via Hume & Barton hwys 31 25
Distance: 643 km
Travelling time: 10 hrs
Heavy transport traffic on Hume Hwy.

MELBOURNE to ADELAIDE
via Western & Dukes hwys 8 1
Distance: 725 km
Travelling time: 8.5 hrs
Most direct route. Set watch back 30 min.
when crossing into S.A.

Smithton
Burnie
Devonport
Launceston
Queenstown
Swansea
TASMANIA
HOBART

HOBART-LAUNCESTON-BURNIE-
QUEENSTOWN-HOBART 1 A10
Distance: 776 km
Travelling time: 10 hrs
Scenic route through rural and mountain country.

HOBART-SWANSEA-LAUNCESTON-
BURNIE-QUEENSTOWN-HOBART A3 1 A10
Distance: 854 km
Travelling time: 13 hrs
Popular touring route offering coastal, rural and
mountain scenery.

ON THE ROAD?

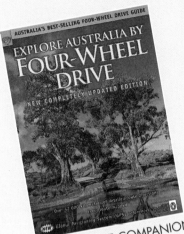

THE COMPLETE COMPANION
TO FOUR-WHEEL DRIVING

CD-ROM WITH
INTERACTIVE MAPPING

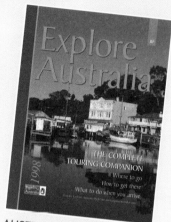

AUSTRALIA'S BEST-SELLING
TRAVEL GUIDE

COMPLETE GUIDES TO TOURING
NEW SOUTH WALES, VICTORIA AND
TASMANIA

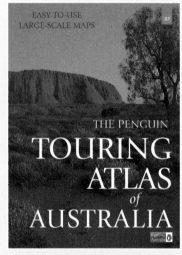

EASY-TO-USE LARGE-SCALE MAPS

THE ESSENTIAL GUIDES TO FISHING
IN QUEENSLAND, NEW SOUTH WALES
AND VICTORIA

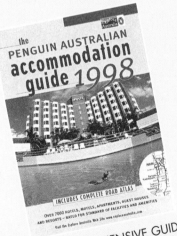

THE COMPREHENSIVE GUIDE
TO ACCOMMODATION IN
AUSTRALIA

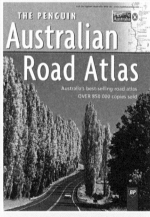

AUSTRALIA'S
MOST COMPREHENSIVE
ROAD ATLAS

SHEET MAPS FOR ALL STATES,
TERRITORIES AND CAPITAL CITIES

Melbourne-Brisbane
via Hume, Newell &
Cunningham Highways 31 39 42 15 15

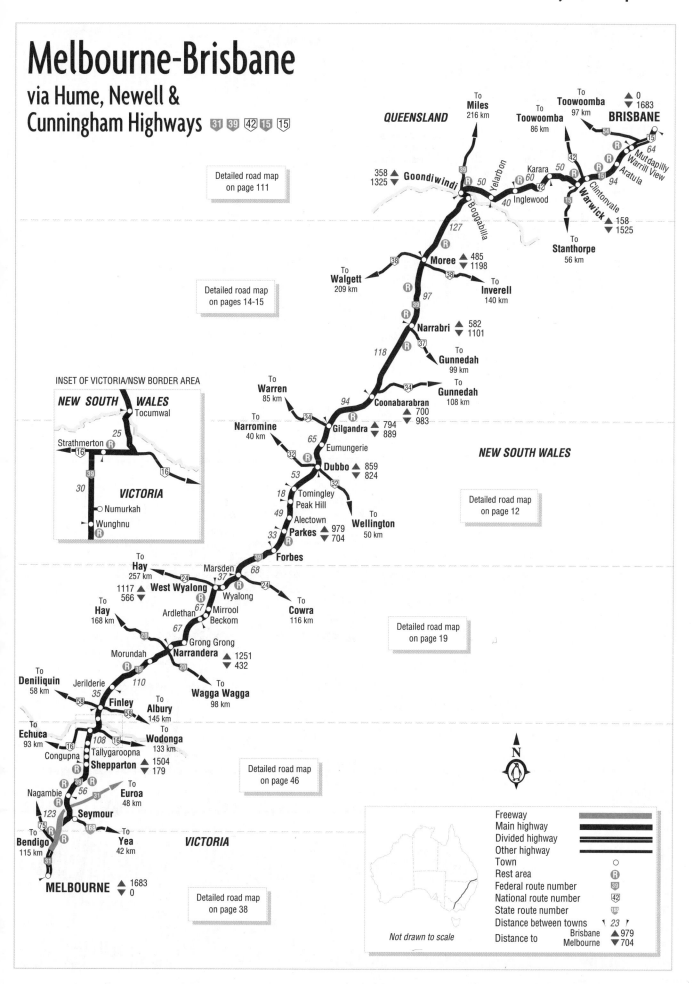

QUEENSLAND

To **Miles** 216 km

To **Toowoomba** 97 km

To **Toowoomba** 86 km

▲ 0
▼ 1683
BRISBANE

358
1325 **Goondiwindi**

Yelarbon 50

Karara 60

Inglewood 40 50 42

54

64
Mutdapilly
Warrill View
Aratula 94

Clintonvale
Warwick 158
1525

Boggabilla 127

To **Stanthorpe** 56 km

Detailed road map on page 111

38 **Moree** 485
1198

To **Walgett** 209 km

To **Inverell** 140 km 38

97

39 **Narrabri** 582
1101

37 To **Gunnedah** 99 km

118

34 To **Gunnedah** 108 km

Detailed road map on pages 14-15

To **Warren** 85 km

94 **Coonabarabran** 700
983

34 **Gilgandra** 794
889

To **Narromine** 40 km 65

Eumungerie

32

NEW SOUTH WALES

Dubbo 859
824

53 32

18 Tomingley
Peak Hill

49 Alectown

33 **Parkes** 979
704

To **Wellington** 50 km

39 **Forbes**

Marsden 68

37 24 To **Cowra** 116 km

Detailed road map on page 12

INSET OF VICTORIA/NSW BORDER AREA

NEW SOUTH WALES
Tocumwal
25
Strathmerton
16
39
30
VICTORIA
Numurkah
Wunghnu

To **Hay** 257 km

24 1117 ▲
566 ▼ **West Wyalong**

Wyalong

Ardlethan 67 Mirrool
Beckom

To **Hay** 168 km

67

20 Grong Grong

Morundah **Narrandera** 1251
432

39 20

Detailed road map on page 19

To **Deniliquin** 58 km

Jerilderie 35 110

58 **Finley**

To **Albury** 145 km
58

To **Wagga Wagga** 98 km

To **Echuca** 93 km

16 108 16

To **Wodonga** 133 km

Congupna Tallygaroopna

Shepparton 1504
179

39 **NEW SOUTH WALES**

Nagambie 56 31

To **Euroa** 48 km

123 **Seymour**

75 168

To **Bendigo** 115 km

To **Yea** 42 km

Detailed road map on page 46

VICTORIA

31 **MELBOURNE** ▲ 1683
▼ 0

Detailed road map on page 38

Legend
Freeway
Main highway
Divided highway
Other highway
Town ○
Rest area (R)
Federal route number 39
National route number 42
State route number 168
Distance between towns ◥ 23 ◤
Distance to | Brisbane ▲ 979
             | Melbourne ▼ 704

Not drawn to scale

N

Adelaide-Darwin
via Stuart Highway 1 87

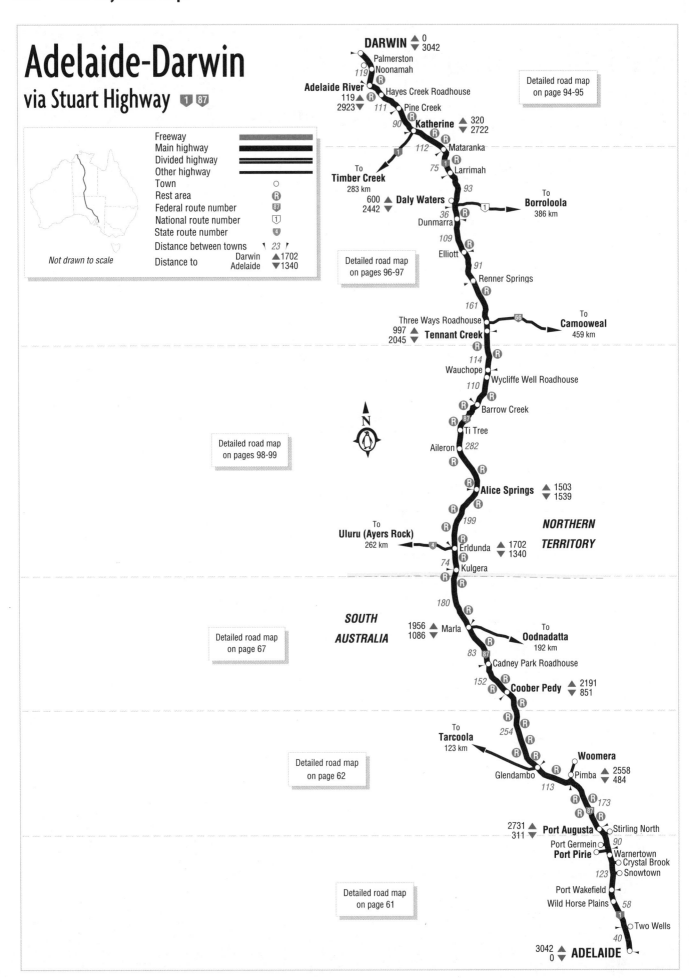

Freeway	
Main highway	
Divided highway	
Other highway	
Town	○
Rest area	R
Federal route number	87
National route number	1
State route number	4
Distance between towns	23
Distance to	Darwin ▲1702
	Adelaide ▼1340

Not drawn to scale

DARWIN ▲ 0 ▼ 3042

Palmerston
119 Noonamah

Adelaide River Hayes Creek Roadhouse
119 ▲
2923 ▼ *111* Pine Creek
90 R
Katherine ▲ 320 ▼ 2722

Detailed road map on page 94-95

112 Mataranka
To **Timber Creek** 283 km
75 Larrimah

93
600 ▲ **Daly Waters** To **Borroloola** 386 km
2442 ▼
36 R
Dunmarra

Detailed road map on pages 96-97

109 R
Elliott
91
Renner Springs

161
Three Ways Roadhouse To **Camooweal** 459 km
997 ▲
2045 ▼ **Tennant Creek**

114 R
Wauchope
110 Wycliffe Well Roadhouse
R
Barrow Creek

Detailed road map on pages 98-99

Ti Tree
Aileron *282*
R
R
Alice Springs ▲ 1503 ▼ 1539
R
199
To **Uluru (Ayers Rock)** 262 km
Erldunda ▲ 1702 ▼ 1340

NORTHERN TERRITORY

74 Kulgera
R

180
R

SOUTH AUSTRALIA

1956 ▲ Marla
1086 ▼

To **Oodnadatta** 192 km

Detailed road map on page 67

83 87
Cadney Park Roadhouse
152 R
Coober Pedy ▲ 2191 ▼ 851
R

R
254 R

To **Tarcoola** 123 km

R
Woomera
Pimba ▲ 2558 ▼ 484
R
Glendambo
113

Detailed road map on page 62

R
173
R 87
2731 ▲ **Port Augusta** Stirling North
311 ▼
Port Germein *90*
Port Pirie Warnertown
Crystal Brook
123 Snowtown

Port Wakefield
Wild Horse Plains *58*

Detailed road map on page 61

1 Two Wells
40
3042 ▲ **ADELAIDE**
0 ▼

THE PENGUIN
Australian
Road Atlas

VIKING

Viking
A division of Penguin Books Australia Ltd
487 Maroondah Highway, PO Box 257
Ringwood, Victoria 3134, Australia
Penguin Books Ltd
Harmondsworth, Middlesex, England
Viking Penguin, a division of Penguin Books USA Inc.
375 Hudson Street, New York, New York 10014, USA
Penguin Books Canada Limited
10 Alcorn Avenue, Toronto, Ontario, Canada M4V 3B2
Penguin Books (N.Z.) Ltd
Cnr Rosedale and Airborne Roads, Albany, Auckland, New Zealand

This seventeenth edition published by Penguin Books Australia Ltd, 1998
First published by George Philip & O'Neil Pty Ltd, 1977
New editions and reprints 1981, 1982, 1983, 1984, 1985, 1986
Sixth edition published by Penguin Books Australia Ltd, 1987
Seventh edition 1988
Eighth edition 1989
Ninth edition 1990
Reprinted 1990
Tenth edition 1991
Eleventh edition 1992
Twelfth edition 1993
Thirteenth edition 1994
Fourteenth edition 1995
Fifteenth edition 1996
Sixteenth edition 1997

Produced by Penguin Cartographic
A division of Penguin Books Australia Ltd
487 Maroondah Highway, Ringwood, Victoria 3134, Australia

Printed and bound in China through Bookbuilders Ltd

ISBN 0 670 87975 4

Publisher's Note: Every effort has been made to ensure that the information in this book is accurate at the time of going to press.
The publisher welcomes information and suggestions for corrections or improvement.
Write to: Managing Editor, Penguin Cartographic, 487 Maroondah Highway, Ringwood, Victoria 3134, Australia.
e-mail: astrid.browne@penguin.com.au

Disclaimer: The publisher cannot accept responsibility for any errors or omissions in this book.
The representation on the maps of any road or track is not necessarily evidence of public right of way.

Photographs
Front cover: New England, New South Wales *Ross Barnett*
Back cover: West MacDonnell Ranges, Northern Territory *Nick Rains/Penguin Books Australia*
Title page: Magnetic Island, Queensland *Gary Lewis/Penguin Books Australia*
Imprint page: Port Douglas, Queensland *Gary Lewis/Penguin Books Australia*
Contents page: Kangaroo Valley, New South Wales *Tourism New South Wales*

Contents

Inside front cover: **Major Highways Route-Planner**

Inside back cover: **Accident Action**

Inter-city Route Maps iv
Sydney–Melbourne via Hume Hwy/Fwy ... v
Sydney–Melbourne via Princes Hwy ... vi
Sydney–Brisbane via Pacific Hwy ... vii
Sydney–Brisbane via New England Hwy ... viii
Melbourne–Adelaide via Western & Dukes Hwys ... ix
Melbourne–Adelaide via Princes Hwy ... x
Melbourne–Brisbane via Hume, Newell
  & Cunningham Hwys ... xi
Adelaide–Darwin via Stuart Hwy ... xii
Perth–Darwin via Brand, North West Coastal,
  Great Northern, Victoria & Stuart Hwys ... xiii
Adelaide–Perth via Eyre & Great Eastern Hwys ... xiv
Adelaide–Sydney via Hume & Sturt Hwys ... xiv
Brisbane–Darwin via Warrego,
  Landsborough, Barkly & Stuart Hwys ... xvi
Brisbane–Cairns via Bruce Hwy ... xvii

Map Symbols xviii

New South Wales
Location Map ... 1
Central Sydney ... 2
Sydney Approach & Bypass Routes ... 3
Sydney & Western Suburbs ... 4
Northern Suburbs, Sydney ... 6
Southern Suburbs, Sydney ... 8
Sydney Region ... 10
Central Eastern New South Wales ... 12
North Eastern New South Wales ... 14
North Western New South Wales ... 16
South Western New South Wales ... 18
South Eastern New South Wales ... 20
Hawkesbury & Central Coast ... 21

Australian Capital Territory
Location Map ... 22
Central Canberra ... 23
Canberra & Northern Suburbs ... 24
Canberra & Southern Suburbs ... 25
Canberra Region ... 26
Australian Capital Territory ... 28

Victoria
Location Map ... 29
Central Melbourne ... 30
Melbourne Approach & Bypass Routes ... 31
Melbourne & Western Suburbs ... 32
Eastern Suburbs, Melbourne ... 34
Southern Suburbs, Melbourne ... 35
Melbourne Region ... 36
Southern Central Victoria ... 38
South Western Victoria ... 40
Central Western Victoria ... 42
North Western Victoria ... 44
North Central Victoria ... 46
North Eastern Victoria ... 48
Yarra Valley Region ... 50

South Australia
Location Map ... 51
Central Adelaide ... 52
Adelaide Approach & Bypass Routes ... 53
Adelaide & Southern Suburbs ... 54
Northern Suburbs, Adelaide ... 56
Adelaide Region, North ... 58
Adelaide Region, South ... 59
South Central South Australia ... 60
Central South Australia ... 62
North Eastern South Australia ... 64
North Western South Australia ... 66
South Western South Australia ... 68
South Eastern South Australia ... 70

Western Australia
Location Map ... 71
Central Perth ... 72
Perth Approach & Bypass Routes ... 73
Perth & Southern Suburbs ... 74
Northern Suburbs, Perth ... 76
Perth & Northern Region ... 78
Southern Region, Perth ... 79
South Western Western Australia ... 80
Central Western Western Australia ... 81
Southern Western Australia ... 82
Central Western Australia ... 84
Northern Western Australia ... 86

Northern Territory
Location Map ... 88
Central Darwin ... 89
Darwin & Northern Suburbs ... 90
North Eastern Suburbs, Darwin ... 91
Darwin Region ... 92
Northern Northern Territory ... 94
Central Northern Territory ... 96
Southern Northern Territory ... 98

Queensland
Location Map ... 100
Central Brisbane ... 101
Brisbane Approach & Bypass Routes ... 102
Gold Coast Approach & Bypass Routes ... 103
Brisbane & Northern Suburbs ... 104
Southern Suburbs, Brisbane ... 106
Brisbane Region ... 108
South Eastern Queensland ... 110
North Eastern Queensland ... 112
Far North Eastern Queensland ... 114
Cape York Peninsula ... 116
Far North Western Queensland ... 117
North Western Queensland ... 118
South Western Queensland ... 120

Tasmania
Location Map ... 122
Central Hobart ... 123
Hobart & Suburbs ... 124
Hobart Region ... 126
Southern Tasmania ... 128
Northern Tasmania ... 130

Index of Place Names 132

Inter-city Route Maps

The following inter-city route maps will help you plan your route between major cities. As well, you can use the maps during your journey, since they provide information on distances between towns along the route, roadside rest areas and road conditions. The map below provides an overview of the routes mapped.

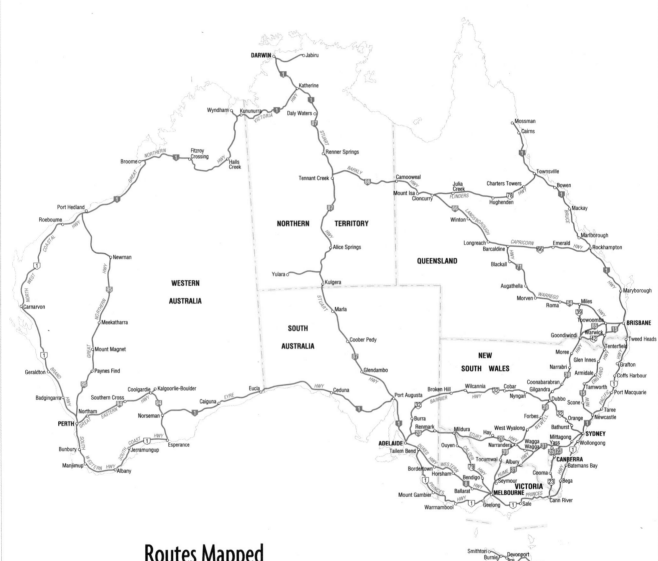

Routes Mapped

Sydney - Melbourne via Highway/Freeway 31 v
Sydney - Melbourne via Highway 1 vi
Sydney - Brisbane via Highways 1 1 vii
Sydney - Brisbane via Highways 1 15 viii
Melbourne - Adelaide via Highways 8 1 ix
Melbourne - Adelaide via Highway 1 1 x
Melbourne - Brisbane via Highways 31 39 42 15 15 xi
Adelaide - Darwin via Highways 1 87 xii
Perth - Darwin via Highway 1 1 xiii
Adelaide - Perth via Highways 1 94 xiv-xv
Adelaide - Sydney via Highways 20 31 xiv-xv
Brisbane - Darwin via Highways 15 54 71 66 87 1 xvi
Brisbane - Cairns via Highway 1 xvii

Sydney-Melbourne
via Hume Highway/Freeway 31

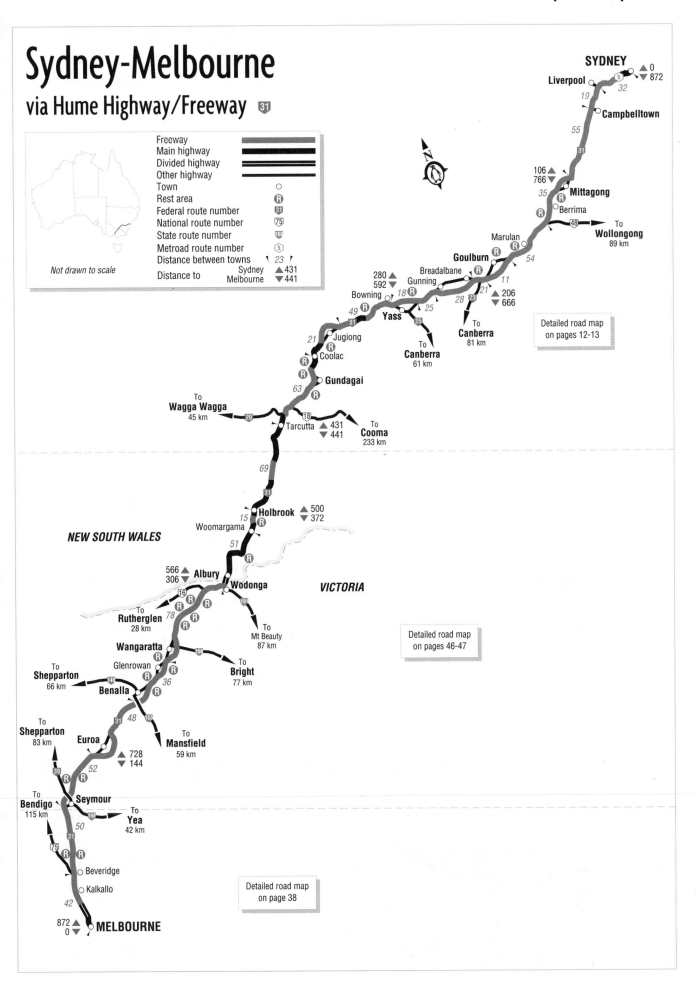

Freeway
Main highway
Divided highway
Other highway
Town
Rest area
Federal route number 31
National route number 75
State route number 160
Metroad route number 5
Distance between towns 23
Distance to Sydney ▲431
Melbourne ▼441

Not drawn to scale

SYDNEY ▲0 ▼872
Liverpool 5 32
19
Campbelltown
55
31
106 ▲ 766 ▼
35 Mittagong
Berrima
To Wollongong 89 km 48
Marulan
54
Goulburn
280 ▲ 592 ▼ Breadalbane
Gunning 11
Bowning 18 21 206 ▲ 666 ▼
49 28 23
Yass
To Canberra 81 km
21 Jugiong
To Canberra 61 km
Coolac
63 Gundagai
To Wagga Wagga 45 km 20
Tarcutta 18 ▲431 ▼441
To Cooma 233 km
69
31
Holbrook ▲500 ▼372
15
Woomargama
NEW SOUTH WALES 51
566 ▲ 306 ▼ Albury
Wodonga VICTORIA
16
To Rutherglen 28 km 78 191
To Mt Beauty 87 km
Wangaratta 156
Glenrowan To Bright 77 km
To Shepparton 66 km 49
36
Benalla
31 48 153
To Shepparton 83 km Euroa To Mansfield 59 km
39 ▲728 ▼144
52
To Bendigo 115 km Seymour
50 160 To Yea 42 km
31
75
Beveridge
Kalkallo
42
872 ▲ 0 ▼ MELBOURNE

Detailed road map on pages 12-13

Detailed road map on pages 46-47

Detailed road map on page 38

Sydney-Melbourne
via Princes Highway ①

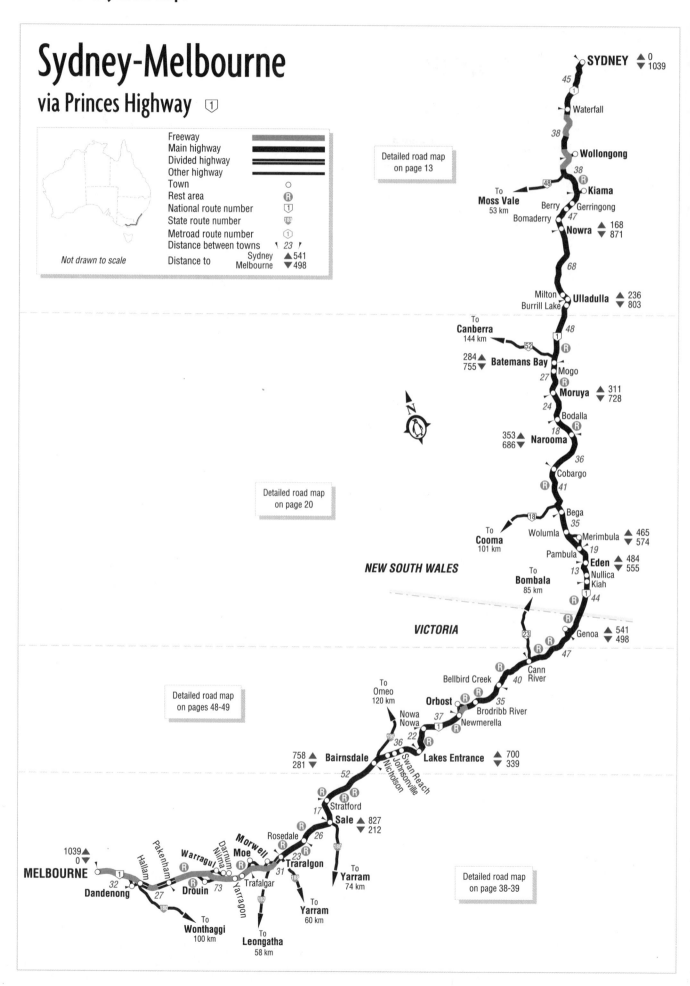

Legend:
- Freeway
- Main highway
- Divided highway
- Other highway
- Town ○
- Rest area Ⓡ
- National route number ①
- State route number 180
- Metroad route number ①
- Distance between towns ↘ 23 ↗
- Distance to Sydney ▲541 Melbourne ▼498

Not drawn to scale

SYDNEY ▲0 ▼1039

45

Waterfall

38

Detailed road map on page 13

Wollongong

38

48 Kiama
Moss Vale Berry Gerringong
To Moss Vale 53 km Bomaderry 47
Nowra ▲168 ▼871

68

Milton Ulladulla ▲236 ▼803
Burrill Lake

To Canberra 144 km 48
52 Ⓡ
284▲ 755▼ Batemans Bay
27 Mogo Ⓡ
Moruya ▲311 ▼728
24 Bodalla Ⓡ
353▲ 686▼ Narooma 18
36

Detailed road map on page 20

Cobargo
Ⓡ 41
18 Bega
To Cooma 101 km Wolumla 35 Merimbula ▲465 ▼574
Pambula 19
NEW SOUTH WALES Eden ▲484 ▼555
To Bombala 85 km 13 Nullica Kiah
Ⓡ ① 44
VICTORIA Ⓡ
23 Ⓡ Genoa ▲541 ▼498
47
Ⓡ Cann River
Bellbird Creek 40
To Omeo 120 km Ⓡ Ⓡ Orbost 35 Brodribb River
Nowa Nowa 37 Newmerella
Detailed road map on pages 48-49 198 22 ① Ⓡ
36 Swan Reach Lakes Entrance ▲700 ▼339
758▲ 281▼ Bairnsdale Johnsonville
52 Nicholson
Ⓡ Ⓡ Ⓡ
17 Stratford
Ⓡ Sale ▲827 ▼212
Rosedale 26
1039▲ 0▼ Pakenham Warragul Moe Morwell 180
MELBOURNE Hallam Nilma 23 Traralgon To Yarram 74 km
① Drouin 31 180
Dandenong 27 Trafalgar 182
180 Yarragon To Yarram 60 km
To Wonthaggi 100 km To Leongatha 58 km Detailed road map on pages 38-39

Sydney-Brisbane
via Pacific Highway 1 1

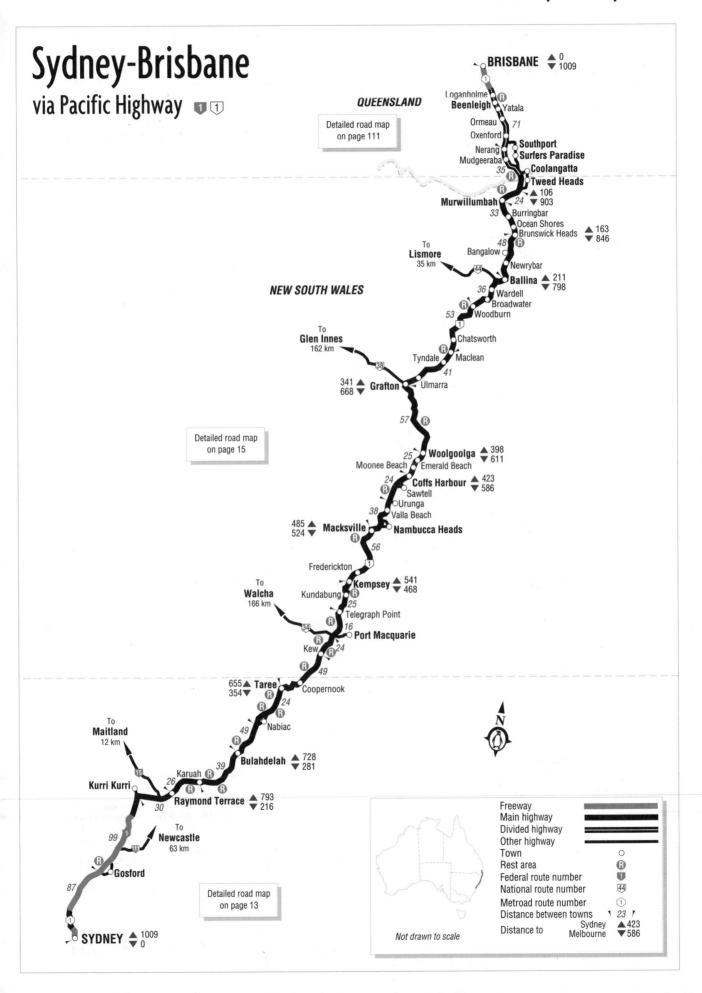

BRISBANE ▲ 0 ▼ 1009

QUEENSLAND

Detailed road map
on page 111

Loganholme
Beenleigh   Yatala
Ormeau   71
Oxenford
Southport
Nerang   Surfers Paradise
Mudgeeraba   Coolangatta
35   Tweed Heads
▲ 106 ▼ 903
24
Murwillumbah   ⓡ
33   Burringbar
Ocean Shores
Brunswick Heads   ▲ 163 ▼ 846
48   ⓡ
To   Bangalow
Lismore   Newrybar
35 km   44   Ballina   ▲ 211 ▼ 798
36   Wardell
NEW SOUTH WALES   Broadwater
53   Woodburn
1   Chatsworth
To   ⓡ
Glen Innes   Maclean
162 km   38   Tyndale
341 ▲   41   Ulmarra
668 ▼   Grafton
57   ⓡ

Detailed road map
on page 15

25   Woolgoolga   ▲ 398 ▼ 611
Moonee Beach   Emerald Beach
24   Coffs Harbour   ▲ 423 ▼ 586
Sawtell
Urunga
38   Valla Beach
485 ▲   Macksville   Nambucca Heads
524 ▼   ⓡ
56
1
Frederickton
Kempsey   ▲ 541 ▼ 468
To   ⓡ
Walcha   Kundabung
166 km   25   Telegraph Point
34   16
ⓡ   Port Macquarie
Kew   ⓡ 24
ⓡ   49
655 ▲   Taree
354 ▼   ⓡ   Coopernook
ⓡ   24
To   49   Nabiac
Maitland   ⓡ
12 km
▲ 728
Karuah   39   Bulahdelah   ▼ 281
15   26
Kurri Kurri   ⓡ   ⓡ
30   Raymond Terrace   ▲ 793 ▼ 216
To
1   Newcastle
99   63 km
11
ⓡ
Gosford
87
N
1
SYDNEY ▲ 1009 ▼ 0

Not drawn to scale

Legend	
Freeway	
Main highway	
Divided highway	
Other highway	
Town	○
Rest area	ⓡ
Federal route number	1
National route number	44
Metroad route number	1
Distance between towns	23
Distance to	Sydney ▲ 423 Melbourne ▼ 586

Detailed road map
on page 13

Sydney-Brisbane
via New England Highway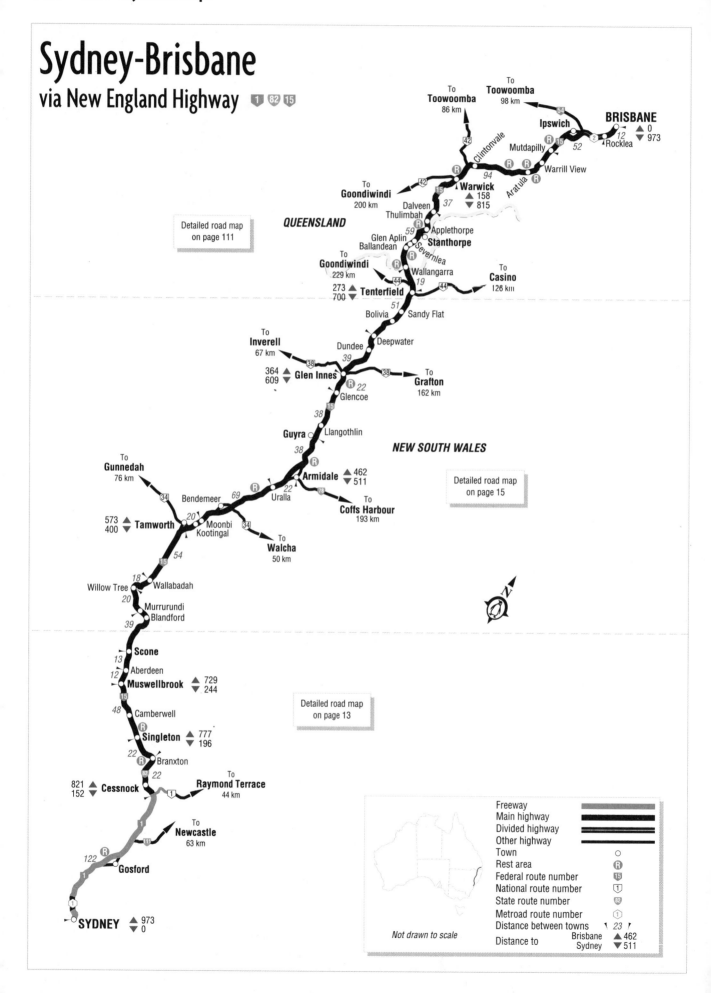

To Toowoomba 86 km

To Toowoomba 98 km

BRISBANE
▲ 0
▼ 973

Ipswich

Rocklea 12

52

2

15

94

Clintonvale

Mutdapilly

Warrill View

Aratula

42

42

15

Warwick ▲ 158 ▼ 815

Dalveen

Thulimbah

37

To Goondiwindi 200 km

QUEENSLAND

Detailed road map on page 111

59

Applethorpe

Glen Aplin

Stanthorpe

Ballandean

Severnlea

Wallangarra

To Goondiwindi 229 km

44

19

273
700 ▲▼ **Tenterfield**

To Casino 126 km

44

Bolivia

51

Sandy Flat

To Inverell 67 km

Dundee

39

Deepwater

38

364
609 ▲▼ **Glen Innes**

38

To Grafton 162 km

22

Glencoe

38

15

Guyra Llangothlin

38

NEW SOUTH WALES

Detailed road map on page 15

462
511 ▲▼ **Armidale**

22

Uralla

76

To Coffs Harbour 193 km

To Gunnedah 76 km

34

Bendemeer

69

573
400 ▲▼ **Tamworth**

20

Moonbi
Kootingal

34

To Walcha 50 km

15

54

18

Willow Tree

Wallabadah

20

Murrurundi
Blandford

39

Scone

13

Aberdeen

12

Muswellbrook ▲ 729 ▼ 244

15

48

Camberwell

Detailed road map on page 13

777
196 ▲▼ **Singleton**

22

Branxton

82

22

To Raymond Terrace 44 km

821
152 ▲▼ **Cessnock**

1

1

To Newcastle 63 km

11

122

Gosford

1

SYDNEY ▲ 973 ▼ 0

	Legend
Freeway	
Main highway	
Divided highway	
Other highway	
Town	○
Rest area	Ⓡ
Federal route number	15
National route number	1
State route number	82
Metroad route number	1
Distance between towns	23
Distance to	Brisbane ▲ 462
	Sydney ▼ 511

Not drawn to scale

Melbourne-Adelaide
via Western & Dukes Highways 🛡8 🛡1

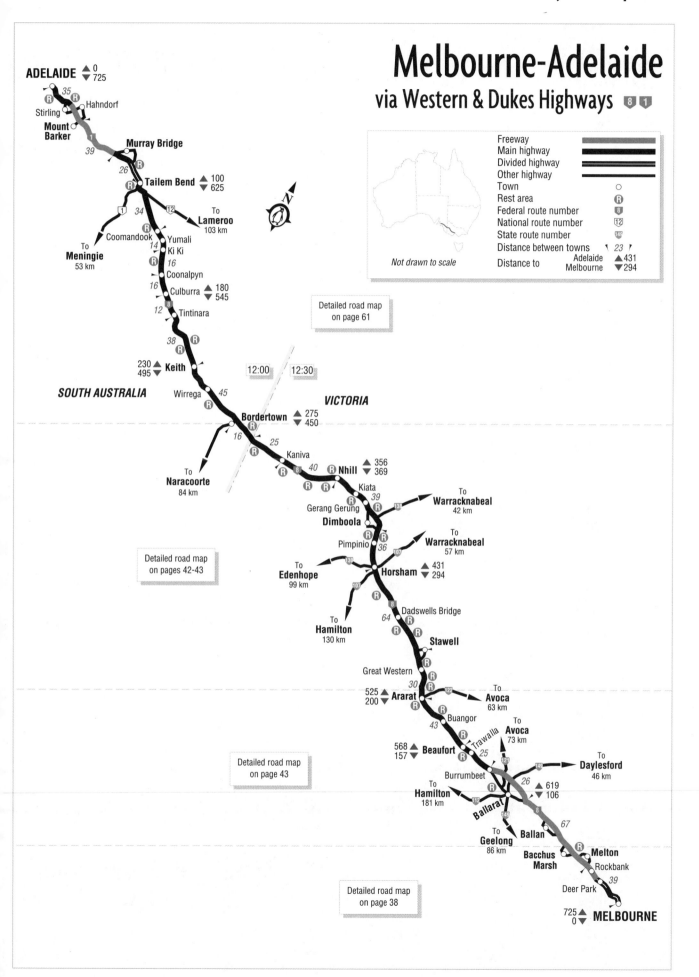

ADELAIDE ▲ 0 ▼ 725

Stirling
Hahndorf
35
Mount Barker
39
Murray Bridge
26
Tailem Bend ▲ 100 ▼ 625
34
To Lameroo 103 km
Coomandook
Yumali
Ki Ki *14*
To Meningie 53 km
Coonalpyn *16*
Culburra ▲ 180 ▼ 545 *16*
Tintinara *12*
Keith ▲ 230 ▼ 495 *38*

SOUTH AUSTRALIA

Wirrega *45*

12:00 | 12:30

VICTORIA

Bordertown ▲ 275 ▼ 450
16
25
Kaniva *40*
To Naracoorte 84 km
Nhill ▲ 356 ▼ 369
Kiata *39*
Gerang Gerung
Dimboola
To Warracknabeal 42 km
Pimpinio *36*
To Warracknabeal 57 km
Edenhope 99 km
To Hamilton 130 km
Horsham ▲ 431 ▼ 294
Dadswells Bridge
64
Stawell
Great Western
30
Ararat ▲ 525 ▼ 200
To Avoca 63 km
Buangor
43
Trawalla *25*
To Avoca 73 km
Beaufort ▲ 568 ▼ 157
To Daylesford 46 km
Burrumbeet
26 ▲ 619 ▼ 106
To Hamilton 181 km
Ballarat
To Geelong 86 km
Ballan
67
Bacchus Marsh
Melton
Rockbank
39
Deer Park
▲ 725 ▼ 0 MELBOURNE

Legend

Freeway	
Main highway	
Divided highway	
Other highway	
Town	○
Rest area	R
Federal route number	8
National route number	12
State route number	149
Distance between towns	23
Distance to	Adelaide ▲ 431
	Melbourne ▼ 294

Not drawn to scale

Detailed road map on page 61

Detailed road map on pages 42-43

Detailed road map on page 43

Detailed road map on page 38

Melbourne-Adelaide
via Princes Highway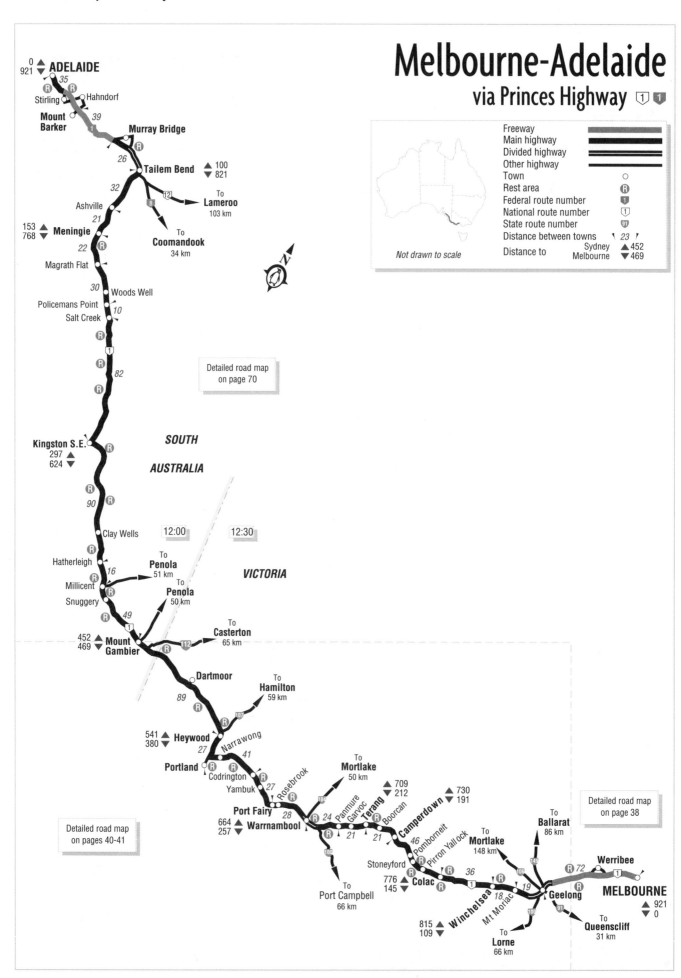

Legend:
- Freeway
- Main highway
- Divided highway
- Other highway
- Town ○
- Rest area ®
- Federal route number
- National route number
- State route number
- Distance between towns 23
- Distance to Sydney ▲ 452 Melbourne ▼ 469

Not drawn to scale

0 ▲
921 ▼ **ADELAIDE**
35

® Stirling ○ Hahndorf ®
Mount Barker
39
Murray Bridge
1 ®
26
Tailem Bend ▲ 100 ▼ 821
32
12
8
To Lameroo 103 km
Ashville ○
21
To Coomandook 34 km
153 ▲
768 ▼ **Meningie** ®
22
Magrath Flat ®
30
Woods Well ○
Policemans Point
Salt Creek ○ 10
®
1 ®
82
®

SOUTH
AUSTRALIA

Kingston S.E. ○ ®
297 ▲
624 ▼
® ®
90
Clay Wells ○
® 12:00 12:30
Hatherleigh ○
Penola 51 km **To Penola**
16
Millicent ○ ®
Snuggery ® **To Penola** 50 km

VICTORIA

® 49
452 ▲ 1
469 ▼ **Mount Gambier** ®
112 **To Casterton** 65 km

Dartmoor ○
To Hamilton 59 km
89
®
® 107
541 ▲ **Heywood** ○
380 ▼
27 Narrawong
41
Portland ® Codrington ○
Yambuk ○ 27 Rosebrook ®
104
Port Fairy 28
664 ▲ 24 Panmure
257 ▼ **Warrnambool** ® Garvoc ○ **Terang**
21 Boorcan ○
100 21 **Camperdown**
46 Pomborneit
Pirron Yallock
Stoneyford ○
776 ▲ ® 36 **Mortlake** 148 km
145 ▼ **Colac** ® 1
To Port Campbell 66 km 18 **Winchelsea** 19
815 ▲ Mt Moriac
109 ▼
100
Lorne 66 km
To Mortlake 50 km
709 ▲
212 ▼
730 ▲
191 ▼
To Ballarat 86 km
149
106
® 72
Werribee ○
® 1
® **Geelong**
MELBOURNE ▲ 921 ▼ 0
To Queenscliff 31 km

Detailed road map on page 70

Detailed road map on page 38

Detailed road map on pages 40-41

Perth-Darwin
via Brand, North West Coastal, Great Northern, Victoria & Stuart Highways ① ①

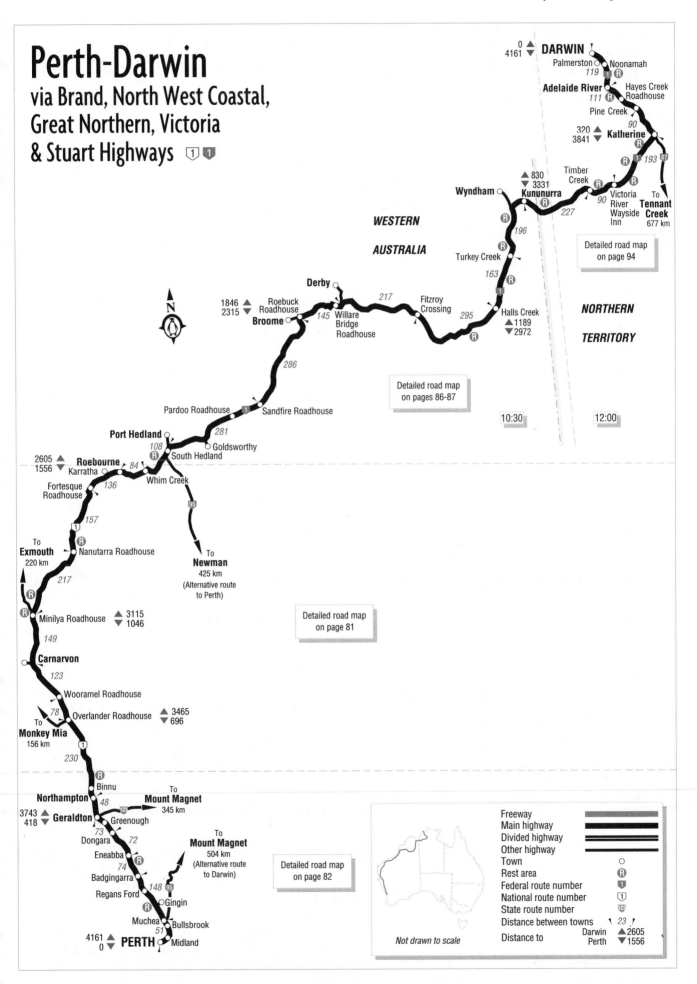

DARWIN
0
4161
Palmerston Noonamah
119
Adelaide River Hayes Creek Roadhouse
111
Pine Creek
90
320 Katherine
3841
193 87
Wyndham Kununurra
830
3331
Timber Creek
227
Victoria River Wayside Inn
196
To Tennant Creek
677 km
Turkey Creek
90
163
Halls Creek
1189
2972
Fitzroy Crossing
295

WESTERN AUSTRALIA

NORTHERN TERRITORY

Derby
1846 Roebuck Roadhouse
2315
217
Broome 145 Willare Bridge Roadhouse

Detailed road map on page 94

Detailed road map on pages 86-87

10:30   12:00

286

Pardoo Roadhouse Sandfire Roadhouse
281
Port Hedland Goldsworthy
108 South Hedland
2605 Roebourne 84
1556 Karratha
Whim Creek
Fortesque Roadhouse 136
157
To Exmouth Nanutarra Roadhouse
220 km
217
Minilya Roadhouse 3115
1046
149
Carnarvon
123
Wooramel Roadhouse
78 Overlander Roadhouse 3465
To 696
Monkey Mia
156 km
230
Binnu
Northampton 48 To Mount Magnet
3743 Geraldton 345 km
418 Greenough
73
Dongara 72
Eneabba
74
Badgingarra
148
Regans Ford Gingin
Muchea Bullsbrook
51
4161 PERTH Midland
0

To Newman
425 km
(Alternative route to Perth)

Detailed road map on page 81

To Mount Magnet
504 km
(Alternative route to Darwin)

Detailed road map on page 82

Freeway	
Main highway	
Divided highway	
Other highway	
Town	○
Rest area	Ⓡ
Federal route number	①
National route number	①
State route number	⑫③
Distance between towns	23
Distance to	Darwin ▲2605
Perth ▼1556	

Not drawn to scale

Adelaide-Perth
via Eyre & Great Eastern Highways 1 94

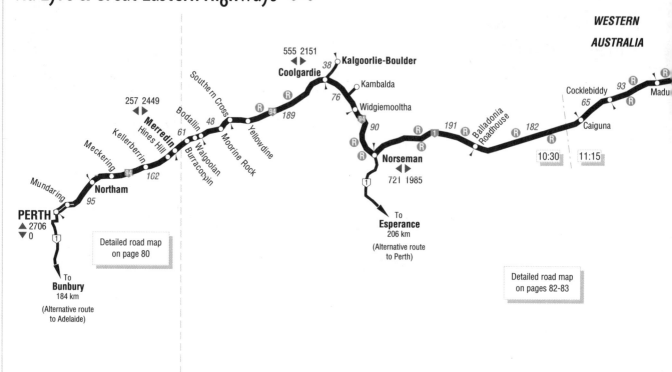

WESTERN AUSTRALIA

555 2151 ◀▶
Coolgardie
Kalgoorlie-Boulder
38

Kambalda

257 2449 ◀▶
Merredin

Southern Cross
Bodallin
48
Yellowdine
94 189

Widgiemooltha

76

Cocklebiddy
65
93 R R
Madu

Hines Hill
61
Walgoolan
Burracoppin
Moorine Rock

94
90

191
Balladonia
Roadhouse
182
Caiguna

Kellerberrin
Meckering
94
162

R
R
1
R

10:30   11:15

Mundaring
95
Northam

R
Norseman
721 1985 ◀▶

1

PERTH
▲ 2706
▼ 0

1

Detailed road map
on page 80

To
Esperance
206 km

(Alternative route
to Perth)

Detailed road map
on pages 82-83

To
Bunbury
184 km

(Alternative route
to Adelaide)

Adelaide-Sydney
via Hume & Sturt Highways 20 31

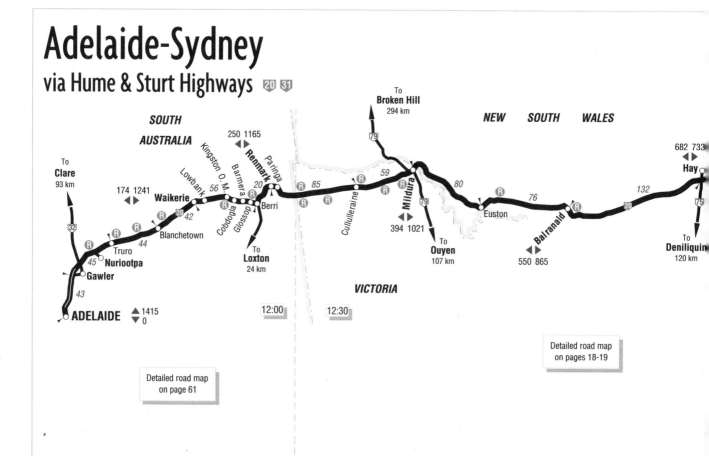

To
Broken Hill
294 km

NEW   SOUTH   WALES

SOUTH
AUSTRALIA

250 1165 ◀▶
Renmark

Paringa

682 733 ◀▶
Hay

To
Clare
93 km

174 1241 ◀▶
Waikerie

Kingston O. M.
Barmera
Lowbank
56
20

Cullulleraine
59
Mildura
80
132

79

42
Cobdogla
Glossop
Berri

R
85
R

R
76
20
75

32
R
R
R
Truro
44
Blanchetown

20
R
R

R
394 1021 ◀▶

R
Euston
79

Balranald
R

To
Deniliquin
120 km

45
Nuriootpa

To
Loxton
24 km

To
Ouyen
107 km

550 865 ◀▶

Gawler

ADELAIDE
▲ 1415
▼ 0

43

VICTORIA

12:00   12:30

Detailed road map
on page 61

Detailed road map
on pages 18-19

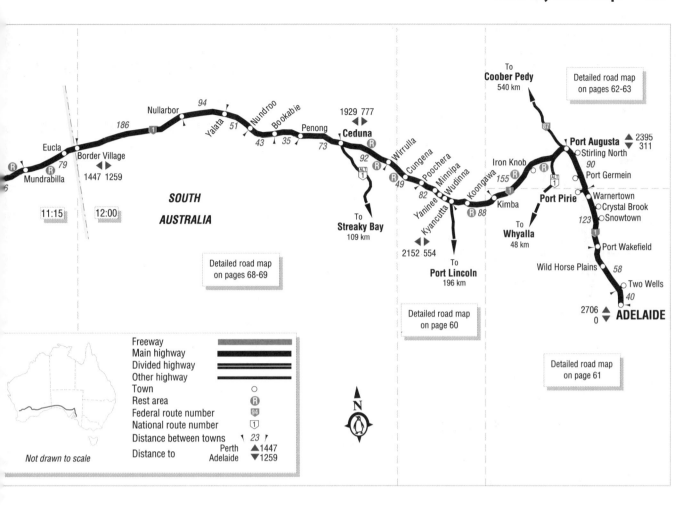

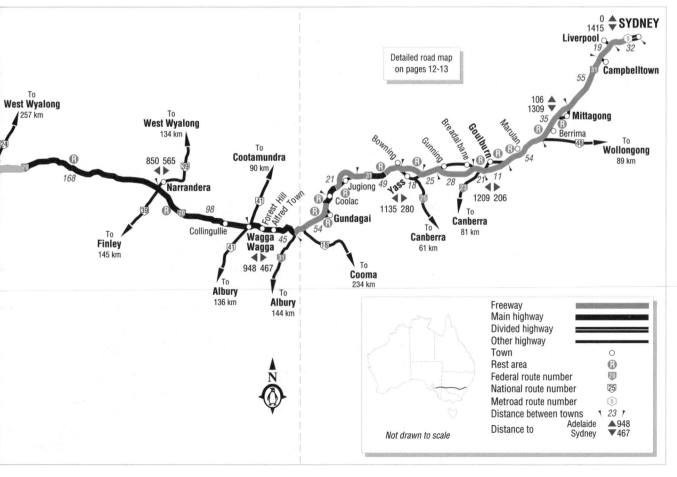

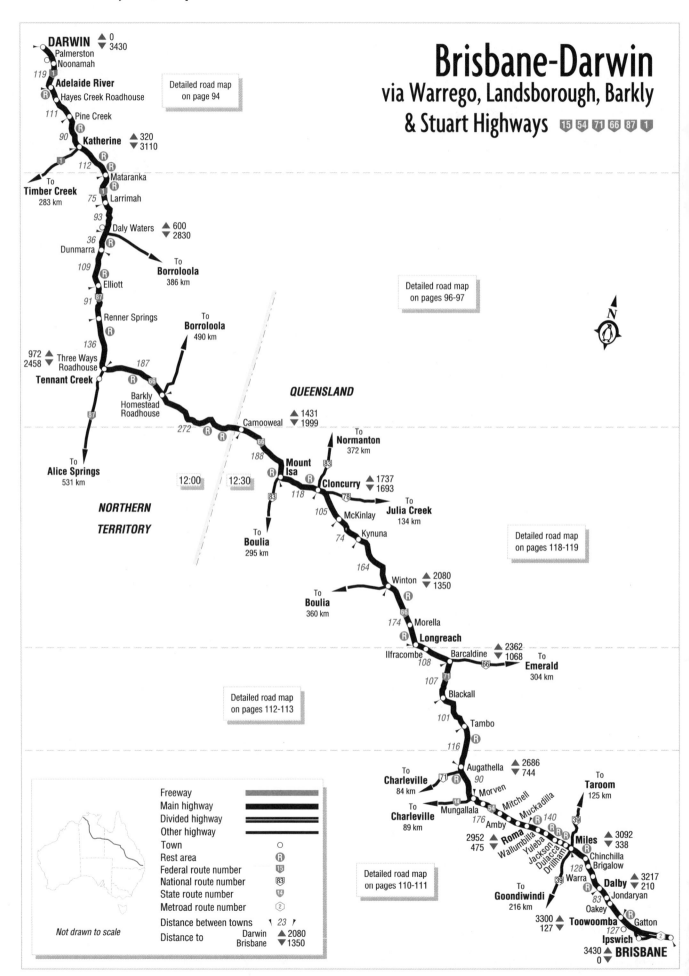

Brisbane-Darwin
via Warrego, Landsborough, Barkly & Stuart Highways 15 54 71 66 87 1

DARWIN ▲ 0 ▼ 3430
Palmerston
Noonamah
119
Adelaide River
Ⓡ Hayes Creek Roadhouse
111
Ⓡ Pine Creek
90
Katherine ▲ 320 ▼ 3110
112
Ⓡ Mataranka
To **Timber Creek** 283 km
75 Larrimah
93
Daly Waters ▲ 600 ▼ 2830
36 Ⓡ
Dunmarra
109 Ⓡ
Elliott
91 87
Ⓡ Renner Springs
136
972 ▲ 2458 ▼ Three Ways Roadhouse
Tennant Creek *187*
Ⓡ 66
Barkly Homestead Roadhouse
87
To **Alice Springs** 531 km

To **Borroloola** 386 km

To **Borroloola** 490 km

NORTHERN TERRITORY

Detailed road map on page 94

Detailed road map on pages 96-97

QUEENSLAND

272 Ⓡ Ⓡ Camooweal ▲ 1431 ▼ 1999
66
188

12:00 12:30

83
To **Boulia** 295 km

Ⓡ **Mount Isa**
Ⓡ **Cloncurry** ▲ 1737 ▼ 1693
118 78
105 McKinlay
74 Kynuna
164

To **Normanton** 372 km
83

To **Julia Creek** 134 km

Winton ▲ 2080 ▼ 1350
Ⓡ
174 66 Morella
Ⓡ **Longreach**
Ilfracombe *108* Barcaldine ▲ 2362 ▼ 1068
107 71 66
Blackall
101
Ⓡ Tambo
116

To **Boulia** 360 km

To **Emerald** 304 km

Detailed road map on pages 112-113

Detailed road map on pages 118-119

Augathella ▲ 2686 ▼ 744
Charleville 84 km 71 Ⓡ *90*
Morven
14
Charleville 89 km Mungallala *176* Mitchell Muckadilla
Amby *140*
2952 ▲ 475 ▼ **Roma** Wallumbilla Yuleba Jackson Ⓡ Ⓡ Ⓡ **Miles** ▲ 3092 ▼ 338
Dulacca Drillham
128 Chinchilla Brigalow
39 Warra Ⓡ **Dalby** ▲ 3217 ▼ 210
Jondaryan
83 Oakey
3300 ▲ 127 ▼ **Toowoomba** *127* Ⓡ Gatton
Ⓡ **Ipswich** 2
3430 ▲ 0 ▼ **BRISBANE**

To **Taroom** 125 km
39

To **Goondiwindi** 216 km

Detailed road map on pages 110-111

N

Legend:
Freeway
Main highway
Divided highway
Other highway
Town ○
Rest area Ⓡ
Federal route number 15
National route number 83
State route number 14
Metroad route number ②
Distance between towns ◣ *23* ◢
Distance to Darwin ▲ 2080 / Brisbane ▼ 1350

Not drawn to scale

Brisbane-Cairns
via Bruce Highway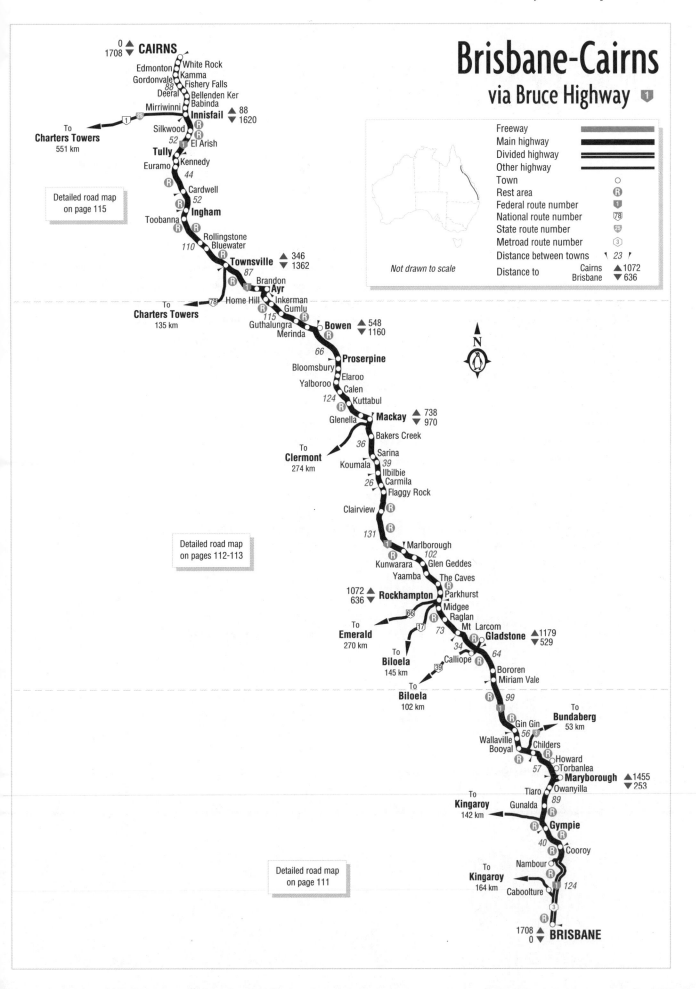

Freeway	
Main highway	
Divided highway	
Other highway	
Town	○
Rest area	Ⓡ
Federal route number	🛡1
National route number	78
State route number	25
Metroad route number	③
Distance between towns	23
Distance to	Cairns ▲1072
	Brisbane ▼636

Not drawn to scale

CAIRNS 0 / 1708

Edmonton
White Rock
Kamma
Gordonvale
Fishery Falls
88
Deeral
Bellenden Ker
Babinda
Mirriwinni
Innisfail ▲88 ▼1620
Silkwood
52
El Arish
Tully
Euramo
Kennedy
44
Cardwell
52
Ingham
Toobanna
Rollingstone
110
Bluewater
Townsville ▲346 ▼1362
87
Brandon
Ayr
Home Hill
Inkerman
Gumlu
115
Guthalungra
Bowen ▲548 ▼1160
Merinda
66
Proserpine
Bloomsbury
Elaroo
Yalboroo
Calen
124
Kuttabul
Glenella
Mackay ▲738 ▼970
Bakers Creek
36
Sarina
39
Koumala
Ilbilbie
26
Carmila
Flaggy Rock
Clairview
131
Marlborough
102
Kunwarara
Glen Geddes
Yaamba
The Caves
1072 ▲ / 636 ▼ **Rockhampton**
Parkhurst
66
Midgee
17
Raglan
73
Mt Larcom
Calliope
Gladstone ▲1179 ▼529
34
64
39
Bororen
Miriam Vale
99
Bundaberg
Gin Gin
56
Wallaville
Childers
Booyal
Howard
57
Torbanlea
Maryborough ▲1455 ▼253
Tiaro
Owanyilla
Gunalda
89
Gympie
40
Cooroy
Nambour
1
Caboolture
124
③
BRISBANE 1708 ▲ / 0 ▼

To **Charters Towers** 551 km

Detailed road map on page 115

To **Charters Towers** 135 km

Detailed road map on pages 112-113

To **Clermont** 274 km

To **Emerald** 270 km

To **Biloela** 145 km

To **Biloela** 102 km

To **Bundaberg** 53 km

To **Kingaroy** 142 km

To **Kingaroy** 164 km

Detailed road map on page 111

N

Map Symbols

Freeway with Federal Route Number		State capital city	**DARWIN**
Freeway under construction		Town, over 50 000 inhabitants	**GEELONG**
Highway, sealed, with National Route Number		Town, 10 000-50 000 inhabitants	**Bairnsdale** ○
Highway, sealed, with Metroad Route Number		Town, 5 000-10 000 inhabitants	**Hamilton** ○
Highway, unsealed, with Tasmania Route Number		Town, 1 000-5 000 inhabitants	Maffra ○
Highway under construction		Town, 200-1 000 inhabitants	Omeo ○
Main road, sealed, with State Route Number		Town, under 200 inhabitants	Eskdale ○
Main road, unsealed		Locality	Bungalla
Main road under construction		Suburb on state and region maps	GLENORCHY
Secondary road, with Tourist Route		Suburb on suburban maps	**Glenorchy**
Secondary road unsealed		Pastoral station homestead	Alroy Downs ▫
Other road, with traffic direction arrow		Closed Aboriginal town	Murgenella ○
Other road, unsealed		Roadhouse	Fortesque Ⓗ
Mall		Commercial airport	✈
Vehicle track		Place of interest	● ■
Walking track		Landmark feature	●
Railway with station	Paratoo	General interest feature	■
Underground railway with station	Flagstaff	Accommodation	▪
Total kilometres between two points	114	Hill, mountain	+
Intermediate kilometres	77	Minesite	⚒
State border		Lighthouse	★
River, waterfall		Route destination	*TO GOULBURN*
Lake		Adjoining page number	45
Intermittent lake		National park	
Aboriginal / Torres Strait Islander land		Other reserve	
Prohibited area		Other named areas	

New South Wales

Location Map

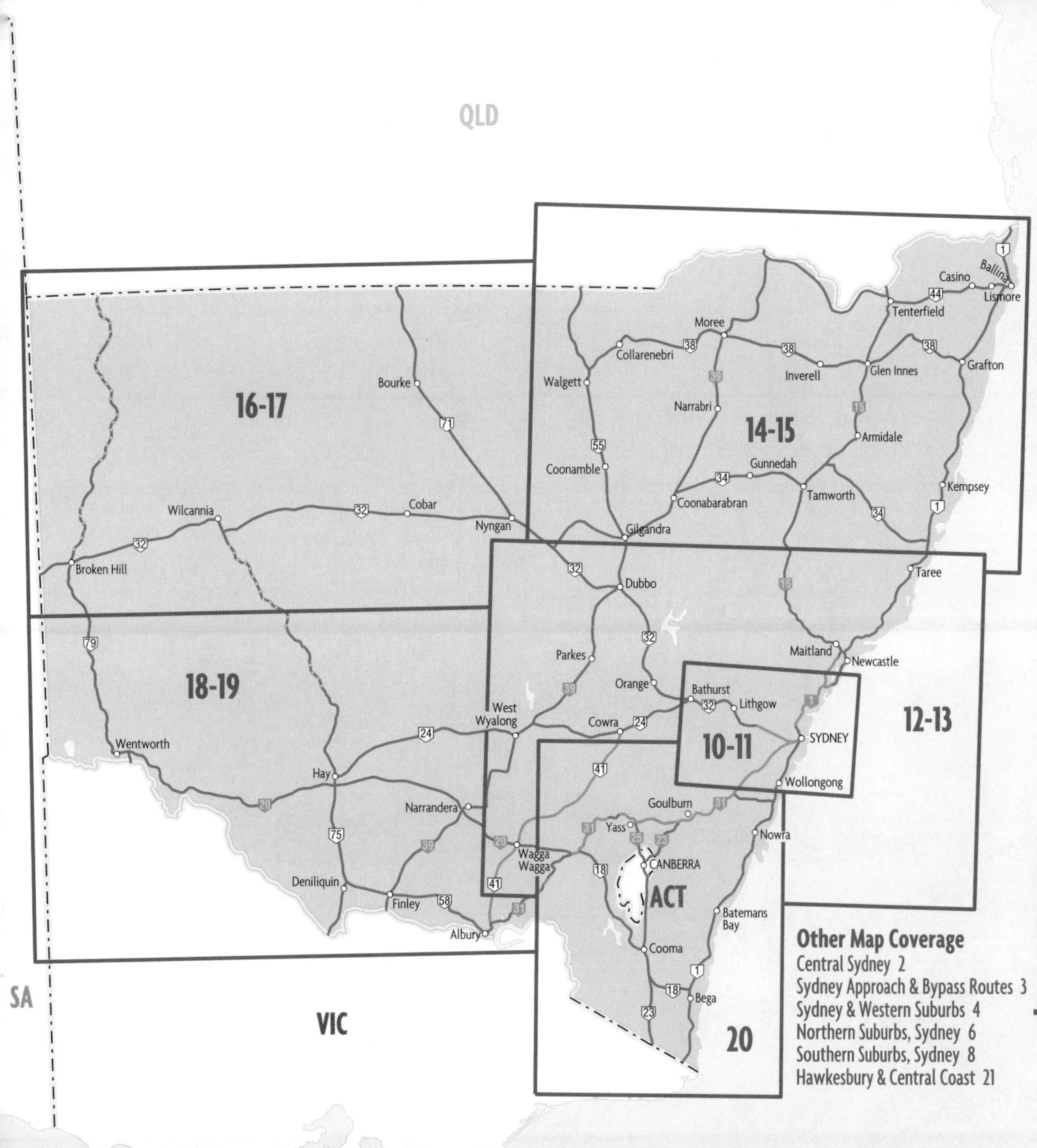

QLD

SA

VIC

16-17

14-15

18-19

12-13

10-11

20

ACT

Ballina
Casino
Lismore
Tenterfield
Moree
Glen Innes
Grafton
Collarenebri
Inverell
Walgett
Armidale
Narrabri
Kempsey
Coonamble
Gunnedah
Bourke
Coonabarabran
Tamworth
Wilcannia
Cobar
Taree
Nyngan
Gilgandra
Broken Hill
Dubbo
Maitland
Newcastle
Parkes
Orange
Bathurst
Lithgow
Wentworth
West Wyalong
Cowra
SYDNEY
Hay
Narrandera
Wollongong
Goulburn
Deniliquin
Wagga Wagga
Yass
Nowra
Finley
Albury
CANBERRA
Batemans Bay
Cooma
Bega

Other Map Coverage

Central Sydney 2
Sydney Approach & Bypass Routes 3
Sydney & Western Suburbs 4
Northern Suburbs, Sydney 6
Southern Suburbs, Sydney 8
Hawkesbury & Central Coast 21

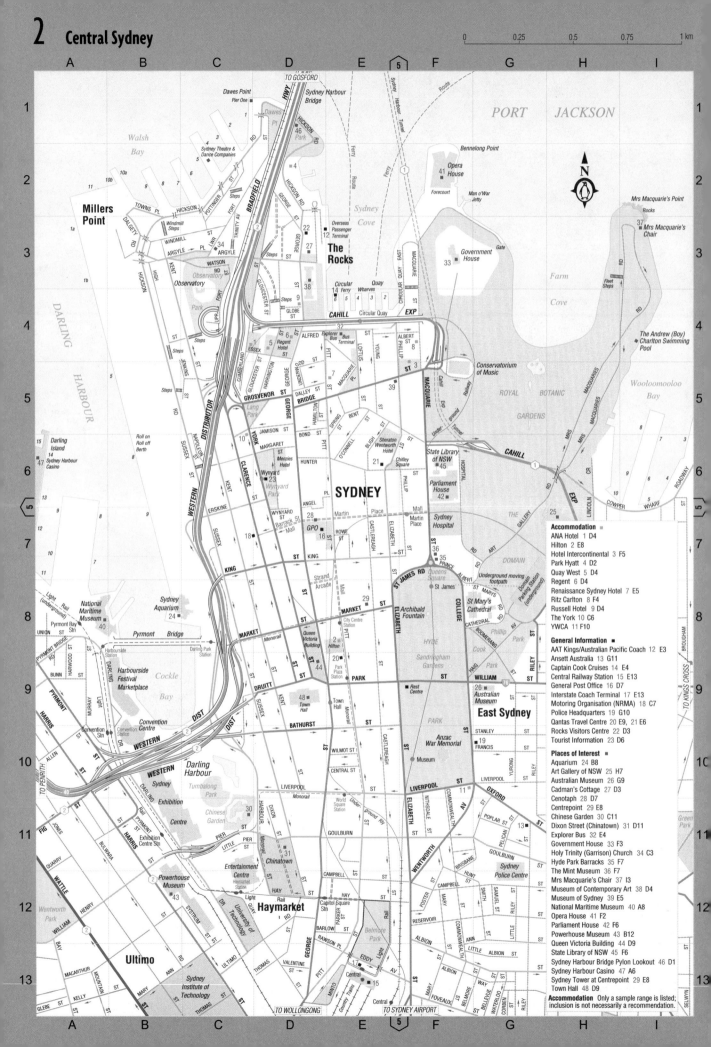

Accommodation
ANA Hotel 1 D4
Hilton 2 E8
Hotel Intercontinental 3 F5
Park Hyatt 4 D2
Quay West 5 D4
Regent 6 D4
Renaissance Sydney Hotel 7 E5
Ritz Carlton 8 F4
Russell Hotel 9 D4
The York 10 C6
YWCA 11 F10

General Information
AAT Kings/Australian Pacific Coach 12 E3
Ansett Australia 13 G11
Captain Cook Cruises 14 E4
Central Railway Station 15 E13
General Post Office 16 D7
Interstate Coach Terminal 17 E13
Motoring Organisation (NRMA) 18 C7
Police Headquarters 19 G10
Qantas Travel Centre 20 E9, 21 E6
Rocks Visitors Centre 22 D3
Tourist Information 23 D6

Places of Interest
Aquarium 24 B8
Art Gallery of NSW 25 H7
Australian Museum 26 G9
Cadman's Cottage 27 D3
Cenotaph 28 D7
Centrepoint 29 E8
Chinese Garden 30 C11
Dixon Street (Chinatown) 31 D11
Explorer Bus 32 E4
Government House 33 F3
Holy Trinity (Garrison) Church 34 C3
Hyde Park Barracks 35 F7
The Mint Museum 36 F7
Mrs Macquarie's Chair 37 I3
Museum of Contemporary Art 38 D4
Museum of Sydney 39 E5
National Maritime Museum 40 A8
Opera House 41 F2
Parliament House 42 F6
Powerhouse Museum 43 B12
Queen Victoria Building 44 D9
State Library of NSW 45 F6
Sydney Harbour Bridge Pylon Lookout 46 D1
Sydney Harbour Casino 47 A6
Sydney Tower at Centrepoint 29 E8
Town Hall 48 D9

Accommodation Only a sample range is listed; inclusion is not necessarily a recommendation.

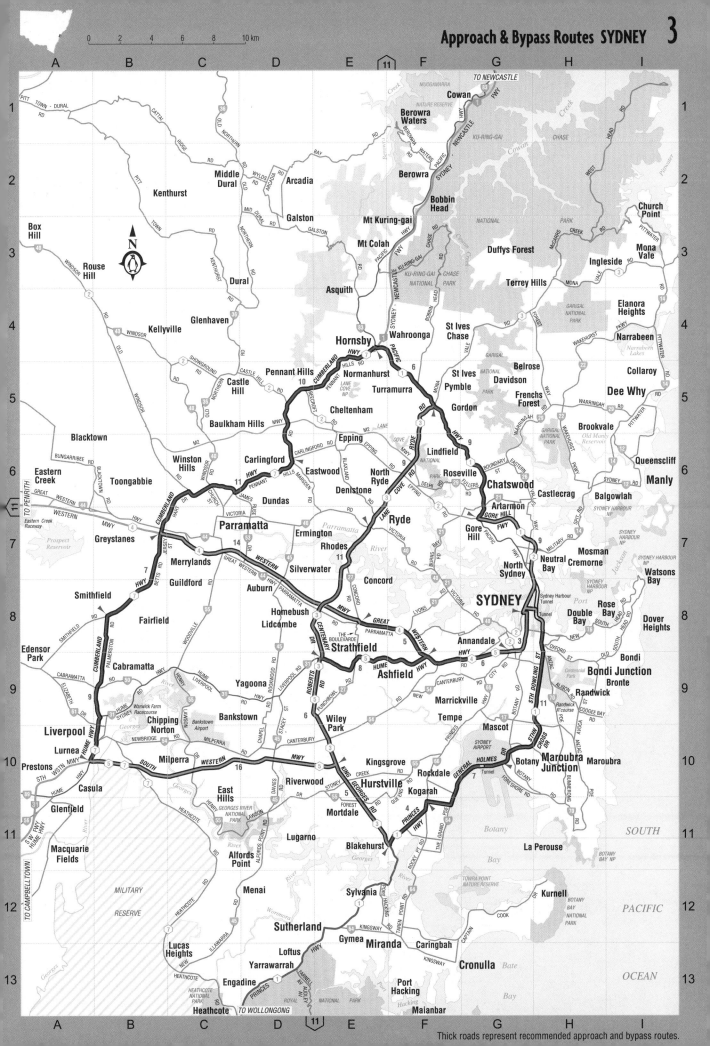

Rogans Hill
Castle Hill
West Pennant Hills
Cumberland State Forest
Koala Park
Berowra Valley Bushland Reserve
Thornleigh
Normanhurst
Sydney Adventist Hospital
Turramurra
Pennant Hills
Lane Cove NP
South Turramurra
Twin Creek Reserve
Pennant Hills Park
Avondale Golf Course
Baulkham Hills
Excelsior Park
Darling Mills State Forest
Beecroft
Pennant Hills Golf Course
Cheltenham
West Pymble
Muirfield Golf Course
North Rocks
Carlingford
Epping
Macquarie University
Winston Hills
Old Toongabbie
Toongabbie
Lake Parramatta Reserve
Dundas Valley
Eastwood
North Ryde
Telopea
Oatlands Golf Course
Denistone
North Ryde G.C.
Macquarie Hospital
Northmead
Pendle Hill
Westmead Hospital
Cumberland Hospital
Wentworthville
Dundas
West Ryde
Parramatta Park & Golf Course
Westmead
Parramatta
Rydalmere
Ryde-Parramatta Golf Course
Meadowbank
Ryde
Melrose Park
Royal Rehab Centre
Mays Hill
Harris Park
Elizabeth Farm
Camellia
Rosehill Racecourse
Ermington
Rhodes
Putney
Rosehill
Showground
Silverwater Corrective Services Complex
Tennyson
Granville
Silverwater
Concord Repatriation General Hospital
Merrylands
Clyde
Clyburn
Main Venue for Olympic Games
Showgrounds
Bicentennial Park
Mortlake
Concord
Guildford
Cabarita
Abbotsford
Auburn
Homebush Bay
State Sports Centre
Concord West
Concord Golf Course
Sydney Wool Centre
North Strathfield
Fairfield
Yennora
Auburn Golf Course
Lidcombe
Flemington
Homebush
Canada Bay
Hudson Park Golf Course
Burwood
Rookwood Cemetery
Chester Hill
Berala
Lidcombe Hospital
Carnarvon Golf Course
Rookwood
Strathfield Golf Course
Strathfield
Villawood
Leightonfield
Carramar
Sefton
Regents Park
Croydon
Lansvale
Bass Hill
Birrong
Chullora
Enfield
Croydon Park
Ashfield
Mirambeena Regional Park
Lansdowne
Ashbury
Georges River
Greenacre
Belfield
Canterbury
Canterbury Racecourse
Motor Racing Circuit
Liverpool Golf Course
Yagoona
Warwick Farm Racecourse
Georges Hall
Crest of Bankstown
Campsie
Hurlstone Park
Mt Lewis
Belmore
Canterbury Hospital
Chipping Norton
Riverwood Golf Course
Bankstown Airport
Condell Park
Bankstown
Punchbowl
Lakemba
Clemton Park
Earlwood

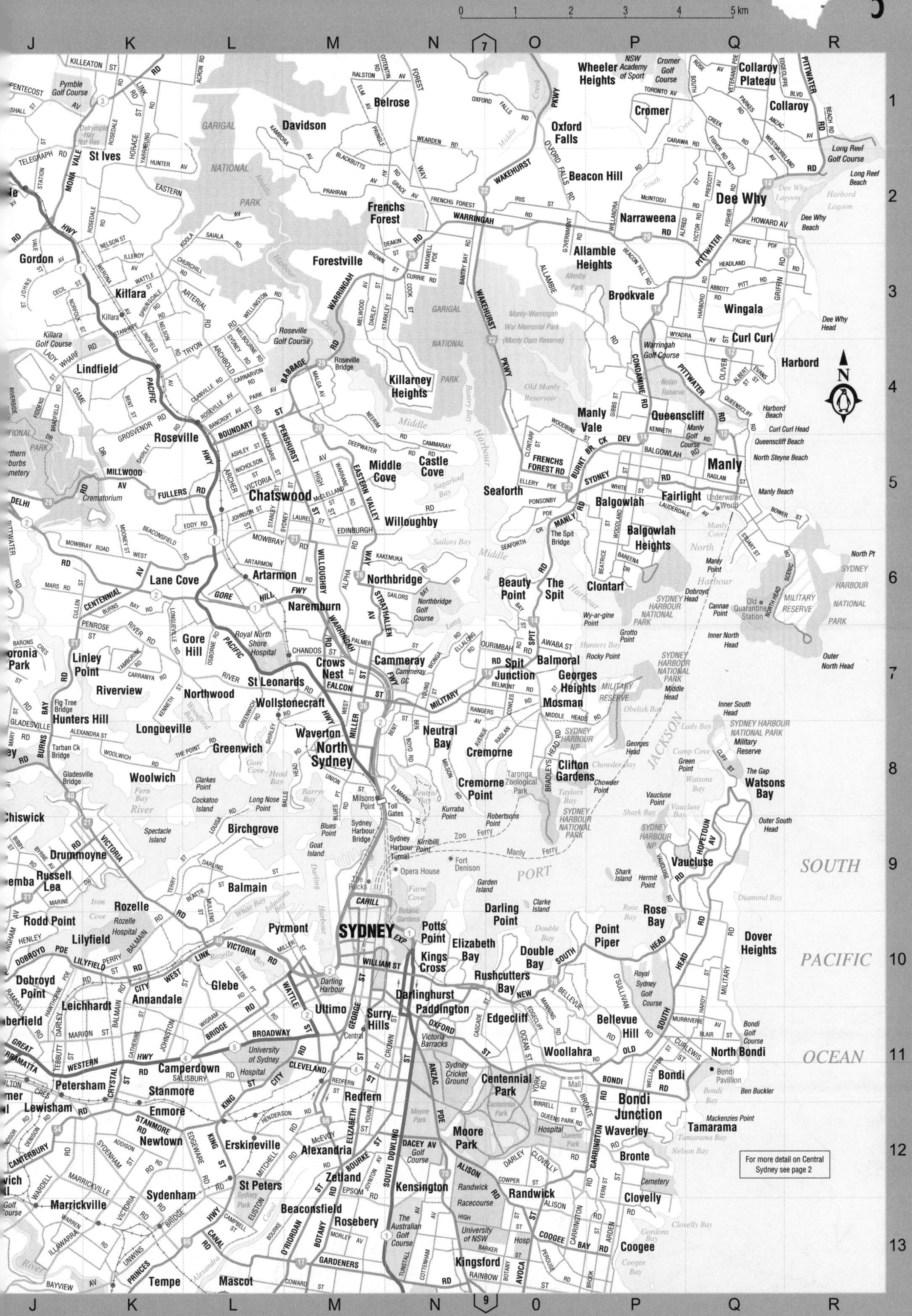

0 1 2 3 4 5 km
J K L M N O P Q R
1 2 3 4 5 6 7 8 9 10 11 12 13
Killeaton St
Pymble Golf Course
St Ives
Mona Vale Rd
Davidson
Belrose
Wheeler Heights
NSW Academy of Sport
Cromer Golf Course
Collaroy Plateau
Collaroy
Cromer
Oxford Falls
Long Reef Golf Course
Long Reef Beach
Garigal National Park
Beacon Hill
Dee Why
Dee Why Lagoon
Dee Why Beach
Harbord Lagoon
Frenchs Forest
Narraweena
Gordon
Forestville
Allambie Heights
Allenby Park
Brookvale
Killara
Wingala
Curl Curl
Dee Why Head
Roseville Golf Course
Roseville Bridge
Manly-Warringah War Memorial Park (Manly Dam Reserve)
Killara Golf Course
Lindfield
Warringah Golf Course
Harbord
Killarney Heights
Old Manly Reservoir
Nolan Reserve
Roseville
Manly Vale
Queenscliff
Manly Golf Course
Harbord Beach
Curl Curl Head
Queenscliff Beach
North Steyne Beach
Chatswood
Middle Cove
Castle Cove
Sugarloaf Bay
Manly
Seaforth
Fairlight
Crematorium
Balgowlah
Underwater World
Manly Beach
Willoughby
Manly Cove
The Spit Bridge
Balgowlah Heights
North Harbour
Sailors Bay
Middle Harbour
Artarmon
Northbridge
Beauty Point
The Spit
Clontarf
Lane Cove
Naremburn
Northbridge Golf Course
Dobroyd Head
Cannae Point
Old Quarantine Station
Military Reserve
Sydney Harbour National Park
North Pt
Wy-ar-gine Point
Grotto Point
Inner North Head
Gore Hill
Royal North Shore Hospital
Hunters Bay
Rocky Point
Outer North Head
Linley Point
Crows Nest
Cammeray
Cammeray GC
Spit Junction
Balmoral
Georges Heights
Middle Head
Riverview
St Leonards
Northwood
Mosman
Inner South Head
Fig Tree Bridge
Hunters Hill
Wollstonecraft
Obelisk Bay
Longueville
Waverton
North Sydney
Neutral Bay
Cremorne
Lady Bay
Camp Cove
Georges Head
Port Jackson
Tarban Ck Bridge
Greenwich
Chowder Bay
Green Point
The Gap
Gladesville Bridge
Woolwich
Clarkes Point
Gore Cove
Head Bay
Clifton Gardens
Watsons Bay
Cremorne Point
Taronga Zoological Park
Chowder Point
Taylors Bay
Cockatoo Island
Long Nose Point
Barrys Bay
Milsons Point
Toll Gates
Kurraba Point
Robertsons Point
Vaucluse Point
Vaucluse Bay
Shark Bay
Chiswick
Spectacle Island
Birchgrove
Blues Point
Sydney Harbour Bridge
Zoo Ferry
Manly Ferry
Outer South Head
Drummoyne
Goat Island
Sydney Harbour Tunnel
Kirribilli Point
Fort Denison
Opera House
Shark Island
Hermit Point
Vaucluse
South Pacific Ocean
Russell Lea
Balmain
The Rocks
Farm Cove
Garden Island
Iron Cove
Rozelle
White Bay
Johnsons Bay
Darling Harbour
Darling Point
Clarke Island
Rose Bay
Diamond Bay
Rodd Point
Rozelle Hospital
Botanic Gardens
Cahill Exp
Lilyfield
Pyrmont
Sydney
Potts Point
Elizabeth Bay
Double Bay
Point Piper
Dover Heights
Kings Cross
Dobroyd Point
Glebe
Darling Harbour
Rushcutters Bay
Royal Sydney Golf Course
Annandale
Leichhardt
Ultimo
Darlinghurst
Paddington
Edgecliff
Bellevue Hill
Surry Hills
Victoria Barracks
Woollahra
Bondi Golf Course
North Bondi
Broadway
University of Sydney
Central
Sydney Cricket Ground
Camperdown
Centennial Park
Bondi
Bondi Pavillion
Ben Buckler
Bondi Bay
Petersham
Hospital
Redfern
Stanmore
Lewisham
Enmore
Moore Park
Bondi Junction
Waverley
Mackenzies Point
Tamarama
Tamarama Bay
Newtown
Erskineville
Alexandria
Queens Park
Nelson Bay
Bronte
For more detail on Central Sydney see page 2
Zetland
Randwick Racecourse
Randwick
Cemetery
Clovelly
Marrickville
Sydenham
St Peters
Sydney Park
Kensington
Beaconsfield
Rosebery
The Australian Golf Course
University of NSW
Clovelly Bay
Gordons Bay
Coogee
Coogee Bay
Kingsford
Tempe
Mascot
Gardeners Rd
Alexandra Canal
Cooks River
Pacific Hwy
Warringah Fwy
Parramatta Rd
Princes Hwy
Military Rd
Pittwater Rd
Wakehurst Pkwy
South Dowling St
Anzac Pde
Old South Head Rd

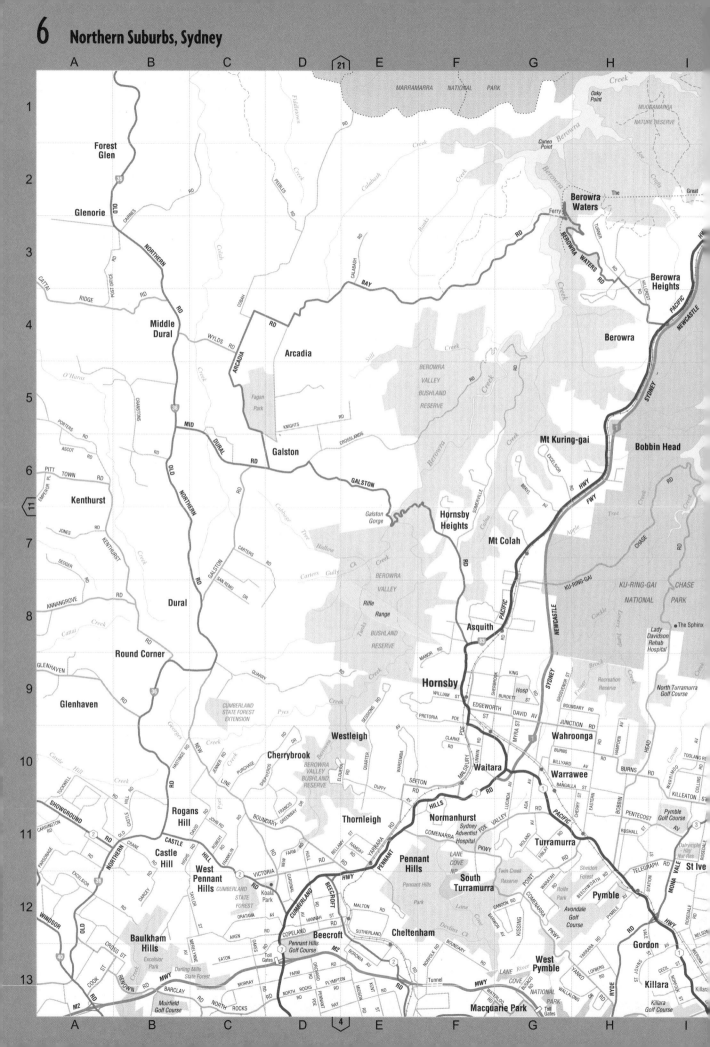

0 1 2 3 4 5 km

J K L M N 21 O P Q R

1
Porto Bay
Gunyah Point
Juno Point
Broken Bay
Ferry
West Head
KU-RING-GAI CHASE NP
Barrenjoey Head
Barrenjoey Lighthouse
Lookout
Shark Rock
North
FWY
83
Walk
VIZE SPUR

2
Jerusalem Bay
CENT SPUR
Cowan Water
Challenger Head
Little Pittwater Bay
Hungry Beach
Great Mackerel Beach
Ferry
Sandy Beach
Barrenjoey Beach
Palm Beach Golf Course
Palm Beach
Palm Beach
Whale Beach
Little Head

3
KU-RING-GAI CHASE
Cowan Point
Hallets Beach
Refuge Bay
KU-RING-GAI CHASE
BARRENJOEY
CYNTHEA
BYNYA
Whale Beach
Whale Beach

4
NATIONAL PARK
PINTA RIDGE
Cowan Creek
Cottage Point
Yeomans Bay
NATIONAL PARK
Longnose Point
Towlers Bay
Careel Bay
Bangalley Head
RIVERVIEW
RIVIERA AV
GEORGE ST
PATRICK
Avalon
CENTRAL
St Michael's Cave
Hole in the Wall

5
Smiths Creek
COTTAGE
POINT
LIBERATOR GENERAL
SAN MARTIN
Taylors Point
Long Beach
Scotland Island
Scotland Island
Refuge Cove
Clareville
HUDSON
Avalon Golf Course
PLATEAU
Avalon Beach
Bilgola Head
BILGOLA RD

6
KU-RING-GAI CHASE
SAN MARTIN DR
LIBERATOR GENERAL
Church Point
MINKARA
BARLY
LENTARA
PITTWATER
Bayview
Newport
IRRUBEL RD
Newport Beach
GLADSTONE ST
MONA
MYOLA RD
Bungan Head

7
NATIONAL PARK
Smiths Creek
Duffys Forest
Terrey Hills Country Club (Golf Course)
BOORALIE
McCARRS
CABBAGE
CICADA
GLEN
WALTER
TREE
SAMUEL ST
Bayview GC
PARK ST
DARLEY
BASSETT
CRESCENT
BARRENJOEY
Bungan Beach
N

8
Waratah Park
NAMBA RD
THIDDUNGRA
TOORONGA
COOYONG RD
Terrey Hills
MYOSRA RD
FOREST RD
MONA VALE
3
Baha'i Temple
POWDER
Ingleside
CHILTERN
LANE COVE RD
3
VINEYARD
WARREN
MAMELL ST
EMMA ST
Mona Vale
Mona Vale Golf Course
Mona Vale Hospital

9
St Ives Showground
Ku-Ring-Gai Wildflower Garden
GARIGAL NATIONAL PARK
Deep Creek
WORKS
INGLESIDE RD
Monash Golf Course
Elanora Golf Course
GARDEN
MACPHERSON RD
Warriewood
ANANA RD
RICKARD RD
JACKSONS
North Narrabeen Reserve
Turimetta Head
PITTWATER RD
Narrabeen Head
SOUTH

10
MONA VALE
3
FOREST WAY
MORGAN RD
Elanora Heights
PKWY
22
WAKEHURST
Narrabeen Lakes
NSW Academy of Sport
Pipeclay Point Reserve
Narrabeen
Narrabeen Beach
OCEAN ST
PITTWATER RD
EDGECLIFFE
PACIFIC

11
Ives rth
GARIGAL NATIONAL PARK
Bore Creek
Middle Harbour
COTTERILL
RALSTON
ELM
OXFORD FALLS RD
Wheeler Heights
Cromer Golf Course
ROSE AV
SOUTH
TORONTO AV
Collaroy Plateau
VETERANS PDE
Collaroy
PARKES RD
ANZAC RD
WESTMORELAND RD
BEACH RD
Collaroy Beach
OCEAN

12
EASTERN
KAMBORA AV
Davidson
Belrose
BLACKBUTTS
WEARDEN RD
PRINGLE AV
Middle Creek
Oxford Falls
OXFORD FALLS RD
Beacon Hill
McINTOSH
CARAWA RD
South Creek
FISHER RD NTH
PRESCOTT
ALFRED
VICTOR
Dee Why
14
Long Reef Golf Course
Long Reef Point
Long Reef Beach
Harbord Lagoon
Dee Why Lagoon
Dee Why Beach

13
PARK
KOOLA
SAIALA
CHURCHILL
ARTERIAL RD
WELLINGTON
TRYON RD
MELBOURNE
Roseville Golf Course
WARRINGAH RD
DEAKIN
BROWN
MAXWELL PDE
CURRIE
COOK ST
STARLEY ST
DARLEY ST
MELWOOD
29
Frenchs Forest
WAKEHURST PKWY
WARRINGAH RD
29
GOVERNMENT RD
Narraweena
BEACON HILL RD
Allambie Heights
ALLAMBIE RD
Allenby Park
Manly-Warringah War Memorial Park (Manly Dam Reserve)
Brookvale
PITTWATER RD
HARBORD RD
ABBOTT RD
PITT ST
GRIFFIN RD
Wingala
HEADLAND RD
PACIFIC
Dee Why PDE
Dee Why Head
Curl Curl
WYADRA AV
Warringah Golf Course
5
29

J K L M N 5 O P Q R

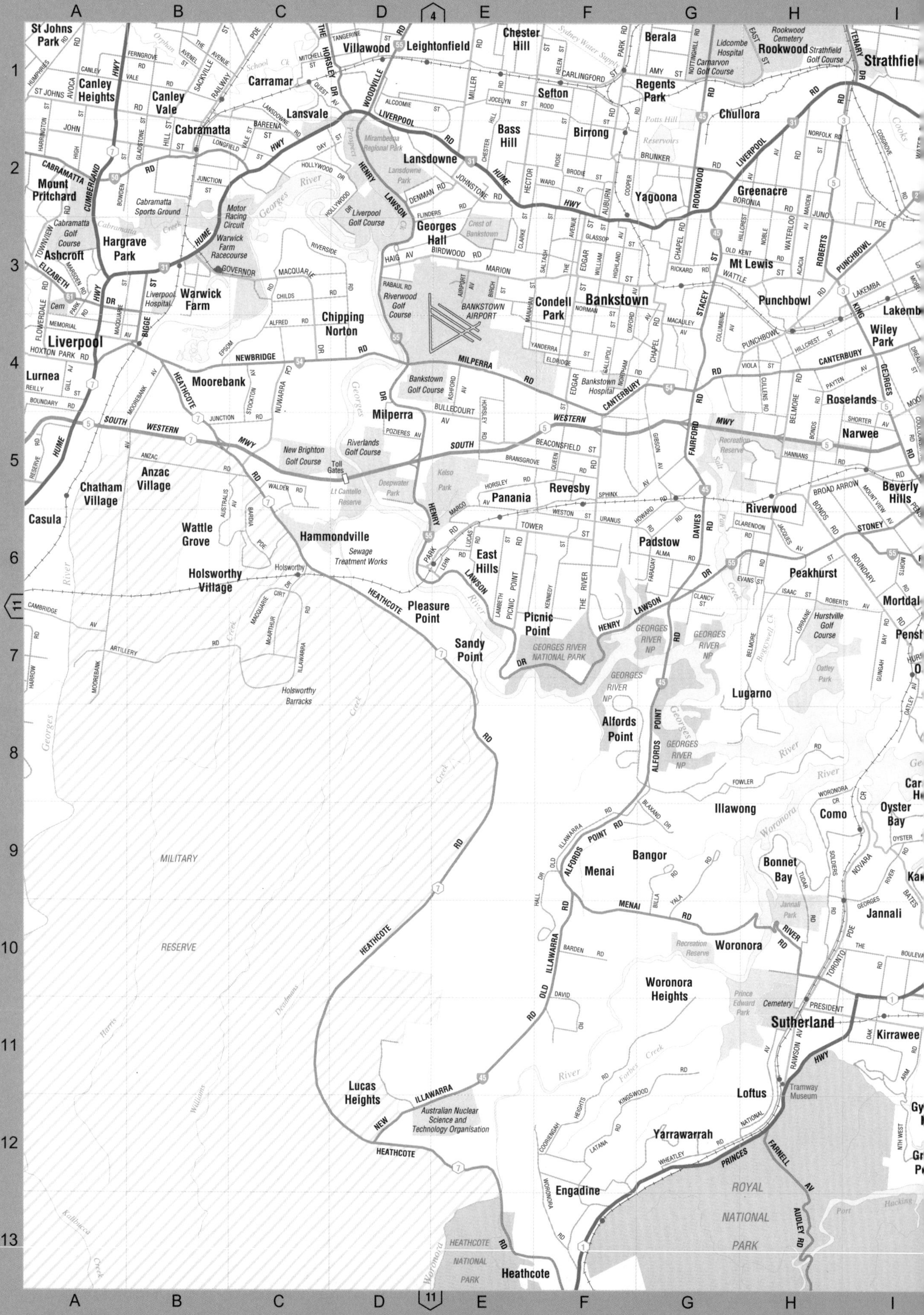

St Johns Park
Canley Heights
Carramar
Villawood
Leightonfield
Chester Hill
Berala
Rookwood
Rookwood Cemetery
Strathfield Golf Course
Strathfiel
Lidcombe Hospital
Camarvon Golf Course
Canley Vale
Lansvale
Sefton
Regents Park
Cabramatta
Bass Hill
Birrong
Chullora
Mount Pritchard
Cabramatta Sports Ground
Lansdowne
Lansdowne Park
Mirambeena Regional Park
Brunker
Yagoona
Greenacre
Ashcroft
Hargrave Park
Motor Racing Circuit
Warwick Farm Racecourse
Liverpool Golf Course
Georges Hall
Crest of Bankstown
Mt Lewis
Warwick Farm
Liverpool Hospital
Governor
Raball Rd Riverwood Golf Course
Birdwood
Condell Park
Bankstown
Punchbowl
Lakemb
Liverpool
Chipping Norton
Bankstown Airport
Wiley Park
Lurnea
Moorebank
Bankstown Golf Course
Milperra
Bankstown Hospital
Roselands
Chatham Village
Anzac Village
New Brighton Golf Course
Milperra
Riverlands Golf Course
Deepwater Park
Kelso Park
Revesby
Narwee
Casula
Wattle Grove
Hammondville
Sewage Treatment Works
Panania
Padstow
Riverwood
Beverly Hills
Holsworthy Village
Holsworthy
Pleasure Point
East Hills
Peakhurst
Mortdal
Hurstville Golf Course
Sandy Point
Picnic Point
Georges River National Park
Georges River NP
Lugarno
Pensh
Oatley Park
Holsworthy Barracks
MILITARY
Alfords Point
Georges River NP
Illawong
Como
Car H
Oyster Bay
RESERVE
Menai
Bangor
Bonnet Bay
Ka
Jannali
Woronora
Woronora Heights
Recreation Reserve
Prince Edward Park
Sutherland
Kirrawee
Gy
Lucas Heights
Australian Nuclear Science and Technology Organisation
Loftus
Tramway Museum
Yarrawarrah
Gr
Engadine
Heathcote
ROYAL NATIONAL PARK

0 1 2 3 4 5 km

J K L M N O P Q R

Enfield
Croydon
Haberfield Leichhardt Annandale
FREDERICK BLAND DARLEY BALMAIN WIGRAM RD
FITZROY RAMSAY MARION ST JOHNSTON BROADWAY
Ashfield Petersham Camperdown WESTERN HWY
Summer Hill Stanmore University of Sydney Salisbury Hospital
Croydon Park Lewisham Enmore Newtown Redfern
Ashbury STANMORE RD Erskineville McEvoy
Canterbury Marrickville St Peters Alexandria
Dulwich Hill Sydenham Zetland
Campsie Hurlstone Park Beaconsfield Rosebery
Earlwood Tempe Mascot Eastlakes
Clemton Park Undercliffe O'RIORDAN Botany
Turrella Arncliffe GARDENERS RD
Bexley North Bardwell Park MARSH ST Daceyville
Kingsgrove Bexley Banksia SYDNEY AIRPORT Pagewood Maroubra Junction Maroubra
Rockdale Kyeemagh Botany Banksmeadow Hillsdale
Hurstville Kogarah St George Hosp Brighton-le-Sands Matraville
Carlton Monterey Chifley Malabar
Allawah Beverley Park Phillip Bay
Connells Point Ramsgate Little Bay La Perouse
Carss Park Sans Souci Dolls Point
Blakehurst Sandringham BOTANY BAY
Sylvania Kurnell
Sylvania Waters Quibray Bay BOTANY BAY NATIONAL PARK
Taren Point
Sylvania Heights Weeney Bay
Miranda Caringbah Woolooware Golf Course Cronulla Golf Course
Wooloware
Yowie Bay Cronulla
Dolans Bay BATE BAY
Lilli Pilli Port Hacking Burraneer OCEAN
Maianbar

Croydon Ashfield Campsie Hurstville Haberfield Leichhardt Annandale Ultimo Surry Hills Paddington Edgecliff Bellevue Hill Woollahra Bondi Bondi Junction Waverley Bronte Clovelly Coogee Randwick Kensington Kingsford Moore Park Centennial Park

SOUTH PACIFIC OCEAN

N

A B C D 12 E F G H I

1

Hill End
Turondale
Wattle Flat
Sofala Historic Town
Palmers Oakey
Capertee
Newnes
GARDENS OF STONE
NATIONAL PARK
PANTONEYS CROWN NATURE RESERVE

2

Mt Wiagdon 1015m
Limekilns
WINBURNDALE NATURE RESERVE
Ben Bullen
GARDENS OF STONE NP
Jews Mtn 1061m
Mt Davidson 1081m
Glow Worm Tunnel
WOLLEM
Wolgan

3

Peel
TURON STATE FOREST
Dark Corner
Cullen Bullen
Angus Place
WINBURNDALE NATURE RESERVE
Portland
Pipers Flat
Lidsdale
GREAT
NATIONAL PARK

4

Dunkeld
MITCHELL HWY
32
Bathurst
Kelso
Glanmire
Sunny Corner
Mt Ovens 1272m
Meadow Flat
GREAT
Wallerawang
Marrangaroo
Bowenfels
Clarence
Newnes Junction
Evans Plains
7
15
13
Walang
Yetholme
33
6
5
7
32
28
Mt Walker 1189m
3
DIVIDING
Wollangambe

TO ORANGE
WESTERN HWY
Mt Panorama Motor Racing Circuit
Orton Park
White Rock
Mount Lambie
4
Rydal
Lithgow
Zig Zag Steam Railway
Bell
Mount Wilson

5

MID WESTERN HWY
24
TO COWRA
SIR JOSEPH BANKS NATURE RESERVE
Perthville
4
Fish
21
WAMBOOL NATURE RESERVE
SUNNY CORNER STATE FOREST
Sodwalls
Lake Lyell
Glenroy
WESTERN
11
Hartley
Hartley Vale
Little Hartley
22
44
40
Mt Tomah Botanic Ga
Georges Plains
6
The Lagoon
5
O'Connell
Locksley
Tarana Quarry
11
Coxs
Mt York
6
8
17

6

Newbridge
Moorilda
12
14
24
Rockley Historic Town
18
Ben Chifley Dam
19
47
Carlwood
LOWES MOUNT STATE FOREST
16
Bonfire Hill 1286m
River
Lowther
31
14
Mount Victoria
Mt Piddington 1078m
BLUE
Blackheath
Mount Blackheath Lookout
18
BLUE MOUN
Perry's Lookdown
Pulpit Rock Reserve & Lookout
Govetts Leap Lookout
Evans Lookout
NATIONAL
Wisemans Creek
26
Lowes Mount
Hazelgrove
7
Hampton
3
Shipley

7

Hobbys Yards
14
15
11
Essington
16
Oberon
13
5
Duckmaloi
28
12
27 JENOLAN STATE FOREST
Gibraltar Rocks 1057m
24
BLACK RANGE
Megalong
Hargreaves Lookout
Explorers Tree
Medlow Bath
32
Wentworth Falls
Leura
Lawson
Haze
Katoomba
Scenic Skyway & Railway
Echo Point
The Three Sisters
Byjaburra
Queen Victoria Hospital
Cataract Falls
Wood
JAMISON VALLEY
Mount-Ha-Ha

8

Trunkey
25
Mount David
28
24
30
Edith
11
19
17
14
Lake Oberon
22
Jenolan Caves
Jenolan Caves
KANANGRA
BLUE MOUNTAINS
NATIONAL
Mt Guouopang 1290m

9

Abercrombie Caves
29
10
Campbells River
Isabella
Shooters Hill
BOYD RANGE
Mt Cloudmaker 1164m
Kanangra Walls
GANGERANG RANGE
SCOTTS MAIN RANGE
BLUE MOUNTAINS
NATIONAL
McMahons Lookout
CATCHMENT AREA
ENTRY PROHIBITE
BURRA STA REC

10

Burraga
Black Springs
Porters Retreat
NATIONAL
Mt Paddin 1210m
PARK
RANGE
GINGRA RANGE
Kowmung River
Green
Butchers
PARK
Burragorang Lookout
Natt

11

Tuena
Limerick
29
38
68
BLUE MOUNTAINS
Mt Werong 1214m
Mt Colong 1047m
Yerranderie Historic Town

12

Peelwood
22
GREAT
NATIONAL PARK
Mt Armstrong 1091m
DIVIDING
BLUE MOUNTAINS
NATIONAL PARK
NATTAI

13

Binda
5
Thalaba
Fullerton
Golspie
Yalbraith
Richlands
GREAT
22
Broughtons Lookout
Wombeyan Caves
Wombeyan Caves
Lords Mountain 845m
Goodmans Ford
29
Bullio
Burragorang Lookout
High Range
Mt Jellore 826m
Tunnel
NATIONAL PARK
THE

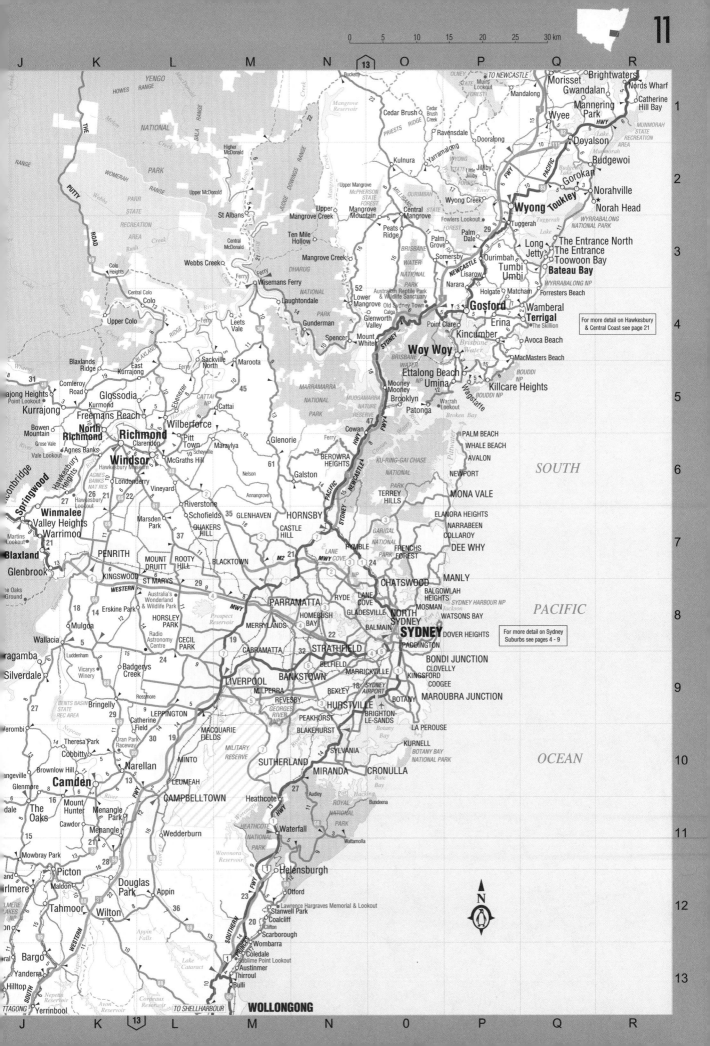

For more detail on Canberra Region see pages 26 & 27

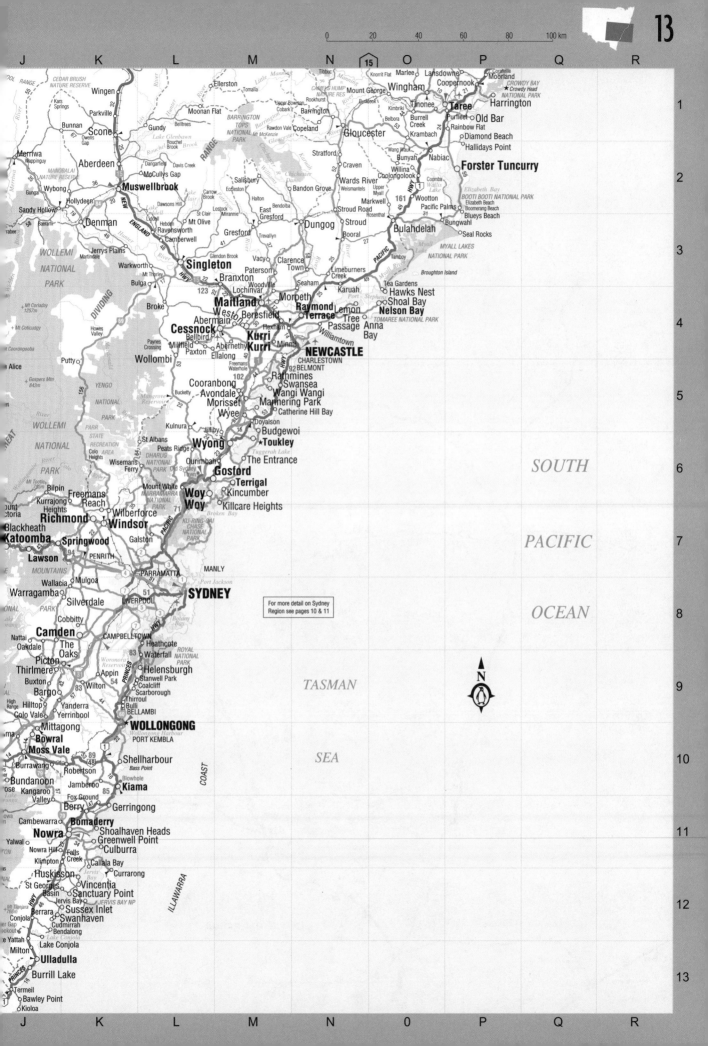

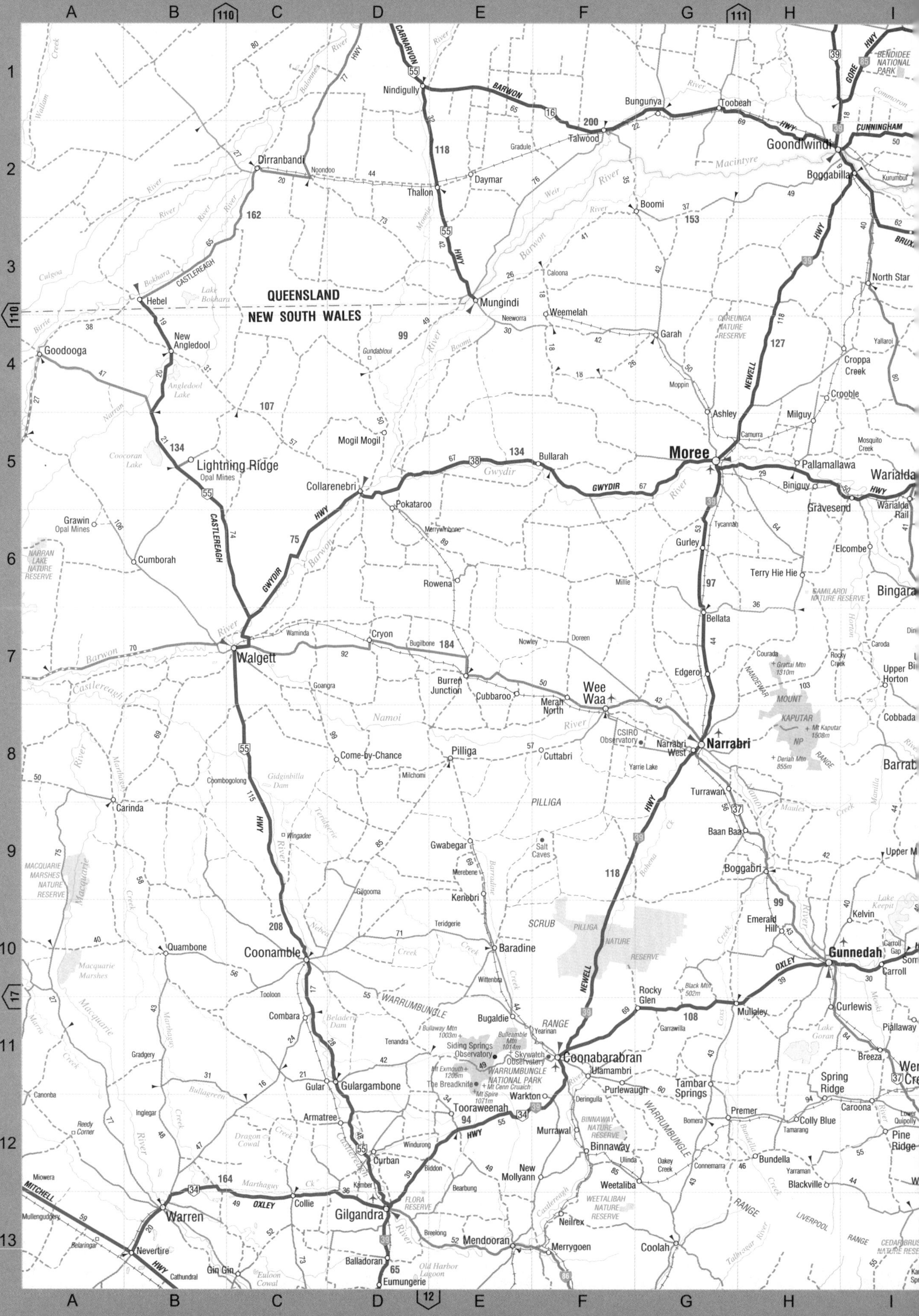

QUEENSLAND
NEW SOUTH WALES

Nindigully
Dirranbandi
Noondoo
Thallon
Daymar
Mungindi
Neeworra
Weemelah
Talwood
Bungunya
Gradule
Toobeah
Goondiwindi
Boggabilla
Kurumbul
North Star
Croppa Creek
Crooble
Yallaroi
Milguy
Ashley
Camurra
Garah
Moppin
Hebel
New Angledool
Goodooga
Lightning Ridge
Opal Mines
Grawin
Opal Mines
Cumborah
Mogil Mogil
Collarenebri
Pokataroo
Merrywinbone
Rowena
Bullarah
Moree
Gurley
Tycannah
Terry Hie Hie
Bellata
Edgeroi
Millie
Doreen
Nowley
Waminda
Cryon
Bugilbone
Burren Junction
Cubbaroo
Meran North
Wee Waa
Narrabri West
Narrabri
CSIRO Observatory
Yarrie Lake
Cuttabri
Pilliga
Milchomi
Come-by-Chance
Coombogolong
Carinda
Quambone
Walgett
Goangra
Gwabegar
Merebene
Gilgooma
Kenebri
Teridgerie
Turrawan
Baan Baa
Boggabri
Upper Horton
Cobbada
Pallamallawa
Warialda
Gravesend
Warialda Rail
Elcombe
Bingara
Kelvin
Emerald Hill
Gunnedah
Carroll
Curlewis
Baradine
Wittenbra
Coonamble
Tooloon
Combara
Tenandra
Yearinan
Bugaldie
Rocky Glen
Garrawilla
Mullaley
Piallaway
Breeza
Spring Ridge
Caroona
Gradgery
Gular
Gulargambone
Armatree
Mt Exmouth
Siding Springs Observatory
Skywatch Observatory
The Breadknife
Mt Cenn Cruaich
Mt Spire
Tooraweenah
Warkton
Coonabarabran
Ulamambri
Purlewaugh
Deringulla
Murrawal
Binnaway
Tambar Springs
Premer
Bomera
Colly Blue
Tamarang
Bundella
Pine Ridge
Blackville
Canonba
Inglegar
Reedy Corner
Mullengudgery
Warren
Collie
Gilgandra
Balladoran
Eumungerie
Curban
Windurong
Biddon
Kember
New Mollyann
Bearburn
Neilrex
Mendooran
Breelong
Old Harbor Lagoon
Merrygoen
Coolah
Weetaliba
Ulinda
Oakey Creek
Connemara
Yarraman
Belaringar
Nevertire
Cathundral
Gin Gin
Euloon Cowal
Miowera

0 20 40 60 80 100 km

J K L M N O P Q R

GREAT

Karara

Inglewood

200 HWY 40

Mt Burrabaranga 794m

Coolmunda Reservoir

Leslie Dam

MAIN RANGE NATIONAL PARK

111

Truck n' Travel Roadhouse

Yangan **Warwick**

Maroon

MT BARNEY NP

Rathdowney

LAMINGTON NP

Springbrook

COOLANGATTA
TWEED HEADS
Fingal

Banora Point

Chinderah
Kingscliff

Cudgen

Bogangar
Hastings Point
Pottsville

1

Tarbon

42

40

21

Tannymorel

Killarney

Queen Mary Falls

88

Legume

55

Woodenbong

Lower Acacia Creek

Hewetsons Mill

Chillingham

Tyalgum

BORDER RANGES NP

Mt Lindesay 1177m

Cougal

WARNING NP

Eungella Siding

Cudgera Creek

Murwillumbah

Stokers Siding

Uki

Billinudgel

Kunghur

New Brighton

Ocean Shores
Brunswick Heads

Tyagarah

2

Beebo

Dumaresq R

Smithlea

Braeside

Pozieres

Cottonvale

Dalveen

The Summit

Applethorpe

Thulimbah

115

Amiens

Pikedale

Mt Bullaganang 629m

Mulli Mulli

Urenville

Grevillia

Rukenvale

Toonumbar

The Risk

Lynchs Ck NP

Wiangaree

Cawongla

Nimbin

Butignbar

Mullumbimby

NIGHTCAP NP

Crabbes Ck

Mooball

Bangalow
Clunes
Newrybar

Byron Bay
Cape Byron
Suffolk Park

Limevale

QUEENSLAND

Texas

229

Bonshaw

Mingoola

24

Stanthorpe

Glen Aplin

Severnlea

Liston

Amosfield

Wylie Creek

Old Bonalbo

Bonalbo

Kyogle

Georgica

Ettrick

Goolmangar

Fairy Hill

Bentley

The Channon

RICHMOND RANGE

Toonumbar Dam

Mummulgum

Lismore

Bexhill

Alphadale

Knockrow

Lennox Head

Wollongbar

3

Smithlea

NEW SOUTH WALES

Ashford

Texas

Ballandean

GIRRAWEEN NP

BALD ROCK NP

SUNDOWN NP

BOONOO BOONOO NATIONAL PARK

Boonoo Boonoo Falls

Pretty Gully

Tabulam

190

Mallanganee

Casino

McKees Hill

Leeville

Tatham

Coraki

Meerschaum Vale

Empire Vale

Wardell

Broadwater

Ballina

44

Pike Creek Reservoir

229

Limestone Caves

The Gulf

Wallangarra

Bluff Rock

Black Swamp

Drake

Sandy Hill

44

Alice

Coombell

Rappville

Mt Belmore 650m

Wyan

New Italy

Woodburn

1

Evans Head

BROADWATER NP

4

Tetman

44

Macintyre Falls

Torrington

Stannum

Deepwater

Bolivia

Sandy Flat

Bu'gilla

Mt Bajimba 1446m

WASHPOOL NATIONAL PARK

Baryulgil

Camira Creek

Whiporie

91

Tabbimoble

BUNDJALUNG NATIONAL PARK

130

Ashford

38 HWY

91

Eromanville

Strathbogie

Dundee

Glen Elgin

GIBRALTAR RANGE NATIONAL PARK

162

Cangai

Copmanhurst

Mt Marsh 501m

Lawrence Road

Chatsworth

Harwood

Lawrence

Seelands

Brushgrove

Tyndale

Ferry

Iluka

Yamba

Angourie

YURAYGIR NATIONAL PARK

Brooms Head

5

Delungra

Graman

Bukkulla

Wellingrove

GWYDIR

Bald Knob

Red Range

MANN RIVER NATURE RESERVE

NYMBOIDA NATIONAL PARK

Newton Boyd

Jackadgery

Ramornie Eatonsville

Waterview Heights

Chambigne

Junction Hill

Grafton

Pillar Valley

YURAYGIR NATIONAL PARK

Minnie Water

6

Inverell

38

Gilgai

Elsmore

Brodies Plains

Stonehenge

Glencoe

Balancing Rock

Furracabad

161

Dalmorton

Buccarumbi

OBX Creek

Coutts Crossing

Power Station

82

Wooli

Lake Hiawatha

Keera

Stannifer

Tingha

Stanborough

The Black Mtn 591m

GUY FAWKES RIVER NATIONAL PARK

Nymboida

Towallum

Glenreagh

Kungala

1

Halfway Creek

Red Rock

North Solitary Island

North West Solitary Island

Arrawarra

Mullaway

Corindi

N

7

Ben Lomond

Wandsworth

Llangothlin

98

Backwater

Marengo

202

MOUNT HYLAND NATURE RESERVE

Mt Hyland 1439m

Billys Creek

Nana Glen

Lower Bucca

SHERWOOD NATURE RESERVE

Woolgoolga

Groper Island

Emerald Beach

Moonee Beach

Korora

South Solitary Island

Penguin

Bundarra

THE BASIN NATURE RESERVE

Guyra

56

Black Mountain

Thunderbolt's Cave

NEW

Clouds Creek

Tyringham

Dundurrabin

Lowanna

Ulong

Coramba

Boambee

Coffs Harbour

SOUTH

8

Woods Reef

Kingstown

Yarrowyck

53

Rockvale

GUY FAWKES RIVER NATURE RESERVE

Hernani

Ebor Falls

CATHEDRAL ROCK NP

Bostobrick

Megan

Thora

Dorrigo

DORRIGO NATIONAL PARK

Bonville

Sawtell

MUTTONBIRD ISLAND NATURE RESERVE

WARRABAH NATIONAL PARK

Armidale

75

Wollomombi

193

Ebor

NEW ENGLAND NATIONAL PARK

Point Lookout

Darkwood

Bellingen

Mylestom

Raleigh

Urunga

9

Uralla

111

Kentucky

Rocky River

Dangarsleigh

Dangars Falls

Hillgrove

Wollomombi Falls

Mihi Falls

Enmore

Jeogla

OXLEY WILD RIVERS NATIONAL PARK

Bowraville

165

Valla Beach

Nambucca Heads

anilla

Watsons Creek

Moonbi

108

Comara

225

Taylors Arm

Macksville

Scotts Head

Warrell Creek

Stuarts Point

10

Moore Creek

Woolbrook

Walcha Road

Walcha

Moona Plains

Apsley Falls

Sterrs Ck Falls

Lower Creek

Bellbrook

Eungai Creek

Warrell Creek

South West Rocks

Jerseyville

HAT HEAD NP

Trial Bay Gaol

worth

Kootingal

15 HWY

Wollun

41

OXLEY

Kangaroo Flat

Kookaburra

Willawarrin

Chybucca

Collombatti

Kinchela

Upper Kinchela

Smithtown

Gladstone

PACIFIC

stdale

Duri

Dungowan

Woolomin

Niangala

258

Brackendale

Yarrowitch

Tia

Tia Falls

WERRIKIMBE NATIONAL PARK

Birdwood

Rollands Plains

Frederickton

Kempsey

Hat Head

11

Chaffey Reservoir

33

Myrtle Scrub

Mt Seaview

34 HWY

Mount Seaview

Ellenborough

Pappinbarra

Telegraph Point

1

Kundabung

LIMEBURNERS CREEK NATURE RESERVE

Point Plomer

Crescent Head

Nundle

156

WALLABADAH NATURE RESERVE

Nowendoc

Bagnoo

Byabarra

Beechwood

Wauchope

Port Macquarie

Lake Innes

OCEAN

12

illow Tree

Barry

Cooplacurripa

Elands

Combeyne

Bulga

Ellenborough Creek

Herons Creek

Kendall

Kew

Lake Cathie

Bonny Hills

North Haven

Dunbogan

Camden Haven

Ardglen

Blandford

WOKO NATIONAL PARK

Caparra

Bobin

Killabakh

Lorne

73

Laurieton

CROWDY BAY NATIONAL PARK

rundi

GREAT DIVIDING RANGE

Tibbuc

Tomalla

Marlee

Knorrit Flat

Cedar Party Creek

Johns River

Lansdowne

Loryville

Moorland

13

Moonan Flat

Rookhurst

CAMELS HUMP NAT RES

Mount George

Wingham

Bretti

Burdekin

Kimbriki

Burrell Creek

Taree

Purfleet

Coopernook

Crowdy Head

Harrington

J K L M N O P Q R

13

A B **120** C D E F **121** G H I

1

QUEENSLAND
NEW SOUTH WALES

Lake Callamulcha

Moombidary

Corner Store
Cameron Corner

Binerah Downs

Adelaide Gate

Hamilton Gate

Waverley Gate

STURT NATIONAL PARK

Warri Warri Gate

Onepah

Berrawinnia Downs

2

Frames

Waka

133

33

55

22

Teurika

Ourimbah

126

Owen Downs

Barrajong

Tibooburra

Pindera Downs

3

Gun Vale

Tilcha Creek

Hewart Downs

40

53

Clifton Downs

Colane

Koridina

Wanaa

Yandama

Depot Glen
Poole's Cairn
Billaboho

Poole's Grave

51

Whyjonta

102 272 79

4

Winnathee

Milparinka

Baronna Downs

Flawker Gate House

Yantara

Petita

The Range

Nantilla

NOCOLECHE
NA

5

Mt Shannon 332m+

MT BROWN RANGE

78

Yantara Lake

Lake Ulenia

Gumpopla

Tarkey

138

Tonga Lake

163

Smithville House

Salt Lake

Lake Bullea

Creek

Yancannia

Ck

Tonga

Mudawowolka Basin

6

Lake Wallace

Pincally

Dalmuir

Cobham

Pulgamurtie

70

Allandy

Questa Park

Glendara

Purnanga

McGurty Hill+

Lake Yantabangee

Big Salt Lake

HWY

59

Kooninberry Mtn+

McCallum Park

Cawnalmurtee

Poloka Lake

Gilpoko Lake

7

Starvation Lake

Turleys Gate

Sanpah

Pine Ridge

339

Packsaddle Roadhouse

65

Pulchra

Oak Vale

Caradoc

Goodwood

Peery Lake

Peri Lake

63

Paddadde

Nundora

Lake Bancannia

NOORTHRANGEE RANGE

24

19

44

32

Peery

Mandalay

8

Pine View

Weshwood Downs

16

CITY

The Selection

Koonawarra

73

Wertago

COTURAUNDEE NATURE RESERVE

Cootawundi

Tarella

White Cliffs
Opal Mines

Momba

Coona Coona

Nine Mile Lakes

Wild Duck

Talalara

Be

MacPhe 275m+

9

Boughams Gate

Teilta

Floods Creek

46

MOOTWINGEE

NATIONAL

BYNGUANO RANGE

Mt Daubeny

93

91

Ulalie

Lake Dick

Oulilla Lake

Marra

Morphetts Creek

BENGORO RANGE

PARK
Aboriginal Historic Site

Mt Murchison 203m+

Hamilton (ruin)

River

137

10

BARRIER RANGE

SILVER

46

61

Jones Lake

Coogee Lake

Comarto

Glenora

Mena Murtee

Wilcannia

BARRIER

Lake Woytchugga

Creek

Lake Gunvulka

Poopelloe Lake

We

Wilangee

102

23

Purnamoota

Cawkers Well

19

HWY **32** RANGE

11

NEW SOUTH WALES
SOUTH AUSTRALIA

Mundi Mundi Plain

Umberumberka Reservoir

Silverton
Historic Town

Stephens Creek

31

Stephens Creek Reservoir

77

HWY

Little Topar Roadhouse

196

32

119

Churinga

Glen Lyon

SCOPES RANGE

Hazel Vale

COBB

MACCULLOCHS

12

Cockburn

BARRIER **32**

49

27

79

Broken Hill

47

Pine

SILVER

Fruit Fly Exclusion Zone Boundary

Kinalung

111

Horse Lake

Box Tank

Four Mile Lake

154

Malta Lake

Pamamaroo Lake

Darling

Tuboowalka

Teryawynia

Cowary

196

178

75

13

Mutooroo

Burta

Ascot Vale

Pine Point

CITY HWY

Cawndilla Lake

KINCHEGA
NATIONAL
PARK

Menindee Lake

Menindee

Seven Mile

Dead Horse Lake

Big Ampi

Amphitheatre Lake

Wallace Lake

Dry Lake

Nyngynderry

Glen Albyn

Glen Ora

Teryaweynya Lake

Victoria Lake

Albemarle

MANARA HILLS

A B C **18** D E F G H I

1 2 3 4 5 6 7 8 9 10 11 12 13

J K 121 L M N O P 110 Q R

0 20 40 60 80 100 km

QUEENSLAND
NEW SOUTH WALES

Lake Numalla

WINYA NAL PARK

rford

ICULGOA FLOODPLAIN NATIONAL PARK

1

Parragundy Gate

Barringun

Jobs Gate

Sharoon

Goodooga

2

MITCHELL

38

Enngonia

Beulah

Neilmongle

27

River

Yantabulla

145

Maureen Joy

42 142

71

Bullaroon

Collerina

Birrie

Bokhara

94

NARRAN LAKE NATURE RESERVE

3

Cuttaburra Basin

River

01

River

213

52

HWY

Lake Coonany

Lake Denman

Fords Bridge

68

62

River

Barwon

97

Bogan

Brewarrina

64

Terewah or Narran Lake

4

57

Creek

Lake Burkanoko

Lake Nichebulka

191

134

Culgoa

Mt Bendemeer 149m

Tarrion

Charlton

Tarcoon

41

70

5

gumbla

Utah Lake

85

Warrego

Darling

101

Mt Burragurry

Talowla Mtn

Toorale East

Mulga

Mt Oxley +309m

OXLEYS TABLELAND

Boorindal

Dwyers

76

Compton Downs

Wave Hill

Wyurta Downs

48

MITCHELL

32

Gongolgon

28

Macquarie

50

6

14

Louth

MT DEERINA

RANGE

RANGE

90

Ben Lomond

Mt Gunderbooka 497m

Mt Wammiga 380m+

104

Creek

43

Byrock

202

34

River

32

25

56

MACQUARIE MARSHES NATURE RESERVE

7

THOOLABOOL RANGE

River

RANKINS

Jinki Lake

Wilga Downs

76

Glenariff

50

71

27

Colossal

Bogan

8

Tilpa Hotel

328

Murtabunna Lake

Mickwilly Lake

96

Mt Booroondara +441m

Mt Buckwaroon 441m

Elura Mine

Dijou Mtn 317m+

159

Mt Merrere 297m

Mt Billagoe 336m+

Coronga Pk 415m

Mulga Dam

Coolabah

71

27

9

260

BARRIER

32

Elsinore

Barnato Lake

84

131

Mount Grenfell Historic Site

Mount Grenfell

Buckwaroon Ck

KIDMAN

55

Mount Drysdale

Girilambone Copper Mine

The Brothers 287m

78

Girilambone

Canonba

Reedy Corner

41

Emmdale Roadhouse

HWY

CSA Copper Mines

Cobar

Boppy Mount

Florida

Summervale

HWY

16

Nyngan

Miowera

10

BARRIER

Peak Gold Mine

McKinnons Gold Project

Canbelego

44

BARRIER

132

43

HWY

Hermidale

32

45

Miandetta

MITCHELL

59

HWY

47

52

Mullengudgery

11

103

KIDMAN

65

Mt Nurri 421m

The Rookery

Buckambool Mtn 407m

Sandy

Creek

65

Mangalore

75

QUANDA NATURE RESERVE

Buddabaddah

Bogan River

Bulbodney

39

12

132

NECKARBOO RANGE

Creek

JACKERMAROO RANGE

Sandy

Creek

Nymagee

31

Nymagee 519m

Ck

THE BALD HILLS

Five Ways

Tottenham

12

20

13

WARNINGS: In outback Australia, long distances separate some towns. Travellers should familiarise themselves with prevailing conditions before departure, and take care to ensure their vehicle is roadworthy and that they carry adequate supplies of petrol, water and food.

In central Australia, rainfall during the "wet" season (Oct-March) can make some roads impassable. Full information on road conditions should be obtained from local authorities before departure.

WAY

Gilgunnia

MERRIMERRIWA RANGE

YATHONG NATURE RESERVE

19

41

Crowl

Creek

TARRAN HILLS

101

Bobadah

Tinda

Yellow Mtn 574m

Meola

Tigers

Albert

J K L M N 19 O P Q R

A B C D 16 E F G H I

1

Mutooroo
Burta
Pine Point
SILVER
Netley
Menindee Lake
Menindee
Cawndilla Lake
KINCHEGA NATIONAL PARK
Tandou Lake
Big Ampi
Wallace Lake
Albemarle
Teryawynia Ck
Glen Ora
Victoria Lake
MANARA HILLS
COBB

2

LANGWELL FLATS
Middle Camp
294
75
Stephens Ck
Redbank Lake
Darling River
Kaleentha Loop
Fruit Fly Exclusion Zone Boundary
Gum Lake
139
Sayers Lake
Manara
Damick
Beilpajah
71

3

Coombah Roadhouse
Coombah Lake
Woolcunda Lake
Popiltah Lake
Popio
Popio Lake
Little Popio
Lake Mindona
Yartla Lake
Darling River
Overnewton
N
133
Mularulu Lake
Corinya
131

4

DANGGALI
CONSERVATION
PARK
Nialia Lake
Wyndham
74
Warrawenia Lake
NEARIE LAKE NATURE RESERVE
Lake Milkengay
Pooncarie
Garnpung Lake
Lake Leaghur
Moornanyah Lake

5

Bunnerungee
79
88
124
Lake Arumpo
MUNGO NATIONAL PARK
Lake Mungo
The Walls of China
Chibnalwood Lakes
The Vale
Hatfield

6

Lake Litra
Lake Victoria
Fletcher Lake
Lake Gol Gol
104
Bunumbar Lake
Oxle

7

Lock 6
Chowilla
Murray River
Lindsay Point
Rufus River
Lock 9
Lock 8
Lock 10
Wentworth
Curlwaa
Dareton
Buronga
Merbein West
Birdwoodton
Merbein South
Merbein
Mildura
Gol Gol
Nicholls Point
Billabong
Irymple
Koorlong
Cardross
Sunny Cliffs
Red Cliffs
Karadoc
MALLEE CLIFFS NATIONAL PARK
Moonlight Lake
Prangle Lakes
69
Pitarpunga Lake
Tin Tin Lake
Penarie
Dundomallee Lake
Ganaway Lake
River
Paringa
Yamba Roadhouse
Taldra
Noora
Morkalla
Karween
Meringur North
Meringur
Cullulleraine
Werrimull
Karawinna
Merrinee
59
53
Yatpool
STURT
117
34
20
STURT
HWY
61
Nangari
Bambill
Carwarp
Nangiloc
Iraak
CALDER
Murray River
80
Lake Benanee
Prill Lake
76
Tunart
Kurnwill
Yarrara
Taplan
Nadda
Meribah
Paruna
SOUTH AUSTRALIA
VICTORIA
Colignan
56
107
HATTAH-KULKYNE NATIONAL PARK
Euston
Robinvale
Balranald
YANGA NATURE RESERVE
211
STUR
Loorica Lake
Lake Talal

8

SUNSET COUNTRY
Rocket Lake
79
Hattah
Beambual River
54
Bannetton
Kyndalyn
MURRAY
Boundary Bend
43
HWY
Weimby
HWY
76

9

Peebinga
PEEBINGA CP
MURRAY - SUNSET NATIONAL PARK
Fruit Fly Exclusion Zone Boundary
Wemen
VICTORIA
109
37
Keelonoong
Goodnight
Kyalite
Natya
HWY
Tooleybuc
VALLEY HWY
84
Moolpa
Perekerten
Lake Lyle
Moulamein

10

Pink Lakes
Mt Gnarr 98m
Kiamil
Ouyen
MALLEE HWY
55
96
112
Mahangatang
Piangil
Wood Wood
Chinkapook
Nyah West
Nyah
Vinifera
Pira
Beverford
Ferry
Lake Wallah
Cunninyeuk
Wakoo Irrigation Area
Linga
Torrita
Walpeup
30
43
Pinnaroo
MALLEE
12
140
Boinka
Underbool
Cowangie
Murrayville
41
MALLEE
Pier Millan
Nandaly
Chillingollah
Woorinen
Swan Hill
Paddlesteamer

11

SCORPION SPRINGS CONSERVATION PARK
70
NGARKAT CP
BIG DESERT
WYPERFELD
Mt Gnarr
Dunt Peak
35
22
Turriff
Speed
Tempy
66
Waitchie
94
79
Lake Tyrrell
Ultima
Lake Boga
Tresco
Mystic Park
16 101
Lake Charm
Murrab
Barha
Koondrook

12

Big Desert Wilderness Park
NATIONAL PARK
For more detailed coverage of localities in Victoria see pages 44 & 45
Patchewollock
Sea Lake
Lascelles
Berriwillock
Woomelang
Culgoa
Lalbert
Ultima
Kerang
Kerang South
Quambatook
26

13

Mt Shaugh 184m
MOUNT SHAUGH CP
WIMMERA
Yaapeet
Kenmare
Rainbow
42
Nethemby
Lake Hindmarsh
Ellam
Brim
107
Beulah
51
Curyo
Nullawil
40
Birchip
106
Dumosa
Wycheproof
Glenloth
Gredgwin
Barraport
Quambatook
Mimmindie
Boort
Durham Ox
Pyra
Mincha

0 20 40 60 80 100 km

J K L M N O P Q R

Column markers: 1 2 3 4 5 6 7 8 9 10 11 12 13

Ivanhoe
Tullamore
Fifield
Condobolin
Ootha
Derriwong
Fairholme
Melrose
Mt Susannah 483m
Derriwong Mtn 414m
YATHONG NATURE RESERVE
KEGINNI RANGE
YARRABUNGARA RANGE
MERRIMERRIWA RANGE
MARODBA RANGE
KAJULIGAN NATURE RESERVE
Conoble Lake
Mossgiel
208
COBB
75
Purcells Lake
Waverley Creek
Willandra Creek
WILLANDRA NATIONAL PARK
Mammarella
Trida
Roto
Warranary Hill 303m
Wee Elwah
Lowlands
Mount Hope
Mt Allen 518m
Matakana
BROKEN RANGE
WALTERS RANGE
Burthong
WALTERS RANGE
Mt Urambie 371m
Mt Tallebung 458m
Tallebung
CREAMY HILLS
Mt Nobby 325m
WOGGOON NATURE RESERVE
Gunebang
Mt Filga 329m
91
MOONEE RANGE
NOMBINNIE NATURE RESERVE
NOMBINNIE NATURE RESERVE
KIDMAN WAY
Warraway Hill 272m
Euabalong West
Euabalong
Lachlan River
Lake Cargelligo
Lake Cargelligo
Burgooney
Tullibigeal
Banar Lake
Bogandillon Swamp
Manna Mtn 552m
Nerang Cowal
Lake Cowal
Hillston
Lake Brewster
LOUGHNAN NAT RES
Boothgandra Mtn
Naradhan
Hannan
Gubbata
Kikoira
Thulloo
Gibsonvale
Ungarie
GUBBATA NATURE RES
Mt Bypalore 422m
Weja
Bena
Winnunga
Wamboyne
Wamboyne Mtn 412m
Corringle
Burcher
Langtree
Goorawin
Merriwagga
Allawah
Girral
Calleen
Wyrra
Marsden
Clear Ridge
Rankins Springs
WESTERN HWY
24
Boundary
Nariah Mtn 481m
Yalgogrin North
Erigolia
Eupalta
Weethalle
West Wyalong
Wyalong
Bland
257
Gunbar
Goolgowi
PULLETOP NAT RES
COCOPARRA NAT RES
COCOPARRA RANGE
Tallimba
LIVE CHARCOAL TANK NAT RES
BODIGOWER NAT RES
Buddigower
Alleena
Barmedman
Booligal
Gunbar South
Tabbita
Barren Box Swamp
Mt Ariah 424m
COCOPARRA NATIONAL PARK
Bingar Mtn 455m
Brogden Mtn 399m
Bolero Mtn 391m
Yalgogrin South
Bellarwi
Reefton
BOGINDEROO NAT RES
BIG BUSH NAT RES
Gidginbung
One Tree
Beelbangera
Yenda
Binya
Tharbogang
Bilbul
Yoogali
Barellan
Kamarah
Mirrool
Beckom
Ariah Park
Quandary
PUCAWAN NAT RES
Griffith
Hanwood
Murrumbidgee Irrigation Area
Moombooldool
Ardlethan
Mt Beckham 374m
Tara
INGALBA NAT RES
Temora
Carrathool
Murrami
Leeton
Yanco
Colinroobie
134
Cowabbie West
Methul
Mimosa
Sebastopol
Maude
Hay
STURT HWY
Bringagee
Willbriggie
Whitton
Wamoon
45
NEWELL
Rannock
North Berry Jerry
168
Darlington Point
Waddi
Tombullen Storage
Dry Lake
Goonerah Lagoon
Cuddell
22
Narrandera
Grong Grong
Matong
Dullah
Ganmain
Marrar
Old Junee
Junee
Booroorban
Robertson Lake
Eurolie Dam
54
Coleambally
Coleambally Irrigation Area
Corobimilla
NARRANDERA NAT RES
Sandigo
Mt Galore 378m
Millwood
Dhurra
Wallacetown
Downside
Hanwood
Wagga Wagga
Wangenella
120
COBB
Yanco Creek
Morundah
Birrego
Widgiewa
Boree Creek
Kywong
143
Currawarna
Collingullie
Oura
Gumly Gumly
Conargo
Coonong
Bundure
Lake Urana
Lake Cullival
Lockhart
Milbrulong
TWE ROCK NAT RES
Osbourne
Kapooka
Uranquinty
Forest Hill
Ladysmith
Alfred Town
Burraboi
Wakool
Dahwilly
Coree South
Jerilderie
Mayrung
Logie Brae
Berrigan Irrigation Area
Myall Plains
Urana
Urangong Creek
Ferndale
Pleasant Hills
Yerong Creek
Henty
Burpandana
Kyeamba
The Rock
Mt Flakney 536m
Mahgoplah
Deniliquin
RIVERINA HWY
Blighty
Finley
NEWELL
Bleasie
Berrigan
203
Oaklands
Rand
Alma Park
Urangeline East
Cookardinia
Little Billabong
Mangandja
Holbrook
151
Bunnaloo
74
Mathoura
BARMAN STATE PARK
Strathmerton
Tocumwal
39
Savernake
Rennie
Coreen
Sangar
Daysdale
Bullanginy
Walbundrie
Walla Walla
Coreen
Geogery
Geogery West
TABLE TOP NAT RES
Cutcairn
Morven
Woomargama
Lankeys Creek
Talmalmo
Leitchville
Gunbower
Womboota
Picola North
Picola
106
Ulupna
Cobram
Barooga
Lowesdale
Buraja
Balldale
Burrumbuttock
Jindera
Howlong
MOUNT LAWSON STATE PARK
Echuca
Moama
Torrumbarry
Barmah
Nathalia
Katunga
VICTORIA
Numurkah
Yarrawonga
Mulwala
Corowa
Wahgunyah
Rutherglen
Albury
Wodonga
Bandiana
Bethanga
Kotupna
Wunghnu
Invergordon
Youanmite
Tungamah
Wilby
Bundalong
Brimin
16
Chiltern
Barnawartha
Chiltern Valley
Bonegilla
Wirlinga
Ettamogah
Bellbrdi
Lake Hume

46 47

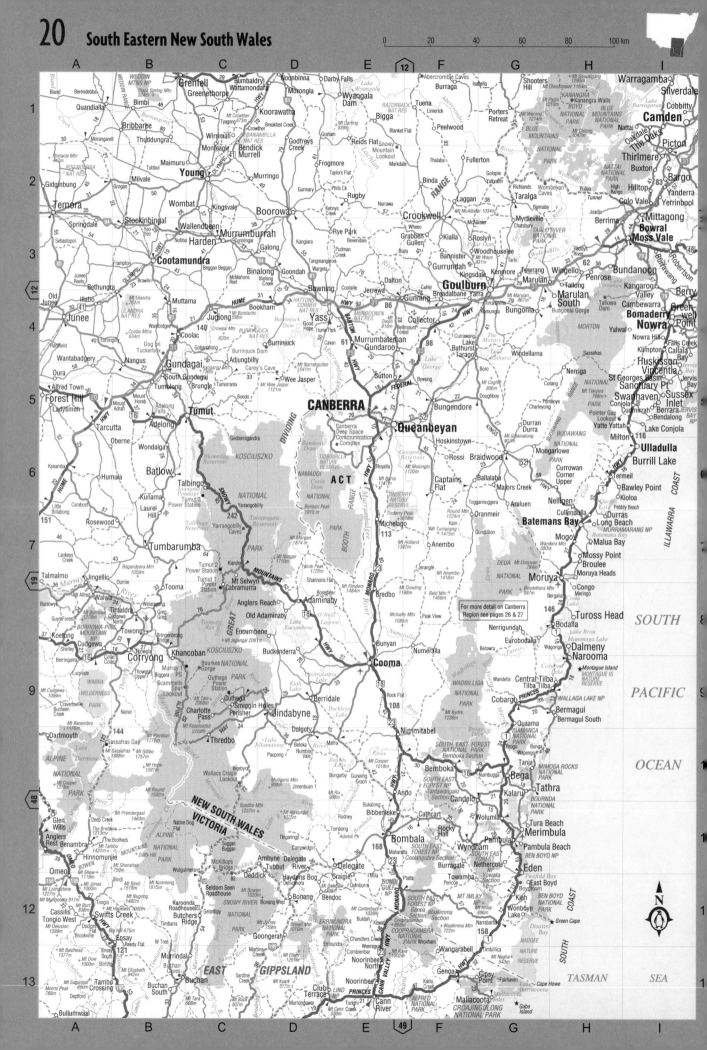

TOURIST INFORMATION:
The Entrance (Memorial Park, Marine Pde)
Gorokan (Wallarah Point Park, Wallarah Rd)
Gosford (200 Mann St)
Terrigal (Rotary Park, Terrigal Dr)

0 2 4 6 8 10 km

PELICAN FEEDING: This unique attraction occurs each afternoon around 3.30pm near the children's playground in the Memorial Park at The Entrance.

NATIONAL PARKS: At **Wyrrabalong** swimming is possible at either Bateau Bay or Tuggerah Beach; waterbirds are a feature. **Bouddi** is renowned for its established walking trails and at Maitland Bay, there is a shipwreck half submerged on the beach. **Brisbane Water** offers spectacular water views and has many fine Aboriginal art sites. Further west, **Dharug** lines the river and has a popular family walking trail.

GREAT NORTH WALK: A section of this 250 km walking track, which runs between Sydney and Newcastle, passes through the region. There are numerous access points, facilities and connections to public transport enabling families, campers and day trippers to enjoy day and weekend walks.

SAFE BOATING:
Tell someone where you are going.
Carry adequate equipment.
Carry effective life jackets.
Carry enough fuel and water.
Ensure engine reliability.
Guard against fire.
Do not overload the craft.
Know the boating rules and local regulations; also distress signals.
Watch the weather.
Do not drink alcohol while boating.

HAWKESBURY RIVER: A magnificent waterway navigable as far as Windsor and further for small craft. There are few settlements along the widest section of the river as most of the shore is protected as part of Brisbane Water and Ku-ring-gai Chase National Parks.

RIVERBOAT POSTMAN: Visitors can join the river mail-boat run which leaves the ferry wharf at Dangar Rd Brooklyn on weekdays. It takes three hours, ferrying mail, groceries and other necessities to residents with no road access.

Wyong
Wyong Creek
Yarramalong
Kulnura
Central Mangrove
Peats Ridge
Mangrove Mountain
Mangrove Creek
Lower Mangrove
Glenworth Valley
Somersby
Palm Grove
Palm Dale
Ourimbah
Lisarow
Niagara Park
Narara
Wyoming
Gosford
Kariong
Point Clare
Tascott
Koolewong
Saratoga
Davistown
Empire Bay
St Huberts Island
Woy Woy
Ettalong Beach
Umina
Wagstaffe
Killcare
Killcare Heights
Kincumber
Green Point
Erina
Wamberal
Terrigal
Matcham
Holgate
Tumbi Umbi
Bateau Bay
Toowoon Bay
Long Jetty
The Entrance
The Entrance North
Forresters Beach
North Avoca
Avoca Beach
MacMasters Beach
Copacabana
Pearl Beach
Patonga
Brooklyn
Mooney Mooney
Mount White
Spencer
Cowan
Berowra Heights
Berowra Waters
Palm Beach
Whale Beach
Avalon
Newport
Newport Beach
Bayview
Mona Vale

Tuggerah Lake
Tuggerah
Lion Island Nature Reserve
Broken Bay
Pittwater
Barrenjoey Lighthouse

TO NEWCASTLE
TO SYDNEY
PACIFIC HWY
SYDNEY NEWCASTLE FWY

TASMAN SEA
SOUTH PACIFIC OCEAN

Australian Capital Territory

Location Map

Other Map Coverage
Central Canberra 23
Canberra Region 26

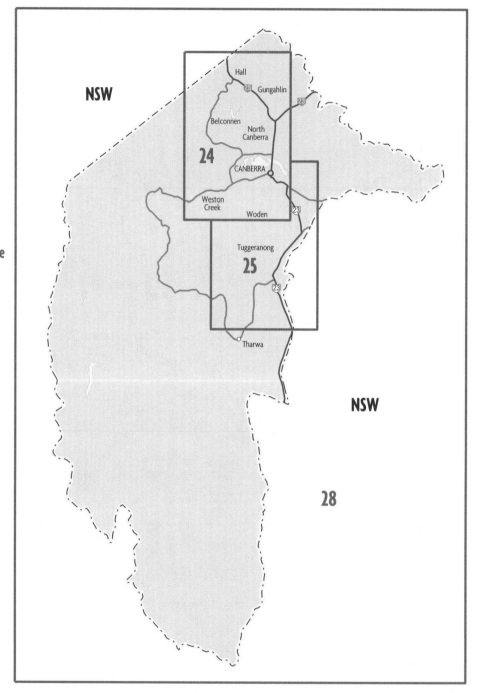

NSW

Hall
Gungahlin
Belconnen
North
Canberra
24
CANBERRA
Weston
Creek
Woden
Tuggeranong
25
Tharwa

NSW

28

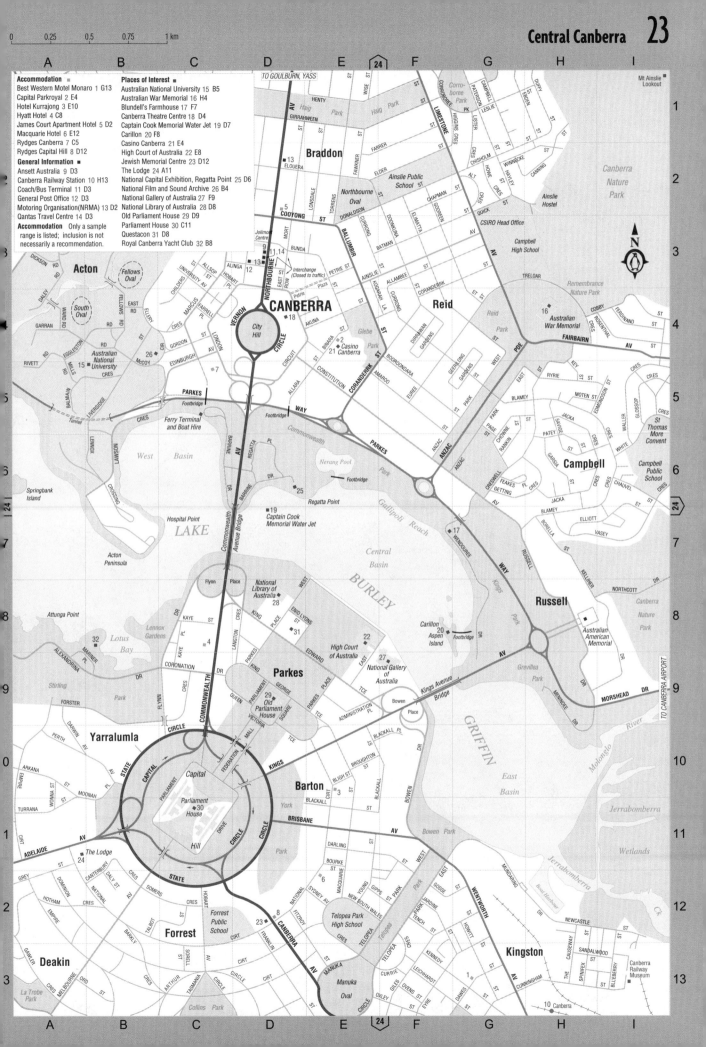

0   1   2   3 km

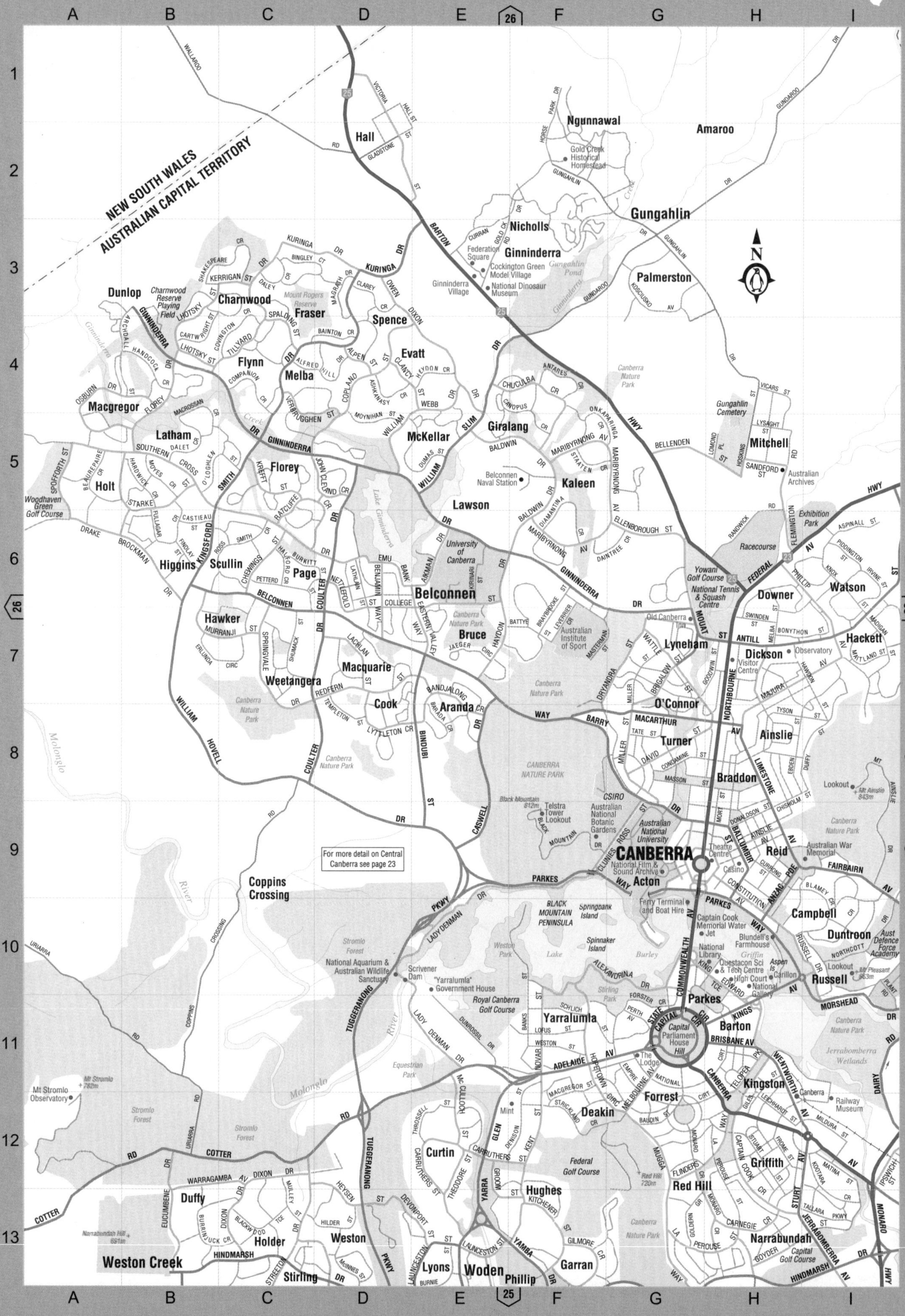

NEW SOUTH WALES
AUSTRALIAN CAPITAL TERRITORY

Hall

Ngunnawal
Amaroo
Gungahlin
Nicholls
Ginninderra
Palmerston
Mitchell

Dunlop
Charnwood
Fraser
Spence
Evatt
Flynn
Melba
McKellar
Giralang
Macgregor
Kaleen
Latham
Florey
Holt
Lawson
Higgins
Scullin
Page
Belconnen
Hawker
Bruce
Weetangera
Macquarie
Cook
Aranda
Downer
Watson
Hackett
Lyneham
Dickson
O'Connor
Turner
Ainslie
Braddon
Reid
CANBERRA
Acton
Campbell
Duntroon
Russell
Coppins
Crossing

For more detail on Central
Canberra see page 23

University
of Canberra

Australian
Institute
of Sport

Telstra
Tower
Lookout
Australian
National
Botanic
Gardens
Australian
National
University
National Film &
Sound Archive

Parkes
Yarralumla
Barton
Kingston
Griffith
Forrest
Deakin
Red Hill
Narrabundah
Hughes
Garran
Curtin
Duffy
Holder
Weston
Stirling
Lyons
Woden
Phillip
Weston Creek

Mt Stromlo
Observatory

National Aquarium &
Australian Wildlife
Sanctuary

Scrivener
Dam
"Yarralumla"
Government House
Royal Canberra
Golf Course

Canberra Nature Park

Australian War
Memorial
Fairbairn

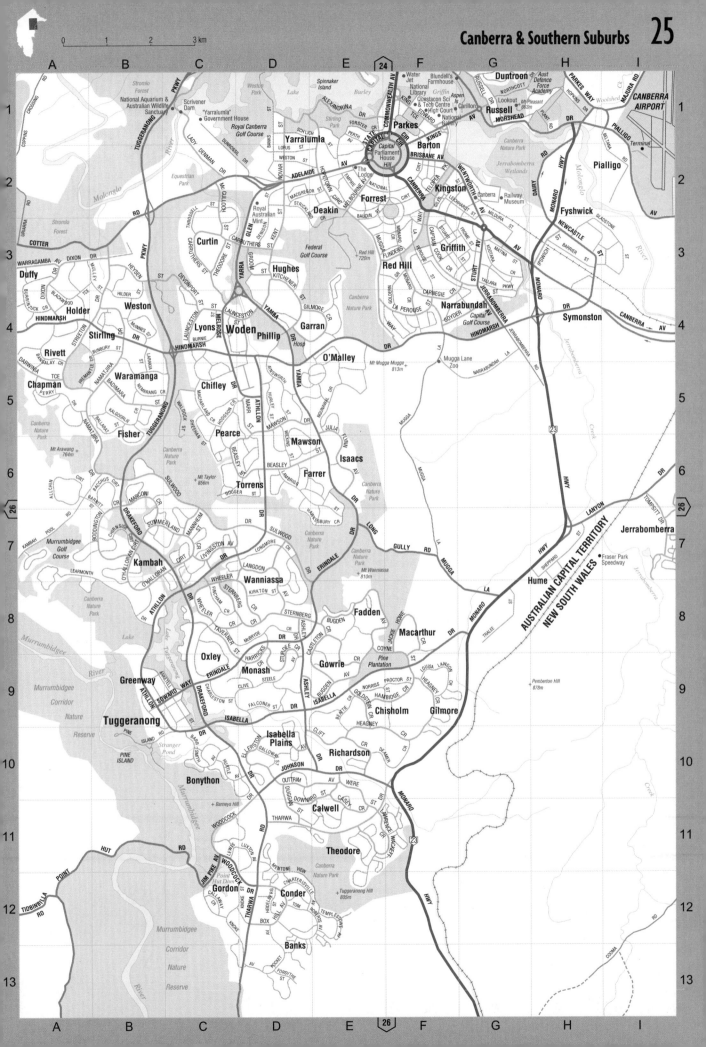

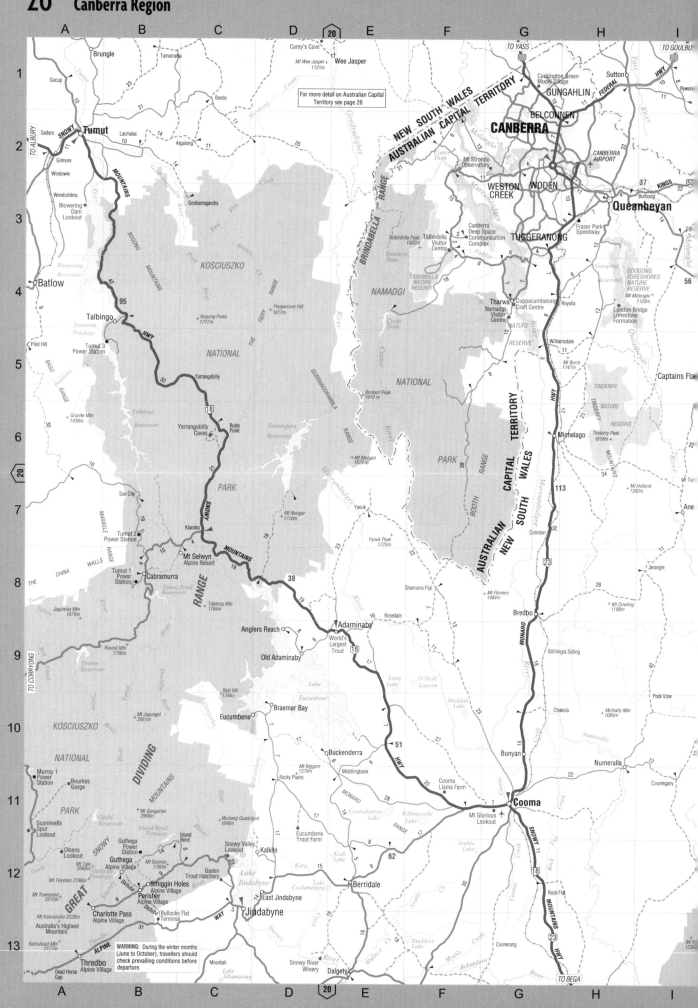

For more detail on Australian Capital
Territory see page 28

WARNING: During the winter months
(June to October), travellers should
check prevailing conditions before
departure.

0 5 10 15 20 km

J K L M N O P Q R

RANGE

KINGS

MORTON

Klimpton TO NOWRA

Callala Bay

Boro

Mt Fairy

Nerriga

Sassafras

+ Mt Sassafras 823m

Huskisson

Tomerong

Vincentia

St Georges Basin

Wandandian

Hyams Beach

Sanctuary Point

JERVIS BAY TERRITORY

Jervis Bay

Green Patch

Butmaroo

Doughboy

HWY

52

Lower Boro

Corang

NATIONAL

+ Mt Tianjara 768m

HWY

Sussex Inlet

endore

22

Charleyong

Tomboye

+ Mt Corang 863m

PARK

Swan Lake

Conjola

Swanhaven

Cudmirrah

Berrara

49

KINGS

DIVIDING

Durran Durra

RIVER

+ Mt Corang

St Georges Basin

PRINCES

Bendalong

Manyana

Cunjurong Point

Lake Conjola

JERVIS BAY NATIONAL PARK

Pointer Gap Lookout

+ Pigeon House Mtn 719m

Yatte Yattah

Narrawallee

Rossi

+ Mt Gillamatong 907m

Braidwood Historic Town

Mongarlowe

BUDAWANG

Milton

COAST

Mollymook

nstown

14

Currockbilly Mtn 823m

NATIONAL

Ulladulla

GREAT

52

23

14

8

Burrill Lake

ILLAWARRA

Ballalaba

11

Majors Creek

Reidsdale

Monga

59

Mt Mogood 391m

Burrill Lake

Currowan Corner Upper

Shallow Crossing

HWY

12

Termeil

DIVIDING

15

Araluen North

Araluen

Bawley Point

MURRAMARANG ABORIGINAL RESERVE

Togannoggera

Round Mtn 1224m

24

HWY

East Lynne

Kioloa

Oranmeir

Nelligen

Benandarah

Pebbly Beach

Kain

16

The Big Hole and Marble Arch Gundillion

Runnyford

PRINCES

Cullendulla

Depot Beach

Durras

+ 1419m

DEUA

Batemans Bay

Shell Museum

Batehaven

Long Beach

MURRAMARANG NATIONAL PARK

Mt Anembo 1416m

Wandera Mtn 580m

Mt Donovan 784m

Mogo

Surf Beach

Batemans Bay

SOUTH

Mtn 5m

NATIONAL

27

Bimbimbie

Malua Bay

Rosedale

Badja Mill

Mogendoura

Tomakin

Mossy Point

Yarragee

Gundary

Mullenderee

Broulee

PACIFIC

Moruya

Moruya Heads

Kiora

The Anchorage

Congo

COAST

OCEAN

PARK

Bergalia

Meringo

Turlinjah

42

Lake Tuross

Tuross Head

Bodalla

Nerrigundah

Potato Point

Eurobodalla

SOUTH

Belowra

Dalmeny

Kianga

Narooma

WADBILLIGA

BODALLA

STATE

Mummuga Lake

Lake Brou

Tilba Valley Vineyard Deer Park

Corunna Lake

Montague Island

MONTAGUE IS NATURE RESERVE

NATIONAL

Yowrie

Wandella

Mt Dromedary Peak Alone 954m

FOREST

Central Tilba Historic Village

Corunna

HWY

Tilba Tilba

GOURA NAT RES

Tilba Tilba Lake

EUROBODALLA NATIONAL PARK

N

PARK

Cobargo

WALLAGA LAKE NP

Wallaga Lake

18

PRINCES

20

Bermagui

Bermagui South

TO BEGA

20

Quaama

BERMAGUEE NATURE RESERVE

J K L M N O P Q R

0   5   10   15   20 km

For more detail on Canberra
Suburbs see pages 24 & 25

CANBERRA

BRINDABELLA RANGE

NEW SOUTH WALES
AUSTRALIAN CAPITAL TERRITORY

Mt Narranguller
1041 m

Murrumbidgee River

Surveyors Hill
736 m

Cockington Green
Model Village

GUNGAHLIN

Talaganda Hill
668 m

Sutton

Lake George

Bywong

BELCONNEN

Lake Ginninderra

Black Mtn
812m

Mt Ainslie
843m

CANBERRA
AIRPORT

Bungendore

Mt Blundall
1047 m

Cotter
Dam

STROMLO
FOREST

Mt Stromlo
Observatory

URIARRA RD

WESTON
CREEK

WODEN

Lake Burley Griffin

KINGS

Queanbeyan

Balcombe Hill
953 m

Radio
Telescope

COTTER

PADDYS RIVER RD

Mt Mugga Mugga
811m

Mt Wanniassa
810m

Burtong

CAPTAINS FLAT

Murrumbidgee River

MURRUMBIDGEE CORRIDOR

Lake Tuggeranong

Fraser Park Speedway

Jerrabomberra Hill
382m

Hoskinstown

TIDBINBILLA
NATURE
RESERVE

Tidbinbilla Peak
1562m

Canberra Deep Space
Communication Complex

TUGGERANONG

Googong
Reservoir

GOOGONG
FORESHORES
NATURE
RESERVE

Mt Molonglo
1120m

Tidbinbilla Visitor
Centre

NATURE

Bendora
Dam

BRINDABELLA RANGE

NAMADGI

Mt Ginini

Gibraltar Falls

RESERVE

Lanyon
Homestead

Royalla

London Bridge
Limestone Formation

CORIN

Tharwa

Cuppacumbalong
Craft Centre

Corin
Dam

Mt McKeahnie

Namadgi
Visitor
Centre

Williamsdale

WILLIAMSDALE RD

Captains Flat

Horseshoe Hill
1143 m

Cooleman Caves

NATIONAL

Bimberi Peak
1910 m

Mt Burra
1147m

TINDERRY
NATURE
RESERVE

Mt Michelago
1090m

GUDGENBY RAMBLA

KOSCIUSZKO

RANGE

Mt Woolpack
1227 m

NATIONAL

PARK

Mt Morgan
1874 m

AUSTRALIAN CAPITAL TERRITORY
NEW SOUTH WALES

Michelago

Tinderry Peak
1618m

Mt Holland
1392 m

PARK

Shanahans Mtn

Anembo

Numerous Timber
Tracks

Yaouk

Sentry Box Mtn
1674m

Colinton

Colinton Hill
1133 m

Yaouk Peak
1725m

YAOUK BILL RANGE

Jerangle

N

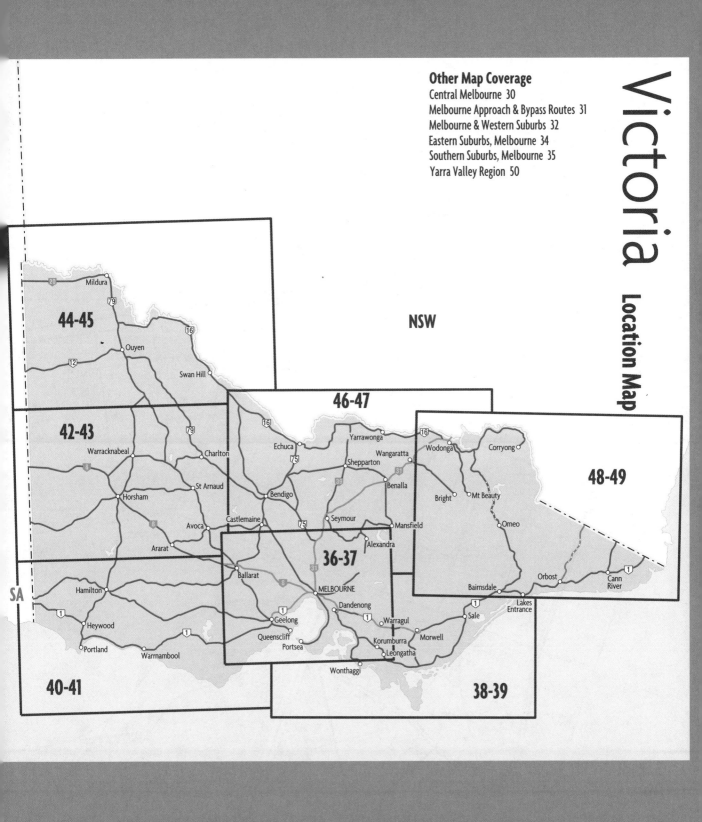

Victoria Location Map

Other Map Coverage
Central Melbourne 30
Melbourne Approach & Bypass Routes 31
Melbourne & Western Suburbs 32
Eastern Suburbs, Melbourne 34
Southern Suburbs, Melbourne 35
Yarra Valley Region 50

NSW

SA

44-45

42-43

46-47

48-49

36-37

40-41

38-39

Mildura
Ouyen
Swan Hill
Warracknabeal
Charlton
Echuca
Yarrawonga
Wangaratta
Wodonga
Corryong
Horsham
St Arnaud
Bendigo
Shepparton
Benalla
Bright
Mt Beauty
Avoca
Castlemaine
Seymour
Mansfield
Omeo
Ararat
Alexandra
Ballarat
MELBOURNE
Bairnsdale
Orbost
Cann River
Hamilton
Dandenong
Sale
Lakes Entrance
Heywood
Geelong
Warragul
Portland
Queenscliff
Portsea
Korumburra
Morwell
Warrnambool
Leongatha
Wonthaggi

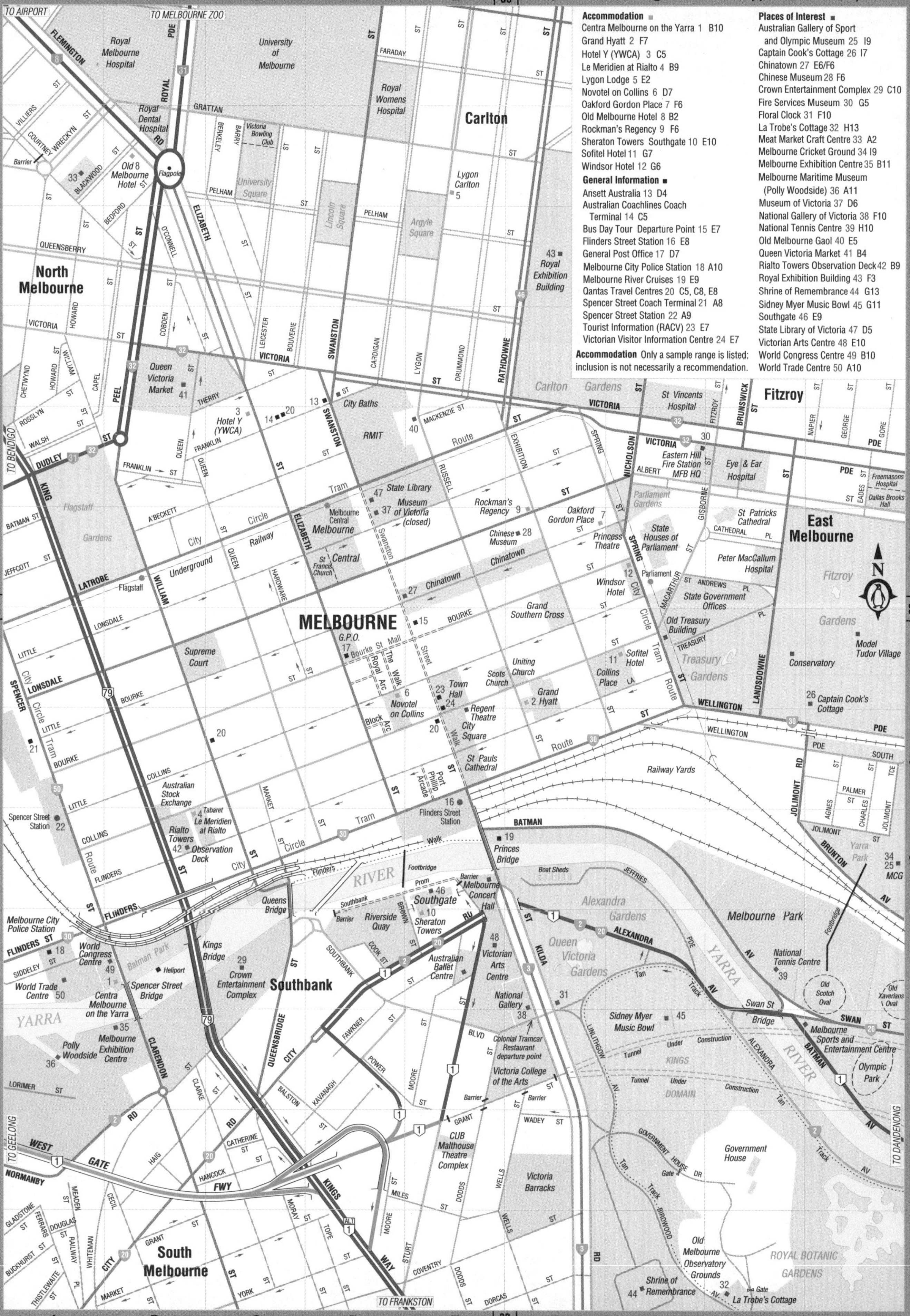

0
0.25
0.5
0.75
1 km
Accommodation
Centra Melbourne on the Yarra 1 B10
Grand Hyatt 2 F7
Hotel Y (YWCA) 3 C5
Le Meridien at Rialto 4 B9
Lygon Lodge 5 E2
Novotel on Collins 6 D7
Oakford Gordon Place 7 F6
Old Melbourne Hotel 8 B2
Rockman's Regency 9 F6
Sheraton Towers Southgate 10 E10
Sofitel Hotel 11 G7
Windsor Hotel 12 G6
General Information
Ansett Australia 13 D4
Australian Coachlines Coach Terminal 14 C5
Bus Day Tour Departure Point 15 E7
Flinders Street Station 16 E8
General Post Office 17 D7
Melbourne City Police Station 18 A10
Melbourne River Cruises 19 E9
Qantas Travel Centres 20 C5, C8, E8
Spencer Street Coach Terminal 21 A8
Spencer Street Station 22 A9
Tourist Information (RACV) 23 E7
Victorian Visitor Information Centre 24 E7
Accommodation Only a sample range is listed; inclusion is not necessarily a recommendation.
Places of Interest
Australian Gallery of Sport and Olympic Museum 25 I9
Captain Cook's Cottage 26 I7
Chinatown 27 E6/F6
Chinese Museum 28 F6
Crown Entertainment Complex 29 C10
Fire Services Museum 30 G5
Floral Clock 31 F10
La Trobe's Cottage 32 H13
Meat Market Craft Centre 33 A2
Melbourne Cricket Ground 34 I9
Melbourne Exhibition Centre 35 B11
Melbourne Maritime Museum (Polly Woodside) 36 A11
Museum of Victoria 37 D6
National Gallery of Victoria 38 F10
National Tennis Centre 39 H10
Old Melbourne Gaol 40 E5
Queen Victoria Market 41 B4
Rialto Towers Observation Deck 42 B9
Royal Exhibition Building 43 F3
Shrine of Remembrance 44 G13
Sidney Myer Music Bowl 45 G11
Southgate 46 E9
State Library of Victoria 47 D5
Victorian Arts Centre 48 E10
World Congress Centre 49 B10
World Trade Centre 50 A10
Carlton
North Melbourne
Fitzroy
East Melbourne
MELBOURNE
Southbank
South Melbourne
TO AIRPORT
TO MELBOURNE ZOO
TO BENDIGO
TO GEELONG
TO FRANKSTON
TO DANDENONG

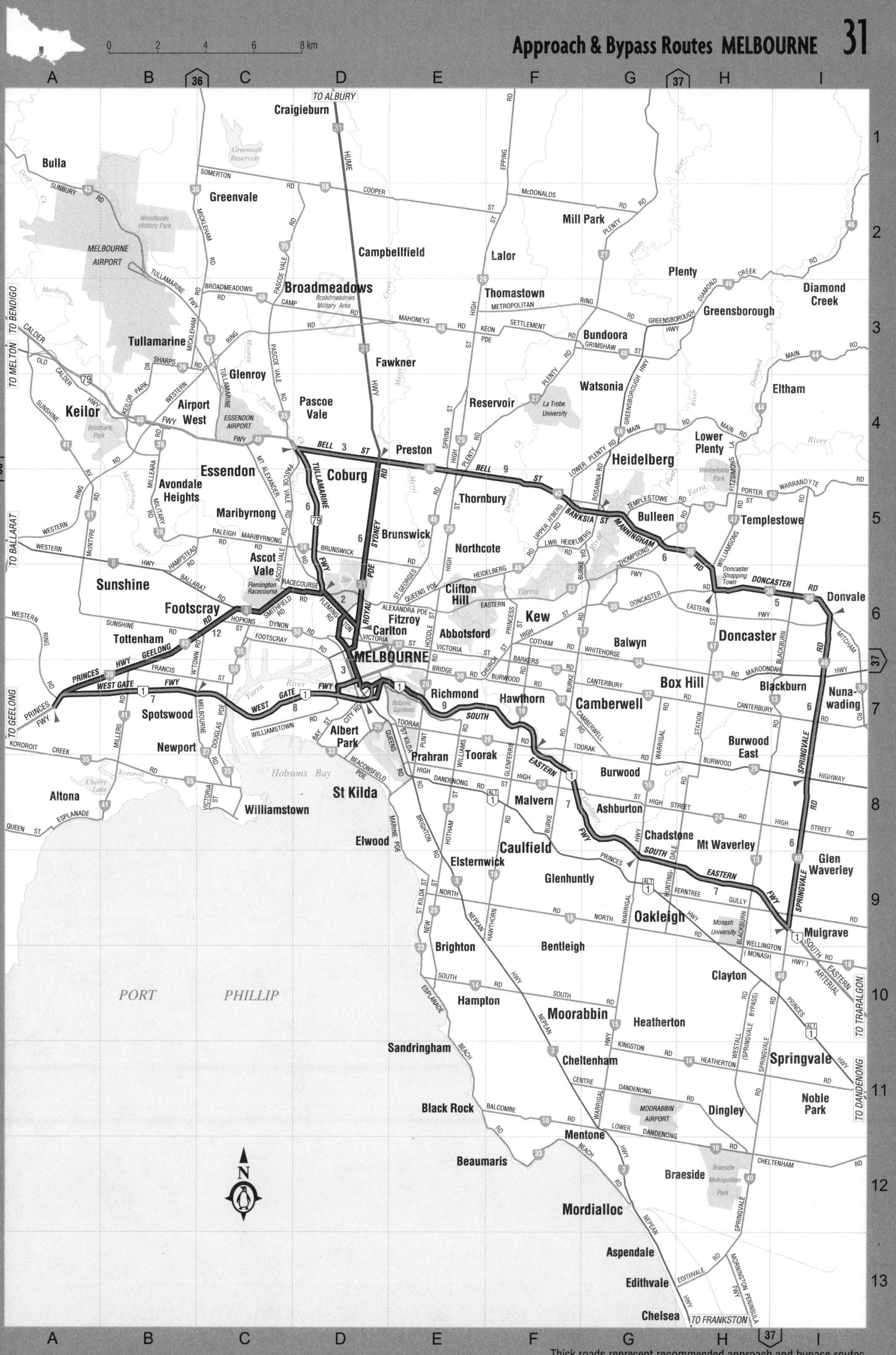

0 2 4 6 8 km
TO ALBURY
Craigieburn
Bulla
Greenvale
Mill Park
Campbellfield
Lalor
MELBOURNE AIRPORT
Broadmeadows
Thomastown
Plenty
Diamond Creek
Greensborough
Tullamarine
Bundoora
Fawkner
Watsonia
Eltham
Glenroy
Keilor
Airport West
Pascoe Vale
Reservoir
La Trobe University
Lower Plenty
Preston
Heidelberg
Essendon
Coburg
Avondale Heights
Thornbury
Bulleen
Templestowe
Maribyrnong
Brunswick
Northcote
Ascot Vale
Flemington Racecourse
Sunshine
Clifton Hill
Donvale
Footscray
Fitzroy
Carlton
Kew
Tottenham
Abbotsford
Balwyn
Doncaster
Doncaster Shopping Town
MELBOURNE
Box Hill
Blackburn
Nunawading
Richmond
Hawthorn
Camberwell
Spotswood
Newport
Albert Park
Prahran
Toorak
Burwood
Burwood East
Altona
Williamstown
Hobsons Bay
St Kilda
Malvern
Ashburton
Chadstone
Mt Waverley
Glen Waverley
Elwood
Caulfield
Elsternwick
Glenhuntly
Oakleigh
Monash University
Mulgrave
Brighton
Bentleigh
Clayton
PORT PHILLIP
Hampton
Moorabbin
Heatherton
Sandringham
Cheltenham
Springvale
Black Rock
Moorabbin Airport
Dingley
Noble Park
Mentone
Beaumaris
Braeside
Braeside Metropolitan Park
Mordialloc
Aspendale
Edithvale
Chelsea
TO FRANKSTON
TO BENDIGO
TO MELTON
TO BALLARAT
TO GEELONG
TO TRARALGON
TO DANDENONG
HUME HWY
SYDNEY RD
BELL ST
TULLAMARINE FWY
WEST GATE FWY
PRINCES HWY
GEELONG RD
SOUTH EASTERN FWY
BANKSIA ST
MANNINGHAM ST
DONCASTER RD
SPRINGVALE RD
ROYAL PDE
NEPEAN HWY
MORNINGTON PENINSULA FWY

0 2 4 6 8 km

J K L M N O P Q R

1 2 3 4 5 6 34 7 8 9 10 11 12 13

Coolaroo
Campbellfield
Epping
Mill Park
South Morang
Kurrak
Wattle Glen
Upfield
Lalor
Plenty
Diamond Creek Reserve
Diamond Creek
Kangaroo Ground
Broadmeadows Military Area
Thomastown
RMIT Bundoora West Campus
Janefield Training Centre
Greensborough
Greensborough Plaza Shopping Centre
Research Park
Research
Warrandyte
Fawkner
Kingsbury
Bundoora
Bundoora Park Golf Course
Bundoora Repatriation Hospital
Grimshaw
Watsonia
St Helena
Greensborough
Montmorency
Eltham
Fawkner Crematorium and Memorial Park
Larundal Psychiatric Hospital
La Trobe University
Macleod Repatriation Hospital
Macleod
Simpson Army Barracks
Yallambie
Heidelberg Golf Course
Lower Plenty
Miniature Steam Trains
Coburg
Pentridge Prison
RMIT Coburg Campus
Reservoir
Preston
Northland Shopping Centre
Olympic Park
Heidelberg West
Rosanna
View Bank
Heidelberg
Rosanna Golf Course
Westerfolds Park
Eltham Lower Park
Warrandyte State Park
Brunswick West
Thornbury
Northcote Municipal Golf Course
Heidelberg Repatriation Hospital
Austin Hospital
Templestowe
Brunswick
Northcote
Ivanhoe
Banksia
John Cain Memorial Park
Bulleen
Lower Templestowe
Flemington
Fitzroy Nth
Parkville
Clifton Hill
Fairfield
Ivanhoe Public Golf Course
Camberwell Golf Course
Yarra Valley Country Club Golf Course
Doncaster
Doncaster East
Park Orchards
Zoological Gardens
Melbourne General Cemetery
Yarra Bend Golf Course
Greenacres Golf Course
Kew Golf Course
Westfield Doncaster Shopping Town
Donvale
Carlton
Collingwood
Abbotsford
Yarra Bend
Kew
Balwyn North
Eastern Golf Course
Doncaster Reserve
MELBOURNE
Richmond
Hawthorn
Balwyn
Box Hill
Nunawading
North Melbourne
Burnley Golf Course
Camberwell
Canterbury
Mont Albert
Box Hill Cemetery
Blackburn
Mitcham
South Melbourne
Kooyong
Surrey Hills
Forest Hill Chase Shopping Centre
Vermont
Port Melbourne
Albert Park
South Yarra
Deakin University Burwood Campus
Box Hill Golf Course
Burwood East
Forest Hill
Middle Park
Prahran
Toorak
Glen Iris
Ashwood
Burwood
Morack Golf Course
St Kilda
Armadale
Ashburton
Mt Waverley
Williamstown
Malvern
Malvern Valley Public Golf Course
Riverdale Golf Course
Syndal The Glen Shopping Centre
Elwood
Caulfield
Glen Huntly
Carnegie
Chadstone
Glen Waverley
Elsternwick
Ormond
Glen Huntly
Murrumbeena
Oakleigh East
Waverley Municipal Golf Course
McKinnon
Oakleigh
Notting Hill
Monash University
Wheelers Hill
Brighton
Bentleigh
Monash Medical Centre
Mulgrave

For more detail on Central Melbourne see page 30

0   2   4   6   8 km

Grid references: A B C D E F G H I / 1 2 3 4 5 6 7 8 9 10 11 12 13

Hurstbridge

Panton Hill

CHERRY TREE RD

Rob Roy

GLEN YARRA

Christmas Hills

STEELS CREEK RD

Historic Gulf Station

OLD HEALESVILLE

Wattle Glen

ST ANDREWS RD

KANGAROO GROUND RD

Watsons Creek

ELTHAM YARRA GLEN RD

ELTHAM

Sugarloaf Reservoir Park

Ridge Park

Melbourne Water

Yarra Glen

Yarra Valley Racing Centre   HEALESVILLE

Yarra Glen Recreation Reserve

YARRA GLEN RD

KANGAROO GROUND

DAWSON

KANGAROO GROUND

WATTLE GLEN

Kangaroo Ground

ELTHAM YARRA GLEN RD

Sugarloaf Reservoir

Maroondah

Yering

HWY

REYNOLDS

MAIN RD

Research

RESEARCH

KANGAROO GROUND RD

WARRANDYTE STATE PARK

Yarra

HENLEY

SKYLINE

COLDSTREAM RD

WEST

LILYDALE AIRFIELD

MACINTYRE

St Huberts RD

MAROONDAH

INGRAMS

Research Park

WARRANDYTE STATE PARK

Creek

PAYNES RD

BRADLEY RD

KILLARA

Coldstream

COLDSTREAM AIRFIELD

Gruyere

JUMPING CREEK RD

Wonga Park

Chirnside Park

SWITCHBACK RD

Chirnside Park Golf Course

BERESFORD

CAVE HILL RD

MELBA HWY

WARBURTON

Warrandyte

WARRANDYTE STATE PARK

WARRANDYTE RD

The 100 Acres

Chirnside Park Shopping Centre

EDWARD

MAROONDAH

Lilydale

HEREFORD

174

Stringybark

YARRA ST

42

REYNOLDS RD

TINDALS RD

HARRIS GULLY

KNEES RD

FALCONER

CROYDON RD WONGA RD

Croydon Hills

YARRA RD

PLYMOUTH

Mooroolbark

BELLARA DR

Barngeong Reserve

MOOROOLBARK

Lilydale Lake

Olinda

33

Park Orchards

OLD WARRANDYTE RD

STINTONS RD

Croydon Golf Course

EXETER RD

MANCHESTER RD

HULL RD

Olinda Reservoir

BIRMINGHAM RD

Mt Evelyn

CLEGG RD

Wandin North

Seville

Donvale

WARRANDYTE RINGWOOD RD

OBAN

WONGA

KENT AV

LINCOLN RD

CROYDON

Croydon

MT DANDENONG

O'Shannassy

Quinn Reserve

SWANSEA RD

Wandin Yallock

SPRINGVALE

PARK

WICKLOW AV

HULL RD

DURHAM RD   CAMBRIDGE

Kilsyth

LIVERPOOL

MT DANDENONG TOURIST RD

YORK

Mt Evelyn Recreation Camp

MONBULK RD

Eastland Shopping Centre

EASTFIELD

Croydon Public Golf Course

Montrose

Views

Department of Conservation and Natural Resources

Kalorama

Silvan

MITCHAM

LOUGHNAN RD

RINGWOOD ST

BEDFORD RD

Ringwood East

DORSET RD

CANTERBURY RD

Bungalook

Mt Dandenong 633m Lookout

Ricketts Sanctuary

RANGES

OLINDA

Melbourne Water Reserve

SEVILLE RD

Melbourne Water Mitcham Reservoir

Mitcham

Ringwood

Heathmont

HEATHERDALE

GREAT RYRIE ST

Ringwood Golf Course

BAYSWATER RD

Eastwood Golf Course

COLCHESTER RD

Burkes Lookout Reserve

DANDENONG RANGES NATIONAL PARK

Olinda Falls

Rhododendron Gardens

Olinda Public Golf Course

RJ Hamer Forest Arboretum

Vermont

Forest Hill

CANTERBURY RD

WANTIRNA RD

Dandenong Creek

MOUNTAIN HWY

POWER RD

Liverpool Road Retarding Basin

MOUNTAIN RD

The Basin

Mt Dandenong

OLINDA

FOREST

TERRARA

BORONIA RD

Morack Golf Course

Bayswater

OLIVE GV

MILLER RD

Olinda

Sassafras

SASSAFRAS RD

PERRINS RD

MONBULK RD

Emerald

Monbulk

Glen Waverley

Waverley Municipal Golf Course

Knox City Shopping Centre

STUD RD

BURWOOD HWY

Wantirna

BORONIA RD

Boronia

ALBERT

FOREST RD

BASIN RD

Lookout Tower One Tree Hill 502m

DANDENONG RANGES NATIONAL PARK

Ferny Creek

Alfred Nicholas Memorial Gardens

SHERBROOKE

Sherbrooke

Monbulk Recreation Reserve

MACCLESFIELD RD

Jells Park Wildlife Lake

HIGH STREET

CATHIES

GEORGE ST

STUD RD (DANDENONG VALLEY HWY)

SCORESBY RD

Tremont

GLENFERN RD

Ferntree Gully

Kallista

The Patch

Wheelers Hill

FERNTREE GULLY

Scoresby

Knoxfield

Caribbean Gardens Caribbean Lake

Knox Park

KELLETTS RD

NAPOLEON RD

Gilbert Park

LYSTERFIELD RD

Upper Ferntree Gully

Upper Ferntree Gully

MONBULK RD

Upwey

DANDENONG RANGES NATIONAL PARK

Sherbrooke Falls

GRANTULLA RD

MONBULK RD

Tecoma

Puffing Billy

Belgrave

Selby

MORRIS RD

0 2 4 6 8 km

33

34

22

PORT PHILLIP

N

Brighton · North Brighton · Middle Brighton · Hampton · Sandringham · Black Rock · Beaumaris · Moorabbin · Highett · Ormond · McKinnon · Bentleigh · Oakleigh · Notting Hill · Wheelers Hill · Scoresby · Knoxfield · Mulgrave · Clayton · Clarinda · Heatherton · Springvale · Cheltenham · Kingston · Mentone · Beaumaris · Mordialloc · Braeside · Dingley · Noble Park · Keysborough · Dandenong · Doveton · Endeavour Hills · Aspendale · Edithvale · Chelsea · Chelsea Heights · Bangholme · Dandenong South · Lyndhurst · Bonbeach · Carrum · Patterson Lakes · Carrum Downs · Skye · Seaford · Kananook · Karingal · Frankston · Langwarrin · Cranbourne South · Amstel Golf Course

Monash University · Monash Medical Centre · Metropolitan Golf Course · Huntingdale Golf Course · Commonwealth Golf Course · Yarra Yarra Golf Course · Southland Shopping Centre · Moorabbin Airport · Spring Valley Golf Course · Kingston Heath Golf Course · Sandown Racecourse and Motor Raceway · Springvale Crematorium & Cemetery · Waverley Park (AFL) · Caribbean Gardens · Caribbean Lake · Churchill National Park · Churchill Park Golf Course · Waverley Golf Course · Moorabbin Municipal Golf Course · Kingswood Golf Course · Braeside Metropolitan Park · Southern Golf Course · Parkmore Shopping Centre · Keysborough Golf Course · Melbourne Water · Gaelic Park Sports Complex · Gas & Fuel Victoria · General Motors · Rossdale Golf Course · Chelsea Golf Course · National Water Sports Centre · Caravan Park · Patterson River Country Club Golf Course · Carrum Downs Recreation Reserve · Long Island Country Club Golf Course · Peninsula Country Club Golf Course · The Pines Flora & Fauna Reserve · Department of Agriculture · Skye Recreation Reserve · Centenary Park Golf Course · Langwarrin Flora & Fauna Reserve · Ballam Park · Frankston Golf Course · Cranbourne

0 10 20 30 km

J	K	L	M	N	O	P	Q	R

1

TO SEYMOUR — 46
TO SEYMOUR
TO MANSFIELD — 47
Yarck
Glenaroua
Kerrisdale 533m
Mt Eaglehawk
Mt Broughton 677m
Highlands
Ghin Ghin
Homewood
Fawcett
Mt Prospect 476m
Koriella
Cathkin 31
GOULBURN
Alexandra
Delatite River
Piries
Boorolite
164
Broadford
Tyaak
Mt Tallarook 806m
Strath Creek
Yea
Moleswoth
6
FRASER NATIONAL PARK
Lake EILDON
Mt Enterprise
Goughs Bay
Macs Cove
Sunday Creek 50
Reedy Creek
Waterford Park
Chevoit
Limestone
VALLEY
Acheron
Thornton
Eildon
Snobs Creek
Eildon STATE
Howqua
Jamieson R.

2

more 41
Clonbinane
Flowerdale
Hazeldene
Break O Day
Murrindindi
Taggerty
26 HWY
Rubicon
11
TORBRECK RANGE
Mt Torbreck 1514m
61
Jamieson
75
Wandong
Heathcote Junction
Mt Caroline 515m
153
41
Devlins Bridge
Rubicon
ROYSTON
Kevington
Ten Mile
Goulburn R.

3

Wallan
Upper Plenty
Mt Disappointment 793m
Glenburn
Mt Bullamite 677m
Buxton
29
Mt Margaret 1573m
Rough Hill 819m
RANGE
Mt Terrible 1335m
Enoch Point
Knockwood
Gaffneys Creek
Beveridge
KINGLAKE
Pheasant Creek
YEA RIVER PARK
Mt Klondyke 869m
CATHEDRAL RANGE STATE PARK
BLUE RANGE
68

4

Kalkallo
Donnybrook
Whittlesea
Woodstock
Humevale
Kinglake West
KINGLAKE NATIONAL PARK
Kinglake
Kinglake East
Castella
Mt Slide
Toolangi
St Fillans
Narbethong
Mt Monda
Marysville
31
Mt Kitchener 960m
Cambarville
A1 Mine Settlement
42
Yan Yean
Arthurs Creek
Mittons Bridge
St Andrews
Steels Creek
Dixons Creek
26
Black Spur
Mt Strickland 1219m
YARRA RANGES
Mt Arnold 1311m
Stockmans Reward
118
Woods Point
Matlock

5

Eden Park
Mernda
Cottles Bridge
Smiths Gully
Christmas Hills
29
Yarra Glen
Yering
Healesville
Healesville Sanctuary
Mt Toole-Be-Wong 792m
Mt Donna Buang 1250m
Cement Ck
POLEY
NATIONAL RANGE PARK
Upper Yarra Dam
McMahons Creek
42
Upper Yarra Reservoir
YARRA RANGES NATIONAL PARK
Jericho
HURSTBRIDGE
SOUTH MORANG
WATTLE GLEN
Watsons Creek
MAROONDAH
22
Coldstream

6

COBURG
HEIDELBERG
TEMPLESTOWE
WARRANDYTE STATE PARK
LILYDALE
CROYDON
Seville
Woori Yallock
Don Valley
Millgrove
Wesburn
Warburton
Big Pats Creek
Mt Horsfall 1134m
For more detail on Yarra Valley Region see page 50
79
KEW
RINGWOOD
Wandin North
Wandin Yallock
25
Launching Place
Yarra Junction
Gladysdale
Mt Baw Baw 1563m
Mt Baw Baw
Alpine Village
39
SCRAY
MELBOURNE
ST KILDA
BOX HILL
39
Olinda STATE FOREST
Silvan
Yellingbo
Hoddles Creek
Three Bridges
Loch Valley
Icy Creek
Fumina

7

CAULFIELD
GLEN WAVERLEY
DANDENONG RANGES NP
Olinda
FERNTREE GULLY
Monbulk
Macclesfield
Nangana
Powelltown
Mt Beenak 743m
42
BLUE RANGE
Alpine Trout Farm
Noojee
OAKLEIGH
UPWEY
BELGRAVE
THE PATCH
Menzies Creek
Avonsleigh
Clematis
Emerald
Cockatoo
Mt Tugwell 353m
Spion Kopje 898m
Nayook
Neerim Junction

8

BRIGHTON
Picnic Point
SPRINGVALE
34
CHURCHILL NP
LYSTERFIELD
Lysterfield Lake Park
Cardinia Reservoir
Gembrook
GEMBROOK PARK
BUNYIP STATE PARK
Gentle Annie 686m
SNAKE RIDGE
Tonimbuk
Tarago Reservoir
Neerim
Neerim East
Neerim South
Hill End
Blue Rock Dam
Mt Tanjil 456m
MOONDARRA
SANDRINGHAM
Ricketts Point
MORDIALLOC
ENDEAVOUR HILLS
Harkaway
Upper Beaconsfield
NEPEAN
DANDENONG
NARRE WARREN
BERWICK
Labertouche
Jindivick
Tarago

9

PHILLIP Bay
CHELSEA
44
Lyndhurst
Beaconsfield
Officer
27
Pakenham
Nar Nar Goon
45
Tynong
Garfield
Bunyip
Iona
Longwarry
Drouin
Drouin South
Rokeby
Buln Buln East
Buln Buln
Shady Creek
Willow Grove
Tanjil South
Westbury
FRANKSTON
SEAFORD
Cranbourne
Clyde
Cardinia
Cora Lynn
Bayles
Warragul
Nilma
Darnum
Yarragon
28
Moe

10

Mornington
Fishermans Beach
Baxter
Pearcedale
Tooradin
Koo-wee-rup
Modella
Ripplebrook
Ellinbank
Trafalgar
Newborough
Coalville
Narracan
Mount Martha
35
Mooroduc
Somerville
52
Warneet
Cannons Creek
Catani
Heath Hill
Athlone
Mt Worth 518m
Allambee
Seaview
MT WORTH STATE PARK
Childers
Thorpdale
TO MORWELL

11

Martha Point
The Briars Homestead
Tyabb
Western Port
Lang Lang
Nyora
Poowong
Poowong East
Trida
Delburn
Safety Beach
romana
Crae
Devilbend Reservoir
Hastings
FRENCH ISLAND STATE PARK
Fairhaven
FRENCH ISLAND
Fairhaven
182
Rosebud
jarook
Red Hill
Balnarring
Crib Point
Tankerton
The Gurdies
Loch
Ranceby
Mount Eccles
Allambee South
Boolarra

12

MORNINGTON PENINSULA NP
Red Hill South
Merricks
Somers
Point Leo
Shoreham
26
Stony Point
Corinella
Grantville
Bena
Woodleigh
46
Korumburra
Coal Creek Historical Village
Ruby
SOUTH GIPPSLAND
Mirboo North
Grand Ridge Brewery
Cowes
Ventnor
Rhyll
Koala Conservation Centre
Churchill Island
Glen Forbes
Kernot
Jumbunna
STRZELECKI
Flinders
West Head
PHILLIP ISLAND NATURE PARK
Bass
Bass Hill
Krowera
Kongwak
Outtrim
Leongatha
Mirboo

13

Seal Rocks
The Nobbies
Penguin Parade
PHILLIP ISLAND
24
Newhaven
San Remo
Cape Woolamai
Kilcunda
Dalyston
TO WONTHAGGI
Powlett River
Wildlife Wonderland Anderson
Archies Creek
Kongwak
Leongatha South
Koonwarra
Dumbalk
Turtons Creek
38
TO INVERLOCH
TO FOSTER
BASS HWY

J	K	L	M	N	O	P	Q	R

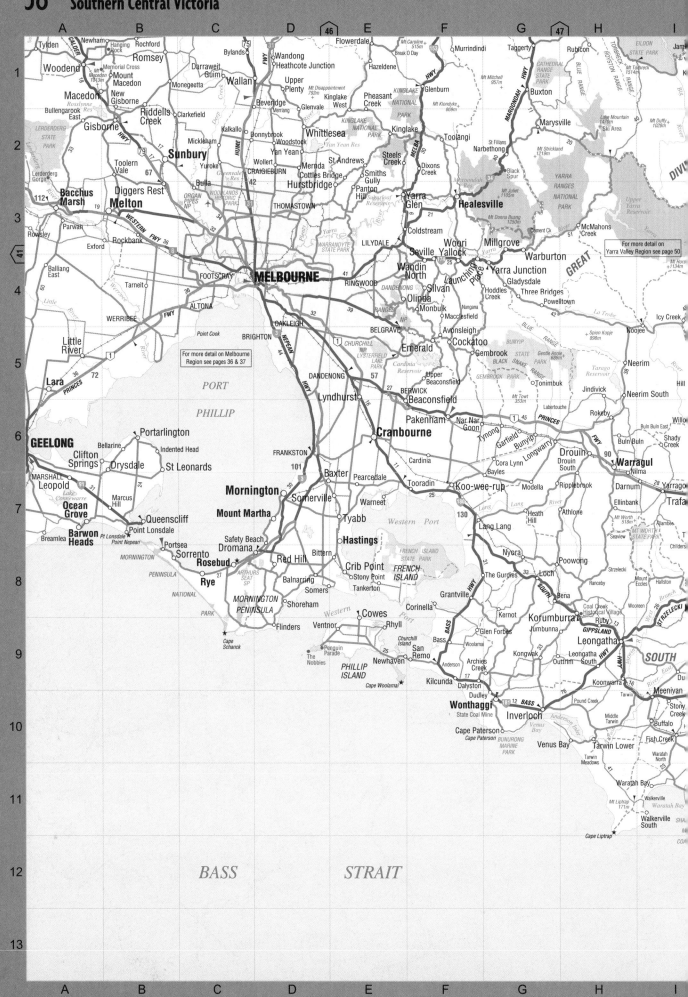

0 10 20 30 40 50 km

J K L M N O P Q R

Column 1

Barfold
Taradale
Langley
Malmsbury

Glenlofty
Lamplough
Majorca
Strathla
Wapeen
Vaughan

Bunji's Shelter
Great Western
Crowlands
Elmhurst
Amphitheatre
Amherst
Talbot
Daisy Hill
Campbelltown
Guildford
Glenluce
Lauriston
Kyneton

Rhymney Reef
Armstrong
Dunneworthy
63
Eversley
Mt Cameron + Dunach 417m
Yandoit
Drummond
Porcupine Ridge
Loddon Falls
Carlsruhe
Woodend

Langi Logan
Ararat
Warrak
Ben Nevis + 877m
Evansford
Clunes
Lawrence
Hepburn Springs
Glenlyon
Tylden

Column 2

Mt Ararat + 616m
Buangor
Raglan
Mt Lonarch
Lexton
Smeaton
Kingston
Daylesford
Bullarto
Trentham
Newbury

Maroona
Beaufort
Trawalla
Burrumbeet
Cardigan Village
Creswick
Newlyn
Rocklyn
Blackwood
Bullengarook East

Column 3

Rossbridge
Middle Creek
91
Nerring
Brewster
BALLARAT
Miners Rest
Nerrina
Spargo Creek
Bolwarrah
Greendale
LERDERDERG STATE PARK

Tatyoon
Yalla Y Poora
Haddon
Sovereign Hill
Bungaree
Wallace
Gordon
Ballan
Blakeville
Myrniong

Column 4

Willaura
Mininera
Snake Valley
Smythesdale
Scarsdale
Buninyong
Napoleons
Ross Creek
Mt Helen
Navigators
Millbrook
Yendon
Mt Egerton
Fiskville
BACCHUS MARSH
Parwan

Wickliffe
Lake Bolac
Westmere
181
Skipton
Linton
Happy Valley
Newtown
Durham Lead
Clarendon
Mt Doran
Glenmore
Rowsley
BRISBANE RANGES NATIONAL PARK

Column 5

Nerrin Nerrin
Mt Hamilton 319m
Mingay
Mt Bute
Piggoreet
Cape Clear
Berringa
Grenville
Elaine
Durdidwarrah
Balliang East
Balliang

Woorndoo
Dundonnell
Illabarook
Dereel
Mt Mercer
Cargerie
86
Woodbourne
Meredith
Anakie Gorge
Steiglitz

Column 6

Darlington
148
Derrinallum
Lismore
Berrybank
Werneth
Warrambine
Lethbridge
Maude
Anakie
Anakie East
Little River
Lara

Cloven Hills
Gnarpurt
Cressy
Duverney
Shelford
Teesdale
Bannockburn
Batesford

Column 7

Portlake
Bookaar
Lake Bookar
Barpinba
Eurack
Inverleigh
GEELONG

Ellerslie
Kolora
Glenormiston
Kariah
Dreeite
Beeac
Lake Murdeduke
Gnarwarre
Fyansford
Ceres
Leopold

Column 8

Noorat
Mt Noorat 313m
Gnotuk
Camperdown
Wool Wool
Alvie
Warrion
Ombersley
Mount Moriac
Moriac
Waurn Ponds
MARSHALL
Ocean Grove

Terang
Boorcan
Cobrico
Pomborneit
Coragulac
Cororooke
Lake Colac
Warncoort
Winchelsea
Modewa
Freshwater Creek
Breamlea
Barwon Heads

Column 9

Garvoc
Dixie
Koallah
Stoneyford
187
COLAC
Birregurra
Bellbrae
Torquay

Panmure
Laang
Mumbli
Swan Marsh
Pirron Yallock
Larpent
Elliminyt
Bambra

Column 10

Ayrford
Glenfyne
Irrewillipe
Yeodene
Deans Marsh
Boonah
Anglesea

Nullawarre
Scotts Creek
Brucknell
Simpson
Kawarren
Barwon Downs
Gerangamete
ANGAHOOK LORNE STATE PARK
Eastern View
Aireys Inlet
Fairhaven

Column 11

Curdie Vale
Nirranda South
66
Timboon
Pascarne
Newfield
Waarre
Carlisle River
CARLISLE STATE PARK
Gellibrand
Forrest
Mt Cowley 657m
Lorne

Peterborough
Port Campbell
Kennedys Creek
Chapple Vale
Wimba
Beech Forest
Separation Creek

Column 12

London Bridge
The Arch
PORT CAMPBELL
Loch Ard Gorge
The Twelve Apostles
Gibson Steps
Princetown
NATIONAL PARK
MELBA GULLY STATE PARK
Yuulong
Lavers Hill
Mt Chapple 550m
Weeaproinah
Tanybryn
Wye River
Kennett River
Cape Patton

Moonlight Head
Point Reginald
Johanna
Glenaire
145
Hordern Vale
Paradise
Skenes Creek
Apollo Bay
Marengo

Column 13

OTWAY NATIONAL PARK
Blanket Bay
Cape Otway

BASS STRAIT

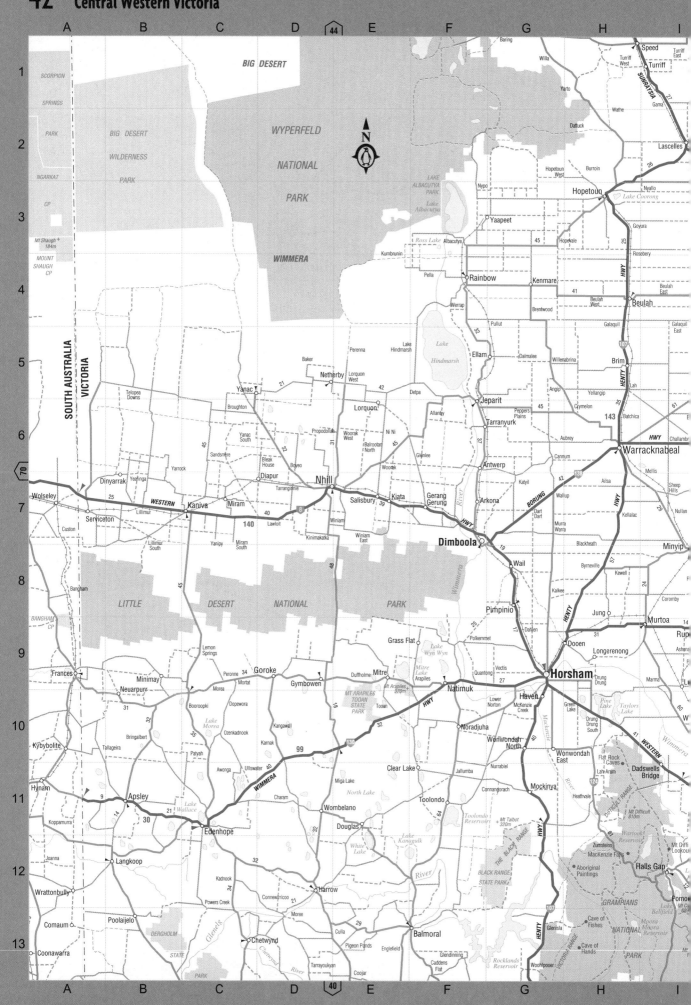

0 10 20 30 40 50 km

VICTORIA

NEW SOUTH WALES

Sea Lake · Long Plains · Gowanford · Ultima · Lake Boga · Lake Barker · Fish Point · Benjeroop · Gonn Crossing · Ballbank · Burraboi · Wakool

Ninda · Boigbeal · Goschen · Lalbert Road · Kunat · Tresco West · Tresco · Lake Tutchewop · Murrabit · Myall · Murray

Green Lake · Berriwillock · Creek Exclusion · Lake Lalbert · Meatian · Mumbel · Mystic Park · VICTORIA · Lake Charm · Capels Crossing · Cullearne · Barham

Banyan · Culgoa · Lalbert · The Marsh · Koorack · Koorack North · Sandhill Lake · Lake Bael Bael · Fairley · Westby · Koondrook · Teal Point · Gannawarra · River

Nelang · Curyo · Sutton · Warne · Cannie · Budgerum · Normanville · Great Spectacle Lake · Kerang · Kerang East · Koroop · Cohuna · McMillans · Mead

Kinnabulla · Marlbed · Jil Jil · Nullawil · Kalpienung · Boundary · Tittybong · Dingwall · Langville · Kerang South · Tragowel · Rowland · Macorna · McMillans · Wee-Wee-Rup · Leitchville

Ballapur · Karyrie · Whirily · Dumosa · Ninyeunook · Quambatook · Lake Meering · Appin · Appin South · Canary Island · Loddon Vale · Mincha · Bald Rock · Mt Hope · Kow Swamp · Gunbower

Birchip · Narraport · Gredgwin · Leaghur State Park · Leaghur · Canary Island South · Gladfield · Pyramid Hill · Terrick Terrick · Sylvaterre

Warmur · Morton Plains · Wycheproof · Fairview · Burgaluke · Barraport · Mimmindie · Yando · Durham Ox · Terrick Terrick State Park · Moloka · Mt Terrick Terrick

Watchem · Corack East · Glenloth · Narrewillock · Boort · Lake Boort · Woolshed Swamp · Yarrawalla South · Mitiamo · Calivil · Prairie · Milloo · Tennyson

Carron · Litchfield · Corack · Banyenong · Wooroonook · Barrakee · Wychitella · Mysia · Fernhurst · Jarklin · Bears Lagoon · Warrauga · Pompapiel · Zone · Dingee · Warragamba

BORUNG · Lake Buloke · Wooroonook Lakes · Charlton · Buckrabanyule · Borung · Korong Vale · Exclusion · Fruit · Fly · Serpentine · Tandarra · Drummartin

Donald · Jeffcott North · Mt Jeffcott 262m · Woosang · Mt Kerang 398m · Fiery Flat · Salisbury West · Kamarooka State Park · Kamarooka

Laen North · Dooboobetic · Yeungroon · Wedderburn · Wedderburn Junction · Mt Korong 425m · Powlett Plains · Glenalbyn · Raywood · Summerfield · Neilborough East

Laen · Cope Cope · Nine Mile · Berrimal · Yowang Hill · Kurracca West · Kooyoora SP · Kurting · Inglewood · Bridgewater on Loddon · Campbells Forest · Sebastian · Wellsford · Whipstick State Park

Rich Avon · Swanwater West · Avon Plains · Swanwater South · Gooroc · Gowar East · Kurracca · Melville Caves · Mt Kooyoora 492m · Wehla · Kingower · Derby · Huntly · Woodvale · Bagshot

Burrereo · Traynors Lagoon · St Arnaud · Logan · Burkes Flat · Rheola · Arnold West · Arnold · Leichhardt · Marong · EAGLEHAWK · Epsom · Fosterville

Banyena · Marnoo · Mitchells Hill · Moolert · Kooreh · Cochranes Creek · Mt Moliagul 527m · McIntyre · Murphys Creek · Llanelly · Newbridge · Woodstock · Maiden Gully · BENDIGO · Longlea

Burrum · Marnoo West · Gre Gre · Beazleys Bridge · Carapooee · Emu · Moliagul · Tarnagulla · Lockwood · Junortoun · Strathfieldsaye · Mandurang

Wallaloo · Kanya · Rostron · Winjallok · Bealiba · Mt Bealiba 488m · Goldsborough · Laanecoorie Reservoir · Laanecoorie · Lockwood South · Ravenswood · Sedgwick · Axe Creek

Callawadda · Wallaloo East · Paradise · Stuart Mill · Archdale · Dunolly · Eddington · Bradford · Ravenswood South · Harcourt North

Deep Lead · Morri Morri · Navarre · Redbank · Moyreisk · Bet Bet · Welshmans Reef · Harcourt · Sutton Grange · Myrtle

Stawell · Campbells Bridge · Tulkara · Landsborough · Moonambel · Barkly · Natte Yallock · Timor West · Bowenvale · Timor · Havelock · Baringhup · Maldon · Barkers Creek · Faraday · Metcalfe

Great Western · Joel Joel · Shays Flat · Warrenmang · Avoca · Tanwood · Rathscar · Bet Bet · Carisbrook · Maryborough · PYRENEES · Paddys Ranges State Park · Daisy Hill · Majorca · Newstead · Castlemaine · Chewton · Campbells Creek · Elphinstone · Barfold

Armstrong · Crowlands · Glenlofty · Elmhurst · Amphitheatre · Lamplough · Amherst · Talbot · Tullaroop Reservoir · Campbelltown · Yapeen · Guildford · Vaughan · Glenluce · Taradale · Langley · Malmsbury

Rhymney Reef · Bunjil's Shelter · Dunneworthy · Eversley · Ben Nevis 877m · Lexton · Evansford · Mt Cameron · Dunach 417m · Strathlea · Sandon · Yandoit · Drummond · Lauriston · Carlsruhe

Ararat · Mt Ararat 618m · Warrak · Mt Buangor 966m · MT BUANGOR STATE PARK · Chute · Waubra · Clunes · Ullina · Smeaton · Kingston · Hepburn Springs · Porcupine Ridge · Denver · Glenlyon · Tylden

Raglan · Buangor · Langi Kal Kal · Mt Misery 724m · Learmonth · Creswick · Coghills Creek · Broomfield · Newlyn · Daylesford · Bullarto · Newbury · Trenthan

Langi-Ghiran State Park · Langi-Ghiran SP

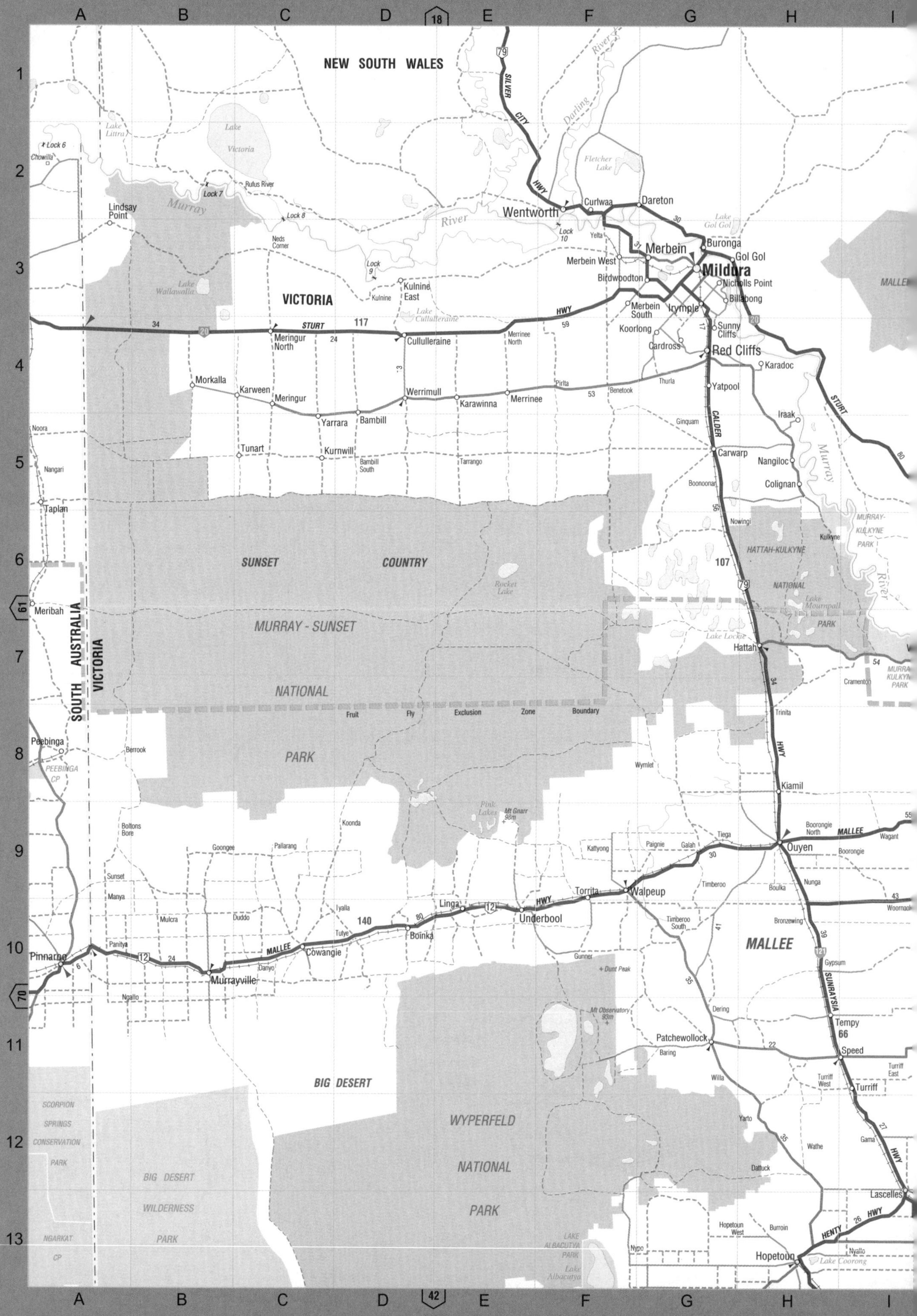

NEW SOUTH WALES

VICTORIA

SOUTH AUSTRALIA

VICTORIA

Column headers: A B C D 18 E F G H I

Row numbers: 1 2 3 4 5 6 7 8 9 10 11 12 13

Lake Littra
Lock 6
Chowilla
Lake Victoria
Lindsay Point
Murray
Lock 7
Rufus River
Lock 8
Neds Corner
Lock 10
Lock 9
Wentworth
SILVER CITY HWY
79
Darling River
Fletcher Lake
Curlwaa
Dareton
30
Yelta
Buronga
Lake Gol Gol
Gol Gol
Merbein
Merbein West
Birdwoodton
Mildura
Nicholls Point
Billabong
Lake Wallawalla
Lake Cullulleraine
Kulnine East
Kulnine
Merbein South
Koorlong
Irymple
Sunny Cliffs
17
20
MALLEE
STURT 117
34
20
Meringur North
24
Cullulleraine
Merrinee North
59
HWY
Cardross
Red Cliffs
Karadoc
Morkalla
Karween
Meringur
Werrimull
Karawinna
Merrinee
Pirita
53
Benetook
Thurla
Yatpool
Iraak
Ginquam
STURT
80
Tunart
Yarrara
Bambill
Kurnwill
Bambill South
Tarrango
Carwarp
Nangiloc
CALDER
Murray
Noora
Nangari
Taplan
Colignan
Boonoonar
56
Nowingi
MURRAY-KULKYNE PARK
Kulkyne
HATTAH-KULKYNE
SUNSET COUNTRY
107
Rocket Lake
NATIONAL
79
Lake Mournpall
River
MURRAY - SUNSET
Meribah
61
NATIONAL
Lake Lockie
Hattah
54
MURRAY KULKYNE PARK
Cramenton
Fruit Fly Exclusion Zone Boundary
34
HWY
Trinita
PARK
Peebinga
Berrook
PEEBINGA CP
Pink Lakes
Mt Gnarr 98m
Wymlet
Kiamil
Boorongie North
Wagant
55
MALLEE
Boltons Bore
Goongee
Pallarang
Koonda
Kattyong
Paignie
Galah
30
Tiega
Ouyen
Boorongie
Sunset
Manya
Iyalla
Torrita
Walpeup
Timberoo
Boulka
Nunga
43
Woomackk
Mulcra
Duddo
Tutye
80
Linga
12
HWY
Underbool
Boinka
140
MALLEE
Cowangie
Danyo
Timberoo South
41
Bronzewing
MALLEE
Pinnaroo
12
24
Panitya
Murrayville
Gunner
Dunt Peak
38
Gypsum
121
SUNRAYSIA
70
Ngallo
Mt Observatory 93m
Dering
Tempy 66
BIG DESERT
Patchewollock
Baring
Speed
22
Turriff East
SCORPION SPRINGS CONSERVATION PARK
WYPERFELD
Willa
Turriff West
Turriff
BIG DESERT
NATIONAL
Yarto
Gama
27
HWY
NGARKAT CP
WILDERNESS
PARK
Dattuck
39
Wathe
Lascelles
PARK
Hopetoun West
Burroin
HENTY
26 HWY
Nypo
Nyallo
Hopetoun
Lake Albacutya
LAKE ALBACUTYA PARK
Lake Coorong

Bottom column markers: A B C D 42 E F G H I

0 10 20 30 40 50 km

J K L M N O P Q R

1

Chibnalwood Lakes

The Vale

Hatfield

2

N

Lake Bungarry

Ryans Lake

3

Moonlight Lake

Prungle Lakes

Oxley

River

NAL PARK

Lachlan

Ita Lake

4

Pitarpunga Lake

Tin Tin Lake

River

Murrumbidgee

Penarie

Ganaway Lake

Dundomalee Lake

5

Lake Benanee

Lake Caringay

Maude

River

ton

binvale

Murrumbidgee

Lake Tala

6

76 HWY

Balranald

STURT HWY

16

Bannerton

Lake Powell Junction

MURRAY

43

Boundary Bend

Loorica Lake

YANGA NATURE RESERVE

76

27

Kyndalyn

90

Weimby

19

Margooya

Yungera

Narrung

Condoulpe

Yanga Lake

Impimi

7

Annuello

Koorkab

Heywood Lake

16

Piambie

Windomal

54

Condouple Lake

84

Koimbo

37

Kenley

Kooloonong

41

Haysdale

Lake Talbetts

Perekerten

Lake Lyle

18

8

Winnambool

109

Goodnight

Kyalite

Moolpa

Bolton

Natya

HWY

Wakool

Edward

18

Prooinga

Manangatang

HWY

41

Tooleybuc

Lake Coonaroop

NEW SOUTH WALES

Moulamein

9

12

Cocamba

Towan

Piangil

Lake Poon Boom

Stony Crossing

Mallan

70

34

23

Wood Wood

Miralie

Lake Poomaho

16

Yarraby

Nyah

Lake Wollare

Cunninyeuk

River

Dhuragoon

Niemur

10

Chinkapook

41

Nyah West

Vinifera

Speewa

Beverford

Woonnen North

Tyntynder Central

Wakool Irrigation Area

37

Jimaringle

24

Daytrap

Ryanby

Chillingollah

Pira

Nowie North

26

Tyntynder South

Nandaly

Lianiduck 93m

Boundary

Woorinen

59

Noorong

27

Burraboi

11

94

Daytrap Corner

Lake Timboram

Swan Hill

Paddlesteamer

Murray

Lake Barker

Fish Point

Ballbank

Wakool

79

Lake Tyrrell

Tyrrell Downs

Waitchie

VICTORIA

32

Lake Boga

Benjeroop

Gonn Crossing

51

Nyarrin

Long Plains

Gowanford

Ultima

Lake Boga

Tresco

101

VALLEY

Lake Tutchewop

Murrabit

31

Wakool

12

Ninda

43

Goschen

Tresco West

16

Myall

32

Sea Lake

43

Lalbert Road

Kunat

Mystic Park

Kangaroo Lake

Culfearne

Barham

HWY

Boigbeat

33

32

Meatian

Mumbel

Beauchamp

Lake Charm

Capels Crossing

Westby

Koondrook

Teal Point

River

13

omelang

Green Lake

Banyan

Berriwillock

Lalbert Creek

Tyrrell Creek

Lalbert

The March

Bael Bael

Fairley

19

River

Gannawarra

Sutton

Culgoa

Warne

29

Koorack

Koorack Sandhill Lake

Sandhill Lake

Lake Bael Bael

26

Kerang HWY

J K L M N O P Q R

43

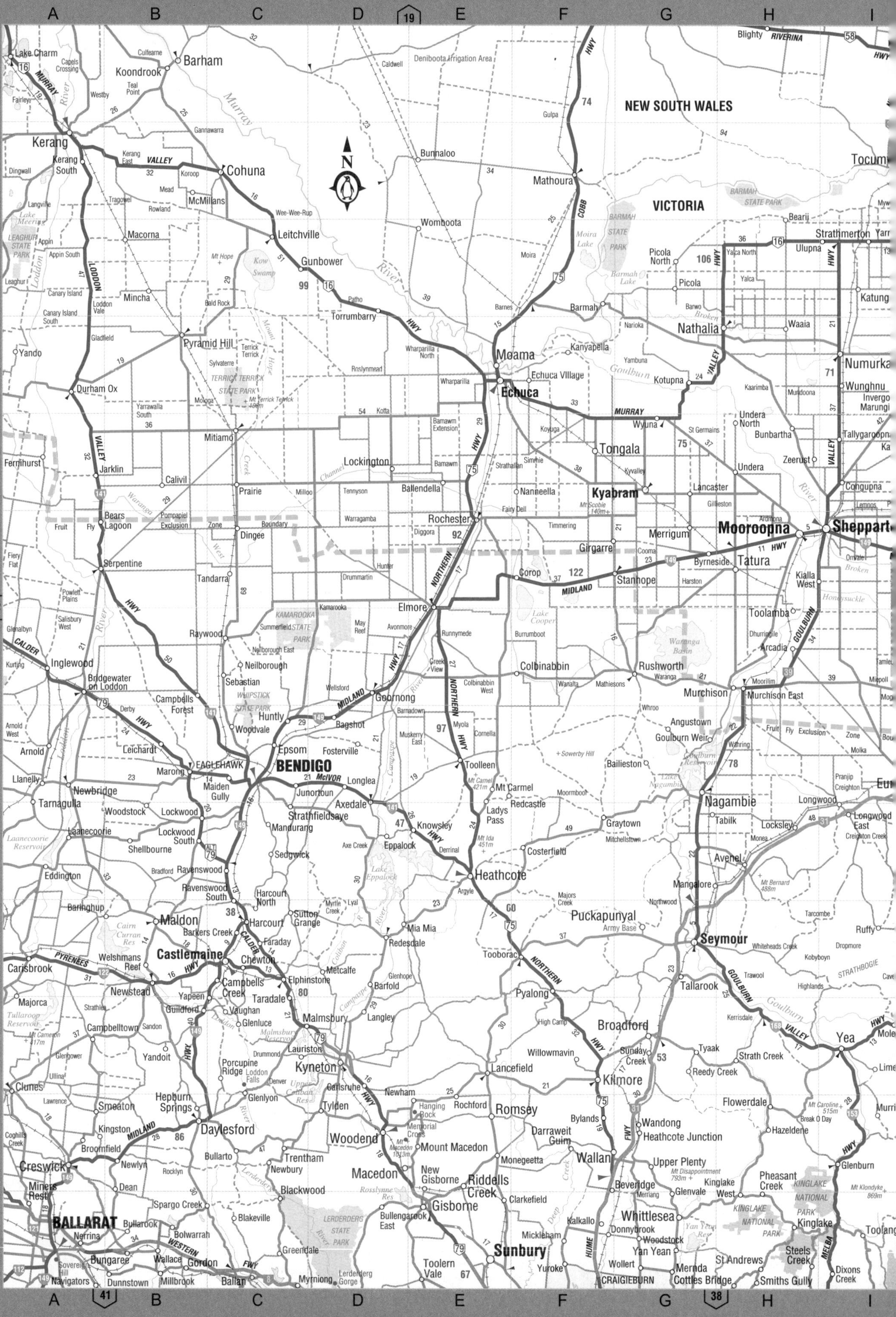
NEW SOUTH WALES
VICTORIA
Lake Charm
Barham
Koondrook
Kerang
Kerang South
Cohuna
Leitchville
Gunbower
Torrumbarry
Bunnaloo
Mathoura
Wombota
Blighty
RIVERINA HWY
Tocumwal
Barmah
Barmah State Park
Strathmerton
Picola North
Picola
Katunga
Nathalia
Waaia
Numurkah
Wunghnu
Invergo
Marungi
Tallygaroopna
Moama
Echuca
Echuca Village
Kanyapella
Kotupna
Wyuna
Tongala
Kyabram
Undera North
Bunbartha
Undera
Zeerust
Congupna
Lancaster
Mooroopna
Shepparton
Merrigum
Girgarre
Tatura
Stanhope
Corop
MIDLAND HWY
Kialla West
Toolamba
Arcadia
Rushworth
Murchison
Murchison East
Colbinabbin
Angustown
Goulburn Weir
Bailieston
Nagambie
Tabilk
Longwood
Avenel
Mangalore
Seymour
Tallarook
Puckapunyal
Graytown
Costerfield
Heathcote
Ladys Pass
Mt Camel
Redcastle
Toolleen
Elmore
Rochester
Lockington
Prairie
Dingee
Tandarra
Mitiamo
Pyramid Hill
Macorna
Mincha
Durham Ox
Jarklin
Calivil
Bears Lagoon
Serpentine
Raywood
Neilborough
Sebastian
Huntly
Goornong
Bagshot
Woodvale
Epsom
BENDIGO
EAGLEHAWK
Marong
Maiden Gully
Junortoun
Longlea
Axedale
Strathfieldsaye
Knowsley
Eppalock
Mandurang
Sedgwick
Inglewood
Bridgewater on Loddon
Campbells Forest
Leichardt
Newbridge
Tarnagulla
Woodstock
Lockwood
Lockwood South
Laanecoorie
Shellbourne
Eddington
Ravenswood
Ravenswood South
Harcourt North
Harcourt
Sutton Grange
Mia Mia
Redesdale
Baringhup
Maldon
Barkers Creek
Castlemaine
Chewton
Faraday
Elphinstone
Metcalfe
Barfold
Welshmans Reef
Carisbrook
PYRENEES HWY
Newstead
Yapeen
Campbells Creek
Taradale
Guildford
Vaughan
Glenluce
Malmsbury
Majorca
Campbelltown
Yandoit
Kyneton
Lauriston
Porcupine Ridge
Tylden
Carlsruhe
Newham
Hepburn Springs
Daylesford
Smeaton
Clunes
Kingston
Creswick
Broomfield
Newlyn
Dean
Woodend
Hanging Rock
Mount Macedon
Trentham
Macedon
New Gisborne
Riddells Creek
Gisborne
Romsey
Rochford
Lancefield
Kilmore
Broadford
Pyalong
Tooborac
Wallan
Wandong
Heathcote Junction
Upper Plenty
Beveridge
Whittlesea
Kinglake
Kinglake West
Glenburn
Yea
Flowerdale
Strath Creek
Sunbury
Clarkefield
Bullengarook East
Blackwood
Spargo Creek
Bullarook
Bolwarrah
BALLARAT
Nerrina
Bungaree
Wallace
Gordon
Ballan
Navigators
Dunnstown
Millbrook
WESTERN FWY
Toolern Vale
Mernda
Cottles Bridge
St Andrews
Smiths Gully
Steels Creek
Dixons Creek
CRAIGIEBURN
Yan Yean
Lerderderg State Park
A B C D E F G H I
1 2 3 4 5 6 7 8 9 10 11 12 13

0 10 20 30 40 50 km

J K L M N O P Q R

NEW SOUTH WALES

VICTORIA

19 Rand
22 Berrigan
Daysdale
Bulgandry
Alma Park
Morven
Culcairn
Holbrook
Savenake
Sangar
RIVERINA
Walbundrie
Walla Walla
Mullengandra
Rennie 37
22
Coreen
Oil Tree Lagoon
45
Brocklesby
Burrumbuttock
Gerogery
Gerogery West
Table Top
TABLE TOP NAT RES
Woomargama
Lowesdale
Baldfy
Fruit Fly
Buraja
13
38
42
53
Barooga
bram
Boomanoomanah Mtn 250m
Murray River
Mulwala
Lake Mulwala
Wahgunyah
Murray River
Howlong
51
Bungowannah
Browns Plains
Barnawartha North
Wirlinga
Ettamogah
Ettamogah Pub
Lake Hume
Wymah
Bungil
Burramine
Yarrawonga 36
Bundalong
Brimin
Corowa
16 133
Rutherglen
HWY
28
16
HUME
Albury
Bellbird
Bethanga
Mt Granya 871m
MT GRANYA STATE PARK
Granya
Bonegilla
Boosey
Katamatite
Bathumi
Esmond
Bundalong South
Boomahnoomoonah
Chiltern Valley
Indigo
Barnawartha
Wodonga
Bandiana
Ebden
Georges Creek
Old Tallangatta
Telford
Burramine South
27 16
VALLEY
Springhurst
Chiltern
Middle Indigo CHILTERN STATE PARK
Baranduda
Huon
Tallangatta
The Cascade
MURRAY VALLEY HWY 120
Bullioh
nite
Tungamah
Youarang
Wilby
Peechelba
Peechelba East
Boralma
68
HUME
Wooragee North
PILOT RANGE
Leneva
Kiewa
Tangambalanga
Tallangatta Valley
Yabba
Noorongong
Almonds
Yeerip
Killawarra
Boorhaman
31
Londrigan
Byawatha
Woolshed
Wooragee
Allans Flat
Osbornes Flat
Kergunyah
Sandy Creek
195
St James
Yundool
Lake Rowan
Bungeet
WARBY RANGE STATE PARK
Mt Warby 500m
Bowser
Eldorado
Carraragarmungee
Reids Ck
Beechworth
Silver Creek
Back Ck
Mt Big Ben 1158m
Kergunyah South
87
Sandy Creek Upper
Gundowring North
Dookie
Devenish
Thoona
Chesney Vale
Taminick
Wangaratta
Tarrawingee
Baarmutha
Hurdle Flat
Stanley
Bruarong
Glen Ck
Mt Stanley 1051m
Gundowring
Tallandoon
Mitta
215
Major Plains
Nooramunga
Mt Major 379m
Goorambat
OVENS
Oxley
Milawa
Markwood
Everton
Whorouly
77
Gapsted
Barwidgee Creek
Mudgegonga
Dederang
Mt Tawonga 1271m
Eskdale
Little Snowy Creek
Mitta Mitta
Glenrowan
KING RIVER
Docker
Greta West
Greta
Meadow Creek
Whorouly South
Bobinawarrah
Merriang
Myrtleford
Rosewhite
Kancoona
KIEWA VALLEY
Benalla
Winton
Lurg
Karn
Molyullah
Ryans Creek
Edi
Edi Upper
Carboor
Ovens
156
Havilah
Eurobin
Coral Bank
Mullindolingong
Tawonga
191
Baddaginnie
Boho
Warrenbayne
Harrys Creek
Marraweeny
Swanpool
Lima
Moorngag
King Valley
Myrrhee
Nug Nug
MOUNT BUFFALO NATIONAL PARK
Anderson Peak 1539m
Mt Buffalo Chalet
Porepunkah
31
Tawonga Gap
Tawonga South
ALPINE
136
et Town
Mt Wombat 539m
Koonda
Tarnook
Strathbogie
Kithbrook
Creek Junction
Boho South
Tatong
Wrightley
Cheshunt
Whitfield
Dandongadale
Eagle Peak 1024m
The Horn 1784m
Bright
Freeburgh
Wandiligong
Mount Beauty
Bogong
NATIONAL
Big River
Mertop
Ancona
Woodfield
MOUNT SAMARIA STATE PARK
Mt Strathbogie 1007m
Barjarg
Tolmie
Powers Lookout
Lake William Hovell
Typo
Mt Warrin 944m
Buckland
Smoko
Kiewa Hydro Electric Scheme
Harrietville
Falls Creek Alpine Village
HIGH PLAINS
RANGE
191
Strathbogie South
Tallangalook
Lake Nillahcootie
Dry Creek
Bonnie Doon
Maindample
Mansfield
164
Merrijig
Mirimbah
Ski Area Mt Stirling
Mt Buller 1804m
Mt Buller Alpine Village
ALPINE
NATIONAL
PARK
Mt Cobbler 1628m
GREAT DIVIDING RANGE
Mt Feathertop 1922m
Mt Hotham 1868m
Hotham Heights Alpine Village
Dinner Plain Alpine Village
111
Mt Tabletop 1588m
DARGO HIGH PLAINS
Cobungra
156
Alexandra
FRASER NATIONAL PARK
Lake Eildon
EILDON STATE PARK
Eildon
Delatite
Piries
Goughs Bay
Macs Cove
Mt McDonald 1625m
Mt Howitt 1742m
Mt Murray 1640m
Mt Phipps 1402m
VALLEY
Thornton
Snobs Creek
Howqua
HOWITT PLAINS
Acheron
Taggerty
Rubicon
EILDON STATE PARK
Jamieson
Mt Torbreck 1514m
Kevington
Mt Terrible 1335m
Mt Birregun 1463m
BLUE RANGE
ROYSTON RANGE
ALPINE
NATIONAL
Mt Kent 1563m
Buxton
CATHEDRAL RANGE STATE PARK
Lake Mountain 1470m Ski Area
Mt Duffy 1028m
Mt Skene 1571m
Crooked River
Dargo
Marysville
Mt Strickland 1219m
Narbethong Black Spur
A1 Mine Settlement
Gaffneys Creek
YARRA RANGES NATIONAL PARK
Mt Temble 1335m
Mt Wellington 1635m
Castle Hill 1448m
PARK
Woods Point
Mt Matlock 1372m
Mt Tamboritha 1640m
Lake Tali Karng
Waterford

38 39

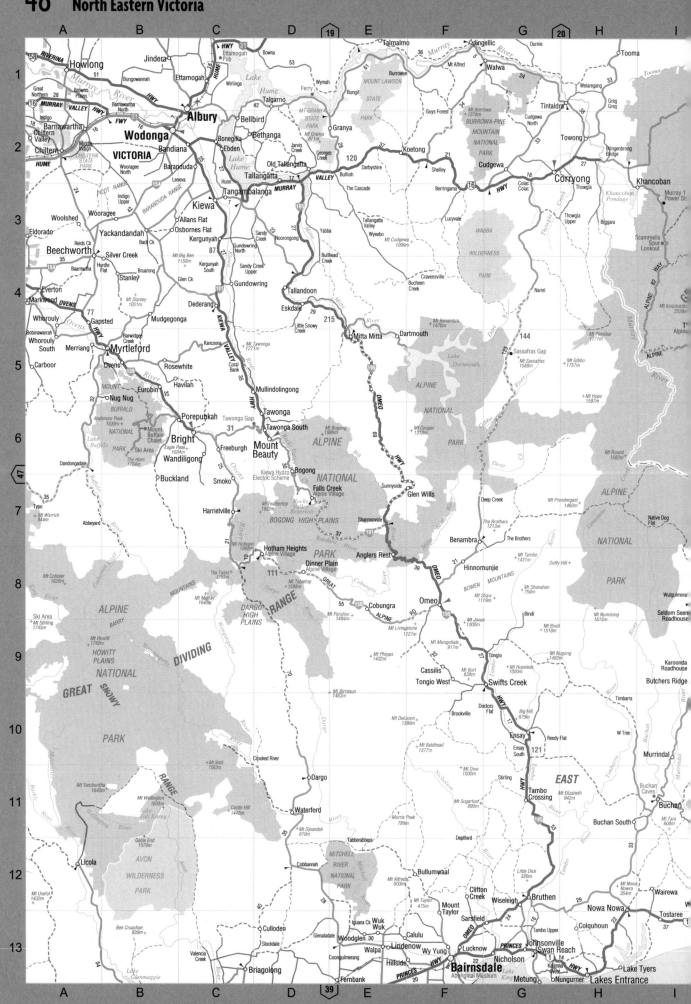

0 10 20 30 40 50 km

J K L M N O P Q R

1 Cabramurra, Tumut Pond Reservoir, Mt Flinders 1484m, Bredbo, Bald Mtn 1469m, Mt Dowling 1198m, Bendethera Caves, DEUA NATIONAL PARK, Bendethera Mtn 987m, Bergalia, Rosedale, Adaminaby, Anglers Reach, Old Adaminaby, Peak View, McInally Mtn 1085m, Bodalla

2 RANGE, KOSCIUSZKO, Mt Jagungal 2061m, Eucumbene, Buckenderra, O'Neill Lagoon, Bunyan, Numeralla, Tuross Falls, WADBILLIGA, Nerrigundah, Belowra, Eurobodalla, Dalmeny, Wagonga, SNOWY MOUNTAINS HWY, MONARO

3 NATIONAL PARK, Guthega, Smiggin Holes, Perisher, Berridale, Cooma, Rock Flat, Yowrie, Wandella, Narooma, Central Tilba, Tilba Tilba, EURO-BODALLA NP, Cootralantra Lake, Kiah Lake, NATIONAL, WALLAGA LAKE NP

4 Lake Jindabyne, Jindabyne, Dalgety, 108, Nimmitabel, Mt Kydra 1236m, Cobargo, Quaama, Brogo, Brogo Dam, Bermagui, Bermagui South, Buckleys Lake, PARK, BIAMANGA NATIONAL PARK

5 Beloka, Maffra, Numbla Vale, Paupong, Mt Cooper 1018m, SOUTH EAST FOREST NATIONAL PARK Bemboka Section, Bemboka, Numbugga, Morgans Crossing, Brogo, Wapengo, Bungai, MIMOSA ROCKS NATIONAL PARK, Lake Jillamatong, Beards Lake

6 Wallace Craigie Lookout, Ingebyra, Mulligans Mtn 908m, Jimenbuen, Gunning Grach, Mt Rix 988m, Ando, SOUTH EAST FORESTS NP Tantawangalo Section, Bimaya, Kameruka, Bega, Tathra, Kalaru, BOURNDA NATIONAL PARK, SOUTH

7 Suggan Buggan, Rodney, Bukalong, Bibbenluke, Cathcart, Black Lake, Rocky Hall, Candelo, Wolumla, Tura Beach, Merimbula, SOUTH EAST FOREST NP Yurrambie Section, Yellow Pinch Dam, PRINCES HWY

8 Tombong, Adams Pk, Tingaringy, Maharatta, SOUTH EAST FOREST NATIONAL PARK Coolangubra Section, Wyndham, Burragate, Nethercote, Pambula, Pambula Beach, BEN BOYD NATIONAL PARK, PACIFIC, Carrowidgin, Bombala, MONARO HWY

9 Ambyne, Tubbut, Deddick, McKillops Bridge, Delegate River, Delegate, Graigie, Mila, Haydens Bog, Mt Delegate 1308m, Quinbura, White Rock Mtn 1069m, SOUTH EAST FOREST, Pericoe, Towamba, MOUNT IMLAY NP, Mt Imlay 886m, Eden, East Boyd, Kiah, Boydtown, OCEAN, SNOWY RIVER, NATIONAL

10 Mt Bowen 1320m, Bonang West, Bonang, Dellicknora, Bendoco, Mt Canterbury 1089m, Buldah, Rockton, Genoa Section, Waalimma Section, Waalimma Mtn 722m, Narrabarba, Green Cape, BEN BOYD NATIONAL PARK, Wonboyn Lake, NADGEE NATURE RESERVE, 158, PARK

11 Brown Mtn 1010m, ERRINUNDRA NATIONAL PARK, Mt Jersey 759m, Goongerah, Martins Creek, Mt Ellery 1291m, Errinundra, Combienbar, Kowat, Cooracambra 958m, COORACAMBRA NATIONAL PARK, Wroxham, Wangarabell, Timbillica, Mt Nagha 543m, Genoa, Gipsy Point, Faihaven, Lake Barracoota, Cape Howe, SOUTH

12 Sardine Creek, Club Terrace, LIND NP, Tonghi Creek, Noorinbee North, Noorinbee, Karlo Creek, Cann River, ALFRED NATIONAL PARK, Mallacoota, Mallacoota Inlet, Gabo Island, CROAJINGOLONG NATIONAL PARK, Mt Kuark 917m, PRINCES, CANN VALLEY HWY, Mt Buck 507m, Murrungowar

13 Orbost, Brodribb River, Cabbage Tree Creek, Bellbird Creek, Mt Cann 530m, Bemm River, Tamboon, CROAJINGOLONG NATIONAL PARK, Little Rame Head, Marlo, Point Ricardo, Cape Conran, Pearl Point, Sydenham Inlet, Tamboon Inlet, Point Hicks (Cape Everard), Rame Head, Wingan Inlet, TASMAN SEA, Lake Corringle, GIPPSLAND, SNOWY RIVER NATIONAL PARK, NEW SOUTH WALES, VICTORIA

N

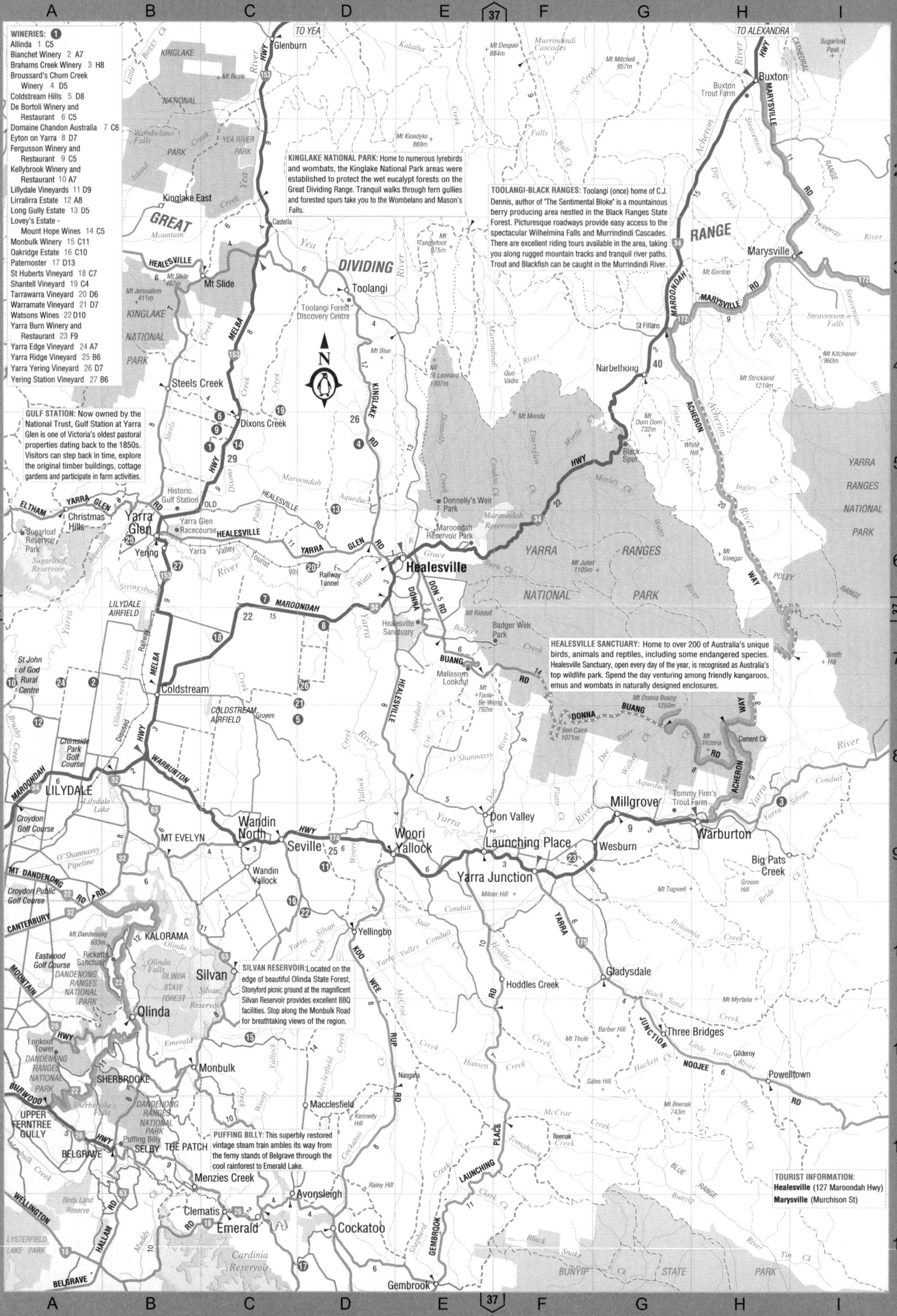

WINERIES:
Allinda 1 C5
Bianchet Winery 2 A7
Brahams Creek Winery 3 H8
Broussard's Chum Creek Winery 4 D5
Coldstream Hills 5 D8
De Bortoli Winery and Restaurant 6 C5
Domaine Chandon Australia 7 C6
Eyton on Yarra 8 D7
Fergusson Winery and Restaurant 9 C5
Kellybrook Winery and Restaurant 10 A7
Lillydale Vineyards 11 D9
Lirralirra Estate 12 A8
Long Gully Estate 13 D5
Lovey's Estate - Mount Hope Wines 14 C5
Monbulk Winery 15 C11
Oakridge Estate 16 C10
Paternoster 17 D13
St Huberts Vineyard 18 C7
Shantell Vineyard 19 C4
Tarrawarra Vineyard 20 D6
Warramate Vineyard 21 D7
Watsons Wines 22 D10
Yarra Burn Winery and Restaurant 23 F9
Yarra Edge Vineyard 24 A7
Yarra Ridge Vineyard 25 B6
Yarra Yering Vineyard 26 D7
Yering Station Vineyard 27 B6
KINGLAKE NATIONAL PARK: Home to numerous lyrebirds and wombats, the Kinglake National Park areas were established to protect the wet eucalypt forests on the Great Dividing Range. Tranquil walks through fern gullies and forested spurs take you to the Wombelano and Mason's Falls.
TOOLANGI-BLACK RANGES: Toolangi (once) home of C.J. Dennis, author of "The Sentimental Bloke" is a mountainous berry producing area nestled in the Black Ranges State Forest. Picturesque roadways provide easy access to the spectacular Wilhelmina Falls and Murrindindi Cascades. There are excellent riding tours available in the area, taking you along rugged mountain tracks and tranquil river paths. Trout and Blackfish can be caught in the Murrindindi River.
GULF STATION: Now owned by the National Trust, Gulf Station at Yarra Glen is one of Victoria's oldest pastoral properties dating back to the 1850s. Visitors can step back in time, explore the original timber buildings, cottage gardens and participate in farm activities.
HEALESVILLE SANCTUARY: Home to over 200 of Australia's unique birds, animals and reptiles, including some endangered species. Healesville Sanctuary, open every day of the year, is recognised as Australia's top wildlife park. Spend the day venturing among friendly kangaroos, emus and wombats in naturally designed enclosures.
SILVAN RESERVOIR: Located on the edge of beautiful Olinda State Forest, Stonyford picnic ground at the magnificent Silvan Reservoir provides excellent BBQ facilities. Stop along the Monbulk Road for breathtaking views of the region.
PUFFING BILLY: This superbly restored vintage steam train ambles its way from the ferny stands of Belgrave through the cool rainforest to Emerald Lake.
TOURIST INFORMATION:
Healesville (127 Maroondah Hwy)
Marysville (Murchison St)
0 2 4 6 8 10 km
TO YEA
TO ALEXANDRA
Glenburn
Buxton
Kinglake East
Mt Slide
Toolangi
Marysville
Narbethong
Steels Creek
Dixons Creek
Yarra Glen
Healesville
Coldstream
LILYDALE
Wandin North
Seville
Woori Yallock
Launching Place
Yarra Junction
Millgrove
Warburton
Wesburn
Don Valley
Yellingbo
Silvan
Olinda
KALORAMA
Monbulk
SHERBROOKE
UPPER FERNTREE GULLY
BELGRAVE
SELBY
THE PATCH
Menzies Creek
Avonsleigh
Clematis
Emerald
Cockatoo
Gembrook
Macclesfield
Hoddles Creek
Gladysdale
Three Bridges
Powelltown
Big Pats Creek
YARRA RANGES NATIONAL PARK
KINGLAKE NATIONAL PARK
GREAT DIVIDING RANGE

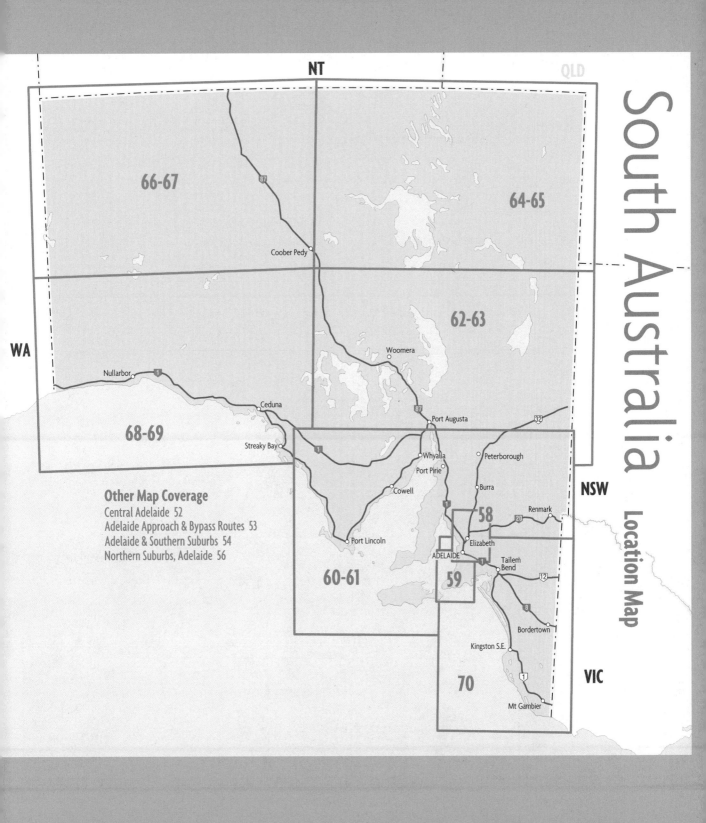

South Australia

Location Map

NT

QLD

66-67

87

64-65

Coober Pedy

62-63

WA

Woomera

Nullarbor

1

Ceduna

87

Port Augusta

32

68-69

Streaky Bay

Whyalla

Peterborough

Port Pirie

NSW

Cowell

Burra

Other Map Coverage
Central Adelaide 52
Adelaide Approach & Bypass Routes 53
Adelaide & Southern Suburbs 54
Northern Suburbs, Adelaide 56

1

Port Lincoln

58

Renmark

20

Elizabeth

ADELAIDE

59

Tailem
Bend

1

60-61

12

8

Bordertown

Kingston S.E.

VIC

70

1

Mt Gambier

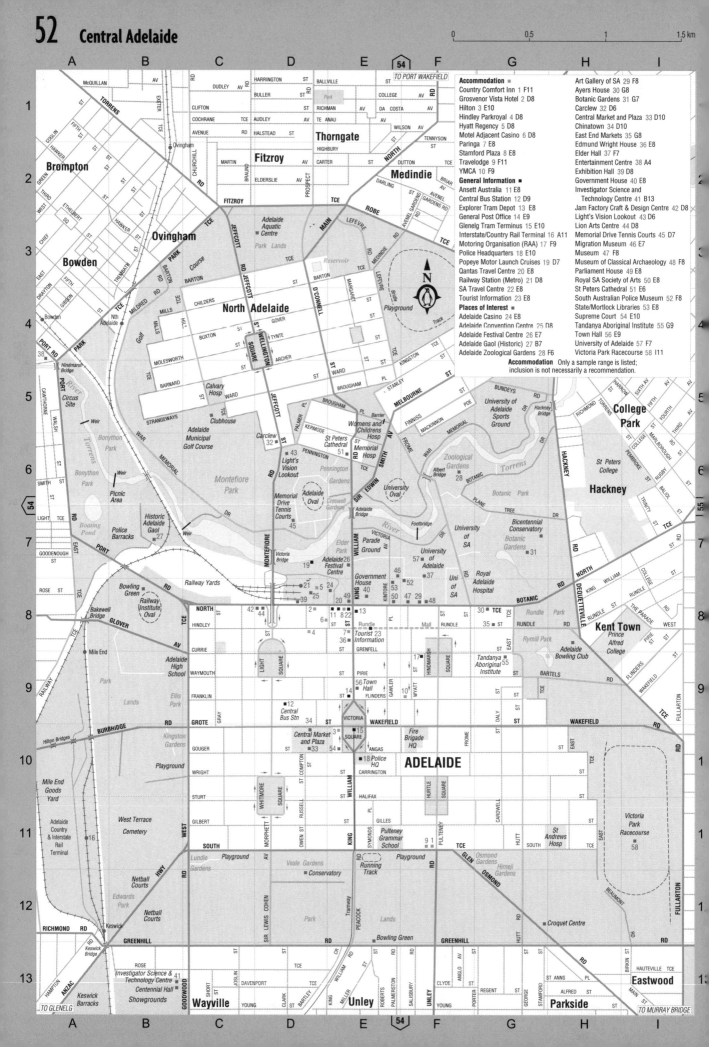

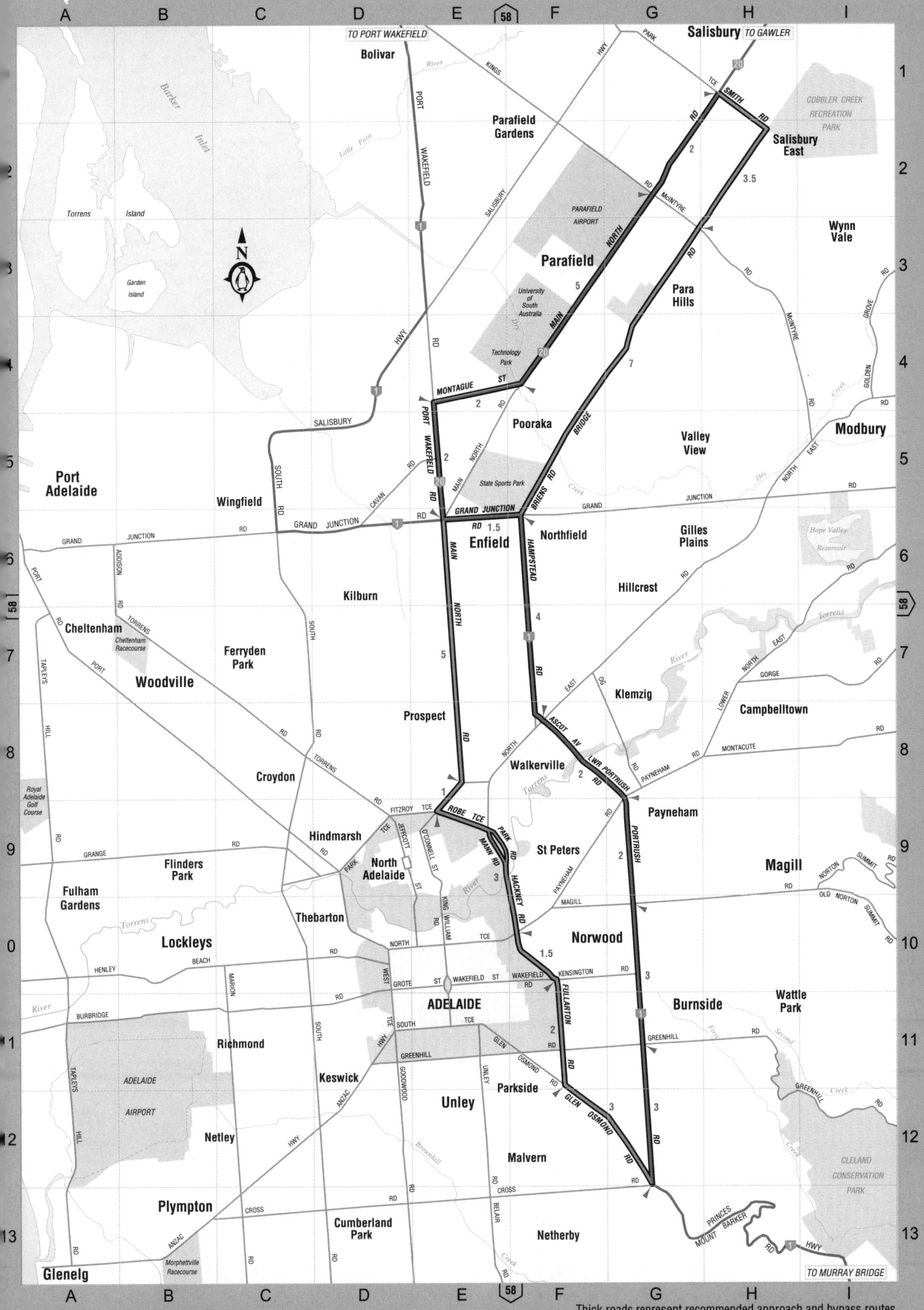

0 1 2 3 4 5 km

A B C D E F G H I

TO PORT WAKEFIELD

58

Bolivar

TO GAWLER

Salisbury

20

SMITH RD

Salisbury East

COBBLER CREEK RECREATION PARK

Parafield Gardens

2

3.5

Wynn Vale

Parafield

PARAFIELD AIRPORT

Para Hills

Modbury

University of South Australia

5

McINTYRE RD

GROVE

GOLDEN

Technology Park

20

MAIN NORTH RD

BRIDGE RD

Valley View

7

MONTAGUE ST

2

Pooraka

Gilles Plains

Hope Valley Reservoir

Port Adelaide

Wingfield

SALISBURY

SOUTH RD

CAVAN RD

PORT WAKEFIELD RD

20

MAIN NORTH RD

GRAND JUNCTION RD 1.5

Enfield

Northfield

HAMPSTEAD RD

Hillcrest

GRAND JUNCTION RD

Cheltenham

58

Cheltenham Racecourse

Kilburn

4

Torrens River

EAST

GORGE

Woodville

Ferryden Park

Prospect

5

MAIN NORTH RD

1

Klemzig

Campbelltown

Croydon

NORTH

ASCOT AV

LWR PORTRUSH RD

2

Walkerville

PAYNEHAM

MONTACUTE

Hindmarsh

FITZROY TCE

ROBE TCE

1

St Peters

Payneham

2

PORTRUSH RD

Magill

Flinders Park

North Adelaide

MANN RD

PARK RD

HACKNEY RD

3

PAYNEHAM RD

MAGILL

NORTON SUMMIT

Fulham Gardens

Thebarton

O'CONNELL ST

KING WILLIAM ST

Torrens

Norwood

OLD NORTON SUMMIT RD

Lockleys

NORTH RD

1.5

WAKEFIELD ST

KENSINGTON RD

Burnside

Wattle Park

ADELAIDE

FULLARTON RD

Richmond

WEST TCE

GROTE ST

SOUTH TCE

GREENHILL RD

2

Greenhill

GREENHILL CREEK

ADELAIDE AIRPORT

Keswick

GOODWOOD RD

ANZAC HWY

Parkside

GLEN OSMOND RD

3

3

Unley

UNLEY RD

GLEN OSMOND

Netley

Malvern

Netherby

Plympton

CROSS RD

BELAIR RD

Cumberland Park

Morphettville Racecourse

PRINCES HWY

MOUNT BARKER RD

CLELAND CONSERVATION PARK

Glenelg

58

TO MURRAY BRIDGE

Torrens Island

Garden Island

Barker Inlet

Royal Adelaide Golf Course

N

Thick roads represent recommended approach and bypass routes.

For more detail on Central Adelaide see page 52

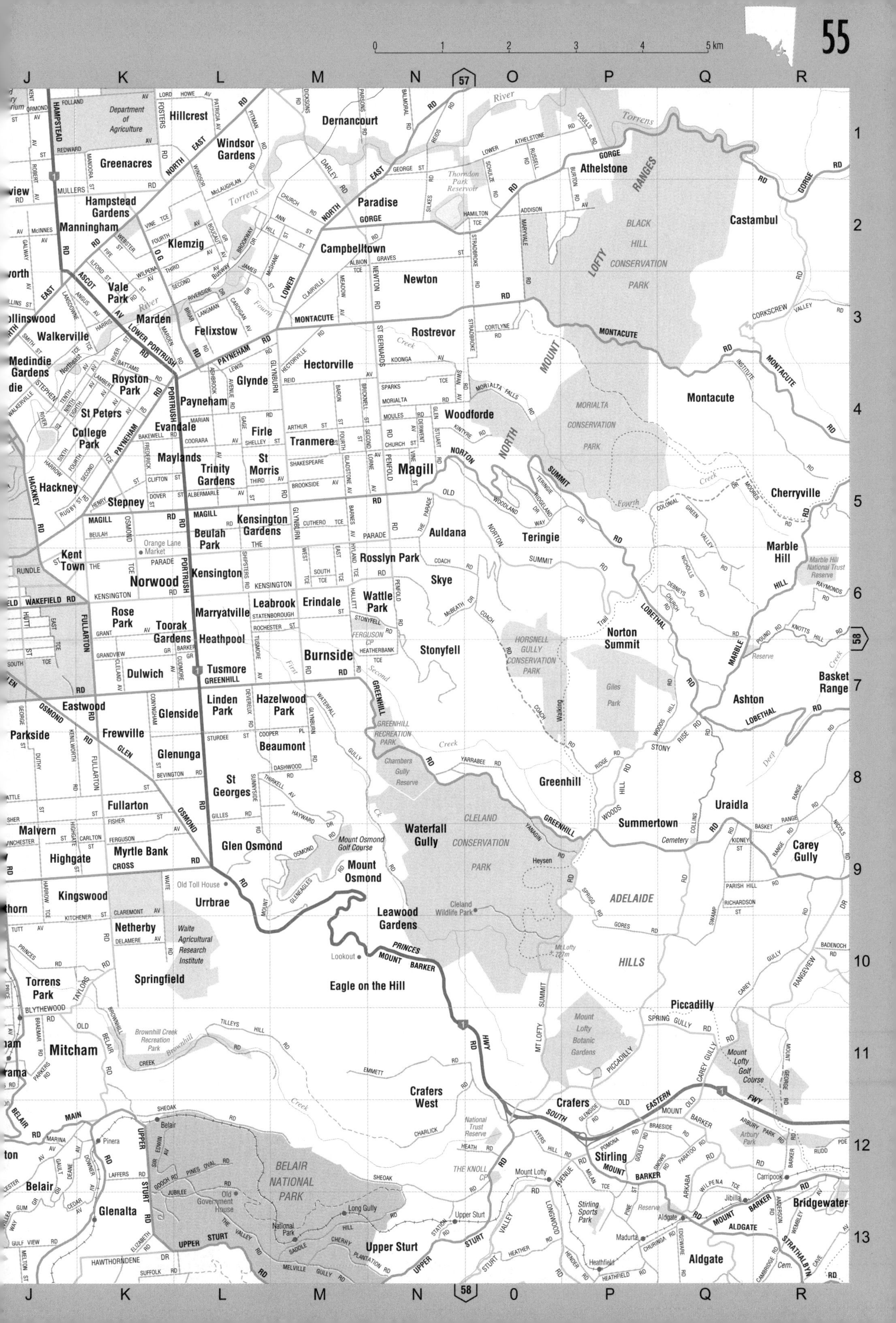

0 1 2 3 4 5 km

J K L M N O P Q R

LOFTY RANGES

Hillcrest
Department of Agriculture
Windsor Gardens
Dernancourt
Torrens River
Greenacres
Hampstead
Hampstead Gardens
Manningham
Klemzig
Campbelltown
Paradise
Newton
Athelstone
Castambul
BLACK HILL CONSERVATION PARK
Vale Park
Marden
Felixstow
Rostrevor
MONTACUTE
Walkerville
Royston Park
Glynde
Hectorville
Woodforde
MOUNT
Montacute
Medindie Gardens
St Peters
College Park
Evandale
Payneham
Firle
Tranmere
Magill
MORIALTA CONSERVATION PARK
NORTH
Cherryville
Hackney
Maylands
Trinity Gardens
St Morris
Auldana
Teringie
Marble Hill
Marble Hill National Trust Reserve
Stepney
Magill
Beulah Park
Kensington Gardens
Rosslyn Park
Skye
SUMMIT
Kent Town
Norwood
Kensington
Marryatville
Leabrook
Erindale
Wattle Park
Stonyfell
HORSNELL GULLY CONSERVATION PARK
Norton Summit
LOBETHAL
Basket Range
Rose Park
Toorak Gardens
Heathpool
Burnside
Ashton
Eastwood
Glenside
Linden Park
Hazelwood Park
Beaumont
Greenhill
Summertown
Uraidla
MARBLE HILL
Parkside
Frewville
Glenunga
St Georges
CLELAND CONSERVATION PARK
Greenhill
Carey Gully
Fullarton
Malvern
Highgate
Myrtle Bank
Glen Osmond
Mount Osmond Golf Course
Waterfall Gully
ADELAIDE HILLS
Kingswood
Urrbrae
Netherby
Waite Agricultural Research Institute
Mount Osmond
Leawood Gardens
Cleland Wildlife Park
Mt Lofty 727m
Piccadilly
Torrens Park
Springfield
PRINCES
Eagle on the Hill
Mount Lofty Botanic Gardens
Mount Lofty Golf Course
Mitcham
Brownhill Creek Recreation Park
Crafers West
Crafers
Stirling
Carripook
Belair
Glenalta
BELAIR NATIONAL PARK
Old Government House
National Park
Long Gully
Upper Sturt
Stirling Sports Park
Aldgate
Bridgewater

River Torrens
Torrens
GORGE

57 58

A B C D E F G H I

1
2
3
4
5
6
7
8
9
10
11
12
13

GULF

ST VINCENT

Outer Harbor

Largs Bay

Semaphore

Semaphore South

Semaphore Park

LEFEVRE PENINSULA

Outer Harbor

Overseas Passenger Terminal

Outer Harbor North Haven Golf Course

North Haven

Osborne

Midlunga

Taperoo

SA Police Academy

STRATHFIELD

Draper

Largs North

Largs Bay

Peterhead

Birkenhead

Exeter

Glanville

Ethelton

Fort Glanville

West Lakes Shore

Delfin Island

West Lakes

Royal Park

Albert Park

Riverside Golf Course

Fishermans Wharf Markets

S.A. Maritime Museum

Port Dock Railway Museum

Commercial Road

Port Adelaide

Queenstown

Alberton

Cheltenham

Cheltenham R'course

Cheltenham Racecourse

Woodville

Rosewater

Pennington

Woodville North

Woodville Gardens

Gillman

North Arm Road

Kapara

Ottoway

Athol Park

Angle Park

Mansfield Park

Greyhound Racing Club

Wingfield

Regency Park

Regency Golf Course

Ferryden Park

Kilburn

Salt Crystallization Pans

BARKER

Torrens Reach

TORRENS ISLAND CONSERVATION PARK

Light Passage

Mutton Cove

Quarantine Station

Australian Submarine Corporation

TORRENS ISLAND

Angas Inlet

Power Station

North Arm Fish Market

MOORHOUSE RD

Garden Island

BARKER INLET

AQUATIC RESERVE

INLET

EASTERN PASSAGE

North Arm Creek

Salt Crystallization Pans

Salt Crystallization Pans

Australian Electric Transport Museum

ST KILDA

Salt Crystallization Pans

Winston Park SA Equestrian Centre

BROOKS

WHITE RD

CASSON

COLEMAN

BARKER

ANJANTO

ROBINSON

PORT

WAKEFIELD

PRINCES

Waterloo Corner

Speed Kartway

GREYHOUND

MUMFORD

ANGLE VALE CR

BURTON

HEASLIP

LIBERATOR

Bolivar Sewage Treatment Works

Bolivar

HODGSON

Para River

Little

JONES RD

RYANS

WHITES

DANIEL

AV

Globe Derby Park Trotting Tracks

SOUTH ROAD CONNECTOR

Dry Creek

Dry Creek

Cava

SALISBURY HWY

MAGAZINE

Dry Creek

CHURCHILL

CAVAN

GRAND

Junction Market

Tube Mills

Black Ath

VICTORIA RD

GOWRIE DR

LADY

MILITARY

ST VINCENT

COMMERCIAL

PORT RD

TAPLEYS HILL RD

GORDON

PORT RD

TORRENS RD

GRAND

JUNCTION

South RD

GRAND RD

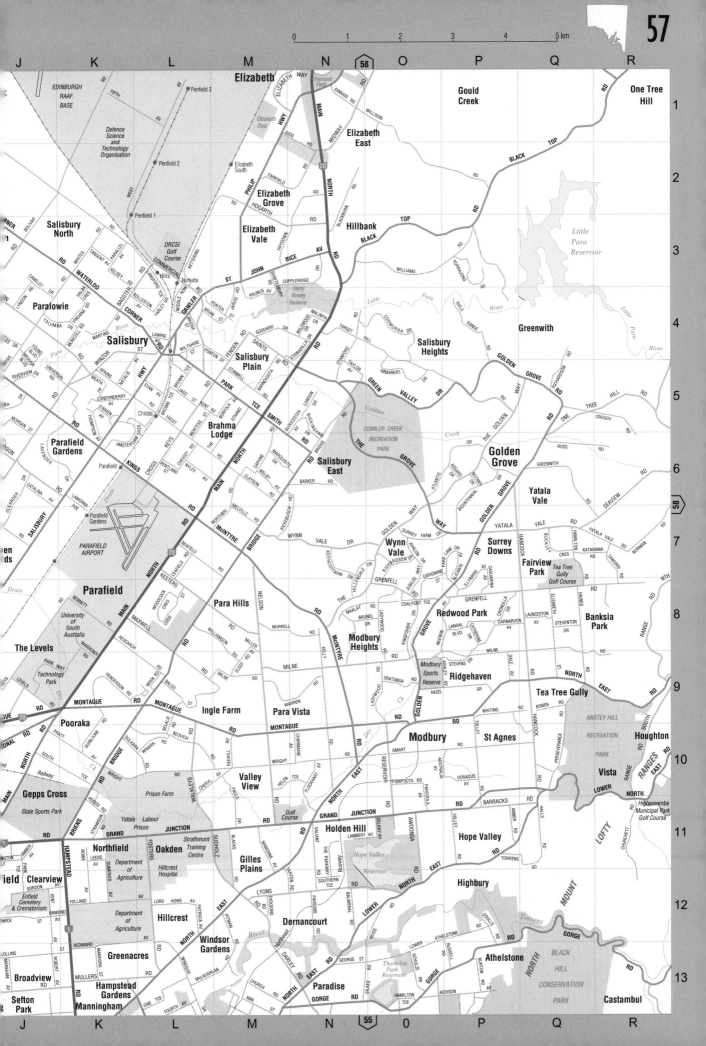

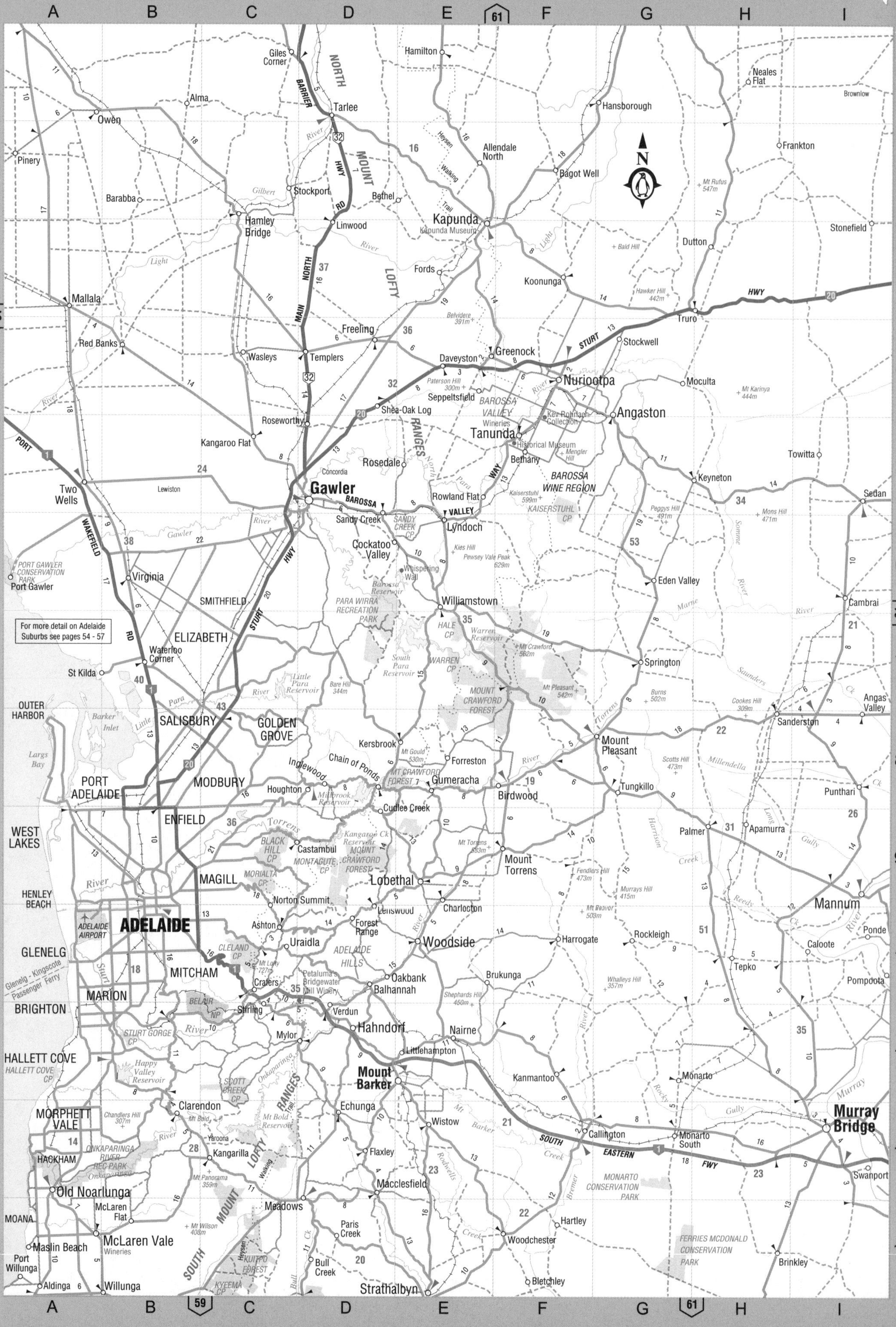

0 5 10 15 20 km

N

A B C D E F G H I

1 2 3 4 5 6 7 8 9 10 11 12 13

Giles Corner, Hamilton, Neales Flat, Brownlow, Alma, Tarlee, Owen, Pinery, Hansborough, Frankton, Barabba, Stockport, Bethel, Allendale North, Bagot Well, Mt Rufus 547m, Hamley Bridge, Linwood, Kapunda, Kapunda Museum, Stonefield, Dutton, Mallala, Fords, Koonunga, Hawker Hill 442m, Truro, HWY, Red Banks, Wasleys, Templers, Freeling, Daveyston, Greenock, Stockwell, Moculta, Mt Karinya 444m, Roseworthy, Shea-Oak Log, Seppeltsfield, Nuriootpa, Kangaroo Flat, Concordia, Rosedale, Tanunda, Angaston, Towitta, Two Wells, Lewiston, Gawler, Sandy Creek, Lyndoch, Bethany, Keyneton, Sedan, Port Gawler, Virginia, Smithfield, Cockatoo Valley, Rowland Flat, Williamstown, Eden Valley, Cambrai, St Kilda, Elizabeth, Waterloo Corner, Springton, Angas Valley, Outer Harbor, Salisbury, Golden Grove, Kersbrook, Forreston, Mount Pleasant, Cookes Hill 309m, Sanderston, West Lakes, Modbury, Inglewood, Houghton, Gumeracha, Birdwood, Tungkillo, Punthari, Port Adelaide, Enfield, Magill, Castambul, Cudlee Creek, Mount Torrens, Palmer, Apamurra, Henley Beach, Norton Summit, Lobethal, Mannum, Adelaide, Adelaide Airport, Ashton, Lenswood, Charleston, Rockleigh, Ponde, Glenelg, Uraidla, Forest Range, Woodside, Harrogate, Tepko, Caloote, Marion, Mitcham, Crafers, Oakbank, Balhannah, Brukunga, Monarto, Pompoota, Brighton, Stirling, Verdun, Hahndorf, Nairne, Kanmantoo, Hallett Cove, Mylor, Littlehampton, Mount Barker, Kanmantoo, Monarto, Murray Bridge, Morphett Vale, Clarendon, Echunga, Wistow, Callington, Monarto South, Hackham, Kangarilla, Flaxley, Macclesfield, Hartley, Swanport, Old Noarlunga, McLaren Flat, Meadows, Woodchester, Brinkley, Moana, Maslin Beach, McLaren Vale, Paris Creek, Bull Creek, Strathalbyn, Bletchley, Port Willunga, Aldinga, Willunga

For more detail on Adelaide Suburbs see pages 54 - 57

0 5 10 15 20 km

58

N

ADELAIDE

ADELAIDE AIRPORT

For more detail on Adelaide Suburbs see pages 54-57

GLENELG

MARION

BRIGHTON

MITCHAM

Ashton
Uraidla
Forest Range
Woodside

CLELAND CP
Mt Lofty 727m
Crafers
Oakbank
Balhannah

BELAIR NP
Stirling
Verdun
Hahndorf
Littlehampton

HALLETT COVE
HALLETT COVE CP

STURT GORGE CP

Happy Valley Reservoir

Mylor

Mount Barker

River

SCOTT CREEK CP

Onkaparinga

MORPHETT VALE
14

Chandlers Hill 307m

River

Clarendon
Mt Bold
Echunga

SOUTH

Jupiter Creek Goldfields

HACKHAM

Mt Bold Reservoir

Wistow

28
Yarooma
Kangarilla
Jupiter Creek

Old Noarlunga

Mt Panorama 359m

LOFTY

Green Hills

Macclesfield

MOANA

McLaren Flat

16

Horsham

Meadows

RANGES

Maslin Beach

McLaren Vale
Wineries

Mt Wilson 408m

Paris Creek

Port Willunga

Prospect Hill

20

Bull Creek

Strathalbyn
Soldiers Memorial Gardens

Aldinga

Willunga

Kuitpo

KUITPO FOREST

RANGES

Aldinga Beach

ALDINGA SCRUB CONSERVATION PARK

6

Dingabledinga

KYEEMA CP

McHarg Creek
Ashbourne

Lookout

Hope Forest

Kuitpo Colony

MT MAGNIFICENT CP

Silver Sands
25

Sellicks Hill

Mt Terrible 386m

Munetta

Yundi

Cole Crossing

Sellicks Beach

Aldinga Bay Lookout

Pages Flat

COX SCRUB CONSERVATION PARK

Sandergrove

Black Hill 73m

Begonia Farm (Open Oct-April)

Mt Cone 415m

Mount Compass

Nangkita

42

34

Myponga Beach

Myponga Reservoir

30

51

Tooperang Trout Farm Tooperang

Fimiss

Lookout

Myponga

24

51

Mosquito Flat

Gilberts

Tonkins Currency Creek Winery

Carrickalinga

14

MYPONGA CONSERVATION PARK

Spring Mtn 418m

SCOTT CONSERVATION PARK

Normanville

Clark Hill 437m

Hindmarsh Falls

Currency

Canoe Tree

Yankalilla

SPRING MOUNTAIN CONSERVATION PARK

Middleton Winery

Currency Creek

Bungala

River

FLEURIEU

35

Glacier Rock

Crows Nest Lookout

Malleebrae Woolshed

Goolwa River

Rapid Bay

Yankalilla Bay

Inman River

Inman Valley

SECOND VALLEY FOREST

19

Hindmarsh Valley

Orimbirra Wildlife Park

Middleton

Cockle Train

19

Goolwa

Narnu Bay

Rapid Bay

35

Mt Hayfield 353m

PENINSULA

SECOND VALLEY FOREST

Back Valley

Greenhills Adventure Park

Hindmarsh Winery

Boomer Beach

Port Elliot

HINDMARSH ISLAND

Second Valley

Bullaparinga Hill 325m

Newland

Victor Harbor

Delamere

12

63

17

SA Whale Centre

Granite Island Fairy Penguins

Encounter Bay

Lookout

Cape Jervis Lighthouse

Sheep Hill 130m

19

Coolawang Ck

Waitpinga

5

Rosetta Head (The Bluff)

Murray Mouth

Cape Jervis

Lands End

Arthur Hill

11

Waitpinga

King Beach West Island WEST ISLAND CONSERVATION PARK

Fishery Beach

TALISKER CP

DEEP CREEK CONSERVATION PARK

Heysen

Walking

Trail

Waitpinga Hill

NEWLAND HEAD CONSERVATION PARK

Porpoise Head

Tunkalilla Beach

Tunk Head

Parsons Beach

Waitpinga Beach

Newland Head

GULF

ST VINCENT

BACKSTAIRS

PASSAGE

Snapper Point

KANGAROO ISLAND

Cape Coutts

DUDLEY

Antechamber Bay

Chapman River

Cape St Albans

60

Moncrieff Bay

Cape Hart CONSERVATION PARK

Cape Willoughby

SOUTHERN OCEAN

PENINSULA

Cape Hart

0 20 40 60 80 100 km

J K L M N O P Q R

63

SOUTH AUSTRALIA
NEW SOUTH WALES

DANGGALI CONSERVATION PARK

1

Hammond
Eurelia
Yalpara
Meadow Downs
Tattuppa Hill 611m
Yunta
Oulnina Hill 710m
Oulnina Park
Oulnina Creek
Wadnaminga
Browns Hill 152m
West Olary Creek

Mt Brown 965m
Horrock's Pass
Wilmington
Willowie
Morchard
Orroroo
Nackara Hill 661m
Dawson
Paratoo
Manunda

BENDA RANGE

Hancocks Lookout
Terka
Booleroo
Pekina Hill 732m
Walloway
Minvalara
Nantabibbie
Nackara
Oodla Wirra
Ocolia Creek

MT REMARKABLE NP
Mt Remarkable 960m
Melrose
Perrcomba
Pekina
Black Rock
Nantabibbie
Ucolta

2

Mambray Creek
Baroota Res
Murray Town
Wirrabara
Hornsdale
Appila
Gumbowie
Peterborough
Terowie
Doughboy Hill 602m
Alderman Reservoir
Wrights Hill 517m
Bolekevie Hill 539m
Ironback Hill 378m
Faraway Hill 216m

TELOWIE GORGE CP
Nelshaby
Napperby
Stone Hut
Mt Lock 733m
Yongala
Mannanarie
Beldie
Whyte Yarcowie
PANDAPPA CONSERVATION PARK

3

Napperby
Laura
Caltowie
Jamestown
Yatina
Tarcowie
Ulooloo
Mount Bryan East
Curoona
Winto Creek

SOUTH AUSTRALIA
NEW SOUTH WALES
18

Warnertown
Gladstone
Huddleston
Georgetown
Canowie
Hallett
Mt Bryan 932m

4

Wandearah
Crystal Brook
Merriton
Narridy
Gulnare
Spalding
Booborowie
Andrews
Leighton
Tracy
Redbanks

CONSERVATION PARK

Clements Gap
Redhill
Koolunga
Yacka
Rochester
Hilltown
Burra
Stein Hill 612m
Burra Creek Gorge

5

Mundoora
Collinsfield
Lake View
Brinkworth
Condowie
Hart
Hanson
Black Springs
Emu Downs
Florieton

Wokurna
Snowtown
Blyth
Sevenhill
Merildin
Brady Creek
Geranium Plain
Morgan
Westons Flat
Cadell
L. Woolpolool

CLARE VALLEY WINE REGION
Clare
Watervale
Leasingham
Manoora
Waterloo
Robertstown
Eba
Qualco
POOGINOOK CONSERVATION PARK
River Murray

6

Lochiel
Nantawarra
Kybunga
Auburn
Point Pass
Australia Plains
Ramco
Cowbank
Barmera
Renmark
Paringa
Lindsay Point

Kulpara
Beaufort
Rhynie
Saddleworth
Julia
Taranna
Peep Hill
Bower
Mount Mary
Waikerie
Kingston-on-Murray
Moorook
Monash
Glossop
Berri
Lyrup

7

Port Clinton
Price
Inkerman
Balaklava
Salter Springs
Giles Corner
Marrabel
Hamley
Riverton
Hampden
Eudunda
Neales Flat
Sutherlands
Blanchetown
New Well
Boolgun
Loveday
Winkie
Loxton

Wild Horse Plains
Bowmans
Erith
Avon
Owen
Alma
Tarlee
Hansborough
Allendale North
Bagot Well
Frankton
Stonefield
Notts Well
Myrla
Pyap
Loxton North
Noora

8

Windsor
Long Plains
Pinery
Hamley Bridge
Kapunda
Dutton
Truro
Stockwell
Sedan
Swan Reach
Bakara
Wunkar
Maggea
Taplan

Dublin
Mallala
Freeling
Greenock
Nuriootpa
Angaston
Keyneton
Black Hill
Wongulla
Kunlara
Galga
Alawoona
Malpas
Meribah

Lower Light
Two Wells
Gawler
Tanunda
Lyndoch
Williamstown
Eden Valley
Springton
Cambrai
Forster
Nildottie
Copeville
Wanbi
Cobera
Paruna

MURRAY-SUNSET NATIONAL PARK
44

9

Port Gawler
Virginia
ELIZABETH
SALISBURY
Birdwood
Mount Pleasant
Tungkillo
Walker Flat
Teal Flat
Purnong
Bowhill
Kalyan
Mindarie
Halidon
Peebinga
Berrook

PORT ADELAIDE
GULF ST VINCENT
ADELAIDE
GLENELG
Kersbrook
Gumeracha
Lobethal
Woodside
Palmer
Apamurra
Younghusband
Coolcha
Perponda
Borrika
Kilpalie
Sandalwood
Karte
Kringin

BILLIATT CONSERVATION PARK

Clarendon
Mount Barker
Balhannah
Hahndorf
Tepko
Mannum
Mypolonga
Field Hill
Perponda
Mindiyarra
Lowaldie
Prieberra Bore
PEEBINGA CP

10

PORT NOARLUNGA
Old Noarlunga
MOANA
McLaren Vale
Meadows
Kangarilla
Macclesfield
Callington
Monarto South
Murray Bridge
Wynarka
Yurgo
Kulkami
Marama
Mulpata
Pinnaroo
Parilla
Lameroo
Murrayville

Aldinga Beach
Sellicks Beach
Willunga
Ashbourne
Woodchester
Strathalbyn
Langhorne Creek
Tailem Bend
Sherlock
Buccleuch
Geranium
Wilkawatt
12 24

11

Normanville
Yankalilla
Myponga
Mount Compass
Nangkita
Finniss
Wellington
Cooke Plains
Malinong
Yumali
Ki Ki
Peake
Jabuk
Parrakie
SCORPION SPRINGS CONSERVATION PARK

Rapid Bay
Second Valley
Port Elliot
Goolwa
Milang
Narrung
Ashville
One Tree Hill 140m
Carcuma
CARCUMA CP
NGARKAT CONSERVATION PARK
BIG DESERT WILDERNESS PARK

DEEP CREEK CP
FLEURIEU PENINSULA
Victor Harbor
Encounter Bay
Lake Alexandrina
Raukkan Aboriginal Settlement
Lake Albert
Waltowa
Meningie
Coonalpyn
Culburra
MOUNT RESCUE CONSERVATION PARK

12

For more detail on Adelaide Region see pages 58 & 59

Noonameena
Camp Coorong
Magrath Flat
Mt Boothby 130m
MOUNT BOOTHBY CP
Tintinara
Coombe
Mt Shaugh 184m
MOUNT SHAUGH CP

SOUTH AUSTRALIA
VICTORIA
42

13

SOUTHERN OCEAN
COORONG NATIONAL PARK
Policemans Point
Salt Creek
Woods Well
PRINCES HWY
Sugarloaf 107m
Wirrega
MESSENT CONSERVATION PARK
Kurfinna
Coombe
Keith
Brimbago

70

J K L M N O P Q R

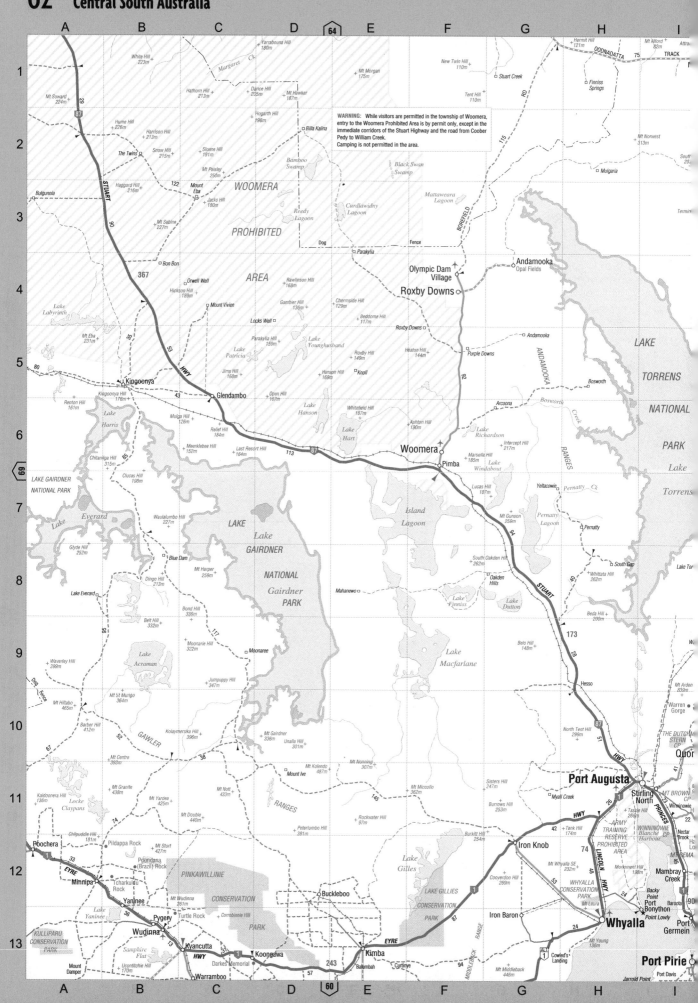

WARNING: While visitors are permitted in the township of Woomera, entry to the Woomera Prohibited Area is by permit only, except in the immediate corridors of the Stuart Highway and the road from Coober Pedy to William Creek. Camping is not permitted in the area.

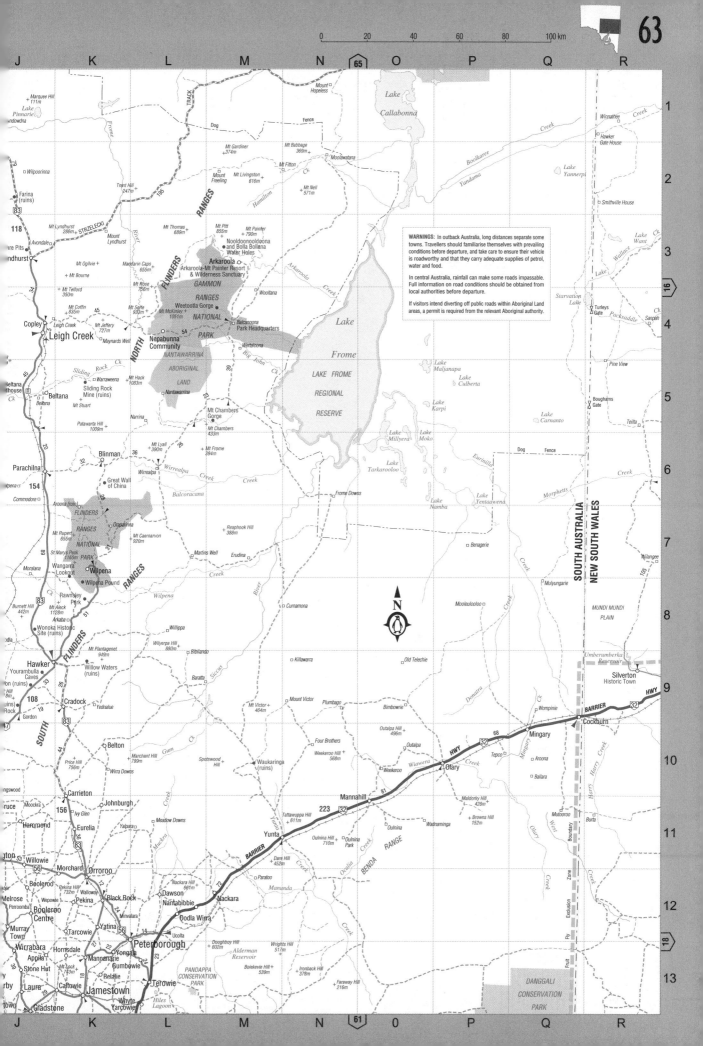

0   20   40   60   80   100 km

WARNINGS: In outback Australia, long distances separate some towns. Travellers should familiarise themselves with prevailing conditions before departure, and take care to ensure their vehicle is roadworthy and that they carry adequate supplies of petrol, water and food.

In central Australia, rainfall can make some roads impassable. Full information on road conditions should be obtained from local authorities before departure.

If visitors intend diverting off public roads within Aboriginal Land areas, a permit is required from the relevant Aboriginal authority.

Mount Hopeless

Lake Callabonna

Winnathee Creek

Hawker Gate House

Wilpoorinna

Lake Yannerpi

Mount Gardiner +374m

Mt Babbage 369m+

Moolawatana

Bookaree

Yandama Creek

Lake Want

Lake Wallace Ck

Farina (ruins)

Mount Freeling

Mt Livingston 616m

Mt Fitton

Mt Neil 571m

Smithville House

Trent Hill 247m+

Dog Ck

Fence

Hamilton

Mt Lyndhurst 286m+ STRZELECKI

Mount Lyndhurst

Mt Thomas 689m+

Mt Pitt 855m+

Mt Painter +790m

Nooldoonooldoona and Bolla Bollana Water Holes

Starvation Lake

118

Avondale

Mt Ogilvie +

+ Mt Bourne

Maandarin Caps + 655m

Arkaroola

Arkaroola-Mt Painter Resort & Wilderness Sanctuary

GAMMON RANGES

Wooltana

Arkaroola Creek

Turleys Gate

Packsaddle

Sanpah Ck

+ Mt Telford 350m

Mt Rose 756m

NATIONAL

Lake

Pine View

Mt Coffin + 835m

Mt Serle 933m

Weetootla Gorge

Mt McKinley + 1051m

PARK

Balcanoona

Frome

Lake Maljanapa

Lake Culberta

Boughams Gate

Copley

Leigh Creek

45

Mt Jeffery 727m

54

Park Headquarters

Lake Karpi

Teilta

Leigh Creek

Maynards Well

Nepabunna Community

NANTAWARRINA

Wertaloona

LAKE FROME

REGIONAL

Lake Karnanto

Mt Stuart

Sliding Rock Ck

Warraweena

Mt Hack 1083m

ABORIGINAL

Big John Ck

RESERVE

Lake Millyera

Lake Moko

Beltana

Sliding Rock Mine (ruins)

LAND

Nantawarrina

Narrina

Mt Chambers Gorge

Lake Tarkarooloo

Lake Namba

Lake Carnanto

Parachilna

Blinman

Mt Lyall +390m

+ Mt Frome 394m

Eurinilla Creek

Dog Fence

154

Great Wall of China

36

Wirrealpa

26

Mt Chambers 433m

Wirrealpa Creek

Lake Yentaawena

Morphetts Ck

Commodore

Aroona (ruin)

FLINDERS

Orapanna

Balcoracana Creek

Frome Downs

Mt Rupert 655m

RANGES

28

Mt Caernarvon 920m

Reaphook Hill + 388m

Benagerie

Moralana

St Marys Peak 1165m +

NATIONAL PARK

31

Martins Well

Mulyungarie

Wangarra Lookout

Wilpena

Erudina

Wilangee

Wilpena Pound

RANGES

Wilpena Creek

Rawnsley Park

Creek

Curnamona

MUNDI MUNDI PLAIN

Burnett Hill 442m

Mt Aleck 1128m

51

Willippa

Mooleulooloo

Arkaba

Mt Plantagenet 949m

Wilyerpa Hill + 880m

Bibliando

Umberumberka Reservoir

Wonoka Historic Site (ruins)

Willow Waters (ruins)

Killawarra

Old Telechie

Silverton Historic Town

Hawker

Yourambulla Caves

Baratta

Sicaus

Donara Ck

BARRIER

HWY

32

108

Cradock

Yednalue

Mt Victor + 464m

Mount Victor

Plumbago

Bimbowrie

Wompinie

Cockburn

Gordon

SOUTH

Belton

Four Brothers

Outalpa Hill 496m

Outalpa

68

Mingary

Aroona

19

Marchant Hill 799m

Spotswood Hill

Weekeroo Hill + 568m

Weekeroo

32

Tepco

Price Hill 756m

Waukaringa (ruins)

Wiawera Ck

Olary

Ballara

Carrieton

Johnburgh

Wirra Downs

Mannahill

81

Maldorky Hill + 428m

Mutooroo

156

Moockra

Ivy Glen

Meadow Downs

223 32

Olnina

Browns Hill 152m

Burta

Hammond

Eurelia

Yalpara

Tattawuppa Hill + 611m

Wadnaminga

Willowie

Morchard

Yunta

Tarata

Oulnina Hill 710m

Oulnina Park

RANGE

Boundary

Murray Town

Booleroo

Pekina Hill 732m

Walloway

Nackara Hill + 661m

Dare Hill + 452m

BENDA

Exclusion Zone

Melrose

Pekina

Black Rock

Dawson

Paratoo

Manunda

Booleroo Centre

Wepowie

Nantabibbie

Oodla Wirra

Murray Town

Yatina

Ucolta

Doughboy Hill + 602m

Alderman Reservoir

Wrights Hill 517m

Wirrabara

Appila

Hornsdale

Mannanarie

Gumbowie

Peterborough

Boieskevie Hill + 539m

Ironback Hill 378m

Faraway Hill 216m

DANGGALI CONSERVATION PARK

Stone Hut

Mt Lock 743m

Beetaloo

PANDAPPA CONSERVATION PARK

Hiles Lagoon

Laura

Caltowie

Jamestown

Whyte Yarcowie

Gladstone

A B C D E F G H I

NORTHERN TERRITORY

SOUTH AUSTRALIA

Mt Wilyunpa 227m

Mount Dare

Mt Apperda 245m

Mt Alinerta 222m

Mirranponga Ponguna Lake

Poeppel C

Larrys Hill 63m

Pitlari 60m

SIMPSON DESERT

Mt Weeahlakiminne 292m

WITJIRA

SIMPSON DESERT

CONSERVATION

PARK

Blood Creek Bore

Mt Hammersley 229m

Dalhousie Springs

NATIONAL

Poolowanna Lake

Mt Crispe 279m

Dalhousie (ruins)

REGIONAL

Beale Hill 53m

Mt Emery 289m

Mt Dillon 234m

PARK

RESERVE

Perra Perra Poolanna Lake

SIMPSON DESERT

Hamilton

Mt Yangalee 244m

WARNING: Visitors planning to enter Desert Parks are required to contact the National Parks and Wildlife Service. A Desert Pass is necessary.

Ephemeral Lakes

SIMPSON

Mount Sarah

Lake Griselda

Mt Sarah 260m

DESERT

Stevenson Creek

REGIONAL

Mt Alexander 285m

Umaroo Lake

Macumba

Macumba

RESERVE

Willawilaninna Lake

River

Pialopotingoona Lake

Pantoowarinna Lake

Warri

Oodnadatta

Mt Carulina 211m

Mt Areebinna 245m

Lake Noalyeana

Millyeewilpa Lake

Peeramudlayeppa Lake

Hanns Hill 238m

Pompapillinna Lake

Stewart Hill 180m

OODNADATTA

Mt Dutton 176m

Warburton

Koolkootinnie Lake

Kalar

Mt Kingston North 209m

Neales

Lake

Arckaringa Creek

Peake Creek

Creek

River

Eyre

LAKE EYRE

Mt Denison 238m

Creek

North

NATIONAL

Lombing Creek

Peake

Ricketts Hill

Umbum Creek

Lake Me

Mount Barry

Lake Conway

Hawker Creek

PARK

Creek

Aimet Creek

TRACK 203

Mt Margaret 412m

Four Hills 106m

LAKE EYRE

NATIONAL

Nilpinna

Davenport

Creek

PARK

WARNING: While visitors are permitted in the township of Woomera, entry to the Woomera Prohibited Area is by permit only, except in the immediate corridors of the Stuart Highway and the road from Coober Pedy to William Creek. Camping is not permitted in the area.

Mt Anna 265m

Douglas

405

ELLIOT PRICE CONSERVATION PARK

Ruby Hill 111m

Lake Cadibarrawirracanna

Anna Creek

William Creek

OODNADATTA

Lake Ellen

Lake Frances

166

Creek

Creek

WOOMERA

Warriner

Lake Eyre South

Lake Frances

STUART HWY

Engenina Creek

Balta Creek

PROHIBITED

Creek

Beresford Hill 71m

127

Coward Springs

LAKE EYRE NATIONAL PARK

Lake Eyre South

Mulle

Campeera Hill 158m

AREA

Hamilton Hill 40m

Curdimurka (ruins)

Welcome or Francos Creek

Mt Woods 170m

Margaret Creek

Bidna Boudna Hill 162m

New Peter Hill 163m

Blanche Cup Mound Springs

Fence

Mt Penrhyn 216m

Mt Purvis 201m

Mt Riddoch 182m

Hermit Hill 121m

Mt Alford 82m

Attrac

Mt Sandy 223m

Brumby Creek

Fence

Yarrabouna Hill 180m

Margaret Creek

TRACK 75

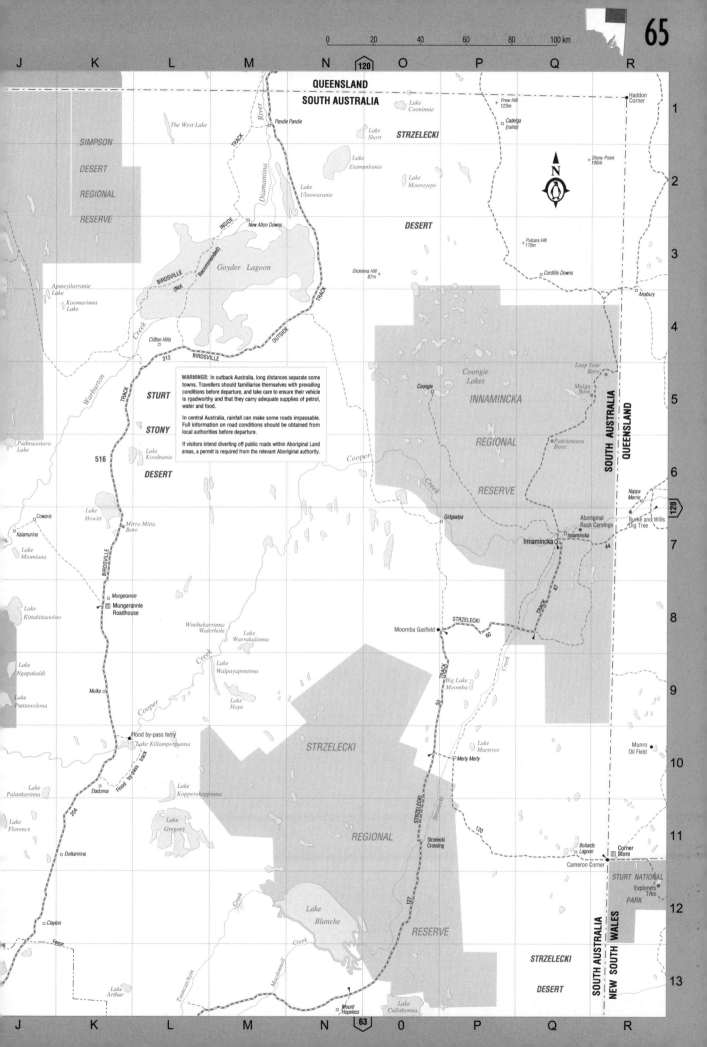

0 20 40 60 80 100 km

J K L M N 120 O P Q R

QUEENSLAND
SOUTH AUSTRALIA

Haddon
Corner

1

Lake
Cooninnie

Frew Hill
123m

The West Lake

Pandie Pandie

STRZELECKI

Cadelga
(ruins)

SIMPSON

Lake
Short

2

DESERT

Lake
Etamanbanie

Stony Point
195m

REGIONAL

Lake
Uloowaranie

DESERT

Lake
Moorayepe

Pulcara Hill
170m

3

RESERVE

New Alton Downs

INSIDE

Goyder Lagoon

Dickinna Hill
87m

Cordillo Downs

Apawyilarranie
Lake

BIRDSVILLE
(Not

Recommended)

Araluru

4

Koomarinna
Lake

TRACK

OUTSIDE

Leap Year
Bore

Clifton Hills

BIRDSVILLE

Coongie
Lakes

Mulga
Bore

Coongie

INNAMINCKA

5

Warburton

312

STURT

INNAMINCKA

QUEENSLAND

Pathraootara
Lake

STONY

REGIONAL

Patchawara
Bore

516

Lake
Koodnanie

SOUTH AUSTRALIA

Cooper

Nappa
Merrie

6

DESERT

RESERVE

Creek

120

Lake
Howitt

Gidgealpa

Aboriginal
Rock Carvings

Burke and Wills
Dig Tree

7

Cowarie

Mirra Mitta
Bore

Innamincka

Kalamurina

BIRDSVILLE

Innamincka

Lake
Miamiana

AA

Mungerannie

Mungerannie
Roadhouse

TRACK

47

STRZELECKI

8

Lake
Kittakittaooloo

Winthekarrinna
Waterhole

Lake
Warrakalanna

Moomba Gasfield

60

Creek

Lake
Ngapakaldi

Lake
Walpayapeninna

TRACK

Big Lake
Moomba

9

Lake
Puntawolona

Mulka

Cooper

Lake
Hope

50

Flood by-pass ferry
Lake Killamperpunna

Lake
Murteree

Munro
Oil Field

10

Lake
Palankarinna

Etadunna

Flood by-pass track

Lake
Kopperekoppinna

Merty Merty

STRZELECKI

11

204

Lake
Gregory

REGIONAL

Strzelecki Crossing

120

Bollards
Lagoon

Corner
Store

Lake
Florence

Cameron Corner

Dulkaninna

STRZELECKI

STURT NATIONAL

Explorers
Tree

PARK

12

Clayton

127

Lake
Blanche

RESERVE

SOUTH AUSTRALIA

NEW SOUTH WALES

Fence

Creek

STRZELECKI

13

Lake
Arthur

Mount
Hopeless

Lake
Callabonna

DESERT

J K L M 63 N O P Q R

WARNINGS: In outback Australia, long distances separate some
towns. Travellers should familiarise themselves with prevailing
conditions before departure, and take care to ensure their vehicle
is roadworthy and that they carry adequate supplies of petrol,
water and food.

In central Australia, rainfall can make some roads impassable.
Full information on road conditions should be obtained from
local authorities before departure.

If visitors intend diverting off public roads within Aboriginal Land
areas, a permit is required from the relevant Aboriginal authority.

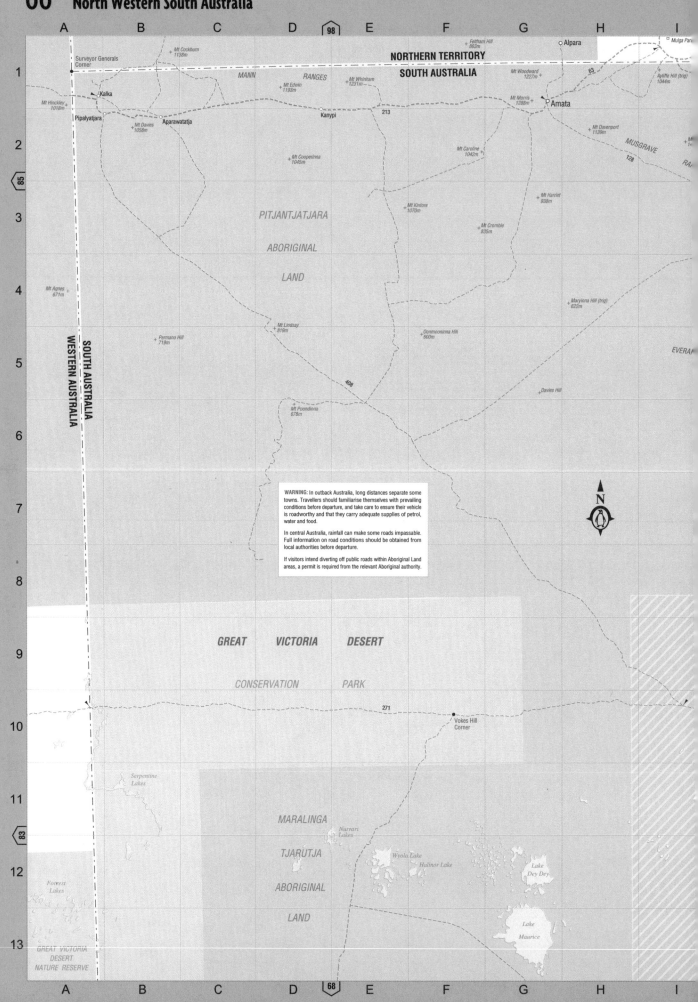

NORTHERN TERRITORY

SOUTH AUSTRALIA

Surveyor Generals
Corner

Mt Hinckley
1018m

Kalka

Pipalyatjara

MANN   RANGES

Mt Cockburn
1138m

Mt Edwin
1193m

Mt Davies
1058m

Aparawatatja

Mt Whinham
1231m

Kanypi

213

Feltham Hill
863m

Alpara

Mt Woodward
1227m

Mt Morris
1288m

Amata

63

Ayliffe Hill (trig)
1044m

Mulga Park

Mt Davenport
1139m

MUSGRAVE

128

RA

PITJANTJATJARA

ABORIGINAL

LAND

Mt Cooperinna
1045m

Mt Kintore
1070m

Mt Caroline
1042m

Mt Harriet
938m

Mt Crombie
835m

Mt Agnes
671m

Permano Hill
719m

Mt Lindsay
819m

Oonmooninna Hill
600m

Maryinna Hill (trig)
622m

EVERAR

408

Davies Hill

Mt Poondinna
678m

WARNING: In outback Australia, long distances separate some
towns. Travellers should familiarise themselves with prevailing
conditions before departure, and take care to ensure their vehicle
is roadworthy and that they carry adequate supplies of petrol,
water and food.

In central Australia, rainfall can make some roads impassable.
Full information on road conditions should be obtained from
local authorities before departure.

If visitors intend diverting off public roads within Aboriginal Land
areas, a permit is required from the relevant Aboriginal authority.

N

GREAT   VICTORIA   DESERT

CONSERVATION   PARK

271

Vokes Hill
Corner

Serpentine
Lakes

MARALINGA

Nurrari
Lakes

TJARUTJA

Wyola Lake

Halinor Lake

Lake
Dey Dey

ABORIGINAL

LAND

Forrest
Lakes

Lake
Maurice

GREAT VICTORIA
DESERT
NATURE RESERVE

SOUTH AUSTRALIA
WESTERN AUSTRALIA

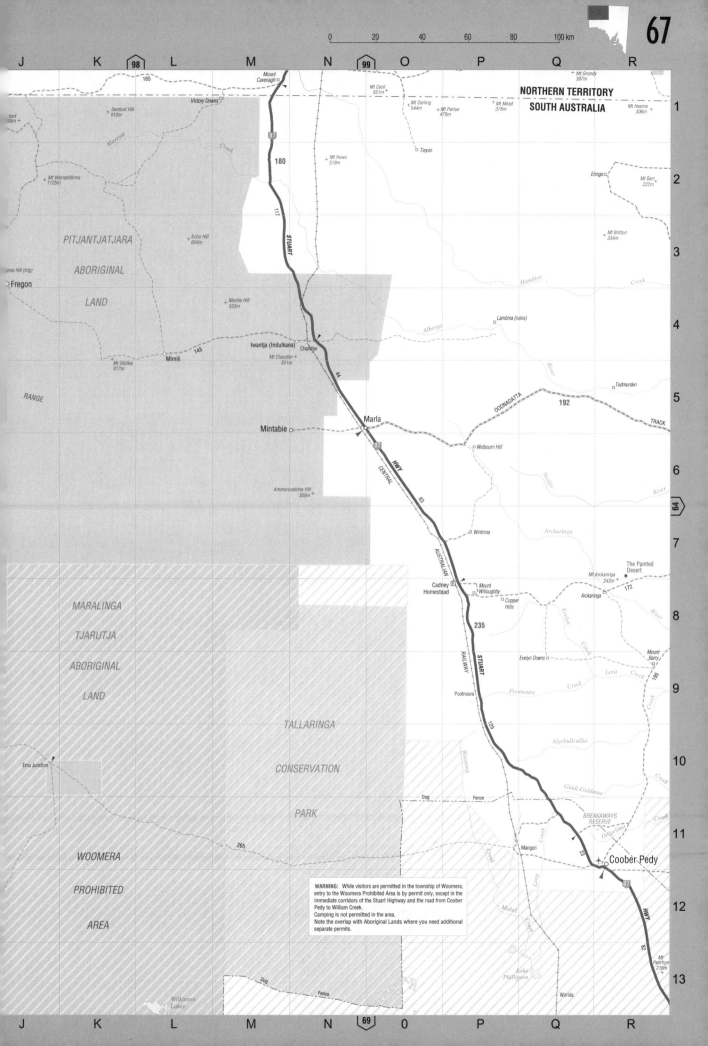

0 20 40 60 80 100 km

J K 98 L M N 99 O P Q R

NORTHERN TERRITORY
SOUTH AUSTRALIA

Mount Cavenagh □

165

Victory Downs □

+ Sentinel Hill 910m

+ Mt Grundy 397m

Mt Darling 544m   + Mt Parlue 478m   + Mt Mead 376m

Mt Hearne 306m

1

180

117

+ Mt Howe 519m

□ Tieyon

Eringa □   + Mt Barr 222m

2

STUART

PITJANTJATJARA

ABORIGINAL

LAND

+ Mt Warrabillinna 1125m

+ Echo Hill 604m

+ Mt Britton 334m

3

○ Fregon

+ Marble Hill 523m

Hamilton   Creek

Alberga   River

Lambina (ruins) □

4

143

Iwantja (Indulkana) ○   Chandler

Mt Chandler + 551m

44

+ Mt Illbillee 917m

Mimili ○

Todmorden □

5

RANGE

OODNADATTA

192

TRACK

Mintabie ○

Marla ○

87

Welbourn Hill □

Neales   River

River

6

HWY

CENTRAL

Ammaroodinna Hill 359m +

83

Arckaringa

64

7

□ Wintinna

+ Mt Arckaringa 243m •

The Painted Desert

AUSTRALIAN

Cadney □ Homestead

+ Mount Willoughby □

Copper Hills □

Arckaringa   172

River

8

235

Evelyn   Creek

STUART

RAILWAY

Evelyn Downs □

Mount Barry

105

9

Pootnoura ○

Pootnoura   Creek

Lora   Creek

129

Algebullcullia

10

Emu Junction ▸

TALLARINGA

CONSERVATION

PARK

Woorong

Giddi-Giddinna   Creek

BREAKAWAYS RESERVE

Oolgelima   Creek

11

265

Dog   Fence

Manguri □

Creek

23

Coober Pedy ○

WOOMERA

PROHIBITED

AREA

WARNING: While visitors are permitted in the township of Woomera, entry to the Woomera Prohibited Area is by permit only, except in the immediate corridors of the Stuart Highway and the road from Coober Pedy to William Creek.
Camping is not permitted in the area.
Note the overlap with Aboriginal Lands where you need additional separate permits.

Long   Creek

87

HWY

12

Mabel   Creek

78

+ Mt Penrhyn 216m

Dog   Fence

Wilkinson Lakes

Lake Phillipson

Wirrida □

13

J K L M N 69 O P Q R

MARALINGA

TJARUTJA

ABORIGINAL

LAND

A   B   C   D   66   E   F   G   H   I

1

GREAT
VICTORIA
DESERT
NATURE
RESERVE

CONSERVATION

PARK

MARALINGA

TJARUTJA

ABORIGINAL

LAND

OOLDEA

RANGE

2

3

Maralinga

SOUTH AUSTRALIA
WESTERN AUSTRALIA

NULLARBOR   PLAIN

Watson   31   Oc

RAILWAY   Fisher   O'Malley

4

83

AUSTRALIA   Cook

TRANS   Denman
Hughes

Deakin

5

NULLARBOR   REGIONAL   RESERVE

125

105

6

NULLARBOR   NATIONAL   PARK

7

94

YALATA

Nullarbor
Roadhouse   ● Whale Watching

ABORIGINAL

Yala

293   55

Lookout

HWY   42

Head
of Bight

LAND   Y
Roa

Agricultural
Check Point   Border
Village   EYRE   89

13   Lookouts

Eucla   Lookouts

EUCLA
NP

Lookouts

8

9

10   GREAT   AUSTRALIAN   BIGHT

11

12   N

13

A   B   C   D   E   F   G   H   I

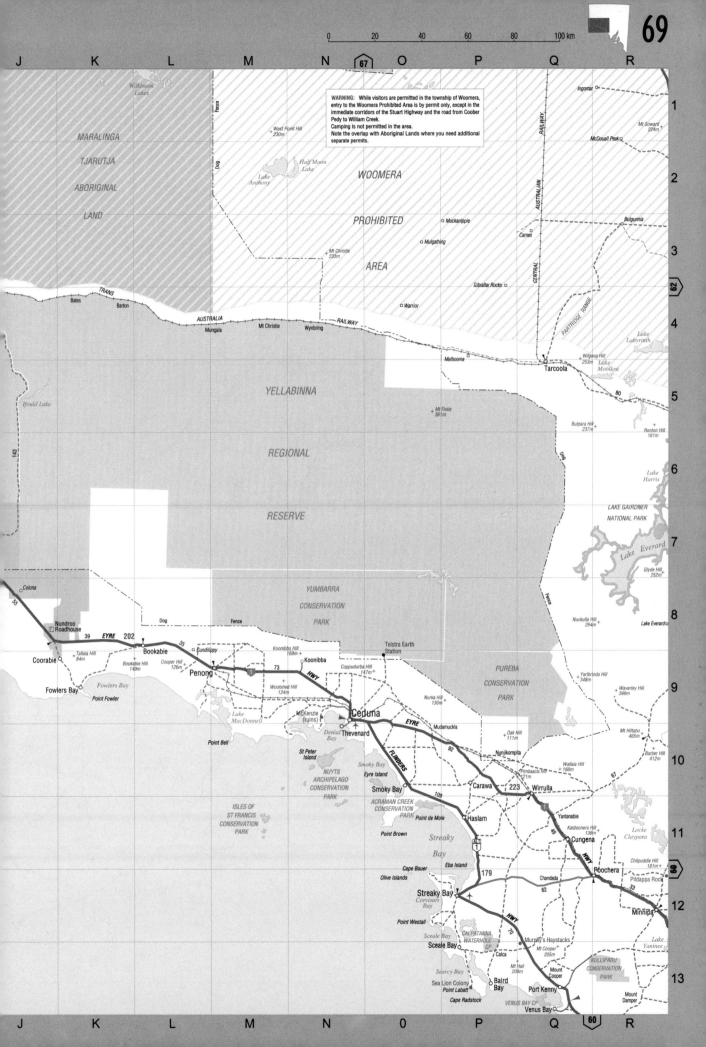

0 20 40 60 80 100 km

61

GULF
ST VINCENT
PORT ADELAIDE
ADELAIDE
GLENELG
PORT NOARLUNGA
Old Noarlunga
MOANA
McLaren Vale
Willunga
Sellicks Beach
Aldinga Beach
Myponga
Normanville
Yankalilla
Rapid Bay
Second Valley
Cape Jervis
Kangaroo Island Vehicular & Passenger Ferry
DEEP CREEK CONSERVATION PARK
FLEURIEU PENINSULA
DUDLEY PENINSULA
Antechamber Bay
Cape St Albans
Cape Willoughby
CAPE HART CONSERVATION PARK
Cape Hart

ELIZABETH
Williamstown
SALISBURY
Kersbrook
Gumeracha
Birdwood
Springton
Mount Pleasant
Tungkillo
Palmer
Apamurra
Lobethal
Woodside
Hahndorf
Balhannah
Mount Barker
Clarendon
Kangarilla
Meadows
Macclesfield
Woodchester
Callington
Monarto South
Strathalbyn
Ashbourne
Belvidere
Langhorne Creek
Finniss
Milang
Mount Compass
Nangkita
Port Elliot
Goolwa
Victor Harbor
Hindmarsh Island
Encounter Bay
Raukkan Aboriginal Settlement
Narrung
NEWLAND HEAD CP
YOUNGHUSBAND
Noonameena
Camp Coorong
Magrath Flat
COORONG
Woods Well
Policemans Point
Salt Creek
NATIONAL PARK PENINSULA

Black Hill
Wongulla
Forster
Nildotte
Teal Flat
Walker Flat
Purnong
Bowhill
Coolcha
Mannum
Mypolonga
Murray Bridge
Monarto
Woods Point
Jervois
Tailem Bend
Wellington
Cooke Plains
Ashville
Malinong
Coomandook
Yumali
Waltowa
Ki Ki
Carcuma
Coonalpyn
Culburra
Tintinara
Keith
Wirrega
Kongal
Buckingham
Willalooka
Padthaway
Wolseley
Bordertown
Mundulla
Western Flat
Keppoch
Wallabrook
Naracoorte
Lucindale
Kingston SE
Reedy Creek
Avenue
Hynam
Kybybolite
Cape Jaffa
Kings Camp
Mount Benson
Boatswain Point
Robe
Nora Creina
Chinaman Wells
Clay Wells
Furner
Beachport
Southend
Rendelsham
Hatherleigh
Mount Burr
Penola
Coonawarra
Nangwarry
Kalangadoo
Tarpeena
Millicent
Snuggery
Tantanoola
Glencoe West
Glencoe
Wandilo
Strathdownie
Mount Gambier
Corattum
Carpenter Rocks
Blackfellow Caves
Nene Valley
Allendale East
Kongorong
Mount Schank
Yahl
Donovans Landing
Port MacDonnell
Nelson

SOUTHERN OCEAN

N

Kunlara
Galga
Wanbi
Alawoona
Malpas
Paruna
Meribah
Copeville
Mindarie
Halidon
Sandalwood
Kilpalie
Borrika
Perponda
Karoonda
Wynarka
Marama
Yurgo
Kulkami
Mulpata
Parilla
Pinnaroo
Lameroo
Parrakie
Wilkawatt
Geranium
Jabuk
Peake
Sherlock
Buccleuch
MALLEE HWY
Kringin
Karte
Peebinga
Bolton's Bore
MURRAY-SUNSET NATIONAL PARK
BILLIATT CONSERVATION PARK
KARTE CP
PEEBINGA CP
SCORPION SPRINGS CONSERVATION PARK
BIG DESERT WILDERNESS PARK
NGARKAT CONSERVATION PARK
MOUNT SHAUGH CP
MOUNT RESCUE CONSERVATION PARK
Apsley
Langkoop
Poolaijelo
Coonawarra
DERGHOLM STATE PARK
Minimay
Neuarpurr
Apsley
LITTLE DESERT NATIONAL PARK
Servicetion
Dinyarrak
SOUTH AUSTRALIA / VICTORIA

DISCOVERY BAY COASTAL PARK
Discovery Bay

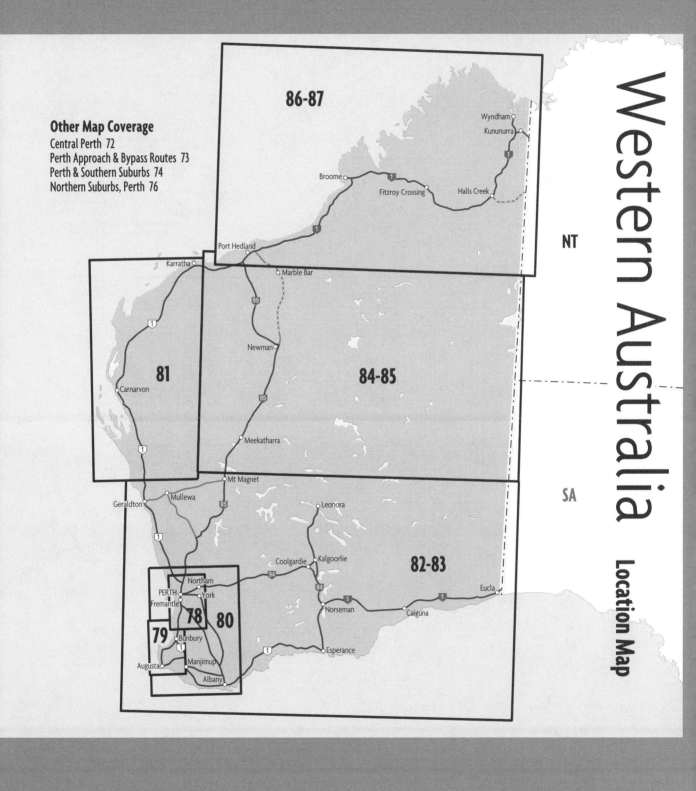

Other Map Coverage

Central Perth 72
Perth Approach & Bypass Routes 73
Perth & Southern Suburbs 74
Northern Suburbs, Perth 76

86-87

Wyndham
Kununurra

Broome
Fitzroy Crossing
Halls Creek

NT

Port Hedland
Karratha
Marble Bar

81

Newman

84-85

Carnarvon

Meekatharra

Mt Magnet

SA

Geraldton
Mullewa

Leonora

Coolgardie
Kalgoorlie

82-83

Eucla

Nortgham
PERTH
Fremantle
York

78
80

Norseman
Caiguna

79
Bunbury

Augusta
Manjimup
Esperance

Albany

Western Australia

Location Map

0 0.25 0.5 0.75 1 km

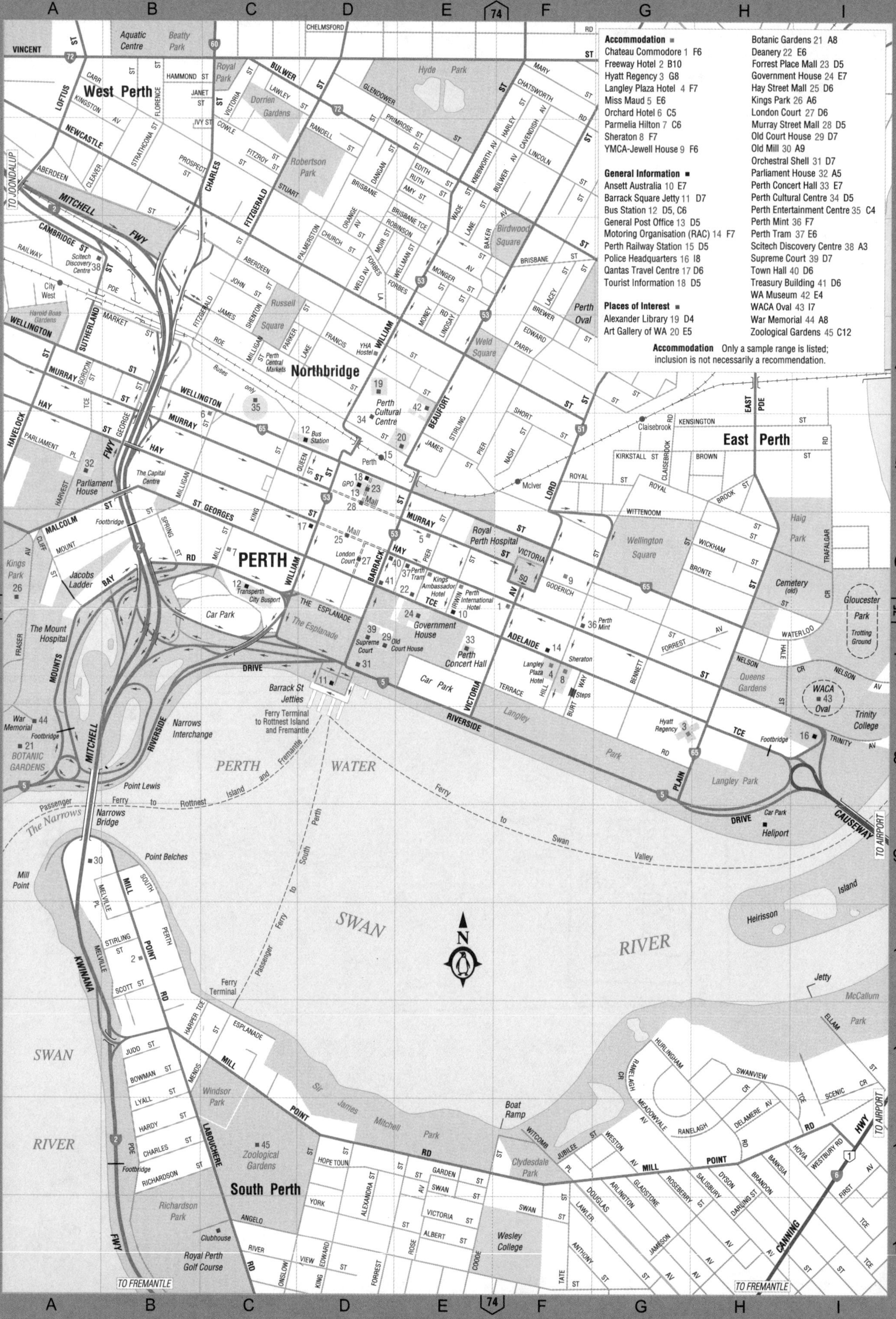

Accommodation
Chateau Commodore 1 F6
Freeway Hotel 2 B10
Hyatt Regency 3 G8
Langley Plaza Hotel 4 F7
Miss Maud 5 E6
Orchard Hotel 6 C5
Parmelia Hilton 7 C6
Sheraton 8 F7
YMCA-Jewell House 9 F6
General Information
Ansett Australia 10 E7
Barrack Square Jetty 11 D7
Bus Station 12 D5, C6
General Post Office 13 D5
Motoring Organisation (RAC) 14 F7
Perth Railway Station 15 D5
Police Headquarters 16 I8
Qantas Travel Centre 17 D6
Tourist Information 18 D5
Places of Interest
Alexander Library 19 D4
Art Gallery of WA 20 E5
Botanic Gardens 21 A8
Deanery 22 E6
Forrest Place Mall 23 D5
Government House 24 E7
Hay Street Mall 25 D6
Kings Park 26 A6
London Court 27 D6
Murray Street Mall 28 D5
Old Court House 29 D7
Old Mill 30 A9
Orchestral Shell 31 D7
Parliament House 32 A5
Perth Concert Hall 33 E7
Perth Cultural Centre 34 D5
Perth Entertainment Centre 35 C4
Perth Mint 36 F7
Perth Tram 37 E6
Scitech Discovery Centre 38 A3
Supreme Court 39 D7
Town Hall 40 D6
Treasury Building 41 D6
WA Museum 42 E4
WACA Oval 43 I7
War Memorial 44 A8
Zoological Gardens 45 C12
Accommodation Only a sample range is listed; inclusion is not necessarily a recommendation.
West Perth
Northbridge
PERTH
East Perth
South Perth
PERTH WATER
SWAN RIVER
Heirisson Island
TO JOONDALUP
TO FREMANTLE
TO AIRPORT

0 1 2 3 4 5 km

TO JOONDALUP TO WANNEROO

Suburbs and localities (north to south, roughly):

Hillarys, Padbury, Kingsley, Landsdale, Lake Goollelal
Sorrento, Duncraig, Greenwood, Marangaroo, Alexander Heights, Cullacabardee, Whiteman Park
Marmion, Waterman, North Beach, Carine, Hamersley, Girrawheen, Koondoola, Ballajura, Whiteman
Trigg, Karrinyup, Balcatta, Nollamara, Mirrabooka, Malaga, Beechboro, West Swan
Stirling, Doubleview, Tuart Hill, Noranda, Morley, Lockridge
Scarborough, Innaloo, Osborne Park, Joondanna, Coolbinia, Dianella, Embleton, Eden Hill
Woodlands, Wembley Downs, Bedford, Inglewood, Bayswater, Bassendean, Ashfield
City Beach, Floreat, Jolimont, Wembley, Lake Monger, North Perth, Mt Lawley, Ascot, Redcliffe, Maylands, Perth Airport
Shenton Park, Subiaco, Mt Claremont, Kings Park, PERTH, East Perth, Burswood, Belmont, Cloverdale, Rivervale
Swanbourne, Karrakatta, Nedlands, Claremont, Crawley, Riverside Dr, Perth Water, Lathlain, Carlisle, Kewdale, Welshpool
Cottesloe, Dalkeith, Swan River, South Perth, Victoria Park, Kensington, St James, Como, Karawara, Bentley, Queens Park, Cannington
Mosman Park, Bicton, Applecross, Manning, Waterford, Riverton, Ferndale, Beckenham
North Fremantle, East Fremantle, Melville, Myaree, Mt Pleasant, Brentwood, Canning River, Lynwood, Langford
Fremantle, O'Connor, Willagee, Winthrop, Bull Creek, Willetton, Thornlie
South Fremantle, Beaconsfield, Kardinya, Bateman, Murdoch University, Leeming
Spearwood, Coolbellup, North Lake, Bibra Lake, Jandakot, Jandakot Airport, Canning Vale, Huntingdale

INDIAN OCEAN

TO MIDLAND
TO KALGOORLIE
TO ARMADALE
TO ALBANY
TO MANDURAH

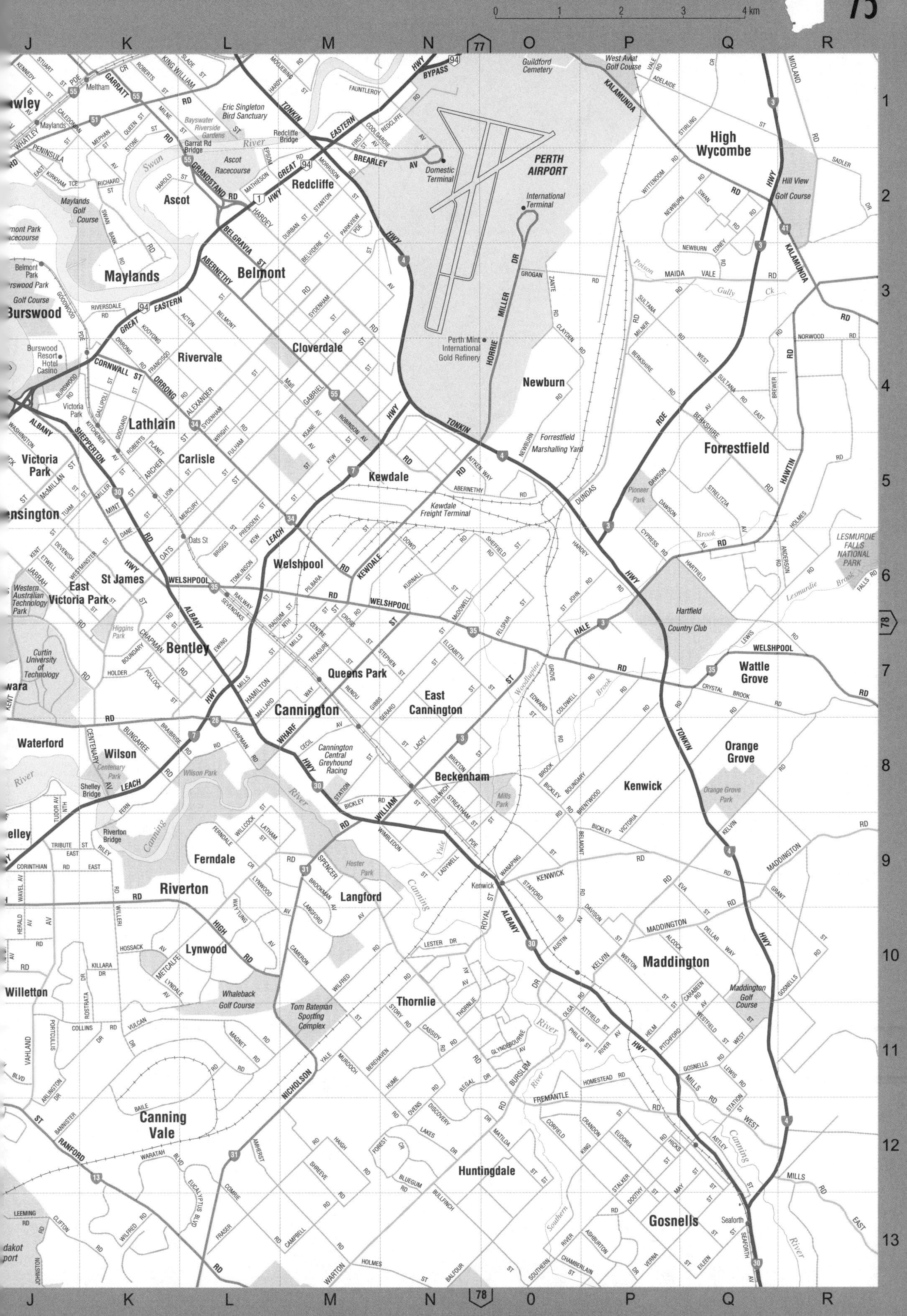

0 1 2 3 4 km

J K L M N O P Q R

1 2 3 4 5 6 7 8 9 10 11 12 13

PERTH AIRPORT
Domestic Terminal
International Terminal

High Wycombe
Hill View Golf Course
West Aviat Golf Course
Guildford Cemetery

Maylands
Ascot
Ascot Racecourse
Maylands Golf Course
Eric Singleton Bird Sanctuary
Bayswater Riverside Gardens
Belmont
Redcliffe
Belmont Park Racecourse

Burswood
Burswood Resort Hotel Casino
Victoria Park
Rivervale
Cloverdale
Newburn
Perth Mint International Gold Refinery
Forrestfield Marshalling Yard
Maida Vale

Lathlain
Carlisle
Kewdale
Kewdale Freight Terminal
Roe
Forrestfield
Pioneer Park

East Victoria Park
St James
Welshpool
Welshpool
Hartfield Country Club
Wattle Grove
Lesmurdie Falls National Park

Western Australian Technology Park
Curtin University of Technology
Bentley
Queens Park
East Cannington
Orange Grove
Orange Grove Park

Waterford
Wilson
Centenary Park
Wilson Park
Cannington
Cannington Central Greyhound Racing
Beckenham
Kenwick
Mills Park

Shelley
Riverton
Riverton Bridge
Shelley Bridge
Ferndale
Langford
Hester Park
Kenwick

Willetton
Lynwood
Whaleback Golf Course
Tom Bateman Sporting Complex
Thornlie
Maddington
Maddington Golf Course

Canning Vale
Huntingdale
Gosnells

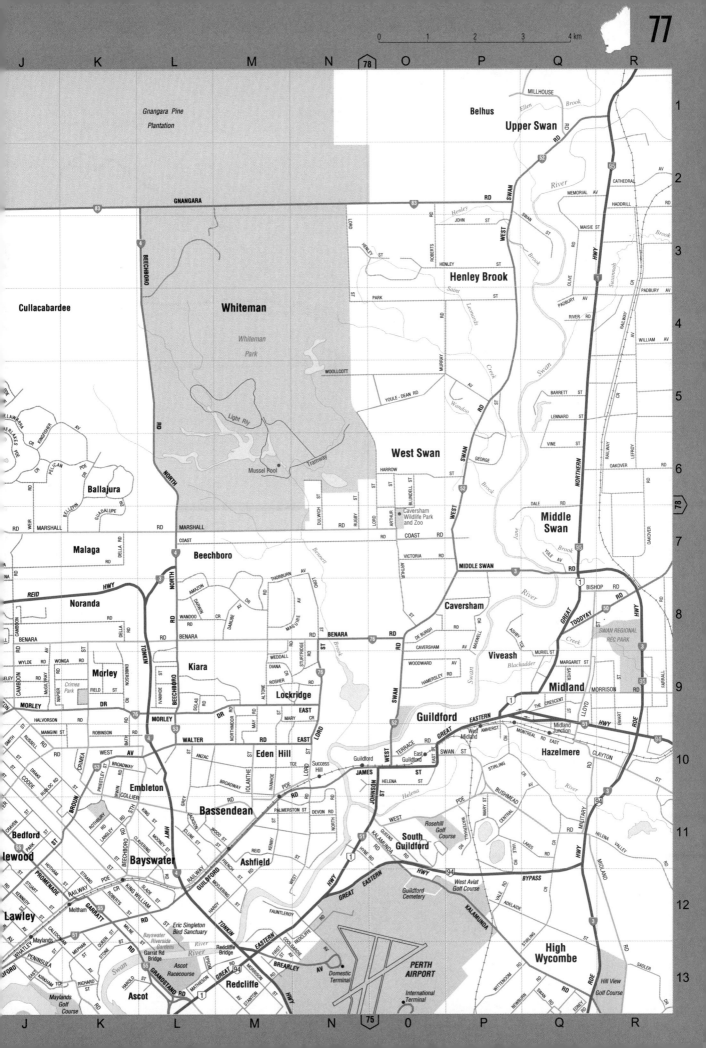

0 5 10 15 20 25 km

TO GERALDTON
TO MOUNT MAGNET

For more detail on Perth
Suburbs see pages 74 - 77

Grid columns: A B C D E F G H I (top and bottom)
Grid rows: 1 2 3 4 5 6 7 8 9 10 11 12 13

Yanchep Beach
Eglinton Rock
YANCHEP NATIONAL PARK
Crystal Cave
Yanchep
Lake Pinjar
Muchea
Kyotmunga
AVON VALLEY NATIONAL PARK
Toodyay
Windmill Hill Cutting
Naggojerring
TO MERREDIN
Quinns Rock
NEERABUP NATIONAL PARK
Bullsbrook
Smiths Hill 361m
MORANGUP NATURE RESERVE
Ringa
Cooringa Winery
27
Northam
Burns
JOONDALUP
WANNEROO
Pearce RAAF Station
51
WALYUNGA NP
Balup
84
Wundowie
Clackline
48
Bakers Hill
Mokine
Camel Farm
MULLALOO
UPPER SWAN
WHITEMAN PARK
SWAN VALLEY WINE REGION
Gidgegannup
HILLARYS
Whitfords Beach
MIRRABOOKA
WHITEMAN
Mount Helena
Chidlow
47
York
York Motor Museum
Sorrento Quay & Underwater World
GUILDFORD
MIDLAND
JOHN FORREST NATIONAL PARK
Mundaring
GREAT EASTERN HWY
DYOTT RANGE
SCARBOROUGH
PERTH AIRPORT
GREENMOUNT NP
Darlington
GOOSEBERRY HILL NP
O'Connor Museum
Mt Talbot 398m
CITY BEACH
PERTH
GREENMOUNT
KALAMUNDA NP
Helena Reservoir
INDIAN
COTTESLOE
CANNINGTON
LESMURDIE FALLS NP
Darling River
Talbot Brook
Passenger Ferry to Rottnest Island
FREMANTLE
MADDINGTON
Cohunu Koala Park
Mt Dale 548m
OCEAN
SPEARWOOD
JANDAKOT
JANDAKOT AIRPORT
Kelmscott Museum
KELMSCOTT
BROOKTON
Adventure World
ARMADALE
ALBANY
Canning Dam
MUNSTER
WATTLEUP
Pioneer Village
Carnac Island
NAVAL BASE
Byford
MILITARY AREA
Cockburn Sound
Garden Island
Kwinana
Rockingham
Mundijong
Tumblegum Farm
Mt Randall 525m
DARLING
BROOKTON
Westdale
Cape Peron
Safety Bay
Mardella
Jarrahdale
Penguin Island
Waikiki
SERPENTINE NATIONAL PARK
Serpentine Dam
Warnbro Beach
Becher Point
Serpentine
Mt Solus 574m
HWY
Peelhurst
Singleton
Keysbrook
Madora
North Dandalup
DARLING RANGE
Halls Head
Mandurah
Boonering Hill 529m
Miami
Peel Inlet
North Yunderup
South Yunderup
Fairbridge Farm School
Florida
Dawesville
Pinjarra
Alcoa Scarp Lookout
South Dandalup Dam
Bannister
Wandering
Melros
Cape Bouvard
YALGORUP NATIONAL PARK
Lake Mealup
Lake McLarty
Meelon
Marrinup
Dwellingup
Etmilyn Etmilyn Forest Tramway
Amphion
Crossman
Dwarda
CAERNARVON HILLS
Coolup
Lane Pool Reserve
Scarp Pool
Nanga
Boddington
Marradong
Lake Clifton
Waroona
Hamel
Waroona Dam
Samson Brook Dam
Mt Keats 474m
Mt Saddleback 75m
Preston Beach
YALGORUP NATIONAL PARK
Wagerup
Yarloop
Logue Brook Dam
Lake Preston
TO BUNBURY
TO BUNBURY
TO ALBANY

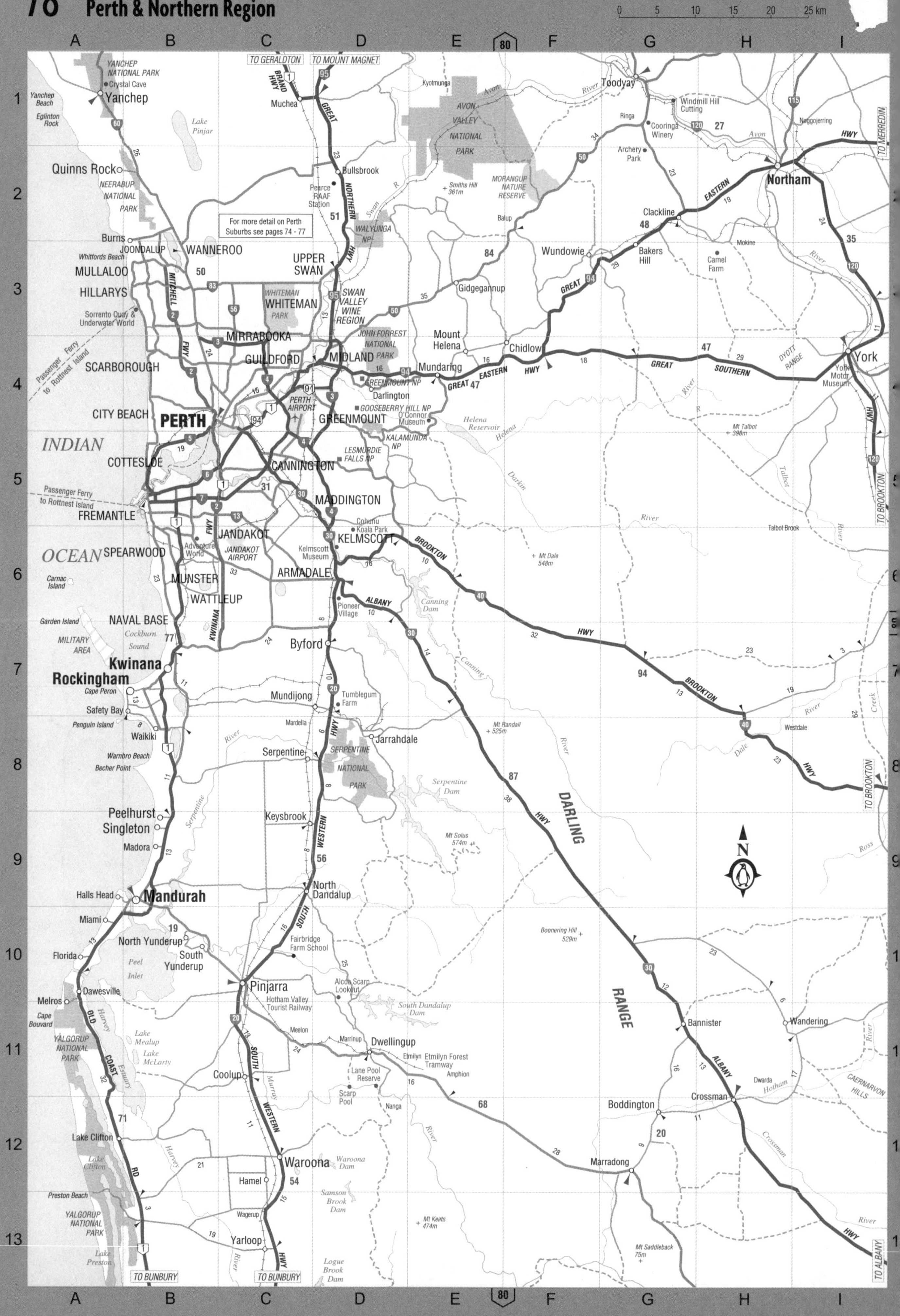

A B C D E F G H I

0 5 10 15 20 25 km

78

INDIAN   OCEAN

1

TO PERTH

YALGORUP NATIONAL PARK

Lake Preston

OLD COAST RD

23

Myalup 5

Binningup 4

37 10

Leschenault Inlet

19

Australind 12

Koombana Bay

Eaton

Bunbury

Picton 13

10

27

HWY 18

Stratham 9

14

Peppermint Grove Beach

TUART FOREST NP

Capel

Wonnerup Ludlow
Wonnerup Beach TUART FOREST NP

10

Ludlow

Abba River

Ruabon

Tutunup

Sabina River

Four Mile Hill

8 BUSSELL

Busselton

HWY Vasse 10

Carbunup River

15 104

Yoongarillup

VASSE 19 58 HWY

WHICHER RANGE

Marybrook

Jindong

Acton Park

Chapman Hill

BUSSELL HWY

20 CARBUNUP

48 10

Yelverton

Metricup

Cowaramup Point
Gracetown 4 8 Cowaramup

Bramley 12

Treeton

Osmington

THE RAPIDS CONSERVATION PARK

Mowen

Mt Yates

Margaret River

Cape Mentelle 4 5
Prevelly

Eagles Heritage

Rosa Glen Pioneer Settlers Memorial

BUSSELL HWY

Witchcliffe

44 10

18

Cape Freycinet

LEEUWIN-NATURALISTE NATIONAL PARK

North Point Boranup

Boranup Lookout

Hamelin Bay East Hill

Hamelin Island
Foul Bay

Cape Hamelin

Hillview Lookout & Golf Course

LEEUWIN-NATURALISTE NATIONAL PARK

Green Hill

Karridale

BUSSELL HWY 10

BROCKMAN

18

Kudardup

SCOTT NATIONAL PARK

Augusta

Flinders Bay

Lighthouse
Cape Leeuwin Matthew Flinders Memorial Seal Island

Flinders Bay

Hardy Inlet

Blackwood River

Scott River

NATURE RESERVE

D'ENTRECASTEAUX NATIONAL PARK

Gingilup Swamps

Lake Quitjup

Lake Jasper

BEEDELUP NP

TO PEMBERTON

80

Cape Naturaliste
Lighthouse and Museum

Sugarloaf Rock

Eagle Bay

Meelup 13

Dunsborough

Quindalup

Yallingup

Canal Rocks

Cape Clairault

LEEUWIN-NATURALISTE NATIONAL PARK

Quinnup

Geographe Bay

16

Geographe Bay

8

Wagerup
Yarloop 19

Logue Brook Dam

Harvey Weir

Harvey 18

Wokalup 19

Stirling Dam

Benger 20

Beela

Worsley Aluminium Refinery

SOUTH WESTERN HWY

43

Brunswick Junction

13

Roelands 19 107

Butekup 5

Waterloo 11

Dardanup

Collie River

Wellington Dam

21 1 10 19

Boyanup 15

Lowden

Donnybrook

SOUTH WESTERN HWY

18 13

Newlands

Kirup 17 Grimwade

Mullalyup 13

Balingup

HWY

TO BRIDGETOWN

Jarrahwood

104 24

VASSE HWY

Nannup 23

WHINSTON HILLS

TO BRIDGETOWN

41

Blackwood River

16

16 BROCKMAN HWY

10

VASSE HWY

10

BROCKMAN HWY

89 13

12 27

The Four Aces

One Tree Bridge

22 10

7

Donnelly River

2

3

4

5

6

7

8

9

10

11

12

13

0   20   40   60   80 km

A   B   C   D   E   F   G   H   I

INDIAN

OCEAN

SOUTHERN   OCEAN

Rottnest Island

PERTH
FREMANTLE
ARMADALE

Kwinana
Rockingham

Mandurah

Bunbury

Busselton

Margaret River

Augusta
Cape Leeuwin

Northam

York

Narrogin

Wagin

Katanning

Collie

Bridgetown

Manjimup

Pemberton

Walpole

Denmark

Albany

Mount Barker

Merredin

For more detail on Perth
Region see pages 78 & 79

N

0   50   100   150   200 km

A   B   C   D   E   F   G   H   I

INDIAN   OCEAN

N

Montebello Islands

Barrow Island
Cape Poivre

Sholl Island

Dolphin Island
Cape Cossigny
Depuch Island
Mundabullangana

Karratha
Enderby Island
Dampier   Wickham   Point Samson
Cape Lambert
Karratha   Cossack
Roadhouse   Roebourne
Mt Negri
176m
Mt Berphus
86m

Whim
Creek   160
Mallina
Yule

Regnard Bay
Cape Preston
104
293
Mt Leopold
290m
Mt Prinsep
99m
Mt Sholl
173m
Mt Oscar
145m
Mt Gick
105m
Mt Constantine
221m
Mt Langebeck
209m
Kangan

Mardie   Mt Potter
98m   Mt McLeodKING
160m
Mt Wohler
255m
Pyramid
ABORIGINAL
LAND
Yandeyarra

Thevenard Island

Fortescue
Roadhouse   Mt Herbert
366m
Mt Leal
372m
Mt Wohler
327m
Mt Richthofen
990m
MILLSTREAM - CHICHESTER
NATIONAL PARK   Mt Francisco
313m
MUNGAROONA
RANGE
NATURE
RESERVE

Beadon Point
Onslow
Yarraloola
Pannawonica   Millstream
Springs   Mt Bilroth
417m   287   Mt Wellard
255m   45   Coolawanya   Hooley
Mulga
Downs

PILBARA

Mt Enid
302m   Mt Florance   HAMERSLEY
Mt McRae
1027m   31   Mt Margaret
879m

WARNING: Entry to Wittenoom
township is not encouraged due
to asbestos dust contamination.   Wittenoom
Hamersley
Hamersley
Gorge

Tom Price   111
Mt Stevenson
1172m   Dales
Gorge
Mt Vigors
1161m
KARIJINI
(HAMERSLEY RANGE)
NATIONAL PARK

Paraburdoo   268   129   136   Mt Tom Price
1072m   50   Mt Bruce
1236m   Marandoo
Juna
Downs

North Murion Island
Wreck of SS "Mildura"
North West Cape
False Island Point
Low Point
Point Murat
Naval Communication Station
Restricted Area
Exmouth   Minderoo   122   Cane River   Red Hill
Mt Rica
565m   Mt Dempster
372m   Mt Elvire
619m
Mt Pyrton
845m   Coolawanya
88   Mt Florance   Mt Margaret
879m   Mulga
Downs

CAPE RANGE
Shothole Canyon
Charles Knife Canyon   Koordarrie   Mt Mary
115m   Mt Stuart
304m   Mt Edith
292m   Mt Brockman
1129m   Mt Samson
1079m   RANGE

Learmonth   103   Nanutarra
Roadhouse   Mount Stuart   Mt Elizabeth
275m   Wyloo   Mt De Courcey
485m   Mt Wall
957m   Mt Turner
1014m   Mt Trevarthon
999m   (HAMERSLEY RANGE)
NATIONAL PARK

Exmouth Gulf   Yanrey   Mt Alexander
410m   Uaroo   Mt Danvers
248m   Mt Clement
358m   Glen Florrie   Kooline   Mt Jope
874m   79   Mt Barricade
1089m

Ningaloo   Giralia   220   217   Marrilla   Nyang   Mt Forrest
145m   Towera   Mt Hamlet
248m   Mt Florry
482m   BARLEE RANGE
NATURE
RESERVE   82

Cardabia
Point Maud
Coral Bay   Winning   Mia Mia   Mt Tucker
265m   Maroonah   Mt Palgrave
704m   Ullawarra   Ashburton Downs   Ashburton
Downs   CAPRICORN

Warroora
Bulbarli Point   Minilya
Roadhouse   Wandagee   Williambury   Lyndon   Edmund   184   Mt Boggola
698m   Mt Bresnahan
683m

Cape Farquhar   Gnaraloo   Minilya   Manberry   Middalya   Mangaroon   Mt Thomson
392m   Wanna   Pingandy   Dooley Downs   Mt Vernon
584m

Red Bluff   149   Cooralya   Mardathuna   Moogooree   Minnie
Creek   Mt Agamemnon
337m   Gifford Creek   Cobra   Mt Augustus
1106m   Mount
Vernon   100

Cape Cuvier   Hill Springs   Eudamullah   Mount Phillips   Mt Phillips
780m   MT AUGUSTUS
NATIONAL PARK   138

H.M.A.S. "Sydney"
Memorial Cairn
Blowholes   Boolathana   Doorawarrah   KENNEDY
RANGE
NATIONAL
PARK   Mt Sandiman
543m   Yinnetharra   Waldburg   Mt Egerton
994m   Woodlands   Mulgul

Carnarvon   173   Meeragoolia   Mooka   Gascoyne Junction   Mt James
602m   Mt James   Mt Gascoyne
789m   Landor   Mt Clere
555m   Mt Labouchere
722m

Gallgiddy   Ella Valla   Yalbalgo   117   Mooloo Downs   Mt Dalgety
520m   Mt Puckford
583m   Mt Marquis
503m   Coolinbah Hill
484m   Milgun

Edaggee   Marron   Pimbee   111   Glenburgh   Yalbra   Errabiddy   337   Yarlanweelor   Mt Fraser
799m

Shark Bay   201   Wahroonga   Carey Downs   Mt Madeline
313m   Innouendy   Mt Gould
710m   Moorarie   Mount Padbury
Cape Peron North
FRANCOIS PERON
NATIONAL PARK   Woorarmel
Roadhouse   Meedo   Gilroyd   Callytharra Springs   Byro   Milly Milly   Mt Nairn
452m   Conical Hill
454m   Mt Hale
732m   Mount
Murchison

Monkey Mia
Dolphin sightings
Faure Island   Gladstone
Yaringa   Woodleigh   Yalardy   Beringarra   Koonmarra

Denham   Hamelin
Pool   Mt Dugel
461m   Weiragoo Hill
474m   Nookawarra   Mt Noonie
512m   Mileura   Belele   Peace Gorge
(The Granites)

Useless Loop
Mine   Eagle Bluff   110 km
Shell Beach   Carbla   Mt Narryer
514m   Manfred   Mt Murchison
503m   Kalli   Coonmarra

Steep Point   Nanga Bay Resort   389   Mount Narryer   Hochsteler Hill
646m   Wilgie Mia Red
Ochre Mine   Meekatharra

Dirk
Hartog
Island   130   Overlander
Roadhouse   144   Muggon   Murchison   Boolardy   Mt Luke
530m   Glen   Beebyn   Yalgowra Hills
586m   Tuckanarra   Karbar

Bernier Island   Gnarrowna Hill
405m   Woolen   NICHOLSON   RANGE   Curdimurka Hill
411m   Coodardy   196

Dorre Island   Billabong
Roadhouse   TOOLONGA
NATURE
RESERVE   Curndiannoo Hill   Cue

Cararrang   Mt Elliot
418m   Tamala   Zuytdorp Cliffs   278   ZUYTDORP
NATURE
RESERVE   Nerren Nerren   New Forest   Twin Peaks   Murgoo   Booltharda Hill
439m   Mt Charles   Taincrow

Kalbarri   KALBARRI
NATIONAL PARK   Eurardy   Coolcalalya   Lake Nerranyne   Pinegrove   Bullardo   Narloo   Mt Farmer   Walga Rock   Lakeside   Wondinong

WEST   COASTAL   HWY   NORTH   WEST   COASTAL   HWY   GREAT   NORTHERN   HWY

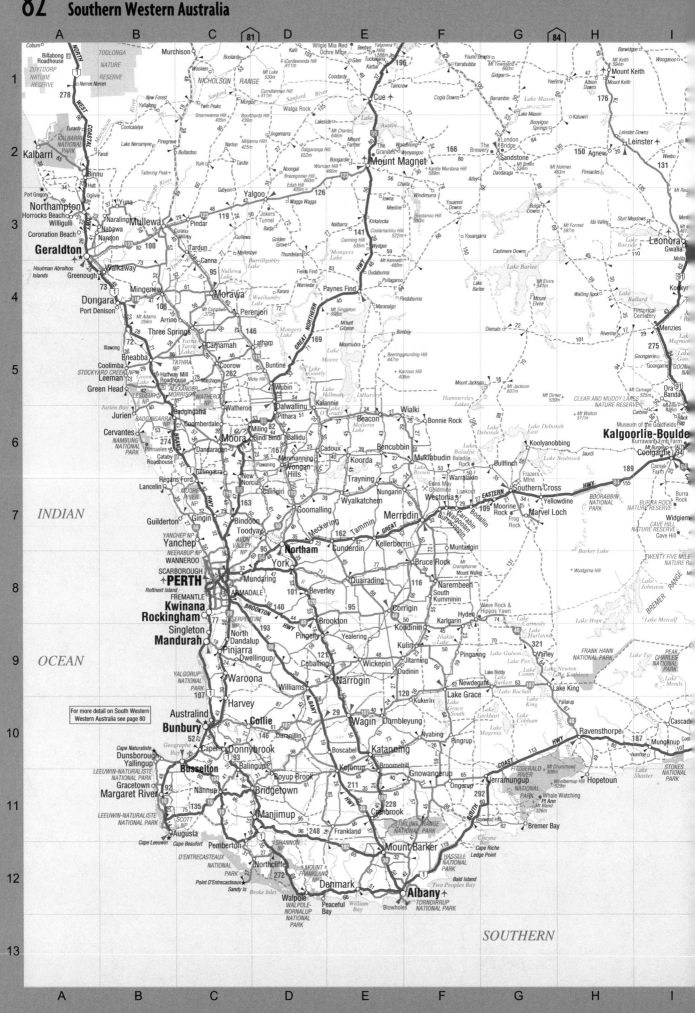

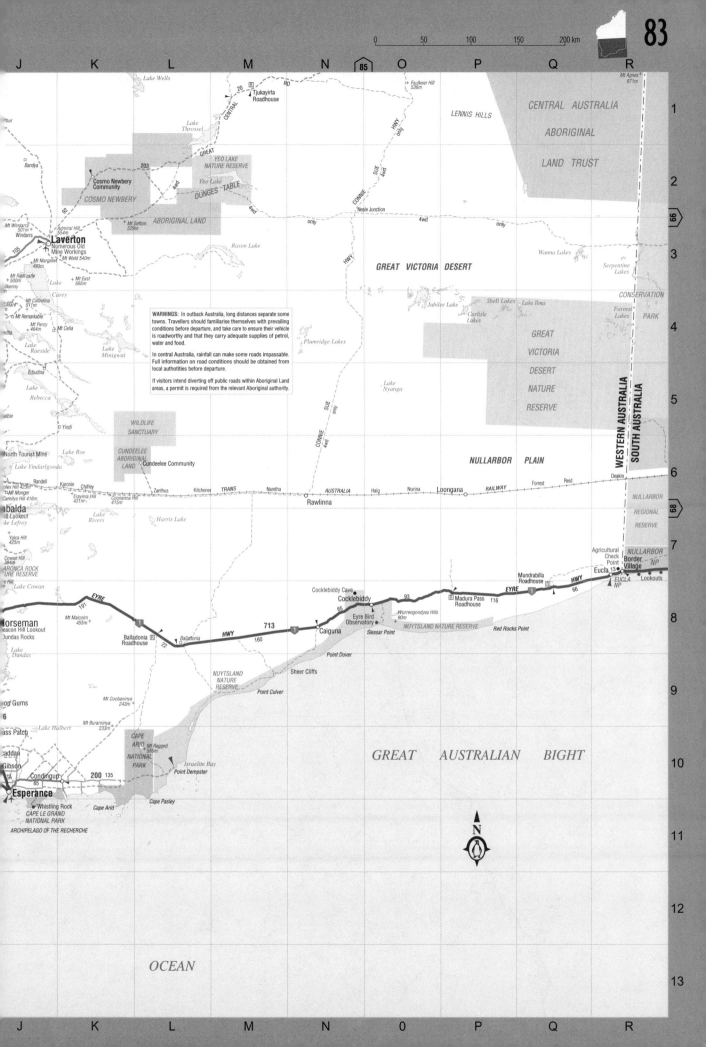

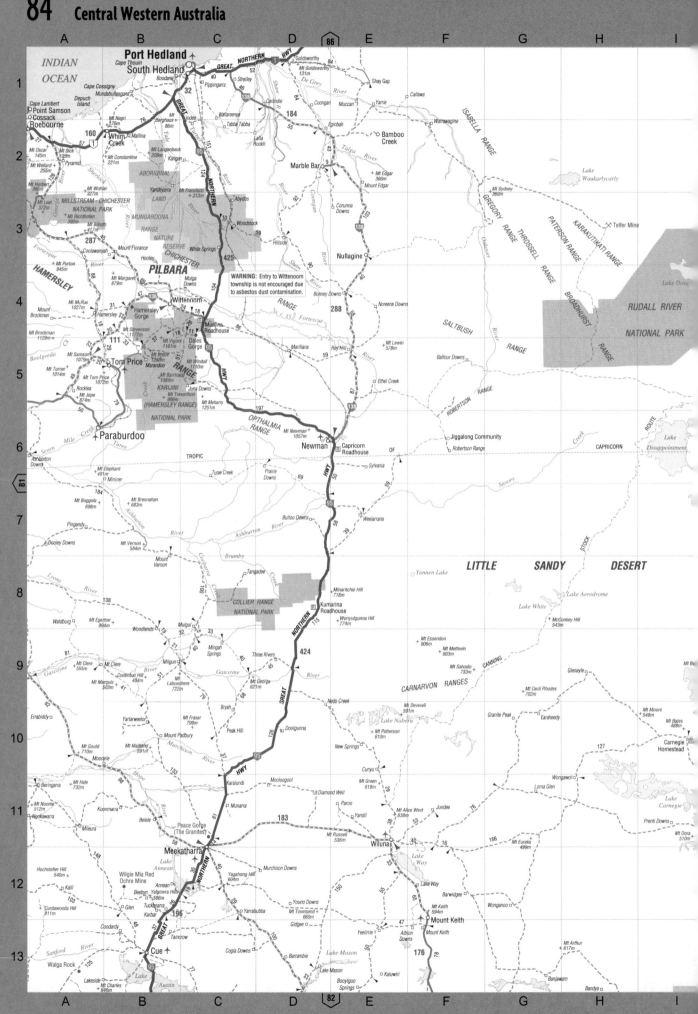

0 50 100 150 200 km

J K L M N O P Q R

87

83

98

66

Mt Cornish +
363m
Mt Crown Head +
419m
Lake Gregory

Mt Romilly +
353m
Mt Elliott +
418m

1

BALGO

Lake Jeavons

ABORIGINAL

Lake Dennis
Lake Lucas

2

ROUTE

Percival Lakes

Tobin Lake

LAND

Lake Wills
Lake Hazlett

3

WARNINGS: In outback Australia, long distances separate some
towns. Travellers should familiarise themselves with prevailing
conditions before departure, and take care to ensure their vehicle
is roadworthy and that they carry adequate supplies of petrol,
water and food.

In central Australia, rainfall can make some roads impassable.
Full information on road conditions should be obtained from
local authotities before departure.

If visitors intend diverting off public roads within Aboriginal Land
areas, a permit is required from the relevant Aboriginal authority.

STOCK

Lake Auld

4

Lake Mackay

che

Lake George

Lake Winfred

CANNING

Gary Junction

5

Mt Webb +
532m

Mt Tietkens +
546m

Ininti

TROPIC

OF

CAPRICORN

Kintore

Mt Leisler +
901m

6

Windy Corner

Lake Macdonald

GIBSON   DESERT

Lake Cobb

CENTRAL AUSTRALIA

Lake Hopkins

WESTERN AUSTRALIA

NORTHERN TERRITORY

7

Mt Madley +
533m

Lake Cohen

McPhersons Pillar +
530m

Mt Taylor +
1001m

Docker River
Community

8

Lake Hancock

GIBSON DESERT

Lake Newell

Lake Earnham

ABORIGINAL LAND TRUST

Lake Jones

Charlies Knob
551m

NATURE RESERVE

Warakurna
Community

Giles
Meteorological
Station

PETERMANN
RANGES

9

HWY

Everard Junction

16

Warakurna
Roadhouse

29

76

Mt William Lambert
517m +

Mt Lampe +
497m

Mt Everard +
544m

452

GUNBARREL

Mt Johnson +
534m

Mt Beadell +
530m

Notabilis Hill +
468m

BAKER

Mt Samuel +
519m

215

336

105

Mt Gosse +
885m

Surveyor
Generals
Corner

GUNBARREL   HWY

Mt Cockburn +
1133m

10

aringo Hill

Thryptomene Hill +
439m

Lake
Breaden

Jackie Junction

JAMIESON

Bentley Hill +
581m

248

Blackstone

RANGE

Mt Scott 668m +

Mt Aloysius +
1085m

Mt Hinckley +
1018m

Kalka

Aparawatatja

SUTHERLAND   RANGE

RANGE

WARBURTON

Mt Harbutt +
558m

RANGE

Mt Rawlinson +
670m

Mt Elvire +
603m

Mt Palgrave +
538m

BARROW RANGE

Mt Cooper +
670m

Pipalyatjara

Mt Davies +
1058m

IDA   RANGE

Mt Worsnop +
461m

Lake Gillen

Boyd
Lagoon

Warburton
Roadhouse

Mt Talbot 623m +

Mt Evaline +
631m

Mt Eliza +
646m

11

Warburton
Aboriginal
Community

RD

HWY

CENTRAL   AUSTRALIA

WESTERN AUSTRALIA

SOUTH AUSTRALIA

Lake Wells

Calachini Hills +
543m

Empress
Spring

565

209

CENTRAL

SUE

4wd

only

Mt Agnes +
671m

12

59

Tjukayirla
Roadhouse

Faulkner Hill +
536m

Permano Hill +
719m +

20

GREAT

LENNIS HILLS

ABORIGINAL   LAND   TRUST

13

Lake Throssel

CONNIE

Yeo Lake
Nature Reserve

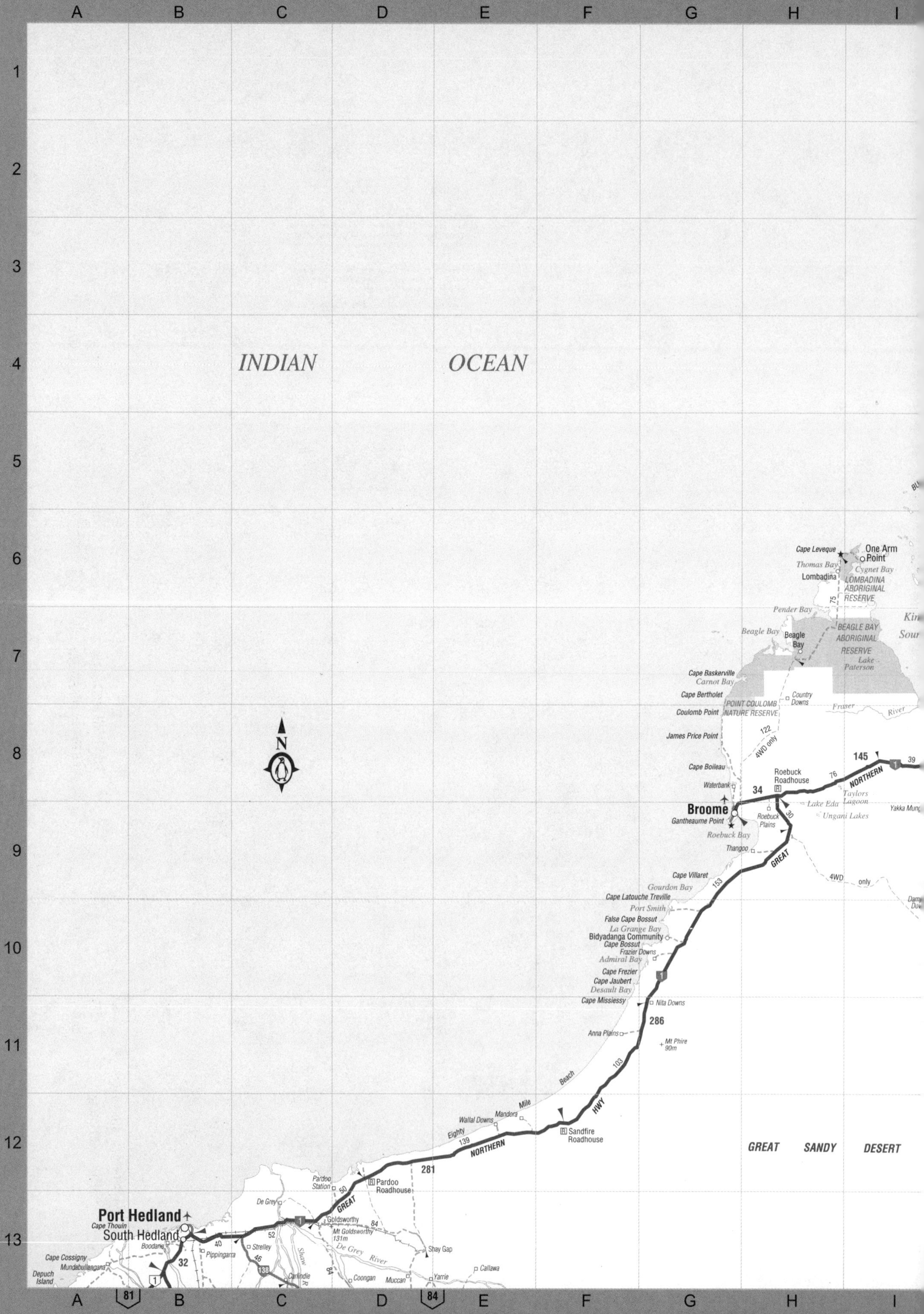

A   B   C   D   E   F   G   H   I

1

2

3

INDIAN　　　　*OCEAN*

4

5

6

Cape Leveque　　One Arm Point
Thomas Bay　　Cygnet Bay
Lombadina　　LOMBADINA ABORIGINAL RESERVE

BLU

King Sour

Pender Bay

Beagle Bay　Beagle Bay　BEAGLE BAY ABORIGINAL RESERVE

7

Lake Paterson

Cape Baskerville
Carnot Bay
Cape Bertholet
Coulomb Point
POINT COULOMB NATURE RESERVE
Country Downs

Fraser River

James Price Point

122

4WD only

8

N

Cape Boileau

Roebuck Roadhouse

145　39

NORTHERN　76

Waterbank

34

Taylors Lagoon

Lake Eda

Yakka Mun

Broome

Roebuck Plains

Ungani Lakes

Gantheaume Point

Roebuck Bay

9

Thangoo

GREAT

4WD only

Cape Villaret
Gourdon Bay

153

Cape Latouche Treville
Port Smith
False Cape Bossut
La Grange Bay
Bidyadanga Community
Cape Bossut
Frazier Downs

Damp Dov

10

Admiral Bay

Cape Frezier
Cape Jaubert
Desault Bay

Cape Missiessy　　Nita Downs

286

Anna Plains　　Mt Phire 90m

11

103

Beach

HWY

GREAT　**SANDY**　**DESERT**

Wallal Downs　Manders
Eighty　Mile
139

Sandfire Roadhouse

12

NORTHERN

281

Pardoo Station
50
Pardoo Roadhouse

GREAT

De Grey

Goldsworthy　84

North Hedland
Cape Thouin
South Hedland
Boodarie
40
52　Mt Goldsworthy 131m
De Grey River
Shay Gap

13

Cape Cossigny
Mundabullangana
Depuch Island
Strelley
Pippingarra
46
Carlindie R
Coongan　Muccan
Yarrie
Callawa

32

138

Shaw R

81　**1**　**84**

A   B   C   D   E   F   G   H   I

0   50   100   150   200 km

TIMOR   SEA

JOSEPH
BONAPARTE
GULF

Cape Londonderry

Cape Talbot

Cape Rulhieres ★

Cape Bernier

Cape Bougainville

Vansittart Bay

Napier Broome Bay

Cape Whiskey

Cape St Lambert

Lacrosse Island

Turtle Point

Admiralty Gulf

Cone Mtn + 178m

KALUMBURU ABORIGINAL LAND

Kalumburu

Mt Casuarina 221m +

Mt Nicholls 143m +

Montague Sound

Mt Connor 312m +

Carson River

Mt Leeming 244m +

OOMBULGURRI

Cambridge Gulf

ORD RIVER NATURE RESERVE

Bonaparte Archipelago

Bigge Island

ADMIRALTY GULF ABORIGINAL LAND

Mitchell Falls

MITCHELL   PLATEAU

Theda

DRYSDALE RIVER NATIONAL PARK

ABORIGINAL LAND

Mt Mongona + 366m

Mt Fraser 366m +

Adolphus Island

Mt Connection + 183m

NOOGOORA BURR QUARANTINE AREA

PARRY'S LAGOON NATURE RESERVE

Kneebone

York Sound

Mt Anderson 485m +

Mitchell River

313

King Edward River +

GARDNER   PLATEAU

Wyndham

69

Mt Cockburn North 671m +

56

Kununurra

MIRIMA (HIDDEN VALLEY) NP

KEEP RIVER NATIONAL PARK

94

Brunswick Bay

Mt Trafalgar 390m +

PRINCE REGENT NATURE

34

El Questro Station tourist resort

41

45

101

36

Newry

Champagny Island

Mt Lyall + 213m

KUNMUNYA ABORIGINAL RESERVE

Mt Hann 779m +

Miners Pool

283

165

Dunham Pilot Dam

Lake Argyle Tourist Village

3A

20

Deception Bay Hall Point

Mt Methuen 427m +

Mt Deborah 399m +

Mt Shadforth 510m +

RESERVE

Drysdale River

66

Dunham River

56

CARR BOYD RANGE

Lake Argyle

The Twins + 318m

Rosewood

Doubtful Bay

Mt Lochee 310m +

Mt Russ 692m +

43

151

Argyle Diamond Mine

Liesdell +

Mt Quirk + 323m

Mt Mary +

Waterloo

Koolan Island Koolan

Collier Bay

Secure Bay

KING

Mt Page + 466m

Mt Blythe + 436m

Mt Lacy 763m +

Mount Elizabeth

Gibb River

27

Bow

Spring Creek

West

Mt Nellie 267m +

Mt Disaster 266m +

Mt Humbert 474m +

TRAINING AREA

Mt Synnott + 488m

Mt Glemont 478m +

Mount Barnett

81

Beverley Springs

Kupingarri Community

Turkey Creek Roadhouse

34

Mt Jarrad + 530m

Texas Downs

Mt John 526m +

Mt Buchanan + 417m

Mistake Creek

TARY

LEOPOLD

Mt Harta

Mt Smith 616m +

Mt Chalmers 704m +

Mt Hart 667m +

Adcock Gorge

Mt House

Warmun Community

Mt Lush 778m +

32

Mt Coghlan + 622m

Nelson Springs

89

Robinson

River

RANGES

365

67

30

Mt House 551m +

22

Mt Clifton 537m +

72

Tableland

VIOLET HILL ABORIGINAL LAND

PURNULULU (BUNGLE BUNGLE) NATIONAL PARK

Mt Panton + 340m

116

by

Napier Downs

WINDJANA GORGE NATIONAL PARK

Mt Herbert + 753m

Mt Ord 937m +

Estaughs

Glenroy

Mt Warton 437m +

Mt Wells + 983m

26

HWY

163

Old Turner

Kirkimble

43

40

46

34

Mt Behn + 344m

Mt Broome 931m +

Millie Windie

Mt Brennan + 532m

Morrington

Fitzroy

River

Ord

Alice Downs

96

Bridge House

41

HWY

54

Blina

30

Ellendale

TUNNEL CREEK NATIONAL PARK

DEVONIAN REEF NATIONAL PARKS

Leopold Downs

Mt Leake + 697m

Mt Laptz + 245m

71

Lansdowne

KING

Springvale

14

Bedford Downs

52

Saunders Creek

Nicholson

HWY

Mount Anderson

59

Camballin

Liveringa

54

30

BROOKING GORGE CP

217

Fossil Downs

GEIKIE GORGE NP

38

LEOPOLD

O'Donnell

RANGES

Mt Barrett 692m +

22

Buntine

Bunda

Myroodah

Mt Wynne + 144m

73

Mt Hardman + 132m

Fitzroy Crossing

Mt Pierre + 203m

Mt Elma 317m +

Mt Amhurst 719m +

Moola Bulla

Halls Creek

Mt Flora + 458m

Flora Valley

80

NOOGOORA BURR QUARANTINE AREA

Quanbun Downs

Jubilee Downs

57

Mt Ball 554m +

Mount Amhurst

16

40

DUNCAN

Wallamunga

Dukes Dome 304m +

Mt Huxley + 537m

Margaret River

NORTHERN

34

55

Ruby Plains

Mt James 175m +

Noonkanbah

Mt Fairbairn 338m +

47

River

DENISON   PLAINS

Birrindudu

Mt Jarlemai 195m +

Mt Fenton 311m +

Mt Tuckfield 187m +

Cadjebut Mine

Mt Ramsay + 421m

Margaret River

Louisa Downs 98

11

GREAT

Mt Any + 268m

Mt Thorlan 263m +

Christmas Creek

32

295

Mary

Wolfe

75

Gordon Downs

Mt Wittenoom 428m +

Cherrabun

Mt Piper + 337m

Bohemia Downs

Mt Dockrell 500m +

WOLFE CREEK METEORITE CRATER RESERVE

Mt Junction + 626m

Lake Merril

Lake Jones

Lake Betty

Lake Mclernon

Mt Josephine 419m +

Sturt Creek

Mt Frederick + 530m

Tilley Claypan

Lake Lanagan

ROUTE

Bililuna Community

STOCK

TANAMI

RD

204

WESTERN AUSTRALIA

NORTHERN TERRITORY

CANNING

Balgo Community

Mt Cornish + 363m

Mt Crown Head 419m +

Lake Gregory

BALGO ABORIGINAL LAND

Mt Romilly + 353m

Mt Elliott + 418m

Lake Jeavons

KIMBERLEY

J   K   L   M   N   O   P   Q   R

85

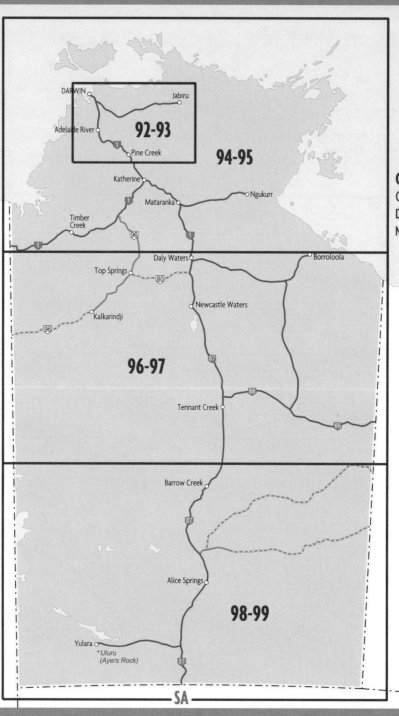

Northern Territory

Location Map

Other Map Coverage
Central Darwin 89
Darwin & Northern Suburbs 90
North Eastern Suburbs, Darwin 91

WA

QLD

SA

DARWIN
Jabiru
Adelaide River
Pine Creek
92-93
94-95
Katherine
Mataranka
Ngukurr
Timber Creek
Daly Waters
Borroloola
Top Springs
Newcastle Waters
Kalkarindji
96-97
Tennant Creek
Barrow Creek
Alice Springs
98-99
Yulara
Uluru
(Ayers Rock)

0   250   500 m

A   B   C   D   E   90   F   G   H   I

1

TO ADELAIDE RIVER
TO DARWIN AIRPORT
HWY

CHARLES

St Johns College

36
Mindil
Beach
Sunset Markets
(May to October)

26

*BOTANIC
GARDENS*

WESTRALIA

Mangroves

Mindil Beach
Reserve

ST

ANNE

Chinese
Cemetery

Boat Ramp

GERANIUM

GILRUTH AV

GARDENS

Gardens
Oval
NTFL

MARIA LIVERIS DR

ATKINS DR

MARIA LIVERIS

Amphitheatre

LAURIE ST

MARY

MEIGS ST

NELSON ST

BEATRICE

FLINDERS

BRENNAN

Mangroves

MGM Grand
Casino

35

MGM
Grand
Darwin

Tennis
Courts

Palmerston
Park Oval

Old
Cemetery

RD

BLAKE

CR

HENRY ST

GOTHENBURG

CR

GUY

CR

Dinah Oval

CHIN

QUAN

GARDENS

Gardens   Park

MELVILLE

HILL ST

ST

JAMES ST

QUEEN ST

CORONATION DR

KING ST

MARGARET

WINSTON

CR

Dinah Beach
Sailing Club

GILRUTH

Golf   Course

GARDENS

HOOD

GARDENS TCE

MIRAMBEENA ST

RAMIREZ

STUART

VOYAGER

DUKE

DINAH

BEACH

Stuart Park

TIGER

RD

FRANCES

Palms
Motel

Frontier
Darwin

McMINN

CASHMAN

FINNISS

Daly Bridge

Small
Boat
Harbour

Lock

BAY

Metro Inn

WOODS

DAY ST

HARVEY

FRANCES

TIGER

Asti
Motel

DASHWOOD

DASHWOOD PL

WOODS

Ti Tree Holiday
Apartments

ST

MAUNA LOA ST

HARRIET

CAVENAGH

Greek
Church

City Gardens
Apartments

Frogshollow
Backpackers

BARNESON

BRENNAN DR

Fishermans Wharf
Ferry Terminal

17

YWCA
11

Elkes
Backpackers

PEARY

SMITH

Marrakai
Apartments

McLACHLAN

SHEPHERD

DARWIN

MANTON ST

GARDINER

CAREY

YMCA
10

DALY RD

DOCTORS RD

GULLY RD

Top End
Hotel

8

MITCHELL

Car Park

Poinciana
Inn

St Marys
Cathedral

Mirambeena
Tourist Resort

3

STOTT

Car Park

FOELSCHE

McMINN

Boat Ramp

25

Aquascene

Darwin
Travelodge

31

McLACHLAN

LINDSAY

WHITFIELD

Tiwi
Lodge

GPO
19

LITCHFIELD

Slipway

1

Darwin
Entertainment
Centre

21
AANT

MOTT

Uniting
Church

SPANN

RSL
Club

Chinese
Temple

28

MAVIE

Deckchair
Cinema

*Doctors
Gully*

Darwin Cinema
Centre

SHACKFORTH

SEARCY

EDMUNDS

All Seasons
Central

AUSTIN

Don
Hotel

Magistrates Court &
Registrar General

Rocks

Cherry Blossom
Motel

Novotel
Atrium

5

PEEL

Holiday Inn

Melaluca
Lodge

9

NUTTALL

Central
Arcade

WEST LA

Austin

Raintree
Park

18

30
Civic
Centre

Stokes
Hill

33
Indo Pacific Marine /
Australian Pearling
Exhibition

Darwin Transit
Centre 16

YHA Backpackers
International

Lyons Cottage
Museum

34

KNUCKEY

NT Tourist
Commission

22

Tamarind
Park

20

6

The
Mall

15

38

YUEN

CHAN

HARRY

42
Tree of
Knowledge

Public
Library

AV

Darwin Harbour
Cruises

14

Walking   Trail

37

Old Admiralty
House

12

23

BENNETT

13

27

Reserve
Bank

CHURCH LA

29

Lameroo Beach

Hotel
Darwin

2

HERBERT

NT
House

Bennett
Park

Law
Court

40
Parliament House,
NT Library,
Supreme Court

Administrators
Office

ESPLANADE

Overland
Telegraph
Memorial

33

Darwin   Harbour

Cliffs

Rocks

39

32
Government
House

HUGHES

KITCHENER

DR

Old Fort
Hill Wharf

Wharf Precinct

43

Fort Hill Wharf

Stokes Hill Wharf

Fort
Hill

Iron Ore Wharf

Land Backed Wharf

PORT   DARWIN

N
[Penguin logo]

Accommodation ■
Beaufort International Hotel 1 B8
Hotel Darwin 2 E10
Mirambeena Tourist Resort 3 D7
MGM Grand Darwin 4 A3
Novotel Atrium 5 C9
Plaza Hotel 6 E10
Poinciana Inn 7 C8
Top End Hotel 8 B7
YHA Backpackers International 9 D9
YMCA 10 B7
YWCA 11 B7

General Information ■
Ansett Australia 12 F10
Bus Terminal 13 F10
Darwin Harbour Cruises 14 I11
Darwin Region Tourism Assoc 15 E9
Darwin Transit Centre (coach) 16 D9
Fishermans Wharf Ferry Terminal 17 I7
Garuda Indonesia Airlines 18 F9
General Post Office 19 E8
Malaysia Airlines 20 E9
Motoring Organisation (AANT) 21 D8
NT Tourist Commission 22 E9

Police Station 23 E10
Qantas Travel Centre 24 F10

Places of Interest ■
Aquascene 25 A7
Botanic Gardens 26 C1
Browns Mart 27 F10
Chinese Temple 28 F9
Christ Church Cathedral 29 F10
Civic Centre 30 G10
Darwin Entertainment Centre 31 C8
Government House 32 F11
Indo Pacific Marine / Australian
   Pearling Exhibition 33 I11
Lyons Cottage Museum 34 D10
MGM Grand Casino 35 A3
Mindil Beach Sunset Markets
   (May to October) 36 A1
Old Admiralty House 37 D10
Old Victoria Hotel 38 E10
Overland Telegraph Memorial 39 F11
Parliament House, NT Library,
   Supreme Court 40 F11
Tour Tub 41 E9
Tree of Knowledge 42 G10
Wharf Precinct 43 H12

Accommodation   Only a sample range is listed;
   inclusion is not necessarily a recommendation.

0   0.25   0.5   0.75   1 km

91

DARWIN AIRPORT

Ludmilla

BAGOT ABORIGINAL RESERVE

RAAF Base

The Narrows

East Point
East Point Military Museum
Rocks
Rocks
East Point Reserve
East Point
Mangroves
Dudley Point
Lake Alexander
Boat Ramp
Mangroves
Mangroves
Creek

Winnellie

Waratah Sports Club
Fannie Bay Racecourse
Richardson Park TCE
Dwyer Park

Rocks
Ross Smith Memorial
Fannie Bay Gaol Museum
ROSS
SMITH AV
Olympic Pool
Waterslide Primary School
Parap

Trailer Boat Club
Boat Ramp
Sailing Club
Vesteys Beach
Skiing and Yachting Area
Boat Ramp
Fannie Bay
Darwin Bowling Club
STUART HWY
Primary School

FANNIE BAY

Water Ski Club
Boat Ramp
Museum and Art Gallery of the Northern Territory
Darwin High School
Sacred Heart College
Mangroves
Sadgroves Creek
Mangroves

Bullocky Point
Rocks

The Gardens
Mindil Beach Sunset Markets (May to October)
Mindil Beach Reserve
Botanic Gardens
St Johns College
Chinese Cemetery
Boat Ramp

Mangroves

MGM Grand Darwin
Gardens Oval NTFL
Old Cemetery
Tennis Courts
Amphitheatre
Stuart Park
Dinah Oval
Dinah Beach

Myilly Point
Rocks
Cullen Bay Marina
Golf Course
Gardens Park
GARDENS
Dinah Beach

Emery Point
Cliffs
Lock
Marina
DARWIN
Small Boat Harbour
Lock

Rocks
Larrakeyah
MILITARY AREA
Daly Bridge
Daly

FRANCES BAY

Elliott Point
Rocks
ESPLANADE
Aquascene
Slipway
Doctors Gully
Bicentennial
Chinese Temple
Deckchair Cinema

Patrol Boat Harbour
Rocks
Rocks
Lyons Cottage Museum
Old Admiralty House
Lameroo Beach
Parliament House
Stokes Hill
Indo Pacific Marine/Australian Pearling Exhibition

Government House
Overland Telegraph Memorial
Fort Hill
Darwin Harbour

For more detail on Central Darwin see page 89

Stokes Hill Wharf
Fort Hill Wharf
Iron Ore Wharf
Land Backed Wharf

PORT   DARWIN

N

0 0.25 0.5 0.75 1 km

TIMOR SEA

BEAGLE GULF

N

Lee Point

Royal Darwin Hospital

Casuarina Beach
Casuarina Coastal Reserve
Dripstone Caves
ROCKLANDS
MAMBULLOO
GARDENS
TIWI
Thri Park
Tiwi Campus NTU
Tiwi
WILLEROO
TROWER RD
Memorial to No. 31 Radar Squadron
Brinkin
OMEO
HIBERNIA CR
BRINKIN
TCE
DR
ERIDUNDA
TROWER RD
Dripstone High School
HENBURY
TAMBLING
DELAMERE
TIWI
FITZMAURICE DR
ROSEWOOD
Nakara
MACREDIE
NAKARA
Nakara Primary School
TCE
V.R.D.
CANARIS
CASTLEREAGH
BONAPARTE
Northern Territory University
BUCHANAN
CAHILL
GOODWIN
ROW LING
LINTON
Swimming Pool Gsell Park
PEREZ
WAN GURI
Wanguri Park
Wanguri Primary School
Wanguri
BATHURST
Leanyer
DRIPSTONE
Casuarina Shopping Square
BRADSHAW
VANDERLIN DR
LEANYER DR
Casuarina
SCRIVEN
ALAWA
Alawa Primary School
STYLES
KLEIN
TCE
Wagaman
Wagaman Primary School
Wagaman Park
JABIRU
BROLGA
Rocks
Picnic Area
Footbridge
Rapid Creek
CASUARINA
ARALIA
NIGHTCLIFF
Nightcliff High School
RYLAND
Rapid Creek
Rossiter Primary School CHRISP
Alawa
STASINOWSKY
ALAWA
LAKESIDE
WACKETT
FRESHWATER
TROWER
Jingili
Casuarina Senior College
PARER
ROTHDALE
MALAY
Wulagi
WULAGI CR
Swimming Pool
Primary School
Sports Oval
Nightcliff
EUGENIA
KURRAJONG
BOUGAINVILLA
SANDALWOOD
CUMMINS
TROWER RD
RYLAND
SPRIGG
MILLNER
Darwin Water Gardens
SANDERS
KNOWLES
Jingili Primary School
Jingili Park
LANYON
Moil Primary School
Moil Park
MOIL
BUCHEN
YANYULA
Yanyula Park
Anula Primary School
Rocks
PROGRESS
TROWER RD
KELSEY
SABINE
FRANCIS
PICKFORD
SCALES
BYRNE
Moil
CIR
YANYULA DR
Jetty Boat Ramp
CASUARINA DR
Coconut Grove
CRAIG
HAZELL
RUNGE
MUSGRAVE
SKELTON ST
Millner Primary School
MILLS
ROBINSON
RYLAND
GULNARE
Orchid Park
Cemetery
BYRNE
LEE POINT
TOLMER
Anula
RD
Darwin Golf Club
BAGOT RD
WARD DR
NATION CR
Caravan Park
HARRIS
TONG LUCK
BRAY SHAW
SHOOBRIDGE
CHIN ST
Millner
RD
McMILLANS
Kimmorley Bridge
Recreation Reserve
ABALA
Marrara Park
CARNOUSTIE CIR
McMILLANS
OLD
Darwin Tennis Centre
Velodrome
COLLOPY
RD
CHARLES
EATON
Marrara Sporting Complex
ABALA
Marrara
NATION CR
DE LATOUR
TOTEM
General Aviation Apron
MURPHY CT
SLADE CT
LORES BONNEY AV
PEDERSON
WRIGLEY
HENRY
NORMAN
BREARLY
DICK WARD DR
BAGOT RD
DARWIN AIRPORT
Darwin Airport Terminal
RPT Apron
LARRIN
McINTOSH
LANCASTER
LESTER
BRAIN
Ludmilla
FITZER
TUDAWALI ST
HARNEY
BENWERRIN
CAMARA
BAGOT ABORIGINAL RESERVE
NADPUR
CARRYING
CALOOLA
RAAF Base
CARDIN
NGIARUK CT
MOSEC
BUKATILLA
COORABIN
CAREELA
CURRINGA
COLLENDINA
DAMALA
COORADILLA
BELLARA
GANDARRA CIR
FANEGANA
Australian Aviation Heritage Centre
DICK WARD DR
Fannie Bay Racecourse
DOUGLAS
Mangroves
Richardson Park
GILBERT
BREWER
LUDMILLA
The Narrows
NARROWS
WELLS
FLEMING
WILMOT
Dwyer Park
BILLEROY
AMAROO
GANDARRA
HWY
WINNELLIE
RD
WINNELLIE
LEE
WITTE
HOOK RD
Rifle Club
Showgrounds
ROSS SMITH
PLAYFORD
CLANCY
FREER
EDWARDS
STRETTON
HUDSON
SADGROVES
REICHARDT
SWEET
BOWEN
COONAWARRA
TANNADICE
BOMBING
CATTERTHUN
ALBATROSS
MENNURR
MATARAM
Winnellie
COONAWARRA
Olympic Pool
Waterslide Primary School
URQUHART
PARAP
GORDON
GREGORY
DRYSDALE
Parap
STUART
BISHOP
REDCAR
STEEL
CATO
COONAWARRA RD
TIGER
BRENNAN
DR
Australian Aviation Heritage Centre

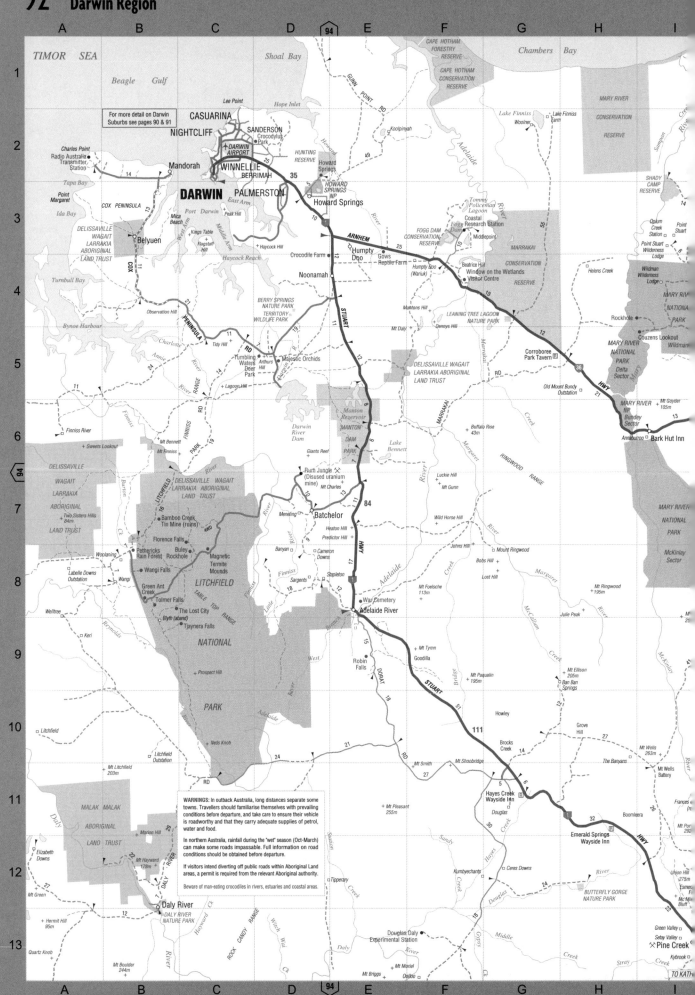

WARNINGS: In outback Australia, long distances separate some towns. Travellers should familiarise themselves with prevailing conditions before departure, and take care to ensure their vehicle is roadworthy and that they carry adequate supplies of petrol, water and food.

In northern Australia, rainfall during the 'wet' season (Oct–March) can make some roads impassable. Full information on road conditions should be obtained before departure.

If visitors intend diverting off public roads within Aboriginal Land areas, a permit is required from the relevant Aboriginal authority.

Beware of man-eating crocodiles in rivers, estuaries and coastal areas.

0 10 20 30 40 km

J K L M N 94 O P Q R

Finke
Bay

POINT STUART
COASTAL RESERVE

CARMOR

PLAIN

Mt Hooper
(Mayambanjdji)

CULALY PLAIN

Oenpelli
(Gunbalanya)

Oenpelli Hill +
(Injalak)

KAKADU

MAGELA PLAIN
(MARNANJ)

Cannon Hill
(Ngamarr-kanangka)

SWIM CREEK
CONSERVATION
RESERVE

Ck

Nardaba

Ubirr Art Site Walk
& Sunset Lookout
Border Store

Ubirr

Cahills Crossing

Munmarlary
(Manmularri)

Diawumba Hill

Mavoamarieprard
Waterhole

Bunga

RANGER

NORTH

ARNHEM

BOGGY PLAIN
(NANJBAGU)

Road impassable
in wet

Mudginberri

MINERAL

LAND

LEASE

Two Mile Hole

Boat
ramp

HWY

8

Jabiru East

ABORIGINAL

Frontier
Kakadu
Village

Bowali Visitor Centre
Park Headquarters

Jabiru
Gagudju
Crocodile Hotel

Ranger Uranium
Mine

LAND

Chirracarwoo
Lagoon

Mt Brockman
289m

Northern
Park Entrance
Station

36

Nourlangie
Billabongs

TRUST

227

58

KOONGARRA
MINERAL LEASE

ARNHEM

Red Lilly
Billabong

Nourlangie
Rock

LAND

JIM

JIM

Alligator
Billabong

Yellow Water
Boardwalk

HWY

Mt Cahill
154m

Koongarra
Nourlangie
Art Site Walk

Cooinda

Namarrgon

Jim Jim Billabong

Spring Peak

Sandy
Billabong

ARNHEM

Mt Basedow
220m

Kunkamoula
Billabong
(Gunkumulu)

Table Top
465m

Adder

Creek

Mundopie Hill

Dird Djahdjam Hill
247m

RD

PLATEAU

Craig Ck

NATIONAL

arris Mine
andoned)

Jim Jim Falls
(Barrkmalam)

Gungural
Recreation
Area

Long
Billabong

Twin Falls
(Gungkurdul)

Goodparla

Maguk Plunge
Pool Walk

Waterfall
Creek
Falls

Mt George
275m

ABORIGINAL

Old Goodparla
(aband)

Road impassable
in wet

LAND

Halfway Peak
217m

Mary River

Bukbukluk Lookout

TRUST

Mt Saunders
304m

Southern Entrance
& Ranger Station

Mt Callanan
318m

Gimbat

Mt Evelyn
365m

Coronation Hill
(Guratba)
300m

Mary River
Roadhouse

HWY

Moline Goldmine

Big Sunday
(Nilyanjurrung)
338m

PARK

Harriet

Mt Gardiner
264m

Coronet Hill
320m

Ngartluk Hill
364m

Cullen

McCarthy Hill

Aston Hill

Ranford Hill

Two Sisters
260m

Ngartluk
Billabongs

ARNHEM LAND ABORIGINAL LAND TRUST

A B C D E F G H I

1

TIMOR

SEA

N

MELVILLE
ISLAND

Cape Van Diemen

Point Jahleel

Vashon Head
Smith Pt   Danger Pt
CROKER
ISLAND
Cape Croker
McCluer Island
Grant Island

2

COBOURG
PENINSULA

Minjilang
Lingi Pt

Port Essington

GURIG NATIONAL PARK

Cape Cockburn

Deception Point
Pularumpi   Milikapiti

BATHURST
ISLAND

TIWI
ABORIGINAL LAND
TRUST

Cape Keith

COBOURG

Greenhill
Island
MARINE

Morse
Island
Endyalgout
Island

PARK

Murgenella
Settlement

Warru

3

Paru
Nguiu   Pickertaramoor

Conder Point

VAN DIEMEN

Cape Gambier

GULF

Mt Pirmain
220m

Cooper

East

4

Beagle
Gulf
Clarence   Strait

Cape Hotham
CAPE HOTHAM
FORESTRY RES

Point Stuart
(Gurnaynjarr)

Field Island

Oenpelli
(Gunbalanya)

Cahills Crossing

Alligator

Mt Howship
+368m

5

For more detail on Darwin
Region see pages 92 & 93

Gunn Point

DARWIN

Mandorah
Belyuen

Radio Australia
Transmitter Station

35
Howard
Springs

Koolpinyah

CAPE HOTHAM
CON RES

L. Finniss

Wooner

MARY RIVER
CONSERVATION
RESERVE

SwimCreek
Plains
Melaleuca

KAKADU
Munmarlary
(Munmularri)

Ubirr Art Site Walk   Ubirr
Sunset Lookout
Border Store

6

Noonamah

ARNHEM

Humpty
Doo (Warluk)

MARRAKAI
CON RES

Helens
Creek

Two Mile Hole

Frontier Kakadu
Village

Nourlangie Rock
Mt Cahill
154m

Jabiru
East
Jabiru

HWY

58

Mt Brockman
289m

Nourlangie
Art Site Walk

Dundee Beach

JOSEPH

BONAPARTE

GULF

Fog Bay

Point Blaze

Finniss River

DELISSAVILLE
WAGAIT
LARRAKIA
ABORIGINAL
LAND TRUST

Darwin
River
Dam

Rum
Jungle

Batchelor

84

MARY
RIVER NP

40

227

Cooinda

37

ARNHEM

KAKADU

LAND

NATIONAL

PLATEAU

Jim Jim Falls
(Barrkmalam)

Twin Falls
(Gungkurdul)

7

North Peron
Island

South Peron
Island

Anson Bay

Wangi
Falls

Banyan

Wangi

Welltree

Keri

Litchfield

Reynolds

LITCHFIELD
NATIONAL
PARK

Litchfield
Outstation

War Cemetery
Adelaide River

Mount Ringwood

MARY
RIVER
NATIONAL
PARK

Mt Masson
243m
Mt George
275m

Goodparla

Mary River

151

PARK

Coronation Hill
(Guratta)
300m

Gimbat

Mt Evelyn
365m

8

Cape Ford

Elizabeth
Downs

Tipperary

MALAK
MALAK
ABORIGINAL
LAND
TRUST

STUART

111

Ban Ban
Springs

The Banyans

Emerald Springs
Wayside Inn

Hayes Creek
Wayside Inn

BUTTERFLY
GORGE NP

Esmeralda
Farm

73

Mary River
Roadhouse

Cape Dombey

DALY   RIVER

PORT   KEATS

Peppimenarti

Daly River

Douglas Daly
Experimental Station

Dollop

Bonalbo

Umbrawarra
Gorge

UMBRAWARRA
GORGE NATURE
PARK

Jindare

Setay Valley

Bonrook

Pine Creek

22

NITMILUK

NATIONAL

PARK

Mt Lambell
317m

Mt Felix
332m

Manyallaluk

BESWICK

9

Pearce Point

Treachery Bay

Swamp Point

Wadeye
Community

MACADAM

RANGE

LAND TRUST

WINGATE

ABORIGINAL

FISH   River

MOUNTAINS

FISH RIVER
FORESTRY
RESERVE

Claravale Station

Morrisons

Claravale

Ferguson

Florina

Marilyum

26

Edith
River

Horseshoe Creek

19

Edith Falls

Helling

90

42

Katherine
Gorge

29

Mt Shepherd
232m

O'Sullivan
House

ABORIGINAL
LAND
TRUST

Beswick

CENTRE

10

Turtle Point

MACADAM

RANGE

Dorisvale

Flora Yards

30

76

Katherine

Tindal

Manbulloo

RAAF
Base

59

Maranboy

Cutta Cutta
Caves Nature
Park

23

112

Barunga

19

Roper

11

NORTHERN TERRITORY
WESTERN AUSTRALIA

Legune

Kneebone

Fitzmaurice

Wombungi

Mt Thymanan
304m

125

66

52

Dry River

King

O'Brien Ck

86

Mataranka

ELSEY
NP

Thermal Pool

Elsey

64

We of the Never
Graves

75

12

87

YAMBARRAN

RANGE

Bradshaw

Victoria

Angalarri

Coolibah

Innesvale

GREGORY
NATIONAL
PARK

24

40

131

Willeroo

28

58

BUNTINE

Gorrie

Western Creek

STUART

Larrimah

168

13

KEEP
RIVER
NATIONAL
PARK

Mt Hensman
384m

Newry

20

PINKERTON

198

73

RANGE

Auvergne

Bulla

Police Station
& Store

Timber
Creek

63

VICTORIA

BUCHANAN

GREGORY
NATIONAL
PARK

Jasper Gorge

Limestone
Gorge

Fitzroy

Coolibah

Victoria River
Wayside Inn

Old Delamere

Delamere

HWY

23

44

96

Gilnockie

Sunday Creek

96

NOTE: Borroloola and Timber Creek, while
located on Aboriginal Land, are open towns.
No entry permit is required.

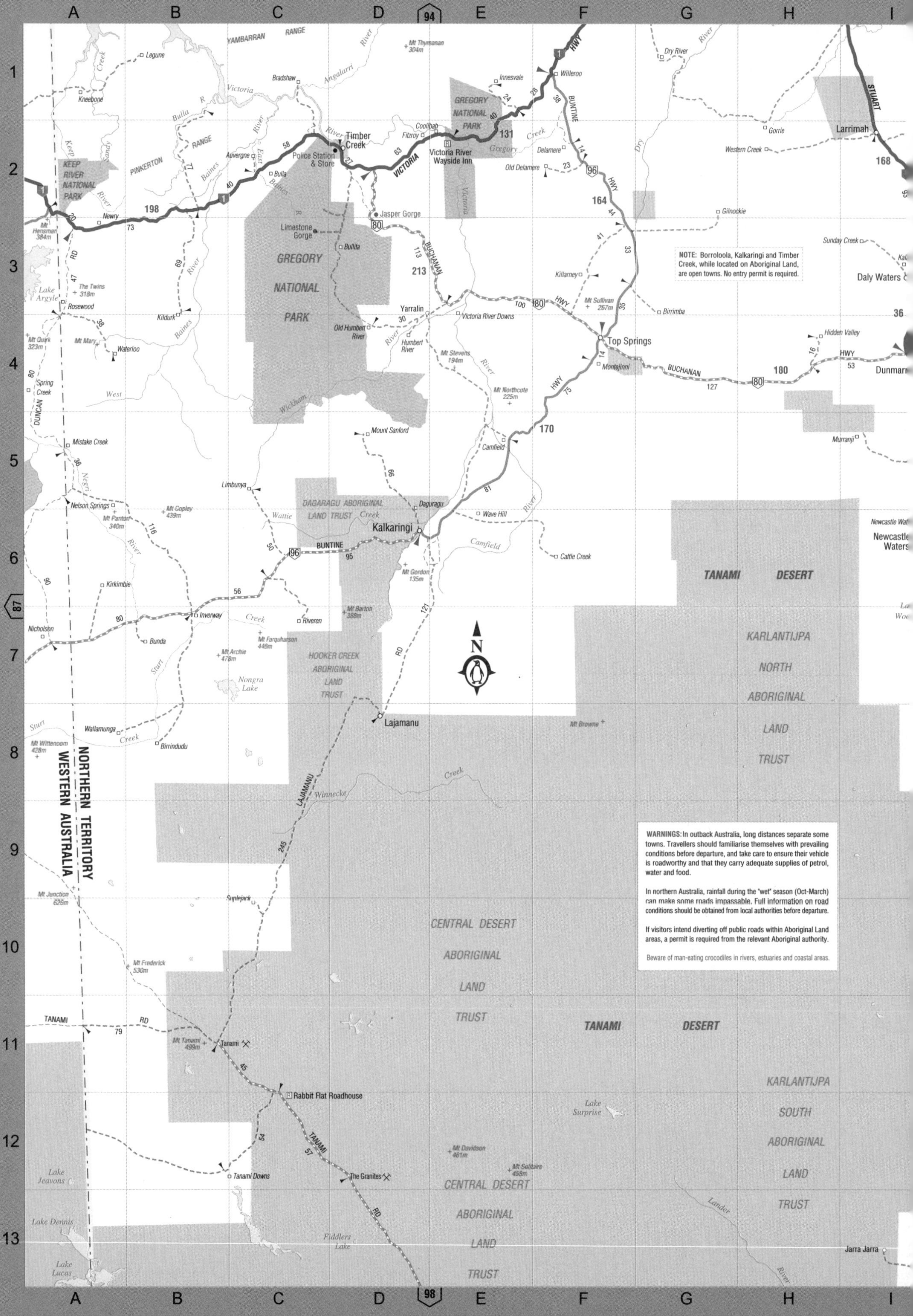

NOTE: Borroloola, Kalkaringi and Timber Creek, while located on Aboriginal Land, are open towns. No entry permit is required.
WARNINGS: In outback Australia, long distances separate some towns. Travellers should familiarise themselves with prevailing conditions before departure, and take care to ensure their vehicle is roadworthy and that they carry adequate supplies of petrol, water and food.
In northern Australia, rainfall during the "wet" season (Oct-March) can make some roads impassable. Full information on road conditions should be obtained from local authorities before departure.
If visitors intend diverting off public roads within Aboriginal Land areas, a permit is required from the relevant Aboriginal authority.
Beware of man-eating crocodiles in rivers, estuaries and coastal areas.
A
B
C
D
E
F
G
H
I
1
2
3
4
5
6
7
8
9
10
11
12
13
94
98
87
YAMBARRAN RANGE
Mt Thymanan 304m
Legune
Dry River
Bradshaw
Angalarri
Innesvale
Willeroo
Victoria
Kneebone
Bulla
PINKERTON RANGE
GREGORY NATIONAL PARK
Timber Creek
Police Station & Store
Coolibah
Fitzroy
Victoria River Wayside Inn
Gorrie
Larrimah
STUART
Western Creek
168
KEEP RIVER NATIONAL PARK
Auvergne
Delamere
Old Delamere
BUNTINE
HWY
VICTORIA
198
Newry
Mt Hensman 384m
Jasper Gorge
Limestone Gorge
Bullita
164
Gilnockie
Sunday Creek
Lake Argyle
The Twins 318m
Rosewood
213
BUCHANAN
Killarney
Daly Waters
Mt Sullivan 267m
Birrimba
Yarralin
Victoria River Downs
Old Humbert River
Humbert River
Kildurk
Mt Quirk 323m
Mt Mary
Waterloo
Top Springs
Hidden Valley
Montejinni
180
Dunmarra
Mt Stevens 194m
Spring Creek
DUNCAN
West
Mt Northcote 225m
Wickham
Mount Sanford
170
Murranji
Mistake Creek
Camfield
Negri
Limbunya
DAGARAGU ABORIGINAL LAND TRUST
Daguragu
Wave Hill
Nelson Springs
Mt Copley 439m
Mt Panton 340m
Wattie Creek
Kalkaringi
Newcastle Waters
Cattle Creek
Mt Gordon 135m
TANAMI DESERT
Kirkimbie
Mt Barton 388m
Inverway
Riveren
Nicholson
Bunda
Mt Farquharson 446m
Mt Archie 476m
HOOKER CREEK ABORIGINAL LAND TRUST
KARLANTIJPA NORTH ABORIGINAL LAND TRUST
Sturt
Nongra Lake
Lajamanu
Wallamunga
Birrindudu
Mt Browne
Mt Wittenoom 428m
NORTHERN TERRITORY
WESTERN AUSTRALIA
LAJAMANU
Winnecke Creek
Mt Junction 625m
Supplejack
CENTRAL DESERT ABORIGINAL LAND TRUST
Mt Frederick 530m
TANAMI RD
Mt Tanami 499m
Tanami
Rabbit Flat Roadhouse
Lake Surprise
KARLANTIJPA SOUTH ABORIGINAL LAND TRUST
Mt Davidson 461m
Mt Solitaire 458m
Tanami Downs
The Granites
Lake Jeavons
Lake Dennis
Lake Lucas
Fiddlers Lake
Lander River
Jarra Jarra

50   100   150 km

J K L 95 M N O P Q R

GULF OF CARPENTARIA

1

SIR EDWARD PELLEW GROUP

West Island

North Island

BARRANYI (NORTH ISLAND) NATIONAL PARK

Hodgson Downs

Maryfield (ruins)

128

Hodgson River

Nutwood Downs

18

Minamia

ALAWA ABORIGINAL LAND TRUST

River

Arnold

River

Cox

Ck

Lagoon

Incumba

NATHAN

RD

207

Nathan River

Rosie

Creek

Lorella Springs

Right

River

Limmen

Bing Bong

SW Is

Centre Island

Vanderlin Island

Manangoora

Borroloola

31

54

Yalco

Creek

2

CARPENTARIA

139

1

273

Amungee Mungee

Tanumbirini

33

October

21

43

Broadmere

Ck

37

Bauhinia Downs

35

Billengarrah

RD

44

BEND

RYANS

113

85

63

Tawallah

NARWINBI ABORIGINAL LAND TRUST

18

Greenbank

43

Doolgarina

24

Seven Emu

26

Pungalina

Spring Creek

3

58

Cape Crawford

Balbirini

HWY

37

Heartbreak Hotel

Mallapunyah

William

River

McArthur

Yalco

River

Newcastle

Creek

Robinson River

Calvert

River

Rocky

Creek

Wollogorang Roadhouse

Westmoreland 117

4

Beetaloo

Kiana

Creek

HWY

115

Glyde

River

Wearyan

River

Foelsche

River

Calvert Hills

Hume

RD

Calvert

Ck

Settlement Creek

Lagoon

5

Ucharonidge

Mungabroom

229

RD

Eva Downs

Wallhallow

Cresswell

Creek

Anthony Lagoon

Cresswell Downs

Benmara

Coanjula

Creek

Nicholson

River

CHINA WALL

WAANYI/GARAWA ABORIGINAL LAND TRUST

6

BARKLY STOCK ROUTE

Tarrabool Lake

377

85

Fish Hole Creek

Springvale

Musselbrook Mining Camp

LAWN HILL NATIONAL PARK

7

8

Renner Springs

Helen Springs

HWY

38

Muckaty

BARKLY

Corella Lake

100

Brunette Downs

Lake Sylvester

100

CONNELLS LAGOON CONSERVATION RESERVE

Mittiebah

RANKEN

Alexandria

Gregory

River

SMITHS RANGE

Hill

Lawn

9

Banka Banka

50

Morphett

136

Attack

Creek

Brunchilly

70

Rockhampton Downs

46

TABLELANDS

76

Playford

77

Buchanan

R

21

Creek

Gallipoli

Norfolk

10

Phillip Creek

29

18

John Flynn Memorial

98

BARKLY

187

66

89

54

Alroy Downs

TABLELAND

Cigarette Hole Creek

RD

98

NORTHERN TERRITORY

QUEENSLAND

Warrego Mine

Warrego

24

25

Three Ways Roadhouse

Tennant Creek

Tennant Creek

Devils Pebbles

31

Barkly Homestead

141

HWY

66

Soudan

31

Avon Downs Police Station

30

27

30

13

Camooweal

CAMOOWEAL CAVES NP

Camooweal Caves

11

87

87

114

122

272

Avon Downs

Lorne

Ranken

River

Six Mile Waterhole

56

URANDANGI RD

118

12

McLaren Creek

52

Kurundi

69

Epenarra

21

Mt Cairns +597m

Big Ranken Waterhole

22 Mile Waterhole

Austral Downs

107

BARKLY

Wooroona

Bullecourt

DEVILS MARBLES CON RES

21

Devils Marbles

Wauchope

Singleton

17

49

Hatches Creek

56

Bullock Waterhole

Mt Michael 243m

TABLELAND

13

Wycliffe Well Roadhouse

Wycliffe Well

61

WARRABRI ABORIGINAL LAND TRUST

21

Ali-Curung

23

Murray Downs

SANDOVER

HWY

21

Lake Nash

J K L M 99 N O P Q R

A B C D E F G H I

96

KARLANTIJPA
SOUTH
ABORIGINAL
LAND
TRUST

TANAMI   DESERT

Rabbit Flat Roadhouse

Lake
Surprise

Mt Davidson
461m

Mt Solitaire
458m

Tanami Downs

The Granites

54
57

TANAMI

CENTRAL   DESERT

ABORIGINAL

LAND

TRUST

Fiddlers
Lake

Lake Jervons
Lake Dennis
Lake Lucas
Lake Hazlett

Jarra Jarra

Willowra

Mt Theo
583m

189

RD

Mt Patricia
577m

PAWA
ABORIGINAL
LAND
TRUST

85

Mt Peake
568m
Old Mount Peake

Mount Barkly

LAKE MACKAY

ABORIGINAL

LAND

TRUST

MALA
ABORIGINAL
LAND
TRUST

Mt Campbell
628m

Mt Leichhardt
1139m

Anningie

Mount
Esther

40

Ti Tree Store &
Police Station

Mt Farewell
603m

Mt Singleton
808m

Mount Doreen

Mt Hardy
840m

YUENDUMU
ABORIGINAL
LAND
TRUST

Coniston

Mt Stafford
1049m

Coniston (ruins)

MOUNT   DENISON

Mount Denison

Mt Gardiner
999m

178   RD

Mt Finniss
978m

12

Ail

31

Mt Nicker
632m

Vaughan Springs

77

28

Yuendumu

38

26

Yuelamu

YALPIRAKINU
ABORIGINAL
LAND
TRUST

Star

Mt Boothby
886m

YUNKANJINI
ABORIGINAL
LAND
TRUST

61

TANAMI

Napperby

Nyirripi

Mt Cockburn
846m

Gurner

Newhaven

Central Mount Wedge

29

Tilmouth Well
Roadhouse

Mt Hammond
750m

98

CSIRO
Experimental Station

Lake
Bennett

118

Mount Wedge

Lake
Lewis

268

RD

Mt Harris
721m

Lake
Mackay

Mt Tietkens
546m

Inini

Pinpirnga

Derwent

Narwietooma

23

Mt Chapple
1166m

39

Amburla

23

Kintore

Tinki

Warren Creek Bore

Mt Liebig

Mt Liebig
1524m

Papunya

Ulambaura

51

51

Milton Park

Mt Leisler
901m

Ilpilla

273

TROPIC   OF   HAASTS   BLUFF   CAPRICORN

Haasts Bluff
1125m

Mt Zeil
1510m

44

Mt Hay
1252m

Hamilton Downs

Lake Macdonald

Ualki

Haasts Bluff

HAASTS   BLUFF   RD

45

37

Redbank
Gorge

Mt Sonder
1380m

Ormiston
Gorge

WEST MACDONNELL
NATIONAL   PARK

Standl
Chas

Serpentine
Gorge

132

DR

Iwupatak

ABORIGINAL

LAND

TRUST

Mt Forbes
762m

WARNING: Visitors planning to travel along Larapinta
Drive through Aboriginal Land require a permit.

TNORALA
(GOSSE BLUFF)
CON RES

Glen Helen

NAMATJIRA

HERMANNSBURG
ABORIGINAL LAND
TRUST

92

Lake Hopkins

124

LARAPINTA
(MEREENIE)

Gosse Bluff

41

DR
(MEREENIE
LOOP)

19

Ipolera

Tjuwanpa
Resource
Centre

24

LARAPINTA

86

DR

127

Hermannsburg

Mt Murray

Lake
Neale

LARAPINTA

Areyonga

WATARRKA
NATIONAL
PARK

Palm
Valley

FINKE
GORGE
NATIONAL
PARK

Wallace Rockhole
Aboriginal
Community

ILLAMURTA SPRINGS
CONSERVATION RES

Jim's Place
Wayside Inn

PETERMANN

ABORIGINAL

Lake
Amadeus

Mt Harris
1067m

Ulpanyali
Kings Canyon
Resort

Kings
Canyon

Lila

MIDDLE RANGE

35

Mt Lewis
808m

Tempe Downs

FWD track

47

Henbury
Meteorite
Craters

29

199

Mt Taylor
1001m

Docker River
Community

LAND

TRUST

Kings Creek Station
(Camping ground)

LURITJA   RD

63

ERNEST

51

GILES

48

RD

Palmer Valley

68

183

231

PETERMANN

RANGES

KATITI ABORIGINAL
LAND TRUST

RD

LIDDLE

50

LURITJA

HILLS

DESERT
RANGE

Desert Oak Hill
624m

GUNBARREL

KERNOT RANGE

18

BASEDOW   RANGE

Imanpa
Community

Mt Gosse
885m

Surveyor Generals
Corner

Mt Olga
1069m

Yulara
Ayers Rock Resort

LASSETER

84

ULURU-KATA TJUTA
NATIONAL PARK

Kata Tjuta
(The Olgas)

41

Uluru
(Ayers Rock)
863m

242

Curtin
Springs

41

11

51

Mt Ebenezer
Roadhouse

HWY

4

55

Erldunda

74

STUART

87

105

Stevensons Pk
1319m

Butlers Dome
1111m

Mygoora
Lake

Mt Connor
863m

Mt Connor (ruins)

68

Lyndvale

Kulgera

Mount
Cavenagh

19

Mt Aloysius
1085m

Mt Hinckley
1018m

Mt Cockburn
1138m

Alpara

Feltham Hill
863m

Mulga Park

63

NORTHERN TERRITORY
SOUTH AUSTRALIA

165

Victory
Downs

Kalka

Pipalyatjara

Mt Davies
1058m

Aparawatatja

MANN

Mt Edwin
1193m

Mt Whinham
1231m

Kanypi

213

RANGES

Mt Woodward
1227m

Mt Morris
1288m

Amata

Ayliffe Hill (High)
1044m

Mt Davenport
1139m

Mt Cuthbert
1035m

Sentinel Hill
910m

66   67

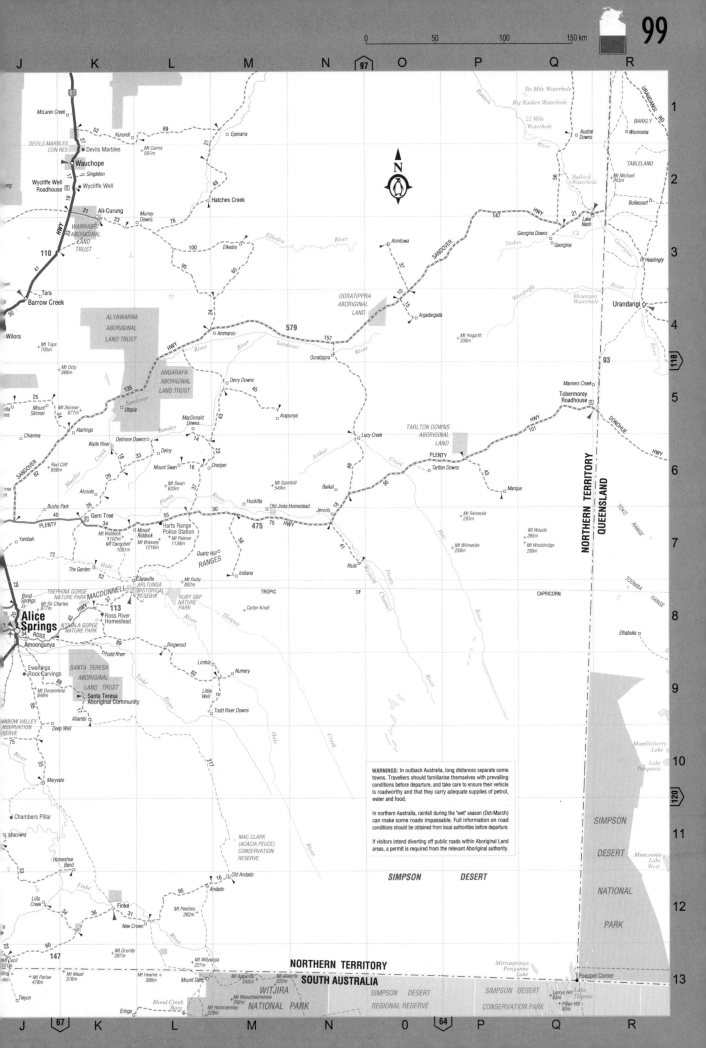

0   50   100   150 km

J   K   L   M   N   97   O   P   Q   R

1

McLaren Creek
52
Kurundi
69
Epenarra
21
DEVILS MARBLES
CON RES
27
Devils Marbles
+ Mt Cairns
597m
Six Mile Waterhole
Big Ranken Waterhole
22 Mile
Waterhole
BARKLY
Wooroona

2

Wauchope
17
Singleton
49
Hatches Creek
TABLELAND
56
Bullock
Waterhole
+ Mt Michael
243m
Bullecourt
Wycliffe Well
Roadhouse
19
Wycliffe Well
147
HWY
27
Lake
Nash

3

21
Ali-Curung
Murray
Downs
23
76
100
Elkedra
Elkedra
River
Annitowa
SANDOVER
Georgina Downs
Stokes
Georgina
Headingly
110
WARRABRI
ABORIGINAL
LAND
TRUST
95
60
37
10

4

41
Tara
Barrow Creek
30
ALYAWARRA
ABORIGINAL
LAND TRUST
24
Ammaroo
579
157
OORATIPPRA
ABORIGINAL
LAND
15
Argadargada
Woodroffe
Mountain
Waterhole
Urandangi
93
118
Wilora
+ Mt Tops
705m

5

+ Mt Octy
696m
135
ANGARAPA
ABORIGINAL
LAND TRUST
Sandover
Derry Downs
45
Arapunya
Ooratippra
+ Mt Hogarth
338m
Manners Creek
Tobermorey
Roadhouse
HWY
101
DONOHUE
HWY
25
Mount
Skinner
+ Mt Skinner
677m
Utopia

6

+ Red Cliff
658m
SANDOVER
82
Chianina
Atartinga
Waite River
Delmore Downs
MacDonald
Downs
14
Delny
Mount Swan
16
Dneiper
+ Mt Sainthill
549m
Baikal
Lucy Creek
TARLTON DOWNS
ABORIGINAL
LAND
PLENTY
Tarlton Downs
43
Marqua
95
18
33
29
Alcoota
37
23
Bundey
48
+ Mt Woods
265m
+ Mt Wooldridge
288m

7

Bushy Park
26
Gem Tree
34
PLENTY
40
Yambah
72
The Garden
52
Mt Riddock
1102m
Mount
Riddock
+ Mt Campbell
1051m
Harts Range
Police Station
+ Mt Brassey
1216m
55
Mt Palmer
1138m
58
RANGES
Quartz Hill
Indiana
30
Huckitta
Old Jinka Homestead
475
75
HWY
Jervois
41
18
Atula
Western
Channel
+ Mt Reinecke
283m
+ Mt Winnecke
258m
Plenty

8

29
Bond
Springs
+ Mt Sir Charles
877m
TREPHINA GORGE
NATURE PARK
MACDONNELL
113
HWY
37
Ross River
Homestead
Claraville
ARLTUNGA
HISTORICAL
RESERVE
+ Mt Ruby
852m
RUBY GAP
NATURE
PARK
TROPIC
OF
CAPRICORN
Alice
Springs
N'DHALA GORGE
NATURE PARK
ROSS
34
Amoongunya
89
Ringwood
+ Carter Knoll
Illogwa
Ethabuka
River

9

Ewaninga
Rock Carvings
88
+ Mt Ooraminna
649m
SANTA TERESA
ABORIGINAL
LAND TRUST
Santa Teresa
Aboriginal Community
Allambi
62
Todd River
Limbla
Numery
Little
Well
Todd River Downs
85

10

RAINBOW VALLEY
CONSERVATION
RESERVE
75
Deep Well
33
Hale
Creek
Mumbleberry
Lake
Lake
Torquinie

11

Chambers Pillar
Idracowra
MAC CLARK
(ACACIA PEUCE)
CONSERVATION
RESERVE
SIMPSON
DESERT
NATIONAL
120

WARNINGS: In outback Australia, long distances separate some towns. Travellers should familiarise themselves with prevailing conditions before departure, and take care to ensure their vehicle is roadworthy and that they carry adequate supplies of petrol, water and food.

In northern Australia, rainfall during the 'wet' season (Oct-March) can make some roads impassable. Full information on road conditions should be obtained from local authorities before departure.

If visitors intend diverting off public roads within Aboriginal Land areas, a permit is required from the relevant Aboriginal authority.

12

53
Horseshoe
Bend
Lilla
Creek
Finke
16
Old Andado
95
Andado
34
36
31
New Crown
Mt Peebles
262m
SIMPSON   DESERT
Muncoonie
Lake West
PARK

13

60
147
Mt Grundy
397m
+ Mt Cecil
551m
+ Mt Parlue
478m
+ Mt Mead
376m
Mt Hearne +
306m
Mount Dare
+ Mt Wilyunpa
227m
NORTHERN TERRITORY
SOUTH AUSTRALIA
Mt Apterda
245m
Mt Aliuerta
222m
Mirranponga
Pongunna
Lake
Poeppel Corner
Tieyon
Eringa
Blood Creek
Bore
Mt Hammersley
229m
Mt Weeahlakiminne
292m
WITJIRA
NATIONAL   PARK
SIMPSON   DESERT
REGIONAL RESERVE
SIMPSON   DESERT
CONSERVATION PARK
Larrys Hill
63m
+ Pillan Hill
60m
Lake
Thomas

J   67   K   L   M   N   64   O   P   Q   R

NORTHERN TERRITORY
QUEENSLAND

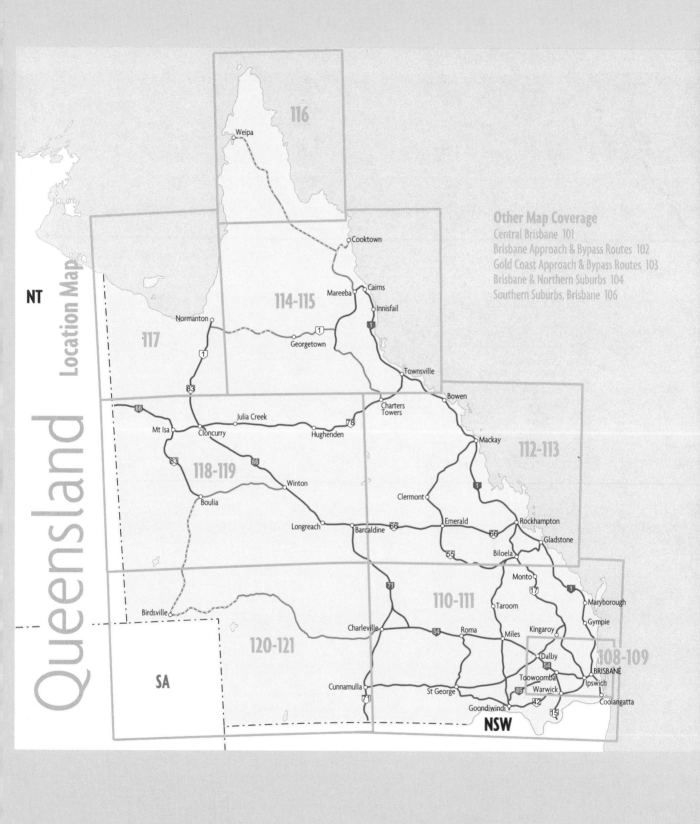

NT

Location Map

Queensland

NSW

SA

116

Weipa

Cooktown

114-115

Mareeba
Cairns
Innisfail

Normanton
Georgetown

Townsville

Bowen

117

1

83

66

Mt Isa
Cloncurry
Julia Creek
Hughenden

Charters
Towers

78

Mackay

112-113

83

118-119

66

Winton

Boulia

Clermont

Emerald

Rockhampton
Gladstone

Longreach
Barcaldine

66

66

55

Biloela

Monto

17

1

Maryborough

71

110-111

Taroom

Gympie

Kingaroy

Birdsville

Charleville

54

Roma

Miles

120-121

Dalby

54

BRISBANE

108-109

Cunnamulla

St George

Toowoomba
Warwick

Ipswich

85

71

Goondiwindi

42

15

Coolangatta

NSW

Other Map Coverage
Central Brisbane 101
Brisbane Approach & Bypass Routes 102
Gold Coast Approach & Bypass Routes 103
Brisbane & Northern Suburbs 104
Southern Suburbs, Brisbane 106

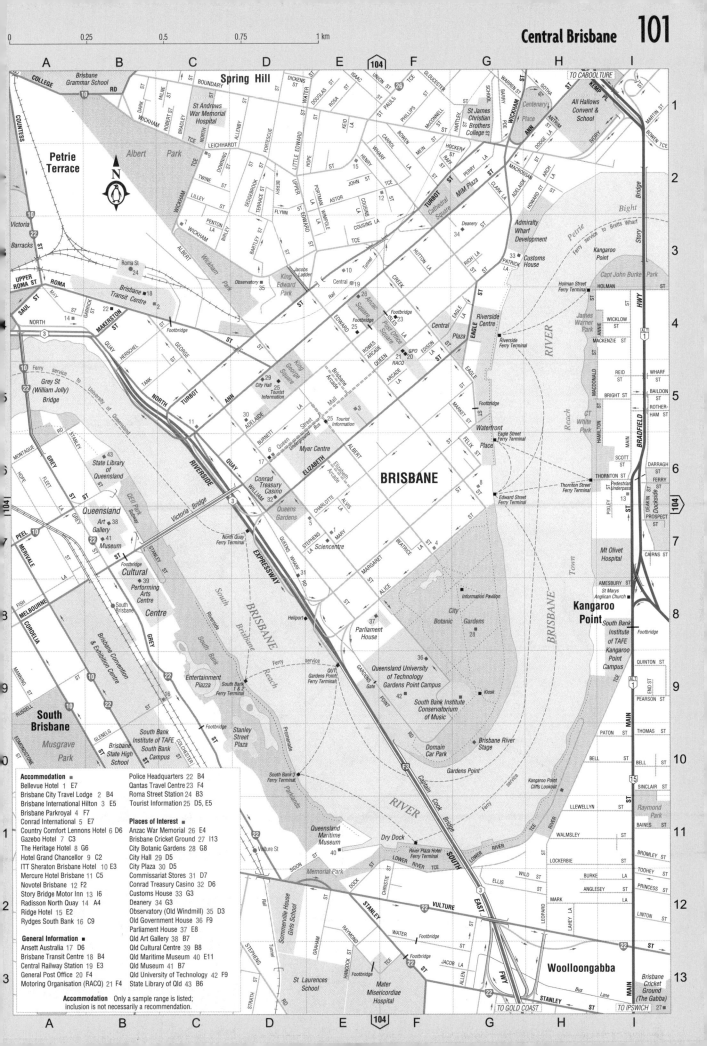

Scale: 0 — 0.25 — 0.5 — 0.75 — 1 km

Spring Hill

Petrie Terrace

Albert Park

Brisbane Grammar School

St Andrews War Memorial Hospital

St James Christian Brothers College

All Hallows Convent & School

Victoria Barracks

Roma St

Brisbane Transit Centre

King Edward Park

Observatory

Admiralty Wharf Development

Customs House

Bight

Kangaroo Point

Capt John Burke Park

James Warner Park

State Library of Queensland

King George Square

City Hall

Brisbane Arcade

Central Plaza

Riverside Centre

RIVER

Reach

CT White Park

Myer Centre

Conrad Treasury Casino

Queens Gardens

BRISBANE

Waterfront Place

Eagle Street

Queensland Art Gallery

Qld Museum

Cultural Centre

Performing Arts Centre

South Bank

Victoria Bridge

North Quay Ferry Terminal

A Sciencentre

Mt Olivet Hospital

Thornton Street Ferry Terminal

Pedestrian Underpass

Kangaroo Point

South Bank Institute of TAFE Kangaroo Point Campus

Brisbane Convention & Exhibition Centre

Entertainment Piazza

South Brisbane Ferry Terminal

Stanley Street Plaza

Parliament House

City Botanic Gardens

Heliport

Information Pavilion

South Brisbane

Musgrave Park

Brisbane State High School

South Bank Institute of TAFE South Bank Campus

Queensland University of Technology Gardens Point Campus

South Bank Institute Conservatorium of Music

Domain Car Park

Brisbane River Stage

Gardens Point

Kangaroo Point Cliffs Lookout

Raymond Park

Queensland Maritime Museum

Dry Dock

River Plaza Hotel Ferry Terminal

RIVER

Sommerville House Girls School

Memorial Park

St Laurences School

Mater Misericordiae Hospital

Woolloongabba

Brisbane Cricket Ground (The Gabba)

TO CABOOLTURE

TO GOLD COAST

TO IPSWICH

Accommodation ■
Bellevue Hotel 1 E7
Brisbane City Travel Lodge 2 B4
Brisbane International Hilton 3 E5
Brisbane Parkroyal 4 F7
Conrad International 5 E7
Country Comfort Lennons Hotel 6 D6
Gazebo Hotel 7 C3
The Heritage Hotel 8 G6
Hotel Grand Chancellor 9 C2
ITT Sheraton Brisbane Hotel 10 E3
Mercure Hotel Brisbane 11 C5
Novotel Brisbane 12 F2
Story Bridge Motor Inn 13 I6
Radisson North Quay 14 A4
Ridge Hotel 15 E2
Rydges South Bank 16 C9

General Information ■
Ansett Australia 17 D6
Brisbane Transit Centre 18 B4
Central Railway Station 19 E3
General Post Office 20 F4
Motoring Organisation (RACQ) 21 F4

Police Headquarters 22 B4
Qantas Travel Centre 23 F4
Roma Street Station 24 B3
Tourist Information 25 D5, E5

Places of Interest ■
Anzac War Memorial 26 E4
Brisbane Cricket Ground 27 I13
City Botanic Gardens 28 G8
City Hall 29 D5
City Plaza 30 D5
Commissariat Stores 31 D7
Conrad Treasury Casino 32 D6
Customs House 33 G3
Deanery 34 G3
Observatory (Old Windmill) 35 D3
Old Government House 36 F9
Parliament House 37 E8
Qld Art Gallery 38 B7
Qld Cultural Centre 39 B8
Qld Maritime Museum 40 E11
Qld Museum 41 B7
Qld University of Technology 42 F9
State Library of Qld 43 B6

Accommodation Only a sample range is listed; inclusion is not necessarily a recommendation.

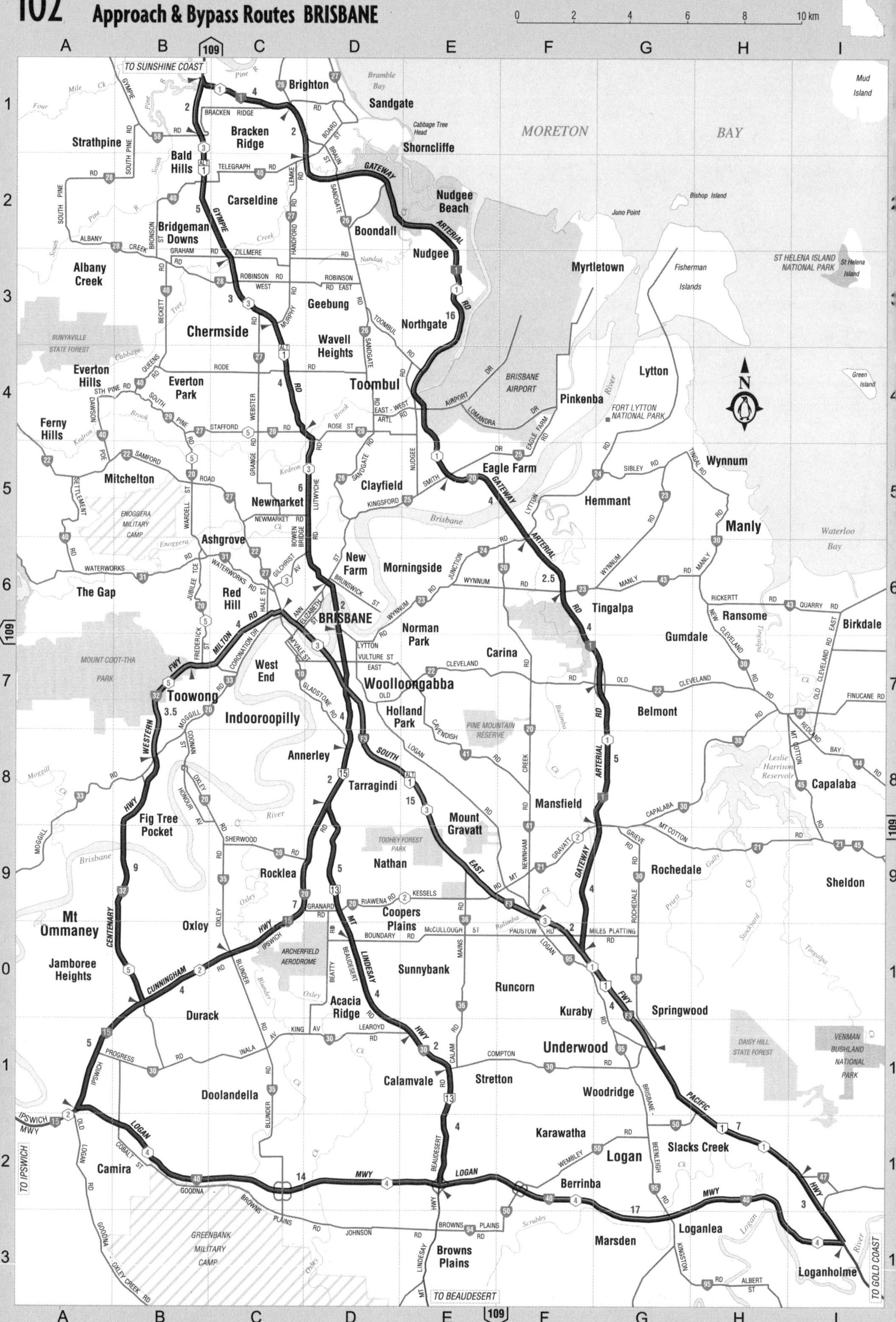

109
TO SUNSHINE COAST

0 2 4 6 8 10 km

A B C D E F G H I

Moreton Bay region map — Brisbane approach and bypass routes.

Place names (north to south, west to east):

Strathpine, Brighton, Sandgate, Bald Hills, Bracken Ridge, Shorncliffe, Mud Island, Carseldine, Bridgeman Downs, Boondall, Nudgee Beach, Nudgee, Myrtletown, Bishop Island, St Helena Island National Park, St Helena Island, Albany Creek, Chermside, Geebung, Wavell Heights, Northgate, Lytton, Green Island, Everton Hills, Everton Park, Toombul, Brisbane Airport, Pinkenba, Fort Lytton National Park, Ferny Hills, Mitchelton, Newmarket, Clayfield, Kingsford, Eagle Farm, Hemmant, Wynnum, Manly, Waterloo Bay, The Gap, Ashgrove, Red Hill, New Farm, Morningside, Tingalpa, Gumdale, Ransome, Birkdale, Mount Coot-Tha Park, Brisbane, Norman Park, Carina, Belmont, Toowong, Indooroopilly, West End, Woolloongabba, Holland Park, Pine Mountain Reserve, Leslie Harrison Reservoir, Capalaba, Fig Tree Pocket, Annerley, Tarragindi, Mount Gravatt, Mansfield, Rochedale, Sheldon, Mt Ommaney, Jamboree Heights, Rocklea, Nathan, Coopers Plains, Runcorn, Kuraby, Springwood, Durack, Oxley, Sunnybank, Acacia Ridge, Calamvale, Stretton, Woodridge, Underwood, Venman Bushland National Park, Daisy Hill State Forest, Doolandella, Karawatha, Logan, Slacks Creek, Camira, Goodna, Browns Plains, Berrinba, Loganlea, Greenbank Military Camp, Marsden, Loganholme, Browns Plains.

TO IPSWICH · TO BEAUDESERT · TO GOLD COAST

Thick roads represent recommended approach and bypass routes.

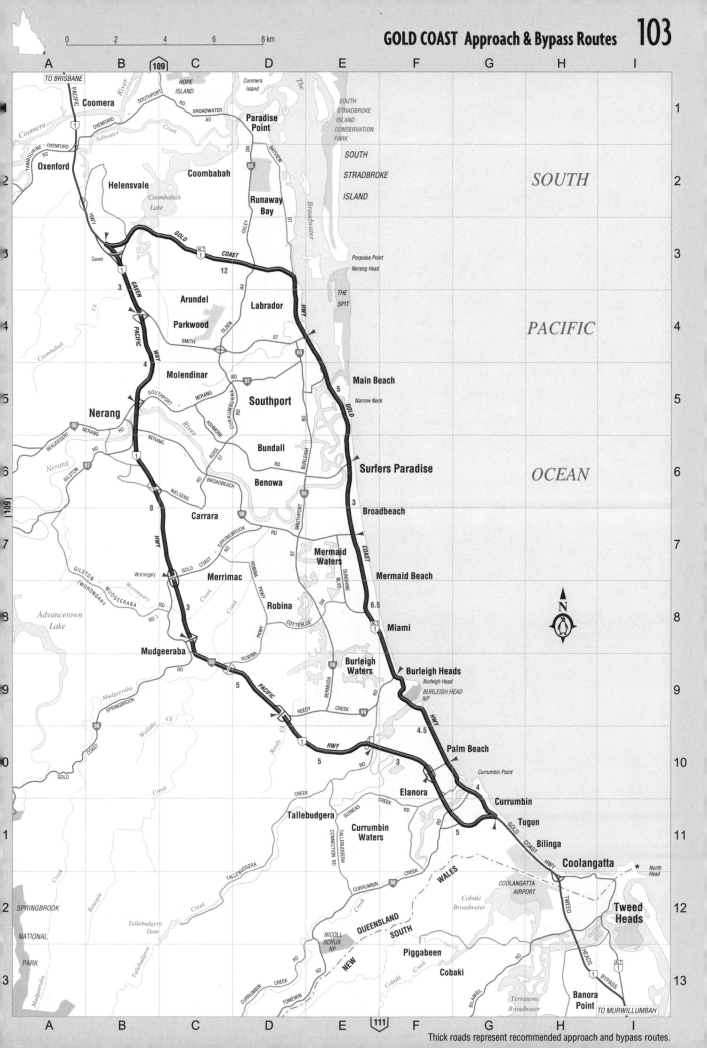

0   2   4   6   8 km

A   B   C   D   E   F   G   H   I

TO BRISBANE

Coomera

HOPE ISLAND

Coomera Island

SOUTH STRADBROKE ISLAND CONSERVATION PARK

PACIFIC

Oxenford

Helensvale

Coombabah

Coombabah Lake

Paradise Point

Runaway Bay

Broadwater

SOUTH STRADBROKE ISLAND

SOUTH

PACIFIC

Gaven

GOLD COAST

Arundel

Parkwood

Labrador

THE SPIT

Porpoise Point
Nerang Head

Molendinar

Southport

Main Beach

Narrow Neck

Nerang

Bundall

OCEAN

Benowa

Surfers Paradise

Carrara

Broadbeach

Mermaid Waters

Merrimac

Robina

Mermaid Beach

Worongary

Miami

Mudgeeraba

Burleigh Waters

Burleigh Heads

Burleigh Head
BURLEIGH HEAD NP

Advancetown Lake

Palm Beach

Currumbin Point

Elanora

Currumbin

Tugun

Tallebudgera

Currumbin Waters

Bilinga

Coolangatta

North Head

WALES

COOLANGATTA AIRPORT

SPRINGBROOK

NATIONAL

Tallebudgera Dam

QUEENSLAND SOUTH

Cobaki Broadwater

Tweed Heads

NICOLL SCRUB NP

Piggabeen

NEW

PARK

Cobaki

Banora Point

Terranora Broadwater

BYPASS

TO MURWILLUMBAH

A   B   C   D   E   F   G   H   I

Thick roads represent recommended approach and bypass routes.

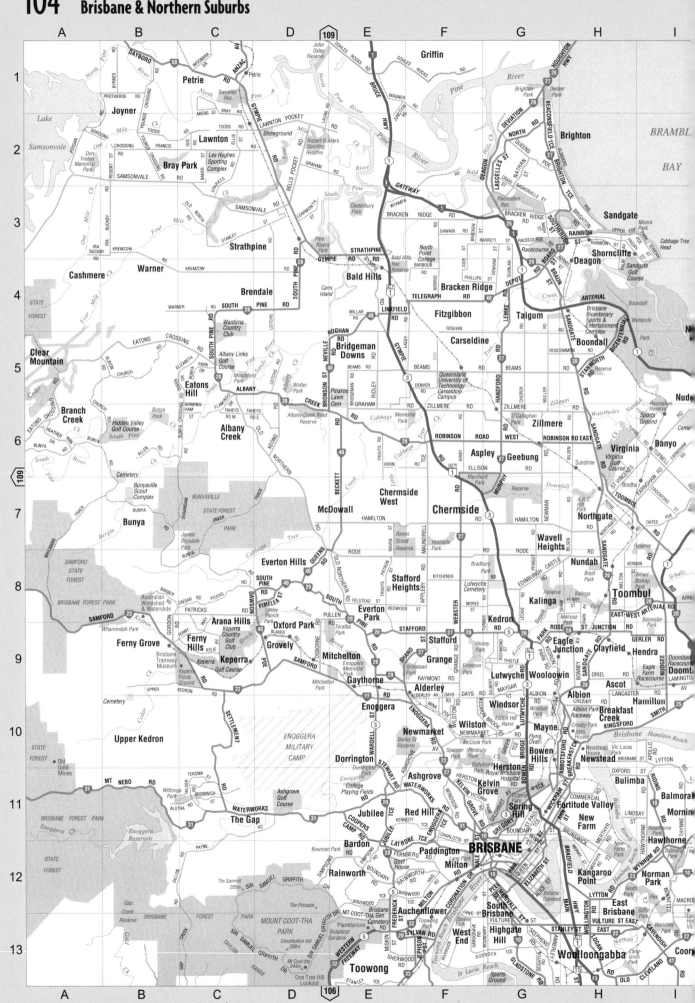

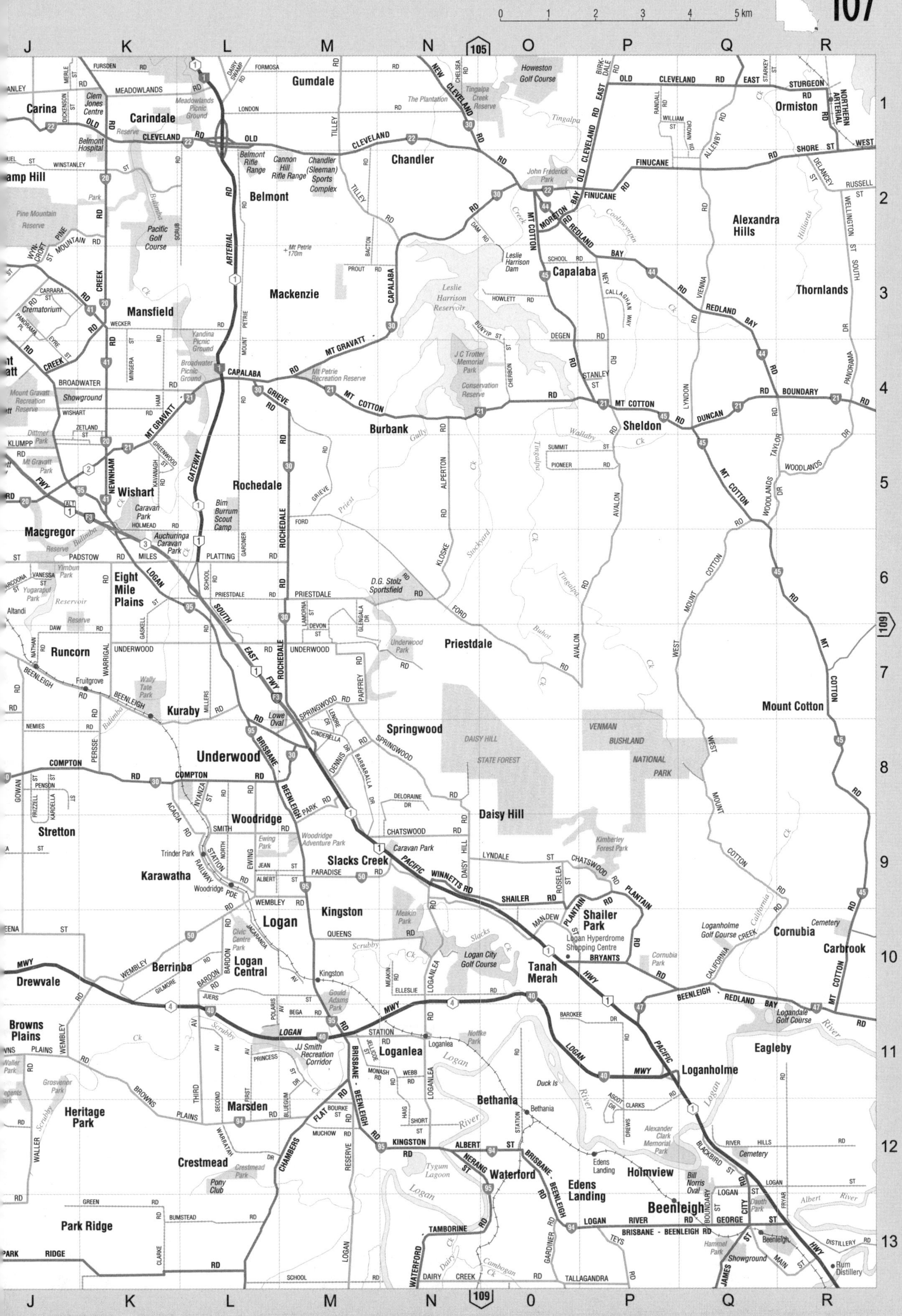

0 1 2 3 4 5 km

Grid columns: J K L M N O P Q R
Grid rows: 1–13

Place names and labels:

Carina, Carindale, Camp Hill, Belmont Hospital, Clem Jones Centre, Meadowlands Picnic Ground, Gumdale, Chandler, Howeston Golf Course, Tingalpa Creek Reserve, The Plantation

Belmont, Belmont Rifle Range, Cannon Hill Rifle Range, Chandler (Sleeman) Sports Complex, John Frederick Park, Finucane, Ormiston, Sturgeon

Pine Mountain Reserve, Pacific Golf Course, Mackenzie, Mt Petrie 170m, Mt Cotton, Leslie Harrison Dam, Capalaba, Alexandra Hills, Thornlands

Crematorium, Mansfield, Broadwater Picnic Ground, Yandina Picnic Ground, Leslie Harrison Reservoir, J C Trotter Memorial Park, Conservation Reserve, Sheldon, Boundary

Mount Gravatt, Mt Gravatt Recreation Reserve, Showground, Wishart, Dittmer Park, Burbank, Mt Petrie Recreation Reserve

Newnham, Wishart, Rochedale, Bim Burrum Scout Camp, Caravan Park, Auchuringa Caravan Park, D.G. Stolz Sportsfield, Priestdale

Macgregor, Yilmbun Park, Yugarapul Park, Eight Mile Plains, Underwood, Underwood Park, Buhot, Mount Cotton

Runcorn, Altandi, Wally Tate Park, Kuraby, Lowe Oval, Springwood, Daisy Hill State Forest, Venman Bushland National Park

Stretton, Trinder Park, Woodridge Adventure Park, Underwood, Woodridge, Slacks Creek, Springwood, Daisy Hill, Kimberley Forest Park

Karawatha, Ewing Park, Kingston, Logan, Shailer Park, Logan Hyperdrome Shopping Centre, Loganholme Golf Course, Cornubia, Carbrook

Drewvale, Berrinba, Logan Central, Kingston, Meakin Park, Logan City Golf Course, Tanah Merah, Cornubia Park, Logandale Golf Course

Browns Plains, Heritage Park, Grosvenor Park, Marsden, Loganlea, JJ Smith Recreation Corridor, Bethania, Loganholme, Eagleby, Alexander Clark Memorial Park, Bill Norris Oval

Crestmead, Grestmead Park, Pony Club, Kingston, Waterford, Tygum Lagoon, Edens Landing, Holmview, Beenleigh

Park Ridge, Beenleigh, Showground, Rum Distillery, Hammel Park

Roads:

Cleveland Rd, Old Cleveland Rd, Mt Gravatt Rd, Mt Cotton Rd, New Cleveland Rd, Redland Bay Rd, Finucane Rd, Northern Arterial, Gateway Fwy, Logan Rd, Pacific Hwy, Pacific Mwy, Beenleigh Rd, Brisbane Rd, Mt Cotton Rd, Loganlea Rd, Chambers Flat Rd, Waterford Tamborine Rd, Brisbane-Beenleigh Rd, Logan River Rd

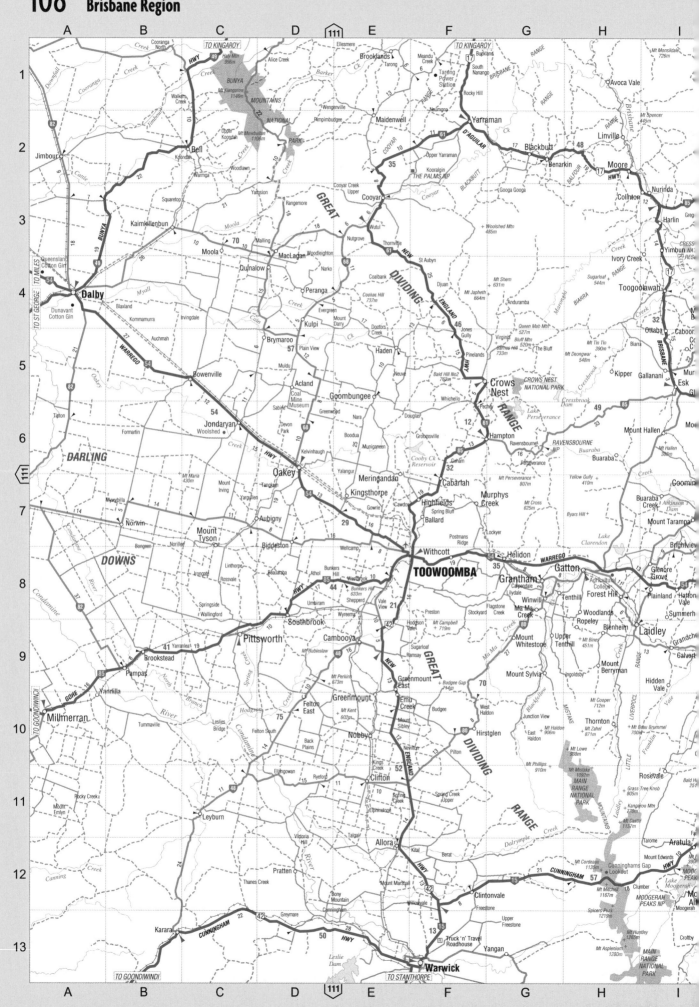

0   10   20   30   40 km

J K L M N O P Q R

1
Cambroon Bridge · Mapleton · Obi Obi · Kureelpa · Bli Bli · TO NOOSA HEADS · Mudjimba · Pacific Paradise
Mt Cabinet 732m · Flaxton · Dulong · Woombye · **Nambour** · Hunchy · Diddillibah · Alexandra Headland
Mt Adelaide 754m · Mapleton Falls NP · Palmwoods · Big Pineapple · **Maroochydore**
CONONDALE NATIONAL PARK · RONDALILLA NP · Witta · Montville · Chevallum · Forest Glen · **Buderim** · **Mooloolaba**
Conondale · Mt Langley 868m · Mt Ramsden 792m · Reesville · Eudlo · Warana

2
North West Mtn 589m · Maleny · Bald Knob 465m · **Mooloolah** · Bokarina · Wurtulla
Bellthorpe · Wootha · Diamond Valley · BULARCHA NP · MOOLOOLAH RIVER NP · CURRIMUNDI LAKE CONSERVATION PARK
Mt Kilcoy · Mt Marysmokes 657m · Booroobin · Long Range Weather Forecasting Observatory · Mt Mellum 404m · Landsborough · Currimundi
Mount Kilcoy · Peachester · Coochin Creek · Commissioners Flat · Beerwah · **Caloundra**
Mt Kilcoy 351m · Stanmore · Mt Beerwah 556m · Mt Coonowrin 375m

3
Kilcoy · D'AGUILAR HWY · Kalangara · GLASS HOUSE MOUNTAINS NP · Glass House Mountains · BRIBIE ISLAND
Winya · Glenfern · Neurum · Durundur · **Woodford** · Beerburrum · BRIBIE ISLAND NATIONAL PARK
Villeneuve · Mt Archer 460m · Bracalba · Mt Tambourin 224m · Donnybrook
D'Aguilar · Delaneys Creek · Mt Delaney 373m

4
Mount Mee · **Elimbah** · White Patch · Banksia Beach
Lake Somerset · Mt Mee 495m · Wamuran Basin · Moodlu · Toorbul · Bellara
Mt Byron 617m · Campbells Pocket · Rocksberg · Abbey Museum · **Bongaree** · **Woorim**
Somerset Dam · Wamuran · Mt Pleasant 524m · **Caboolture** · Skirmish Point · North Point · Cape Moreton

5
Crossdale · Mount Pleasant · Morayfield · Beachmere · Bulwer · MORETON ISLAND · MORETON ISLAND NATIONAL PARK
Dayboro · BURPENGARY · Deception Bay · Cowan Cowan Point · Mt Tempest 280m
Bryden · Upper Laceys Creek · **Narangba** · Alma Park Zoo · **DECEPTION BAY** · **SOUTH**
Dundas · Mt Sim Jue 611m · Kobble · Dakabin · SCARBOROUGH

6
D'AGUILAR NATIONAL PARK · Mt Samson 742m · Lakeside Racing Circuit · **Kallangur** · **REDCLIFFE** · Tangalooma · Moreton Island Tourist Resort
Mt Glorious · Mt Lawson 473m · Mount Samson · **PETRIE** · MARGATE · MORETON · **PACIFIC**
Hydro Power Station · Upper Cedar Creek · STRATHPINE · Bramble Bay · For more detail on Brisbane Suburbs see pages 104-107
Mount Nebo · Yugar · Closeburn · SANDGATE

7
CABBAGE TREE RANGE · Samford · Highvale · **CHERMSIDE** · Mud Island · BAY · Kooringal
BRISBANE FOREST PARK · NEWMARKET · BRISBANE AIRPORT · Fisherman Islands · St Helena Island · Green Island · South Passage
Lake Manchester · Fernvale · Fairmeview · Wanora · St Helens · ST HELENA ISLAND NP · **Amity Point**

8
BRISBANE · **WYNNUM** · **MANLY** · Rocky Point · Capt Cook Memorial · **Point Lookout**
Marburg · INDOOROOPILLY · **WOOLLOONGABBA** · Waterloo Bay · WELLINGTON POINT · Ormiston House · **OCEAN**
Haigslea · Mt Crosby · Peel Island · Historical Cemetery · Blue Lake Beach
Borallon · CAPALABA · **CLEVELAND** · Old Court House · **Dunwich** · Mt Hardgrave 219m · BLUE LAKE NATIONAL PARK

9
IPSWICH · IPSWICH BYPASS · SUNNYBANK · Blue Lake · **NORTH STRADBROKE ISLAND**
Walloon · SOUTHERN HWY · LOGAN · **WOODRIDGE** · **VICTORIA POINT** · Ibis Lagoon · Eighteen Mile Swamp
Ebenezer · Swanbank Power Station · GREENBANK MILITARY CAMP · **LOGAN** · DAISY HILL STATE FOREST · **REDLAND BAY** · Macleay Island
Loamside · Ripley · Purga

10
Flinders · Mt Goolman 454m · BETHANIA · WATERFORD · **LOGANHOLME** · Russell Island · Native Companion Lagoon
Peak Crossing · Mt Blaine 457m · **BEENLEIGH** · Alberton Rum Distillery · Rocky Point · SOUTH STRADBROKE ISLAND
Harrisville · Flinders Peak 679m · North Maclean · **YATALA** · Cabbage Tree Point · Steiglitz
Limestone Ridge · Mt Elliot 436m · Wolfdene · Woongoolba · Norwell · Jacobs Well

11
Warrill View · Munbilla · Mt Joyce 465m · Jimboomba · Kagaru · Cedar Grove · Ormeau · SOUTH STRADBROKE ISLAND CONSERVATION PARK
Roadvale · Milbong · Woodhill · Veresdale · **Tamborine** · Dreamworld · **Coomera** · Couran
Kalbar · Kulgun · Woolabra Farmworld · Gleneagle · North Tamborine · Upper Coomera · Movie World · Currigee
Mt May 357m · Eagle Heights · Movie World · **Oxenford** · Sanctuary Cove

12
Templin · Coulson · Bromelton · TAMBORINE NATIONAL PARK · Mount Tamborine · Maudsland · Sea World · Fishermans Wharf · GOLD COAST
Boonah · Milford · **Beaudesert** · Boys Town · Wongalepong · Benobble · **Nerang** · MAIN BEACH · **SOUTHPORT**
Bunburra · Sugarloaf 408m · Josephville · Canungra · Mt Nathan 938m · **SURFERS PARADISE** · BROADBEACH · Conrad Jupiters Casino

13
Cannon Creek · Kooralbyn · Laravale · Advancetown Lake · Advancetown · Gilston · Gold Coast War Memorial & Skirmish
Knapps Peak 645m · Mt Mahomet 445m · Kerry · Tabooba · Flying Fox · Wrapungar · **Mudgeeraba** · BURLEIGH HEADS · BURLEIGH HEAD NP
Maroon · TO WOODENBONG · LAMINGTON NP · Beechmont · SPRINGBROOK NP · TO TWEED HEADS

A B C D 112 E F 113 H I

1

Blackall
Allandale
Birkhead
Dawson Castlevale DEVELOPMENTAL RD 208
Spring Creek
Mt Catherine 627m
55 DAWSON
Rolleston
Bauhinia
FITZROY DEV RD
Mt Hope 352m 74 19
LANDSBOROUGH 101
Barcoo River
Barcoo River
302
CARNARVON RANGE
Consuelo
Fairfield
Mt Boordomen 330m

2

MATILDA 217
42
Tambo
BUCKLAND TABLELAND
CARNARVON NATIONAL PARK
Mt Playfair
Mt Hutton 699m
Mt Faraday 790m
Mt Hornet 920m
Mt Acland 975m
Carnarvon NATIONAL PARK
Carnarvon Gorge
NUGA NUGA NP
Lake Nuga Nuga
CARNARVON DEV RD 41 69
Mt Nicholson 769m

WARREGO RANGE
Sumnervale
HWY
Caldervale
GREAT
MURPHY
Mt King 807m
TABLELAND
110 CARNARVON
EXPEDITION NATIONAL PARK
Mt Weldon 660m
Mt Round 460m

3

75
71
116
Milray
Woolga
River
Mt Ogilby 700m
DIVIDING
103
Mt Comball 354m
EXPEDITION NATIONAL PARK
Broadmere
LYND RANGE
Dawson

4

SCRUBBY CREEK RECREATION RESERVE
Langlo Downs
87
Augathella
CHESTERTON RANGE
101
RANGE
Mt Hutton 914m
Injune
Gunnewin
53

5

ADAVALE
Langlo Crossing
Box Creek
84
71
90
54
Mt Boyd 614m
Mt Hotspur 699m
71
Bymount
71 DEVELOPMENTAL RD
Durham Downs
82

CHARLEVILLE RD
Langlo River
Charleville
89
14
Morven
WARREGO
44 Mungallala
Mitchell
HWY
18 Roma
Muggleton

6

Royal Flying Doctor Base & Visitors Centre
Sommariva
176
54
45 Womalilla
Amby
Muckadilla 87
Roma 41
Wallumbilla 54 Yuleba
Jack

121
R
Cooladdi Roadhouse
73
Boatman Bore
Bonus Downs
55 45

7

Coolabah
Guestling
99
49
206
Creek
Albany Downs
33 HWY

8

HWY
199
Wyandra
71
Balonne River
210
Surat
194
SURAT
87 Glenl
Coalb

9

Koroit Opal Field
Coongoola
Clifton
87
Begonia
Binda
Lake Kajarabie
116 CARNARVON
Cotea Ck
Rocky Crossing

MITCHELL (MATILDA)
Glendilla
54
THRUSHTON NATIONAL PARK
Alton
Flinton 182
MOO

10

Cunnamulla
49
134 BALONNE
291
45 HWY 48 112
Bollon
66
Boolba
St George
St George Irrigation Area
49
114
ALTON NATIONAL PARK

MITCHELL 49
Charlotte Plains
Warrego
CARNARVON HWY
55
44
77
Nindigully
BARWON
165 16 200
Bur

11

118
71
Noorama Sports Centre
Warrego River
Culgoa
27 Dirranbandi
Noondoo 20
44 Daymar 76
Thallon
118
Gradule
Talwood

12

Tinpenburra
CULGOA FLOODPLAIN NATIONAL PARK
Culgoa
162
Bokhara
CASTLEREAGH
Lake Bokhara
Moonie River
55 HWY
42
26 Caloona
41 Boo

QUEENSLAND
NEW SOUTH WALES
Jobs Gate
Hebel
38
Mungindi
Neeworra
Weemelah
18

13

Sharoon
Barringun
HWY
71
Neilmongle
Goodooga
47
19 New Angledool
20
Angledool Lake
Gundabloui
30
18 18

A B 17 C D E F 14 H I

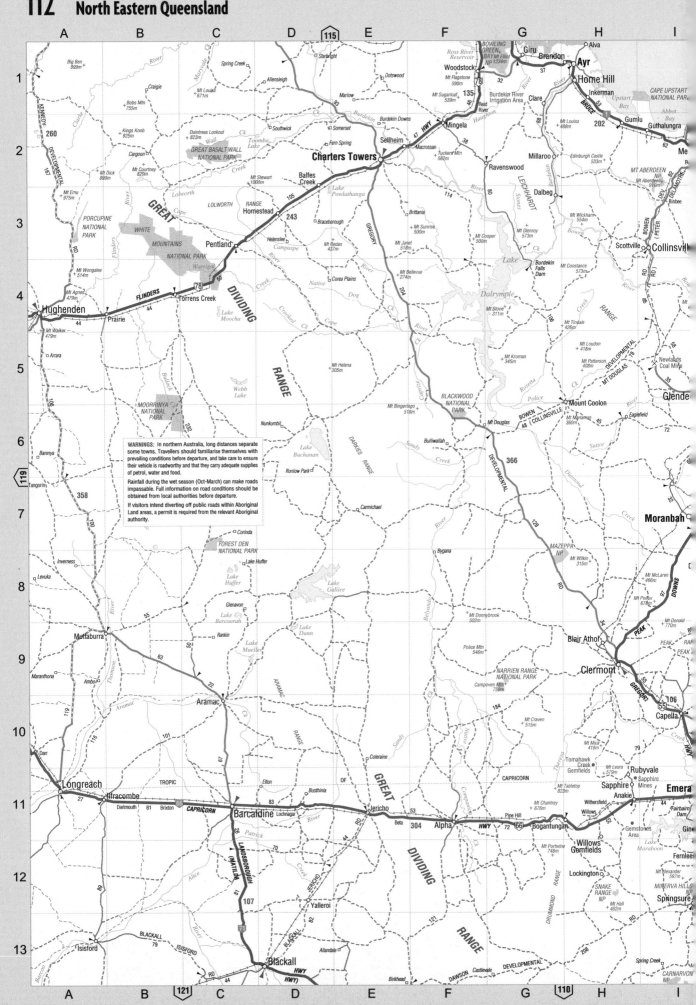

CORAL SEA

SOUTH

PACIFIC

OCEAN

N

THE WHITSUNDAYS

Gloucester Island
Dingo Beach
DRYANDER NP
Hayman Island
Earlando
Hook Island
Cannonvale Airlie Beach
Shute Harbour
Whitsunday Island
WHITSUNDAY ISLANDS NP
Hamilton Island
Proserpine
CONWAY NP
Lindeman Island
190
Shaw Island
Repulse Bay
Midge Point
SMITH ISLANDS NATIONAL PARK
Bloomsbury
Mt Crompton +792m
Elaroo
SOUTH CUMBERLAND ISLANDS NATIONAL PARK
Yalboroo
HWY
Seaforth Ball Bay
Brampton Island
Calen
Cape Hillsborough
Keswick Is
Scawfell Island
Mount Ossa
Kuttabul
St Bees Island
Shoal Point
Eungella NATIONAL PARK
Mount Charlton
Bucasia
Walkerston
Farleigh
Slade Point
Eungella
33
Mackay
Miran Marian
Bakers Creek
Finch Hatton
46
Eton
Half Tide
HOMEVALE NATIONAL PARK
20
Grasstree
Sarina Beach
Sarina
Armstrong Beach
Homevale
56
Half Creek
Koumala
CAPE PALMERSTON NATIONAL PARK
50
Mt Fort Cooper 528m
Nebo
Mt White 594m
Ilbilbie
NORTHUMBERLAND
274 57
Coppabella
14
29
Mt Scott +852m
Carmila
Flaggy Rock
WEST HILL NP
Middle Island
Mt Orange 530m
MtCoxendean 480m
Saltbush Park
334
Clairview
White Bluff Mtn 522m
South Island
REEF
Quail Island
Stanage
Broad Sound
FITZROY River
Leichhardt Downs
Railheston
Mt Edward +171m
Mt Price 164m
Townshend Is
CAPRICORN
Dysart
Bar Mtn 308m
Mt Joss +421m
St Lawrence
Mt Phillip 393m
Mt Wellington 528m
Mt Westall +550m
Stephens
Mt Buffalo 518m
Ogmore
Double Island +747m
Pine Mtn 375m
Shoalwater Bay
Middlemount
SARINA RD
Mt Bora +350m
Glenprairie
Mt Muigrave 655m
Mt Atherton 438m
24
Mt Magog 575m
MILITARY TRAINING AREA
CHANNEL
Tieri
MAY DOWNS 72
82
BRUCE
Manly
Marlborough
79
Kunwarara
BYFIELD NATIONAL PARK
119
Junee
HWY
Merimal
Oaky Creek Mine
Mt Gardiner 450m +
Clifton
Fitzroy
Glen Geddes
Farnborough
KEPPEL ISLANDS NATIONAL PARK
Fairhill
Royles
Apis Creek
River
Yaamba
Mt White Mine
Arizona
Milman
Yeppoon
Great Keppel Island
Enshan Mine
Burkan
South Yaamba
The Caves
Mulambin
Kinka
Telson
Ridgelands
Parkhurst
Emu Park
TROPIC
Round Mtn 746m
ROCKHAMPTON
Tungamull
Keppel Sands
CURTIS
Nogoa
Dalma
Gracemere
Joskeleigh
OF
Comet
FOLEYVALE ABORIGINAL COMMUNITY
Kabra
75
Warren
Midgee
Broadmount
Heron Island
CAPRICORN
CAPRICORN
Bluff
Sorrel Hills
Wycarbah
Stanwell
Port Alma
CURTIS ISLAND NP
66
Gobwarra
Westwood
Bouldercombe
Mt Barker 161m
CAPRICORN CAYS NATIONAL PARK
Blackwater
Dingo
270
Gogango
36
Baijol
Marmor
Southend
Blackwater Mine
Duaringa
66
Mount Morgan
Raglan
Scrubby Mtn 933m
Namoi Hills
Wallaroo
Mt Battery 486m
LEICHHARDT
107
Ambrose
CURTIS CHANNEL
BLACKDOWN TABLELAND NATIONAL PARK
Mt Success 490m
Coomooboolaroo
Dululu
Mt Hope 458m
Mount Larcom
33
Yarwun
Gladstone
Bonnie Doon
South Blackwater Mine
50
Wowan
145
Vimy
Cedric Mtn 622m
Boyne Island
Lady Musgrave Island
Struan
Mt Dawson 317m
Lancefield
Mt Redshirt 597m
BURNETT
102
Calliope
Tannum Sands
Benaraby
EURIMBULA NP
WOORABINDA ABORIGINAL COMMUNITY
RANGE RD
Mt Ramsay 445m
39
HWY
Turkey Beach
Bustard Bay
92
Rannes
DAWSON
66
Barmundu
Seventeen Seventy
Baralaba
40
Googven
Mt Dromedary +477m
Agnes Water
EXPEDITION
Jambin
Argoon
Specimen Hill 671m
BRUCE
EURIMBULA NP
DEVELOPMENTAL
53
17
Calide
Bororen
DEEPWATER NATIONAL PARK
CARNARVON RANGE
DAWSON
Callide Coal Mine & Power Station
KROOMBIT TOPS NATIONAL PARK
Nagoorin
Miriam Vale
DAWSON HWY
46 39
Biloela
Callide Dam
Mt Graarbi 600m
Uboba
110
Rolleston
Banana
Thangool
111

0   25   50   75   100 km

WARNINGS: In northern Australia, long distances separate some towns. Travellers should familiarise themselves with prevailing conditions before departure, and take care to ensure their vehicle is roadworthy and that they carry adequate supplies of petrol, water and food.

Rainfall during the wet season (Oct-March) can make roads impassable. Full information on road conditions should be obtained from local authorities before departure.

If visitors intend diverting off public roads within Aboriginal Land areas, a permit is required from the relevant Aboriginal authority.

Beware of man-eating crocodiles in rivers and estuaries.

GULF

OF

CARPENTARIA

CAPE

YORK

PENINSULA

ABORIGINAL LAND

MITCHELL-ALICE RIVERS NATIONAL PARK

STAATEN RIVER NATIONAL PARK

Pormpuraaw Aboriginal Community

Kowanyama Aboriginal Community

Wallaby Island

Rutland Plains

Inkerman

Dorunda

Delta Downs

Point Burrowes

Fitzmaurice Point

Karumba

Barge Service Karumba to Weipa

Normanton

Mutton Hole

Shady Lagoon

Glenore Crossing

Magowra

Burke & Wills Cairn

Middle Point

Rocky Lake

Manrika Lake

Inverleigh

Macalister

Bang Bang Jump Up Rock Formation

Bang Bang

Donors Hill

Neumayer Valley

Wondoola

Iffley

Muggera Lagoon

GULF

SAVANNAH

Burke & Wills Roadhouse

Boomarra

Canobie

Taldora

Croydon

Coralie

Alehvale

Claraville

Esmeralda

Momba

Templeton

Mittagong

Racecourse Lagoon

Inorunie

Chadshunt

Gilbert River

Kutchera

Mt Turner 457m+

Georgetown

Forsayth

Goldsmiths

Cobbold Gorge

Robin Hood

Agate Creek Gemfields

Bairds Table Mountain 914m

Gleniora

Nara

Victoria Vale

Pelham

Perry Vale

Gorge Creek

Abingdon Downs

Huonfels

Tallaroo Hot

Dagworth

Mt Campbell 366m+

Vanlee

Strathmore

Miranda Downs

Fourteen Mile

Musgrave Station

Hann River Roadhouse & Camping

New Strathgordon

Strathmay

Strathaven

New Dixie

Oroners Outstation

Seefton

Killarney

Kimba

Pinnacles

King River

Strathleven

King Junction

Palme

Koolatah

Dunbar

Drumduff

Windermere Lagoon

Purumu Lagoon

Mosquito Lagoon

Twelve Mile Lagoon

Kingfish Lagoon

Highbury Lagoon

Longreach Lagoon

Dinner Camp Lagoon

Bulimba

Wal

BULLE NATI PA

GREAT DIVIDING

PENINSULA

BURKE DEVELOPMENTAL

NEWCASTLE

GREGORY RANGE

WILLS

BURKE DEVELOPMENTAL (MATILDA)

227

307

81

44

105

86

48

80

171

176

30

41

25

68

60

75

51

73

69

70

114

577

80

90

67

61

95

95

195

134

132

162

83

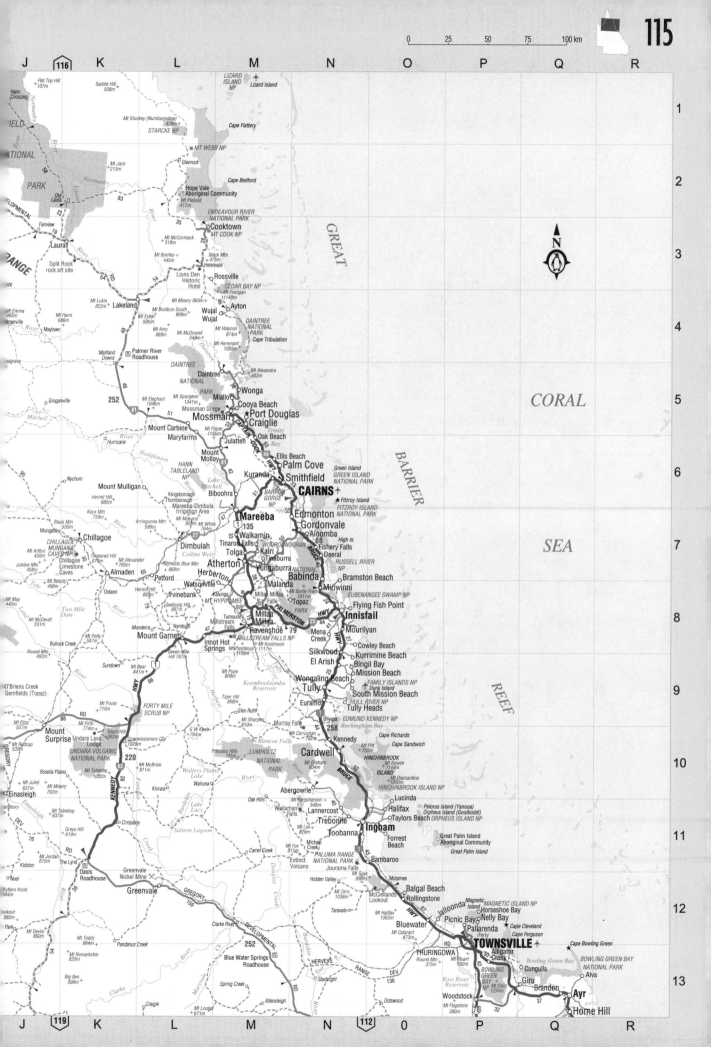

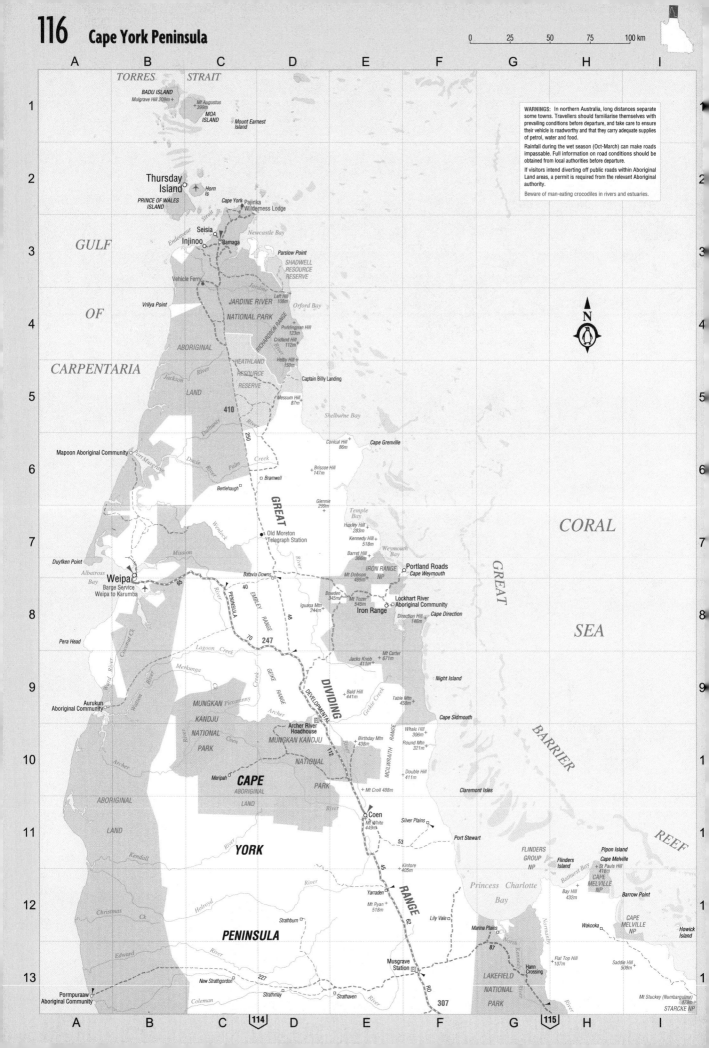

0   25   50   75   100 km

TORRES STRAIT

BADU ISLAND
Mulgrave Hill 209m +

Mt Augustus
+ 399m

MOA
ISLAND

Mount Earnest
Island

Thursday
Island

Horn
Is

PRINCE OF WALES
ISLAND

Cape York
Pajinka
Wilderness Lodge

Seisia
Injinoo
Bamaga

Newcastle Bay

Parslow Point

SHADWELL
RESOURCE
RESERVE

Vehicle Ferry

Jardine

Left Hill
108m

Orford Bay

JARDINE RIVER

NATIONAL PARK

RICHARDSON RANGE

Purklingman Hill
123m

Cridland Hill
112m +

Helby Hill +
150m

ABORIGINAL

HEATHLAND
RESOURCE
RESERVE

Captain Billy Landing

Messum Hill
87m

Shelburne Bay

LAND

Jackson

River

Dulhunty

410

250

River

Palm

Creek

Conical Hill +
86m

Cape Grenville

GULF

OF

CARPENTARIA

Mapoon Aboriginal Community

Port Musgrave

Ducie

River

Briscoe Hill
147m +

Bramwell

Bertiehaugh

Glennie
299m
+

Temple
Bay

Haxley Hill
283m +

Wenlock

GREAT

Old Moreton
Telegraph Station

Kennedy Hill +
518m

Weymouth
Bay

Mission

River

Batavia Downs

Barret Hill
366m +

IRON RANGE
NP

Portland Roads
Cape Weymouth

Duyfken Point

Albatross
Bay

Weipa

Barge Service
Weipa to Karumba

65

PENINSULA

40

EMBLEY

RANGE

48

Bowden
345m +

Mt Dobson
495m +

Mt Tozer
545m +

Lockhart River
Aboriginal Community

Iron Range

Cape Direction

Iguana Mtn
244m +

Direction Hill +
146m

CORAL

GREAT

Pera Head

Lagoon

Creek

70

247

Jacks Knob
411m +

Mt Carter
+ 671m

Coconut Ck

Merkunga

GENKE

RANGE

Night Island

SEA

Ward

River

Watson

River

Aurukun
Aboriginal Community

MUNGKAN

KANDJU

Piccaninny

Archer

Creek

DIVIDING

DEVELOPMENTAL

Bald Hill
441m +

Genke

Creek

Table Mtn
458m +

Cape Sidmouth

BARRIER

NATIONAL

PARK

Coen

Archer River
Roadhouse

MUNGKAN KANDJU

NATIONAL

112

Whale Hill
306m +

Round Mtn
321m +

MCILWRAITH

RANGE

Birthday Mtn
438m +

Double Hill
411m +

Claremont Isles

Archer

River

Meripah

CAPE

ABORIGINAL

PARK

+ Mt Croll 488m

Coen
Mt White
449m +

Silver Plains

Port Stewart

FLINDERS
GROUP
NP

Flinders
Island

Pipon Island
Cape Melville

+ St Pauls Hill
418m

REEF

Kendall

LAND

River

53

Kintore
+ 405m

CAPE
MELVILLE
NP

Ballurst Bay

Bay Hill
432m

Barrow Point

YORK

45

Yarraden

Normanby

Princess Charlotte

Bay

Wakooka

CAPE
MELVILLE
NP

ABORIGINAL

Mt Ryan +
518m

RANGE

62

Lily Vale

Marina Plains

Flat Top Hill
+ 107m

Howick
Island

Christmas

Ck

Strathburn

PENINSULA

Holroyd

River

New Strathgordon

227

Strathmay

Coleman

River

Strathaven

River

Musgrave
Station

RD

87

North

LAKEFIELD

NATIONAL

PARK

Kennedy

Hann
Crossing

Saddle Hill
508m

Pormpuraaw
Aboriginal Community

Edward

River

307

River

Mt Stuckey (Numbargulme)
479m +

STARCKE NP

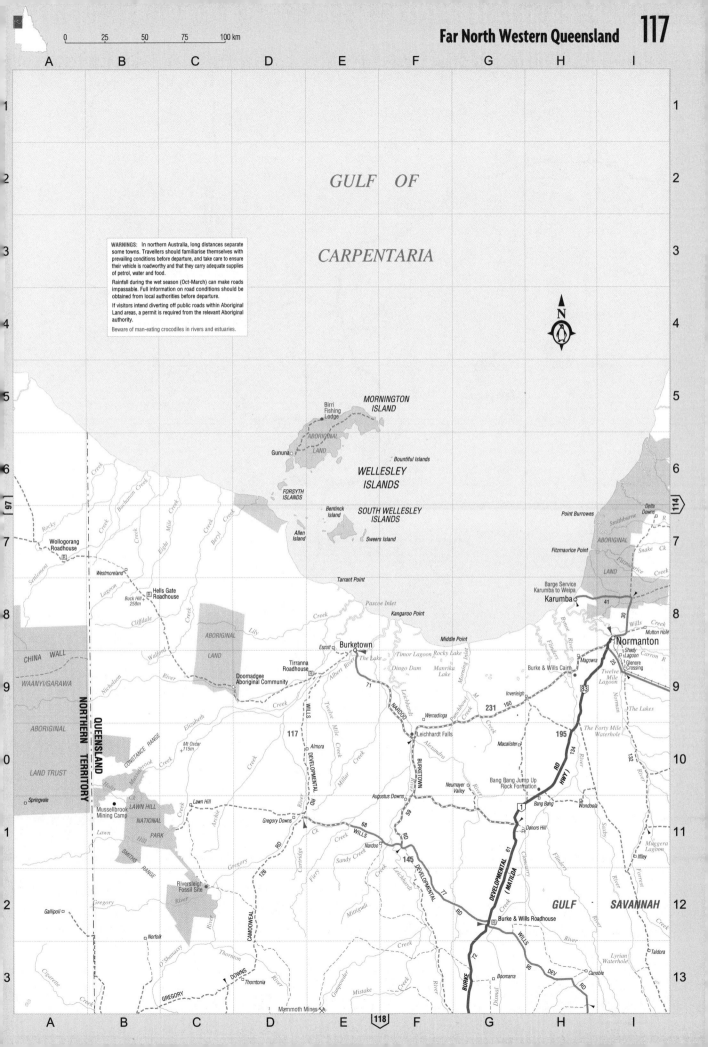

WARNINGS: In northern Australia, long distances separate some towns. Travellers should familiarise themselves with prevailing conditions before departure, and take care to ensure their vehicle is roadworthy and that they carry adequate supplies of petrol, water and food.

Rainfall during the wet season (Oct-March) can make roads impassable. Full information on road conditions should be obtained from local authorities before departure.

If visitors intend diverting off public roads within Aboriginal Land areas, a permit is required from the relevant Aboriginal authority.

Beware of man-eating crocodiles in rivers and estuaries.

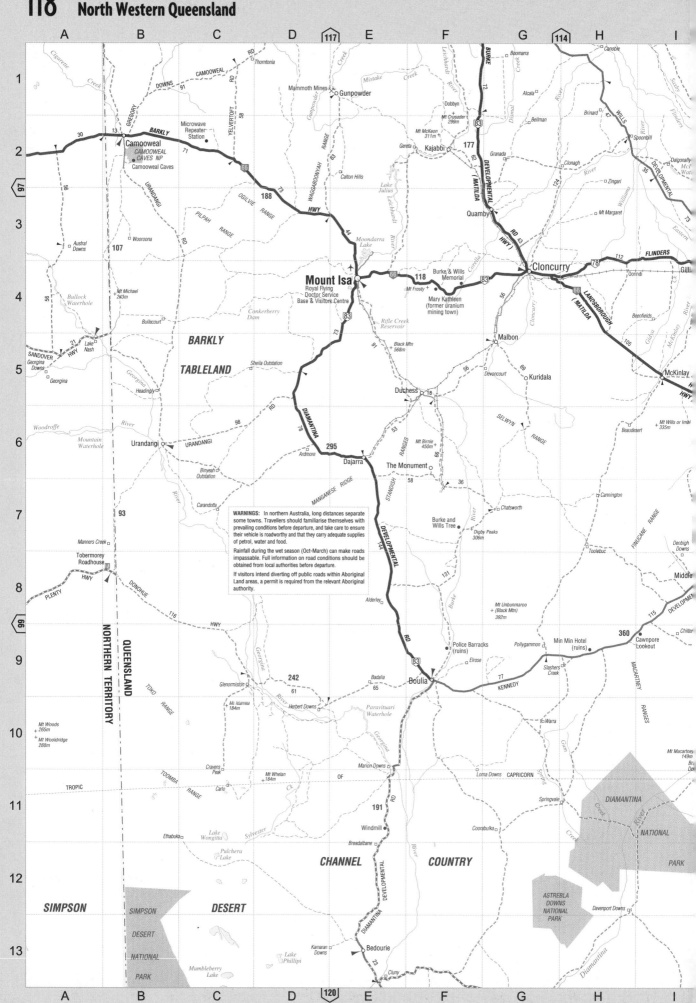

WARNINGS: In northern Australia, long distances separate some towns. Travellers should familiarise themselves with prevailing conditions before departure, and take care to ensure their vehicle is roadworthy and that they carry adequate supplies of petrol, water and food.

Rainfall during the wet season (Oct-March) can make roads impassable. Full information on road conditions should be obtained from local authorities before departure.

If visitors intend diverting off public roads within Aboriginal Land areas, a permit is required from the relevant Aboriginal authority.

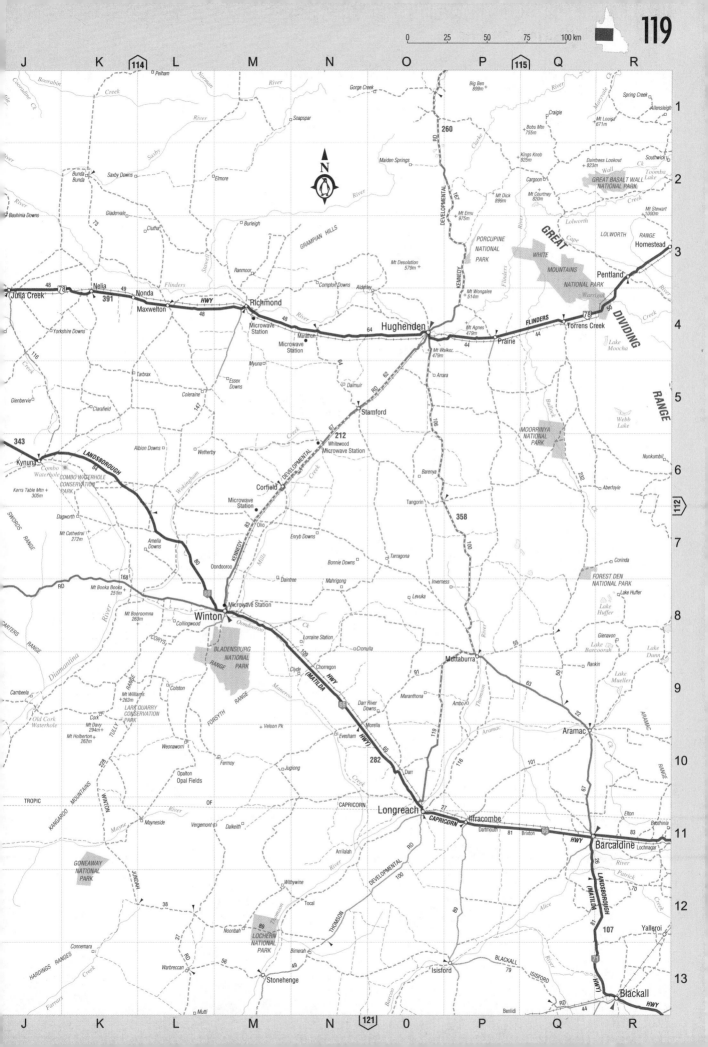

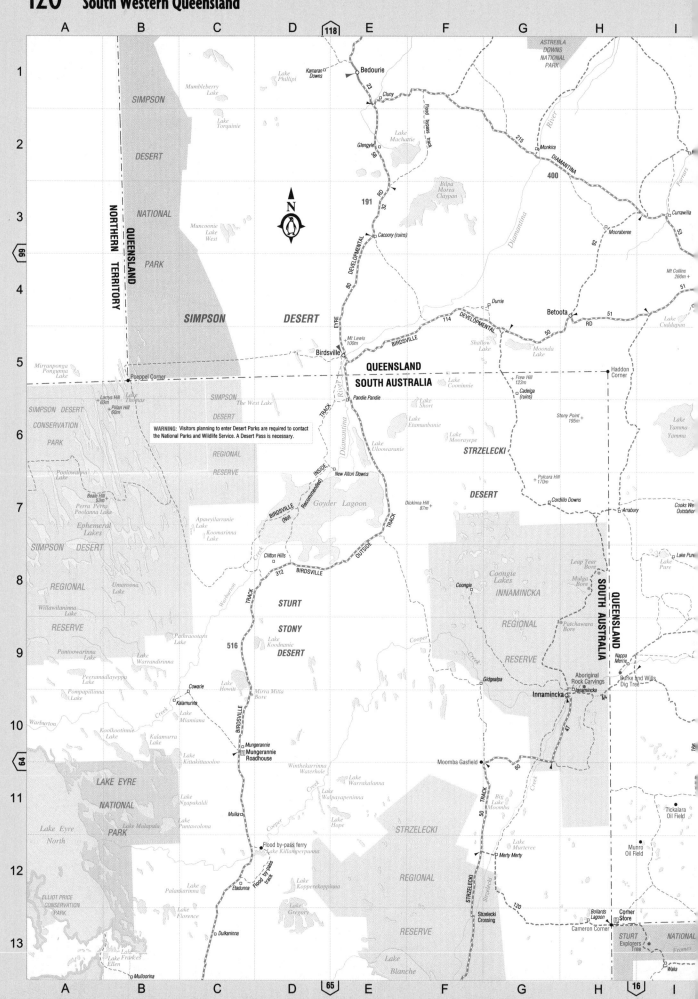

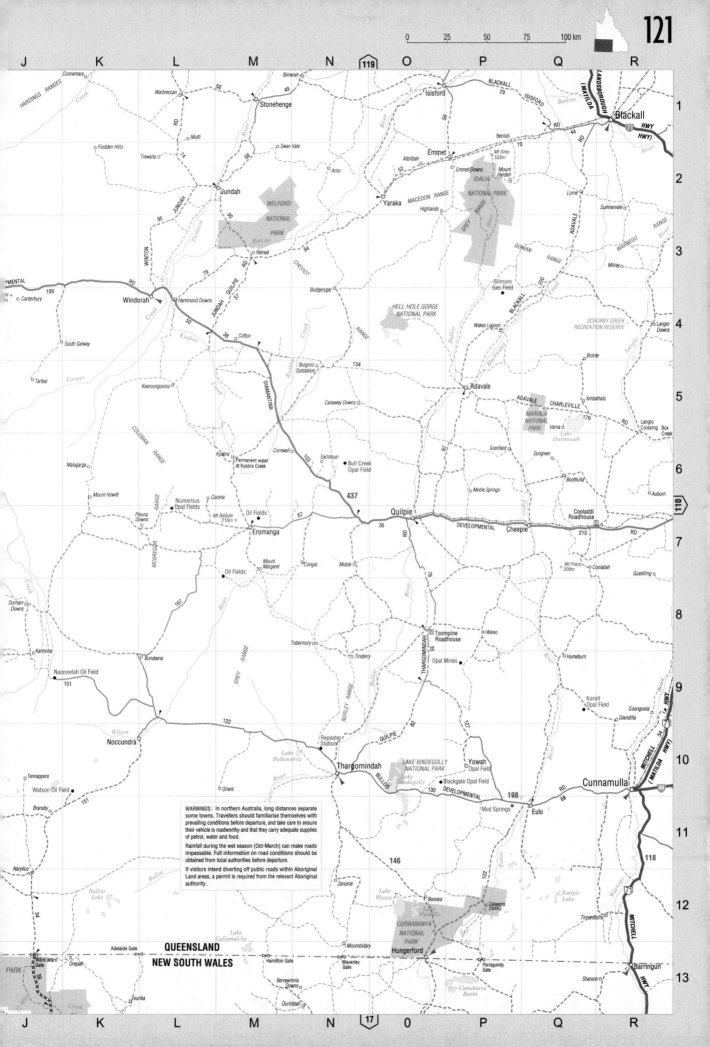

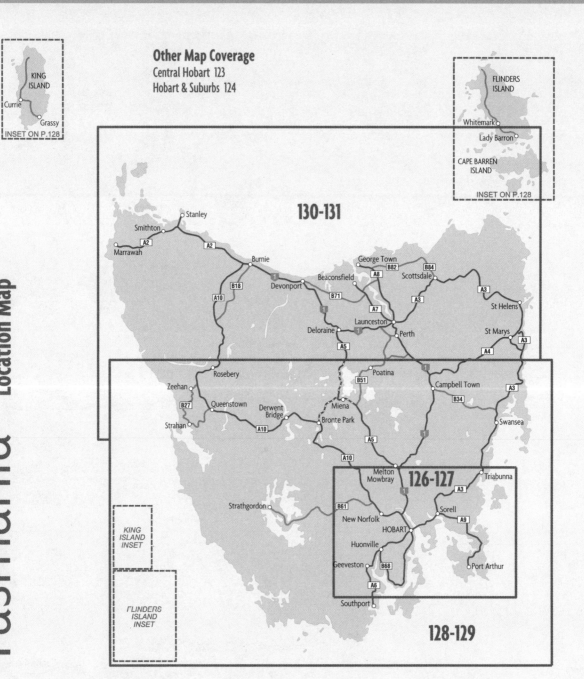

Tasmania

Location Map

Other Map Coverage
Central Hobart 123
Hobart & Suburbs 124

KING ISLAND
Currie
Grassy
INSET ON P.128

FLINDERS ISLAND
Whitemark
Lady Barron
CAPE BARREN ISLAND
INSET ON P.128

130-131

Stanley
Smithton
A2
Marrawah
A2
Burnie
George Town
B82
Scottsdale
B84
A8
Beaconsfield
A3
St Helens
B18
Devonport
B71
A3
A10
A7
Launceston
Deloraine
Perth
St Marys
A5
A4
A3

Rosebery
Poatina
Zeehan
B51
Campbell Town
A3
B27
Queenstown
Derwent Bridge
Miena
B34
Strahan
A10
Bronte Park
Swansea
A5

Strathgordon
A10
Melton Mowbray
126-127
Triabunna
B61
A3
New Norfolk
Sorell
A9
HOBART
Huonville
Geeveston
B68
Port Arthur
A6
Southport

128-129

KING ISLAND INSET

FLINDERS ISLAND INSET

0   0.25   0.5   0.75   1 km

Glebe

124

Queens
Domain

TO TASMAN BRIDGE
TO HOBART AIRPORT

A3

27

Tattersalls Hobart
Aquatic Centre

Cenotaph
AV

26 Penitentiary Chapel
& Courts
(National Trust HQ)

TAFE
Technical
College

Ambulance
HQ

Rose
Garden

A3

18 Cenotaph

Fire Brigade

Railway
Roundabout
Fountain

ABC Radio, Television
& Administration

BROOKER AV

A6

TAFE
Technical
College

15 Tigerline
Terminal

Magistrates
Court

Police
Headquarters

13

Wapping
Residential
Neighbourhood

A6

21
Gasworks
Shopping
Village

Railway
Goods
Yard

Theatre
32 Royal

Royal Hobart Hospital

Car Park

Railway
Freight
Terminal

Queen Alexandra
Maternity
Hospital

City Hall

5 Hotel
Grand
Chancellor

Multi Storey
Car Park

Multi Storey
Car Park

Bathurst Street
Post Office

Car Park

Centre for
the Arts

A6

8 Ansett
Australia

14

HOBART

30 State Library
& Museum of
Fine Arts

31 Tasmanian
Museum
& Art Gallery

Victoria
Dock

Swing Bridge

Fishermans
Market

Macquarie

12
Metro City Bus
Terminus

GPO
10

33 Town Hall

19
Constitution
Dock

Wharf

SULLIVANS

Multi Storey
Car Park

17

Cat and
Fiddle Arcade

St Davids
Cathedral

Franklin
20 Square

16 Tourist
Information

Lift
Bridge

COVE

Country
Comfort 3
Hadleys
Hotel

A6

Hobart
City Council
Customer Service
Centre

Elizabeth Street Pier

Government
Offices

Franklin Wharf
Cruise Centre

Ferry

Commonwealth
Law Courts

Brooke Street
Pier 9

Cadbury Cruise & Derwent River
ferry departure point

Passenger
Bellerive

Hobart 4
Macquarie

Parliament
House
25

Parliament
Square

Watermans Dock

Murray Street Pier

Commonwealth
Government
Centre

28

Princes   Wharf

CASTRAY

ESPLANADE

CSIRO

St Davids
Park

Supreme
Court

National Trust 24
Shop

29

SALAMANCA

Salamanca
Market

Salamanca
Arts Centre

22

Kellys Steps

Lenna
6 of Hobart

Princes
Park

St Helens
Hospital

A6

7
Salamanca
Inn

Tourist
Information
Signboard

Battery Point

B68

34

Barton 1
Cottage

Maritime
Museum

Colville
Cottage

23

TO WREST POINT HOTEL-CASINO

Streets: CAMPBELL ST, SHORT ST, GLEBE ST, ABERDEEN ST, DAVIES AV, BROOKER AV, EDWARD ST, PATRICK ST, ARGYLE ST, LIVERPOOL ST, TASMAN HWY, CENOTAPH AV, BRISBANE ST, BRISBANE LA, Steps, MELVILLE ST, ELIZABETH ST, MISTRAL, CAMPBELL ST, SUN ST, SACKVILLE ST, EVANS ST, BATHURST ST, CRITERION, WELLINGTON CT, Bank Arcade, Kemp ST, ARGYLE ST, MARKET PL, HUNTER ST, MURRAY ST, MATHERS LA, Arcade, ELIZABETH Mall, LORGS PL, MACQUARIE ST, WATCHORN ST, Cat & Fiddle, HARRINGTON LA, Murray PL, COLLINS ST, COLLINS CT, TRAFALGAR PL, DESPARD ST, MORRISON ST, BROOKE ST, Franklin, LIVERPOOL ST, VICTORIA ST, Centrepoint Arcade, SALAMANCA PL, CASTRAY ESPLANADE, COLLINS ST, BARRACK ST, MACQUARIE ST, DAVEY ST, SANDY ST, HEATHFIELD AV, WILMOT ST, RETREAT, McGREGOR ST, RUNNYMEDE ST, BATTERY SQ, GLADSTONE ST, KIRKSWAY PL, BAY ST, MONTPELIER ST, KNOPWOOD ST, HAMPDEN RD, ELLERSLIE RD, JAMES ST, STOWELL AV, KELLY ST, ARTHURS CIRCUS, SOUTH ST, FRANCIS ST, CASTRAY ESPLANADE, SECHERON RD, FINLAY ST, CLARKE AV, NEWCASTLE ST, LOGAN ST, DE WITT ST, WATERLOO CR, COLVILLE ST, MONA ST, ARTHUR ST

N

Accommodation ■
Barton Cottage 1 F13
Colville Cottage 2 H13
Country Comfort Hadleys Hotel 3 C7
Hobart Macquarie 4 B9
Hotel Grand Chancellor 5 F5
Lenna of Hobart 6 H11
Salamanca Inn 7 E10

General Information ■
Ansett Australia 8 C6
Derwent River Cruises 9 F8
General Post Office 10 E6
Hobart Transit Centre 11 A10
Metro City Bus Terminus 12 D6
Police Headquarters 13 D4
Qantas Travel Centre 14 C6
Tigerline Terminal 15 E3
Tourist Information 16 E7

Accommodation Only a sample
range is listed; inclusion is not
necessarily a recommendation.

Places of Interest ■
Cat and Fiddle Arcade 17 C6/7
Cenotaph 18 H3
Constitution Dock 19 F6
Franklin Square 20 E7
Gasworks Shopping Village 21 G4
Kellys Steps 22 G10
Maritime Museum 23 I13
National Trust Shop 24 E10
Parliament House 25 E9
Penitentiary Chapel & Courts
   (National Trust HQ) 26 C2
Queens Domain 27 E1
St Davids Park 28 D9
Salamanca Place 29 F10
State Library/Allport Library
   and Museum of Fine Arts 30 A6
Tasmanian Museum & Art Gallery 31 E6
Theatre Royal 32 E4
Town Hall 33 E6
Van Diemen's Land
   Folk Museum (Narryna) 34 E12

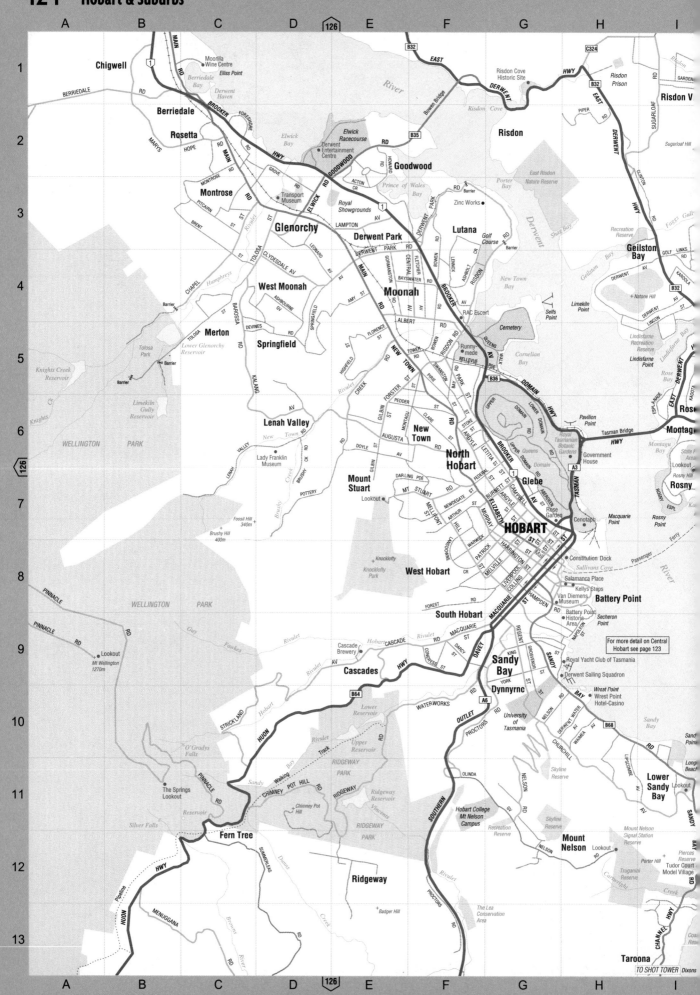

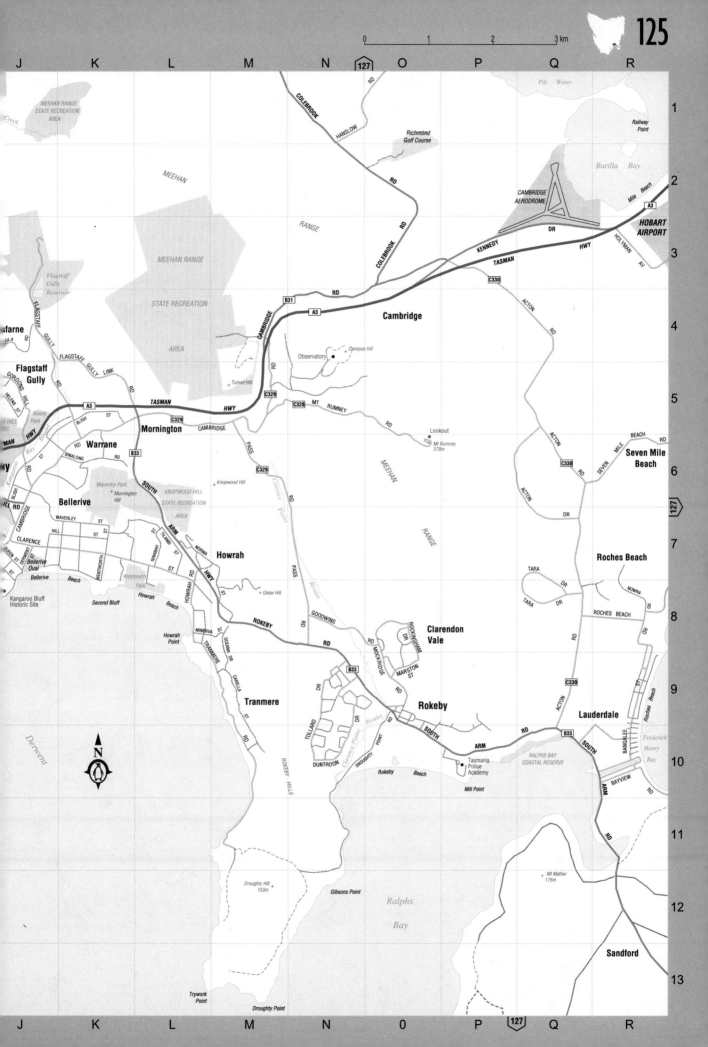

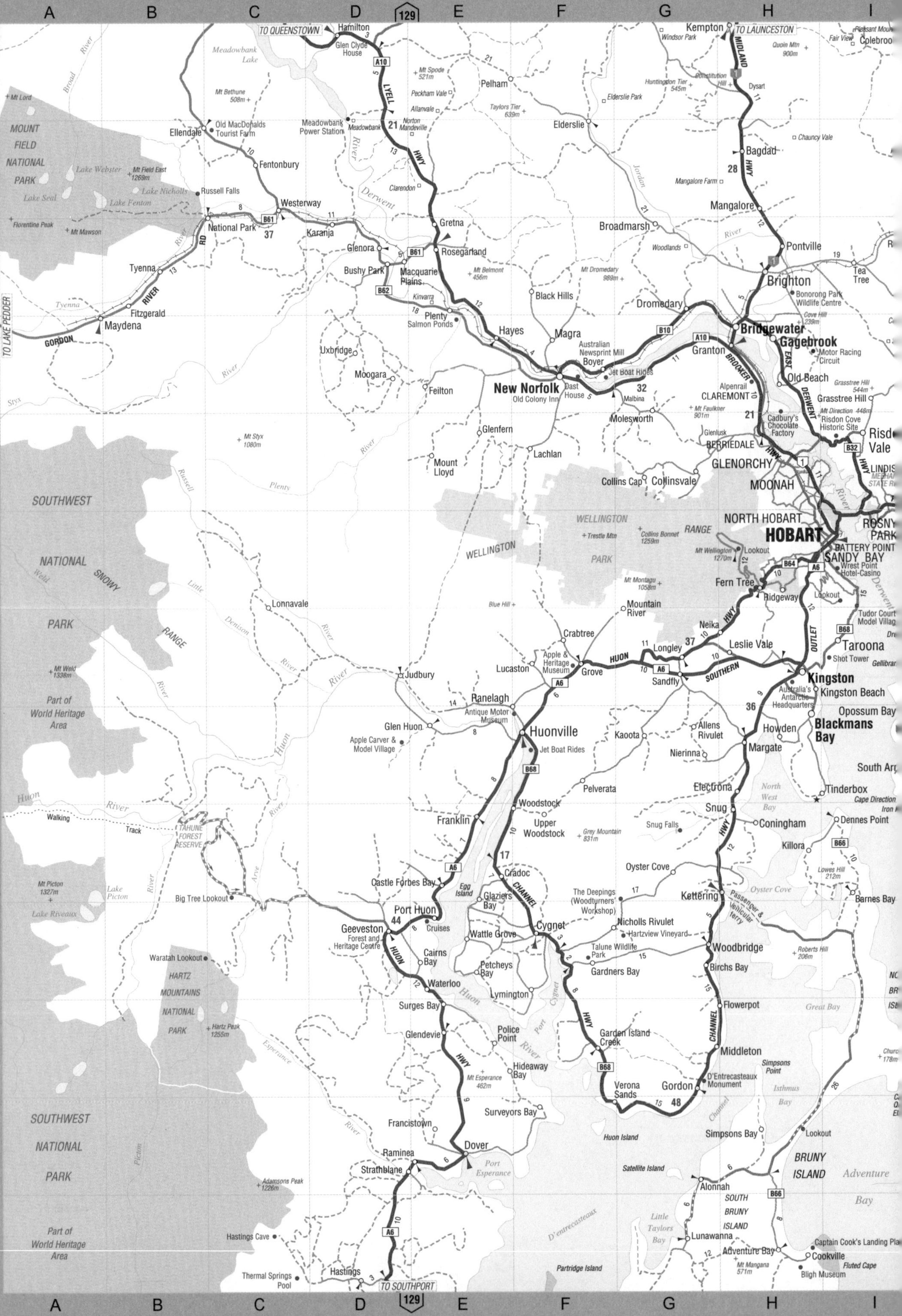

TO QUEENSTOWN

Grid columns: A B C D E F G H I
Grid rows: 1–13

Hamilton · Glen Clyde House · Mt Spode 521m · Pelham · Windsor Park · Kempton · **TO LAUNCESTON** · Fair View · Colebrook

Mt Bethune 508m · Old MacDonalds Tourist Farm · Peckham Vale · Allanvale · Norton Mandeville · Taylors Tier 639m · Eldersife Park · Huntington Tier 545m · Constitution Hill · Quoin Mtn 900m · Dysart · Pleasant Mount · Colebroo

Ellendale · Meadowbank Power Station · Meadowbank · Elderslie · Chauncy Vale · Bagdad

MOUNT FIELD NATIONAL PARK · Lake Webster · Mt Field East 1269m · Fentonbury · Clarendon · Jordan · Mangalore Farm · 28

Lake Nicholls · Russell Falls · Westerway · Karanja · Gretna · Broadmarsh · Mangalore · Pontville · Tea Tree

Lake Seal · Florentine Peak · Mt Mawson · National Park · B61 · 37 · Glenora · Rosegarland · Woodlands · Brighton · Bonorong Park Wildlife Centre

Tyenna · Bushy Park · Macquarie Plains · Mt Belmont 456m · Black Hills · Mt Dromedary 989m · Dromedary · Bridgewater · Gagebrook · Cove Hill 239m · Motor Racing Circuit · Risd

TO LAKE PEDDER · Fitzgerald · Maydena · GORDON · Kinvarra · Plenty Salmon Ponds · Hayes · Magra · Australian Newsprint Mill · Boyer · Granton · Alpenrail · CLAREMONT · Mt Faulkner 901m · Cadbury's Chocolate Factory · Old Beach · Grasstree Hill 544m · Grasstree Hill · Mt Direction 448m · Risdon Cove Historic Site

New Norfolk · Old Colony Inn · Oast House · Jet Boat Rides · 32 · Malbina · Molesworth · BERRIEDALE · Glenlusk · 21 · Risdon · Vale · B32

Mt Styx 1080m · Uxbridge · Moogara · Feilton · Glenfern · Lachlan · Mount Lloyd · Collins Cap · Collinsvale · GLENORCHY · MOONAH · ROSNY PARK · LINDIS

SOUTHWEST NATIONAL PARK · SNOWY RANGE · WELLINGTON PARK · WELLINGTON RANGE · Collins Bonnet 1259m · Trestle Mtn · NORTH HOBART · HOBART · BATTERY POINT · SANDY BAY

Mt Weld 1398m · Lonnavale · Denison · Blue Hill · Mountain River · Mt Wellington 1270m · Lookout · Wrest Point Hotel-Casino

Part of World Heritage Area · Judbury · Crabtree · Lucaston · Apple & Heritage Museum · Grove · Longley · Neika · Leslie Vale · Fern Tree · Ridgeway · Lookout · Tudor Court Model Village · Taroona · Shot Tower · Gellibrar

Ranelagh · Antique Motor Museum · Sandfly · Kingston · Kingston Beach · Opossum Bay

Glen Huon · Apple Carver & Model Village · Huonville · Jet Boat Rides · Kaoota · Allens Rivulet · Australia's Antarctic Headquarters · Howden · Margate · BLACKMANS BAY · South Ar

Walking Track · TAHUNE FOREST RESERVE · Franklin · Woodstock · Pelverata · Nierinna · Electrona · Snug · North West Bay · Tinderbox · Cape Direction · Iron

Mt Picton 1327m · Lake Picton · Big Tree Lookout · Upper Woodstock · Grey Mountain 831m · Snug Falls · Coningham · Killora · Dennes Point · Barnes Bay

Lake Riveaux · Arve · Castle Forbes Bay · Cradoc · Glaziers Bay · Egg Island · The Deepings (Woodturners' Workshop) · Oyster Cove · Kettering · Passenger & Vehicular Ferry · Lowes Hill 212m

Waratah Lookout · Geeveston Forest and Heritage Centre · Port Huon · Cruises · Cairns Bay · Wattle Grove · Cygnet · Nicholls Rivulet · Hartzview Vineyard · Woodbridge · Birchs Bay · Roberts Hill 206m · B66

HARTZ MOUNTAINS NATIONAL PARK · Hartz Peak 1255m · Waterloo · Petcheys Bay · Lymington · Talune Wildlife Park · Gardners Bay · Flowerpot · Great Bay

Surges Bay · Glendevie · Police Point · Garden Island Creek · Middleton · Simpsons Point · Chur 178m

Esperance · Mt Esperance 462m · Hideaway Bay · Verona Sands · Gordon · 48 · D'Entrecasteaux Monument · Isthmus Bay

SOUTHWEST NATIONAL PARK · Adamsons Peak 1226m · Francistown · Surveyors Bay · Huon Island · Simpsons Bay · BRUNY ISLAND · Adventure Bay

Raminea · Dover · Port Esperance · Satellite Island · Alonnah · SOUTH BRUNY ISLAND · Lookout

Part of World Heritage Area · Strathblane · Hastings Cave · Little Taylors Bay · Lunawanna · Adventure Bay · Mt Mangana 571m · Captain Cook's Landing Pla · Fluted Cape · Cookville · Bligh Museum

Thermal Springs Pool · Hastings · **TO SOUTHPORT** · Partridge Island · D'entrecasteaux

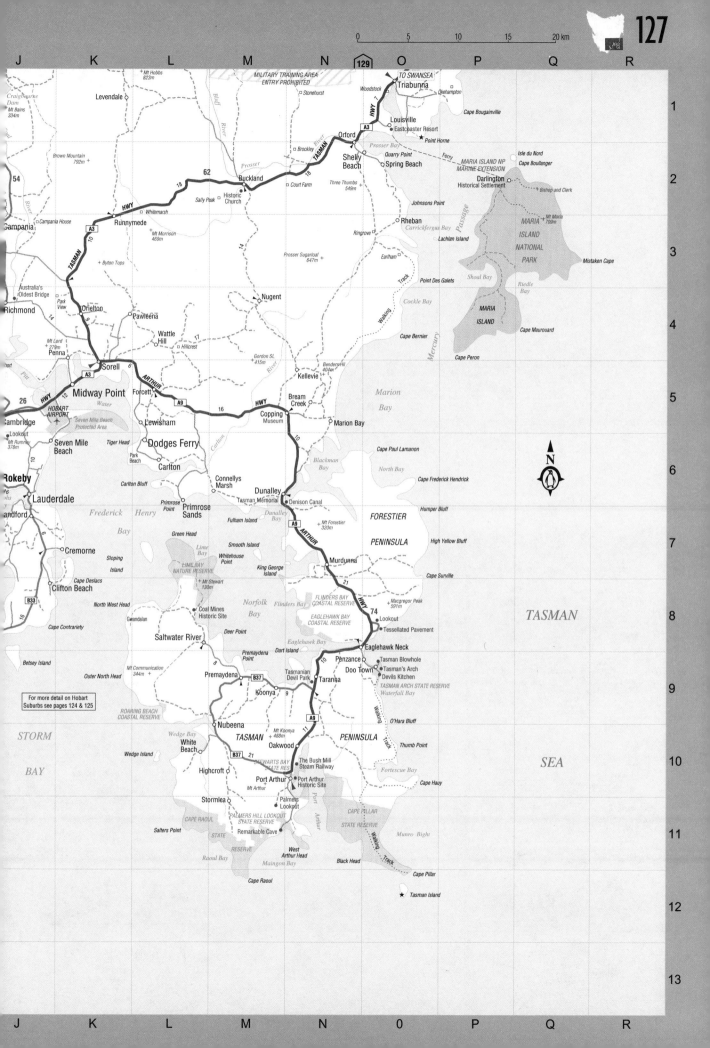

Craigbourne
Dam
Mt Bains
334m +

Levendale

Mt Hobbs
823m +

MILITARY TRAINING AREA
ENTRY PROHIBITED

129

TO SWANSEA
Triabunna

Woodstock

Stonehurst

Okehampton

Cape Bougainville

Brown Mountain
792m +

HWY
7

Louisville
Eastcoaster Resort

Point Horne

Cape Boullanger
Isle du Nord

1

54

Campania House

62

Buckland

Brockley

A3

Orford

Prosser Bay

Quarry Point
Spring Beach

MARIA ISLAND NP
MARINE EXTENSION

Darlington
Historical Settlement

Bishop and Clerk

2

Runnymede

HWY

Whitemarsh

Sally Peak

Historic
Church

Court Farm

Shelly
Beach

Three Thumbs
549m

Johnsons Point

Mt Maria
709m +

MARIA
ISLAND
NATIONAL
PARK

A3

10

Mt Morrison
469m +

14

Prosser Sugarloaf
647m

Rheban

Carrickfergus Bay

Ringrove

Lachlan Island

Mistaken Cape

3

Australia's
Oldest Bridge

Park
View

Byton Tops +

Nugent

Earlham

Point Des Galets

Shoal Bay

Riedle
Bay

Richmond

Orielton

Pawleena

Walking

MARIA
ISLAND

Cape Maurouard

4

Mt Lord
279m +
Penna

Wattle
Hill

Hillcrest

17

Gordon SL
415m

Kellevie

Benders Hill
404m

Cape Bernier

Cape Peron

Campania

A3

Sorell

6

ARTHUR

Forcett

A9

16

HWY

Copping
Museum

Bream
Creek

Marion Bay

Marion
Bay

Passage

Mercury

5

26

HWY

Midway Point

Lewisham

Marion Bay

10

Blackman
Bay

Cape Paul Lamanon

North Bay

Cape Frederick Hendrick

6

HOBART
AIRPORT

Seven Mile Beach
Protected Area

Dodges Ferry

Tiger Head

Carlton

Rokeby

Lauderdale

Cremorne

Clifton Beach

B33

Park
Beach

Carlton Bluff

Connellys
Marsh

Dunalley

Tasman Memorial

Denison Canal

Humper Bluff

FORESTIER
PENINSULA

High Yellow Bluff

7

Frederick

Henry

Bay

Primrose
Point

Primrose
Sands

Green Head

Fulham Island

Dunalley
Bay

A9

ARTHUR

Mt Forestier
320m

Seven Mile
Beach

Lime
Bay

LIME BAY
NATURE RESERVE

Smooth Island

Whitehouse
Point

King George
Island

Murdunna

Cape Surville

TASMAN

8

Betsey Island

Sloping
Island

North West Head

Mt Stewart
130m +

Norfolk
Bay

Flinders Bay

FLINDERS BAY
COASTAL RESERVE

EAGLEHAWK BAY
COASTAL RESERVE

21

HWY
74

Lookout

Tessellated Pavement

Macgregor Peak
591m +

Cape Deslacs

Cape Contrariety

Gwandalan

Coal Mines
Historic Site

Deer Point

Eaglehawk Bay

Dart Island

Eaglehawk Neck

Penzance

Tasman Blowhole

9

Saltwater River

Premaydena
Point

Doo Town

Tasman's Arch
Devils Kitchen

TASMAN ARCH STATE RESERVE
Waterfall Bay

Premaydena

B37

Koonya

Tasmanian
Devil Park

Taranna

10

9

O'Hara Bluff

Outer North Head

Mt Communication
344m +

ROARING BEACH
COASTAL RESERVE

Nubeena

TASMAN

Oakwood

A9

11

PENINSULA

Thumb Point

STORM

Wedge Bay

White
Beach

Mt Koonya
488m +

The Bush Mill
Steam Railway

SEA

10

B37

21

Highcroft

STEWARTS BAY
STATE RES

Fortescue Bay

Cape Hauy

Wedge Island

Port Arthur

Port Arthur
Historic Site

Mt Arthur

Port

Stormlea

Palmers
Lookout

PALMERS HILL LOOKOUT
STATE RESERVE

CAPE PILLAR
STATE RESERVE

Munro Bight

11

BAY

Salters Point

CAPE RAOUL

STATE

Remarkable Cave

Arthur

Walking Track

West
Arthur Head

Black Head

Cape Pillar

12

RESERVE

Raoul Bay

Maingon Bay

Cape Raoul

Tasman Island

13

For more detail on Hobart
Suburbs see pages 124 & 125

N

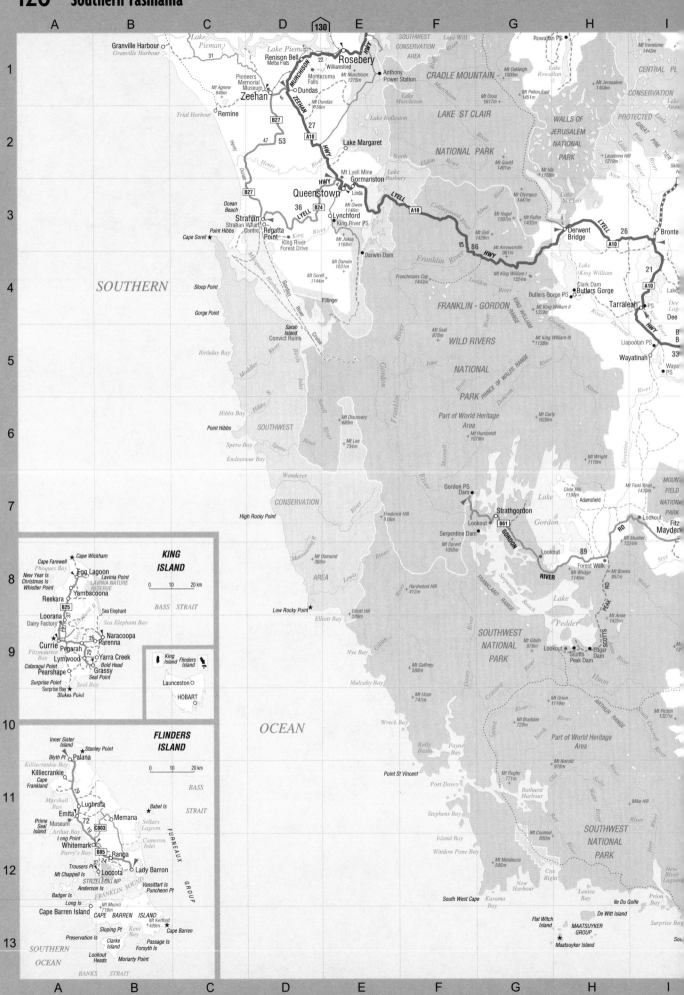

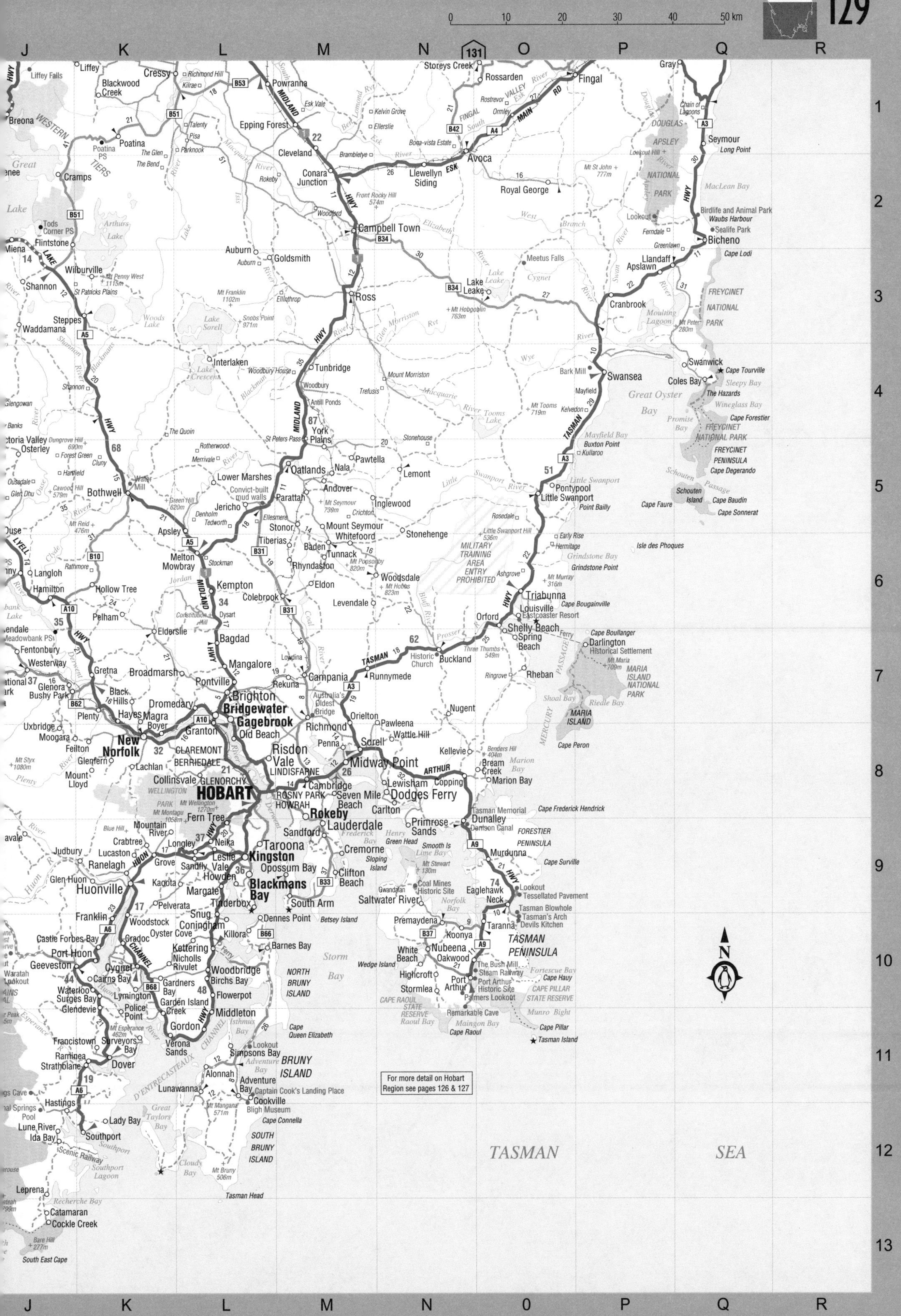

0 10 20 30 40 50 km
J K L M N O P Q R
1 2 3 4 5 6 7 8 9 10 11 12 13
131
Liffey
Liffey Falls
Blackwood Creek
Cressy
Richmond Hill
Kilrae
B53
Powranna
Breona
WESTERN
TIERS
Poatina
Poatina PS
The Glen
The Bend
Talenty
Pisa
Parknook
Epping Forest
Esk Vale
Kelvin Grove
Ellerslie
Cleveland
Conara Junction
Brambletye
Storeys Creek
Rossarden
Fingal
Rostrevor
Ormley
VALLEY
FINGAL
MAIN RD
Bona-vista Estate
Avoca
Llewellyn Siding
ESK
Royal George
Gray
Chain of Lagoons
DOUGLAS-APSLEY NATIONAL PARK
Lookout Hill
Mt St John 777m
Seymour
Long Point
MacLean Bay
Birdlife and Animal Park
Waubs Harbour
Sealife Park
Bicheno
Cape Lodi
Lookout
Ferndale
Greenlawn
Great Lake
Cramps
Tods Corner PS
Arthurs Lake
Flintstone
Miena
Wilburville
Mt Penny West 1115m
Shannon
St Patricks Plains
Front Rocky Hill 574m
Woodford
Campbell Town
Elizabeth
B34
Auburn
Goldsmith
Mt Franklin 1102m
Ellinthorp
Ross
Lake Leake
Meetus Falls
Cygnet
Llandaff
Apslaw
Cranbrook
FREYCINET NATIONAL PARK
Moulting Lagoon
Mt Peter 280m
Steppes
Waddamana
Woods Lake
Lake Sorell
Snobs Point 971m
Mt Hobgoblin 763m
Glen Morriston
Interlaken
Lake Crescent
Woodbury House
Tunbridge
Mount Morriston
Woodbury
Antill Ponds
Trefusis
Macquarie
Tooms Lake
Mt Tooms 719m
Bark Mill
Swansea
Mayfield
Kelvedon
Swanwick
Cape Tourville
Coles Bay
Sleepy Bay
The Hazards
Great Oyster Bay
Wineglass Bay
Cape Forestier
Promise Bay
FREYCINET NATIONAL PARK
FREYCINET PENINSULA
Cape Degerando
Shannon
Glengowan
The Quoin
Dungrove Hill 690m
Victoria Valley
Osterley
Forest Green
Cluny
Hartfield
Rotherwood
Merrivale
St Peters Pass
York Plains
Stonehouse
Pawtella
Oatlands
Nala
Lemont
Lower Marshes
Convict-built mud walls
Parattah
Andover
Mayfield Bay
Buxton Point
Kullaroo
Little Swanport
Pontypool
Little Swanport
Point Bailly
Schouten Passage
Schouten Island
Cape Baudin
Cape Sonnerat
Cape Faure
Ousedale
Glen Dhu
Cawood Hill 579m
Bothwell
Water Mill
Green Hill 620m
Jericho
Denholm
Tedworth
Ellesmere
Mt Seymour 739m
Crichton
Inglewood
Mount Seymour
Whitefoord
Stonehenge
Rosedale
Little Swanport Hill 536m
Early Rise
Hermitage
Grindstone Bay
Grindstone Point
Isle des Phoques
MILITARY TRAINING AREA ENTRY PROHIBITED
Mt Reid 476m
Ouse
LYELL
Apsley
Melton Mowbray
Stockman
Tiberias
Stonor
Baden
Tunnack
Mt Pooanby 820m
Rhyndaston
Woodsdale
Mt Hobbs 823m
Ashgrove
Mt Murray 316m
B10
Rathmore
Langloh
Hamilton
Hollow Tree
Jordan
Kempton
Colebrook
Eldon
Levendale
Triabunna
Cape Bougainville
Louisville
Eastcoaster Resort
Orford
Shelly Beach
Spring Beach
Pelham
Constitution Hill
Dysart
Eldershe
Bagdad
Prosser
Bluff River
Three Thumbs 549m
Cape Boullanger
Darlington
Historical Settlement
Mt Maria 709m
MARIA ISLAND NATIONAL PARK
Meadowbank Lake
Fentonbury
Westerway
Gretna
Broadmarsh
Mangalore
Lowdina
Campania
Historic Church
Buckland
TASMAN
Runnymede
Ringrove
Rheban
Shoal Bay
Riedle Bay
MARIA ISLAND
Glenora
Bushy Park
Black Hills
Dromedary
Pontville
Brighton
Bridgewater
Gagebrook
Rekuna
Australia's Oldest Bridge
Orielton
Pawleena
Wattle Hill
Nugent
MERCURY PASSAGE
Cape Peron
Uxbridge
Plenty
Hayes
Magra
Boyer
Granton
Old Beach
Richmond
Moogara
Feilton
New Norfolk
CLAREMONT
BERRIEDALE
Risdon Vale
LINDISFARNE
Penna
Sorell
Midway Point
Kellevie
Benders Hill 404m
Bream Creek
Marion Bay
Mt Styx 1080m
Glenfern
Lachlan
Mount Lloyd
Collinsvale
GLENORCHY
HOBART
WELLINGTON PARK
Mt Wellington 1270m
Mt Montagu 1058m
ROSNY PARK
HOWRAH
Cambridge
Seven Mile Beach
Lewisham
Dodges Ferry
Copping
ARTHUR
Carlton
Tasman Memorial
Cape Frederick Hendrick
Fern Tree
Blue Hill
Mountain River
Crabtree
Rokeby
Lauderdale
Sandford
Frederick Henry Bay
Primrose Sands
Dunalley
Denison Canal
FORESTIER PENINSULA
Judbury
Lucaston
Longley
Neika
Taroona
Kingston
Green Head
Smooth Is
Lime Bay
Cremorne
Sloping Island
Murdunna
Cape Surville
Ranelagh
HUON
Grove
Sandfly
Leslie Vale
Howden
Opossum Bay
Clifton Beach
Mt Stewart 130m
Glen Huon
Huonville
Kaoota
Margate
Blackmans Bay
B33
Gwandalan
Coal Mines Historic Site
Saltwater River
Norfolk Bay
Eaglehawk Neck
Lookout
Tessellated Pavement
Pelverata
Tinderbox
South Arm
Tasman Blowhole
Tasman's Arch
Devils Kitchen
Franklin
Woodstock
Snug
Coningham
Dennes Point
Betsey Island
Premaydena
Taranna
Castle Forbes Bay
Cradoc
Oyster Cove
Kilorra
B66
B37
Koonya
TASMAN PENINSULA
Port Huon
Kettering
Nicholls Rivulet
Barnes Bay
Storm Bay
White Beach
Nubeena
Oakwood
Geeveston
Cygnet
CHANNEL
Woodbridge
Birchs Bay
Wedge Island
The Bush Mill Steam Railway
Fortescue Bay
Cape Hauy
Waratah Lookout
Cairns Bay
Gardners Bay
NORTH BRUNY ISLAND
Highcroft
Port Arthur
Port Arthur Historic Site
Palmers Lookout
CAPE PILLAR STATE RESERVE
Waterloo
Surges Bay
Lymington
B68
Garden Island Creek
Flowerpot
Stormlea
CAPE RAOUL STATE RESERVE
Raoul Bay
Glendevie
Police Point
Middleton
Remarkable Cave
Maingon Bay
Cape Raoul
Munro Bight
Mt Esperance 462m
Esperance
Gordon
Verona Sands
Isthmus Bay
Cape Queen Elizabeth
Cape Pillar
Tasman Island
Francistown
Surveyors Bay
Lookout
Simpsons Bay
Adventure Bay
BRUNY ISLAND
Ramiea
Strathblane
Dover
D'ENTRECASTEAUX
For more detail on Hobart Region see pages 126 & 127
Alonnah
Adventure Bay
Hastings
Lunawanna
Captain Cook's Landing Place
Cookville
Bligh Museum
Mt Mangana 571m
Cape Connella
Hastings Cave
Thermal Springs Pool
Lady Bay
Great Taylors Bay
Lune River
Ida Bay
Southport
SOUTH BRUNY ISLAND
Scenic Railway
Southport Lagoon
Cloudy Bay
Mt Bruny 506m
TASMAN
SEA
Tasman Head
Leprena
Recherche Bay
Catamaran
Cockle Creek
Bare Hill 277m
South East Cape

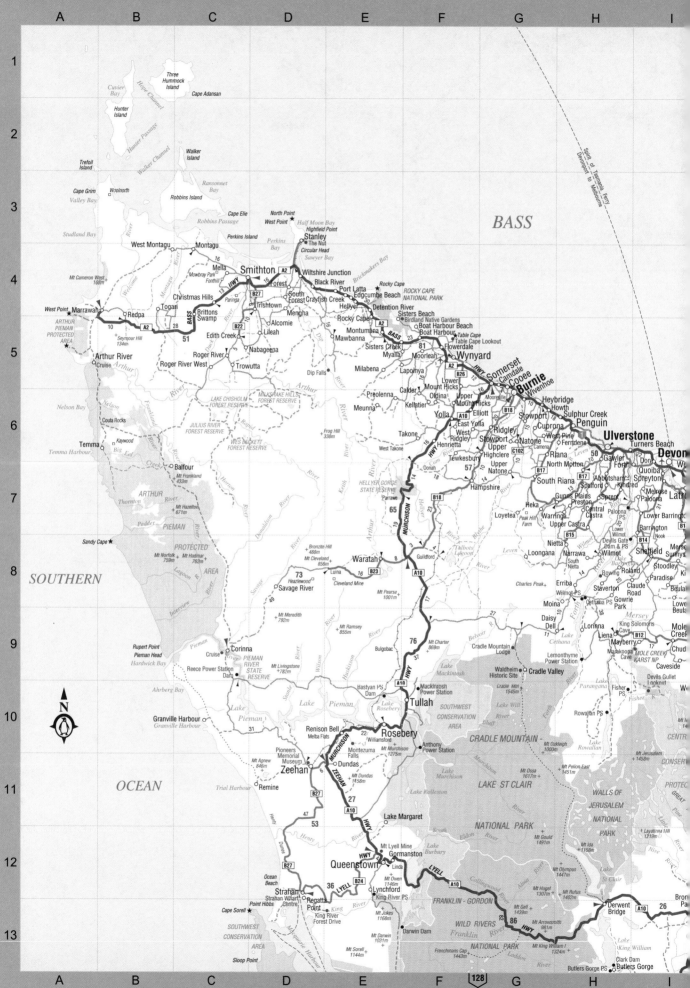

0 10 20 30 40 50 km

J K L M N O P Q R

STRAIT

FLINDERS ISLAND
Ranga Lady Barron
Loccota B85
Trousers Pt
Mt Chappell Is
STRZELECKI NATIONAL PARK
Adelaide Bay
Great Dog Is
Vansittart Is
Puncheon Pt
Badger Is Anderson Is FRANKLIN SOUND

Long Is
Cape Barren Island Mt Munro 716m
CAPE BARREN ISLAND
Kent Bay
Mt Kerford 499m

Preservation Is
Clarke Island Forsyth Is Passage Is
Sloping Pt

Lookout Heads Moriarty Point

BANKS STRAIT

Cape Portland Swan Island
Vinegar Hill 52m Little Mussleroe Bay
Waterhouse Island Mussleroe Bay
Waterhouse Point Cape Naturaliste
Croppies Point Cape Portland
Ninth Island Petal Point
WATERHOUSE PROTECTED AREA Waterhouse Great Musselroe Bay
West Sandy Cape East Sandy Cape Ringarooma Bay Icena
Tenth Island Anderson Bay Tomahawk Rushy Lagoon
Stony Head Boobyalla Mt William 216m
Five Mile Bluff Waterhouse MOUNT WILLIAM NATIONAL PARK
Lulworth Noland Bay Bridport Gladstone Eddystone Point
Low Head Weymouth Eddystone Point
West Head Low Head Beechford Bellingham South Mount Cameron
Greens Beach Back Creek B82 Ansons Bay
Badger Head Leura Pipers Wineries Forester Ansons Bay
Kelso Lefroy River Pipers Brook B84 Winnaleah Herrick The Gardens
George Town Mt Horror 686m Pioneer Moorina Bay of Fires
ASBESTOS RANGE NATIONAL PARK Lavender Farm North Scottsdale Telita Derby Branxholm
Port Sorell Clarence Point The Glen Glen Retreat Golconda Scottsdale Kamena Tulendeena Weldborough
Beauty Point Bell Bay A8 Tunnel Mt Stronach 497m Tonganah Lottah
Beaconsfield Rowella Kayena Lower Bangor Wyena Nabowla Lietinna Springfield Cuckoo Ledgerwood Goulds Country
Flowery Gully Sidmouth Hillwood Mount Direction North Lilydale Lisle West Scottsdale Cuckoo Hill 732m Ringarooma Goshen
Holwell Devot Robigana Turners Marsh Karoola Lilydale SOUTH SPRINGFIELD FOREST PARK Priory Binalong Bay
Sassafras East Winkleigh Exeter Turners Marsh Lalla Underwood South Springfield Talawa Pyengana St Helens Point
West Frankford Glengarry Gravelly Beach Lanena Myrtle Bank Mt Arthur 1187m Mt Maurice 1120m Alberton St Columba Falls St Helens Akaroa
Frankford Rosevears Dilston Patersonia Targa Diddleum Plains Trenah Mt Victoria 1208m Stieglitz
Notley Hills Legana Bridgenorth ROCHERLEA St Patricks River Tayene Mt Saddleback 1277m Parnella St Helens Island
Birralee Rosevale MOWBRAY Nunamara Mt Barrow 1413m Mt Young 903m Parkside Dianas Basin
Reedy Marsh Selbourne Glenburn Corra Linn Burns Creek Upper Esk Beaumaris
Weetah Glenvista LAUNCESTON Musselboro ROSES TIER Mt Nicholas 869m Scamander
Deloraine Hagley RIVERSIDE Rejbia White Hills Whistloca Roses Tier Mathinna Upper Scamander
Exton Westwood TREVALLYN Country Club Casino Carr Villa Tower Hill Cornwall Falmouth
Red Hills Westbury Hadspen Entally House Blessington Alpine Village Four Mile Creek
Osmaston Carrick Breadalbane English Town BEN LOMOND NATIONAL PARK St Marys
Quamby Brook Whitemore Glengre Pateena Hampden Legges Tor 1575m Mangana Gray
Golden Valley Cluan Bishopsbourne Perth Western Junction Deddington Storeys Creek B42 Fingal TASMAN
Bracknell Oaks Foiberry Evandale Nile Rossarden Fingal Cornwall
Jackeys Marsh Longford Symmons Plains Raceway Royal George Rostrevor Ormley
Liffey Richmond Hill Powranna Kelvin Grove Avoca Chain of Lagoons
Liffey Falls Kilraa Esk Vale Ellerslie DOUGLAS APSLEY NATIONAL PARK
Blackwood Creek Cressy Bona-vista Estate Seymour Long Point
Breona Epping Forest Brambletye Llewellyn Siding Lookout Hill
Poatina Cleveland Front Rocky Hill 574m Royal George Mt St John 777m Lookout
Poatina PS Conara Junction Woodford Birdlife and Animal Park
The Glen Parknook Ferndale Waubs Harbour
Cramps The Bend Greenlawn Sealife Park
Liawenee Campbell Town Meetus Falls Bicheno
Tods Corner PS Auburn Goldsmith Lake Leake Llandaff Cape Lodi
Flintstone Lake Leake Apslawn
Miena Shannon Mt Franklin 1102m Ellinthorp Mt Hobgoblin 763m Cranbrook FREYCINET NATIONAL PARK
Wilburville St Patricks Plains Snobs Point 971m Moulting Lagoon Mt Peter 280m
Waddamana Interlaken Woodbury House Mount Morriston Swansea Swanwick Cape Tourville
Steppes Woodbury Trefusis Bark Mill Coles Bay Sleepy Bay
Lake Echo PS Glengowan Antill Ponds Mayfield The Hazards Great Oyster Bay

SEA

TASMAN

129

Index of Place Names

A1 Mine Settlement Vic. 37 R4, 39 J2, 47 M13
Abbeyard Vic. 47 O9, 48 A7
Abbotsford NSW 4 I8
Abbotsford Vic. 33 L8
Abbotsham Tas. 130 H7
Abercorn Qld 111 M3
Aberdeen NSW 13 K2
Aberfeldy Vic. 39 J3
Abergowrie Qld 115 N10
Abermain NSW 13 M4
Abernethy NSW 13 M4
Acacia Ridge Qld 106 H7
Acheron Vic. 37 O2, 47 J11
Acland Qld 108 D5
Acton ACT 23 A3, 24 G9
Acton Park WA 79 E8
Adaminaby NSW 20 D8, 26 E9, 49 L1
Adamsfield Tas. 128 H7
Adavale Qld 121 P5
Addington Vic. 36 B2
Adelaide SA 52, 54 I6, 58 B10, 59 E1, 61 K9, 70 A1
Adelaide Hills SA 58 D10
Adelaide River NT 92 E8, 94 E7
Adelong NSW 12 D13, 20 B5
Adjungbilly NSW 12 E12, 20 C4
Advancetown Qld 109 N13
Adventure Bay Tas. 126 H13, 129 L11
Agery SA 60 I6
Agnes Vic. 39 J10
Agnes Banks NSW 11 K6
Agnes Water Qld 113 Q13
Agnew WA 82 H2
Aileron NT 98 I6
Ailsa Vic. 42 H7
Ainslie ACT 24 H8
Aireys Inlet Vic. 36 E12, 41 P10
Airlie Beach Qld 113 K3
Airly Vic. 39 N5
Airport West Vic. 32 H4
Akaroa Tas. 131 R8
Alawa NT 91 F4
Alawoona SA 61 Q8, 70 H1
Albacutya Vic. 42 F3
Albany WA 80 H13, 82 F12
Albany Creek Qld 104 C6
Albert NSW 12 B3, 17 R13, 19 R1
Albert Park SA 54 D2, 56 E13
Albert Park Vic. 33 K10
Alberton Qld 109 N10
Alberton SA 54 D1, 56 D12
Alberton Tas. 131 O8
Alberton Vic. 39 L9
Albion Qld 104 H10
Albury NSW 19 Q13, 47 P4, 48 C1
Alcomie Tas. 130 D5
Alderley Qld 104 F9
Aldersyde WA 80 G5
Aldgate SA 55 Q13
Aldinga SA 58 A13, 59 F4
Aldinga Beach SA 59 E4, 61 K10, 70 B3
Alectown NSW 12 D4
Alexander Heights WA 76 H4
Alexander Morrison National Park WA 82 B5
Alexandra Vic. 37 O1, 47 J11
Alexandra Headland Qld 109 N1
Alexandra Hills Qld 107 Q2
Alexandria NSW 5 M12, 9 O2
Alford SA 60 I5
Alfords Point NSW 8 F8
Alfred Cove WA 74 E9
Alfred National Park Vic. 20 F13, 49 O11
Alfred Town NSW 12 C12, 19 R10, 20 A5
Algester Qld 106 H8
Ali-Curung NT 97 K13, 99 K2
Alice NSW 15 O4, 111 P13
Alice Creek Qld 108 D1
Alice Springs NT 99 J8
Allambee Vic. 37 Q11, 38 I7
Allambee South Vic. 37 Q12, 38 I8
Allambie Heights NSW 5 O3, 7 N12
Allanby Vic. 42 F6
Allans Flat Vic. 47 P5, 48 B3
Allansford Vic. 40 I9
Allanson WA 80 D8
Allawah NSW 9 K7

Allawah NSW 19 M6
Alleena NSW 12 A9, 19 Q6
Allenby Gardens SA 54 F4
Allendale East SA 70 H12
Allendale North SA 58 E2, 61 L7
Allens Rivulet Tas. 126 G8
Allies Creek Qld 111 M5
Alligator Creek Qld 115 P13
Allora Qld 108 E12, 111 N10
Alma SA 58 B1, 61 L7
Alma Park NSW 19 P12, 47 O1
Almaden Qld 115 K7
Almonds Vic. 47 L5
Alonnah Tas. 126 G12, 129 L11
Aloomba Qld 115 N7
Alpara NT 66 G1, 98 E13
Alpha Qld 112 F11
Alphadale NSW 15 Q3
Alpine National Park Vic. 20 B11, 39 L1, 47 O12, 48 D6
Alstonville NSW 15 Q3, 111 Q12
Alton Qld 110 I10
Alton National Park Qld 110 I10
Altona Vic. 32 F10, 36 I7, 38 C4
Altona Meadows Vic. 32 E12
Alva Qld 112 H1, 115 Q13
Alvie Vic. 36 A10, 41 N8
Alyangula NT 95 O9
Amaroo ACT 24 G2
Amata SA 66 G1, 98 E13
Ambrose Qld 113 O12
Amby Qld 110 F6
Ambyne Vic. 20 D11, 49 K8
American River SA 60 I12
Amherst Vic. 36 B1, 41 N1, 43 N12
Amiens Qld 15 M2, 111 N12
Amity Point Qld 109 P7
Amoongunya NT 99 J8
Amosfield NSW 15 M2, 111 O12
Amphion WA 78 E11, 80 D6
Amphitheatre Vic. 41 M1, 43 M12
Anakie Qld 112 H11
Anakie Vic. 36 F7, 41 Q6
Anakie East Vic. 36 F7, 41 Q6
Anakie Junction Vic. 36 F7
Ancona Vic. 47 K10
Andamooka SA 62 G4
Anderson Vic. 37 M13, 38 F9
Ando NSW 20 E10, 49 N6
Andover Tas. 129 M5
Andrews SA 61 L4
Anduramba Qld 108 G4
Anembo NSW 20 F7, 26 I7, 28 I11
Angas Valley SA 58 I8
Angaston SA 58 G4, 61 M8
Angip Vic. 42 G5
Angle Park SA 56 G11
Anglers Reach NSW 20 D8, 26 D9, 49 K1
Anglers Rest Vic. 20 A11, 48 E8
Anglesea Vic. 36 E12, 41 Q9
Angourie NSW 15 Q5
Angus Place NSW 10 F3, 12 I6
Angustown Vic. 46 G8
Anna Bay NSW 13 N4
Annandale NSW 5 K10, 9 M1
Annangrove NSW 11 M6
Annerley Qld 106 H3
Annuello Vic. 45 J7
Ansons Bay Tas. 131 R6
Anstead Qld 106 A6
Antill Ponds Tas. 129 M4, 131 M13
Antwerp Vic. 42 F6
Anula NT 91 I7
Anzac Village NSW 8 B5
Apamurra SA 58 H9, 61 M9, 70 D1
Aparawatatja SA 66 B2, 85 R11, 98 B13
Apollo Bay Vic. 41 N12
Appila SA 61 K2, 63 J13
Appin NSW 11 L12, 13 K9
Appin Vic. 43 O4, 46 A3
Appin South Vic. 43 P4, 46 A3
Apple Tree Creek Qld 111 O3
Apple Tree Flat NSW 12 H4
Applecross WA 74 G8

Applethorpe Qld 15 M2, 111 N12
Apslawn Tas. 129 P3, 131 Q12
Apsley Tas. 129 L5
Apsley Vic. 42 B11, 70 I9
Araluen NSW 20 G6, 27 L6
Araluen North NSW 27 L6
Aramac Qld 112 C10, 119 Q10
Aramara Qld 111 O4
Arana Hills Qld 104 C9
Aranda ACT 24 E8
Arapiles Vic. 42 F9
Ararat Vic. 41 K2, 43 K13
Aratula Qld 108 I12, 111 O10
Arcadia NSW 6 D4
Arcadia Vic. 46 H7
Archdale Vic. 43 M10
Archer River Roadhouse Qld 116 D9
Archerfield Qld 106 G6
Archies Creek Vic. 37 N13, 38 G9
Ardath WA 80 I4
Ardeer Vic. 32 F7
Ardglen NSW 15 J13
Ardlethan NSW 12 A10, 19 Q7
Ardmona Vic. 46 H6
Ardmory Qld 109 J7
Ardno Vic. 40 A5, 70 I12
Ardross WA 74 G9
Ardrossan SA 61 J7
Areegra Vic. 42 I6
Areyonga NT 98 G9
Argalong NSW 26 B2
Argoon Qld 111 K1, 113 N13
Argyle Vic. 46 E9
Ariah Park NSW 12 B9, 19 Q7
Aringa Vic. 40 G9
Arkaroola SA 63 M3
Arkona Vic. 42 F7
Armadale Vic. 33 M10
Armadale WA 78 C6, 80 C4, 82 C8
Armatree NSW 14 D12
Armidale NSW 15 L9
Armstrong Vic. 41 K1, 43 K12
Armstrong Beach Qld 113 L6
Armytage Vic. 36 C10
Arncliffe NSW 9 L4
Arnhem Land NT 93 R3, 95 K6
Arno Bay SA 60 F5
Arnold Vic. 43 O9, 46 A8
Arnold West Vic. 43 O9, 46 A8
Arrawarra NSW 15 P7
Arrilalah Qld 119 N11
Arrino WA 82 C4
Artarmon NSW 5 L6
Arthur River Tas. 130 A5
Arthur River WA 80 F8
Arthurs Creek Vic. 37 L4
Arthurton SA 60 I7
Arthurville NSW 12 F3
Asbestos Range National Park Tas. 131 J6
Ascot Qld 104 H9
Ascot Vic. 36 C3
Ascot WA 75 K2, 77 K13
Ascot Park SA 54 G11
Ascot Vale Vic. 33 J7
Ashbourne SA 59 H5, 61 L10, 70 C3
Ashburton Vic. 33 N11
Ashbury NSW 4 I12, 9 K2
Ashcroft NSW 8 A3
Ashens Vic. 42 I9
Ashfield NSW 4 H11, 9 K1
Ashfield WA 77 M11
Ashford NSW 15 K4, 111 L13
Ashford SA 54 H8
Ashgrove Qld 104 F11
Ashley NSW 14 G4, 111 J13
Ashton SA 55 Q7, 58 C10, 59 H1
Ashville SA 61 M11, 70 D3
Ashwood Vic. 33 O11
Aspendale Vic. 35 D6
Aspley Qld 104 F6
Asquith NSW 6 F8
Astrebla Downs National Park Qld 118 G12, 120 G1
Athelstone SA 55 P1, 57 P13
Atherton Qld 115 M7

Athlone Vic. 37 O10, 38 H7
Athol Qld 108 D8
Athol Park SA 56 F11
Attadale WA 74 E9
Attunga NSW 15 J10
Attwood Vic. 32 I2
Aubigny Qld 108 C7
Aubrey Vic. 42 G6
Auburn NSW 4 D9
Auburn SA 61 L6
Auburn Tas. 129 L3, 131 M12
Auburn River National Park Qld 111 L4
Auchenflower Qld 104 E12, 106 E1
Auchmah Qld 108 B5
Audley NSW 11 N10
Augathella Qld 110 C5
Augusta WA 79 C13, 80 B11, 82 B11
Auldana SA 55 N5
Aurukun Aboriginal Community Qld 116 A9
Austinmer NSW 11 M13
Australia Plains SA 61 M6
Australind WA 79 G4, 80 C8, 82 C10
Avalon NSW 7 Q4, 11 P6, 21 H12
Avenel Vic. 46 H9
Avenue SA 70 G9
Avoca Tas. 129 N1, 131 O11
Avoca Vic. 43 M12
Avoca Beach NSW 11 Q4, 21 H6
Avoca Vale Qld 108 H1
Avon SA 61 K7
Avon Plains Vic. 43 K8
Avon Valley National Park WA 78 E1, 80 D2, 82 C7
Avondale NSW 13 M5
Avondale Qld 111 O2
Avondale Heights Vic. 32 H6
Avonmore Vic. 46 D7
Avonsleigh Vic. 37 M7, 38 F5, 50 C12
Awonga Vic. 42 C11
Axe Creek Vic. 43 R10, 46 D9
Axedale Vic. 46 D9
Ayers Rock *see* Uluru NT
Ayers Rock Resort *see* Yulara NT
Ayr Qld 112 H1, 115 Q13
Ayrford Vic. 41 J10
Ayton Qld 115 M4

Baan Baa NSW 14 H9
Baandee WA 80 H2
Baarmutha Vic. 47 O6, 48 A4
Babakin WA 80 I4
Babinda Qld 115 N7
Bacchus Marsh Vic. 36 G5, 38 A3, 41 R4
Back Creek Tas. 131 L6
Back Creek Vic. 47 P5, 48 B3
Back Plains Qld 108 D10
Back Valley SA 59 F8
Backwater NSW 15 M7
Baddaginnie Vic. 47 K7
Baden Tas. 129 M6
Badgerys Creek NSW 11 K9
Badgingarra WA 82 B6
Badgingarra National Park WA 82 B6
Badja Mill NSW 27 J9
Badjaling WA 80 G4
Bael Bael Vic. 43 O2, 45 O13
Baerami NSW 13 J3
Bagdad Tas. 126 H2, 129 L7
Bagnoo NSW 15 N12
Bagot Well SA 58 F2, 61 M7
Bagshot Vic. 43 R9, 46 D8
Bailieston Vic. 46 G8
Baird Bay SA 69 P13
Bairnsdale Vic. 39 P4, 48 F13
Bajool Qld 113 O11
Bakara SA 61 O8
Baker Vic. 42 D5
Bakers Creek Qld 113 L5
Bakers Hill WA 78 G3, 80 E3
Bakers Swamp NSW 12 F4
Baking Board Qld 111 K7
Balaklava SA 61 K6
Balcatta WA 76 E8
Bald Hills Qld 104 E4
Bald Knob NSW 15 M6
Bald Knob Qld 109 L2
Bald Rock Vic. 43 Q5, 46 B3
Bald Rock National Park NSW 15 M3, 111 N12
Baldry NSW 12 E4
Balfes Creek Qld 112 D2

Balfour Tas. 130 B7
Balga WA 76 G7
Balgal Beach Qld 115 O12
Balgo Community WA 87 P12
Balgowan SA 60 H7
Balgowlah NSW 5 P5
Balgowlah Heights NSW 5 P6, 11 O8
Balhannah SA 58 D10, 59 I1, 61 L9, 70 C2
Balingup WA 79 I8, 80 D9, 82 C11
Balintore Vic. 36 B11
Balkuling WA 80 F4
Ball Bay Qld 113 K4
Balladonia Roadhouse WA 83 L8
Balladoran NSW 12 E1, 14 D13
Ballajura WA 77 K6
Ballalaba NSW 12 H13, 20 F6, 27 K5
Ballan Vic. 36 F4, 41 Q4, 46 C13
Ballandean Qld 15 M3, 111 N12
Ballangeich Vic. 40 I8
Ballapur Vic. 43 J4
Ballarat Vic. 36 C4, 41 O3, 46 A13
Ballard Qld 108 F7
Ballark Vic. 36 D5
Ballaying WA 80 G8
Ballbank NSW 18 I11, 43 P1, 45 P11
Balldale NSW 19 P12, 47 N2
Ballendella Vic. 46 E5
Balliang Vic. 36 F6, 41 R5
Balliang East Vic. 36 G6, 38 A4, 41 R5
Ballidu WA 82 D6
Ballimore Vic. 12 F2
Ballina NSW 15 Q3, 111 R12
Balmain NSW 5 L9, 11 O8
Balmattum Vic. 47 J8
Balmoral NSW 5 O7, 11 J13
Balmoral Qld 104 I11
Balmoral Vic. 40 E2, 42 F13
Balnarring Vic. 37 K11, 38 D8
Balook Vic. 39 K8
Balranald NSW 18 H8, 45 N6
Balrootan North Vic. 42 E6
Balumbah SA 60 F3, 62 E13
Balup WA 78 E2, 80 D3
Balwyn Vic. 33 N8
Balwyn North Vic. 33 O7
Bamaga Qld 116 C3
Bamawm Vic. 46 E5
Bamawm Extension Vic. 46 E5
Bambaroo Qld 115 O11
Bambill Vic. 18 B8, 44 D4
Bambill South Vic. 44 D5
Bamboo Creek WA 84 E2
Bambra Vic. 36 D11, 41 P9
Bamganie Vic. 36 D7, 41 P6
Banana Qld 111 J1, 113 N13
Bancroft Qld 111 M2
Bandiana Vic. 19 Q13, 47 P4, 48 C2
Bandon Vic. 12 E6
Bandon Grove NSW 13 M2
Banealla SA 61 P13, 70 G5
Bangalow NSW 15 Q2, 111 Q12
Bangerang Vic. 42 I6
Bangham SA 42 A8, 70 I7
Bangholme Vic. 35 G7
Bangor NSW 8 F9
Bangor Tas. 131 L7
Banks ACT 25 D13
Banksia NSW 9 L5
Banksia Beach Qld 109 N4
Banksia Park SA 57 Q8
Banksmeadow NSW 9 P5
Bankstown NSW 4 D13, 8 F3, 11 M9
Bannaby NSW 12 I10, 20 G2
Bannerton Vic. 18 F9, 45 J6
Bannister NSW 12 H10, 20 F3
Bannister WA 78 G11, 80 E6
Bannockburn Vic. 36 E8, 41 Q7
Banora Point NSW 15 Q1, 111 Q11
Banyan Vic. 43 J2, 45 J13
Banyena Vic. 43 J8
Banyenong Vic. 43 L6
Banyo Qld 104 I6
Barabba SA 58 B2
Baradine NSW 14 E10
Barakula Qld 111 K6
Baralaba Qld 113 M13
Baranduda Vic. 47 P4, 48 C2
Barcaldine Qld 112 C11, 119 Q11
Bardon Qld 104 E12

Bardwell Park NSW 9 L4
Barellan NSW 19 P7
Barfold Vic. 41 R1, 43 R12, 46 D10
Bargara Qld 111 O2
Bargo NSW 11 J13, 13 J9, 20 I2
Barham NSW 18 I12, 43 Q2, 45 Q13, 46 B1
Baring Vic. 42 G1, 44 G11
Baringhup Vic. 43 P11, 46 B10
Barjarg Vic. 47 L10
Bark Hut Inn NT 92 I6
Barkers Creek Vic. 43 Q11, 46 C10
Barkly Vic. 43 L11
Barkly Homestead NT 97 N11
Barkstead Vic. 36 E3
Barmah Vic. 19 K13, 46 F3
Barmedman Vic. 12 B9, 19 R7
Barmera SA 61 P7
Barmundu Qld 113 P13
Barnadown Vic. 46 D8
Barnawartha Vic. 19 P13, 47 O4, 48 A2
Barnawartha North Vic. 47 O4, 48 B1
Barnes NSW 19 K13, 46 E3
Barnes Bay Tas. 126 I9, 129 L10
Barongarook Vic. 36 B12
Barongarook West Vic. 36 A12, 41 N9
Barooga NSW 19 M13, 47 J3
Baroota SA 61 J2, 62 I12
Barossa Valley SA 58 E4
Barpinba Vic. 36 B9, 41 N7
Barraba NSW 14 I8
Barrage SA 59 I8, 61 M11, 70 C4
Barrakee Vic. 43 M6
Barramunga Vic. 36 B13
Barranyi (North Island) National Park NT 95 P12, 97 P1
Barraport Vic. 18 H13, 43 N5
Barringo Vic. 36 H3
Barrington NSW 13 N1
Barrington Tas. 130 I7
Barrington Tops National Park NSW 13 M1
Barringun NSW 17 N1, 110 A13, 121 R13
Barrogan NSW 12 F6
Barron Gorge National Park Qld 115 M6
Barrow Creek NT 99 J4
Barry NSW 12 G7, 15 K12
Barrys Reef Vic. 36 F3
Bartle Frere National Park *see* Wooroonooran National Park
Barton ACT 23 D10, 24 H11, 25 F2
Barton SA 69 K4
Barunga NT 94 H10
Barunga Gap SA 61 J5
Barwidgee Creek Vic. 47 O7, 48 B5
Barwo Vic. 46 G3
Barwon Downs Vic. 36 C12, 41 O10
Barwon Heads Vic. 36 G10, 38 A7, 41 R8
Baryulgil NSW 15 O4, 111 P13
Basket Range SA 55 R7
Bass Vic. 37 M13, 38 F9
Bass Hill NSW 4 C12, 8 E2
Bassendean WA 77 L11
Batchelor NT 92 D7, 94 E7
Batchica Vic. 42 H6
Bateau Bay NSW 11 Q3, 21 H3
Batehaven NSW 27 N7
Bateman WA 74 G11
Batemans Bay NSW 20 H7, 27 N7
Bates SA 69 K4
Batesford Vic. 36 F9, 41 Q7
Bathumi Vic. 47 L3
Bathurst NSW 10 B4, 12 H6
Batlow NSW 12 D13, 20 B6, 26 A4
Battery Point Tas. 123 F11, 124 H8, 126 I6
Bauhinia Qld 110 I1
Baulkham Hills NSW 4 C3, 6 B12
Bauple Qld 111 P5
Baw Baw National Park Vic. 39 J5
Bawley Point NSW 13 J13, 20 H6, 27 P5
Baxter Vic. 37 K10, 38 D7
Bayles Vic. 37 N10, 38 G7
Baynton Vic. 36 H1
Bayswater Vic. 34 C10
Bayswater WA 77 K11
Bayview NSW 7 P7, 21 H13
Beachmere Qld 109 M5
Beachport SA 70 F10
Beacon WA 82 E6
Beacon Hill NSW 5 O2, 7 N12
Beaconsfield NSW 5 M13, 9 O3

133

Beaconsfield Tas. 131 K7
Beaconsfield Vic. 37 M8, 38 E6
Beaconsfield WA 74 C11
Beagle Bay WA 86 H7
Bealiba Vic. 43 N10
Bearbung NSW 14 E12
Beardmore Vic. 39 K4
Beargamil NSW 12 D5
Bearii Vic. 19 L13, 46 H3
Bears Lagoon Vic. 43 P7, 46 A6
Beatrice Hill NT 92 F4
Beauaraba Qld 108 D8
Beauchamp Vic. 43 N2, 45 N12
Beaudesert Qld 109 L12, 111 P10
Beaufort SA 61 J6
Beaufort Vic. 41 M3
Beaumaris Tas. 131 Q9
Beaumaris Vic. 35 B5
Beaumont SA 55 L8
Beauty Point NSW 5 O6
Beauty Point Tas. 131 K6
Beazleys Bridge Vic. 43 L9
Beckenham WA 75 N8
Beckom NSW 12 A9, 19 Q7
Bedford WA 77 J11
Bedgerebong NSW 12 C6
Bedourie Qld 118 E13, 120 E1
Beeac Vic. 36 B10, 41 N8
Beebo Qld 15 J2, 111 L12
Beech Forest Vic. 41 N11
Beechboro WA 77 L7
Beechford Tas. 131 L6
Beechmont Qld 109 M13
Beechwood NSW 15 O12
Beechworth Vic. 47 O6, 48 A3
Beecroft NSW 4 F3, 6 D12
Beedelup National Park WA 79 H13, 80 C11
Beela WA 79 H3, 80 C7
Beelbangera NSW 19 N7
Beenak Vic. 50 F12
Beenleigh Qld 107 P13, 109 M10, 111 Q10
Beerburrum Qld 109 M3
Beerwah Qld 109 M3, 111 P7
Bega NSW 20 G10, 49 Q6
Beggan Beggan NSW 12 E10, 20 C3
Beilpajah NSW 18 I2
Belair SA 55 J12
Belair National Park SA 55 M12, 58 B10, 59 G1, 70 B2
Belalie SA 61 L3, 63 K13
Belbora NSW 13 O1
Belconnen ACT 24 E6, 26 G1, 28 E3
Beldon WA 76 B1
Belfield NSW 4 G12, 9 J2, 11 N9
Belgrave Vic. 34 F13, 37 L7, 38 E5, 50 A12
Belhus WA 77 P1
Belka WA 80 I3
Bell NSW 10 H5
Bell Qld 108 C2, 111 M7
Bell Bay Tas. 131 K6
Bellambi NSW 13 K9
Bellara Qld 109 N4
Bellarine Vic. 36 H9, 38 B6
Bellarwi NSW 12 B9, 19 Q7
Bellata NSW 14 G7
Bellbird NSW 13 L4
Bellbird Vic. 19 Q13, 47 Q4, 48 C2
Bellbird Creek Vic. 49 L12
Bellbowrie Qld 106 A6
Bellbrae Vic. 36 F11, 41 Q9
Bellbrook NSW 15 N10
Bellellen Vic. 41 J1, 43 J12
Bellenden Ker National Park see Wooroonooran National Park
Bellerive Tas. 125 K6
Bellevue Hill NSW 5 P11, 9 R1
Bellingen NSW 15 P8
Bellingham Tas. 131 M6
Bellmount Forest NSW 12 G11, 20 E4
Bellthorpe Qld 109 K2
Belltrees NSW 13 L1
Belmont NSW 13 M5
Belmont Qld 107 L2
Belmont WA 75 L3
Belmore NSW 4 H13, 9 J3
Belmunging WA 80 F3
Beloka NSW 20 D10, 49 L5
Belowra NSW 20 G8, 27 K11, 49 P2
Belrose NSW 5 M1, 7 L11

Beltana SA 63 J5
Beltana Roadhouse SA 63 J5
Belton SA 63 K10
Belvidere SA 61 L10, 70 C3
Belyuen NT 92 B3, 94 D6
Bemboka NSW 20 F10, 49 P5
Bemm River Vic. 49 M13
Ben Boyd National Park NSW 20 G11, 49 Q8
Ben Bullen NSW 10 F2, 12 I5
Ben Lomond NSW 15 L7
Ben Lomond National Park Tas. 131 O9
Bena NSW 12 A7, 19 Q4
Bena Vic. 37 O12, 38 G8
Benalla Vic. 47 K7
Benambra Vic. 20 A11, 48 F7
Benandarah NSW 27 N6
Benaraby Qld 113 P12
Benarkin Qld 108 G2
Bencubbin WA 82 E6
Bendalong NSW 13 J12, 20 I5, 27 Q3
Bendemeer NSW 15 K10
Bendick Murrell NSW 12 E9, 20 C1
Bendidee National Park Qld 14 I1, 111 K11
Bendigo Vic. 43 R9, 46 C8
Bendoc Vic. 20 D12, 49 L9
Bendolba NSW 13 M2
Beneree NSW 12 F6
Benetook Vic. 44 F4
Benger WA 79 H3, 80 C7
Bengworden Vic. 39 P5
Beni NSW 12 F2
Benjeroop Vic. 43 O1, 45 O12
Benlidi Qld 119 P13, 121 P1
Benobble Qld 109 M12
Bentleigh Vic. 33 M13, 35 B1
Bentley NSW 15 P3
Bentley WA 75 K7
Benwerrin Vic. 36 D12, 41 P10
Berala NSW 4 D11, 8 G1
Berambing NSW 10 I5
Berat Qld 108 F12
Beremboke Vic. 36 F6
Berendebba NSW 12 C8, 20 A1
Beresfield NSW 13 M4
Bergalia NSW 20 G8, 27 M9, 49 R1
Bermagui NSW 20 H9, 27 M13, 49 R4
Bermagui South NSW 20 H9, 27 M13, 49 R4
Berowra NSW 6 H4
Berowra Heights NSW 6 I3, 11 N6, 21 D13
Berowra Waters NSW 6 H2, 21 C13
Berrara NSW 13 J12, 20 I5, 27 Q3
Berri SA 61 Q7
Berridale NSW 20 D9, 26 E12, 49 L4
Berriedale Tas. 124 B2, 126 G5, 129 L8
Berrigan NSW 19 N12, 47 K1
Berrima NSW 13 J10, 20 H3
Berrimah NT 92 C2
Berrimal Vic. 43 M8
Berrinba Qld 107 K10
Berringa Vic. 36 B6, 41 O5
Berringama Vic. 20 A9, 48 F3
Berriwillock Vic. 18 F12, 43 K2, 45 K13
Berrook Vic. 44 A8, 61 R9, 70 I1
Berry NSW 13 K11, 20 I4
Berrybank Vic. 36 A8, 41 M6
Berwick Vic. 37 M8, 38 E5
Bessiebelle Vic. 40 F8
Bet Bet Vic. 43 O11
Beta Qld 112 E11
Bete Bolong Vic. 49 J12
Bethanga Vic. 19 Q13, 47 Q4, 48 C2
Bethania Qld 107 O12, 109 M10
Bethany SA 58 F5
Bethel SA 58 D2
Bethungra NSW 12 C11, 20 B4
Betoota Qld 120 H4
Beulah Tas. 130 I8
Beulah Vic. 18 E13, 42 H4
Beulah East Vic. 42 I4
Beulah Park SA 55 L5
Beulah West Vic. 42 H4
Bevendale NSW 12 F10, 20 E3
Beverford Vic. 18 H10, 45 N10
Beveridge Vic. 37 J3, 38 D1, 46 F12
Beverley SA 54 F3
Beverley WA 80 F4, 82 D8
Beverley East WA 80 F4
Beverley Park NSW 9 L7
Beverly Hills NSW 8 I5

Bexhill NSW 15 Q3
Bexley NSW 9 K5, 11 N9
Bexley North NSW 9 J4
Beyal Vic. 43 J5
Biala NSW 12 G10, 20 E3
Biamanga National Park NSW 20 G10, 49 Q5
Biarra Qld 108 H5
Bibbenluke NSW 20 E11, 49 N7
Biboohra Qld 115 M6
Bicheno Tas. 129 Q2, 131 Q12
Bicton WA 74 D8
Biddeston Qld 108 D7
Biddon NSW 14 D12
Bidyadanga Community WA 86 G10
Big Pats Creek Vic. 37 O6, 50 H9
Bigga NSW 12 G8, 20 E1
Biggara NSW 20 B9, 48 H3
Biggenden Qld 111 N4
Bilbarin WA 80 H4
Bilbul NSW 19 O7
Bilgola NSW 7 Q5
Billabong Vic. 18 D7, 44 G3
Billabong Roadhouse WA 81 C12, 82 A1
Billaricay WA 80 I5
Billilingra Siding NSW 26 G9
Billiluna Community WA 87 P11
Billimari NSW 12 E7
Billinudgel NSW 15 Q2, 111 Q11
Billys Creek NSW 15 O7
Biloela Qld 111 K1, 113 N13
Bilpin NSW 11 J5, 13 J6
Bilyana Qld 115 N9
Bimbaya NSW 49 P6
Bimbi NSW 12 D8, 20 B1
Bimbimbie NSW 27 N8
Binalong NSW 12 E10, 20 D3
Binalong Bay Tas. 131 R8
Binbee Qld 112 I3
Binda NSW 10 A13, 12 G9, 20 F2
Bindi Vic. 20 B12, 48 G8
Bindi Bindi WA 82 D6
Bindle Qld 110 G9
Bindoon WA 80 D2, 82 C7
Bingara NSW 14 I6
Bingera Qld 111 O2
Bingil Bay Qld 115 N9
Binginwarri Vic. 39 K9
Biniguy NSW 14 H5
Binjour Qld 111 M4
Binnaway NSW 14 F12
Binningup WA 79 G3, 80 C7
Binnu WA 82 A2
Binnum SA 70 H8
Binya NSW 19 O7
Birchgrove NSW 5 L9
Birchip Vic. 18 F13, 43 K4
Birchs Bay Tas. 126 G10, 129 L10
Birdsville Qld 120 E5
Birdwood NSW 15 N11
Birdwood SA 58 F8, 61 L9, 70 C1
Birdwoodton Vic. 18 D7, 44 G3
Birkdale Qld 105 P12
Birkenhead SA 56 C10
Birralee Tas. 131 K8
Birrego NSW 19 O10
Birregurra Vic. 36 C11, 41 O9
Birriwa NSW 12 G2
Birrong NSW 4 D12, 8 F2
Bishopsbourne Tas. 131 L9
Bittern Vic. 37 K11, 38 E8
Black Bobs Tas. 128 I5
Black Forest SA 54 H9
Black Hill SA 61 N8, 70 E1
Black Hills Tas. 126 F3, 129 K7
Black Mountain NSW 15 L8
Black River Tas. 130 D4
Black Rock SA 61 L2, 63 K12
Black Rock Vic. 35 A4
Black Springs NSW 10 D8, 12 H8
Black Springs SA 61 L5
Black Swamp NSW 15 N4, 111 O13
Blackall Qld 110 A1, 112 D13, 119 R13, 121 R1
Blackburn Vic. 33 Q9
Blackbutt Qld 108 G2, 111 O7
Blackdown Tableland National Park Qld 113 K12
Blackfellow Caves SA 70 G12
Blackheath NSW 10 H6, 13 J7
Blackheath Vic. 42 H7
Blackmans Bay Tas. 126 H8, 129 L9

Blackstone WA 85 P10
Blacktown NSW 11 L7
Blackville NSW 14 H12
Blackwarry Vic. 39 L8
Blackwater Qld 113 K11
Blackwood Vic. 36 F3, 41 Q3, 46 C13
Blackwood Creek Tas. 129 K1, 131 K10
Blackwood National Park Qld 112 F5
Bladensburg National Park Qld 119 M8
Blair Athol Qld 112 H9
Blair Athol SA 54 I1, 56 I12
Blairgowrie Vic. 36 I11
Blakehurst NSW 9 J8, 11 N10
Blakeville Vic. 36 F3, 41 Q3, 46 C13
Blampied Vic. 36 D2
Blanchetown SA 61 N7
Bland NSW 12 B8, 19 R6, 20 A1
Blandford NSW 15 J13
Blanket Flat NSW 12 G9, 20 E1
Blaxland NSW 11 J7
Blaxland Qld 108 B4
Blaxlands Ridge NSW 11 K5
Blayney NSW 12 G6
Bleak House Vic. 42 D6
Blenheim Qld 108 H9
Blessington Tas. 131 N9
Bletchley SA 58 F13
Bli Bli Qld 109 N1, 111 Q7
Blighty NSW 19 L12, 46 H1
Blinman SA 63 K6
Bloomsbury Qld 113 J4
Blow Clear NSW 12 B7, 19 Q5
Blowclear NSW 12 C5
Blue Lake National Park Qld 109 P9
Blue Mountains NSW 20 H1
Blue Mountains National Park NSW 10 G8, 12 I8,
   13 J7, 20 G1
Blue Water Springs Roadhouse Qld 115 M13
Bluewater Qld 115 O12
Blueys Beach NSW 13 P2
Bluff Qld 113 K11
Bluff Beach SA 60 H8
Bluff Rock NSW 15 M4, 111 N13
Blyth SA 61 K5
Boambee NSW 15 P8
Boat Harbour Tas. 130 F5
Boat Harbour Beach Tas. 130 F5
Boatswain Point SA 70 F9
Bobadah NSW 17 P13
Bobbin Head NSW 6 H6
Bobin NSW 15 N13
Bobinawarrah Vic. 47 N7, 48 A5
Bobs Creek Vic. 47 M10
Bochara Vic. 40 F5
Bodalla NSW 20 H8, 27 M10, 49 R2
Bodallin WA 82 F7
Boddington WA 78 G12, 80 E6
Bogan Gate NSW 12 C5
Bogangar NSW 15 Q1, 111 R11
Bogantungan Qld 112 H11
Boggabilla NSW 14 I2, 111 K12
Boggabri NSW 14 H9
Bogolong NSW 12 D8
Bogong Vic. 47 Q9, 48 D6
Boho Vic. 47 J8
Boho South Vic. 47 K8
Boigbeat Vic. 43 K2, 45 K12
Boinka Vic. 18 C10, 44 D10
Boisdale Vic. 39 M5
Bokarina Qld 109 N2
Bolgart WA 80 E1
Bolinda Vic. 36 I3
Bolivar SA 56 H4
Bolivia NSW 15 M4, 111 N13
Bollon Qld 110 E10
Bolton Vic. 45 K8
Boltons Bore Vic. 44 A9, 61 R10, 70 I2
Bolwarra Vic. 40 D9
Bolwarrah Vic. 36 E4, 41 P3, 46 B13
Bomaderry NSW 13 K11, 20 I4
Bombala NSW 20 E11, 49 N7
Bomera NSW 14 G12
Bonalbo NSW 15 O3, 111 P12
Bonang Vic. 20 D12, 49 L9
Bonang West Vic. 20 D12, 49 K9
Bonbeach Vic. 35 D8
Bondi NSW 5 P11, 9 R1
Bondi Gulf National Park NSW 20 E12, 49 N8
Bondi Junction NSW 5 P11, 9 R2, 11 O9

Bondo NSW 12 E12, 20 C5, 26 C1
Bonegilla Vic. 19 Q13, 47 Q4, 48 C2
Boneo Vic. 37 J12
Bongaree Qld 109 N5, 111 Q8
Bongeen Qld 108 B8
Bonnet Bay NSW 8 H9
Bonnie Doon Vic. 47 K10
Bonnie Rock WA 82 F6
Bonny Hills NSW 15 O12
Bonshaw NSW 15 K4, 111 M13
Bonville NSW 15 P8
Bony Mountain Qld 108 D12
Bonython ACT 25 C10
Booborowie SA 61 L4
Boobyalla Tas. 131 P5
Boodua Qld 108 E6
Bookaar Vic. 41 L7
Bookabie SA 69 L8
Bookham NSW 12 E11, 20 D4
Bool Lagoon SA 70 H9
Boolading WA 80 E8
Boolarra Vic. 37 R12, 39 J8
Boolba Qld 110 F10
Booleroo SA 61 K1, 63 J12
Booleroo Centre SA 61 K2, 63 J12
Boolgun SA 61 O7
Booligal NSW 19 K6
Boolite Vic. 43 J7
Boomahnoomoonah Vic. 47 L4
Boomerang Beach NSW 13 P2
Boomi NSW 14 G2, 110 I12
Boomleera NT 92 H11
Boonah Qld 109 J12, 111 P10
Boonah Vic. 36 D12, 41 P10
Boondall Qld 104 H5
Boonoo Boonoo NSW 15 N3, 111 O12
Boonoo Boonoo National Park NSW 15 N3, 111 O12
Boonoonar Vic. 44 G5
Boorabbin National Park WA 82 H7
Booragoon WA 74 G10
Booral NSW 13 N3
Boorcan Vic. 41 K8
Boorhaman Vic. 47 M5
Boorindal NSW 17 O6
Boorolite Vic. 37 R1
Boorongie Vic. 44 I9
Boorongie North Vic. 44 H9
Booroobin Qld 109 L2
Booroopki Vic. 42 C10
Booroorban NSW 19 K9
Boorowa NSW 12 F10, 20 D2
Boosey Vic. 47 J4
Booti Booti National Park NSW 13 P2
Booyal Qld 111 N3
Boppy Mount NSW 17 O10
Borallon Qld 109 K8
Boralma Vic. 47 M5
Borambil NSW 12 I1
Boraning WA 80 E7
Boranup WA 79 B12
Borden WA 80 I10
Border Ranges National Park NSW 15 O1, 111 P11
Border Store NT 93 Q2, 94 H5
Border Village SA 68 B8, 83 R7
Bordertown SA 70 H6
Boree NSW 12 F6
Boree Creek NSW 19 P10
Boro NSW 12 H12, 20 G5, 27 K1
Boronia Vic. 34 D11
Boronia Heights Qld 106 I13
Boronia Park NSW 5 J7
Bororen Qld 111 M1, 113 P13
Borrika SA 61 O9, 70 F2
Borroloola NT 95 O13, 97 O3
Borung Vic. 43 O6
Boscabel WA 80 F9, 82 E10
Bostobrick NSW 15 O8
Botany NSW 9 O5, 11 O9
Botany Bay National Park NSW 9 P10, 11 O10
Bothwell Tas. 129 K5
Bouddi National Park NSW 11 P5, 21 H7
Bouldercombe Qld 113 N11
Boulia Qld 118 F9
Boulka Vic. 44 H9
Boundain WA 80 G6
Boundary Bend Vic. 18 G9, 45 L7
Bourke NSW 17 N5
Bournda National Park NSW 20 G10, 49 R6

Bow NSW 13 J2
Bow Bridge Roadhouse WA 80 F13
Bowan Park NSW 12 F6
Bowden SA 52 A3, 54 H4
Bowelling WA 80 E8
Bowen Qld 113 J2
Bowen Hills Qld 104 G10
Bowen Mountain NSW 11 J5
Bowenfels NSW 10 H8
Bowenvale Vic. 43 O11
Bowenville Qld 108 C5, 111 M8
Bower SA 61 N6
Boweya Vic. 47 L5
Bowhill SA 61 N9, 70 E1
Bowling Alley Point NSW 15 K12
Bowling Green Bay National Park Qld 112 G1,
   115 Q13
Bowmans SA 61 K6
Bowna NSW 19 Q13, 47 Q3, 48 D1
Bowning NSW 12 F11, 20 D4
Bowral NSW 13 J10, 20 I3
Bowraville NSW 15 O9
Bowser Vic. 47 M5
Box Creek Qld 110 A5, 121 R5
Box Hill Vic. 33 O8
Box Tank NSW 16 D12
Boxwood Vic. 47 K5
Boxwood Hill WA 82 F11
Boyanup WA 79 G6, 80 C8
Boyeo Vic. 42 D6
Boyer Tas. 126 F4, 129 K8
Boyland Qld 109 M12
Boyne Island Qld 113 P12
Boys Town Qld 109 L12
Boyup Brook WA 80 E9, 82 D11
Bracalba Qld 109 L4
Bracken Ridge Qld 104 F4
Brackendale NSW 15 L11
Bracknell Tas. 131 K10
Braddon ACT 23 E2, 24 H8
Bradford Vic. 43 P10, 46 B9
Bradvale Vic. 36 A6, 41 M5
Brady Creek SA 61 M6
Braefield NSW 15 J12
Braeside Qld 15 M1, 111 N11
Braeside Vic. 35 D5
Brahma Lodge SA 57 M5
Braidwood NSW 12 H13, 20 G6, 27 L4
Bramfield SA 60 B5
Bramley WA 79 B9
Brampton Island Qld 113 L4
Bramston Beach Qld 115 N8
Branch Creek Qld 104 A6
Brandon Qld 112 H1, 115 Q13
Branxholm Tas. 131 O7
Branxholme Vic. 40 E6
Branxton NSW 13 M3
Brawlin NSW 12 D11, 20 B3
Bray Junction SA 70 F10
Bray Park Qld 104 B2
Braybrook Vic. 32 G7
Breadalbane NSW 12 H11, 20 F4
Breadalbane Tas. 131 M9
Break O Day Vic. 37 M2, 38 E1, 46 H12
Breakfast Creek NSW 12 E8, 20 D1
Breakfast Creek NSW 12 I3
Breakfast Creek Qld 104 H10
Bream Creek Tas. 127 N5, 129 O8
Breamlea Vic. 36 G11, 38 A7, 41 R8
Brecon SA 70 G6
Bredbo NSW 20 E8, 26 G8, 49 N1
Breelong NSW 12 F1, 14 D13
Breeza NSW 14 I11
Bremer Bay WA 82 G11
Brendale Qld 104 C4
Brentwood SA 60 H9
Brentwood Vic. 42 G4
Brentwood WA 74 H10
Breona Tas. 129 J1, 131 J10
Bretti NSW 15 M13
Brewarrina NSW 17 Q5
Brewongle NSW 10 D5
Brewster Vic. 36 A3, 41 N3
Briagolong Vic. 39 N4, 48 C13
Bribbaree NSW 12 C9, 20 B1
Bribie Island National Park Qld 109 N3
Bridge Inn Vic. 43 J11
Bridgeman Downs Qld 104 E5
Bridgenorth Tas. 131 L8

Bridgetown WA 80 D10, 82 D11
Bridgewater SA 55 R13
Bridgewater Tas. 126 H4, 129 L7
Bridgewater on Loddon Vic. 43 P9, 46 A7
Bridport Tas. 131 N6
Brigalow Qld 111 L7
Bright Vic. 47 P8, 48 C6
Brighton Qld 104 H2
Brighton SA 54 D13, 58 A11, 59 E2
Brighton Tas. 126 H3, 129 L7
Brighton Vic. 33 L13, 35 A1, 37 J7, 38 C5
Brighton-Le-Sands NSW 9 M6, 11 N9
Brightview Qld 108 I7
Brightwaters NSW 11 Q1
Brim Vic. 18 E13, 42 H5
Brimbago SA 61 P13, 70 H6
Brimboal Vic. 40 C3
Brimin Vic. 19 O13, 47 M4
Bringagee NSW 19 M8
Bringalbert Vic. 42 B10, 70 I8
Bringelly NSW 11 K9
Bringenbrong Bridge NSW 20 B8, 48 H2
Brinkin NT 91 E2
Brinkley SA 58 H13
Brinkworth SA 61 K5
Brisbane Qld 101, 104 F12, 109 L8, 111 P9
Brisbane Ranges National Park Vic. 36 F6, 41 Q5
Brisbane Water National Park NSW 11 O4, 21 D9
Brit Brit Vic. 40 E3
Brittons Swamp Tas. 130 C4
Brixton Qld 112 B11, 119 Q11
Broad Arrow WA 82 I5
Broadbeach Qld 109 O13
Broadford Vic. 37 K1, 46 G11
Broadmarsh Tas. 126 G3, 129 L7
Broadmeadows Vic. 33 J2
Broadview SA 55 J2, 57 J13
Broadwater NSW 15 Q3, 111 Q13
Broadwater Vic. 40 G7
Broadwater National Park NSW 15 Q4, 111 Q13
Brocklehurst NSW 12 E2
Brocklesby NSW 19 P12, 47 O2
Brockman National Park WA 80 D11
Brodies Plains NSW 15 K6
Brodribb River Vic. 49 K12
Brogo NSW 20 G10, 49 Q5
Broke NSW 13 L4
Broken Hill NSW 16 B12
Bromelton Qld 109 L12
Brompton SA 52 A2, 54 H4
Bronte NSW 5 P12, 9 R2
Bronte Park Tas. 128 I3, 130 I13
Bronzewing Vic. 44 H10
Brookfield Qld 106 A3
Brooklands Qld 108 E1, 111 N7
Brooklyn NSW 11 O5, 21 E11
Brooklyn Vic. 32 F8
Brooklyn Park SA 54 F6
Brocks Creek NT 92 G10
Brookton WA 80 F5, 82 D8
Brookvale NSW 5 P3, 7 N13
Brookville Vic. 20 A12, 39 Q1, 48 F10
Broome WA 86 G9
Broomehill WA 80 H9, 82 E11
Broomfield Vic. 36 D2, 41 P2, 43 P13, 46 A12
Brooms Head NSW 15 Q6
Brooweena Qld 111 O4
Broughton Vic. 42 C6
Broula NSW 12 E8
Broulee NSW 20 H7, 27 N8
Brownlow SA 58 I1, 61 M7
Brownlow Hill NSW 11 J10
Browns Plains Qld 107 J11
Browns Plains Vic. 47 O3, 48 A1
Bruarong Vic. 47 P6, 48 B4
Bruce ACT 24 E7
Bruce SA 63 J11
Bruce Rock WA 80 I3, 82 F8
Brucefield SA 60 I5
Brucknell Vic. 41 K10
Brukunga SA 58 E10
Brungle NSW 12 D12, 20 C5, 26 A1
Brunswick Vic. 33 K6
Brunswick Heads NSW 15 Q2, 111 Q12
Brunswick Junction WA 79 H4, 80 C7
Brunswick West Vic. 33 J6
Bruny Island Tas. 126 H12, 129 M11
Brushgrove NSW 15 P5

Bruthen Vic. 39 Q3, 48 G12
Bryden Qld 109 J6
Brymaroo Qld 108 D5, 111 N8
Buangor Vic. 41 L2, 43 L13
Buaraba Qld 108 H6
Buaraba Creek Qld 108 I7
Bucasia Qld 113 L5
Bucca Qld 111 O2
Buccarumbi NSW 15 N6
Buccleuch SA 61 O11, 70 F3
Buchan Vic. 20 B13, 48 I11
Buchan South Vic. 20 B13, 48 H11
Bucheen Creek Vic. 20 A9, 48 F4
Buckenderra NSW 20 D8, 26 D10, 49 L2
Bucketty NSW 11 N1, 13 L5
Buckingham SA 70 H6
Buckingham WA 80 E8
Buckland Qld 108 F1
Buckland Tas. 127 M2, 129 N7
Buckland Vic. 47 P9, 48 B7
Buckleboo SA 60 E2, 62 D12
Buckley Vic. 36 E10
Buckleys Swamp Vic. 40 G6
Buckrabanyule Vic. 43 N6
Budawang National Park NSW 12 I13, 20 H5, 27 N4
Buddabaddah NSW 12 A1, 17 R11
Buddigower NSW 12 A8, 19 Q6
Buderim Qld 109 N1, 111 Q7
Budgee Qld 108 F10
Budgee Budgee NSW 12 H3
Budgeree Vic. 39 J8
Budgeree East Vic. 39 J8
Budgerum Vic. 43 N3, 45 N13
Budgewoi NSW 11 Q2, 13 M5
Buffalo Vic. 38 I10
Bugaldie NSW 14 E11
Bugilbone NSW 14 D7
Builyan Qld 111 M1
Bukalong NSW 20 E11, 49 N6
Bukkulla NSW 15 K5
Bulahdelah NSW 13 O3
Bulart Vic. 40 F4
Buldah Vic. 20 E12, 49 M9
Bulga NSW 13 L3, 15 N12
Bulgandramine NSW 12 D3
Bulgandry NSW 19 P12, 47 O1
Bulgobac Tas. 130 E9
Bulimba Qld 104 H11
Bull Creek SA 58 D13, 59 H4
Bull Creek WA 74 H10
Bull Island SA 70 G8
Bulla Vic. 36 I5, 38 C3
Bullaburra NSW 10 I7
Bullarah NSW 14 F5
Bullaring WA 80 H5
Bullarook Vic. 36 D4, 41 P3, 46 B13
Bullarto Vic. 36 F3, 41 Q2, 43 Q13, 46 C12
Bullarto South Vic. 36 F3
Bulleen Vic. 33 O6
Bullengarook Vic. 36 G4
Bullengarook East Vic. 36 G3, 38 A2, 41 R3, 46 D13
Bulleringa National Park Qld 114 I8
Bullfinch WA 82 G6
Bullhead Creek Vic. 47 R6, 48 D3
Bulli NSW 11 M13, 13 K9
Bullio NSW 10 G13, 12 I9, 20 II2
Bullioh Vic. 47 R5, 48 E2
Bullock Creek Qld 115 J8
Bullsbrook WA 78 D2, 80 D3
Bullumwaal Vic. 20 A13, 39 P3, 48 F12
Buln Buln Vic. 37 P9, 38 H6
Buln Buln East Vic. 37 Q9, 38 I6
Bulwer Qld 109 P5
Bulyee WA 80 G5
Bumbaldry NSW 12 E8, 20 C1
Bumberry NSW 12 E6
Bumbunga SA 61 K5
Bunbartha Vic. 46 H5
Bunburra Qld 109 J12
Bunbury WA 79 F4, 80 C8, 82 C10
Bundaberg Qld 111 O2
Bundaburrah NSW 12 C7
Bundalaguah Vic. 39 M6
Bundalong Vic. 19 O13, 47 L3
Bundalong South Vic. 19 O13, 47 L4
Bundanoon NSW 13 J10, 20 H3
Bundarra NSW 15 K7
Bundeena NSW 11 O11

Bundella NSW 14 H12
Bunding Vic. 36 E4
Bundjalung National Park NSW 15 Q4, 111 Q13
Bundook NSW 13 N1, 15 M13
Bundoora Vic. 33 N3
Bundure NSW 19 N10
Bunga NSW 20 G10, 49 R5
Bungador Vic. 43 L13
Bungal Vic. 36 E5, 41 P4
Bungarby NSW 20 E10, 49 M6
Bungaree Vic. 36 D4, 41 P3, 46 B13
Bungeet Vic. 47 L5
Bungendore NSW 12 H12, 20 F5, 27 J2, 28 I3
Bungil Vic. 47 R3, 48 E1
Bungle Bungle National Park see Purnululu National Park
Bungonia NSW 12 I11, 20 G4
Bungowannah NSW 19 P13, 47 O3, 48 B1
Bungulla NSW 15 M4, 111 N13
Bungulla WA 80 H3
Bunguluke Vic. 43 M5
Bungunya Qld 14 G1, 110 I11
Bungwahl NSW 13 O3
Buninyong Vic. 36 C5, 41 O4
Bunkers Hill Qld 108 D8
Bunnaloo NSW 19 K12, 46 E2
Bunnan NSW 13 K1
Buntine WA 82 D5
Bunya Qld 104 B7
Bunya Mountains National Park Qld 108 C1, 111 N7
Bunyah NSW 13 O2
Bunyan NSW 20 E8, 26 G10, 49 N2
Bunyip Vic. 37 O9, 38 G6
Buraja NSW 19 O12, 47 M2
Burbank Qld 107 M4
Burbong NSW 26 I3, 28 H4
Burcher NSW 12 B7, 19 R5
Burekup WA 79 H4, 80 C8
Burgooney NSW 19 P4
Burke & Wills Roadhouse Qld 114 B12, 117 G12
Burkes Flat Vic. 43 N9
Burketown Qld 117 E8
Burleigh Head National Park Qld 109 O13
Burleigh Heads Qld 109 O13, 111 Q10
Burnbank Vic. 36 A1
Burnett Heads Qld 111 O2
Burnie Tas. 130 G6
Burns WA 78 A2
Burns Creek Tas. 131 N9
Burnside SA 55 M7
Burnt Yards NSW 12 F7
Buronga NSW 18 D7, 44 G3
Burpengary Qld 109 L5, 111 P8
Burra SA 61 L5
Burra Creek Gorge SA 61 M5
Burraboi NSW 19 J11, 43 R1, 45 R11
Burracoppin WA 82 F7
Burraga NSW 10 B9, 12 H8, 20 F1
Burragate NSW 20 F11, 49 P8
Burramine Vic. 47 K3
Burramine South Vic. 47 K4
Burrandana NSW 12 B13, 19 R11
Burraneer NSW 9 L13
Burrawang NSW 13 J10, 20 I3
Burraway NSW 12 D1
Burrell Creek NSW 13 O1, 15 N13
Burren Junction NSW 14 E7
Burrereo Vic. 43 J8
Burrill Lake NSW 13 J13, 20 I6, 27 P4
Burringbar NSW 15 Q2, 111 Q11
Burringurrah WA 81 G8
Burrinjuck NSW 12 E11, 20 D4
Burroin Vic. 42 H2, 44 H13
Burrowa-Pine Mountain National Park Vic. 20 A8, 48 F2
Burrowye Vic. 20 A8, 48 E1
Burrum Vic. 43 J9
Burrum Coast National Park Qld 111 O3
Burrum Heads Qld 111 P3
Burrum River National Park Qld 111 P3
Burrumbeet Vic. 36 B3, 41 N3
Burrumboot Vic. 46 F7
Burrumbuttock NSW 19 P12, 47 P2
Burswood WA 75 J3
Burton SA 57 J3
Burwood NSW 4 H10
Burwood Vic. 33 O10
Burwood East Vic. 33 P10

Bushfield Vic. 40 I9
Bushy Park Tas. 126 D3, 129 J7
Bushy Park Vic. 39 M5
Busselton WA 79 D7, 80 B9, 82 C10
Butchers Ridge Vic. 20 C12, 48 I9
Bute SA 61 J5
Butler Tanks SA 60 E6
Butlers Gorge Tas. 128 H4, 130 H13
Buxton NSW 11 J12, 13 J9, 20 I2
Buxton Qld 111 P3
Buxton Vic. 37 O3, 38 G1, 47 J12, 50 H1
Byabarra NSW 15 O12
Byaduk Vic. 40 F6
Byaduk North Vic 40 F6
Byawatha Vic. 47 N5
Byfield National Park Qld 113 O9
Byford WA 78 D7, 80 D4
Bylands Vic. 37 J2, 38 C1, 46 F12
Bylong NSW 12 I3
Bymount Qld 110 G5
Byrneside Vic. 46 G6
Byrnestown Qld 111 N4
Byrneville Vic. 42 H8
Byrock NSW 17 P7
Byron Bay NSW 15 R2, 111 R12
Bywong NSW 12 G12, 20 F5, 26 I1, 28 H2

Cabarita NSW 4 H9
Cabarlah Qld 108 F7, 111 N9
Cabawin Qld 111 K8
Cabbage Tree Creek Vic. 49 K12
Cabbage Tree Point Qld 109 O10
Caboolture Qld 109 M4, 111 P8
Caboonbah Qld 108 I5
Cabramatta NSW 8 B2, 11 M8
Cabramurra NSW 20 C8, 26 B8, 49 J1
Caddens Flat Vic. 40 F2, 42 F13
Cadell SA 61 O6
Cadney Homestead SA 67 P8
Cadoux WA 82 D6
Cahills Crossing NT 93 Q2, 94 H5
Caiguna WA 83 N8
Cairns Qld 115 N6
Cairns Bay Tas. 126 E10, 129 K10
Calamvale Qld 106 I9
Calca SA 69 P13
Calder Tas. 130 F6
Caldwell NSW 19 J12, 46 D1
Calen Qld 113 K4
Calga NSW 11 O4, 21 C7
Calingiri WA 80 E1, 82 D7
Caliph SA 61 P8
Calivil Vic. 43 Q6, 46 B5
Callala Bay NSW 13 K11, 20 I4, 27 R1
Callawadda Vic. 43 J10
Calleen NSW 12 A7, 19 Q5
Callide Qld 111 K1, 113 N13
Callignee Vic. 39 K8
Callignee North Vic. 39 L8
Callington SA 58 F12, 61 M10, 70 D2
Calliope Qld 113 P12
Caloona NSW 14 F3, 110 I12
Caloote SA 58 I10
Caloundra Qld 109 N2, 111 Q7
Caltowie SA 61 K3, 63 K13
Calulu Vic. 39 P4, 48 E13
Calvert Qld 108 I9
Calvert Vic. 41 J3
Calwell ACT 25 E11
Camballin WA 87 J9
Cambarville Vic. 37 P4
Camberwell NSW 13 L3
Camberwell Vic. 33 N9
Cambewarra NSW 13 J11, 20 I4
Cambooya Qld 108 E9
Cambrai SA 58 I6, 61 M8
Cambrian Hill Vic. 36 C4
Cambridge Tas. 125 O4, 127 J5, 129 M8
Cambroon Bridge Qld 109 K1
Camburinga NT 95 O6
Camdale Tas. 130 G5
Camden NSW 11 K10, 13 K8, 20 I1
Camden Park SA 54 F9
Camellia NSW 4 D7
Camena Tas. 130 G6
Camira Qld 106 D10
Camira Creek NSW 15 P4, 111 P13
Cammeray NSW 5 M7

Camooweal Qld 97 R11, 118 B2
Camooweal Caves National Park Qld 97 R11, 118 B2
Camp Coorong SA 61 M12, 70 D4
Camp Hill Qld 105 J13, 107 J2
Campania Tas. 127 J3, 129 M7
Campbell ACT 23 H6, 24 H10
Campbell Town Tas. 129 M2, 131 N12
Campbellfield Vic. 33 K2
Campbells Bridge Vic. 43 J11
Campbells Creek Vic. 43 Q12, 46 C10
Campbells Forest Vic. 43 Q9, 46 B7
Campbells Pocket Qld 109 L4
Campbells River NSW 10 C9
Campbelltown NSW 11 L10, 13 K8
Campbelltown SA 55 M2
Campbelltown Vic. 36 D1, 41 P1, 43 P12, 46 A11
Camperdown NSW 5 K11, 9 M1
Camperdown Vic. 41 L8
Campsie NSW 4 H13, 9 J3
Camurra NSW 14 H5
Canada Bay NSW 4 H10
Canary Island Vic. 43 P4, 46 A3
Canary Island South Vic. 43 O5, 46 A3
Canbelego NSW 17 O10
Canberra ACT 12 F12, 20 D5, 23, 24 G9, 26 G2, 28 F3
Candelo NSW 20 G10, 49 P6
Cangai NSW 15 O5
Cania Gorge National Park Qld 111 L2
Caniambo Vic. 47 J6
Canimble NSW 12 E7
Canley Heights NSW 8 A1
Canley Vale NSW 8 B1
Cann River Vic. 20 E13, 49 N11
Canna WA 82 C4
Cannawigara SA 70 H6
Cannie Vic. 43 M3, 45 M13
Canning Qld 109 M5
Canning Vale WA 75 K12
Cannington WA 75 L7, 78 C5
Cannon Creek Qld 109 J13
Cannon Hill Qld 105 J11
Cannons Creek Vic. 37 L10
Cannonvale Qld 113 K3
Cannum Vic. 42 G6
Canomodine NSW 12 F6
Canonba NSW 14 A12, 17 R9
Canowie SA 61 L4
Canowindra NSW 12 E7
Canterbury NSW 4 I12, 9 K2
Canterbury Vic. 33 O9
Canunda National Park SA 70 G11
Canungra Qld 109 M12
Capalaba Qld 107 O3, 109 N8
Caparra NSW 15 N13
Cape Arid National Park WA 83 K10
Cape Barren Island Tas. 128 A13, 131 Q2
Cape Borda SA 60 F12
Cape Bridgewater Vic. 40 C9
Cape Clear Vic. 36 B6, 41 N5
Cape Crawford NT 97 M4
Cape Jervis SA 59 B9, 61 J11, 70 A4
Cape Le Grand National Park WA 83 J11
Cape Melville National Park Qld 116 H12
Cape Palmerston National Park Qld 113 L6
Cape Paterson Vic. 38 G10
Cape Range National Park WA 81 B3
Cape Tribulation National Park see Daintree National Park
Cape Upstart National Park Qld 112 I1
Cape York Peninsula Qld 114 G2, 116 C10
Capel WA 79 F6, 80 C8, 82 C10
Capella Qld 112 I10
Capels Crossing Vic. 43 P2, 45 P13, 46 A1
Capertee NSW 10 E1, 12 I5
Capricorn Roadhouse WA 84 E6
Captain Billy Landing Qld 116 D5
Captains Flat NSW 12 H13, 20 F6, 26 I5, 28 I8
Carabost NSW 20 A6
Caragabal NSW 12 C8
Caralue SA 60 E4
Caralulup Vic. 36 B1
Caramut Vic. 40 I6
Carapooee Vic. 43 M9
Carapook Vic. 40 D4
Caravan Head NSW 8 I8
Carawa SA 69 P10
Carboor Vic. 47 N7, 48 A5

Carbrook Qld 107 R10
Carbunup River WA 79 C8
Carcoar NSW 12 G7
Carcuma SA 61 O12, 70 F4
Cardigan Village Vic. 36 B3, 41 O3
Cardinia Vic. 37 M9, 38 F6
Cardross Vic. 18 D7, 44 G4
Cardwell Qld 115 N10
Careel Bay NSW 7 Q4
Carey Gully SA 55 R9
Cargerie Vic. 36 D6, 41 P5
Cargo NSW 12 F6
Carina Qld 105 J13, 107 J1
Carinda NSW 14 A8
Carindale Qld 105 K13, 107 K1
Carine WA 76 D7
Caringbah NSW 9 K11
Carisbrook Vic. 43 O11, 46 A10
Carlisle WA 75 L5
Carlisle River Vic. 36 A13, 41 M10
Carlsruhe Vic. 36 G2, 41 R2, 43 R13, 46 D11
Carlton NSW 9 K7
Carlton Tas. 127 L6, 129 N8
Carlton Vic. 30 E2, 33 K8
Carlwood NSW 10 E6
Carmila Qld 113 L7
Carnamah WA 82 C5
Carnarvon WA 81 B8
Carnarvon National Park Qld 110 D2, 110 F2, 112 I13
Carnegie Vic. 33 N12
Carnegie Homestead WA 84 I10
Carngham Vic. 36 B4
Caroda NSW 14 I7
Carole Park Qld 106 D9
Caroline SA 40 A6, 70 I12
Caroling WA 80 G4
Caroona NSW 14 I12
Carpa SA 60 F5
Carpendale Qld 108 G8
Carpendeit Vic. 41 L9
Carpenter Rocks SA 70 G12
Carrabin WA 82 F7
Carrajung Vic. 39 L8
Carrajung South Vic. 39 L8
Carramar NSW 4 A11, 8 C1
Carranballac Vic. 41 L4
Carraragarmungee Vic. 47 N5
Carrathool NSW 19 M7
Carrick Tas. 131 L9
Carrickalinga SA 59 D6
Carrieton SA 63 K10
Carroll NSW 14 I10
Carroll Gap NSW 14 I10
Carron Vic. 43 J6
Carrow Brook NSW 13 L2
Carrowidgin NSW 20 D11, 49 L8
Carrum Vic. 35 D9
Carrum Downs Vic. 35 G10
Carseldine Qld 104 F5
Carss Park NSW 9 K7
Cartmeticup WA 80 G8
Carwarp Vic. 18 D8, 44 G5
Cascade WA 82 I10
Cascades Tas. 124 E9
Cashmere Qld 104 A4
Cashmore Vic. 40 D9
Casino NSW 15 P3, 111 P12
Cassilis NSW 12 I1
Cassilis Vic. 20 A12, 48 F9
Castambul SA 55 Q2, 57 R13, 58 D9
Castella Vic. 37 M4, 50 C3
Casterton Vic. 40 C4
Castle Cove NSW 5 N5
Castle Forbes Bay Tas. 126 E9, 129 K10
Castle Hill NSW 4 D1, 6 B11, 11 M7
Castlemaine Vic. 43 Q11, 46 C10
Casuarina NT 91 G4, 92 C2
Casula NSW 8 A6
Cataby Roadhouse WA 82 B6
Catamaran Tas. 129 J13
Catani Vic. 37 N10
Cathcart NSW 20 F11, 49 O7
Cathedral Rock National Park NSW 15 N8
Catherine Field NSW 11 K10
Catherine Hill Bay NSW 11 R1, 13 M5
Cathkin Vic. 37 N1
Cathundral NSW 12 C1, 14 B13

Cattai NSW 11 M5
Cattai National Park NSW 11 L5
Catumnal Vic. 43 N5
Caulfield Vic. 33 M11
Cavan NSW 12 F11, 20 E4
Cavan SA 56 I10
Caveat Vic. 46 I10
Cavendish Vic. 40 F3
Caveside Tas. 130 I9
Cawdor NSW 11 K11
Cawdor Qld 108 E7
Cawongla NSW 15 P2, 111 Q12
Cecil Park NSW 11 L8
Cecil Plains Qld 111 M9
Cedar Bay National Park Qld 115 M3
Cedar Brush NSW 11 O1
Cedar Brush Creek NSW 11 O1
Cedar Grove Qld 109 L11
Cedar Party Creek NSW 15 N13
Ceduna SA 69 N9
Cement Creek Vic. 37 O5, 38 G3, 50 H8
Centennial Park NSW 5 O11, 9 Q1
Central Castra Tas. 130 H7
Central Colo NSW 11 K4
Central McDonald NSW 11 M3
Central Mangrove NSW 11 O2, 21 B4
Central Tilba NSW 20 H9, 27 M12, 49 R3
Ceratodus Qld 111 L3
Ceres NSW 12 D2
Ceres Vic. 36 F9, 41 Q8
Cervantes WA 82 B6
Cessnock NSW 13 M4
Chadstone Vic. 33 O12
Chain of Ponds SA 58 D8
Chakola NSW 26 G10
Challambra Vic. 42 I6
Chambigne NSW 15 O6
Chandada SA 60 A1, 69 Q12
Chandler Qld 105 N13, 107 N2
Chandler SA 67 N4
Chandlers Creek Vic. 20 E12, 49 M10
Channel Country Qld 118 D12
Chapel Hill Qld 106 D3
Chapman ACT 25 A5
Chapman River SA 59 A11
Chapple Vale Vic. 41 L11
Charam Vic. 42 D11
Charleston SA 58 E9
Charlestown NSW 13 N5
Charley Creek Vic. 36 A13
Charleville Qld 110 B6
Charleyong NSW 12 I12, 20 G5, 27 M2
Charlotte Pass NSW 20 C9, 26 A12, 49 J4
Charlton NSW 17 Q5
Charlton Vic. 43 M6
Charnwood ACT 24 C3
Charters Towers Qld 112 E2
Chatham Village NSW 8 A5
Chatsbury NSW 12 I10, 20 G3
Chatswood NSW 5 L5, 11 O8
Chatsworth NSW 15 Q5
Chatsworth Vic. 40 I6
Cheepie Qld 121 Q7
Cheesemans Creek NSW 12 F5
Chelmer Qld 106 E3
Chelsea Vic. 35 D8, 37 K8
Chelsea Heights Vic. 35 F7
Cheltenham NSW 4 G3, 6 E12
Cheltenham SA 54 D1, 56 E13
Cheltenham Vic. 35 C3
Chepstowe Vic. 36 A4
Cherbourg Aboriginal Community Qld 111 N6
Chermside Qld 104 F7, 109 L7
Chermside West Qld 104 E7
Cherokee Vic. 36 H2
Cherrybrook NSW 6 D10
Cherryville SA 55 R5
Cheshunt Vic. 47 N9
Chesney Vale Vic. 47 L6
Chester Hill NSW 4 C11, 8 E1
Chesterton Range National Park Qld 110 E6
Chetwynd Vic. 40 C2, 42 C13
Chevallum Qld 109 M1
Chevoit Vic. 37 M1
Chewton Vic. 43 Q11, 46 C10
Chidlow WA 78 F4, 80 D3
Chifley ACT 25 C5
Chifley NSW 9 Q6

Chifley WA 83 K6
Chigwell Tas. 124 A1
Childers Qld 111 O3
Childers Vic. 37 Q11, 38 I8
Chillagoe Qld 115 K7
Chillagoe-Mungana Caves National Park Qld 115 J7
Chillingham NSW 15 Q1
Chillingollah Vic. 18 G10, 45 L10
Chiltern Vic. 19 P13, 47 O4, 48 A2
Chiltern Valley Vic. 19 P13, 47 N4, 48 A2
Chinaman Wells SA 70 F10
Chinchilla Qld 111 K7
Chinderah NSW 15 Q1, 111 Q11
Chinkapook Vic. 18 F10, 45 K10
Chintin Vic. 36 I3
Chipping Norton NSW 4 A13, 8 C4
Chirnside Park Vic. 34 D6
Chisholm ACT 25 E9
Chiswick NSW 5 J9
Chittering WA 80 D2
Chorregon Qld 119 N9
Christmas Hills Tas. 130 C4
Christmas Hills Vic. 34 E1, 37 L5, 50 A5
Chudleigh Tas. 130 I9
Chullora NSW 4 E11, 8 G1
Church Point NSW 7 O5
Churchill Vic. 39 K8
Churchill National Park Vic. 35 I3, 37 L7, 38 E5
Churchlands WA 74 D1, 76 D12
Chute Vic. 41 M2, 43 M13
City Beach WA 74 C3, 78 A4
Clackline WA 78 G2, 80 E3
Clairview Qld 113 L7
Clandulla NSW 12 I4
Clapham SA 55 J11
Clare Qld 112 G1
Clare SA 61 L5
Claremont Tas. 126 G4, 129 L8
Claremont WA 74 D5
Clarence NSW 10 G4
Clarence Park SA 54 H9
Clarence Point Tas. 131 K6
Clarence Town NSW 13 N3
Clarendon NSW 11 K6
Clarendon Qld 109 J7
Clarendon SA 58 B12, 59 G3, 61 K10, 70 B2
Clarendon Vic. 36 D5, 41 P4
Clarendon Vale Tas. 125 O8
Clareville NSW 7 Q5
Clarinda Vic. 35 D2
Clarkefield Vic. 36 I3, 38 B2
Clarkes Hill Vic. 36 D3
Clarkfield Vic. 46 E13
Claude Road Tas. 130 H8
Clay Wells SA 70 G10
Clayfield Qld 104 H9
Claypans SA 61 N9, 70 E1
Clayton Qld 111 O2
Clayton Vic. 35 E2
Clear Lake Vic. 42 F11
Clear Mountain Qld 104 A5
Clear Ridge NSW 12 B7, 19 R5
Clearview SA 57 J12
Clematis Vic. 37 M7, 50 C13
Clements Gap SA 61 J4
Clemton Park NSW 4 H13, 9 J3
Clermont Qld 112 H9
Cleve SA 60 F5
Cleveland Qld 109 O8
Cleveland Tas. 129 M1, 131 M11
Clifton NSW 11 M12
Clifton Qld 108 E11, 111 N10
Clifton Beach Tas. 127 J8, 129 M9
Clifton Creek Vic. 39 Q3, 48 F12
Clifton Gardens NSW 5 O8
Clifton Hill Vic. 33 L7
Clifton Springs Vic. 36 H9, 38 A6
Clinton Centre SA 61 J7
Clintonvale Qld 108 F12, 111 O10
Clonbinane Vic. 37 K2
Cloncurry Qld 118 G4
Clontarf NSW 5 P6
Closeburn Qld 109 L6
Clouds Creek NSW 15 O7
Clovelly NSW 5 P13, 9 R3, 11 O9
Clovelly Park SA 54 G13
Cloven Hills Vic. 41 L7
Cloverdale WA 75 M4

Cloyna Qld 111 N5
Cluan Tas. 131 K9
Club Terrace Vic. 20 D13, 49 M11
Clumber Qld 108 H12
Clunes NSW 15 Q3, 111 Q12
Clunes Vic. 36 C2, 41 O2, 43 O13, 46 A11
Clybucca NSW 15 O10
Clyde Vic. 37 L9
Clydebank Vic. 39 N6
Clydesdale Vic. 36 E1
Coal Creek Qld 108 I5
Coalbank Qld 108 E4
Coalcliff NSW 11 M12, 13 K9
Coaldale NSW 15 O5
Coalstoun Lakes Qld 111 N4
Coalstoun Lakes National Park Qld 111 N4
Coalville Vic. 37 R10
Cobains Vic. 39 N6
Cobar NSW 17 N10
Cobargo NSW 20 G9, 27 L13, 49 Q4
Cobark NSW 13 M1, 15 L13
Cobaw Vic. 36 E1
Cobbadah NSW 14 I8
Cobbannah Vic. 39 N3, 48 D12
Cobbitty NSW 11 K10, 13 K8, 20 I1
Cobbora NSW 12 G2
Cobden Vic. 41 K9
Cobdogla SA 61 P7
Cobera SA 61 P8, 70 G1
Cobram Vic. 19 M13, 47 J3
Cobrico Vic. 41 K9
Cobungra Vic. 47 R11, 48 E8
Coburg Vic. 33 K5, 37 J5
Cocamba Vic. 45 K9
Cochranes Creek Vic. 43 N9
Cockaleechie SA 60 D7
Cockatoo Vic. 37 M7, 38 F5, 50 D13
Cockatoo Valley SA 58 D6
Cockburn SA 16 A12, 63 Q9
Cockle Creek Tas. 129 J13
Cocklebiddy WA 83 O8
Coconut Grove NT 91 B6
Cocoparra National Park NSW 19 O6
Codrington Vic. 40 F9
Coen Qld 116 E11
Coffin Bay SA 60 C8
Coffin Bay National Park SA 60 B7
Coffs Harbour NSW 15 P8
Coghills Creek Vic. 36 C2, 41 O2, 43 O13, 46 A12
Cohuna Vic. 19 J12, 43 Q3, 46 C2
Coimadai Vic. 36 G4
Colac Vic. 36 B11, 41 N9
Colac Colac Vic. 20 A9, 48 G2
Colbinabbin Vic. 46 F7
Colbinabbin West Vic. 46 E7
Coldstream Vic. 34 G5, 37 M5, 38 E3, 50 B7
Coleambally NSW 19 N9
Colebrook Tas. 126 I1, 129 M6
Coledale NSW 11 M13
Coleraine Vic. 40 E4
Coles Bay Tas. 129 Q4, 131 Q13
Coleyville Qld 108 I10
Colignan Vic. 18 E8, 44 H5
Colinroobie NSW 19 P8
Colinton NSW 26 G7, 28 F12
Colinton Qld 108 I3
Collarenebri NSW 14 D5
Collaroy NSW 5 Q1, 7 P11, 11 P7, 12 I2
Collaroy Plateau NSW 5 Q1, 7 P11
Collector NSW 12 H11, 20 F4
College Park SA 52 H5, 55 K4
Collerina NSW 17 P4
Collie NSW 14 C13
Collie WA 80 D8, 82 C10
Collie Burn WA 80 D8
Collie Cardiff WA 80 D8
Collier Range National Park WA 84 C8
Collingullie NSW 12 A12, 19 Q10
Collingwood Vic. 33 L8
Collins Cap Tas. 126 G5
Collinsfield SA 61 K4
Collinsvale Tas. 126 G5, 129 L8
Collinsville Qld 112 I3
Collinswood SA 55 J3
Collombatti Rail NSW 15 O10
Colly Blue NSW 14 H12
Colo NSW 11 L4
Colo Heights NSW 11 K3, 13 K6
Colo Vale NSW 13 J9, 20 I2

Colonel Light Gardens SA 54 I11
Colquhoun Vic. 39 R4, 48 H13
Colton SA 60 B4
Comara NSW 15 N9
Comaum SA 40 A2, 42 A13, 70 I10
Combara NSW 14 H7
Combienbar Vic. 20 E13, 49 M10
Comboyne NSW 15 N12
Come-by-Chance NSW 14 D8
Comet Qld 113 J11
Comleroy Road NSW 11 K5
Commissioners Flat Qld 109 L3
Como NSW 8 H9
Como WA 74 I6
Compton Downs NSW 17 P6
Conara Junction Tas. 129 M2, 131 N11
Conargo NSW 19 L11
Concord NSW 4 H8
Concordia SA 58 D5
Condah Vic. 40 E6
Condamine Qld 111 J7
Condell Park NSW 4 C13, 8 F3
Conder ACT 25 D12
Condingup WA 83 K10
Condobolin NSW 12 A5, 19 Q3
Condoulpe NSW 18 H9, 45 N7
Condowie SA 61 K5
Congo NSW 20 H8, 27 N9
Congupna Vic. 46 I5
Conimbla National Park NSW 12 E7
Coningham Tas. 129 L10
Conjola NSW 13 J12, 20 I5, 27 P3
Conmurra SA 70 G9
Connangorach Vic. 42 F11
Connells Point NSW 9 J7
Connellys Marsh Tas. 127 M6
Connemarra NSW 14 G12
Connewarre Vic. 36 F10
Connewirricoo Vic. 40 D1, 42 D12
Conondale Qld 109 K1
Conondale National Park Qld 109 J1, 111 O7
Conway National Park Qld 113 K3
Coober Pedy SA 67 R11
Coobowie SA 60 I10
Coochin Creek Qld 109 M3
Cooee Tas. 130 G5
Cooeeinbardi Qld 109 J4
Coogee NSW 5 P13, 9 R3, 11 O9
Coojar Vic. 40 E2, 42 E13
Cook ACT 24 D8
Cook SA 68 E4
Cookamidgera NSW 12 D5
Cookardinia NSW 19 Q12
Cooke Plains SA 61 N11, 70 E3
Cooks Gap NSW 12 H2
Cooktown Qld 115 L3
Cookville Tas. 126 H13, 129 L11
Coolabah NSW 17 P8
Coolac NSW 12 D11, 20 B4
Cooladdi Roadhouse Qld 110 A7, 121 Q7
Coolah NSW 12 H1, 14 G13
Coolalie NSW 12 F11, 20 E3
Coolamon NSW 12 B11, 19 Q9
Coolana Qld 109 J8
Coolangatta Qld 15 Q1, 111 Q11
Coolaroo Vic. 33 J1
Coolatai NSW 15 J4, 111 L13
Coolbellup WA 74 E12
Coolbinia WA 76 H11
Coolcha SA 61 N9, 70 E1
Coolgardie WA 82 I6
Coolimba WA 82 B5
Coolongolook NSW 13 O2
Cooloola National Park see Great Sandy National
  Park
Cooltong SA 61 Q6
Coolum Beach Qld 111 Q6
Coolup WA 78 C11, 80 C6
Cooma NSW 20 E9, 26 G11, 49 M3
Cooma Vic. 46 G6
Coomalbidgup WA 82 I10
Coomandook SA 61 N11, 70 E3
Coomba NSW 13 O2
Coombah Roadhouse NSW 18 C2
Coombe SA 61 P13, 70 G5
Coombell NSW 15 P3, 111 P13
Coomberdale WA 82 C6
Coombogolong NSW 14 B8
Coomera Qld 109 N11

Coominglah Qld 111 L2
Coominya Qld 108 I7, 111 O9
Coomoora Vic. 36 E2
Coonabarabran NSW 14 F11
Coonalpyn SA 61 O12, 70 F4
Coonamble NSW 14 C10
Coonarr Qld 111 O2
Coonawarra SA 40 A2, 42 A13, 70 H10
Coonerang NSW 26 G13
Coongulla Vic. 39 L5
Coongulmerang Vic. 39 O4, 48 E13
Coonong NSW 19 O10
Coonooer Bridge Vic. 43 M8
Coopernook NSW 13 P1, 15 O13
Coopers Creek Vic. 39 K5
Coopers Plains Qld 106 I6
Cooplacurripa NSW 15 M12
Coopracambra National Park Vic. 20 E12, 49 N10
Coorabie SA 69 K9
Cooran Qld 111 P6
Cooranbong NSW 13 M5
Cooranga North Qld 108 B1
Coorong National Park SA 61 M12, 70 D5
Coorow WA 82 C5
Cooroy Qld 111 P6
Coorparoo Qld 104 I13, 106 I1
Cooya Beach Qld 115 M5
Cooyal NSW 12 H3
Cooyar Qld 108 E3, 111 N7
Cooyar Creek Upper Qld 108 E3
Cope Cope Vic. 43 L7
Copeland NSW 13 N1
Copeville SA 61 O9, 70 F1
Copley SA 63 J4
Copmanhurst NSW 15 O5
Copocabana NSW 21 H7
Coppabella Qld 113 J7
Copping Tas. 127 N5, 129 N8
Coppins Crossing ACT 24 C9
Cora Lynn Vic. 37 N9, 38 G6
Corack Vic. 43 K6
Corack East Vic. 43 K6
Coradgery NSW 12 C4
Coragulac Vic. 36 A10, 41 N8
Coraki NSW 15 Q3, 111 Q13
Coral Bank Vic. 47 Q7, 48 C5
Coral Bay WA 81 B5
Coralville NSW 13 P1, 15 O13
Coramba NSW 15 P8
Corang NSW 12 I12, 20 G5, 27 N2
Corattum SA 70 H12
Cordalba Qld 111 O3
Cordering WA 80 E8
Coree South NSW 19 M11
Coreen NSW 19 O12, 47 M2
Corfield Qld 119 M6
Corinda Qld 106 F5
Corindhap Vic. 36 C7, 41 O5
Corindi NSW 15 P7
Corinella Vic. 37 M12, 38 F8
Corinna Tas. 130 C9
Cornella Vic. 46 E8
Corner Store Qld 16 A1, 65 R11, 120 H13
Cornubia Qld 107 R10
Cornwall Tas. 131 Q10
Corny Point SA 60 G4
Corobimilla NSW 19 O9
Coromby Vic. 42 I8
Coronation Beach WA 82 A3
Corop Vic. 46 F6
Cororooke Vic. 36 A11, 41 N8
Corowa NSW 19 O13, 47 M3
Corra Linn Tas. 131 M9
Corrigin WA 80 H5, 82 E8
Corringle NSW 12 B7, 19 R5
Corringle Vic. 49 J13
Corroboree Park Tavern NT 92 G5
Corryong Vic. 20 B8, 48 G2
Corunna NSW 27 M12
Cosgrove Vic. 47 J5
Cosmo Newbery Community WA 83 K2
Cossack WA 81 G1, 84 A1
Costerfield Vic. 46 F9
Cottesloe WA 74 B6, 78 A5
Cottles Bridge Vic. 37 L4, 38 E2, 46 H13
Cottonvale Qld 15 M2, 111 N11
Couangalt Vic. 36 H4
Cougal NSW 15 P1

Coulson Qld 109 J12
Coulta SA 60 C7
Countegany NSW 26 I11
Courada NSW 14 H7
Couran Qld 109 O11
Couta Rocks Tas. 130 B6
Coutts Crossing NSW 15 P6
Cow Flat NSW 10 B6
Cowabbie West NSW 12 A10, 19 Q8
Cowan NSW 7 J1, 11 N5, 21 D12
Cowandilla SA 54 F6
Cowangie Vic. 18 B10, 44 C10
Cowaramup WA 79 C9, 80 A9
Cowell SA 60 G5
Cowes Vic. 37 L12, 38 E8
Cowled's Landing SA 60 H3, 62 G13
Cowley Beach Qld 115 N8
Cowper NSW 15 P5
Cowra NSW 12 F8
Cowwarr Vic. 39 L6
Coyrecup WA 80 H9
Crabbes Creek NSW 15 Q2, 111 Q11
Crabtree Tas. 126 F7, 129 K9
Cracow Qld 111 K3
Cradle Mountain-Lake St Clair National Park Tas.
  128 F1, 130 F10
Cradle Valley Tas. 130 G9
Cradoc Tas. 126 E9, 129 K10
Cradock SA 63 K9
Crafers SA 55 O12, 58 C10, 59 H1
Crafers West SA 55 N11
Craigie NSW 20 E12, 49 M8
Craigie WA 76 B2
Craigieburn Vic. 37 J4, 38 C2, 46 F13
Craiglie Qld 115 M5
Cramenton Vic. 44 I7
Cramps Tas. 129 J2, 131 K11
Cranbourne Vic. 37 L9, 38 E6
Cranbourne South Vic. 35 H13
Cranbrook Tas. 129 P3, 131 P12
Cranbrook WA 80 H11, 82 E11
Craven NSW 13 N2
Cravensville Vic. 20 A9, 48 F4
Crawford Qld 111 N6
Crawley WA 74 F5
Crayfish Creek Tas. 130 E4
Creek Junction Vic. 47 K9
Creek View Vic. 46 E7
Creighton Vic. 46 I8
Creighton Creek Vic. 46 I9
Cremorne NSW 5 N8
Cremorne Tas. 127 K7, 129 M9
Cremorne Point NSW 5 N8
Crescent Head NSW 15 P11
Cressbrook Lower Qld 108 I4
Cressy Tas. 129 L1, 131 L10
Cressy Vic. 36 B8, 41 N6
Crestmead Qld 107 L12
Creswick Vic. 36 C3, 41 O2, 43 O13, 46 A12
Crib Point Vic. 37 L11, 38 E8
Croajingolong National Park Vic. 20 F13, 49 P12
Croftby Qld 108 I13
Crohamhurst Qld 109 L2
Cromer NSW 5 P1, 7 N11
Crooble NSW 14 H4, 111 K13
Crooked River Vic. 39 N1, 47 Q13, 48 D10
Crookwell NSW 12 H10, 20 F2
Croppa Creek NSW 14 I4, 111 K13
Crossdale Qld 109 J5
Crossley Vic. 40 H9
Crossman WA 78 H12, 80 E6
Crow Mountain NSW 15 J8
Crowdy Bay National Park NSW 13 P1, 15 O13
Crower SA 70 G9
Crowlands Vic. 41 L1, 43 L12
Crows Nest NSW 5 M7
Crows Nest Qld 108 F5, 111 N8
Crows Nest National Park Qld 108 G5
Crowther NSW 12 E9, 20 C1
Croxton East Vic. 40 G5
Croydon NSW 4 H11, 9 J1
Croydon Qld 114 F10
Croydon SA 54 G3
Croydon Vic. 34 C8, 37 L6
Croydon Hills Vic. 34 C7
Croydon Park NSW 4 H11, 9 J2
Croydon Park SA 54 G2
Crymelon Vic. 42 H6

139

Cryon NSW 14 D7
Crystal Brook SA 61 J4
Cuballing WA 80 G6, 82 E9
Cubbaroo NSW 14 E7
Cuckoo Tas. 131 N7
Cudal NSW 12 F6
Cuddell NSW 19 O9
Cudgee Vic. 40 I9
Cudgen NSW 15 Q1, 111 Q11
Cudgera Creek NSW 15 Q1
Cudgewa Vic. 20 A8, 48 G2
Cudgewa North Vic. 20 B8, 48 G2
Cudlee Creek SA 58 D9
Cudmirrah NSW 13 J12, 20 I5, 27 Q3
Cue WA 81 H13, 82 E1, 84 B13
Culbin WA 80 F7
Culburra NSW 13 K11
Culburra SA 61 O12, 70 F5
Culcairn NSW 19 Q12, 47 Q1
Culfearne Vic. 43 P2, 45 Q13, 46 B1
Culgoa Vic. 18 G12, 43 L3, 45 L13
Culgoa Floodplain National Park Qld 17 Q1, 110 D12
Culla Vic. 40 D2, 42 E13
Cullacabardee WA 77 J4
Cullen Bullen NSW 10 F3, 12 I6
Cullendulla NSW 20 H7, 27 O6
Culler NSW 12 G11, 20 F3
Culloden Vic. 39 N4, 48 D13
Cullulleraine Vic. 18 C7, 44 D4
Cumberland Park SA 54 H9
Cumborah NSW 14 B6
Cummins SA 60 D7
Cumnock NSW 12 F4
Cundare Vic. 36 A9
Cundeelee Community WA 83 L6
Cunderdin WA 80 G3, 82 E7
Cungena SA 60 A1, 69 Q11
Cungulla Qld 115 Q13
Cunjurong Point NSW 27 Q3
Cunliffe SA 60 I6
Cunnamulla Qld 110 A10, 121 R10
Cunningar NSW 12 E10, 20 C3
Cunningham Qld 108 D12
Cunningham SA 60 I7
Cunninyeuk NSW 18 H10, 45 O10
Cuprona Tas. 130 G6
Curara WA 82 C3
Curban NSW 14 D12
Curdie Vale Vic. 41 J10
Curl Curl NSW 5 Q3, 7 O13
Curlewis NSW 14 H11
Curlwaa NSW 18 D6, 44 F2
Currabubula NSW 15 J11
Curramulka SA 60 I8
Currarong NSW 13 K12
Currawang NSW 12 H11, 20 F4
Currawarna NSW 12 A12, 19 Q10
Currawinya National Park Qld 17 J1, 121 O12
Currency Creek SA 59 H7
Currie Tas. 128 A9
Currigee Qld 109 O12
Currimundi Qld 109 N2
Currowan Corner Upper NSW 12 I13, 20 H6, 27 N5
Currumbin Qld 111 Q10
Curtin ACT 24 E12, 25 C3
Curtin Springs NT 98 F12
Curtinye SA 60 F3, 62 E13
Curtis Island National Park Qld 113 P11
Curyo Vic. 18 F12, 43 J3
Custon SA 42 A7, 70 I7
Cuttabri NSW 14 F8
Cygnet Tas. 126 F10, 129 K10
Cygnet River SA 60 I12
Cynthia Qld 111 L3

D'Aguilar Qld 109 L4
D'Aguilar National Park Qld 109 K6
D'Entrecasteaux National Park WA 79 F13, 80 C11, 82 C12
Daceyville NSW 9 P4
Dadswells Bridge Vic. 42 I11
Dahlen Vic. 42 G9
Dahwilly NSW 19 K11
Daintree Qld 115 M5
Daintree National Park Qld 115 L5, 115 M4
Daisy Dell Tas. 130 H9
Daisy Hill Qld 107 O9

Daisy Hill Vic. 41 O1, 43 O12
Dajarra Qld 118 E6
Dakabin Qld 109 M6
Dalbeg Qld 112 G3
Dalby Qld 108 A4, 111 M8
Dalgety NSW 20 D10, 26 E13, 49 L4
Dalkeith WA 74 E7
Dallarnil Qld 111 N3
Dalma Qld 113 N11
Dalmalee Vic. 42 G5
Dalmeny NSW 20 H8, 27 N11, 49 R2
Dalmorton NSW 15 N6
Dalton NSW 12 G11, 20 E3
Dalveen Qld 15 M2, 111 N11
Dalwallinu WA 82 D5
Daly River NT 92 B12, 94 D8
Daly Waters NT 96 I3
Dalyston Vic. 37 N13, 38 F9
Dalyup WA 83 J10
Dampier WA 81 G1
Dandaloo NSW 12 C2
Dandaragan WA 82 C6
Dandenong Vic. 35 G5, 37 K8, 38 D5
Dandenong Ranges Vic. 34 F11
Dandenong Ranges National Park Vic. 34 F10, 37 L6, 38 E4, 50 A11
Dandenong South Vic. 35 H6
Dandongadale Vic. 47 O8, 48 A6
Dangarfield NSW 13 L2
Dangarsleigh NSW 15 L9
Dangin WA 80 G4
Danyo Vic. 44 C10
Darby Falls NSW 12 F8, 20 D1
Darbyshire Vic. 48 E2
Dardadine WA 80 F7
Dardanup WA 79 G5, 80 C8
Dareton NSW 18 D6, 44 F2
Dargo Vic. 39 O2, 47 R13, 48 D11
Dark Corner NSW 10 E3, 12 I6
Darkan WA 80 E8
Darke Peak SA 60 E4
Darkwood NSW 15 O8
Darley Vic. 36 G5
Darling Downs Qld 108 B6, 111 M9
Darling Point NSW 5 O10
Darlinghurst NSW 5 N10
Darlington Tas. 127 P2, 129 P7
Darlington Vic. 41 K7
Darlington WA 78 D4, 80 D3
Darlington Point NSW 19 N8
Darnick NSW 18 H2
Darnum Vic. 37 Q10, 38 I7
Daroobalgie NSW 12 D6
Darr Qld 112 A10, 119 O10
Darra Qld 106 E7
Darraweit Guim Vic. 37 J3, 38 C1, 46 F12
Darriman Vic. 39 M9
Dart Dart Vic. 42 G7
Dartmoor Vic. 40 C6
Dartmouth Qld 112 B11, 119 P11
Dartmouth Vic. 20 A10, 48 E5
Darwin NT 89, 90 E10, 92 C3, 94 D5
Dattuck Vic. 42 H2, 44 H12
Daveyston SA 58 E4
Davidson NSW 5 M1, 7 K11
Davis Creek NSW 13 L2
Davistown NSW 21 G7
Daw Park SA 54 H11
Dawes Qld 111 L2
Dawesville WA 78 A10, 80 C6
Dawson SA 61 M2, 63 L12
Dawson Vic. 39 L5
Dawsons Hill NSW 13 L2
Dayboro Qld 109 L5
Daylesford Vic. 36 E2, 41 Q2, 43 Q13, 46 B12
Daymar Qld 14 E2, 110 H12
Daysdale NSW 19 O12, 47 M1
Daytrap Vic. 45 J10
Daytrap Corner Vic. 45 J10
Dead Horse Gap NSW 26 A13
Deagon Qld 104 H4
Deakin ACT 23 A13, 24 F12, 25 E2
Deakin WA 68 A5, 83 R6
Dean Vic. 36 D3, 41 P3, 46 B12
Deanmill WA 80 D10
Deans Marsh Vic. 36 D12, 41 O9
Deception Bay Qld 109 M5, 111 Q8
Deddick Vic. 20 C11, 49 J8
Deddington Tas. 131 N10

Dederang Vic. 47 Q6, 48 C4
Dee Lagoon Tas. 128 I4
Dee Why NSW 5 Q2, 7 O12, 11 P7
Deep Creek Vic. 20 A11, 48 F7
Deep Lead Vic. 43 J11
Deepwater NSW 15 M5
Deepwater National Park Qld 111 N1, 113 Q13
Deer Park Vic. 32 D6
Deeral Qld 115 N7
Delamere SA 59 C8
Delaneys Creek Qld 109 L4
Delatite Vic. 37 R1, 47 L11
Delburn Vic. 37 R11, 39 J8
Delegate NSW 20 E11, 49 M8
Delegate River Vic. 20 D11, 49 L8
Dellicknora Vic. 20 D12, 49 K8
Deloraine Tas. 131 J9
Delta Qld 112 I2
Delungra NSW 15 J6
Delvine Vic. 39 O5
Denham WA 81 B10
Deniliquin NSW 19 L11
Denistone NSW 4 G5
Denman NSW 13 K3
Denman SA 68 D4
Denmark WA 80 G13, 82 E12
Dennes Point Tas. 126 I9, 129 L10
Dennington Vic. 40 H9
Denver Vic. 36 F2, 41 Q2, 43 Q13, 46 C11
Depot Beach NSW 27 O6
Deptford Vic. 20 A13, 39 Q3, 48 F11
Derby Tas. 131 O7
Derby WA 43 P9, 46 B8
Derby WA 87 J7
Dereel Vic. 36 C6, 41 O5
Dergholm Vic. 40 B3
Dering Vic. 44 G11
Deringulla NSW 14 F12
Dernancourt SA 55 M1, 57 M12
Derrinal Vic. 46 E9
Derrinallum Vic. 41 L6
Derriwong NSW 12 B5, 19 R3
Derwent Bridge Tas. 128 H3, 130 H13
Derwent Park Tas. 124 E3
Detention River Tas. 130 E4
Detpa Vic. 42 F5
Deua National Park NSW 20 G7, 27 K8, 49 P1
Devenish Vic. 47 K5
Devlins Bridge Vic. 37 M3
Devoit Tas. 131 L7
Devon Vic. 39 L9
Devon Park Qld 108 D6
Devon Park SA 54 H3
Devonian Reef National Parks WA 87 L8
Devonport Tas. 130 I6
Dewars Pool WA 80 E2
Dharug National Park NSW 11 N3, 13 L6, 21 A9
Dhulura NSW 12 B12, 19 Q10
Dhuragoon NSW 19 J10, 45 Q10
Dhurringile Vic. 46 H7
Diamantina National Park Qld 118 H11
Diamond Beach NSW 13 P1
Diamond Creek Vic. 33 Q2
Diamond Valley Qld 109 M2
Dianella WA 76 I9
Diapur Vic. 42 D7
Dickson ACT 24 H7
Diddleum Plains Tas. 131 N8
Didillibah Qld 109 N1
Digby Vic. 40 D5
Diggers Rest Vic. 36 I4, 38 B3
Diggora Vic. 46 E6
Dilkoon NSW 15 P5
Dilston Tas. 131 L8
Dimboola Vic. 42 F7
Dimbulah Qld 115 L7
Dingabledinga SA 59 G4
Dingee Vic. 43 Q7, 46 C6
Dingley Vic. 35 E4
Dingo Qld 113 L11
Dingo Beach Qld 113 J2
Dingup WA 80 D10
Dingwall Vic. 43 O3, 46 A2
Dinmont Vic. 41 N11
Dinner Plain Vic. 47 R10, 48 D8
Dinninup WA 80 E9
Dinoga NSW 14 I7
Dinyarrak Vic. 42 B7, 70 I6
Direk SA 57 J1

Dirranbandi Qld 14 C2, 110 G12
Dixie Vic. 41 K9
Dixons Creek Vic. 37 M4, 38 F2, 46 I13, 50 C5
Djuan Qld 108 F4
Dobbyn Qld 118 F1
Dobroyd Point NSW 5 J10
Docker Vic. 47 M7
Docker River Community NT 85 R9, 98 A11
Doctors Creek Qld 108 E4
Doctors Flat Vic. 20 A12, 39 Q1, 48 F10
Dodges Ferry Tas. 127 L6, 129 N8
Dolans Bay NSW 9 K12
Dolls Point NSW 9 M8
Don Tas. 130 I6
Don Valley Vic. 37 N6, 50 E9
Donald Vic. 43 K7
Doncaster Vic. 33 P7
Doncaster East Vic. 33 Q7
Dongara WA 82 B4
Donnybrook Qld 109 N4
Donnybrook Vic. 37 J4, 38 C2, 46 F13
Donnybrook WA 79 H6, 80 C8, 82 C10
Donovans Landing SA 40 A7, 70 I12
Donvale Vic. 33 R7, 34 A8
Doo Town Tas. 127 O9
Dooboobetic Vic. 43 L7
Doodlakine WA 80 H2
Dooen Vic. 42 H9
Dookie Vic. 47 J5
Doolandella Qld 106 F9
Doomben Qld 104 I9
Dooralong NSW 11 P1
Dopewora Vic. 42 C10
Doreen NSW 14 F7
Dorodong Vic. 40 B2, 70 I10
Dorrigo NSW 15 O8
Dorrigo National Park NSW 15 O8
Dorrington Qld 104 E10
Double Bay NSW 5 O10
Doubleview WA 76 C10
Doughboy NSW 12 H12, 20 G5, 27 K2
Douglas Qld 108 E6
Douglas Vic. 42 E11
Douglas Park NSW 11 K12
Douglas-Apsley National Park Tas. 129 P1, 131 Q11
Dover Tas. 126 E12, 129 K11
Dover Heights NSW 5 Q10, 11 O8
Doveton Vic. 35 I5
Dowerin WA 80 F1
Dowlingville SA 61 J7
Downer ACT 24 H6
Downside NSW 12 B12, 19 R10
Doyalson NSW 11 Q1, 13 M5
Drake NSW 15 N3, 111 O12
Dreeite Vic. 36 A9, 41 N8
Drewvale Qld 107 J10
Drik Drik Vic. 40 C7
Drillham Qld 111 J7
Dripstone NSW 12 F4
Dromana Vic. 37 J11, 38 D8
Dromedary Tas. 126 G3, 129 L7
Dropmore Vic. 46 I10
Drouin Vic. 37 P9, 38 H6
Drouin South Vic. 37 P10, 38 H6
Drumborg Vic. 40 D7
Drummartin Vic. 43 R7, 46 D6
Drummond Vic. 36 F1, 41 Q1, 43 Q12, 46 C11
Drummoyne NSW 5 J9
Drung Drung Vic. 42 H9
Drung Drung South Vic. 42 H10
Dry Creek SA 56 H10
Dry Creek Vic. 47 K9
Dryander National Park Qld 113 J2
Drysdale Vic. 36 H9, 38 B6
Drysdale River National Park WA 87 O3
Duaringa Qld 113 M11
Dubbo NSW 12 E2
Dubelling WA 80 G4
Dublin SA 61 K7
Duchess Qld 118 F5
Duckmaloi NSW 10 E7
Duddo Vic. 44 C10
Dudinin WA 80 H6
Dudley Vic. 38 G10
Dudley Park SA 54 H2
Duffholme Vic. 42 E9
Duffy ACT 24 B13, 25 A3
Duffys Forest NSW 7 K7

Dulacca Qld 111 J7
Dularcha National Park Qld 109 M2
Dullah NSW 12 A11, 19 Q9
Dulong Qld 109 M1
Dululu Qld 113 N12
Dulwich SA 55 K7
Dulwich Hill NSW 5 J12, 9 L2
Dumbalk Vic. 37 Q13, 38 I9
Dumberning WA 80 F7
Dumbleyung WA 80 H8, 82 E10
Dumosa Vic. 18 G13, 43 L4
Dunach Vic. 36 B1, 41 O1, 43 O12
Dunalley Tas. 127 M6, 129 N9
Dunbogan NSW 15 O12
Duncraig WA 76 C5
Dundas NSW 4 E6
Dundas Qld 109 J6
Dundas Tas. 128 D1, 130 E11
Dundas Valley NSW 4 E5
Dundee NSW 15 M5
Dundee Beach NT 94 C6
Dundinin WA 82 E9
Dundonnell Vic. 41 K6
Dundurrabin NSW 15 O7
Dunedoo NSW 12 G1
Dungog NSW 13 N3
Dungowan NSW 15 K11
Dunk Island Qld 115 O9
Dunkeld NSW 10 B4, 12 H6
Dunkeld Vic. 40 H4
Dunlop ACT 24 A3
Dunmarra NT 96 I4
Dunmore NSW 12 C4
Dunmore Vic. 40 G7
Dunneworthy Vic. 41 K1, 43 K12
Dunnstown Vic. 36 D4, 41 P3, 46 B13
Dunolly Vic. 43 O10
Dunorlan Tas. 131 J8
Dunrobin Vic. 40 C4
Dunsborough WA 79 C7, 80 B9, 82 B10
Duntroon ACT 24 I10, 25 G1
Dunwich Qld 109 P8, 111 Q9
Durack Qld 106 F8
Dural NSW 6 B8
Duranillin WA 80 F8, 82 D10
Durdidwarrah Vic. 36 E6, 41 Q5
Durham Lead Vic. 36 C5, 41 O4
Durham Ox Vic. 18 I13, 43 P5, 46 A4
Duri NSW 15 J11
Durong Qld 111 M6
Durran Durra NSW 12 I12, 20 G5, 27 L3
Durras NSW 20 H7, 27 O6
Durundur Qld 109 K3
Dutson Vic. 39 N7
Dutton SA 58 H3, 61 M7
Dutton Park Qld 106 G2
Duverney Vic. 36 B8, 41 N6
Dwarda WA 78 H11, 80 E6
Dwellingup WA 78 D11, 80 D6, 82 C9
Dwyers NSW 17 O6
Dynnyrne Tas. 124 G10
Dysart Qld 113 J9
Dysart Tas. 126 H1

Eagle Bay WA 79 B6, 80 A8
Eagle Farm Qld 105 J9
Eagle Heights Qld 109 N12
Eagle Junction Qld 104 G9
Eagle On The Hill SA 55 M10
Eagle Point Vic. 39 Q5
Eagleby Qld 107 Q11
Eaglehawk Vic. 43 Q9, 46 B8
Eaglehawk Neck Tas. 127 N8, 129 O9
Earlando Qld 113 J2
Earlston Vic. 47 J7
Earlwood NSW 4 I13, 9 K3
East Boyd NSW 20 G12, 49 Q8
East Brisbane Qld 104 H12, 106 H1
East Cannington WA 75 N7
East Fremantle WA 74 C10
East Gresford NSW 13 M3
East Haldon Qld 108 G10
East Hills NSW 8 E6
East Jindabyne NSW 26 D12
East Kurrajong NSW 11 L5
East Lynne NSW 27 O6
East Melbourne Vic. 30 I6
East Perth WA 72 H5, 74 I3
East Point NT 90 C2

East Sydney NSW 2 G9
East Victoria Park WA 75 J6
East Yolla Tas. 130 F6
Eastern View Vic. 36 E12, 41 P10
Eastlakes NSW 9 O4
Eastwood NSW 4 G5
Eastwood SA 52 I13, 55 J7
Eaton WA 79 G4, 80 C8
Eatons Hill Qld 104 C5
Eatonsville NSW 15 O6
Eba SA 61 N6
Ebden Vic. 47 Q4, 48 C2
Ebenezer NSW 11 L5
Ebenezer Qld 109 J9
Ebor NSW 15 N8
Eccleston NSW 13 M2
Echuca Vic. 19 K13, 46 E4
Echuca Village Vic. 19 K13, 46 F4
Echunga SA 58 D12, 59 I3
Eddington Vic. 43 O10, 46 A9
Eddystone Point Tas. 131 R6
Eden NSW 20 G11, 49 Q8
Eden Hill WA 77 M10
Eden Hills SA 54 H13
Eden Park Vic. 37 K3
Eden Valley SA 58 G6, 61 M8
Edenhope Vic. 42 C11
Edens Landing Qld 107 O12
Edgcumbe Beach Tas. 130 E4
Edgecliff NSW 5 O11, 9 Q1
Edgecombe Vic. 36 G1
Edgeroi NSW 14 G7
Edgewater WA 76 D1
Edi Vic. 47 N7
Edi Upper Vic. 47 N8
Edillilie SA 60 D7
Edith NSW 10 E8, 12 I7
Edith Creek Tas. 130 C5
Edith River NT 94 F9
Edithburgh SA 60 I10
Edithvale Vic. 35 D7
Edmonton Qld 115 N7
Edmund Kennedy National Park Qld 115 N9
Edwardstown SA 54 G11
Egg Lagoon Tas. 128 A8
Eidsvold Qld 111 M3
Eight Mile Plains Qld 107 K6
Eildon Vic. 37 P2, 47 K11
Einasleigh Qld 115 J10
Ejanding WA 80 F1
Ekibin Qld 106 H3
El Arish Qld 115 N9
Elaine Vic. 36 D6, 41 P5
Elands NSW 15 N12
Elaroo Qld 113 J4
Elbow Hill SA 60 G5
Elcombe NSW 14 I6
Elderslie Tas. 126 F1, 129 K7
Eldon Tas. 129 M6
Eldorado Vic. 47 N5, 48 A3
Electrona Tas. 126 H8
Elimbah Qld 109 M4, 111 P8
Elizabeth SA 57 M1, 58 B7, 61 L8, 70 C1
Elizabeth Bay NSW 5 N10
Elizabeth Beach NSW 13 P2
Elizabeth East NSW 57 N1
Elizabeth Grove SA 57 M2
Elizabeth Town Tas. 131 J8
Elizabeth Vale SA 57 M3
Ellalong NSW 13 L4
Ellam Vic. 18 D13, 42 G5
Ellangowan Qld 108 D11
Ellen Grove Qld 106 E9
Ellenborough NSW 15 N12
Ellendale Tas. 126 B2, 129 J7
Ellerslie Vic. 41 J8
Ellerston NSW 13 L1, 15 K13
Ellesmere Qld 108 E1
Elliminyt Vic. 36 B11, 41 N9
Ellinbank Vic. 37 P10, 38 H7
Elliott NT 97 J6
Elliott Tas. 130 F6
Elliott Heads Qld 111 O2
Ellis Beach Qld 115 M6
Elliston SA 60 A5
Elmhurst Vic. 41 L1, 43 L12
Elmore Vic. 46 E6
Elong Elong NSW 12 F2

Elphinstone Qld 108 E11
Elphinstone Vic. 43 R12, 46 C10
Elsey National Park NT 94 I11
Elsinore NSW 17 L10
Elsmore NSW 15 K6
Elsternwick Vic. 33 L12
Eltham NSW 15 Q3, 111 Q12
Eltham Vic. 33 Q4
Elwomple SA 61 N10, 70 E3
Elwood Vic. 33 K11
Embleton WA 77 K10
Emerald Qld 112 I11
Emerald Vic. 37 M7, 38 F5, 50 C13
Emerald Beach NSW 15 P7
Emerald Hill NSW 14 H10
Emerald Springs Wayside Inn NT 92 H11, 94 F8
Emita Tas. 128 A11
Emmaville NSW 15 L5
Emmdale Roadhouse NSW 17 J10
Emmet Qld 121 P2
Empire Bay NSW 21 G8
Empire Vale NSW 15 Q3, 111 Q13
Emu Vic. 43 M9
Emu Bay SA 60 H11
Emu Creek Qld 108 E10
Emu Downs SA 61 M5
Emu Junction SA 67 J10
Emu Park Qld 113 O10
Endeavour Hills Vic. 35 I4, 37 L8
Endeavour River National Park Qld 115 L3
Eneabba WA 82 B5
Enfield NSW 4 H11, 9 J1
Enfield SA 57 J12, 58 B9
Enfield Vic. 36 C6, 41 O5
Engadine NSW 8 F12
Englefield Vic. 40 E2, 42 E13
English Town Tas. 131 N9
Enmore NSW 5 K12, 9 M2, 15 M9
Enngonia NSW 17 N2
Enoch Point Vic. 37 R3
Enoggera Qld 104 E10
Ensay Vic. 20 B12, 39 R1, 48 G10
Ensay South Vic. 20 A13, 39 Q1, 48 G10
Eppalock Vic. 46 D9
Epping NSW 4 G4
Epping Vic. 33 M1
Epping Forest Tas. 129 M1, 131 M11
Epsom Vic. 43 R9, 46 C8
Ercildoun Vic. 36 B3
Erica Vic. 39 J5
Erigolia NSW 19 O6
Erikin WA 80 H3
Erina NSW 11 P4, 21 G6
Erindale SA 55 M6
Erith SA 61 K7
Erldunda NT 98 I11
Ermington NSW 4 F7
Erobin Qld 105 Q10
Eromanga Qld 121 M7
Erriba Tas. 130 H8
Erringibba National Park Qld 111 J8
Errinundra Vic. 20 D12, 49 L10
Errinundra National Park Vic. 20 D12, 49 L10
Erskine Park NSW 11 L8
Erskineville NSW 5 L12, 9 N2
Esk Qld 108 I5, 111 O8
Eskdale Vic. 47 R6, 48 D4
Esmond Vic. 19 O13, 47 L4
Esperance WA 83 J10
Essendon Vic. 32 I5
Essington NSW 10 C7
Ethelton SA 56 C11
Etmilyn WA 78 E11
Eton Qld 113 K5
Ettalong Beach NSW 11 P5, 21 G8
Ettamogah NSW 19 Q13, 47 P3, 48 C1
Ettrick NSW 15 P2, 111 P12
Euabalong NSW 19 P3
Euabalong West NSW 19 O3
Euchareena NSW 12 G4
Eucla WA 68 A8, 83 R7
Eucla National Park WA 68 A8, 83 R7
Eucumbene NSW 20 D8, 26 D10, 49 K2
Eudlo Qld 109 M1
Eudunda SA 61 M6
Eugowra NSW 12 E6
Eujinyn WA 80 I3
Eulo Qld 121 Q11

Eumundi Qld 111 P6
Eumungerie NSW 12 E1, 14 D13
Eungai Creek NSW 15 O10
Eungella NSW 15 Q1
Eungella Qld 113 J5
Eungella National Park Qld 113 J4
Eurack Vic. 36 B9, 41 O7
Euramo Qld 115 N9
Euratha NSW 19 P6
Eurelia SA 61 K1, 63 K11
Euri Creek Qld 112 I2
Eurimbula National Park Qld 113 Q12
Eurobodalla NSW 20 G8, 27 M11, 49 R2
Eurobodalla National Park NSW 27 N12, 49 R3
Euroa Vic. 46 I8
Eurobin Vic. 47 P7, 48 B5
Eurong Qld 111 Q4
Eurongilly NSW 12 C11, 20 A4
Euston NSW 18 F8, 45 J6
Evandale SA 55 K4
Evandale Tas. 131 M9
Evans Head NSW 15 Q4, 111 Q13
Evans Plains NSW 10 B4
Evansford Vic. 36 B2, 41 N1, 43 N12
Evatt ACT 24 D4
Everard Junction WA 85 L9
Evergreen Qld 108 D4
Eversley Vic. 41 L1, 43 L12
Everton Vic. 47 N6, 48 A4
Everton Hills Qld 104 D8
Everton Park Qld 104 E8
Ewens Ponds SA 70 H13
Exeter NSW 56 C11
Exeter Tas. 131 L7
Exford Vic. 36 H5, 38 B3
Exmouth WA 81 C3
Expedition National Park Qld 110 H3
Exton Tas. 131 K9
Eyre Peninsula SA 60 C6

Fadden ACT 25 E8
Fairfield NSW 4 A10
Fairfield Qld 106 G2
Fairfield Vic. 33 M7
Fairhaven Vic. 20 G13, 36 E12, 37 L11, 41 P10, 49 Q11
Fairholme NSW 12 B6, 19 R4
Fairley Vic. 43 O3, 45 O13, 46 A1
Fairlight NSW 5 P5
Fairneyview Qld 109 J8
Fairview Vic. 43 M5
Fairview Park SA 57 Q7
Fairy Dell Vic. 46 E5
Fairy Hill NSW 15 P3, 111 P12
Falls Creek NSW 13 K11, 20 I4
Falls Creek Vic. 47 R9, 48 D7
Falmouth Tas. 131 Q9
Family Islands National Park Qld 115 O9
Fannie Bay NT 90 D6
Faraday Vic. 43 Q11, 46 C10
Farleigh Qld 113 K5
Farnborough Qld 113 O10
Farnham NSW 12 G4
Farrell Flat SA 61 L5
Farrer ACT 25 D6
Fassifern Valley Qld 109 J12
Faulconbridge NSW 11 J7
Fawcett Vic. 37 O1
Fawkner Vic. 33 K4, 37 J5
Feilton Tas. 126 E4, 129 K8
Felixstow SA 55 L3
Felton East Qld 108 D10, 111 N10
Felton South Qld 108 C10
Fentonbury Tas. 126 C2, 129 J7
Fentons Creek Vic. 43 N8
Fern Hill Vic. 36 G2
Fern Tree Tas. 124 C12, 126 H6, 129 L9
Fernbank Vic. 39 O5, 48 E13
Ferndale NSW 15 P11
Ferndale WA 75 L9
Ferndene Tas. 130 H6
Fernihurst Vic. 43 O6, 46 A5
Fernlees Qld 112 I12
Ferntree Gully Vic. 34 D12, 37 L7
Fernvale Qld 109 J7, 111 P9
Ferny Creek Vic. 34 E12
Ferny Grove Qld 104 B9
Ferny Hills Qld 104 C9
Ferryden Park SA 54 G2, 56 G13

Fields Find WA 82 D4
Fiery Flat Vic. 43 O7, 46 A6
Fifield NSW 12 B4, 19 R2
Fig Tree Pocket Qld 106 D4
Finch Hatton Qld 113 J5
Findon SA 54 E4
Fine Flower Creek NSW 15 O5
Fingal Qld 15 Q1
Fingal Tas. 129 P1, 131 P10
Finke NT 99 K12
Finke Gorge National Park NT 98 H9
Finley NSW 19 M12, 46 I1
Finniss SA 59 I6, 61 L11, 70 C3
Firle SA 55 L4
Fish Creek Vic. 38 I10
Fish Point Vic. 43 O1, 45 O11
Fisher ACT 25 B5
Fisher SA 68 G4
Fishermans Bend Vic. 33 J9
Fishery Falls Qld 115 N7
Fiskville Vic. 36 F5, 41 Q4
Fitzgerald Tas. 126 B3, 128 I7
Fitzgerald River National Park WA 82 G11
Fitzgibbon Qld 104 F4
Fitzroy SA 52 D2, 54 H3
Fitzroy Vic. 30 H4, 33 K8
Fitzroy Crossing WA 87 L9
Fitzroy Island National Park Qld 115 N7
Fitzroy North Vic. 33 K7
Five Dock NSW 5 J10
Five Ways NSW 12 A2, 17 Q12
Flaggy Rock Qld 113 L7
Flagstaff Gully Tas. 125 J5
Flagstone Creek Qld 108 G8
Flamingo Beach Vic. 39 O7
Flaxley SA 58 D12, 59 I3
Flaxton Qld 109 M1
Fleming ton Vic. 33 J7
Fleurieu Peninsula SA 59 E7, 61 K12, 70 A4
Flinders Qld 109 K10
Flinders Vic. 37 J12, 38 D9
Flinders Bay WA 79 C13
Flinders Chase National Park SA 60 F13
Flinders Group National Park Qld 116 G11
Flinders Island Tas. 128 B10, 131 R1
Flinders Park SA 54 F5
Flinders Ranges SA 63 K9
Flinders Ranges National Park SA 63 K7
Flinton Qld 110 I10
Flintstone Tas. 129 J2, 131 K12
Floreat WA 74 D2, 76 D13
Florey ACT 24 C5
Florida NSW 17 O10
Florida WA 78 A10
Florieton SA 61 N5
Flowerdale Tas. 130 F5
Flowerdale Vic. 37 L2, 38 E1, 46 H12
Flowerpot Tas. 126 H11, 129 L10
Flowery Gully Tas. 131 K7
Flying Fish Point Qld 115 N8
Flying Fox Qld 109 M13
Flynn ACT 24 C4
Flynn Vic. 39 L7
Flynns Creek Vic. 39 K7
Foleyvale Aboriginal Community Qld 113 M11
Footscray Vic. 32 I8, 37 J6, 38 C4
Forbes NSW 12 D6
Forcett Tas. 127 L5
Fords SA 58 E3
Fords Bridge NSW 17 M4
Forest Tas. 130 D4
Forest Den National Park Qld 112 C7, 119 Q7
Forest Glen NSW 6 A2
Forest Glen Qld 109 M1
Forest Hill NSW 12 B12, 19 R10, 20 A5
Forest Hill Qld 108 H8
Forest Hill Vic. 33 R10, 34 A10
Forest Lake Qld 106 E9
Forest Range SA 58 D10, 59 I1
Forest Reefs NSW 12 G6
Forestdale Qld 106 G11
Forester Tas. 131 O6
Forestville NSW 5 M3, 7 K13
Forge Creek Vic. 39 P5
Formartin Qld 108 B6
Forrest ACT 23 C12, 24 G12, 25 E2
Forrest Vic. 36 B13, 41 O10
Forrest WA 83 Q6
Forrest Beach Qld 115 O11

Forresters Beach NSW 11 Q4, 21 H4
Forrestfield WA 75 Q5
Forreston SA 58 E8
Forsayth Qld 114 I11
Forster SA 61 N8, 70 E1
Forster NSW 13 P2
Fortescue Roadhouse WA 81 F2
Forth Tas. 130 H6
Fortitude Valley Qld 104 H11
Forty Mile Scrub National Park Qld 115 L9
Foster Vic. 39 J10
Fosterville Vic. 43 R9, 46 D8
Four Mile Creek Tas. 131 Q10
Fowlers Bay SA 69 K9
Fox Ground NSW 13 K11
Framlingham Vic. 41 J8
Frampton NSW 12 C10, 20 B3
Frances SA 42 A9, 70 I8
Francistown Tas. 126 E12, 129 K11
Francois Peron National Park WA 81 B9
Frank Hann National Park WA 82 H9
Frankford Tas. 131 K8
Frankland WA 80 F11, 82 E11
Franklin Tas. 126 E9, 129 K10
Franklin-Gordon Wild Rivers National Park Tas.
  128 F4, 130 F13
Franklinford Vic. 36 E1
Frankston Vic. 35 D12, 37 K9, 38 D6
Frankton SA 58 H2, 61 M7
Fraser ACT 24 C3
Fraser Island Qld 111 Q3
Fraser National Park Vic. 37 P1, 47 K11
Frederickton NSW 15 O10
Freeburgh Vic. 47 Q8, 48 C6
Freeling SA 58 D4, 61 L7
Freemans Reach NSW 11 L5, 13 K7
Freemans Waterhole NSW 13 M5
Freestone Qld 108 F12
Fregon SA 67 J3
Fremantle WA 74 B11, 78 A5, 80 C4, 82 B8
French Island Vic. 37 M11, 38 E8
Frenchs Forest NSW 5 M2, 7 L12, 11 O7
Freshwater Creek Vic. 36 F10, 41 Q8
Frewville SA 55 K8
Freycinet National Park Tas. 129 Q4, 131 Q12
Frogmore NSW 12 F9, 20 D2
Fryerstown Vic. 36 F1
Fulham SA 54 D6
Fulham Vic. 39 M6
Fulham Gardens SA 54 D5
Fullarton SA 55 K8
Fullerton NSW 10 C12, 12 H9, 20 F2
Fumina Vic. 37 Q7
Furner SA 70 G10
Furracabad NSW 15 L6
Fyansford Vic. 36 F9, 41 Q7
Fyshwick ACT 25 H2

Gadara NSW 26 A2
Gaffneys Creek Vic. 37 R4, 39 J2, 47 M13
Gagebrook Tas. 126 H4, 129 L7
Galah Vic. 44 G9
Galaquil Vic. 42 H4
Galaquil East Vic. 42 I4
Galga SA 61 O8, 70 F1
Galiwinku NT 95 M5
Gallanani Qld 108 I5
Gallangowan Qld 111 O6
Galong NSW 12 E10, 20 D3
Galston NSW 6 D6, 11 N6, 13 L7
Gama Vic. 42 I1, 44 I12
Gammon Ranges National Park SA 63 L3
Ganmain NSW 12 A11, 19 Q9
Gannawarra Vic. 43 Q3, 45 Q13, 46 B2
Gapsted Vic. 47 O7, 48 A4
Gapuwiyak NT 95 N5
Garah NSW 14 G4, 110 I13
Garden Island Creek Tas. 126 F11, 129 K11
Gardens of Stone National Park NSW 10 F1, 12 I5
Gardners Bay Tas. 126 F10, 129 K10
Garema NSW 12 D7
Garfield Vic. 37 O9, 38 G6
Garibaldi Vic. 36 C5, 41 O4
Garigal National Park NSW 5 L1, 7 M8, 11 O7
Garland NSW 12 F7
Garra NSW 12 F5
Garran ACT 24 F13, 25 D4
Garrawilla NSW 14 G11
Garvoc Vic. 41 J9

Gary Junction WA 85 M4
Gascoyne Junction WA 81 D8
Gatton Qld 108 H8, 111 O9
Gatum Vic. 40 F3
Gawler SA 58 D5, 61 L8
Gawler Tas. 130 H6
Gayndah Qld 111 N4
Gaythorne Qld 104 E9
Gazette Vic. 40 G6
Geebung Qld 104 G6
Geelong Vic. 36 F9, 38 A6, 41 R7
Geeralying WA 80 F7
Geeveston Tas. 126 D10, 129 K10
Geham Qld 108 F6
Geikie Gorge National Park WA 87 M9
Geilston Bay Tas. 124 H3
Gelantipy Vic. 20 C12, 48 I9
Gellibrand Vic. 36 A13, 41 N10
Gelliondale Vic. 39 L10
Gem Tree NT 99 K7
Gembrook Vic. 37 N8, 38 F5, 50 E13
Genoa Vic. 20 F13, 49 P11
George Town Tas. 131 K6
Georges Creek Vic. 47 R4, 48 D2
Georges Hall NSW 4 B13, 8 D3
Georges Heights NSW 5 O7
Georges Plains NSW 10 B5, 12 H6
Georges River National Park NSW 8 F7, 11 M9
Georgetown Qld 114 I10
Georgetown SA 61 K4
Georgica NSW 15 P2, 111 Q12
Gepps Cross SA 57 J10
Geraldton WA 82 A3
Gerang Gerung Vic. 42 F7
Gerangamete Vic. 36 B12, 41 O10
Geranium SA 61 P11, 70 G3
Geranium Plain SA 61 M6
Gerogery NSW 19 Q12, 47 P2
Gerogery West NSW 19 Q13, 47 P2
Gerringong NSW 13 K11
Geurie NSW 12 F3
Gheringhap Vic. 36 F9
Ghin Ghin Vic. 37 M1
Gibraltar Range National Park NSW 15 M5
Gibson WA 83 J10
Gibsonvale NSW 19 P5
Gidgegannup WA 78 E3, 80 D3
Gidginbung NSW 12 B9, 19 R7, 20 A2
Giffard Vic. 39 N8
Gilbert River Qld 114 G10
Gilberts SA 59 I6
Gilderoy Vic. 50 H11
Giles Corner SA 58 C1, 61 L7
Gilgai NSW 15 K6
Gilgandra NSW 14 D13
Gilgooma NSW 14 D9
Gilgunnia NSW 17 N13, 19 N1
Gilles Plains SA 57 M11
Gilliat Qld 118 I4
Gillieston Vic. 46 G5
Gillingarra WA 82 C6
Gillman SA 56 F10
Gilmore ACT 25 F9
Gilmore NSW 26 A2
Gilston Qld 109 N13
Gin Gin NSW 12 D1, 14 C13
Gin Gin Qld 111 N2
Gindie Qld 112 I11
Gingin WA 80 C2, 82 C7
Ginninderra ACT 24 E3
Ginquam Vic. 44 G5
Gippsland Lakes Vic. 39 R5
Gipsy Point Vic. 20 G13, 49 P11
Giralang ACT 24 E5
Girgarre Vic. 46 F7
Girilambone NSW 17 Q9
Girral NSW 12 A7, 19 Q5
Girraween National Park Qld 15 M3, 111 N12
Girrawheen WA 76 F6
Giru Qld 112 G1, 115 Q13
Gisborne Vic. 36 H3, 38 B2, 46 E13
Gladesville NSW 4 I7, 11 N8
Gladfield Vic. 43 P5, 46 A4
Gladstone NSW 15 P10
Gladstone Qld 113 P12
Gladstone SA 61 K3, 63 J13
Gladstone Tas. 131 P6
Gladstone WA 81 C10
Gladysdale Vic. 37 N6, 38 G4, 50 G10

Glamis NSW 15 M12
Glamorganvale Qld 109 J8
Glandore SA 54 G9
Glanmire NSW 10 C4
Glanville SA 56 B11
Glass House Mountains Qld 109 M3, 111 P7
Glass House Mountains National Park Qld 109 L3
Glaziers Bay Tas. 126 E9
Glebe NSW 5 L10
Glebe Tas. 123 C1, 124 G7
Glen Tas. 131 L7
Glen Alice NSW 13 J5
Glen Aplin Qld 15 M3, 111 N12
Glen Creek Vic. 47 P6, 48 C4
Glen Elgin NSW 15 M5
Glen Esk Qld 108 I5
Glen Forbes Vic. 37 N12, 38 F9
Glen Geddes Qld 113 N10
Glen Helen NT 98 H8
Glen Huntly Vic. 33 N12
Glen Huon Tas. 126 E7, 129 K9
Glen Innes NSW 15 L6
Glen Iris Vic. 33 N10
Glen Osmond SA 55 L9
Glen Waverley Vic. 33 R12, 34 A12, 37 L7
Glen Wills Vic. 20 A11, 48 F7
Glenaire Vic. 41 M12
Glenaladale Vic. 39 O4, 48 D13
Glenalbyn Vic. 43 O8, 46 A7
Glenalta SA 55 K13
Glenariff NSW 17 P8
Glenaroua Vic. 37 J1
Glenbrae Vic. 36 A2
Glenbrook NSW 11 J7
Glenburn Vic. 37 M3, 38 F1, 46 I12, 50 C1
Glenburnie SA 40 A6, 70 I12
Glencoe NSW 15 L7
Glencoe SA 70 H11
Glencoe West SA 70 H11
Glendalough WA 74 F1, 76 F12
Glendambo SA 62 C5
Glendaruel Vic. 36 B2, 41 N2, 43 N13
Glenden Qld 112 I5
Glendevie Tas. 126 E11, 129 K10
Glendinning Vic. 40 F2, 42 F13
Glendon Brook NSW 13 L3
Gleneagle Qld 109 L12
Glenelg SA 54 C11, 58 A10, 59 E1, 61 K9, 70 B2
Glenelg North SA 54 C9
Glenelg South SA 54 D11
Glenfern Qld 109 J3
Glenfern Tas. 126 E5, 129 K8
Glenfyne Vic. 41 K9
Glengarry Tas. 131 K8
Glengarry Vic. 39 K6
Glengower Vic. 36 C1, 41 O1, 43 O12, 46 A11
Glengowrie SA 54 E11
Glenhaven NSW 6 A9, 11 M7
Glenhope Vic. 46 D10
Glenisla Vic. 40 G2, 42 G13
Glenlee Vic. 42 F6
Glenlofty Vic. 41 L1, 43 L12
Glenloth Vic. 18 G13, 43 M5
Glenluce Vic. 36 F1, 41 Q1, 43 Q12, 46 C11
Glenlusk Tas. 126 G5
Glenlyon Vic. 36 F2, 41 Q2, 43 Q13, 46 C11
Glenmaggie Vic. 39 L5
Glenmore NSW 11 J10
Glenmore Vic. 36 F5, 41 Q4
Glenmorgan Qld 110 I8
Glenora Tas. 126 D3, 129 J7
Glenorchy Tas. 124 D3, 126 H5, 129 L8
Glenorchy Vic. 43 J11
Glenore Tas. 131 K9
Glenore Crossing Qld 114 C9, 117 I9
Glenore Grove Qld 108 I8
Glenorie NSW 6 A2, 11 M6
Glenormiston Vic. 41 K8
Glenreagh NSW 15 P7
Glenrowan Vic. 47 M6
Glenroy NSW 10 G5
Glenroy SA 70 H10
Glenroy Vic. 32 I4
Glenside SA 55 K7
Glenunga SA 55 K8
Glenvale Vic. 37 K3, 38 D1, 46 G13
Glenworth Valley NSW 11 O4, 21 B8
Glossodia NSW 11 K5

Glossop SA 61 Q7
Gloucester NSW 13 N1
Glynde SA 55 L4
Gnangara WA 76 G1
Gnarming WA 80 I5
Gnarpurt Vic. 41 M6
Gnarwarre Vic. 36 E9, 41 Q8
Gnotuk Vic. 41 L8
Gnowangerup WA 80 I9, 82 F11
Goangra NSW 14 C7
Gobarralong NSW 12 D12, 20 C4
Gobondery NSW 12 C4
Gobur Vic. 47 J10
Gocup NSW 26 A1
Godfreys Creek NSW 12 F9, 20 D1
Gogango Qld 113 M11
Gol Gol NSW 18 D7, 44 G3
Golconda Tas. 131 M7
Gold Coast Qld 109 O13, 111 R10
Golden Beach Vic. 39 O7
Golden Grove SA 57 P6, 58 C8
Golden Valley Tas. 131 J9
Goldsborough Vic. 43 N10
Goldsmith Tas. 129 L3, 131 M12
Goldsworthy (abandoned) WA 84 D1, 86 C13
Gollan NSW 12 G2
Golspie NSW 10 D13, 12 H9, 20 G2
Goneaway National Park Qld 119 K11
Gongolgon NSW 17 Q6
Gonn Crossing NSW 18 I11, 43 P1, 45 P12
Goobarragandra NSW 12 E13, 20 C6, 26 C3
Good Hope NSW 12 F11, 20 D4
Goodilla NT 92 F9
Goodmans Ford NSW 10 F13
Goodna Qld 106 C9
Goodnight NSW 18 G9, 45 M8
Goodooga NSW 14 A4, 17 R2, 110 E13
Goodwood Qld 111 O3
Goodwood SA 54 H8
Goodwood Tas. 124 E2
Googa Googa Qld 108 G3
Goolgowi NSW 19 M6
Goolma NSW 12 G3
Goolmangar NSW 15 Q3
Gooloogong NSW 12 E7
Goolwa SA 59 I7, 61 L11, 70 C3
Goomalibee Vic. 47 K6
Goomalling WA 80 F1, 82 D7
Goombungee Qld 108 E5, 111 N8
Goomeri Qld 111 O5
Goon Nure Vic. 39 P5
Goondah NSW 12 F11, 20 D3
Goondiwindi Qld 14 H2, 111 K11
Goondooloo SA 61 O9, 70 F1
Goongarrie WA 82 I5
Goongarrie National Park WA 82 I5
Goongee Vic. 44 B9, 61 R10
Goongerah Vic. 20 D12, 49 K10
Goonumbla NSW 12 D5
Gooram Vic. 47 J9
Goorambat Vic. 47 K6
Goorawin NSW 19 M5
Goornong Vic. 46 D7
Gooroc Vic. 43 L7
Gooseberry Hill National Park WA 78 D4
Goovigen Qld 113 N13
Goowarra Qld 113 L11
Gorae Vic. 40 D8
Gorae West Vic. 40 D8
Gordon ACT 25 D12
Gordon NSW 5 J3, 6 H13
Gordon SA 63 J9
Gordon Tas. 126 G11, 129 L11
Gordon Vic. 36 E4, 41 Q3, 46 B13
Gordonvale Qld 115 N7
Gore Hill NSW 5 L7
Gormandale Vic. 39 L7
Gormanston Tas. 128 E3, 130 E12
Gorokan NSW 11 Q2
Goroke Vic. 42 D9
Goschen Vic. 43 M1, 45 N12
Gosford NSW 11 P4, 13 L6, 21 F6
Goshen Tas. 131 Q8
Gosnells WA 75 P13
Gosse SA 60 G12
Goughs Bay Vic. 37 Q1, 47 L11
Goulburn NSW 12 H11, 20 G3
Goulburn River National Park NSW 12 H2
Goulburn Weir Vic. 46 G8

Gould Creek SA 57 P1
Goulds Country Tas. 131 P7
Gowanford Vic. 43 L1, 45 L11
Gowangardie Vic. 47 J6
Gowar East Vic. 43 M8
Gowrie ACT 25 E9
Gowrie Qld 108 E7
Gowrie Park Tas. 130 H8
Goyura Vic. 42 H3
Grabben Gullen NSW 12 G10, 20 F3
Grabine NSW 12 F8
Gracemere Qld 113 N11
Gracetown WA 79 B9, 80 A9, 82 B11
Graceville Qld 106 E4
Gradgery NSW 14 B11
Gradule Qld 14 E2, 110 H11
Grafton NSW 15 P6
Graham NSW 12 F9, 20 D1
Graman NSW 15 J5
Grampians National Park Vic. 40 H1, 42 H12
Grandchester Qld 108 I9
Grange Qld 104 F9
Grange SA 54 C4
Grantham Qld 108 G8, 111 O9
Granton Tas. 126 H4, 129 L8
Grantville Vic. 37 N12, 38 F8
Granville NSW 4 C8
Granville Harbour Tas. 128 B1, 130 C10
Granya Vic. 19 R13, 47 R4, 48 E2
Grass Flat Vic. 42 F9
Grass Patch WA 83 J10
Grassdale Vic. 40 E5
Grassmere Vic. 40 I9
Grasstree Qld 113 L5
Grasstree Hill Tas. 126 I4
Grassy Tas. 128 A9
Gravelly Beach Tas. 131 L7
Gravesend NSW 14 I5
Grawin NSW 14 A6
Grawlin Plains NSW 12 D6
Gray Tas. 129 Q1, 131 Q10
Grays Point NSW 8 I12
Graytown Vic. 46 F9
Gre Gre Vic. 43 K9
Great Barrier Reef Qld 113 M2, 115 N3
Great Basalt Wall National Park Qld 112 C2, 119 R2
Great Keppel Island Qld 113 P10
Great Northern Vic. 47 N3, 48 A1
Great Ocean Road Vic. 36 D13, 41 N12
Great Palm Island Aboriginal Community Qld 115 O11
Great Sandy National Park Qld 111 Q3, 111 Q5
Great Western Vic. 41 J1, 43 J12
Gredgwin Vic. 18 H13, 43 N4
Green Fields SA 57 J7
Green Head WA 82 B5
Green Hill Creek Vic. 36 A1
Green Hills NSW 15 I3
Green Island National Park Qld 115 N6
Green Lake Vic. 42 H10
Green Lake Vic. 43 J2, 45 K12
Green Patch NSW 27 R2
Green Point NSW 21 G6
Greenacre NSW 4 E12, 8 H2
Greenacres SA 55 K2, 57 K13
Greenbushes WA 80 D9
Greendale Vic. 36 F4, 41 Q3, 46 C13
Greenethorpe NSW 12 E8, 20 C1
Greenhill SA 55 O8
Greenhills WA 80 F3
Greenmantle NSW 12 G8
Greenmount Qld 108 E10, 111 N10
Greenmount Vic. 39 L9
Greenmount WA 78 D4
Greenmount East Qld 108 E9
Greenmount National Park WA 78 D4
Greenock SA 58 E4, 61 L7
Greenough WA 82 A4
Greens Beach Tas. 131 K6
Greensborough Vic. 33 P3, 37 K5
Greenslopes Qld 106 H2
Greenvale Qld 115 L12
Greenwald Vic. 40 C7
Greenway ACT 25 B9
Greenways SA 70 G10
Greenwell Point NSW 13 K11, 20 I4
Greenwich NSW 5 L8
Greenwith SA 57 Q4

Greenwood Qld 108 D6
Greenwood WA 76 D5
Greg Greg NSW 20 B8, 48 H1
Gregors Creek Qld 108 I3
Gregory National Park NT 94 C13, 94 E12, 96 C3, 96 E1
Grenfell NSW 12 D8, 20 B1
Grenville Vic. 36 C6, 41 O5
Gresford NSW 13 M3
Greta Vic. 47 M7
Greta West Vic. 47 M7
Gretna Tas. 126 E3, 129 K7
Grevillia NSW 15 O2, 111 P11
Greymare Qld 108 D13
Griffin Qld 104 F1
Griffith ACT 24 H12, 25 F3
Griffith NSW 19 N7
Grimwade WA 79 I7, 80 D9
Gringegalgona Vic. 40 E3
Gritjurk Vic. 40 E4
Grogan NSW 12 C9, 20 B2
Grong Grong NSW 12 A11, 19 P9
Groomsville Qld 108 F6
Grose Vale NSW 11 J6
Grosvenor Qld 111 M4
Grove Tas. 126 F7, 129 K9
Grove Hill NT 92 H10
Grovely Qld 104 D9
Gruyere Vic. 34 I5, 37 M5, 50 C8
Gubbata NSW 19 P5
Guilderton WA 80 B2, 82 C7
Guildford NSW 4 B8
Guildford Tas. 130 F8
Guildford Vic. 36 E1, 41 Q1, 43 Q12, 46 B11
Guildford WA 77 O9, 78 C4
Gular NSW 14 C11
Gulargambone NSW 14 D11
Gulf Creek NSW 15 J7
Gulf Savannah Qld 114 B12, 117 H12
Gulgong NSW 12 H2
Gullewa WA 82 C3
Gulnare SA 61 K4
Gulpa NSW 19 K12, 46 F1
Guluguba Qld 111 J6
Gum Creek SA 61 L5
Gum Lake NSW 18 F2
Gumble NSW 12 E5
Gumbowie SA 61 L2, 63 K13
Gumdale Qld 105 M12, 107 M1
Gumeracha SA 58 E8, 61 L9, 70 C1
Gumlu Qld 112 H2
Gumly Gumly NSW 12 B12, 19 R10
Gunalda Qld 111 P5
Gunbar NSW 19 M6
Gunbar South NSW 19 M6
Gunbower Vic. 19 J13, 43 R4, 46 C3
Gundagai NSW 12 D12, 20 B5
Gundaring WA 80 G8
Gundaroo NSW 12 G11, 20 E4
Gundary NSW 27 M8
Gunderman NSW 11 N4
Gundiah Qld 111 P5
Gundillion NSW 20 F7, 27 K7
Gundowring Vic. 47 Q6, 48 C4
Gundowring North Vic. 47 Q6, 48 C3
Gundy NSW 13 L1
Gunebang NSW 19 P3
Gungahlin ACT 24 G2, 26 G1, 28 F2
Gungal NSW 13 J2
Gunnary NSW 12 F9, 20 D2
Gunnedah NSW 14 H10
Gunner Vic. 44 F10
Gunnewin Qld 110 G5
Gunning NSW 12 G11, 20 E4
Gunning Grach NSW 20 E10, 49 M6
Gunningbland NSW 12 C5
Gunns Plains Tas. 130 G7
Gunpowder Qld 118 E1
Gununa Qld 117 D6
Gunyah Vic. 39 J9
Gurig National Park NT 94 G3
Gurley NSW 14 G6
Gurrai SA 61 Q10, 70 H2
Gurrundah NSW 12 G10, 20 F3
Guthalungra Qld 112 I2
Guthega NSW 20 C9, 26 B12, 49 J4
Guy Fawkes River National Park NSW 15 N7
Guyong NSW 12 G6
Guyra NSW 15 L8

Guys Forest Vic. 20 A8, 48 F2
Gwabegar NSW 14 E9
Gwalia WA 82 I3
Gwandalan NSW 11 R1
Gwandalan Tas. 127 K8, 129 N9
Gwelup WA 76 D8
Gymbowen Vic. 42 D9
Gymea Bay NSW 8 I12
Gympie Qld 111 P6
Gypsum Vic. 44 H10

Haasts Bluff NT 98 G8
Haberfield NSW 5 J11, 9 L1
Hackett ACT 24 I7
Hackham SA 58 A12, 59 F3
Hackney SA 52 H6, 55 J5
Haddon Vic. 36 B4, 41 O3
Haden Qld 108 E5, 111 N8
Hadspen Tas. 131 L9
Hagley Tas. 131 K9
Hahndorf SA 58 D11, 59 I2, 61 L9, 70 C2
Haig WA 83 O6
Haigslea Qld 109 J8
Hail Creek Qld 113 J6
Halbury SA 61 K6
Half Tide Qld 113 L5
Halfway Creek NSW 15 P7
Halfway Mill Roadhouse WA 82 B5
Halidon SA 61 P9, 70 G1
Halifax Qld 115 O11
Hall ACT 24 D2
Hallett SA 61 L4
Hallett Cove SA 58 A11, 59 E2
Hallidays Point NSW 13 P2
Halls Creek WA 87 P9
Halls Gap Vic. 40 I1, 42 I12
Halls Head WA 78 A9
Hallston Vic. 37 Q12, 38 I8
Halton NSW 13 M2
Hamel WA 78 C12, 80 C6
Hamersley WA 76 F7
Hamersley Range WA 81 G3, 84 A4
Hamersley Range National Park WA see **Karijini**
National Park
Hamilton Qld 104 H10
Hamilton SA 58 E1, 61 L7
Hamilton Tas. 126 D1, 129 J6
Hamilton Vic. 40 F5
Hamilton Hill WA 74 C12
Hamilton Island Qld 113 K3
Hamley Bridge SA 58 C2, 61 L7
Hammond SA 61 K1, 63 J11
Hammondville NSW 8 C6
Hampden SA 61 M6
Hampshire Tas. 130 F7
Hampstead Gardens SA 55 K2, 57 K13
Hampton NSW 10 F6, 12 I7
Hampton Qld 108 F6, 111 N8
Hampton Vic. 35 A2
Hann Crossing Qld 116 G13
Hann River Roadhouse Qld 114 I1
Hann Tableland National Park Qld 115 L6
Hannahs Bridge NSW 12 H1
Hannan NSW 19 O5
Hansborough SA 58 G1, 61 M7
Hanson SA 61 L5
Hanwood NSW 19 N7
Happy Valley SA 60 G10
Happy Valley Vic. 36 B5, 41 N4, 45 J6
Harbord NSW 5 Q4
Harcourt Vic. 43 Q11, 46 C10
Harcourt North Vic. 43 Q11, 46 C10
Harden NSW 12 E10, 20 C3
Hardwicke Bay SA 60 H9
Harefield NSW 12 C12, 19 R10, 20 A4
Harford Tas. 131 J7
Hargrave Park NSW 8 A3
Hargraves NSW 12 H4
Harkaway Vic. 37 M8
Harlin Qld 108 I3, 111 O7
Harrietville Vic. 47 Q9, 48 C7
Harrington NSW 13 P1, 15 O13
Harris Park NSW 4 C7
Harrismith WA 80 H6
Harrisville Qld 109 J10
Harrogate SA 58 F10
Harrow Vic. 40 D1, 42 D12
Harrys Creek Vic. 47 J8
Harston Vic. 46 G6

Hart SA 61 K5
Hartley NSW 10 G5, 12 I6
Hartley SA 58 F13
Hartley Vale NSW 10 G5
Hartz Mountains National Park Tas. 126 B10,
129 J10
Harvey WA 79 H2, 80 C7, 82 C10
Harwood NSW 15 Q5
Haslam SA 69 P11
Hassell National Park WA 80 I12, 82 F12
Hastings Tas. 126 D13, 129 J12
Hastings Vic. 37 L11, 38 E7
Hastings Point NSW 15 Q1, 111 R11
Hat Head NSW 15 P10
Hat Head National Park NSW 15 P10
Hatches Creek NT 97 M13, 99 L2
Hatfield NSW 18 H6, 45 O1
Hatherleigh SA 70 G11
Hattah Vic. 18 E9, 44 H7
Hattah-Kulkyne National Park Vic. 18 D8, 44 H6
Hatton Vale Qld 108 I8
Havelock Vic. 43 O11
Haven Vic. 42 G10
Havilah Vic. 47 P7, 48 B5
Hawker ACT 24 B7
Hawker SA 63 J9
Hawkesbury Heights NSW 11 K6
Hawkesbury Region NSW 21
Hawkesdale Vic. 40 H7
Hawks Nest NSW 13 O4
Hawley Beach Tas. 131 J6
Hawthorn SA 55 J9
Hawthorn Vic. 33 L9
Hawthorne Qld 104 I12
Hay NSW 19 K8
Haydens Bog Vic. 20 D12, 49 L8
Hayes Tas. 126 E4, 129 K7
Hayes Creek Wayside Inn NT 92 G11, 94 E8
Hayman Island Qld 113 K2
Haymarket NSW 2 D12
Haysdale Vic. 45 L8
Hazel Park Vic. 39 J10
Hazelbrook NSW 10 I7
Hazeldene Qld 109 J4
Hazeldene Vic. 37 L2, 38 E1, 46 H12
Hazelgrove NSW 10 E6
Hazelmere WA 77 Q10
Hazelwood Vic. 39 J7
Hazelwood Park SA 55 L7
Healesville Vic. 37 N5, 38 F3, 50 E6
Heartbreak Hotel NT 97 N4
Heath Hill Vic. 37 O10, 38 G7
Heathcote NSW 8 E13, 11 M11, 13 L8
Heathcote Vic. 46 E9
Heathcote Junction Vic. 37 K2, 38 D1, 46 G12
Heathcote National Park NSW 8 E13, 11 M11
Heatherton Vic. 35 D3
Heathfield Vic. 40 B4, 70 I11
Heathmere Vic. 40 D8
Heathmont Vic. 34 C10
Heathpool SA 55 L6
Heathvale Vic. 42 H11
Heathwood Qld 106 F10
Hebden NSW 13 L3
Hebel Qld 14 B3, 110 F13
Hectorville SA 55 M4
Hedley Vic. 39 K10
Heidelberg Vic. 33 N5
Heidelberg West Vic. 33 N5
Heka Tas. 130 G7
Helensburgh NSW 11 M11, 13 L9
Helenvale Qld 115 L3
Helidon Qld 108 G8
Hell Hole Gorge National Park Qld 121 O4
Helling NT 94 G9
Hells Gate Roadhouse Qld 117 B8
Hellyer Tas. 130 E4
Hellyer Tas. 130 E4
Hemmant Qld 105 L10
Hendon SA 54 D2
Hendra Qld 104 H9
Henley NSW 5 J8
Henley Beach SA 54 B5, 58 A9
Henley Brook WA 77 P3
Henrietta Tas. 130 F6
Hensley Park Vic. 40 G4
Henty NSW 12 A13, 19 Q11
Henty Vic. 40 D5
Hepburn Springs Vic. 36 E2, 41 Q2, 43 Q13, 46 B12
Herberton Qld 115 M8

Heritage Park Qld 107 J12
Hermannsburg NT 98 H9
Hermidale NSW 17 P10
Hernani NSW 15 N8
Heron Island Qld 113 Q11
Herons Creek NSW 15 O12
Herrick Tas. 131 P6
Herston Qld 104 G11
Hervey Bay Qld 111 P3
Hesket Vic. 36 H2
Hesso SA 62 H9
Hewetsons Mill NSW 15 N2
Hexham NSW 13 M4
Hexham Vic. 41 J7
Heybridge Tas. 130 G6
Heyfield Vic. 39 L5
Heywood Vic. 40 D8
Hiamdale Vic. 39 L7
Hiawatha Vic. 39 K9
Hidden Vale Qld 108 I9
Hidden Valley National Park WA see Mirima
National Park
Hideaway Bay Tas. 126 E11
Higgins ACT 24 B6
High Camp Vic. 36 I1, 46 F11
High Range NSW 10 H13, 13 J9, 20 H2
High Wycombe WA 75 Q1, 77 Q13
Highbury SA 57 P12
Highbury WA 80 G7
Highclere Tas. 130 G6
Highcroft Tas. 127 M10, 129 N10
Higher McDonald NSW 11 M2
Highett Vic. 35 B3
Highfields Qld 108 F7
Highgate SA 55 J9
Highgate WA 74 I2, 76 I13
Highgate Hill Qld 104 G13, 106 G1
Highlands Vic. 37 M1, 46 H10
Highvale Qld 109 K8
Hilgay Vic. 40 D4
Hill End NSW 10 A1, 12 G5
Hill End Vic. 37 R8, 38 I5
Hillarys WA 76 A3, 78 A3
Hillbank SA 57 N3
Hillcrest SA 55 L1, 57 L12
Hillcrest Vic. 36 B4
Hillgrove NSW 15 M9
Hillman WA 80 F8
Hillsdale NSW 9 P5
Hillside Vic. 39 P4, 48 F13
Hillston NSW 19 M4
Hilltop NSW 11 J13, 13 J9, 20 I2
Hilltown SA 61 L5
Hillwood Tas. 131 L7
Hilton SA 54 G7
Hilton WA 74 D12
Hinchinbrook Island National Park Qld 115 O10
Hindmarsh SA 54 G4
Hindmarsh Island SA 59 I8, 70 C4
Hindmarsh Valley SA 59 G7
Hines Hill WA 80 I2
Hinnomunjie Vic. 20 A11, 48 F8
Hirstglen Qld 108 F10
Hobart Tas. 123, 124 G7, 126 H6, 129 L8
Hobbys Yards NSW 10 A7, 12 G7
Hoddle Vic. 38 I10
Hoddles Creek Vic. 37 N6, 38 G4, 50 F10
Hodgson Vale Qld 108 E9
Holbrook NSW 19 R12, 47 R1
Holden Hill SA 57 N11
Holder ACT 24 C13, 25 A4
Holgate NSW 11 P4, 21 G5
Holland Park Qld 106 I3
Hollow Tree Tas. 129 K6
Holly WA 80 G9
Hollydeen NSW 13 K2
Holmview Qld 107 P12
Holmwood NSW 12 F7
Holsworthy Village NSW 8 B6
Holt ACT 24 A5
Holwell Tas. 131 K7
Home Hill Qld 112 H1, 115 Q13
Homebush NSW 4 G10
Homebush Bay NSW 4 F9, 11 N8
Homecroft Vic. 42 I6
Homerton Vic. 40 E8
Homestead Qld 112 D3, 119 R3
Homevale National Park Qld 113 J5
Homewood Vic. 37 M1

Honiton SA 60 I10
Hook Island Qld 113 K2
Hope Forest SA 59 G5
Hope Vale Aboriginal Community Qld 115 L2
Hope Valley SA 57 P11
Hopetoun Vic. 18 E12, 42 H3, 44 H13
Hopetoun WA 82 H11
Hopetoun West Vic. 42 G2, 44 G13
Hopevale Vic. 42 G3
Hoppers Crossing Vic. 32 B11, 36 H7
Hordern Vale Vic. 41 M12
Hornsby NSW 6 F9, 11 N7
Hornsby Heights NSW 6 F7
Hornsdale SA 61 K2, 63 K13
Horrocks Beach WA 82 A3
Horse Lake NSW 16 D12
Horsham SA 59 H4
Horsham Vic. 42 G9
Horsley Park NSW 11 L8
Hoskinstown NSW 12 H13, 20 F6, 27 J3, 28 I5
Hotham Heights Vic. 47 Q10, 48 D8
Hotspur Vic. 40 D6
Houghton SA 57 R10, 58 D8
Hove SA 54 E13
Howard Qld 111 P3
Howard Springs NT 92 D3, 94 E5
Howard Springs National Park NT 92 D3
Howden Tas. 126 H8, 129 L9
Howes Valley NSW 13 K4
Howley NT 92 G10
Howlong NSW 19 P13, 47 O3, 48 A1
Howqua Vic. 37 R2, 47 L11
Howrah Tas. 125 M7, 129 M8
Howth Tas. 130 G6
Hoya Qld 109 J12
Hoyleton SA 61 K6
Huddleston SA 61 K3
Hughenden Qld 112 A4, 119 O4
Hughes ACT 24 F13, 25 D3
Hughes SA 68 C5
Hull River National Park Qld 115 N9
Hume ACT 25 H7
Hume Park NSW 12 F11, 20 D4
Humevale Vic. 37 L3
Humpty Doo NT 92 E3, 94 E6
Humula NSW 12 C13, 20 A6
Hunchy Qld 109 M1
Hungerford Qld 17 J1, 121 O13
Hunter Vic. 46 D6
Hunters Hill NSW 5 J7
Hunterston Vic. 39 M9
Huntingdale WA 75 N12
Huntly Vic. 43 R9, 46 C8
Huon Vic. 47 Q5, 48 C2
Huonville Tas. 126 F8, 129 K9
Hurdle Flat Vic. 47 O6, 48 A4
Hurlstone Park NSW 4 I13, 9 K3
Hurstbridge Vic. 34 A1, 37 L5, 38 E3
Hurstville NSW 9 J6, 11 N9
Huskisson NSW 13 K12, 20 I5, 27 R1
Hutt WA 82 A2
Hyams Beach NSW 27 R2
Hyde Park SA 54 I8
Hyden WA 82 F8
Hynam SA 42 A11, 70 I9

Icy Creek Vic. 37 Q7, 38 I4
Ida Bay Tas. 129 J12
Idalia National Park Qld 121 P2
Iguana Creek Vic. 39 O4, 48 E13
Ilbilbie Qld 113 L6
Ilford NSW 12 I5
Ilfracombe Qld 112 A11, 119 P11
Illabarook Vic. 36 B6, 41 N5
Illabo NSW 12 C11, 20 A4
Illalong Creek NSW 12 E11, 20 D3
Illawarra Vic. 43 J11
Illawarra Coast NSW 13 K12, 20 I7, 27 P6
Illawong NSW 8 G9
Illawong WA 82 B5
Illowa Vic. 40 H9
Iluka NSW 15 Q5
Imanpa Community NT 98 H11
Imbil Qld 111 P6
Impimi NSW 18 H9, 45 O7
Inala Qld 106 F8
Indented Head Vic. 36 I9, 38 B6
Indigo Vic. 47 N4, 48 A2
Indigo Upper Vic. 47 O5, 48 B3

Indooroopilly Qld 106 E2, 109 L8
Ingebyra NSW 20 C10, 49 J5
Ingham Qld 115 N11
Ingle Farm SA 57 L9
Inglegar NSW 14 B12
Ingleside NSW 7 O7
Inglewood Qld 15 K1, 111 L11
Inglewood SA 58 D8
Inglewood Tas. 129 N5
Inglewood Vic. 43 O8, 46 A7
Inglewood WA 77 J11
Ingliston Vic. 36 F5
Ingoldsby Qld 108 H9
Injinoo Qld 116 C3
Injune Qld 110 G5
Inkerman Qld 112 H1
Inkerman SA 61 J7
Inman Valley SA 59 E7
Innaloo WA 76 D10
Innamincka SA 65 Q7, 120 H10
Innes National Park SA 60 G10
Innisfail Qld 115 N8
Innot Hot Springs Qld 115 L8
Interlaken Tas. 129 L4, 131 L13
Inverell NSW 15 K6
Invergordon Vic. 19 M13, 46 I4
Inverleigh Vic. 36 E9, 41 P7
Inverloch Vic. 38 G10
Iona Vic. 37 O9
Ipolera NT 98 G9
Ipswich Qld 109 J9, 111 P9
Iraak Vic. 18 E8, 44 H5
Irishtown Tas. 130 D4
Iron Baron SA 60 H2, 62 G13
Iron Knob SA 60 H1, 62 G12
Iron Range Qld 116 E8
Iron Range National Park Qld 116 E7
Irongate Qld 108 C8
Ironside Qld 106 F2
Irrewarra Vic. 36 B11
Irrewillipe Vic. 36 A12, 41 M9
Irvinebank Qld 115 L8
Irvingdale Qld 108 C4
Irymple Vic. 18 D7, 44 G3
Isaacs ACT 25 E6
Isabella NSW 10 C9, 12 H8, 20 F1
Isabella Plains ACT 25 D10
Isisford Qld 112 A13, 119 P13, 121 O1
Isla Gorge National Park Qld 111 J3
Island Bend NSW 26 C11
Ivanhoe NSW 19 J2
Ivanhoe Vic. 33 M6
Ivory Creek Qld 108 I3
Iwantja (Indulkana) SA 67 N4
Iwupataka NT 98 I8

Jabiru NT 93 P4, 94 H6
Jabiru East NT 93 Q4, 94 H6
Jabuk SA 61 O11, 70 F3
Jack River Vic. 39 K9
Jackadgery NSW 15 O5
Jackeys Marsh Tas. 131 J10
Jackie Junction WA 85 N10
Jackson Qld 110 I7
Jacobs Well Qld 109 O11
Jacobs Well WA 80 F4
Jalloonda Qld 115 O12
Jallumba Vic. 42 F11
Jaloran WA 80 G7
Jamberoo NSW 13 K10
Jambin Qld 113 N13
Jamboree Heights Qld 106 C6
Jamestown SA 61 L3, 63 K13
Jamieson Vic. 37 R2, 38 I1, 47 L12
Jancourt East Vic. 41 L9
Jandakot WA 74 I13, 78 C6
Jandowae Qld 111 L7
Jannali NSW 8 I10
Jardee WA 80 D11
Jardine River National Park Qld 116 C4
Jarklin Vic. 43 P6, 46 A5
Jarra Jarra NT 96 I13, 98 I2
Jarrahdale WA 78 D8, 80 D5
Jarrahmond Vic. 49 J12
Jarrahwood WA 79 G8, 80 C9
Jarvis Creek Vic. 47 R4, 48 D2
Jaurdi WA 82 H6
Jeeralang North Vic. 39 K8
Jeffcott Vic. 43 L7

Jeffcott North Vic. 43 L6
Jemalong NSW 12 C6
Jennacubbine WA 80 E2
Jeogla NSW 15 M9
Jeparit Vic. 42 F6
Jerangle NSW 20 F7, 26 I8, 28 I13
Jericho Qld 112 E11
Jericho Tas. 129 L5
Jericho Vic. 37 R5, 39 J3
Jerilderie NSW 19 M11
Jerrabomberra NSW 25 I7
Jerramungup WA 82 G11
Jerrawa NSW 12 G11, 20 E4
Jerrys Plains NSW 13 K3
Jerseyville NSW 15 P10
Jervis Bay JBT 13 K12, 20 I5, 27 R2
Jervis Bay National Park JBT 13 K12, 27 R2
Jervis Bay National Park NSW 13 K12, 27 R2
Jervois SA 61 N10, 70 E3
Jetsonville Tas. 131 N6
Jiggalong Community WA 84 F6
Jil Jil Vic. 43 K3
Jilliby NSW 11 P2, 13 M6, 21 D1
Jimaringle NSW 19 J11, 45 R10
Jimboomba Qld 109 M11, 111 P10
Jimbour Qld 108 A2, 111 M7
Jimenbuen NSW 20 D10, 49 L6
Jimna Qld 109 J1
Jim's Place Wayside Inn NT 98 I9
Jindabyne NSW 20 D9, 26 C12, 49 K4
Jindalee Qld 106 C5
Jindera NSW 19 P13, 47 P3, 48 B1
Jindivick Vic. 37 P8, 38 H5
Jindong WA 79 D8
Jingalup WA 80 F10
Jingellic NSW 20 A8, 48 F1
Jingili NT 91 F5
Jitarning WA 80 I6, 82 F9
Joadja NSW 13 J10, 20 H2
Joanna SA 40 A1, 42 A12, 70 I9
Joel Joel Vic. 43 K11
Johanna Vic. 41 M12
John Forrest National Park WA 78 D3
Johnburgh SA 63 K11
Johns River NSW 15 O13
Johnsonville Vic. 39 Q4, 48 G13
Jolimont WA 74 E2
Jondaryan Qld 108 C6, 111 M8
Jones Gully Qld 108 F5
Joondalup WA 78 B1
Joondanna WA 76 G11
Josbury WA 80 F7
Josephville Qld 109 L12
Joskeleigh Qld 113 O11
Joyner Qld 104 B1
Jubilee Qld 104 E11
Jubuck WA 80 H5
Judbury Tas. 126 D7, 129 K9
Jugiong NSW 12 E11, 20 C4
Julatten Qld 115 M6
Julia SA 61 M6
Julia Creek Qld 119 J4
Jumbuk Vic. 39 K8
Jumbunna Vic. 37 O12, 38 G9
Junction Hill NSW 15 P6
Junction View Qld 108 G10
Jundah Qld 121 M2
Junee NSW 12 C11, 19 R9, 20 A4
Junee Reefs NSW 12 C11, 20 A3
Jung Vic. 42 H8
Junortoun Vic. 43 R10, 46 C8
Jupiter Creek SA 59 H3
Jura WA 80 I3
Jurien WA 82 B6
Jurunjung Vic. 36 H4

Kaarimba Vic. 46 H4
Kabra Qld 113 N11
Kadina SA 60 I6
Kadnook Vic. 40 C1, 42 C12
Kadungle NSW 12 C4
Kagaru Qld 109 L11
Kaglan WA 80 I12
Kaimkillenbun Qld 108 B3, 111 M8
Kain NSW 20 F7, 27 J6
Kainton SA 61 J6
Kairi Qld 115 M7
Kajabbi Qld 118 F2
Kakadu National Park NT 93 O2, 94 G5

Kalamunda National Park WA 78 D5
Kalangadoo SA 70 H11
Kalangara Qld 109 K3
Kalannie WA 82 D6
Kalaru NSW 20 G10, 49 Q6
Kalbar Qld 109 J11, 111 P10
Kalbarri WA 81 C13, 82 A2
Kalbarri National Park WA 81 C13, 82 A1
Kaleen ACT 24 F5
Kaleentha Loop NSW 18 F1
Kalgoorlie-Boulder WA 82 I6
Kalimna West Vic. 39 R4, 48 G13
Kalinga Qld 104 G8
Kalka SA 66 A1, 85 R11, 98 B13
Kalkallo Vic. 37 J4, 38 C2, 46 F13
Kalkaringi NT 96 D6
Kalkee Vic. 42 G8
Kalkite NSW 26 D12
Kallangur Qld 109 M6
Kallaroo WA 76 A2
Kallista Vic. 34 G12
Kalorama Vic. 34 G9, 50 B10
Kalpienung Vic. 43 M3
Kalpowar Qld 111 M2
Kalumburu WA 87 N2
Kalunga Qld 115 M8
Kalyan SA 61 O9, 70 F1
Kamarah NSW 12 A9, 19 P7
Kamarooka Vic. 43 R8, 46 D6
Kambah ACT 25 B7
Kambalda WA 83 J7
Kamballup WA 80 I11
Kamber NSW 14 D12
Kameruka NSW 49 P6
Kamona Tas. 131 O7
Kanangra Boyd National Park NSW 10 F9, 12 I8,
   20 H1
Kanawalla Vic. 40 G4
Kancoona Vic. 47 P7, 48 C5
Kandos NSW 12 I4
Kangarilla SA 58 C12, 59 G3, 61 L10, 70 B2
Kangaroo Flat NSW 15 M11
Kangaroo Flat SA 58 C5
Kangaroo Ground Vic. 33 R2, 34 A3
Kangaroo Island SA 59 A11, 60 F11
Kangaroo Point Qld 101 H8, 104 H12
Kangaroo Valley NSW 20 I3
Kangarooby NSW 12 E7
Kangawall Vic. 42 D10
Kangiara NSW 12 F10, 20 D3
Kaniva Vic. 42 C7
Kanmantoo SA 58 F11
Kanumbra Vic. 47 J10
Kanya Vic. 43 K10
Kanyapella Vic. 19 K13, 46 F4
Kanypi SA 66 D2, 98 C13
Kaoota Tas. 126 G8, 129 L9
Kapinnie SA 60 C6
Kapooka NSW 12 B12, 19 R10
Kapunda SA 58 E3, 61 L7
Karabeal Vic. 40 G4
Karadoc Vic. 18 E7, 44 H4
Karalundi WA 84 C11
Karanja Tas. 126 D3
Karara Qld 15 L1, 108 B13, 111 M11
Karatta SA 60 G13
Karawara WA 75 J7
Karawatha Qld 107 K9
Karawinna Vic. 18 C8, 44 E4
Kardinya WA 74 E11
Kareela NSW 8 I9
Kariah Vic. 41 L8
Karijini (Hamersley Range) National Park WA
   81 I5, 84 B5
Karingal Vic. 35 F12
Kariong NSW 21 E7
Karkoo SA 60 D6
Karlgarin WA 82 F9
Karlo Creek Vic. 20 F13, 49 O11
Karn Vic. 47 L7
Karnak Vic. 42 D10
Karonie WA 83 K6
Karoola Tas. 131 M7
Karoonda SA 61 O10, 70 F2
Karoonda Roadhouse Vic. 20 C12, 48 I9
Karrakatta WA 74 D5
Karratha WA 81 G1
Karratha Roadhouse WA 81 G1
Karridale WA 79 C12, 80 B10

Karrinyup WA 76 C8
Kars Springs NSW 13 J1, 14 I13
Karte SA 61 Q10, 70 H2
Karuah NSW 13 N3
Karumba Qld 114 B8, 117 H8
Karween Vic. 18 B8, 44 C4
Karyrie Vic. 43 K4
Katamatite Vic. 19 M13, 47 J4
Katandra Vic. 46 I5
Katanning WA 80 H9, 82 E10
Kata Tjuta NT 98 D11
Katherine NT 94 G10
Katoomba NSW 10 H7, 13 J7
Kattyong Vic. 44 F9
Katunga Vic. 19 M13, 46 I3
Katyil Vic. 42 G7
Kawarren Vic. 36 B12, 41 N10
Kayena Tas. 131 K7
Kealba Vic. 32 F5
Kedron Qld 104 G8
Keep River National Park NT 87 R5, 94 A13, 96 A2
Keera NSW 15 J7
Keilor Vic. 32 G4
Keilor Downs Vic. 32 F4
Keilor East Vic. 32 H5
Keilor Park Vic. 32 H4
Keith SA 61 P13, 70 G6
Kellalac Vic. 42 H7
Kellatier Tas. 130 F6
Kellerberrin WA 80 H3, 82 E7
Kellevie Tas. 127 N5, 129 N8
Kelmscott WA 78 D6
Kelso NSW 10 B4
Kelso Tas. 131 K6
Kelvin NSW 14 I10
Kelvin Grove Qld 104 F11
Kelvin View Vic. 47 J9
Kelvinhaugh Qld 108 D6
Kempsey NSW 15 O11
Kempton Tas. 126 H1, 129 L6
Kendall NSW 15 O12
Kendenup WA 80 H11
Kenebri NSW 14 E9
Kenilworth Qld 111 P7
Kenley Vic. 45 M7
Kenmare Vic. 18 D13, 42 G4
Kenmore NSW 12 H10, 20 G3
Kenmore Qld 106 C3
Kenmore Hills Qld 106 B2
Kennedy Qld 115 N10
Kennedy Range National Park WA 81 D8
Kennedys Creek Vic. 41 L11
Kennett River Vic. 41 O11
Kennys Creek NSW 12 F10, 20 D2
Kensington NSW 5 N12, 9 P2
Kensington SA 55 L6
Kensington WA 75 J5
Kensington Gardens SA 55 L5
Kent Town SA 52 H8, 55 J6
Kentbruck Vic. 40 C8
Kenthurst NSW 6 A6
Kentucky NSW 15 L9
Kenwick WA 75 P8
Keperra Qld 104 C9
Keppel Islands National Park Qld 113 P10
Keppel Sands Qld 113 O10
Keppoch SA 70 H8
Kerang Vic. 18 I12, 43 P3, 45 P13, 46 A2
Kerang East Vic. 43 P3, 46 B2
Kerang South Vic. 18 I12, 43 P3, 46 A2
Kergunyah Vic. 47 Q5, 48 C3
Kergunyah South Vic. 47 P6, 48 C4
Kernot Vic. 37 N12, 38 G8
Kerrabee NSW 13 J3
Kerrie Vic. 36 I2
Kerrisdale Vic. 37 L1, 46 H11
Kerrs Creek NSW 12 G5
Kerry Qld 109 L13
Kersbrook SA 58 E8, 61 L9, 70 C1
Keswick SA 54 H7
Kettering Tas. 126 H9, 129 L10
Kevington Vic. 37 R3, 38 I1, 47 L12
Kew NSW 15 O12
Kew Vic. 33 M8
Kewdale WA 75 M5
Kewell Vic. 42 H8
Keyneton SA 58 H5, 61 M8
Keysborough Vic. 35 F4
Keysbrook WA 78 C9, 80 D5

Khancoban NSW 20 B9, 48 H3
Ki Ki SA 61 O11, 70 F4
Kiah NSW 20 G12, 49 Q9
Kialla NSW 12 H10, 20 F3
Kialla West Vic. 46 H6
Kiama NSW 13 K10
Kiamil Vic. 18 E10, 44 H8
Kiana SA 60 C8
Kiandra NSW 20 C7, 26 C7
Kianga NSW 27 N11
Kiara WA 77 L9
Kiata Vic. 42 E7
Kidman Park SA 54 D5
Kidston Qld 115 J11
Kielpa SA 60 E4
Kiewa Vic. 47 Q5, 48 C3
Kikoira NSW 19 P5
Kilburn SA 54 H1, 56 H12
Kilcoy Qld 109 J3, 111 P7
Kilcunda Vic. 37 M13, 38 F9
Kilkenny SA 54 F2
Kilkerran SA 60 I7
Kilkivan Qld 111 O5
Killabakh NSW 15 N13
Killara NSW 5 K3, 6 H13
Killarney Qld 15 N1, 111 O11
Killarney Vic. 40 H9
Killarney Heights NSW 5 N4
Killawarra Vic. 47 L5
Killcare NSW 21 G8
Killcare Heights NSW 11 P5, 13 M6, 21 H8
Killiecrankie Tas. 128 A11
Killora Tas. 126 H9, 129 L10
Kilmany Vic. 39 M6
Kilmany South Vic. 39 M6
Kilmore Vic. 37 J2, 46 F11
Kilpalie SA 61 O9, 70 G2
Kilsyth Vic. 34 E8
Kimba SA 60 F3, 62 E13
Kimberley Tas. 130 I8
Kimberley, The WA 87 L6
Kimbriki NSW 13 O1, 15 N13
Kinalung NSW 16 D12
Kinchega National Park NSW 16 D13, 18 D1
Kinchela NSW 15 P10
Kincumber NSW 11 P4, 13 M6, 21 G7
Kindred Tas. 130 H7
King Island Tas. 128 B8
King River WA 80 H13
King Valley Vic. 47 N8
Kingaroy Qld 111 N6
Kinglake Vic. 37 M4, 38 E2, 46 H13
Kinglake Central Vic. 37 L3
Kinglake East Vic. 37 M3, 50 B2
Kinglake National Park Vic. 37 L4, 38 E1, 46 H12,
   50 B1
Kinglake West Vic. 37 L3, 38 E1, 46 H13
Kingoonya SA 62 B5
Kingower Vic. 43 O9
Kings Camp SA 70 E9
Kings Canyon Resort NT 98 F9
Kings Creek Qld 108 E10
Kings Cross NSW 5 N10
Kings Plains National Park NSW 15 K5
Kingsborough Qld 115 L6
Kingsbury Vic. 33 M4
Kingscliff NSW 15 Q1, 111 R11
Kingscote SA 60 I12
Kingsdale NSW 12 H11, 20 G3
Kingsford NSW 5 N13, 9 P3, 11 O9
Kingsgrove NSW 9 J5
Kingsley WA 76 D4
Kingsthorpe Qld 108 E7, 111 N9
Kingston ACT 23 G13, 24 H11, 25 F2
Kingston NSW 15 K8
Kingston Qld 107 M10
Kingston Tas. 126 H7, 129 L9
Kingston Vic. 36 D2, 41 P2, 43 P13, 46 A12
Kingston Beach Tas. 126 H7
Kingston-on-Murray SA 61 P7
Kingston S.E. SA 70 F8
Kingsvale NSW 12 E10, 20 C2
Kingswood NSW 11 K8
Kingswood SA 55 J9, 63 J10
Kinimakatka Vic. 42 D7
Kinka Qld 113 O10
Kinnabulla Vic. 43 J4
Kintore NT 85 R6, 98 B7
Kioloa NSW 13 J13, 20 H6, 27 P6

147

Kiora NSW 27 M9
Kipper Qld 108 H5
Kirkstall Vic. 40 H8
Kirrawee NSW 8 I11
Kirup WA 79 H7, 80 C9
Kital Qld 108 F12
Kitchener WA 83 L6
Kithbrook Vic. 47 J9
Klemzig SA 55 K2
Klimpton NSW 13 K11, 20 I4, 27 Q1
Knebsworth Vic. 40 F7
Knockrow NSW 15 Q3, 111 Q12
Knockwood Vic. 37 R3
Knorrit Flat NSW 13 O1, 15 M13
Knowsley Vic. 46 E9
Knoxfield Vic. 34 B13, 35 I1
Koallah Vic. 41 L9
Kobble Qld 109 L6
Kobyboyn Vic. 46 H10
Koetong Vic. 20 A8, 48 E2
Kogan Qld 111 L8
Kogarah NSW 9 L6
Koimbo Vic. 45 K8
Kojonup WA 80 G9, 82 E11
Koloona NSW 15 J6
Kolora Vic. 41 K8
Kommamurra Qld 108 B4
Komungla NSW 12 H11, 20 G4
Konagaderra Vic. 36 I4
Kondalilla National Park Qld 109 L1
Kondinin WA 80 I5, 82 F9
Kongal SA 70 H6
Kongorong SA 70 H12
Kongwak Vic. 37 O13, 38 G9
Konnongorring WA 80 F1
Konong Wootong Vic. 40 D3
Konong Wootong North Vic. 40 D3
Koo-wee-rup Vic. 37 M10, 38 F7
Kookaburra NSW 15 N10
Kookynie WA 82 I4
Koolan WA 87 J5
Koolewong NSW 21 F7
Kooloonong Vic. 18 G9, 45 L8
Koolunga SA 61 K4
Koolyanobbing WA 82 G6
Koolywurtie SA 60 I8
Koonda Vic. 44 D9, 47 J7
Koondah Qld 108 B2
Koondoola WA 76 I6
Koondrook Vic. 18 I12, 43 Q2, 45 Q13, 46 B1
Koongarra NT 93 P5
Koongawa SA 60 D3, 62 C13
Koonibba SA 69 N9
Koonoomoo Vic. 47 J2
Koonunga SA 58 F3
Koonwarra Vic. 37 P13, 38 H9
Koonya Tas. 127 M9, 129 N10
Koorack Koorack Vic. 43 N2, 45 N13
Kooralbyn Qld 109 K13
Kooralgin Qld 108 F2
Koorawatha NSW 12 E8, 20 C1
Koorda WA 82 E6
Kooreh Vic. 43 M9
Kooringal Qld 109 P7
Koorkab Vic. 45 L7
Koorlong Vic. 18 D7, 44 G4
Kootingal NSW 15 K10
Kooyong Vic. 33 M9
Koppamurra SA 42 A11, 70 I9
Koppio SA 60 D7
Korbel WA 80 I3
Koriella Vic. 37 O1
Korobeit Vic. 36 F4
Koroit Vic. 40 H9
Korong Vale Vic. 43 O7
Koroop Vic. 43 Q3, 46 B2
Korora NSW 15 P8
Korumburra Vic. 37 O12, 38 H8
Korweinguboora Vic. 36 E3
Kosciuszko National Park NSW 12 E13, 20 C6, 26 A10, 28 A10, 49 J2
Kotta Vic. 46 D4
Kotupna Vic. 19 L13, 46 G4
Koumala Qld 113 L6
Kowanyama Aboriginal Community Qld 114 D3
Kowat Vic. 20 E12, 49 N10
Koyuga Vic. 46 F5
Krambach NSW 13 O1
Kringin SA 61 Q9, 70 H2

Krongart SA 70 H11
Kroombit Tops National Park Qld 111 L1, 113 O13
Krowera Vic. 37 O12
Ku-ring-gai Chase National Park NSW 6 H8, 7 N3, 11 O6, 13 L7, 21 F11
Kudardup WA 79 C12
Kuitpo SA 59 G4
Kuitpo Colony SA 59 H5
Kukerin WA 80 I7, 82 F10
Kulgera NT 98 I12
Kulgun Qld 109 J11
Kulikup WA 80 E9
Kulin WA 80 I6, 82 F9
Kulkami SA 61 P10, 70 G2
Kulkyne Vic. 44 H6
Kulnine Vic. 44 D3
Kulnine East Vic. 18 C7, 44 D3
Kulnura NSW 11 O2, 13 L5, 21 A2
Kulpara SA 61 J6
Kulpi Qld 108 D4, 111 N8
Kulwin Vic. 44 I9
Kulyalling WA 80 F5
Kumarina Roadhouse WA 84 D8
Kumarl WA 83 J9
Kumbarilla Qld 111 L8
Kumbia Qld 111 N7
Kumorna SA 61 P13, 70 G5
Kunama NSW 20 B6
Kunat Vic. 43 N1, 45 N12
Kundabung NSW 15 O11
Kungala NSW 15 P7
Kunghur NSW 15 P2
Kunjin WA 80 H5
Kunlara SA 61 O8, 70 F1
Kununoppin WA 80 H1
Kununurra WA 87 Q5
Kunwarara Qld 113 N9
Kupingarri Community WA 87 M7
Kuraby Qld 107 K7
Kuranda Qld 115 M6
Kuridala Qld 118 G5
Kuringup WA 80 I8
Kurmond NSW 11 K5
Kurnbrunin Vic. 42 E4
Kurnell NSW 9 P9, 11 O10
Kurnwill Vic. 18 B8, 44 C5
Kurraca Vic. 43 N8
Kurraca West Vic. 43 N8
Kurrajong NSW 11 K5
Kurrajong Heights NSW 11 J5
Kurralta Park SA 54 G8
Kurri Kurri NSW 13 M4
Kurrimine Beach Qld 115 N9
Kurting Vic. 43 O8, 46 A7
Kurumbul Qld 14 I2, 111 K12
Kuttabul Qld 113 K5
Kweda WA 80 G5
Kwinana WA 78 B7, 80 C4, 82 C8
Kwolyin WA 80 H3
Kyabram Vic. 46 G5
Kyalite NSW 18 H9, 45 N8
Kyancutta SA 60 C3, 62 C13
Kybunga SA 61 K6
Kybybolite SA 42 A10, 70 I8
Kyeamba NSW 12 C13, 19 R11, 20 A6
Kyeemagh NSW 9 M5
Kyndalyn Vic. 18 F9, 45 K7
Kyneton Vic. 36 G1, 41 R1, 43 R12, 46 D11
Kynuna Qld 119 J6
Kyogle NSW 15 P2, 111 P12
Kyotmunga WA 78 E1, 80 D2
Kyup Vic. 40 F4
Kyvalley Vic. 46 G5
Kywong NSW 19 P10

La Perouse NSW 9 P8, 11 O10
Laanecoorie Vic. 43 P10, 46 A9
Laang Vic. 41 J9
Labertouche Vic. 37 O9, 38 G6
Lachlan Tas. 126 F5, 129 K8
Lacmalac NSW 26 B2
Lady Barron Tas. 128 B12, 131 R1
Lady Bay Tas. 129 K12
Lady Musgrave Island Qld 113 R12
Ladys Pass Vic. 46 E8
Ladysmith NSW 12 C12, 19 R10, 20 A5
Laen Vic. 43 J7
Laen North Vic. 43 J7
Laggan NSW 12 H9, 20 F2

Lah Vic. 42 H5
Lah-Arum Vic. 42 H11
Laheys Creek NSW 12 G2
Laidley Qld 108 H9, 111 O9
Lajamanu NT 96 D8
Lake Bathurst NSW 12 H11, 20 F4
Lake Biddy WA 82 G9
Lake Bindegolly National Park Qld 121 O11
Lake Boga Vic. 18 H11, 43 N1, 45 N11
Lake Bolac Vic. 41 J5
Lake Buloke Vic. 43 K7
Lake Burley Griffin ACT 23 C7, 24 F10, 25 D1
Lake Cargelligo NSW 19 O4
Lake Cathie NSW 15 O12
Lake Charm Vic. 18 H12, 43 O2, 45 O13, 46 A1
Lake Clifton WA 78 A12, 80 C6
Lake Condon Vic. 40 E7
Lake Conjola NSW 13 J12, 20 I5, 27 Q3
Lake Cowal NSW 12 B7, 19 R5
Lake Eyre National Park SA 64 I8, 120 B11
Lake Gairdner National Park SA 62 C7, 69 R7
Lake Grace WA 82 F9
Lake Hindmarsh Vic. 42 E5
Lake King WA 82 G9
Lake Leake Tas. 129 O3, 131 O12
Lake Margaret Tas. 128 E2, 130 E11
Lake Marmal Vic. 43 N6
Lake Meering Vic. 43 O4
Lake Mountain Vic. 38 H2
Lake Mundi Vic. 40 B4, 70 I11
Lake Poomaho NSW 18 H10, 45 N9
Lake Powell Junction Vic. 45 K6
Lake Rowan Vic. 47 K5
Lake Torrens National Park SA 62 I5
Lake Tyers Vic. 48 H13
Lake View SA 61 K4
Lakefield National Park Qld 115 J1, 116 G13
Lakeland Qld 115 K4
Lakemba NSW 4 G13, 8 I3
Lakes Entrance Vic. 39 R5, 48 H13
Lakesland NSW 11 J12
Lal Lal Vic. 36 D5, 41 P4
Lalbert Vic. 18 G12, 43 M2, 45 M13
Lalbert Road Vic. 43 M1, 45 M12
Lalla Tas. 131 M7
Lallat Vic. 43 J9
Lallat North Vic. 43 J8
Lalor Vic. 33 M2
Lameroo SA 61 Q11, 70 H3
Lamington National Park Qld 15 P1, 109 M13, 111 P11
Lamplough Vic. 36 A1, 41 M1, 43 N12
Lancaster Vic. 46 G5
Lancefield Vic. 36 I2, 46 E11
Lancelin WA 80 B1, 82 B7
Landsborough Qld 109 M2, 111 P7
Landsborough Vic. 43 L11
Landsdale WA 76 H3
Lane Cove NSW 5 K6, 11 N8
Lane Cove National Park NSW 4 H3, 5 J4, 6 F11, 11 N7
Lanena Tas. 131 L7
Lang Lang Vic. 37 N10, 38 F7
Langford WA 75 M9
Langhorne Creek SA 61 M10, 70 D3
Langi Kal Kal Vic. 36 A3, 41 N2
Langi Logan Vic. 41 K2, 43 K13
Langkoop Vic. 40 B1, 42 B12, 70 I9
Langley Vic. 36 G1, 41 R1, 43 R12, 46 D11
Langlo Crossing Qld 110 A5, 121 R5
Langloh Tas. 129 J6
Langsborough Vic. 39 L10
Langtree NSW 19 M5
Langville Vic. 43 O4, 46 A2
Langwarrin Vic. 35 G13
Lankeys Creek NSW 19 R12, 20 A7
Lannercost Qld 115 N11
Lansdowne NSW 4 B12, 8 D2, 13 P1, 15 O13
Lansvale NSW 4 A11, 8 C1
Lapoinya Tas. 130 E5
Lara Vic. 36 G8, 38 A5, 41 R6
Lara Lake Vic. 36 F8
Larapinta Qld 106 H10
Laravale Qld 109 L13
Largs Bay SA 56 B9
Largs North SA 56 C9
Larpent Vic. 36 A11, 41 N9
Larrakeyah NT 90 B10
Larras Lee NSW 12 F5

Larrimah NT 94 I12, 96 I2
Lascelles Vic. 18 E12, 42 I2, 44 I12
Latham ACT 24 B5
Latham WA 82 D5
Lathlain WA 75 K4
Latrobe Tas. 130 I7
Lauderdale Tas. 125 Q9, 127 J6, 129 M9
Laughtondale NSW 11 M4
Launceston Tas. 131 L8
Launching Place Vic. 37 N6, 38 F4, 50 E9
Laura Qld 115 K3
Laura SA 61 K3, 63 J13
Laurel Hill NSW 20 B7
Laurieton NSW 15 O13
Lauriston Vic. 36 F1, 41 R1, 43 R12, 46 C11
Lavers Hill Vic. 41 M11
Laverton Vic. 32 D11
Laverton WA 83 J3
Lawgi Qld 111 L1
Lawler Vic. 43 J7
Lawloit Vic. 42 D7
Lawn Hill National Park Qld 97 R8, 117 B11
Lawnton Qld 104 C2
Lawrence NSW 15 P5
Lawrence Vic. 36 C2, 41 O2, 43 O13, 46 A12
Lawrence Road NSW 15 P5
Lawrenny Tas. 129 J6
Lawson ACT 24 E5
Lawson NSW 10 I7, 13 J7
Le Roy Vic. 39 K8
Leabrook SA 55 L6
Leadville NSW 12 H1
Leaghur Vic. 43 O4, 46 A3
Leanyer NT 91 I3
Learmonth Vic. 36 B3, 41 O2, 43 O13
Learmonth WA 81 B4
Leasingham SA 61 L6
Leawood Gardens SA 55 N9
Lebrina Tas. 131 M7
Ledge Point WA 80 B1
Lee Point NT 91 I1
Leederville WA 74 G1, 76 G13
Leeman WA 82 B5
Leeming WA 74 I13
Leeton NSW 19 O8
Leets Vale NSW 11 M4
Leeuwin-Naturaliste National Park WA 79 B11,
   80 A9, 82 A11
Leeville NSW 15 P3
Lefroy Tas. 131 L6
Legana Tas. 131 L8
Legerwood Tas. 131 O7
Legume NSW 15 N1, 111 O11
Leichardt Vic. 43 P9, 46 B8
Leichhardt NSW 5 J10, 9 L1
Leigh Creek SA 63 J4
Leighton SA 61 L5
Leightonfield NSW 4 B11, 8 D1
Leinster WA 82 H2
Leitchville Vic. 19 J13, 43 R4, 46 C3
Lemana Tas. 129 H11, 131 J9
Lemnos Vic. 46 I5
Lemon Springs Vic. 42 C9
Lemon Tree Passage NSW 13 N4
Lemont Tas. 129 N5
Lenah Valley Tas. 124 D6
Leneva Vic. 47 P5, 48 B2
Lennox Head NSW 15 R3, 111 R12
Lenswood SA 58 D10
Leonards Hill Vic. 36 E3
Leongatha Vic. 37 P13, 38 H9
Leongatha South Vic. 37 P13, 38 H9
Leonora WA 82 I3
Leopold Vic. 36 G10, 38 A7, 41 R8
Leppington NSW 11 L9
Leprena Tas. 129 J12
Leslie Vale Tas. 126 H7, 129 L9
Leslies Bridge Qld 108 C10
Lesmurdie Falls National Park WA 75 R6, 78 D5
Lesueur National Park WA 82 B5
Lethbridge Vic. 36 E7, 41 Q6
Leumeah NSW 11 L10
Leura NSW 10 H7
Levendale Tas. 127 K1, 129 M6
Lewis Ponds NSW 12 G6
Lewisham NSW 5 J12, 9 L2
Lewisham Tas. 127 L5, 129 N8
Lewiston SA 58 B5
Lexton Vic. 36 A2, 41 N2, 43 N13

Leyburn Qld 108 C11, 111 M10
Liawenee Tas. 129 J2, 131 J11
Licola Vic. 39 L3, 48 A12
Lidcombe NSW 4 E10
Liddell NSW 13 L3
Lidsdale NSW 10 F4, 12 I6
Liena Tas. 130 H9
Lietinna Tas. 131 N7
Lietpar Vic. 44 I9
Liffey Tas. 129 K1, 131 K10
Lightning Ridge NSW 14 B5
Lileah Tas. 130 D5
Lilli Pilli NSW 9 K13
Lillicur Vic. 36 A1
Lillimur Vic. 42 B7
Lillimur South Vic. 42 B7, 70 I7
Lilydale Qld 108 G8
Lilydale Tas. 131 M7
Lilydale Vic. 34 F6, 37 L6, 38 E3, 50 A8
Lilyfield NSW 5 J10
Lima Vic. 47 K8
Limeburners Creek NSW 13 N3
Limekilns NSW 10 D2, 12 H5
Limerick NSW 10 A11, 12 G8, 20 F1
Limestone Vic. 37 N2, 46 I11
Limestone Ridge Qld 109 K11
Limevale Qld 15 K2, 111 M12
Lincoln National Park SA 60 E9
Lincolnfields SA 61 J5
Lind National Park Vic. 20 E13, 49 M11
Linda Tas. 128 E3, 130 E12
Lindeman Island Qld 113 K3
Linden NSW 11 J7
Linden Park SA 55 L7
Lindenow Vic. 39 P4, 48 E13
Lindfield NSW 5 J4
Lindisfarne Tas. 125 J4, 126 I5, 129 L8
Lindsay Vic. 40 A4, 70 I11
Lindsay Point Vic. 18 A7, 44 A3, 61 R6
Lindum Qld 105 L9
Linga Vic. 18 C10, 44 E10
Linley Point NSW 5 J7
Linthorpe Qld 108 C8
Linton Vic. 36 B5, 41 N4
Linville Qld 108 H2, 111 O7
Linwood SA 58 D3
Lipson SA 60 E7
Lisarow NSW 11 P3, 21 F4
Lisle Tas. 131 M7
Lismore NSW 15 Q3, 111 Q12
Lismore Vic. 41 M6
Liston NSW 15 M2, 111 O12
Litchfield Vic. 43 J6
Litchfield National Park NT 92 C8, 94 D7
Lithgow NSW 10 G5, 12 I6
Littabella National Park Qld 111 O1
Little Bay NSW 9 Q7
Little Billabong NSW 19 R12, 20 A6
Little Desert National Park Vic. 42 B8, 70 I7
Little Hard Hills Vic. 36 C6
Little Hartley NSW 10 G5
Little Jilliby NSW 11 P2, 21 D1
Little Mussleroe Bay Tas. 131 Q4
Little River Vic. 36 G7, 38 A5, 41 R6
Little Snowy Creek Vic. 47 R7, 48 D4
Little Swanport Tas. 129 O5
Little Topar Roadhouse NSW 16 D11
Littlehampton SA 58 E11, 59 I2
Liverpool NSW 8 A4, 11 M9, 13 K8
Lizard Island National Park Qld 115 M1
Llandaff Tas. 129 P3, 131 Q12
Llandeilo Vic. 36 E4
Llanelly Vic. 43 O9, 46 A8
Llangothlin NSW 15 L7
Llewellyn Siding Tas. 129 N2, 131 N11
Llowalong Vic. 39 M5
Loamside Qld 109 K9
Lobethal SA 58 E9, 61 L9, 70 C1
Loccota Tas. 128 B12, 131 Q1
Loch Vic. 37 O12, 38 G8
Loch Sport Vic. 39 P6
Loch Valley Vic. 37 Q6
Lochaber SA 70 H8
Lochern National Park Qld 119 M12
Lochiel SA 61 J6
Lochinvar NSW 13 M4
Lochnagar Qld 112 D11, 119 R11
Lock SA 60 D4
Lockhart NSW 19 P10

Lockhart River Aboriginal Community Qld 116 E8
Lockington Qld 112 H12
Lockington Vic. 46 D5
Lockleys SA 54 D6
Lockridge WA 77 M9
Locksley NSW 10 D5, 12 H6
Locksley Vic. 46 H9
Lockwood Vic. 43 Q10, 46 B9
Lockwood South Vic. 43 Q10, 46 B9
Lockyer Qld 108 G7
Loddon Vale Vic. 43 P5, 46 A3
Loftus NSW 8 H11
Logan Qld 107 L10, 109 M9, 111 P9
Logan Vic. 43 N9
Logan Central Qld 107 L10
Loganholme Qld 107 Q11, 109 N10
Loganlea Qld 107 N11
Logie Brae NSW 19 M11
Lombadina WA 86 H6
Londonderry NSW 11 K6
Londrigan Vic. 47 N5
Long Beach NSW 20 H7, 27 O7
Long Flat NSW 15 N12
Long Jetty NSW 11 Q3, 21 H3
Long Plains SA 61 K7
Long Plains Vic. 43 K1, 45 K11
Long Pocket Qld 106 F3
Longerenong Vic. 42 H9
Longford Tas. 131 L9
Longford Vic. 39 N7
Longlea Vic. 43 R10, 46 D8
Longley Tas. 126 G7, 129 L9
Longreach Qld 112 A11, 119 O11
Longueville NSW 5 K8
Longwarry Vic. 37 O9, 38 G6
Longwood Vic. 46 I9
Longwood East Vic. 46 I9
Lonnavale Tas. 126 C6, 129 J9
Loongana Tas. 130 G8
Loongana WA 83 P6
Loorana Tas. 128 A9
Lorinna Tas. 130 H9
Lorne Vic. 36 D13, 41 P10
Lorquon Vic. 42 E6
Lorquon West Vic. 42 E5
Lostock NSW 13 L2
Lota Qld 105 N11
Lottah Tas. 131 P7
Louisville Tas. 127 O1, 129 O6
Louth NSW 17 L7
Louth Bay SA 60 D8
Loveday SA 61 P7
Low Head Tas. 131 K6
Lowaldie SA 61 O10, 70 F2
Lowan Vale SA 70 H6
Lowanna NSW 15 P8
Lowbank SA 61 P6
Lowden WA 79 I6, 80 D8
Lowdina Tas. 127 J2, 129 M7
Lower Acacia Creek NSW 15 N2
Lower Barrington Tas. 130 I7
Lower Beulah Tas. 130 I8
Lower Boro NSW 27 L1
Lower Bucca NSW 15 P7
Lower Creek NSW 15 N9
Lower Glenelg National Park Vic. 40 B7
Lower Light SA 61 K8
Lower Mangrove NSW 11 N4, 21 A8
Lower Marshes Tas. 129 L5
Lower Mookerawa NSW 12 G4
Lower Mount Hicks Tas. 130 F5
Lower Norton Vic. 42 G10
Lower Plenty Vic. 33 P5, 37 K5
Lower Quipolly NSW 14 I12
Lower Sandy Bay Tas. 124 I11
Lower Templestowe Vic. 33 P6
Lower Turners Marsh Tas. 131 L7
Lower Wilmot Tas. 130 H7
Lowes Mount NSW 10 D6
Lowesdale NSW 19 O12, 47 M2
Lowlands NSW 19 M3
Lowmead Qld 111 N1
Lowood Qld 109 J7, 111 P9
Lowther NSW 10 F6
Loxton SA 61 Q7
Loxton North SA 61 Q7
Loy Yang Vic. 39 K7
Loyetea Tas. 130 G7
Lubeck Vic. 42 I9

Lucas Heights NSW 8 D11
Lucaston Tas. 126 F7, 129 K9
Lucinda Qld 115 O11
Lucindale SA 70 G9
Lucknow NSW 12 G6
Lucknow Vic. 39 Q4, 48 F13
Lucky Bay SA 60 G5
Lucyvale Vic. 20 A9, 48 F3
Luddenham NSW 11 K9
Ludlow WA 79 E7
Ludmilla NT 90 G2, 91 B9
Lue NSW 12 I3
Lugarno NSW 8 G7
Lughrata Tas. 128 A11
Luina Tas. 130 E8
Lumholtz National Park Qld 115 M10
Lunawanna Tas. 126 G13, 129 L11
Lune River Tas. 129 J12
Lurg Vic. 47 L7
Lurnea NSW 8 A4
Lutana Tas. 124 F3
Lutwyche Qld 104 G9
Lyal Vic. 43 R11, 46 D10
Lymington Tas. 126 F10, 129 K10
Lymwood Tas. 128 A9
Lynchford Tas. 128 E3, 130 E12
Lynchs Creek NSW 15 P2
Lyndhurst NSW 12 F7
Lyndhurst SA 63 J3
Lyndhurst Vic. 35 H8, 37 L8, 38 E5
Lyndoch SA 58 E6, 61 L8
Lyneham ACT 24 G7
Lynton SA 55 J12
Lynwood WA 75 L10
Lyons ACT 24 E13, 25 C4
Lyons Vic. 40 D7
Lyonville Vic. 36 F3
Lyrup SA 61 Q7
Lysterfield Vic. 37 L7
Lytton Qld 105 M8

Ma Ma Creek Qld 108 G8
Maaoope SA 70 H10
Maaroom Qld 111 P4
McAlinden WA 80 E8
Macalister Qld 111 L8
McAllister NSW 12 H10, 20 F3
Macarthur ACT 25 F8
MacArthur Vic. 40 F7
Macclesfield SA 58 D12, 59 I3, 61 L10, 70 C2
Macclesfield Vic. 37 M7, 38 F4, 50 D12
McCrae Vic. 37 J11
McCullys Gap NSW 13 L2
McDowall Qld 104 D7
Macedon Vic. 36 H3, 38 A1, 46 D12
McGillivray SA 60 H12
McGraths Hill NSW 11 L6
Macgregor ACT 24 A4
Macgregor Qld 107 J6
McHarg Creek SA 59 H5
McIntyre Vic. 43 O9
Mackay Qld 113 L5
McKees Hill NSW 15 P3
McKellar ACT 24 E5
Mackenzie Qld 107 L3
McKenzie Creek Vic. 42 G10
McKinlay Qld 118 I5
McKinnon Vic. 33 M13, 35 C1
Macks Creek Vic. 39 L9
Macksville NSW 15 P9
MacLagan Qld 108 D3, 111 N8
McLaren Flat SA 58 B13, 59 F4
McLaren Vale SA 58 A13, 59 F4, 61 K10, 70 B2
Maclean NSW 15 P5
Macleod Vic. 33 N4
McLoughlins Beach Vic. 39 M9
McMahons Creek Vic. 37 P5, 38 H3
McMahons Reef NSW 12 E11, 20 C3
MacMasters Beach NSW 11 P4, 21 H7
McMillans Vic. 18 I12, 43 Q3, 46 B2
Macorna Vic. 18 I13, 43 P4, 46 B3
McPhail NSW 12 D3
Macquarie ACT 24 D7
Macquarie Fields NSW 11 L10
Macquarie Park NSW 4 I3, 6 G13
Macquarie Plains Tas. 126 D3
Macrossan Qld 112 F2
Macs Cove Vic. 37 R1, 47 L11

Madalya Vic. 39 K9
Maddington WA 75 P10, 78 D5
Madora WA 78 B9
Madura Pass Roadhouse WA 83 P8
Mafeking Vic. 40 I3
Maffra NSW 20 D10, 49 M5
Maffra Vic. 39 M5
Maffra West Upper Vic. 39 M4
Maggea SA 61 O7
Magill SA 55 N5, 58 C9
Magnetic Island National Park Qld 115 P12
Magpie Vic. 36 C4
Magra Tas. 126 F4, 129 K7
Magrath Flat SA 61 N12, 70 E5
Maharatta NSW 20 E11, 49 N8
Maianbar NSW 9 L13
Maiden Gully Vic. 43 Q9, 46 C8
Maidenwell Qld 108 E2, 111 N7
Maidstone Vic. 32 I7
Mailors Flat Vic. 40 I9
Maimuru NSW 12 D9, 20 C2
Main Beach Qld 109 O12, 111 Q10
Main Range National Park Qld 15 N1, 108 H11, 111 O10
Maindample Vic. 47 K10
Maitland NSW 13 M4
Maitland SA 60 I7
Major Plains Vic. 47 K6
Majorca Vic. 36 C1, 41 O1, 43 O12, 46 A10
Majors Creek NSW 12 H13, 20 G6, 27 K5
Majors Creek Vic. 46 F9
Malabar NSW 9 Q6
Malaga WA 77 K7
Malanda Qld 115 M7
Malbina Tas. 126 G4
Malbon Qld 118 G5
Malcolm WA 82 I3
Maldon NSW 11 K12
Maldon Vic. 43 P11, 46 B10
Maleny Qld 109 L2, 111 P7
Malinong SA 61 N11, 70 E3
Mallacoota Vic. 20 G13, 49 Q11
Mallala SA 58 A3, 61 K7
Mallan NSW 18 I10, 45 O9
Mallanganee NSW 15 O3, 111 P12
Mallee Cliffs National Park NSW 18 E7, 44 I3
Malling Qld 108 D3
Malmsbury Vic. 36 G1, 41 R1, 43 R12, 46 C11
Malpas SA 61 Q8, 70 H1
Malua Bay NSW 20 H7, 27 O7
Malvern SA 55 J9
Malvern Vic. 33 M11
Malyalling WA 80 G6
Mambray Creek SA 61 J2, 62 I12
Manangatang Vic. 18 F10, 45 K9
Manara NSW 18 G2
Mandagery NSW 12 D6
Mandalong NSW 11 P1
Mandorah NT 92 B2, 94 D5
Mandurah WA 78 B9, 80 C5, 82 C9
Mandurang Vic. 43 R10, 46 C9
Mangalo SA 60 F4
Mangalore NSW 17 P11
Mangalore Tas. 126 H2, 129 L7
Mangalore Vic. 46 G9
Mangana Tas. 131 P10
Mangoplah NSW 12 B13, 19 Q11
Mangrove Creek NSW 11 N3, 21 A6
Mangrove Mountain NSW 11 O3, 21 A4
Manguri SA 67 Q11
Manildra NSW 12 F5
Manilla NSW 15 J9
Maningrida NT 95 K5
Manjimup WA 80 D10, 82 D11
Manly NSW 5 Q5, 11 P7, 13 L7
Manly Qld 105 N10, 109 N8
Manly Vale NSW 5 O4
Manly West Qld 105 N10
Manmanning WA 82 D6
Mannahill SA 63 O11
Mannanarie SA 61 L2, 63 K13
Mannerim SA 36 H10
Mannering Bay NSW 11 Q1
Mannering Park NSW 11 Q1, 13 M5
Mannibadar Vic. 36 A6, 41 N5
Manning WA 74 I8
Manningham SA 55 K2, 57 K13
Manns Beach Vic. 39 L10
Mannum SA 58 I9, 61 M9, 70 D1

Manoora SA 61 L6
Mansfield Qld 107 K3
Mansfield Vic. 47 L10
Mansfield Park SA 54 F1, 56 G12
Mantung SA 61 P8
Manumbar Qld 111 O6
Many Peaks Qld 111 M1
Manya Vic. 44 A9, 61 R10, 70 I2
Manyana NSW 27 Q3
Manypeaks WA 80 I12
Mapleton Qld 109 L1
Mapleton Falls National Park Qld 109 L1
Mapoon Aboriginal Community Qld 116 B6
Maralinga SA 68 H3
Marama SA 61 P10, 70 G2
Maranboy NT 94 H10
Marangaroo WA 76 G5
Marathon Qld 119 N4
Maraylya NSW 11 M6
Marbelup WA 80 H13
Marble Bar WA 84 D2
Marble Hill SA 55 R6
Marburg Qld 109 J8
Marchagee WA 82 C5
Marcus Hill Vic. 36 H10, 38 B7
Mardella WA 78 C8, 80 D5
Marden SA 55 K3
Mareeba Qld 115 M7
Marengo NSW 15 N7
Marengo Vic. 41 N12
Margaret River WA 79 C10, 80 A10, 82 B11
Margate Qld 109 N6
Margate Tas. 126 H8, 129 L9
Margooya Vic. 45 J7
Maria Island National Park Tas. 127 Q3, 129 P7
Mariala National Park Qld 121 Q5
Marian Qld 113 K5
Maribyrnong Vic. 32 I6
Marion SA 54 F12, 58 A10, 59 F1
Marion Bay SA 60 G10
Marion Bay Tas. 127 N5, 129 O8
Markdale NSW 12 G9, 20 E2
Markwell NSW 13 O2
Markwood Vic. 47 N6, 48 A4
Marla SA 67 N5
Marlbed Vic. 43 K4
Marlborough Qld 113 M9
Marlee NSW 13 O1, 15 N13
Marleston SA 54 G8
Marlo Vic. 49 J13
Marma Vic. 42 I9
Marmion WA 76 B6
Marmor Qld 113 O11
Marnoo Vic. 43 K9
Marnoo West Vic. 43 J9
Marong Vic. 43 Q9, 46 B8
Maroochydore Qld 109 N1, 111 Q7
Maroon Qld 15 O1, 109 J13, 111 P11
Maroona Vic. 41 J3
Maroota NSW 11 M4
Maroubra NSW 9 Q5
Maroubra Junction NSW 9 Q5, 11 O9
Marp Vic. 40 B6
Marrabel SA 61 L6
Marradong WA 78 G12, 80 E6
Marramarra National Park NSW 6 E1, 11 N5, 13 L6, 21 A11
Marrangaroo NSW 10 F4
Marrar NSW 12 B11, 19 R9
Marrara NT 91 H8
Marrawah Tas. 130 B4
Marraweeny Vic. 47 J8
Marree SA 62 I1, 64 I13
Marrickville NSW 5 J13, 9 L3, 11 N9
Marrinup WA 78 D11, 80 D6
Marryatville SA 55 L6
Marsden NSW 12 B7, 19 R5
Marsden Qld 107 L12
Marsden Park NSW 11 L7
Marshall Vic. 36 F10, 38 A7, 41 R8
Martindale NSW 13 K3
Martins Creek Vic. 20 C13, 49 K10
Marulan NSW 12 I11, 20 G3
Marulan South NSW 12 I11, 20 H4
Marungi Vic. 46 I4
Marvel Loch WA 82 G7
Mary River National Park NT 92 H6, 92 I4
Mary River Roadhouse NT 93 L11, 94 G8
Maryborough Qld 111 P4

150

Maryborough Vic. 43 O11
Marybrook WA 79 C7
Maryfarms Qld 115 L5
Marysville Vic. 37 O4, 38 G2, 47 J13, 50 I3
Maryvale NSW 12 F3
Mascot NSW 5 L13, 9 N3
Maslin Beach SA 58 A13, 59 E4
Massey Vic. 43 K6
Matakana NSW 19 N3
Mataranka NT 94 I11
Matcham NSW 11 P4, 21 G5
Matheson NSW 15 L6
Mathiesons Vic. 46 F7
Mathinna Tas. 131 P9
Mathoura NSW 19 K12, 46 F2
Matlock Vic. 37 R5, 39 J3
Matong NSW 12 A11, 19 Q9
Matraville NSW 9 Q6
Maude NSW 19 J8, 45 R5
Maude Vic. 36 E7, 41 Q6
Maudsland Qld 109 N12
Mawbanna Tas. 130 E5
Mawson ACT 25 D6
Mawson WA 80 G4
Maxwelton Qld 119 L4
May Reef Vic. 46 D7
Mayanup WA 80 E9
Mayberry Tas. 130 I9
Maydena Tas. 126 A4, 128 I7
Mayfield Tas. 131 P13
Maylands SA 55 K4
Maylands WA 75 K3
Mayne Qld 104 G10
Mayrung NSW 19 L11
Mays Hill NSW 4 B7
Maytown Qld 115 J4
Mazeppa National Park Qld 112 G7
Mead Vic. 43 Q3, 46 B2
Meadow Creek Vic. 47 N7
Meadow Flat NSW 10 E4
Meadowbank NSW 4 G6
Meadows SA 58 D13, 59 H3, 61 L10, 70 C2
Meandarra Qld 111 J8
Meander Tas. 131 J10
Meandu Creek Qld 108 F1
Meatian Vic. 43 M2, 45 M12
Meckering WA 80 F3, 82 D7
Medindie SA 52 E2, 55 J4
Medindie Gardens SA 55 J3
Medlow Bath NSW 10 H6
Meeandah Qld 105 J9
Meekatharra WA 81 I11, 84 C12
Meelon WA 78 C11, 80 D6
Meelup WA 79 B6
Meenar WA 80 F2
Meeniyan Vic. 38 I10
Meerlieu Vic. 39 O5
Meerschaum Vale NSW 15 Q3, 111 Q12
Megalong NSW 10 G7
Megan NSW 15 O8
Melba ACT 24 C4
Melba Flats Tas. 128 D1, 130 D10
Melbourne Vic. 30, 33 K9, 37 J6, 38 D4
Mella Tas. 130 C4
Mellis Vic. 42 I6
Melros WA 78 A10
Melrose NSW 12 A4, 19 Q2
Melrose SA 61 J2, 63 J12
Melrose Tas. 130 I7
Melrose Park NSW 4 G7
Melrose Park SA 54 H10
Melton SA 61 J6
Melton Vic. 36 H5, 38 B3
Melton Mowbray Tas. 129 L6
Melton South Vic. 36 H5
Melville WA 74 E10
Melville Forest Vic. 40 F3
Memana Tas. 128 B11
Memerambi Qld 111 N6
Mena Creek Qld 115 N8
Mena Park Vic. 36 A4
Menai NSW 8 F9
Menangle NSW 11 K11
Menangle Park NSW 11 K11
Mendooran NSW 12 G1, 14 E13
Mengha Tas. 130 D4
Menindee NSW 16 E13, 18 E1
Meningie SA 61 M12, 70 D4
Menora WA 76 H11

Mentone Vic. 35 C4
Menzies WA 82 I4
Menzies Creek Vic. 37 M7, 50 B12
Mepunga East Vic. 41 J10
Mepunga West Vic. 40 I9
Merah North NSW 14 F7
Merbein Vic. 18 D7, 44 G3
Merbein South Vic. 18 D7, 44 F3
Merbein West Vic. 19 D7, 44 F3
Mercunda SA 61 O8
Merebene NSW 14 E9
Meredith Vic. 36 E6, 41 P5
Meribah SA 18 A9, 44 A6, 61 R8, 70 I1
Merildin SA 61 L5
Merimal Qld 113 N10
Merimbula NSW 20 G11, 49 Q7
Merinda Qld 112 I2
Meringandan Qld 108 E7
Meringo NSW 20 H8, 27 N9
Meringur Vic. 18 B8, 44 C4
Meringur North Vic. 18 B7, 44 C4
Merino Vic. 40 D5
Mernda Vic. 37 K4, 38 D2, 46 G13
Merredin WA 80 I2, 82 F7
Merriang Vic. 37 K3, 38 D2, 46 G13, 47 O7, 48 A5
Merricks Vic. 37 K12
Merrigum Vic. 46 G6
Merrijig Vic. 47 M10
Merrinee Vic. 18 C7, 44 E4
Merrinee North Vic. 44 E4
Merriton SA 61 J4
Merriwa NSW 13 J2
Merriwagga NSW 19 M5
Merrygoen NSW 12 G1, 14 F13
Merrylands NSW 4 B8, 11 M8
Merrywinbone NSW 14 D6
Merseylea Tas. 130 I8
Merton Tas. 124 C5
Merton Vic. 47 J10
Metcalfe Vic. 43 R11, 46 D10
Methul NSW 12 A10, 19 Q8
Metricup WA 79 C8
Metung Vic. 39 R5, 48 G13
Meunna Tas. 130 E6
Mia Mia Vic. 46 D10
Miallo Qld 115 M5
Miami WA 78 A10
Miandetta NSW 17 Q10
Michael Creek Qld 115 N11
Michelago NSW 20 E7, 26 G6, 28 F10
Mickleham Vic. 37 J4, 38 C2, 46 F13
Middle Cove NSW 5 M5
Middle Creek Vic. 41 L2
Middle Dural NSW 6 B4
Middle Indigo Vic. 47 O4, 48 A2
Middle Park Qld 106 C6
Middle Park Vic. 33 J10
Middle River SA 60 G12
Middle Swan WA 77 Q7
Middle Tarwin Vic. 38 H10
Middlemount Qld 113 K9
Middlepoint NT 92 F3
Middleton Qld 118 I8
Middleton SA 59 H7
Middleton Tas. 126 G11, 129 L11
Middlingbank NSW 26 E11
Midge Point Qld 113 K4
Midgee Qld 113 N11
Midland WA 77 Q9, 78 D4
Midway Point Tas. 127 K5, 129 M8
Miena Tas. 129 J2, 131 J12
Miepoll Vic. 46 I7
Miga Lake Vic. 42 E11
Mil Lel SA 40 A5, 70 I12
Mila NSW 20 E12, 49 N8
Milabena Tas. 130 E5
Milang SA 61 L11, 70 C3
Milawa Vic. 47 N6
Milbong Qld 109 K11
Milbrulong NSW 12 A13, 19 P10
Milchomi NSW 14 D8
Mildura Vic. 18 D7, 44 G3
Mile End SA 54 G6
Miles Qld 111 K7
Milford Qld 109 J12
Milguy NSW 14 H5, 111 K13
Milikapiti NT 94 D3
Miling WA 82 C6
Milingimbi NT 95 L5

Mill Park Vic. 33 N1
Millaa Millaa Qld 115 M8
Millaroo Qld 112 G2
Millbrook Vic. 36 E4, 41 P3, 46 B13
Millers Point NSW 2 A2
Millfield NSW 13 L4
Millgrove Vic. 37 N6, 38 G3, 50 G9
Millicent SA 70 G11
Millie NSW 14 F6
Millmerran Qld 108 A10, 111 M10
Millner NT 91 D7
Milloo Vic. 43 R7, 46 C5
Millstream-Chichester National Park WA 81 H2, 84 A3
Millstream Falls National Park Qld 115 M8
Millswood SA 54 I8
Millthorpe NSW 12 G6
Milltown Vic. 40 E7
Millwood NSW 12 A12, 19 Q9
Milman Qld 113 N10
Milparinka NSW 16 C4
Milperra NSW 8 D5, 11 M9
Miltalie SA 60 G4
Milton NSW 13 J13, 27 P4
Milton Qld 104 F12
Milvale NSW 12 D9, 20 B2
Milyakburra NT 95 O8
Mimili SA 67 L4
Mimmindie Vic. 18 H13, 43 O5
Mimosa NSW 12 B10, 19 R8
Mimosa Rocks National Park NSW 20 G10, 49 R5
Minamia NT 95 K13, 97 K2
Minbrie SA 60 G4
Mincha Vic. 18 I13, 43 P4, 46 B3
Mindarie SA 61 P9, 70 G1
Minden Qld 109 J8
Mindiyarra SA 61 O9, 70 F2
Miners Rest Vic. 36 C3, 41 O3, 46 A13
Minerva Hills National Park Qld 112 I12
Mingary SA 63 Q10
Mingay Vic. 41 L5
Mingela Qld 112 F2
Mingenew WA 82 B4
Mingoola NSW 15 L3, 111 M13
Minhamite Vic. 40 H7
Minilya Roadhouse WA 81 B6
Minimay Vic. 42 B9, 70 I8
Mininera Vic. 41 K4
Minjilang NT 94 H2
Minlaton SA 60 I9
Minmi NSW 13 M4
Minnie Water NSW 15 Q6
Minniging WA 80 F6
Minnipa SA 60 B2, 62 A12, 69 R12
Minnivale WA 80 G1
Minore NSW 12 E2
Mintabie SA 67 N5
Mintaro SA 61 L6
Minto NSW 11 L10
Minvalara SA 61 L2, 63 K12
Minyip Vic. 42 I8
Miowera NSW 14 A12, 17 R10
Miralie Vic. 45 M9
Miram Vic. 42 C7
Miram South Vic. 42 C7
Miranda NSW 9 J11, 11 N10
Mirani Qld 113 K5
Mirannie NSW 13 M2
Mirboo Vic. 37 R13, 39 J9
Mirboo North Vic. 37 R12, 38 I8
Miriam Vale Qld 111 M1, 113 Q13
Mirima (Hidden Valley) National Park WA 87 R5
Mirimbah Vic. 47 N11
Miriwinni Qld 115 N8
Mirmgadja Village NT 95 M6
Mirrabooka WA 76 I8, 78 C4
Mirranatwa Vic. 40 H3
Mirrool NSW 12 A9, 19 Q7
Missabotti NSW 15 O9
Mission Beach Qld 115 N9
Mitcham SA 55 J11, 58 B10, 59 G1
Mitcham Vic. 33 R9, 34 A9
Mitchell ACT 24 H5
Mitchell Qld 110 F6
Mitchell Park SA 54 G12
Mitchell River National Park Vic. 39 O3, 48 E12
Mitchell-Alice Rivers National Park Qld 114 E3
Mitchells Hill Vic. 43 K9
Mitchellstown Vic. 46 F9

Mitchelton Qld 104 D9
Mitiamo Vic. 43 Q6, 46 C5
Mitre Vic. 42 E9
Mitta Mitta Vic. 47 R7, 48 E5
Mittagong NSW 13 J10, 20 I2
Mittons Bridge Vic. 37 L4
Mittyack Vic. 45 J9
Miva Qld 111 O5
Moama NSW 19 K13, 46 E4
Moana SA 58 A13, 59 E4, 61 K10, 70 B2
Mockinya Vic. 42 G11
Moculta SA 58 G4
Modbury SA 57 O10, 58 B8
Modbury Heights SA 57 N8
Modella Vic. 37 O10, 38 G7
Modewarre Vic. 36 E10, 41 P8
Moe Vic. 37 R10, 39 J7
Mogendoura NSW 27 M8
Moggill Qld 106 A8
Mogil Mogil NSW 14 D5
Moglonemby Vic. 46 I7
Mogo NSW 20 H7, 27 N7
Mogriguy NSW 12 E2
Mogumber WA 80 D1
Moil NT 91 G6
Moina Tas. 130 H8
Moira NSW 19 K13, 46 F3
Mokepilly Vic. 40 I1, 43 J12
Mokine WA 78 H2, 80 E3
Mole Creek Tas. 130 I9
Mole Creek Karst National Park Tas. 130 I9
Mole River NSW 15 M4, 111 N13
Molesworth Tas. 126 G4
Molesworth Vic. 37 N1, 46 I11
Moliagul Vic. 43 N10
Molka Vic. 46 I8
Mollongghip Vic. 36 D3
Mollymook NSW 27 P4
Mologa Vic. 43 Q6, 46 B4
Molong NSW 12 F5
Moltema Tas. 131 J8
Molyullah Vic. 47 L7
Mona SA 61 J5
Mona Vale NSW 7 P7, 11 P6, 21 H13
Monarto SA 58 G11
Monarto South SA 58 G12, 61 M10, 70 D2
Monash ACT 25 D9
Monash SA 61 Q7
Monbulk Vic. 34 G12, 37 M7, 38 F4, 50 B11
Monea Vic. 46 H9
Monegeetta Vic. 36 I3, 38 B1, 46 E12
Monga NSW 27 M5
Mongarlowe NSW 12 I13, 20 G6, 27 M4
Monkey Mia WA 81 B10
Montacute SA 55 Q4
Montagu Tas. 130 C4
Montagu Bay Tas. 124 I6
Montana Tas. 131 J9
Monteagle NSW 12 E9, 20 C1
Monterey NSW 9 M7
Montgomery Vic. 39 N6
Montmorency Vic. 33 P4
Monto Qld 111 M2
Montrose Tas. 124 C3
Montrose Vic. 34 F9
Montumana Tas. 130 E5
Montville Qld 109 M1
Mooball NSW 15 Q2, 111 Q11
Moockra SA 63 J11
Moodlu Qld 109 L4
Moogara Tas. 126 D4, 129 J8
Moogerah Qld 108 I12
Moogerah Peaks National Park Qld 108 I12
Moola Qld 108 C3, 111 M8
Moolerr Vic. 43 L9
Mooloolaba Qld 109 N1, 111 Q7
Mooloolah Qld 109 M2
Mooloolah River National Park Qld 109 N2
Moolpa NSW 18 H9, 45 O8
Moombooldool NSW 19 P7
Moombra Qld 108 I6
Moona Plains NSW 15 M10
Moonah Tas. 124 E4, 126 H5
Moonambel Vic. 43 M11
Moonan Flat NSW 13 L1, 15 K13
Moonbah NSW 26 C13
Moonbi NSW 15 K10
Moondarra Vic. 39 J6
Moonee Beach NSW 15 P8

Moonee Ponds Vic. 32 I6
Mooney Mooney NSW 11 O5, 21 D10
Moonford Qld 111 L2
Moonie Qld 111 K9
Moonta SA 60 I6
Moonta Bay SA 60 I6
Moora WA 82 C6
Moorabbin Vic. 35 B2
Mooralla Vic. 40 G3
Moore Qld 108 H2, 111 O7
Moore Creek NSW 15 J10
Moore Park NSW 5 N12, 9 P2
Moore Park Qld 111 O2
Moore River National Park WA 80 C1, 82 C7
Moorebank NSW 8 B4
Mooreville Tas. 130 G6
Moorilda NSW 10 A6, 12 G7
Moorilim Vic. 46 H7
Moorina Tas. 131 P7
Moorine Rock WA 82 G7
Moorland NSW 13 P1, 15 O13
Moorlands SA 61 N10, 70 E3
Moorleah Tas. 130 F5
Moormbool Vic. 46 F8
Moorngag Vic. 47 L8
Moorooduc Vic. 37 K10
Moorook SA 61 P7
Moorooka Qld 106 G4
Moorookyle Vic. 36 D2
Mooroolbark Vic. 34 E7
Mooroopna Vic. 46 H6
Moorowie SA 60 H10
Moorrinya National Park Qld 112 B5, 119 Q5
Moorumbine WA 80 G5
Mootwingee National Park NSW 16 E8
Moppin NSW 14 G4, 111 J13
Moranbah Qld 112 I7
Morangarell NSW 12 C9, 20 A1
Morawa WA 82 C4
Morayfield Qld 109 M5
Morchard SA 61 K1, 63 K12
Mordialloc Vic. 35 C6, 37 J8
Morea Vic. 42 C9
Moree NSW 14 G5
Moree Vic. 40 D1, 42 D13
Morella Qld 119 O10
Moreton Island National Park Qld 109 P5, 111 Q8
Morgan SA 61 N6
Morgans Crossing NSW 49 P6
Moriac Vic. 36 E10, 41 Q8
Moriarty Tas. 131 J7
Morisset NSW 11 Q1, 13 M5
Morkalla Vic. 18 B7, 44 B4, 61 R7
Morley WA 77 K9
Morningside Qld 104 I11
Mornington Tas. 125 L5
Mornington Vic. 37 K10, 38 D7
Mornington Peninsula Vic. 37 J12, 38 C8
Mornington Peninsula National Park Vic. 36 H11, 37 J12, 38 B8
Morongla NSW 12 F8, 20 D1
Morpeth NSW 13 M4
Morphett Vale SA 58 A12, 59 F3
Morphettville SA 54 F11
Morri Morri Vic. 43 K10
Morrisons Vic. 36 E6
Mortat Vic. 42 C9
Mortchup Vic. 36 A5, 41 M4
Mortdale NSW 8 I6
Mortlake NSW 4 H8
Mortlake Vic. 41 J7
Morton National Park NSW 13 J11, 20 H4, 27 O2
Morton Plains Vic. 43 K5
Morundah NSW 19 O9
Moruya NSW 20 H7, 27 M8
Moruya Heads NSW 20 H7, 27 N8
Morven NSW 19 Q12, 47 Q1
Morven Qld 110 D6
Morwell Vic. 39 J7
Morwell National Park Vic. 39 J8
Mosman NSW 5 O7, 11 O8
Mosman Park WA 74 B7
Mosquito Creek NSW 14 I5
Mosquito Flat SA 59 H6
Moss Vale NSW 13 J10, 20 I3
Mossgiel NSW 19 J3
Mossman Qld 115 M5
Mossy Point NSW 20 H7, 27 N8
Moulamein NSW 18 I10, 45 P9

Moulyinning WA 80 H7
Mount Aberdeen National Park Qld 112 H2
Mount Adrah NSW 12 C12, 20 B5
Mount Alford Qld 108 I12, 111 P10
Mount Alfred Vic. 20 A8, 48 F1
Mount Augustus National Park WA 81 F7
Mount Barker SA 58 E11, 59 I2, 61 L10, 70 C2
Mount Barker WA 80 H12, 82 E12
Mount Barney National Park Qld 15 O1, 111 P11
Mount Bauple National Park Qld 111 O5
Mount Baw Baw Vic. 37 R7, 39 J4
Mount Beauty Vic. 47 Q8, 48 D6
Mount Beckworth Vic. 36 B2
Mount Benson SA 70 F9
Mount Beppo Qld 108 I4
Mount Berryman Qld 108 H9
Mount Best Vic. 39 J9
Mount Bruce SA 70 G10
Mount Bryan SA 61 L4
Mount Bryan East SA 61 M4
Mount Buffalo National Park Vic. 47 O7, 48 B5
Mount Buller Vic. 47 N11
Mount Burr SA 70 G11
Mount Bute Vic. 36 A7, 41 M5
Mount Carbine Qld 115 L5
Mount Carmel Vic. 46 E8
Mount Charlton Qld 113 K5
Mount Christie SA 69 M4
Mount Claremont WA 74 C3
Mount Colah NSW 6 F7
Mount Compass SA 59 G5, 61 K10, 70 B3
Mount Cook National Park Qld 115 L3
Mount Coolon Qld 112 H5
Mount Cooper SA 60 A3, 69 Q13
Mount Cotton Qld 107 Q7
Mount Cottrell Vic. 36 H6
Mount Damper SA 60 B3, 62 A13, 69 R13
Mount Dandenong Vic. 34 F10
Mount Darry Qld 108 E4
Mount David NSW 10 C8, 12 H7
Mount Direction Tas. 131 L7
Mount Donna Buang Vic. 38 G3
Mount Doran Vic. 36 D5, 41 P4
Mount Druitt NSW 11 L7
Mount Drysdale NSW 17 N9
Mount Duneed Vic. 36 F10
Mount Ebenezer Roadhouse NT 98 H11
Mount Eccles Vic. 37 Q12, 38 H8
Mount Eccles National Park Vic. 40 F7
Mount Edwards Qld 108 I12
Mount Egerton Vic. 36 E5, 41 Q4
Mount Emlyn Qld 108 A11
Mount Emu Vic. 36 A5, 41 M4
Mount Evelyn Vic. 34 G7, 50 B9
Mount Fairy NSW 27 K1
Mount Field National Park Tas. 126 A2, 128 I7
Mount Forbes Qld 109 J10
Mount Frankland National Park WA 80 F12, 82 D12
Mount Franklin Vic. 36 E2
Mount Gambier SA 70 H12
Mount Garnet Qld 115 L8
Mount George NSW 13 O1, 15 N13
Mount Gravatt Qld 107 J4
Mount Gunderbooka NSW 17 M7
Mount Hallen Qld 108 I6
Mount Hawthorn WA 76 G12
Mount Helen Vic. 36 C4, 41 O4
Mount Helena WA 78 E3, 80 D3
Mount Hope NSW 19 N2
Mount Hope SA 60 C6
Mount Horeb NSW 12 D12, 20 B5
Mount Hotham Vic. 47 Q10, 48 D8
Mount Hunter NSW 11 K10
Mount Hypipamee National Park Qld 115 M8
Mount Imlay National Park NSW 20 F12, 49 P9
Mount Irvine NSW 10 I4
Mount Irving Qld 108 C7
Mount Isa Qld 118 E4
Mount Kaputar National Park NSW 14 H7
Mount Keith WA 82 H1, 84 F12
Mount Kilcoy Qld 109 J2
Mount Kosciuszko NSW 20 C9, 26 A13
Mount Kuring-gai NSW 6 G6
Mount Lambie NSW 10 E4
Mount Larcom Qld 113 O12
Mount Lawley WA 75 J1, 77 J12
Mount Lewis NSW 4 E13, 8 G3
Mount Liebig NT 98 E7

Mount Lloyd Tas. 126 E5, 129 K8
Mount Lonarch Vic. 41 M1, 43 M13
Mount Macedon Vic. 36 H3, 38 B1, 46 E12
Mount Magnet WA 82 E2
Mount Marshall Qld 108 E12
Mount Martha Vic. 37 J10, 38 D7
Mount Mary SA 61 N6
Mount McIntyre SA 70 H11
Mount Mee Qld 109 K4
Mount Mercer Vic. 36 C6, 41 O5
Mount Molloy Qld 115 M6
Mount Morgan Qld 113 N11
Mount Moriac Vic. 36 E10, 41 Q8
Mount Muirhead SA 70 G11
Mount Mulligan Qld 115 L6
Mount Nebo Qld 109 K7
Mount Nelson Tas. 124 E7
Mount Olive NSW 13 L3
Mount Ommaney Qld 106 C6
Mount Osmond SA 55 M9
Mount Ossa Qld 113 K4
Mount Perry Qld 111 N3
Mount Pleasant Qld 109 K5
Mount Pleasant SA 58 G8, 61 M9, 70 D1
Mount Pleasant WA 74 G8
Mount Pritchard NSW 8 A2
Mount Rat SA 60 I8
Mount Remarkable National Park SA 61 J1, 62 I12
Mount Richmond Vic. 40 C8
Mount Richmond National Park Vic. 40 C8
Mount Rowan Vic. 36 C3
Mount St Gwinear Vic. 39 J4
Mount Samson Qld 109 L6
Mount Schank SA 70 H12
Mount Seaview NSW 15 M12
Mount Selwyn NSW 20 C7, 26 C8
Mount Seymour Tas. 129 M5
Mount Sibley Qld 108 E10
Mount Slide Vic. 37 M4, 50 C3
Mount Spec/Crystal Creek Nat. Pk see Paluma
  Range Nat. Pk
Mount Stirling Vic. 47 N11, 48 A9
Mount Stuart Tas. 124 E7
Mount Surprise Qld 115 J10
Mount Sylvia Qld 108 G9
Mount Tamborine Qld 109 N12
Mount Tarampa Qld 108 I7
Mount Taylor Vic. 39 P4, 48 F13
Mount Thorley NSW 13 L3
Mount Torrens SA 58 F9
Mount Tyson Qld 108 C7
Mount Victoria NSW 10 H6, 13 J7
Mount Walker Qld 108 I10
Mount Walker WA 82 F8
Mount Wallace Vic. 36 F5, 41 Q4
Mount Walsh National Park Qld 111 N4
Mount Warning National Park NSW 15 Q1,
  111 Q11
Mount Waverley Vic. 33 P11
Mount Webb National Park Qld 115 L2
Mount Wedge SA 60 B4
Mount Wells Battery NT 92 I11
Mount White NSW 11 O4, 13 L6, 21 C9
Mount Whitestone Qld 108 G9
Mount William National Park Tas. 131 Q6
Mount Wilson NSW 10 H5
Mountain River Tas. 126 G7, 129 K9
Moura Qld 111 J1
Mourilyan Qld 115 N8
Moutajup Vic. 40 G4
Mowbray Tas. 131 L8
Mowbray Park NSW 11 J11
Mowen WA 79 C10
Moyhu Vic. 47 M7
Moyreisk Vic. 43 M10
Moyston Vic. 41 J2, 43 J13
Muchea WA 78 C1, 80 D2
Muckadilla Qld 108 G6
Mudamuckla SA 69 O10
Mudgee NSW 12 H3
Mudgeeraba Qld 109 O13, 111 Q10
Mudgegonga Vic. 47 P6, 48 B4
Mudginberri NT 93 Q3
Muggleton Qld 110 H6
Mukinbudin WA 82 F6
Mulambin Qld 113 O10
Mulcra Vic. 44 B10, 61 R10, 70 I2
Muldu Qld 108 D5
Mulgildie Qld 111 M2

Mulgoa NSW 11 K8, 13 K8
Mulgrave Vic. 33 R13, 35 G1
Mullaley NSW 14 H11
Mullaloo WA 76 A1, 78 A3
Mullalyup WA 79 I8, 80 D9
Mullaway NSW 15 P7
Mullenderee NSW 27 N8
Mullengandra NSW 19 Q13, 47 Q3
Mullengudgery NSW 14 A13, 17 R11
Mullewa WA 82 B3
Mulli Mulli NSW 15 O2, 111 P11
Mullindolingong Vic. 47 Q8, 48 C5
Mullion Creek NSW 12 G5
Mullumbimby NSW 15 Q2, 111 Q12
Mulpata SA 61 P10, 70 G2
Mulwala NSW 19 N13, 47 L3
Mumballup WA 80 D8
Mumbannar Vic. 40 B6, 70 I12
Mumbel Vic. 43 M2, 45 M12
Mumbil NSW 12 F4
Mumblin Vic. 41 K9
Mummulgum NSW 15 O3, 111 P12
Munbilla Qld 109 J11
Mundaring WA 78 E4, 80 D3, 82 C8
Mundijong WA 78 D7, 80 D5
Mundoona Vic. 46 H4
Mundoora SA 61 J4
Mundrabilla Roadhouse WA 83 Q8
Mundubbera Qld 111 M4
Mundulla SA 70 H7
Munetta SA 59 F5
Mungala SA 69 L4
Mungallala Qld 110 E6
Mungana Qld 115 J7
Mungar Qld 111 P4
Mungerannie Roadhouse SA 65 K8, 120 C10
Mungeribar NSW 12 D2
Mungery NSW 12 D3
Mungindi NSW 14 E3, 110 H13
Mungkan Kandju National Park Qld 116 D10
Munglinup WA 82 I10
Mungo National Park NSW 18 G5
Mungungo Qld 111 M2
Muniganeen Qld 108 E6
Munjina Roadhouse WA 84 C4
Munro Vic. 39 N5
Munster WA 78 B6
Muntadgin WA 82 F7
Muradup WA 80 F9
Murarrie Qld 105 K11
Murchison Vic. 46 H7
Murchison WA 81 E12, 82 C1
Murchison East Vic. 46 H7
Murdinga SA 60 D5
Murdoch WA 74 G12
Murdunna Tas. 127 N7, 129 O9
Murga NSW 12 E6
Murgenella Settlement NT 94 H3
Murgheboluc Vic. 36 E9
Murgon Qld 111 N6
Murninnie Beach SA 60 H3
Murphys Creek Qld 108 F7, 111 N9
Murphys Creek Vic. 43 O9
Murra Warra Vic. 42 G7
Murrabit Vic. 18 I11, 43 P1, 45 P12
Murramarang National Park NSW 27 O7
Murrawal NSW 14 F12
Murray Bridge SA 58 I12, 61 M10, 70 D2
Murray River National Park SA 18 A7, 61 Q7
Murray Town SA 61 K2, 63 J12
Murray-Sunset National Park Vic. 18 B9, 44 C7,
  61 R8, 70 I1
Murrayville Vic. 18 B11, 44 B10, 61 R10
Murrindal Vic. 20 C13, 48 I10
Murrindindi Vic. 37 N2, 38 F1, 46 I12
Murringo NSW 12 E9, 20 C2
Murroon Vic. 36 C12, 41 O10
Murrumba Vic. 18 I5
Murrumbateman NSW 12 F11, 20 E4
Murrumbeena Vic. 33 N12
Murrumburrah NSW 12 E10, 20 C3
Murrungowar Vic. 20 D13, 49 K12
Murrurundi NSW 15 J13
Murtoa Vic. 42 I9
Murwillumbah NSW 15 Q1, 111 Q11
Musgrave Station Qld 114 H1, 116 F13
Musk Vic. 36 E2
Musk Vale Vic. 36 E2
Muskerry East Vic. 46 D8

Musselboro Tas. 131 N9
Mussleroe Bay Tas. 131 Q4
Muston SA 60 I12
Muswellbrook NSW 13 K2
Mutarnee Qld 115 O12
Mutdapilly Qld 109 J10
Muttaburra Qld 112 B9, 119 P9
Muttama NSW 12 D11, 20 B4
Myall Vic. 43 P2, 45 P12
Myall Lakes National Park NSW 13 O3
Myall Mundi NSW 12 C1
Myall Plains NSW 19 N11
Myalla Tas. 130 E5
Myalup WA 79 G2, 80 C7
Myamyn Vic. 40 E7
Myaree WA 74 F10
Myaring Vic. 40 B5
Mylestom NSW 15 P8
Mylor SA 58 D11, 59 H2
Myola Vic. 46 E8
Mypolonga SA 61 N9, 70 D2
Myponga SA 59 E6, 61 K11, 70 B3
Myponga Beach SA 59 D6
Myrla SA 61 P7
Myrniong Vic. 36 F4, 41 R4, 46 C13
Myrrhee Vic. 47 M8
Myrtle Bank SA 55 K9
Myrtle Bank Tas. 131 M7
Myrtle Creek Vic. 43 R11, 46 D10
Myrtle Scrub NSW 15 M11
Myrtleford Vic. 47 O7, 48 B5
Myrtletown Qld 105 L6
Myrtleville NSW 12 I10, 20 G3
Mysia Vic. 43 O6
Mystic Park Vic. 18 H11, 43 O2, 45 O12
Mywee Vic. 46 I2
Mywybilla Qld 108 B7

Nabageena Tas. 130 C5
Nabawa WA 82 B3
Nabiac NSW 13 O2
Nabowla Tas. 131 N7
Nackara SA 61 M2, 63 M12
Nadda SA 18 A8, 61 Q8
Nagambie Vic. 46 G8
Nagoorin Qld 111 M1, 113 P13
Nailsworth SA 55 J3
Nairne SA 58 E11
Nakara NT 91 G2
Nala Tas. 129 M5
Nalinga Vic. 47 J6
Nalya WA 80 G5
Namadgi National Park ACT 12 F13, 20 D6, 26 E4,
  28 B7
Nambour Qld 109 M1, 111 P7
Nambrok Vic. 39 M6
Nambucca Heads NSW 15 P9
Nambung National Park WA 82 B6
Nana Glen NSW 15 P7
Nanango Qld 111 N7
Nanarup WA 80 I13
Nandaly Vic. 18 F11, 45 J10
Nandi Qld 111 M8
Nanga WA 78 D12, 80 D6
Nangalala NT 95 L5
Nangana Vic. 37 N7, 38 F4, 50 E11
Nangar National Park NSW 12 E6
Nangari SA 18 A8, 44 A5, 61 R8
Nangeenan WA 80 I2
Nangiloc Vic. 18 E8, 44 H5
Nangkita SA 59 H5, 61 L10, 70 C3
Nangus NSW 12 C12, 20 B5
Nangwarry SA 70 H11
Nanneella Vic. 46 F5
Nannup WA 79 G10, 80 C10, 82 C11
Nanson WA 82 A3
Nantabibbie SA 61 M2, 63 L12
Nantawarra SA 61 K6
Nanutarra Roadhouse WA 81 E4
Napoleons Vic. 36 C5, 41 O4
Napperby SA 61 J3, 63 J13
Nar Nar Goon Vic. 37 N9, 38 F6
Nara Qld 108 E6
Naracoopa Tas. 128 B9
Naracoorte SA 70 H9
Naradhan NSW 19 O5
Naraling WA 82 B3
Narangba Qld 109 M5
Narara NSW 11 P3, 21 E5

153

Narbethong Vic. 37 N4, 38 G2, 47 J13, 50 G4
Nareen Vic. 40 D3
Narellan NSW 11 K10
Narembeen WA 82 F8
Naretha WA 83 M6
Nariel Vic. 20 B9, 48 G4
Naringal Vic. 41 J9
Narioka Vic. 46 G4
Narko Qld 108 D4
Narnu Bay SA 59 I8
Narooma NSW 20 H9, 27 N11, 49 R2
Narrabarba NSW 20 G12, 49 P9
Narrabeen NSW 7 P10, 11 P7
Narrabri NSW 14 G8
Narrabri West NSW 14 G8
Narrabundah ACT 24 H13, 25 F4
Narracan Vic. 37 R11, 39 J7
Narrandera NSW 19 P9
Narraport Vic. 43 K5
Narrawa NSW 12 G10, 20 E2
Narrawa Tas. 130 H8
Narrawallee NSW 27 P3
Narraweena NSW 5 P2, 7 N12
Narrawong Vic. 40 E8
Narre Warren Vic. 37 L8
Narrewillock Vic. 43 M5
Narrldy SA 61 K4
Narrien Range National Park Qld 112 G9
Narrikup WA 80 H12
Narrogin WA 80 G6, 82 E9
Narromine NSW 12 D2
Narrung SA 61 M11, 70 D3
Narrung Vic. 45 L7
Narwee NSW 8 I5
Nashdale NSW 12 F6
Nathalia Vic. 19 L13, 46 H4
Nathan Qld 106 I5
Natimuk Vic. 42 F9
National Park Tas. 126 C2, 129 J7
Native Dog Flat Vic. 20 B11, 48 I7
Natone Tas. 130 G6
Nattai NSW 10 I11, 13 J8
Nattai National Park NSW 10 I12, 13 J9, 20 H2
Natte Yallock Vic. 43 M11
Natural Arch National Park see Springbrook
  National Park
Natya Vic. 18 G9, 45 L8
Naval Base WA 78 A6
Navarre Vic. 43 L10
Navigators Vic. 36 D4, 41 P4, 46 A13
Nayook Vic. 37 P7
Neale Junction WA 83 N2
Neales Flat SA 58 H1, 61 M7
Nebo Qld 113 K6
Nectar Brook SA 61 J1, 62 I11
Nedlands WA 74 E6
Neds Corner Vic. 44 C3
Needles Tas. 131 J9
Neerabup National Park WA 78 A2, 80 C3, 82 B8
Neerdie Qld 111 P5
Neerim Vic. 37 P8, 38 H5
Neerim East Vic. 37 Q8
Neerim Junction Vic. 37 P7
Neerim South Vic. 37 P8, 38 H5
Neeworra NSW 14 E4, 110 H13
Neika Tas. 126 H7, 129 L9
Neilborough Vic. 43 Q8, 46 C7
Neilborough East Vic. 43 Q8, 46 C7
Neilmongle NSW 17 Q2, 110 D13
Neilrex NSW 14 F13
Nelia Qld 119 K4
Nelligen NSW 20 H6, 27 N6
Nelly Bay Qld 115 P12
Nelshaby SA 61 J3, 63 J13
Nelson NSW 11 M6
Nelson Vic. 40 A7, 70 I13
Nelson Bay NSW 13 O4
Nelungaloo NSW 12 D5
Nene Valley SA 70 H12
Nepabunna Community SA 63 L4
Nerang Qld 109 N12, 111 Q10
Nerriga NSW 12 I12, 20 H5, 27 N1
Nerrigundah NSW 20 G8, 27 L10, 49 Q2
Nerrin Nerrin Vic. 41 K5
Nerrina Vic. 36 D4, 41 O3, 46 A13
Nerring Vic. 36 A3, 41 M3
Netherby SA 55 K10
Netherby Vic. 18 C13, 42 D5

Nethercote NSW 20 G11, 49 Q8
Netley SA 54 F8
Neuarpurr Vic. 42 B10, 70 I8
Neumgna Qld 108 F1
Neurea NSW 12 F4
Neuroodla SA 63 J8
Neurum Qld 109 K3
Neutral Bay NSW 5 N8
Neuve Qld 108 E5
Nevertire NSW 12 C1, 14 B13
Neville NSW 12 G7
Nevilton Qld 108 E10
New Angledool NSW 14 B4, 110 F13
New Brighton NSW 15 Q2
New England NSW 15 M7
New England National Park NSW 15 N9
New Farm Qld 104 I11
New Gisborne Vic. 36 H3, 38 B1, 46 E12
New Italy NSW 15 Q4, 111 Q13
New Mollyann NSW 14 F12
New Norcia WA 80 D1, 82 C6
New Norfolk Tas. 126 F4, 129 K8
New Residence SA 61 P7
New Town Tas. 124 F6
New Well SA 61 O7
Newborough Vic. 37 R10, 39 J7
Newbridge NSW 10 A6, 12 G7
Newbridge Vic. 43 P10, 46 A8
Newburn WA 75 O4
Newbury Vic. 36 F3, 41 Q2, 43 Q13, 46 C12
Newcastle NSW 13 N4
Newcastle Waters NT 96 I6
Newdegate WA 82 G9
Newell, The NSW 14 F10
Newfield Vic. 41 K10
Newham Vic. 36 H2, 38 B1, 46 E12
Newhaven Vic. 37 M13, 38 E9
Newland SA 59 G8
Newlands WA 79 H7, 80 D9
Newlyn Vic. 36 D3, 41 P2, 43 P13, 46 B12
Newman WA 84 D6
Newmarket Qld 104 E10, 109 L7
Newmerella Vic. 49 J13
Newnes NSW 10 G1, 13 J5
Newnes Junction NSW 10 G4
Newport NSW 7 P6, 11 P6, 21 H12
Newport Vic. 32 H10
Newport Beach NSW 7 Q6, 21 H12
Newry Vic. 39 M5
Newrybar NSW 15 Q3, 111 Q12
Newstead Qld 104 H10
Newstead Vic. 43 P12, 46 B10
Newton SA 55 N3
Newton Boyd NSW 15 N6
Newtown NSW 5 K12, 9 M2
Newtown Vic. 36 B5, 41 N4
Ngallo Vic. 44 A11, 70 I3
Ngapal SA 61 L6
Nguiu NT 94 D4
Ngukurr NT 95 L10
Ngunnawal ACT 24 F2
Nhill Vic. 42 D7
Nhulunbuy NT 95 P5
Ni Ni Vic. 42 E6
Niagara Park NSW 21 E5
Niangala NSW 15 K11
Nicholls ACT 24 F3
Nicholls Point Vic. 18 D7, 44 G3
Nicholls Rivulet Tas. 126 F10, 129 K10
Nicholson Vic. 39 Q4, 48 G13
Niddrie Vic. 32 H5
Niemur NSW 19 J10, 45 Q10
Nierinna Tas. 126 G8
Nietta Tas. 130 H8
Nightcap National Park NSW 15 Q2
Nightcliff NT 91 A5, 92 C2
Nildottie SA 61 N8, 70 E1
Nile Tas. 131 M10
Nilma Vic. 37 P10, 38 H6
Nimbin NSW 15 Q2, 111 Q12
Nimmitabel NSW 20 E10, 49 N5
Ninda Vic. 43 J1, 45 J11
Nindigully Qld 14 D1, 110 H11
Nine Mile Vic. 43 M7
Ninnes SA 61 J6
Ninyeunook Vic. 43 M5
Nipan Qld 111 J2
Nippering WA 80 H8
Nirranda Vic. 41 J10

Nirranda South Vic. 41 J10
Nitmiluk National Park NT 94 G9
Nobby Qld 108 E10, 111 N10
Noble Park Vic. 35 F4
Noccundra Qld 121 L10
Noggojerring WA 78 I1, 80 E2
Nollamara WA 76 H9
Nonda Qld 119 K4
Noojee Vic. 37 Q7, 38 I4
Nook Tas. 130 I8
Nookanellup WA 80 G9
Noonamah NT 92 E4, 94 E6
Noonameena SA 61 M12, 70 D4
Noonbinna NSW 12 E8, 20 D1
Noondoo Qld 14 C2, 110 G12
Noora SA 18 A8, 44 A5, 61 R7
Nooramunga Vic. 47 K6
Noorat Vic. 41 K8
Noorinbee Vic. 20 E13, 49 N11
Noorinbee North Vic. 20 E13, 49 N11
Noorong NSW 18 I11, 45 P11
Noorongong Vic. 47 Q5, 48 D3
Noosa Heads Qld 111 Q6
Nora Creina SA 70 F10
Noradjuha Vic. 42 F10
Norah Head NSW 11 Q2
Norahville NSW 11 Q2
Noranda WA 77 K8
Nords Wharf NSW 11 R1
Norillee Qld 108 B7
Norman Park Qld 104 I12
Normanhurst NSW 4 G1, 6 F11
Normanton Qld 114 C8, 117 I8
Normanville SA 59 D7, 61 K11, 70 B3
Normanville Vic. 43 N3
Nornakin WA 80 H4
Nornalup WA 80 F13
Norseman WA 83 J8
North Adelaide SA 52 C4, 54 H5
North Avoca NSW 21 H6
North Beach SA 60 I5
North Beach WA 76 B8
North Berry Jerry NSW 12 B11, 19 R9
North Bondi NSW 5 Q11
North Brighton SA 54 D12
North Bruny Island Tas. 129 M10
North Dandalup WA 78 C9, 80 D5, 82 C9
North Fremantle WA 74 A9
North Haven NSW 15 O12
North Haven SA 56 C6
North Hobart Tas. 124 F6, 126 H6
North Lake WA 74 F13
North Lilydale Tas. 131 M7
North Maclean Qld 109 L10
North Melbourne Vic. 30 A3
North Motton Tas. 130 H7
North Perth WA 74 H1, 76 H13
North Richmond NSW 11 K5
North Rocks NSW 4 D4
North Ryde NSW 4 I5
North Scottsdale Tas. 131 N6
North Shields SA 60 D8
North Star NSW 14 I3, 111 K12
North Stradbroke Island Qld 109 P9, 111 R9
North Sydney NSW 5 M8, 11 O8
North Yunderup WA 78 B10, 80 C5
Northam WA 78 H2, 80 E3, 82 D7
Northampton WA 82 A3
Northbridge NSW 5 M6
Northbridge WA 72 C4, 74 H2
Northcliffe WA 80 D12, 82 D12
Northcote Vic. 33 L7
Northdown Tas. 131 J6
Northfield SA 57 K11
Northgate Qld 104 H7
Northmead NSW 4 C5
Northwood NSW 5 L7
Northwood Vic. 46 G10
Norton Summit SA 55 P6, 58 C9
Norwell Qld 109 N10
Norwin Qld 108 B7
Norwood SA 55 K6
Notley Hills Tas. 131 K8
Notting WA 80 I5
Notting Hill Vic. 33 P13, 35 E1
Notts Well SA 61 O7
Novar Gardens SA 54 E9
Nowa Hill NSW 13 J11, 20 I4
Nowa Nowa Vic. 48 H12

Nowendoc NSW 15 L12
Nowie North Vic. 45 M10
Nowingi Vic. 44 G6
Nowley NSW 14 E7
Nowra NSW 13 K11, 20 I4
Nubba NSW 12 D10, 20 B3
Nubeena Tas. 127 M10, 129 N10
Nudgee Qld 104 I5
Nudgee Beach Qld 104 I5
Nug Nug Vic. 47 O8, 48 B5
Nuga Nuga National Park Qld 110 G2
Nugent Tas. 127 M4, 129 N7
Nulla Vale Vic. 36 I1
Nullan Vic. 42 I7
Nullarbor National Park SA 68 C7, 83 R7
Nullarbor Roadhouse SA 68 G7
Nullawarre Vic. 41 J10
Nullawil Vic. 18 G12, 43 L4
Numbla Vale NSW 20 D10, 49 L5
Numbugga NSW 20 G10, 49 P6
Numbulwar NT 95 N9
Numeralla NSW 20 F8, 26 H10, 49 O2
Numurkah Vic. 19 M13, 46 I4
Nunamara Tas. 131 M8
Nunawading Vic. 33 Q8
Nundah Qld 104 H8
Nundle NSW 15 K12
Nundroo Roadhouse SA 69 J8
Nunga Vic. 44 H9
Nungarin WA 80 I1
Nungurner Vic. 39 R5, 48 G13
Nunjikompita SA 69 P10
Nurina WA 83 O6
Nurinda Qld 108 I3
Nuriootpa SA 58 F4, 61 M8
Nurom SA 61 J3
Nurrabiel Vic. 42 G11
Nutfield Vic. 37 L4
Nutgrove Qld 108 E3
Nyabing WA 80 I8, 82 F10
Nyah Vic. 18 G10, 45 M10
Nyah West Vic. 18 G10, 45 M10
Nyallo Vic. 42 I3, 44 I13
Nyarrin Vic. 45 J11
Nyirripi NT 98 D6
Nymagee NSW 17 O12
Nymboida NSW 15 O7
Nymboida National Park NSW 15 N6
Nymbool Qld 115 L8
Nyngan NSW 17 R10
Nyora Vic. 37 O11, 38 G8
Nypo Vic. 42 F3, 44 F13

O'Connell NSW 10 C5
O'Connor ACT 24 G8
O'Connor WA 74 D11
O'Malley ACT 25 E4
O'Malley SA 68 G4
Oak Beach Qld 115 M6
Oak Park Vic. 32 I4
Oakbank SA 58 D10, 59 I1
Oakdale NSW 11 J11, 13 J8, 20 I1
Oakden SA 57 L11
Oakey Qld 108 D6, 111 N9
Oakey Creek NSW 14 G12
Oaklands NSW 19 O11
Oaklands SA 60 I9
Oaklands Park SA 54 F12
Oakleigh Vic. 33 O12, 35 D1, 38 D4
Oakleigh East Vic. 33 O12
Oaks Tas. 131 L9
Oakvale Vic. 43 N4
Oakwood Tas. 127 N10, 129 N10
Oasis Roadhouse Qld 115 K11
Oatlands Tas. 129 M5
Oatley NSW 8 I7
Ob Flat SA 70 H12
Oberne NSW 12 C13, 20 A6
Oberon NSW 10 E7, 12 I7
Obi Obi Qld 109 L1
Obley NSW 12 E4
OBX Creek NSW 15 O6
Ocean Grove Vic. 36 G10, 38 A7, 41 R8
Ocean Shores NSW 15 Q2, 111 Q12
Ockley WA 80 G6
Oenpelli (Gunbalanya) NT 93 R1, 94 I5
Officer Vic. 37 M9
Ogilvie WA 82 A3

Ogmore Qld 113 M9
Olary SA 63 P10
Old Adaminaby NSW 20 D8, 26 D9, 49 K1
Old Bar NSW 13 P1
Old Beach Tas. 126 H4, 129 L8
Old Bonalbo NSW 15 O2, 111 P12
Old Junee NSW 12 C11, 19 R9, 20 A4
Old Noarlunga SA 58 A12, 59 F3, 61 K10, 70 B2
Old Tallangatta Vic. 47 R4, 48 D2
Old Toongabbie NSW 4 B5
Old Warrah NSW 14 I12
Oldina Tas. 130 F6
Olinda NSW 12 I4
Olinda Vic. 34 F11, 37 M7, 38 E4, 50 B11
Olio Qld 119 M7
Olympic Dam Village SA 62 F4
Ombersley Vic. 36 C10, 41 O8
Omeo Vic. 20 A12, 48 F8
Ondit Vic. 36 B10
One Arm Point WA 86 I6
One Tree NSW 19 K7
One Tree Hill SA 57 R1
Ongerup WA 82 F11
Onslow WA 81 D3
Oodla Wirra SA 61 M2, 63 L12
Oodnadatta SA 64 B6
Ooldea SA 68 I4
Ooma Creek NSW 12 D7
Ooma North NSW 12 D7
Oonah Tas. 130 F7
Oondooroo Qld 119 L7
Oorindi Qld 118 H4
Ootann Qld 115 K8
Ootha NSW 12 B5, 19 R3
Opalton Qld 119 L10
Ophir NSW 12 G5
Opossum Bay Tas. 126 I8, 129 M9
Ora Banda WA 82 I5
Orange NSW 12 G6
Orange Grove WA 75 Q8
Orangeville NSW 11 J10
Oranmeir NSW 20 F7, 27 K6
Orbost Vic. 49 J12
Orchid Beach Qld 111 Q2
Orford Tas. 127 N1, 129 O6
Orford Vic. 40 G8
Organ Pipes National Park Vic. 32 E1, 36 I5, 38 C3
Orielton Tas. 127 K4, 129 M7
Ormeau Qld 109 N11
Ormiston Qld 105 R13, 107 R1
Ormond Vic. 33 M12, 35 B1
Orpheus Island National Park Qld 115 O11
Orroroo SA 61 L1, 63 K12
Orrvale Vic. 46 I6
Orton Park NSW 10 B4
Osborne SA 56 D7
Osborne Park WA 76 F11
Osbornes Flat Vic. 47 P5, 48 B3
Osbourne NSW 12 A13, 19 P11
Osmaston Tas. 131 K9
Osmington WA 79 D9, 80 B9
Osterley Tas. 129 J5
Otford NSW 11 M12
Ottaba Qld 108 I5
Ottoway SA 56 F11
Otway National Park Vic. 41 N12
Oura NSW 12 C12, 19 R10, 20 A5
Ourimbah NSW 11 P3, 13 M6, 21 E4
Ournie NSW 20 B8, 48 G1
Ouse Tas. 129 J6
Outer Harbor SA 56 C5, 58 A7
Outtrim Vic. 37 O13, 38 G9
Ouyen Vic. 18 E10, 44 H9
Ovens Vic. 47 O7, 48 B5
Overland Corner SA 61 P6
Overlander Roadhouse WA 81 C11
Ovingham SA 52 B3
Owanyilla Qld 111 P4
Owen SA 58 A1, 61 K7
Owens Gap NSW 13 K1
Oxenford Qld 109 N12, 111 Q10
Oxford Falls NSW 5 O1, 7 N11
Oxford Park Qld 104 D9
Oxley ACT 25 C9
Oxley NSW 18 I7, 45 Q3
Oxley Qld 106 E6
Oxley Vic. 47 M6
Oxley Wild Rivers National Park NSW 15 M10
Oyster Bay NSW 8 I9

Oyster Cove Tas. 126 G9, 129 L10
Ozenkadnook Vic. 42 C10

Paaratte Vic. 41 K10
Pacific Palms NSW 13 P2
Pacific Paradise Qld 109 N1
Packsaddle Roadhouse NSW 16 C7
Padbury WA 76 B3
Paddington NSW 5 N11, 9 P1, 11 O8
Paddington Qld 104 F12
Paddys River NSW 12 I10, 20 H3
Padstow NSW 8 G6
Padthaway SA 70 H7
Page ACT 24 C6
Pages Flat SA 59 F5
Pagewood NSW 9 P5
Paignie Vic. 44 G9
Pajinka Wilderness Lodge Qld 116 C2
Pakenham Vic. 37 M9, 38 F6
Palana Tas. 128 A10
Palgarup WA 80 D10
Pallamallawa NSW 14 H5
Pallara Qld 106 G9
Pallarang Vic. 44 C9
Pallarenda Qld 115 P12
Pallarup WA 82 H10
Palm Beach NSW 7 Q2, 11 P5, 21 H11
Palm Cove Qld 115 M6
Palm Dale NSW 11 P3, 21 E3
Palm Grove NSW 11 P3, 21 D4
Palm Valley see Finke Gorge National Park
Palmer SA 58 H9, 61 M9, 70 D1
Palmer River Roadhouse Qld 115 K4
Palmers Island NSW 15 Q5
Palmers Oakey NSW 10 D2, 12 I5
Palmerston ACT 24 G3
Palmerston NT 92 D3
Palmerville Qld 115 J4
Palmwoods Qld 109 M1
Palmyra WA 74 D10
Paloona Tas. 130 I7
Paluma Range National Park Qld 115 N11
Pambula NSW 20 G11, 49 Q7
Pambula Beach NSW 20 G11, 49 Q7
Pampas Qld 108 B9, 111 M10
Panania NSW 8 E5
Panitya Vic. 44 A10, 61 R10, 70 I2
Panmure Vic. 41 J9
Pannawonica WA 81 F3
Panorama SA 55 J11
Pantapin WA 80 H3
Panton Hill Vic. 34 C1, 37 L5, 38 E3
Pappinbarra NSW 15 N12
Papunya NT 98 G7
Para Hills SA 57 M8
Para Vista SA 57 M9
Paraburdoo WA 81 H5, 84 A6
Parachilna SA 63 J6
Paradise SA 55 M2, 57 N13
Paradise Tas. 130 I8
Paradise Vic. 43 K10
Paradise Vic. 41 N12
Paradise Beach Vic. 39 O7
Parafield SA 57 K8
Parafield Gardens SA 57 J6
Paralowie SA 57 J4
Parap NT 90 E6, 91 A13
Parattah Tas. 129 M5
Pardoo Roadhouse WA 86 D12
Parenna Tas. 128 A9
Parilla SA 61 Q10, 70 H3
Paringa SA 18 A7, 61 Q6
Paris Creek SA 58 D13, 59 I4
Park Holme SA 54 F11
Park Orchards Vic. 33 R7, 34 A7
Park Ridge Qld 107 J13
Parkers Corner Vic. 39 J5
Parkes ACT 23 D9, 24 G11, 25 F1
Parkes NSW 12 D5
Parkham Tas. 131 J8
Parkhurst Qld 113 N10
Parkinson Qld 106 I10
Parkside SA 52 H13, 55 J8
Parkside Tas. 131 Q8
Parkville NSW 13 K1
Parkville Vic. 33 K7
Parkwood Vic. 40 E4
Parndana SA 60 H12
Parnella Tas. 131 R8

Parrakie SA 61 P11, 70 G3
Parramatta NSW 4 C6, 11 M8, 13 L7
Parrawe Tas. 130 E7
Paru NT 94 D4
Paruna SA 18 A9, 61 Q8, 70 H1
Parwan Vic. 36 G5, 38 A3, 41 R4
Pasadena SA 54 H12
Paschendale Vic. 40 D4
Pascoe Vale Vic. 33 J4
Paskeville SA 61 J6
Pastoria Vic. 36 H1
Pata SA 61 Q8
Patchewollock Vic. 18 D11, 44 G11
Pateena Tas. 131 L9
Paterson NSW 13 M3
Patersonia Tas. 131 M8
Patho Vic. 46 D3
Patonga NSW 11 O5, 21 F10
Patrick Estate Qld 109 J7
Patterson Lakes Vic. 35 E9
Patyah Vic. 42 C10
Paupong NSW 20 D10, 49 K5
Pawleena Tas. 127 K4, 129 N7
Pawtella Tas. 129 M5
Paxton NSW 13 L4
Payneham SA 55 L4
Paynes Crossing NSW 13 L4
Paynes Find WA 82 E4
Paynesville Vic. 39 Q5
Paytens Bridge NSW 12 D7
Peaceful Bay WA 80 F13, 82 D12
Peachester Qld 109 L2
Peak Charles National Park WA 82 I9
Peak Crossing Qld 109 K10, 111 P10
Peak Downs Qld 112 I8
Peak Hill NSW 12 D4
Peak Hill WA 84 C10
Peak Range National Park Qld 112 I9
Peak View NSW 20 F8, 26 I10, 49 O1
Peake SA 61 O11, 70 F3
Peakhurst NSW 8 H6, 11 N9
Pearce ACT 25 C5
Pearcedale Vic. 37 L10, 38 E7
Pearl Beach NSW 21 F10
Pearshape Tas. 128 A9
Peats Ridge NSW 11 O3, 13 L6, 21 B4
Pebbly Beach NSW 20 H6, 27 O6
Pechey Qld 108 F6
Peebinga SA 18 A9, 44 A8, 61 R9, 70 I1
Peechelba Vic. 47 M4
Peechelba East Vic. 47 M4
Peel NSW 10 C3, 12 H6
Peelhurst WA 78 B9, 80 C5
Peelwood NSW 10 A11, 12 G8, 20 F1
Peep Hill SA 61 M6
Pegarah Tas. 128 A9
Pekina SA 61 K2, 63 K12
Pelham Tas. 126 E1, 129 K6
Pella Vic. 42 F4
Pelverata Tas. 126 F8, 129 K9
Pemberton WA 80 D11, 82 C11
Pembroke NSW 15 O12
Penarie NSW 18 H7, 45 N4
Pendle Hill NSW 4 A6
Penguin Tas. 130 H6
Penna Tas. 127 K4, 129 M8
Pennant Hills NSW 4 G1, 6 E11
Penneshaw SA 61 J12
Pennington SA 54 E1, 56 E12
Pennyroyal Vic. 36 C12
Penola SA 40 A3, 70 I10
Penong SA 69 M9
Penrith NSW 11 K7, 13 K7
Penrose NSW 13 J10, 20 H3
Penshurst NSW 8 I7
Penshurst Vic. 40 H6
Pentland Qld 112 C3, 119 R3
Penwortham SA 61 L6
Penzance Tas. 127 O9
Peppermint Grove WA 74 C7
Peppers Plains Vic. 42 G6
Peppimenarti NT 94 C9
Peranga Qld 108 D4
Peregian Beach Qld 111 Q6
Perekerten NSW 18 I9, 45 P8
Perenjori WA 82 C4
Perenna Vic. 42 E5
Pericoe NSW 20 F12, 49 P8
Perisher NSW 20 C9, 26 B12, 49 J4

Peronne Vic. 42 C9
Perponda SA 61 O9, 70 F2
Perroomba SA 61 K2, 63 J12
Perry Bridge Vic. 39 O6
Perseverance Qld 108 G6
Perth Tas. 131 L9
Perth WA 72, 78 B4, 80 C3, 82 B8
Perthville NSW 10 B5, 12 H6
Petal Point Tas. 131 P5
Petcheys Bay Tas. 126 E10
Peterborough SA 61 L2, 63 L13
Peterborough Vic. 41 K11
Peterhead SA 56 C10
Petersham NSW 5 J11, 9 L1
Petersville SA 60 I7
Petford Qld 115 L7
Petrie Qld 104 C1, 109 L6
Petrie Terrace Qld 101 A2
Pheasant Creek Vic. 37 L3, 38 E1, 46 H13
Phillip ACT 24 F13, 25 D4
Phillip Bay NSW 9 Q7
Phillip Island Vic. 37 L13, 38 E9
Phils Creek NSW 12 F9, 20 E2
Piallaway NSW 14 I11
Pialligo ACT 25 H2
Piambie Vic. 45 M7
Piangil Vic. 18 G10, 45 M9
Plawaning WA 82 D6
Piccadilly SA 55 Q10
Pickertaramoor NT 94 D4
Picnic Bay Qld 115 P12
Picnic Point NSW 8 E7
Picola Vic. 19 L13, 46 G3
Picola North Vic. 19 L13, 46 G3
Picton NSW 11 J11, 13 K9, 20 I2
Picton WA 79 G4
Pier Millan Vic. 18 F10, 45 J10
Piesseville WA 80 G7
Pigeon Ponds Vic. 40 E2, 42 E13
Piggoreet Vic. 36 B5, 41 N4
Pikedale Qld 15 L2, 111 M12
Pilbara, The WA 81 I3, 84 B4
Pilcherra Bore SA 61 P10, 70 G2
Pillar Valley NSW 15 P6
Pilliga NSW 14 E8
Pillinger Tas. 128 E4
Pilot Hill NSW 26 A5
Pilton Qld 108 F10
Pimba SA 62 F6
Pimpimbudgee Qld 108 D2
Pimpinio Vic. 42 G8
Pindar WA 82 C3
Pine Creek NT 92 I13, 94 F8
Pine Hill Qld 112 G11
Pine Lodge Vic. 46 I5
Pine Point SA 60 I8
Pine Ridge NSW 14 I12
Pinelands Qld 108 F5
Pinery SA 58 A2, 61 K7
Pingaring WA 82 F9
Pingelly WA 80 F5, 82 D9
Pingrup WA 82 F10
Pinjarra WA 78 C10, 80 C6, 82 C9
Pinjarra Hills Qld 106 B5
Pinkenba Qld 105 K8
Pinnaroo SA 18 A11, 44 A10, 61 R10, 70 I3
Pioneer Tas. 131 P6
Pioneer Bend SA 60 H12
Pipalyatjara SA 66 B2, 85 R11, 98 B13
Pipers Brook Tas. 131 M6
Pipers Creek Vic. 36 G2
Pipers Flat NSW 10 E3
Pipers River Tas. 131 L6
Pira Vic. 18 G10, 45 M10
Piries Vic. 37 R1, 47 L11
Pirlta Vic. 44 F4
Pirron Yallock Vic. 36 A11, 41 M9
Pithara WA 82 D6
Pitt Town NSW 11 L6
Pittong Vic. 36 A5, 41 M4
Pittsworth Qld 108 C9, 111 N9
Plain View Qld 108 D5
Plainland Qld 108 I8
Platts NSW 20 F12, 49 N8
Pleasant Hills NSW 12 A13, 19 P11
Pleasure Point NSW 8 D6
Plenty Tas. 126 E3, 129 K7
Plenty Vic. 33 O2
Plympton SA 54 F8

Plympton Park SA 54 F10
Poatina Tas. 129 K1, 131 K11
Point Clare NSW 11 P4, 21 F7
Point Cook Vic. 32 D13
Point Leo Vic. 37 K12
Point Lonsdale Vic. 36 H11, 38 B7
Point Lookout Qld 109 Q8, 111 R9
Point Pass SA 61 M6
Point Piper NSW 5 P10
Point Samson WA 81 G1, 84 A1
Point Turton SA 60 H9
Pokataroo NSW 14 D5
Police Point Tas. 126 E11, 129 K11
Policemans Point SA 61 N13, 70 E5
Polkemmet Vic. 42 F9
Pomborneit Vic. 41 M9
Pomona Qld 111 P6
Pomonal Vic. 40 I1, 42 I12
Pompapiel Vic. 43 Q7, 46 B6
Pompoota SA 58 I10
Ponde SA 58 I10
Pondooma SA 60 G4
Pontville Tas. 126 H3, 129 L7
Pontypool Tas. 129 O5
Poochera SA 60 A1, 62 A12, 69 R12
Pooginagoric SA 70 H7
Poolaijelo Vic. 40 B2, 42 B13, 70 I10
Poona National Park Qld 111 P4
Pooncarie NSW 18 E4
Poonindie SA 60 D8
Pooraka SA 57 K9
Pootilla Vic. 36 D3
Pootnoura SA 67 P9
Poowong Vic. 37 O11, 38 G8
Poowong East Vic. 37 P11
Popanyinning WA 80 F6
Porcupine National Park Qld 112 A3, 119 P3
Porcupine Ridge Vic. 36 E2, 41 Q1, 43 Q13,
   46 C11
Porepunkah Vic. 47 P8, 48 C6
Pormpuraaw Aboriginal Community Qld 114 D1,
   116 A13
Porongurup WA 80 H12
Porongurup National Park WA 80 H12
Port Adelaide SA 56 D11, 58 A8, 61 K9, 70 A1
Port Albert Vic. 39 L10
Port Alma Qld 113 O11
Port Arthur Tas. 127 N10, 129 N10
Port Augusta SA 62 I11
Port Bonython SA 60 I2, 62 I12
Port Broughton SA 61 J4
Port Campbell Vic. 41 K11
Port Campbell National Park Vic. 41 K11
Port Clinton SA 61 J7
Port Davis SA 60 I3, 61 I3, 62 I13
Port Denison WA 82 B4
Port Douglas Qld 115 M5
Port Elliot SA 59 H8, 61 L11, 70 C3
Port Fairy Vic. 40 G9
Port Franklin Vic. 39 J10
Port Gawler SA 58 A6, 61 K8
Port Germein SA 61 J2, 62 I13
Port Gibbon SA 60 G5
Port Gregory WA 82 A3
Port Hacking NSW 9 K13
Port Hedland WA 84 C1, 86 B13
Port Hughes SA 60 I6
Port Huon Tas. 126 E10, 129 K10
Port Julia SA 60 I8
Port Kembla NSW 13 K10
Port Kenny SA 60 A3, 69 Q13
Port Latta Tas. 130 E4
Port Lincoln SA 60 D8
Port MacDonnell SA 70 H13
Port Macquarie NSW 15 P12
Port Melbourne Vic. 33 J10
Port Minlacowie SA 60 H9
Port Neill SA 60 E6
Port Noarlunga SA 61 J10, 70 A2
Port Pirie SA 61 J3, 62 I13
Port Rickaby SA 60 H8
Port Sorell Tas. 131 J6
Port Stephens NSW 13 N4
Port Victoria SA 60 H7
Port Vincent SA 60 I9
Port Wakefield SA 61 J6
Port Welshpool Vic. 39 K10
Port Willunga SA 58 A13, 59 E4
Portarlington Vic. 36 H9, 38 B6

Porters Retreat NSW 10 D10, 12 H8, 20 G1
Portland NSW 10 E3, 12 I6
Portland Vic. 40 D9
Portland Roads Qld 116 F7
Portsea Vic. 36 I11, 38 B8
Postmans Ridge Qld 108 F7
Potato Point NSW 27 N10
Potts Point NSW 5 N10
Pottsville NSW 15 Q1, 111 R11
Pound Creek Vic. 38 H10
Powelltown Vic. 37 O7, 38 G4, 50 H11
Powers Creek Vic. 40 C1, 42 C12
Powlett Plains Vic. 43 P8, 46 A6
Powlett River Vic. 37 N13
Powranna Tas. 129 L1, 131 M10
Pozieres Qld 15 M2, 111 N11
Prahran Vic. 33 L10
Prairie Qld 112 B4, 119 P4
Prairie Vic. 43 Q6, 46 C5
Pranjip Vic. 46 I8
Pratten Qld 108 D12, 111 N10
Precipice National Park Qld 111 J3
Premaydena Tas. 127 M9, 129 N10
Premer NSW 14 G12
Preolenna Tas. 130 E6
Preston Qld 108 F8
Preston Tas. 130 H7
Preston Vic. 33 L5
Pretty Gully NSW 15 N3, 111 O12
Prevelly WA 79 B10
Price SA 61 J7
Priestdale Qld 107 N7
Primrose Sands Tas. 127 L6, 129 N9
Princetown Vic. 41 L11
Priors Pocket Qld 106 B8
Priory Tas. 131 Q8
Prooinga Vic. 45 K8
Propodollah Vic. 42 D6
Proserpine Qld 113 J3
Prospect SA 54 I3
Prospect Hill SA 59 H4
Proston Qld 111 N5
Puckapunyal Vic. 46 G10
Pudman Creek NSW 12 F10, 20 E3
Pularumpi NT 94 C3
Pullabooka NSW 12 C7
Pullenvale Qld 106 A5
Pullut Vic. 42 G4
Punchbowl NSW 4 F13, 8 H3
Punchmirup WA 80 G9
Punthari SA 58 I8
Pura Pura Vic. 41 L5
Puralka Vic. 40 B6, 70 I12
Purfleet NSW 13 P1, 15 N13
Purga Qld 109 K10
Purlewaugh NSW 14 F11
Purnim Vic. 40 I9
Purnong SA 61 N9, 70 E1
Purnululu (Bungle Bungle) National Park WA
    87 Q8
Putney NSW 4 H7
Pyalong Vic. 37 J1, 46 F10
Pyap SA 61 Q7
Pyengana Tas. 131 P8
Pygery SA 60 C2, 62 B13
Pymble NSW 5 J2, 6 H12, 11 N7
Pyramid Hill Vic. 18 I13, 43 Q5, 46 B4
Pyrmont NSW 5 L10

Quaama NSW 20 G9, 27 L13, 49 Q4
Quairading WA 80 G4, 82 E8
Quakers Hill NSW 11 L7
Qualco SA 61 O6
Quambatook Vic. 18 H12, 43 N4
Quambone NSW 14 B10
Quamby Qld 118 G3
Quamby Brook Tas. 131 J9
Quandary NSW 12 B9, 19 R7
Quandialla NSW 12 C8, 20 A1
Quantong Vic. 42 F9
Queanbeyan NSW 12 G13, 20 E5, 26 H3, 28 G4
Queens Park WA 75 M7
Queenscliff NSW 5 P4
Queenscliff Vic. 36 H10, 38 B7
Queensport Qld 105 J10
Queenstown SA 54 D1, 56 D12
Queenstown Tas. 128 E3, 130 E12
Quellington WA 80 F3
Quilpie Qld 121 O7

Quinalow Qld 108 D4
Quinburra NSW 20 E12, 49 M9
Quindalup WA 79 C7
Quindanning WA 80 E7
Quinninup WA 80 D11
Quinns Rock WA 78 A2, 80 C3
Quinnup WA 79 B8
Quirindi NSW 15 J12
Quoiba Tas. 130 I7
Quorn SA 62 I10

RAAF Base NT 90 I3, 91 D11
Rabbit Flat Roadhouse NT 96 C12, 98 C1
Raglan Qld 113 O11
Raglan Vic. 41 M2, 43 M13
Railton Tas. 130 I8
Rainbow Vic. 18 D13, 42 F4
Rainbow Beach Qld 111 Q5
Rainbow Flat NSW 13 P1
Rainworth Qld 104 E12
Raleigh NSW 15 P8
Raluana Vic. 43 J9
Ramco SA 61 O6
Raminea Tas. 126 E12, 129 K11
Ramingining NT 95 L5
Ramornee Bridge NSW 15 O6
Ramsay Qld 108 E9
Ramsgate NSW 9 L7
Ranceby Vic. 37 P12, 38 H8
Rand NSW 19 P12, 47 N1
Randell WA 83 J6
Randwick NSW 5 O12, 9 Q3
Ranelagh Tas. 126 E7, 129 K9
Ranga Tas. 128 B12, 131 Q1
Rangemore Qld 108 D3
Rankins Springs NSW 19 O6
Rannes Qld 113 M12
Rannock NSW 12 B10, 19 R8
Ransome Qld 105 N12
Rapid Bay SA 59 C8, 61 J11, 70 A3
Rapid Creek NT 91 C4
Rappville NSW 15 P4, 111 P13
Rathdowney Qld 15 P1, 111 P11
Rathmines NSW 13 M5
Rathscar Vic. 43 N11
Raukan Aboriginal Settlement SA 61 M11, 70 D3
Ravensbourne Qld 108 G6
Ravensbourne National Park Qld 108 G6
Ravensdale NSW 11 O1
Ravenshoe Qld 115 M8
Ravensthorpe WA 82 H10
Ravenswood Qld 112 G2
Ravenswood Vic. 43 Q10, 46 C9
Ravenswood South Vic. 43 Q11, 46 C10
Ravensworth NSW 13 L3
Rawdon Vale NSW 13 M1
Rawlinna WA 83 N6
Rawson Vic. 39 J5
Raymond Terrace NSW 13 N4
Raywood Vic. 43 Q8, 46 C7
Red Banks SA 58 B4
Red Cliffs Vic. 18 D7, 44 G4
Red Hill ACT 24 G13, 25 F3
Red Hill Qld 104 F11
Red Hill Vic. 37 J11, 38 D8
Red Hill South Vic. 37 K11
Red Hills Tas. 131 J9
Red Jacket Vic. 39 J3
Red Range NSW 15 M6
Red Rock NSW 15 Q7
Redbank Qld 106 A9
Redbank Vic. 43 M11
Redbanks SA 61 M5
Redcastle Vic. 46 E8
Redcliffe Qld 109 N6, 111 Q8
Redcliffe WA 75 M2, 77 M13
Redesdale Vic. 46 D10
Redfern NSW 5 M11, 9 O1
Redhill SA 61 J4
Redland Bay Qld 109 O9, 111 Q9
Redmond WA 80 H12
Redpa Tas. 130 B4
Redwood Park SA 57 P8
Reedy Creek SA 70 F8
Reedy Creek Vic. 37 K2, 46 G11
Reedy Dam Vic. 42 I4
Reedy Flat Vic. 20 B12, 39 R1, 48 G10
Reedy Marsh Tas. 131 J8
Reefton NSW 12 B9, 19 R7

Reekara Tas. 128 A8
Reesville Qld 109 L2
Regans Ford WA 80 C1, 82 C7
Regatta Point Tas. 128 D3, 130 D12
Regency Park SA 54 G1, 56 H12
Regents Park NSW 4 D11, 8 G1
Reid ACT 23 F4, 24 H9
Reid WA 83 Q6
Reid River Qld 112 F1
Reids Creek Vic. 47 O5, 48 A3
Reids Flat NSW 12 F9, 20 E1
Reidsdale NSW 27 L5
Rekuna Tas. 126 I3, 129 M7
Relbia Tas. 131 M9
Remine Tas. 128 C2, 130 D11
Rendelsham SA 70 G11
Renison Bell Tas. 128 D1, 130 E10
Renmark SA 61 Q6
Renner Springs NT 97 J8
Rennie NSW 19 O12, 47 L2
Renown Park SA 54 H3
Research Vic. 33 R3, 34 A4
Reservoir Vic. 33 L4
Retreat Tas. 131 M6
Revesby NSW 8 F5, 11 M9
Rheban Tas. 127 O3, 129 O7
Rheola Vic. 43 O9
Rhodes NSW 4 G7
Rhymney Reef Vic. 41 J1, 43 J13
Rhyndaston Tas. 129 M6
Rhynie SA 61 L6
Riana Tas. 130 G6
Rich Avon Vic. 43 K8
Richardson ACT 25 E10
Richlands NSW 10 E13, 12 H9, 20 G2
Richlands Qld 106 E9
Richmond NSW 11 K6
Richmond Qld 119 M4
Richmond SA 54 F7
Richmond Tas. 127 J4, 129 M7
Richmond Vic. 33 L9
Riddells Creek Vic. 36 H3, 38 B1, 46 E12
Ridgehaven SA 57 P9
Ridgelands Qld 113 N10
Ridgeway Tas. 124 E12, 126 H6
Ridgley Tas. 130 G6
Ridleyton SA 54 G4
Riggs Creek Vic. 47 J8
Ringa WA 78 G1, 80 E2
Ringarooma Tas. 131 O7
Ringwood Vic. 34 B9, 37 L6, 38 E4
Ripley Qld 109 K9
Ripplebrook Vic. 37 O10, 38 G7
Risdon Tas. 124 G2
Risdon Vale Tas. 124 I1, 126 I5, 129 L8
Riverhills Qld 106 C7
Riverside Tas. 131 L8
Riverstone NSW 11 L6
Riverton SA 61 L6
Riverton WA 75 K9
Rivervale WA 75 L4
Riverview NSW 5 K7
Riverwood NSW 8 H5
Rivett ACT 25 A4
Roadvale Qld 109 J11, 111 P10
Rob Roy Vic. 34 D1
Robe SA 70 F9
Robertson NSW 13 K10, 20 I3
Robertson Qld 106 I5
Robertstown SA 61 M6
Robigana Tas. 131 L7
Robinvale Vic. 18 F8, 45 J6
Rochedale Qld 107 L5
Rocherlea Tas. 131 L8
Roches Beach Tas. 125 R7
Rochester SA 61 K5
Rochester Vic. 46 E6
Rochford Vic. 36 H2, 38 B1, 46 E12
Rock Flat NSW 20 E9, 26 G12, 49 N4
Rockbank Vic. 32 A4, 36 H5, 38 B3
Rockdale NSW 9 L5
Rockhampton Qld 113 N11
Rockingham WA 78 B7, 80 C4, 82 C8
Rocklea Qld 106 G5
Rockleigh SA 58 G10
Rockley NSW 10 B7, 12 H7
Rocklyn Vic. 36 E3, 41 P2, 43 P13, 46 B12
Rocksberg Qld 109 L5

Rockvale NSW 15 M8
Rocky Cape Tas. 130 E4
Rocky Cape National Park Tas. 130 F4
Rocky Creek NSW 14 H7
Rocky Creek Qld 108 A11
Rocky Crossing Qld 110 I10
Rocky Dam NSW 15 J4, 111 K13
Rocky Glen NSW 14 G11
Rocky Gully WA 80 F11
Rocky Hall NSW 20 F11, 49 O7
Rocky Hill Qld 108 F1
Rocky Plains NSW 26 D11
Rocky River NSW 15 K9
Rocky River SA 60 F13
Rodd Point NSW 5 J10
Rodney NSW 20 E11, 49 M7
Roebourne WA 81 G1, 84 A2
Roebuck Roadhouse WA 86 H8
Roelands WA 79 H4, 80 C8
Rogans Hill NSW 4 D1, 6 B11
Roger Corner SA 60 I9
Roger River Tas. 130 C5
Roger River West Tas. 130 C5
Rokeby Tas. 125 O9, 127 J6, 129 M8
Rokeby Vic. 37 P9, 38 H6
Rokewood Vic. 36 B7, 41 O6
Rokewood Junction Vic. 36 B6, 41 N5
Roland Tas. 130 H8
Rollands Plains NSW 15 O11
Rolleston Qld 110 G1, 113 J13
Rollingstone Qld 115 O12
Roma Qld 110 H6
Romsey Vic. 36 I2, 38 B1, 46 E12
Rookhurst NSW 13 N1, 15 L13
Rookwood NSW 4 F11, 8 H1
Rooty Hill NSW 11 L7
Ropeley Qld 108 H9
Roper River Bar NT 95 K10
Roper River Store NT 95 K10
Rosa Glen WA 79 C10, 80 B10
Rosanna Vic. 33 O5
Rose Bay NSW 5 P9
Rose Bay Tas. 124 I6
Rose Park SA 55 K6
Rosebery NSW 5 M13, 9 O3
Rosebery Tas. 128 E1, 130 E10
Rosebery Vic. 42 H4
Rosebery East Vic. 42 I3
Rosebrook Vic. 40 H9
Rosebud Vic. 37 J11, 38 C8
Rosedale NSW 20 D8, 26 E8, 49 L1
Rosedale NSW 27 N7
Rosedale Qld 111 N2
Rosedale SA 58 E5
Rosedale Vic. 39 L7
Rosegarland Tas. 126 E3
Rosehill NSW 4 D7
Roselands NSW 8 H4
Roseneath Vic. 40 B3
Rosenthal NSW 13 N3
Roses Tier Tas. 131 O9
Rosetta Tas. 124 B2
Rosevale Qld 108 I11, 111 O10
Rosevale Tas. 131 K8
Rosevears Tas. 131 L8
Roseville NSW 5 K5
Rosewater SA 56 E12
Rosewhite Vic. 47 P7, 48 B5
Rosewood NSW 20 B7
Rosewood Qld 109 J9, 111 P9
Roseworthy SA 58 D5, 61 L8
Roslyn NSW 12 H10, 20 F3
Roslynmead Vic. 46 D4
Rosny Tas. 124 I7
Rosny Park Tas. 125 J6, 126 I6, 129 M8
Ross Tas. 129 M3, 131 N12
Ross Creek Vic. 36 C4, 41 O4
Ross River Homestead NT 99 K8
Rossarden Tas. 129 O1, 131 O10
Rossbridge Vic. 41 J3
Rossi NSW 12 H13, 20 F6, 27 J4
Rosslyn Park SA 55 M6
Rossmore NSW 11 L9
Rossvale Qld 108 C8
Rossville Qld 115 L3
Rostrevor SA 55 N3
Rostron Vic. 43 L10
Roto NSW 19 M3
Rottnest Island WA 80 B4, 82 B8

Rouchel Brook NSW 13 L2
Round Corner NSW 6 B9
Rowella Tas. 131 K7
Rowena NSW 14 E6
Rowland Vic. 43 Q4, 46 B2
Rowland Flat SA 58 E5
Rowsley Vic. 36 F5, 38 A3, 41 R4
Roxby Downs SA 62 F4
Royal George Tas. 129 O2, 131 P11
Royal National Park NSW 8 G12, 11 N11, 13 L8
Royal Park SA 54 D2, 56 D13
Royalla NSW 12 G13, 20 E6, 26 H4, 28 F7
Royston Park SA 55 K4
Rozelle NSW 5 K9
Ruabon WA 79 F7
Rubicon Vic. 37 P2, 38 H1, 47 K12
Ruby Vic. 37 P12, 38 H9
Rubyvale Qld 112 H11
Rudall SA 60 E5
Rudall River National Park WA 84 H4
Ruffy Vic. 46 I10
Rufus River NSW 18 B6, 44 C2
Rugby NSW 12 F9, 20 E2
Rukenvale NSW 15 P2, 111 P11
Rules Point NSW 26 C6
Runcorn Qld 107 J7
Running Stream NSW 12 I5
Runnyford NSW 27 M6
Runnymede Tas. 127 K3, 129 M7
Runnymede Vic. 46 E7
Rupanyup Vic. 42 I9
Rupanyup North Vic. 42 I8
Rupanyup South Vic. 42 I9
Rushcutters Bay NSW 5 N10
Rushworth Vic. 46 G7
Russell ACT 23 H8, 24 I10, 25 G1
Russell Lea NSW 5 J9
Russell River National Park Qld 115 N7
Rutherglen Vic. 19 O13, 47 N4
Ryanby Vic. 45 L10
Ryans Creek Vic. 47 M8
Rydal NSW 10 F5, 12 I6
Rydalmere NSW 4 D6
Ryde NSW 4 H6, 11 N8
Rye Vic. 36 I11, 38 C8
Rye Park NSW 12 F10, 20 D3
Ryeford Qld 108 D11
Rylstone NSW 12 I4
Ryton Vic. 39 J9

Sabine Qld 108 D6
Sackville North NSW 11 L4
Saddleworth SA 61 L6
Safety Bay WA 78 B7
Safety Beach Vic. 37 J11, 38 D7
St Agnes SA 57 P10
St Albans NSW 11 M2, 13 L6
St Albans Vic. 32 E5, 36 I6
St Andrews Vic. 38 E2, 46 H13
St Arnaud Vic. 43 L9
St Aubyn Qld 108 F4
St Clair NSW 13 L3
St Fillans Vic. 37 N4, 38 G2, 47 J13, 50 G4
St George Qld 110 G10
St Georges SA 55 L8
St Georges Basin NSW 13 K12, 20 I5, 27 Q2
St Germains Vic. 46 G5
St Helena Island National Park Qld 105 P6, 109 N7
St Helens Tas. 131 Q8
St Helens Vic. 40 G8
St Huberts Island NSW 21 G8
St Ives NSW 5 K1, 6 I11
St Ives North NSW 7 J10
St James Vic. 47 K5
St James WA 75 K6
St Johns Park NSW 8 A1
St Kilda SA 58 A7
St Kilda Vic. 33 K11, 37 J7
St Kilda East Vic. 33 L11
St Lawrence Qld 113 L8
St Leonards NSW 5 L7
St Leonards Vic. 36 I9, 38 B6
St Lucia Qld 106 F2
St Marys NSW 11 L8
St Marys SA 54 H12
St Marys Tas. 131 Q10
St Morris SA 55 L5
St Patricks River Tas. 131 M8
St Peters NSW 5 L12, 9 N2

St Peters SA 55 K4
Sale Vic. 39 N6
Salisbury NSW 13 M2
Salisbury Qld 106 H5
Salisbury SA 57 K4, 58 B8, 61 K8, 70 C1
Salisbury Vic. 42 E7
Salisbury East SA 57 N6
Salisbury Heights SA 57 O4
Salisbury North SA 57 J3
Salisbury Plain SA 57 M4
Salisbury West Vic. 43 P8, 46 A7
Sallys Corner NSW 13 J10
Sallys Flat NSW 12 H5
Salmon Gums WA 83 J9
Salt Creek SA 61 N13, 70 E6
Salter Springs SA 61 L6
Saltwater River Tas. 127 L8, 129 N9
Samford Qld 109 L7, 111 P9
San Remo Vic. 37 M13, 38 F9
Sanctuary Point NSW 13 K12, 20 I5, 27 R2
Sandalwood SA 61 P9, 70 G1
Sandergrove SA 59 I5
Sanderson NT 92 C2
Sanderston SA 58 H8
Sandfire Roadhouse WA 86 F12
Sandfly Tas. 126 G7, 129 L9
Sandford Tas. 125 R13, 127 J7, 129 M9
Sandford Vic. 40 D4
Sandgate Qld 104 H3, 109 M6
Sandhill Lake Vic. 43 O3, 45 O13
Sandigo NSW 19 P9
Sandilands SA 60 I8
Sandon Vic. 36 D1, 41 P1, 43 P12, 46 B11
Sandringham NSW 9 L8
Sandringham Vic. 35 A3, 37 J8
Sandsmere Vic. 42 C6
Sandstone WA 82 G2
Sandy Bay Tas. 124 G9, 126 I6
Sandy Creek SA 58 D6
Sandy Creek Vic. 47 Q5, 48 D3
Sandy Creek Upper Vic. 47 Q6, 48 C4
Sandy Flat NSW 15 M4, 111 N13
Sandy Hill NSW 15 N3, 111 O13
Sandy Hollow NSW 13 J2
Sandy Point NSW 8 E7
Sandy Point Vic. 38 I11
Sangar NSW 19 N12, 47 L1
Sans Souci NSW 9 L8
Santa Teresa Aboriginal Community NT 99 K9
Sapphire NSW 15 K6
Sapphire Qld 112 H11
Sapphiretown SA 60 I12
Sarah Island Tas. 128 D5
Saratoga NSW 21 G7
Sardine Creek Vic. 20 C13, 49 J11
Sarina Qld 113 L6
Sarina Beach Qld 113 L5
Sarsfield Vic. 39 Q4, 48 G13
Sassafras NSW 13 J11, 20 H4, 27 O1
Sassafras Tas. 131 J7
Sassafras Vic. 34 F11
Sassafras East Tas. 131 J7
Savage River Tas. 130 D8
Savenake NSW 19 N12, 47 L2
Sawtell NSW 15 P8
Sayers Lake NSW 18 G2
Scaddan WA 83 J10
Scamander Tas. 131 Q9
Scarborough NSW 11 M12, 13 K9
Scarborough Qld 109 N6
Scarborough WA 76 B10, 78 A4, 82 C8
Scarsdale Vic. 36 B5, 41 N4
Sceale Bay SA 69 P13
Scheyville NSW 11 L6
Schofields NSW 11 L7
Scone NSW 13 K1
Scoresby Vic. 34 B13, 35 H1
Scotland Island NSW 7 P5
Scotsburn Vic. 36 D5, 41 P4
Scott National Park WA 79 D12, 80 B11, 82 C11
Scotts Creek Vic. 41 K10
Scotts Head NSW 15 P9
Scottsdale Tas. 131 N7
Scottville Qld 112 I3
Scullin ACT 24 B6
Sea Elephant Tas. 128 B8
Sea Lake Vic. 18 F11, 43 J1, 45 J12
Seabird WA 80 B1
Seacombe Vic. 39 O6

Seaford Vic. 35 E10, 37 K9
Seaforth NSW 5 O5
Seaforth Qld 113 K4
Seaham NSW 13 N4
Seal Rocks NSW 13 P3
Seaspray Vic. 39 N8
Seaton SA 54 D3
Seaton Vic. 39 L5
Seaview Vic. 37 P11, 38 H7
Sebastian Vic. 43 Q8, 46 C7
Sebastopol NSW 12 C10, 19 R8, 20 A3
Sebastopol Vic. 36 C4
Second Valley SA 59 C8, 61 J11, 70 A3
Sedan SA 58 I5, 61 M8
Sedgwick Vic. 43 R10, 46 C9
Seelands NSW 15 P6
Sefton NSW 4 C11, 8 F1
Sefton Park SA 55 J2, 57 J13
Seisia Qld 116 C3
Selbourne Tas. 131 K8
Selby Vic. 34 G13, 50 B12
Seldom Seen Roadhouse Vic. 20 C12, 48 I8
Sellheim Qld 112 E2
Sellicks Beach SA 59 E5, 61 K10, 70 B2
Sellicks Hill SA 59 E5
Semaphore SA 56 B10
Semaphore Park SA 54 A1, 56 B12
Semaphore South SA 56 B11
Separation Creek Vic. 41 O11
Seppeltsfield SA 58 E4, 61 L8
Serpentine Vic. 43 P7, 46 A6
Serpentine WA 78 C8, 80 D5
Serpentine National Park WA 78 D8, 80 D5, 82 C8
Serviceton Vic. 42 A7, 70 I7
Seven Hills Qld 105 J12
Seven Mile Beach Tas. 125 R6, 127 J6, 129 M8
Sevenhill SA 61 L5
Seventeen Mile Rocks Qld 106 D6
Seventeen Seventy Qld 113 Q13
Severnlea Qld 15 M2, 111 N12
Seville Vic. 34 I7, 37 M6, 38 F4, 50 C9
Seymour Tas. 129 Q1, 131 Q11
Seymour Vic. 46 G10
Shackleton WA 80 H3
Shadforth NSW 12 G6
Shady Creek Vic. 37 Q9, 38 I6
Shailer Park Qld 107 P10
Shallow Crossing NSW 27 N5
Shannon Tas. 129 J3, 131 J12
Shannon WA 80 E11
Shannon National Park WA 80 E11, 82 D11
Shannons Flat NSW 20 D7, 26 F8
Shannonvale Vic. 48 E7
Sharps Well SA 61 J5
Shay Gap (abandoned) WA 84 E1, 86 D13
Shays Flat Vic. 43 L11
Shea-Oak Log SA 58 D4
Sheans Creek Vic. 47 J9
Sheep Hills Vic. 42 I7
Sheffield Tas. 130 I8
Sheldon Qld 107 P4
Shelford Vic. 36 D8, 41 P6
Shellbourne Vic. 43 P10, 46 B9
Shelley Vic. 20 A8, 48 F2
Shelley WA 75 J9
Shellharbour NSW 13 K10
Shelly Beach Tas. 127 O2, 129 O7
Shenton Park WA 74 D3
Sheoaks Vic. 36 E7, 41 Q6
Shepherds Flat Vic. 36 E2
Shepparton Vic. 46 I6
Shepperd Qld 108 E8
Sherbrooke Vic. 34 F12, 50 A11
Sheringa SA 60 B5
Sherlock SA 61 O10, 70 F3
Sherwood Qld 106 E4
Shipley NSW 10 G6
Shirley Vic. 41 L3
Shoal Bay NSW 13 O4
Shoal Point Qld 113 L5
Shoalhaven Heads NSW 13 K11
Shooters Hill NSW 10 E9, 12 I8, 20 G1
Shoreham Vic. 37 K12, 38 D8
Shorncliffe Qld 104 H3
Shotts WA 80 D8
Shute Harbour Qld 113 K3
Sidmouth Tas. 131 K7
Sidonia Vic. 36 H1
Silkwood Qld 115 N8

Silvan Vic. 34 I10, 37 M6, 38 F4, 50 C10
Silver Creek Vic. 47 O6, 48 B4
Silver Sands SA 59 E5
Silverdale NSW 11 J9, 13 K8, 20 I1
Silverton NSW 16 B11, 63 R9
Silverwater NSW 4 E8
Simmie Vic. 46 F5
Simpson Vic. 41 L10
Simpson Desert SA 118 A12
Simpson Desert National Park Qld 99 R11, 118 B12, 120 B1
Simpsons Bay Tas. 126 H12, 129 L11
Singleton NSW 13 L3
Singleton WA 78 B9, 80 C5, 82 C9
Sinnamon Park Qld 106 D5
Sisters Beach Tas. 130 E5
Sisters Creek Tas. 130 E5
Skenes Creek Vic. 41 O12
Skipton Vic. 41 M4
Skye SA 55 N6
Skye Vic. 35 G11
Slacks Creek Qld 107 M9
Slade Point Qld 113 L5
Slaty Creek Vic. 43 M8
Smeaton Vic. 36 D2, 41 P2, 43 P13, 46 A12
Smiggin Holes NSW 20 C9, 26 B12, 49 J4
Smith Islands National Park Qld 113 L4
Smithfield Qld 15 K3, 115 M6
Smithfield SA 58 C6
Smithlea Qld 111 L12
Smiths Gully Vic. 37 L4, 38 E2, 46 H13
Smithton Tas. 130 C4
Smithtown NSW 15 P10
Smithville SA 61 P10, 70 G2
Smoko Vic. 47 Q9, 48 C7
Smoky Bay SA 69 O10
Smythesdale Vic. 36 B5, 41 N4
Snake Range National Park Qld 112 H12
Snake Valley Vic. 36 B4, 41 N4
Snobs Creek Vic. 37 P2, 47 K11
Snowtown SA 61 J5
Snowy River National Park Vic. 20 C12, 49 J9
Snug Tas. 126 H9, 129 L10
Snuggery SA 70 G11
Sodwalls NSW 10 F5
Sofala NSW 10 C1, 12 H5
Somers Vic. 37 K12, 38 D8
Somersby NSW 11 O3, 21 D5
Somerset Tas. 130 G5
Somerset Dam Qld 109 J4
Somerton NSW 14 I10
Somerton Park SA 54 C12
Somerville Vic. 37 L10, 38 E7
Sommariva Qld 110 C6
Sorell Tas. 127 K5, 129 M8
Sorrento Vic. 36 I11, 38 B8
Sorrento WA 76 A5
South Arm Tas. 126 I8, 129 M9
South Bindoon WA 80 D2
South Brisbane Qld 101 A9, 104 G12, 106 G1
South Bruny Island Tas. 129 L12
South Coast NSW 20 H13, 27 O11
South Cumberland Islands National Park Qld 113 M4
South East Forest National Park NSW 20 F10, 49 O5
South Forest Tas. 130 D4
South Fremantle WA 74 C12
South Guildford WA 77 O11
South Gundagai NSW 12 D12, 20 B5
South Hedland WA 84 C1, 86 B13
South Hobart Tas. 124 F9
South Kilkerran SA 60 I7
South Kumminin WA 80 I4, 82 F8
South Melbourne Vic. 30 B13, 33 K9
South Mission Beach Qld 115 N9
South Morang Vic. 33 O1, 37 K5
South Mount Cameron Tas. 131 P6
South Nanango Qld 108 F1
South Nietta Tas. 130 H8
South Perth WA 72 C12, 74 H5
South Riana Tas. 130 G7
South Springfield Tas. 131 N7
South Stirling WA 80 I11
South Stradbroke Island Qld 109 O11, 111 Q10
South Turramurra NSW 4 H2, 6 F12
South West Rocks NSW 15 P10
South Yaamba Qld 113 N10
South Yarra Vic. 33 L10

South Yunderup WA 78 B10, 80 C5
Southbank Vic. 30 C10
Southbrook Qld 108 D8, 111 N9
Southend Qld 113 P12
Southend SA 70 G11
Southern Cross Vic. 40 H9
Southern Cross WA 82 G7
Southport Qld 109 O12
Southport Tas. 129 K12
Southwest National Park Tas. 126 A5, 128 F9
Southwood National Park Qld 111 J10
Spalding SA 61 L4
Spalford Tas. 130 H7
Spargo Creek Vic. 36 E3, 41 Q3, 46 B13
Spearwood WA 78 A6
Speed Vic. 18 E11, 42 H1, 44 I11
Speewa Vic. 45 N10
Spence ACT 24 D4
Spencer NSW 11 N4, 21 B9
Spicers Creek NSW 12 G3
Spit Junction NSW 5 O7
Spotswood Vic. 32 H9
Sprent Tas. 130 H7
Spreyton Tas. 130 I7
Spring Beach Tas. 127 O2, 129 O7
Spring Bluff Qld 108 F7
Spring Creek Qld 108 E11
Spring Creek Upper Qld 108 F11
Spring Hill NSW 12 G6
Spring Hill Qld 101 C1, 104 G11
Spring Hill Vic. 36 F2
Spring Ridge NSW 12 G2
Spring Ridge NSW 14 H12
Springbrook Qld 15 Q1, 111 P11
Springbrook National Park Qld 109 N13
Springdale NSW 12 C10, 20 A3
Springfield SA 55 K10
Springfield Tas. 124 D5, 131 N7
Springfield Vic. 36 I2
Springhurst Vic. 47 N4
Springmount Vic. 36 D3
Springside Qld 108 C8, 111 M9
Springsure Qld 112 I12
Springton SA 58 G7, 61 M8, 70 D1
Springvale Vic. 35 F3, 37 K7
Springwood NSW 11 J7, 13 J7
Springwood Qld 107 N8
Squaretop Qld 108 B3
Staaten River National Park Qld 114 G5
Stafford Qld 104 F9
Stafford Heights Qld 104 E8
Stamford NSW 119 N5
Stanage Qld 113 M7
Stanborough NSW 15 J7
Stanhope Vic. 46 G6
Stanley Tas. 130 D3
Stanley Vic. 47 O6, 48 B4
Stanmore NSW 5 K11, 9 M1
Stanmore Qld 109 L3
Stannifer NSW 15 K6
Stannum NSW 15 M5, 111 N13
Stansbury SA 60 I9
Stanthorpe Qld 15 M2, 111 N12
Stanwell Qld 113 N11
Stanwell Park NSW 11 M12, 13 K9
Starcke National Park Qld 115 L1, 116 I13
Staughton Vale Vic. 36 F6
Stavely Vic. 40 I4
Staverton Tas. 130 H8
Stawell Vic. 43 J11
Steels Creek Vic. 37 M4, 38 E2, 46 H13, 50 B4
Steiglitz Qld 109 O10
Steiglitz Vic. 36 E7, 41 Q5
Stenhouse Bay SA 60 G10
Stephens Creek NSW 16 B11
Stepney SA 55 K5
Steppes Tas. 129 K3, 131 K13
Stieglitz Tas. 131 R8
Stirling ACT 24 C13, 25 B4
Stirling SA 55 P12, 58 C11, 59 H1
Stirling Vic. 20 A13, 39 Q2, 48 G11
Stirling WA 76 E10
Stirling North SA 60 I1, 62 I11
Stirling Range National Park WA 80 H11, 82 E11
Stockdale Vic. 39 N4, 48 D13
Stockinbingal NSW 12 C10, 20 B3
Stockmans Reward Vic. 37 Q4
Stockport SA 58 C2
Stockwell SA 58 G4, 61 M7

159

Stockyard Qld 108 F8
Stockyard Hill Vic. 41 L3
Stokers Siding NSW 15 Q1, 111 Q11
Stokes SA 60 D7
Stokes Bay SA 60 H11
Stokes National Park WA 82 I10
Stone Hut SA 61 K3, 63 J13
Stonefield SA 58 I3, 61 M7
Stonehaven Vic. 36 F9
Stonehenge NSW 15 L6
Stonehenge Qld 119 M13, 121 M1
Stonehenge Tas. 129 N5
Stones Corner Qld 106 H2
Stoneyford Vic. 41 M9
Stonor Tas. 129 M5
Stony Creek Vic. 38 I10
Stony Crossing NSW 18 H10, 45 N9
Stony Point Vic. 37 L11, 38 E8
Stonyfell SA 55 N7
Stoodley Tas. 130 I8
Store Creek NSW 12 G4
Storeys Creek Tas. 129 O1, 131 O10
Stormlea Tas. 127 M11, 129 N10
Stowport Tas. 130 G6
Stowport Upper Tas. 130 G6
Stradbroke Vic. 39 M8
Stradbroke West Vic. 39 M7
Strahan Tas. 128 D3, 130 D12
Strangways Vic. 36 E1
Stratford NSW 13 N2
Stratford Vic. 39 N5
Strath Creek Vic. 37 L1, 46 H11
Strathalbyn SA 58 E13, 59 I4, 61 L10, 70 C3
Strathallan Vic. 46 E5
Stratham WA 79 F5, 80 C8
Strathblane Tas. 126 D12, 129 K11
Strathbogie NSW 15 K5
Strathbogie Vic. 47 J9
Strathbogie South Vic. 47 J9
Strathdownie Vic. 40 B5, 70 I11
Stratherne WA 80 G5
Strathewen Vic. 37 L4
Strathfield NSW 4 G11, 8 I1, 11 N8
Strathfieldsaye Vic. 43 R10, 46 C9
Strathgordon Tas. 128 G7
Strathkellar Vic. 40 G5
Strathlea Vic. 36 D1, 41 P1, 43 P12, 46 A11
Strathmerton Vic. 19 M13, 46 I3
Strathmore Vic. 32 I5
Strathpine Qld 104 C3, 109 L6, 111 P8
Streaky Bay SA 69 P12
Streatham Vic. 41 K4
Streton WA 80 H5
Stretton Qld 107 J9
Strickland Tas. 129 J5
Stroud NSW 13 N3
Stroud Road NSW 13 N2
Strzelecki Vic. 37 P11, 38 H8
Strzelecki Crossing SA 65 O11, 120 F13
Strzelecki National Park Tas. 128 A12, 131 Q1
Stuart Mill Vic. 43 M10
Stuart Park NT 89 F4, 90 G9
Stuart Town NSW 12 G4
Stuarts Point NSW 15 P10
Sturt National Park NSW 16 A2, 65 R12, 120 I13
Subiaco WA 74 F3
Sue City NSW 26 B7
Suffolk Park NSW 15 R2
Sugarloaf Qld 108 F9
Suggan Buggan Vic. 20 C11, 49 J7
Sulphur Creek Tas. 130 H6
Summer Hill NSW 5 J11, 9 L2
Summerfield Vic. 43 Q8, 46 C7
Summerholm Qld 108 I8
Summertown SA 55 P8
Summervale NSW 17 Q10
Sumner Qld 106 C6
Sunbury Vic. 36 I4, 38 B2, 46 E13
Sunday Creek Vic. 37 K1, 46 G11
Sundown National Park Qld 15 L3, 111 M12
Sunny Cliffs Vic. 18 D7, 44 G4
Sunny Corner NSW 10 E3
Sunnybank Qld 106 I7, 109 M9
Sunnyside NSW 15 M4, 111 N13
Sunnyside Tas. 130 I8
Sunnyside Vic. 48 E7
Sunnyvale SA 60 I6
Sunset Vic. 44 A9, 61 R10, 70 I2
Sunshine Vic. 32 G7

Sunshine Coast Qld 109 O1, 111 R6
Surat Qld 110 H8
Surf Beach NSW 27 N7
Surfers Paradise Qld 109 O13, 111 Q10
Surges Bay Tas. 126 E11, 129 K10
Surprise Bay Tas. 128 A9
Surrey Downs SA 57 P8
Surrey Hills Vic. 33 O9
Surry Hills NSW 5 M11, 9 P1
Surveyors Bay Tas. 126 F12, 129 K11
Sussex Inlet NSW 13 K12, 20 I5, 27 Q2
Sutherland NSW 8 H11, 11 M10
Sutherlands SA 61 M6
Sutton NSW 12 G12, 20 E5, 26 H1, 28 G2
Sutton Vic. 43 K3, 45 K13
Sutton Grange Vic. 43 R11, 46 C10
Swan Hill Vic. 18 H11, 45 N11
Swan Marsh Vic. 41 M9
Swan Reach SA 61 N8
Swan Reach Vic. 39 R4, 48 G13
Swan Valley WA 78 D3
Swanbourne WA 74 B4
Swanhaven NSW 13 J12, 20 I5, 27 Q2
Swanpool Vic. 47 L8
Swanport SA 58 I12
Swansea Tas. 129 P4, 131 P13
Swanwater South Vic. 43 L8
Swanwater West Vic. 43 K8
Swanwick Tas. 129 Q4, 131 Q13
Swifts Creek Vic. 20 A12, 39 Q1, 48 G9
Sydenham NSW 5 K12, 9 M3
Sydenham Vic. 32 D3
Sydney NSW 2, 5 M10, 11 O8, 13 L8
Sydney Harbour National Park NSW 5 P7, 11 P8
Sylvania NSW 9 J9, 11 N10
Sylvania Heights NSW 9 J10
Sylvania Waters NSW 9 K9
Sylvaterre Vic. 43 Q5, 46 C4
Symonston ACT 25 H4

Taabinga Qld 111 N6
Tabbara Vic. 49 K12
Tabberabbera Vic. 39 O3, 48 E12
Tabbimoble NSW 15 Q4, 111 Q13
Tabbita NSW 19 N6
Tabilk Vic. 46 G9
Table Top NSW 19 Q13, 47 Q3
Tabooba Qld 109 L13
Tabor Vic. 40 G6
Tabulam NSW 15 O3, 111 O12
Taggerty Vic. 37 O2, 38 G1, 47 J12
Tahara Vic. 40 E5
Tahara Bridge Vic. 40 D5
Tahmoor NSW 11 J12
Taigum Qld 104 G4
Tailem Bend SA 61 N10, 70 E3
Takone Tas. 130 F6
Talawa Tas. 131 O8
Talbingo NSW 12 E13, 20 C6, 26 B4
Talbot Vic. 36 B1, 41 N1, 43 O12
Talbot Brook WA 78 H5, 80 E4
Taldra SA 18 A7, 61 Q7
Talgai Qld 108 E11
Talgarno Vic. 19 Q13, 47 Q4, 48 D1
Talia SA 60 A3
Tallageira Vic. 42 A10, 70 I8
Tallandoon Vic. 47 Q6, 48 D4
Tallangalook Vic. 47 K9
Tallangatta Vic. 47 Q5, 48 D2
Tallangatta Valley Vic. 47 R5, 48 E3
Tallarook Vic. 46 G10
Tallebung NSW 19 P2
Tallimba NSW 12 A8, 19 Q6
Tallong NSW 12 I11, 20 H3
Tallygaroopna Vic. 46 I5
Talmalmo NSW 19 R13, 20 A7, 48 E1
Talwood Qld 14 F2, 110 I11
Tamarama NSW 5 Q12
Tamarang NSW 14 H12
Tambar Springs NSW 14 G11
Tambaroora NSW 12 G5
Tambellup WA 80 H10
Tambo Qld 110 B2
Tambo Crossing Vic. 20 B13, 39 Q2, 48 G11
Tambo Upper Vic. 39 R4, 48 G13
Tamboon Vic. 49 N13
Tamborine Qld 109 M11, 111 Q10
Tamborine National Park Qld 109 N11
Tamboy NSW 13 O3

Taminick Vic. 47 L6
Tamleugh Vic. 47 J7
Tamleugh North Vic. 47 J7
Tamleugh West Vic. 46 I7
Tammin WA 80 G3, 82 E7
Tamrookum Qld 109 L13
Tamworth NSW 15 J11
Tanah Merah Qld 107 O10
Tanami NT 96 B11
Tandarra Vic. 43 Q7, 46 C6
Tangalooma Qld 109 P6
Tangambalanga Vic. 47 Q5, 48 C3
Tangkam Qld 108 D7
Tangmangaroo NSW 12 F10, 20 D3
Tangorin Qld 112 A7, 119 O6
Tanja NSW 20 G10, 49 R5
Tanjil Bren Vic. 37 R7, 39 J4
Tanjil South Vic. 37 R9, 39 J6
Tankerton Vic. 37 L12, 38 E8
Tannum Sands Qld 113 P12
Tannymorel Qld 15 N1, 111 O11
Tansey Qld 111 N5
Tantanoola SA 70 G11
Tanunda SA 58 F5, 61 L8
Tanwood Vic. 43 M11
Tanybryn Vic. 41 N11
Taperoo SA 56 D8
Taplan SA 18 A8, 44 A5, 61 R8
Tara NSW 12 A10, 19 Q8
Tara NT 99 J4
Tara Qld 111 K8
Taradale Vic. 36 F1, 41 R1, 43 R12, 46 C11
Tarago NSW 12 H12, 20 F4
Tarago Vic. 37 P9
Taralga NSW 12 I9, 20 G2
Tarampa Qld 109 J7
Tarana NSW 10 E5
Tarana Quarry NSW 10 E5
Taranna Tas. 127 N9, 129 O10
Tarcombe Vic. 46 H10
Tarcoola SA 69 Q5
Tarcoon NSW 17 P6
Tarcowie SA 61 K2, 63 K12
Tarcutta NSW 12 C13, 20 A5
Tardun WA 82 C3
Taree NSW 13 P1, 15 N13
Taren Point NSW 9 K10
Targa Tas. 131 M8
Tarilta Vic. 36 E1
Taringa Qld 106 E2
Tarlee SA 58 D1, 61 L7
Tarlo NSW 12 I10, 20 G3
Tarlo River National Park NSW 12 I10, 20 G3
Tarnagulla Vic. 43 O10, 46 A8
Tarneit Vic. 32 B9, 36 H6, 38 B4
Tarnma SA 61 L6
Tarnook Vic. 47 K7
Tarome Qld 108 I12
Tarong Qld 108 E1
Taroom Qld 111 J4
Taroona Tas. 124 H13, 126 I7, 129 L9
Tarpeena SA 70 H11
Tarra-Bulga National Park Vic. 39 K8
Tarragal Vic. 40 C9
Tarragindi Qld 106 H4
Tarraleah Tas. 128 I4
Tarranginnie Vic. 42 D7
Tarrango Vic. 44 E5
Tarranyurk Vic. 42 F6
Tarraville Vic. 39 L10
Tarrawingee Vic. 47 N6
Tarrayoukyan Vic. 40 D2, 42 D13
Tarrenlea Vic. 40 E5
Tarrington Vic. 40 G5
Tarrion NSW 17 Q5
Tarwin Vic. 38 H10
Tarwin Lower Vic. 38 H10
Tarwin Meadows Vic. 38 H10
Tarwonga WA 80 F7
Tascott NSW 21 F7
Tasman Peninsula Tas. 127 M10, 129 O10
Tatham NSW 15 P3
Tathra NSW 20 G10, 49 R6
Tathra National Park WA 82 C5
Tatong Vic. 47 L8
Tatura Vic. 46 H6
Tatyoon Vic. 41 K3
Tawonga Vic. 47 Q8, 48 D6
Tawonga South Vic. 47 Q8, 48 D6

Tayene Tas. 131 N8
Taylors Arm NSW 15 O9
Taylors Beach Qld 115 O11
Taylors Flat NSW 12 F9, 20 E2
Taylors Lakes Vic. 32 E3
Taylorville SA 61 O6
Tea Gardens NSW 13 O4
Tea Tree Tas. 126 I3
Tea Tree Gully SA 57 Q9
Teal Flat SA 61 N9, 70 E1
Teal Point Vic. 43 P2, 45 P13, 46 B1
Tecoma Vic. 34 F13
Teddywaddy Vic. 43 M6
Teesdale Vic. 36 D8, 41 P7
Telegraph Point NSW 15 O11
Telford Vic. 47 K4
Telita Tas. 131 O7
Telopea NSW 4 D5
Telopea Downs Vic. 42 B5, 61 R13, 70 I6
Temma Tas. 130 B6
Temora NSW 12 C10, 19 R8, 20 A2
Tempe NSW 5 K13, 9 M3
Templers SA 58 D4, 61 L7
Templestowe Vic. 33 Q6, 37 K6
Templin Qld 109 J12
Tempy Vic. 18 E11, 44 H11
Ten Mile Vic. 37 R3
Ten Mile Hollow NSW 11 N3
Tenandra NSW 14 D11
Tennant Creek NT 97 K10
Tennyson NSW 4 I8
Tennyson Qld 106 F4
Tennyson SA 54 B3
Tennyson Vic. 43 R7, 46 D5
Tenterden WA 80 H11
Tenterfield NSW 15 M4, 111 N13
Tenth Island Tas. 131 L5
Tenthill Qld 108 G8
Tepko SA 58 H10, 61 M9, 70 D2
Terang Vic. 41 K8
Teridgerie NSW 14 E10
Teringie SA 55 O5
Terip Terip Vic. 46 I10
Terka SA 61 J1, 63 J12
Termeil NSW 13 J13, 20 H6, 27 O5
Terowie NSW 12 C3
Terowie SA 61 L3, 63 L13
Terrey Hills NSW 7 L8, 11 O6
Terrick Terrick Vic. 43 Q5, 46 C4
Terrigal NSW 11 Q4, 13 M6, 21 H5
Terry Hie Hie NSW 14 H6
Tewantin Qld 111 Q6
Tewinga NSW 15 O9
Tewkesbury Tas. 130 F6
Texas Qld 15 K3, 111 M12
Thalaba NSW 10 B13, 12 G9, 20 F2
Thalia Vic. 43 L5
Thallon Qld 14 E2, 110 H12
Thanes Creek Qld 108 C12
Thangool Qld 111 K1, 113 N13
Tharbogang NSW 19 N7
Thargomindah Qld 121 N10
Tharwa ACT 26 G4, 28 E7
The Anchorage NSW 27 N9
The Basin Vic. 34 E11
The Bluff Qld 108 G5
The Brothers Vic. 20 A11, 48 G7
The Cascade Vic. 47 R5, 48 E3
The Caves Qld 113 N10
The Channon NSW 15 Q2
The Cove Vic. 41 J10
The Entrance NSW 11 Q3, 13 M6, 21 H2
The Entrance North NSW 11 Q3, 21 H2
The Gap Qld 104 C11
The Gap Vic. 36 H4
The Gardens NT 89 C3, 90 D8
The Gardens Tas. 131 R7
The Glen Tas. 131 L7
The Granites NT 96 D12, 98 D2
The Gulf NSW 15 L4, 111 M13
The Gums Qld 111 K8
The Gurdies Vic. 37 N11, 38 G8
The Heart Vic. 39 N6
The Highlands Vic. 36 G5
The Lagoon NSW 10 B5
The Lakes National Park Vic. 39 Q5
The Levels SA 57 J8
The Lynd Qld 115 K11
The Monument Qld 118 F6

The Narrows NT 90 H5, 91 C12
The Oaks NSW 11 J11, 13 J8, 20 I1
The Palms National Park Qld 108 F2
The Patch Vic. 34 H12, 37 M7, 50 B12
The Pines SA 60 H9
The Risk NSW 15 P2, 111 P11
The Rock NSW 12 B13, 19 Q11
The Rocks NSW 2 D3
The Sisters Vic. 41 J8
The Spit NSW 5 O6
The Summit Qld 15 M2, 111 N12
The Vale NSW 18 H5, 45 O1
Thebarton SA 54 G5
Theodore ACT 25 E11
Theodore Qld 111 J2
Theresa Park NSW 11 K10
Thevenard SA 69 N10
Thirlmere NSW 11 J12, 13 J9, 20 I2
Thirlmere Lakes National Park NSW 11 J12
Thirlstane Tas. 131 J7
Thirroul NSW 11 M13, 13 K9
Thomas Plains SA 61 J6
Thomastown Vic. 33 M2, 37 K5, 38 D3
Thoona Vic. 47 L5
Thora NSW 15 O8
Thornborough Qld 115 L6
Thornbury Vic. 33 L6
Thorneside Qld 105 O11
Thorngate SA 52 D1
Thornlands Qld 107 R3
Thornleigh NSW 4 F1, 6 E11
Thornlie WA 75 N11
Thornton Qld 108 H10, 111 O10
Thornton Vic. 37 P2, 47 K11
Thornville Qld 108 E3
Thorpdale Vic. 37 R11, 38 I7
Thowgla Vic. 20 B8, 48 H3
Thowgla Upper Vic. 20 B9, 48 H3
Thredbo NSW 20 C10, 26 A13, 48 I5
Three Bridges Vic. 37 O7, 38 G4, 50 G11
Three Springs WA 82 C4
Three Ways Roadhouse NT 97 K10
Thrington SA 60 I6
Thrushton National Park Qld 110 E9
Thuddungra NSW 12 D9, 20 B1
Thulimbah Qld 15 M2, 111 N12
Thulloo NSW 12 A7, 19 P5
Thuringowa Qld 115 O13
Thurla Vic. 44 G4
Thursday Island Qld 116 B2
Ti Tree NT 98 I5
Ti Tree Store & Police Station NT 98 I5
Tia NSW 15 M11
Tiaro Qld 111 P4
Tibbuc NSW 13 N1, 15 M13
Tiberias Tas. 129 M6
Tibooburra NSW 16 D3
Tichborne NSW 12 D5
Tickera SA 60 I5
Tidal River Vic. 39 J12
Tiega Vic. 44 G9
Tieri Qld 113 J10
Tilba Tilba NSW 20 H9, 27 M12, 49 R3
Tilmouth Well Roadhouse NT 98 H6
Tilpa NSW 17 J8
Timbarra Vic. 20 B12, 48 H10
Timber Creek NT 94 D13, 96 D2
Timberoo Vic. 44 G9
Timberoo South Vic. 44 G10
Timbillica NSW 20 G13, 49 P10
Timboon Vic. 41 K10
Timmering Vic. 46 F6
Timor Vic. 43 O11
Timor West Vic. 43 N11
Tin Can Bay Qld 111 P5
Tinaburra Qld 115 M7
Tinamba Vic. 39 M5
Tinaroo Falls Qld 115 M7
Tincurrin WA 80 H7
Tindal NT 94 G10
Tinderbox Tas. 126 I8, 129 L9
Tingalpa Qld 105 L12
Tingaringy NSW 20 D11, 49 K7
Tingha NSW 15 K7
Tingoora Qld 111 N6
Tinonee NSW 13 O1, 15 N13
Tintaldra Vic. 20 B8, 48 H1
Tintinara SA 61 O12, 70 F5
Tiparra West SA 60 I7, 60 I7

Tipton Qld 108 A6, 111 M8
Tirranaville NSW 12 H11, 20 G4
Tirranna Roadhouse Qld 117 E9
Tittybong Vic. 43 M3, 45 M13
Tiwi NT 91 G1
Tjukayirla Roadhouse WA 83 M1, 85 L12
Tjuwanpa Resource Centre NT 98 H9
Tocal Qld 119 N12
Tocumwal NSW 19 M12, 46 I2
Togari Tas. 130 B4
Toggannoggera NSW 20 F6, 27 K6
Toiberry Tas. 131 L9
Tolga Qld 115 M7
Tolmie Vic. 47 M9
Tom Price WA 81 H4, 84 B5
Tomahawk Tas. 131 O5
Tomakin NSW 27 N8
Tomalla NSW 13 M1, 15 L13
Tomaree National Park NSW 13 O4
Tombong NSW 20 E11, 49 M7
Tomboye NSW 12 I12, 20 G5, 27 M2
Tomerong NSW 27 Q1
Tomingley NSW 12 D3
Tongala Vic. 46 F5
Tonganah Tas. 131 N7
Tonghi Creek Vic. 20 E13, 49 M12
Tongio Vic. 20 A12, 48 G9
Tongio West Vic. 20 A12, 48 F9
Tonimbuk Vic. 37 O8, 38 G5
Tooan Vic. 42 E10
Toobanna Qld 115 N11
Toobeah Qld 14 G1, 111 J11
Tooborac Vic. 46 F10
Toodyay WA 78 G1, 80 E2, 82 D7
Toogong NSW 12 E6
Toogoolawah Qld 108 I4, 111 O8
Toogoom Qld 111 P3
Tookayerta SA 61 P8
Toolamba Vic. 46 H7
Toolangi Vic. 37 M4, 38 F2, 46 I13, 50 D3
Toolern Vale Vic. 36 H4, 38 B2, 46 E13
Tooleybuc NSW 18 G10, 45 M9
Toolibin WA 80 H6
Tooligie SA 60 D5
Toolleen Vic. 46 E8
Toolondo Vic. 42 F11
Toolong Vic. 40 G9
Tooloom NSW 15 N2, 111 O12
Tooloon NSW 14 C10
Tooma NSW 20 B8, 48 H1
Toombul Qld 104 H8
Toombullup Vic. 47 M9
Toompine Roadhouse Qld 121 O8
Toongabbie Vic. 39 L6
Toongi NSW 12 E3
Toonumbar NSW 15 O2, 111 P12
Tooperang SA 59 H6
Toora Vic. 39 J10
Tooradin Vic. 37 M10, 38 F7
Toorak Vic. 33 M10
Toorak Gardens SA 55 K6
Tooraweenah NSW 14 E12
Toorbul Qld 109 N4
Toorongo Vic. 37 Q6
Tootgarook Vic. 36 I11
Tootool NSW 12 A12, 19 Q10
Toowong Qld 104 E13, 106 E2
Toowoomba Qld 108 F8, 111 N9
Toowoon Bay NSW 11 Q3, 21 H3
Top Springs NT 96 F4
Topaz Qld 115 M8
Torbanlea Qld 111 P3
Torndirrup National Park WA 80 I13, 82 F12
Torquay Vic. 36 F11, 41 Q9
Torrens ACT 25 D6
Torrens Creek Qld 112 B4, 119 Q4
Torrens Park SA 55 J10
Torrensville SA 54 G6
Torrington NSW 15 L4, 111 N13
Torrita Vic. 18 D10, 44 F9
Torrumbarry Vic. 19 J13, 46 D3
Tostaree Vic. 48 I13
Tottenham NSW 12 B2, 17 R12
Tottenham Vic. 32 G8
Toukley NSW 11 Q2, 13 M6
Tourello Vic. 36 C2
Towallum NSW 15 O7
Towamba NSW 20 F12, 49 P8

Towan Vic. 45 L9
Towaninny Vic. 43 M3
Tower Hill Tas. 131 P9
Tower Hill Vic. 40 H9
Towitta SA 58 I5
Townsville Qld 115 P12
Towong Vic. 20 B8, 48 H2
Towrang NSW 12 I10, 20 G3
Tracy SA 61 M4
Trafalgar Vic. 37 R10, 38 I7
Tragowel Vic. 43 P3, 46 B2
Trangie NSW 12 C1
Tranmere SA 55 M4
Tranmere Tas. 125 M9
Traralgon Vic. 39 K7
Traralgon South Vic. 39 K7
Trawalla Vic. 36 A3, 41 M3
Trawool Vic. 46 H10
Trayning WA 80 H1, 82 E7
Traynors Lagoon Vic. 43 K8
Trebonne Qld 115 N11
Treeton WA 79 C9, 80 B9
Tremont Vic. 34 E12
Trenah Tas. 131 O8
Trentham Vic. 36 F3, 41 R2, 43 R13, 46 C12
Trentham East Vic. 36 G3
Tresco Vic. 18 H11, 43 O1, 45 O12
Tresco West Vic. 43 N1, 45 N12
Trevallyn NSW 13 M3
Trevallyn Tas. 131 L8
Trewalla Vic. 40 D9
Trewilga NSW 12 D4
Triabunna Tas. 127 O1, 129 O6
Trida NSW 19 L3
Trida Vic. 37 P11
Trigg WA 76 B9
Trinita Vic. 44 H8
Trinity Gardens SA 55 L5
Trowutta Tas. 130 C5
Truck 'n' Travel Roadhouse Qld 15 M1, 108 F13
Truganina Vic. 32 D9
Trundle NSW 12 C4
Trunkey NSW 10 A8, 12 G7
Truro SA 58 G3, 61 M7
Tuan Qld 111 P4
Tuart Forest National Park WA 79 F6
Tuart Hill WA 76 F10
Tubbul NSW 12 D9, 20 B2
Tubbut Vic. 20 D11, 49 K8
Tucklan NSW 12 G2
Tuena NSW 10 A10, 12 G8, 20 F1
Tuggerah NSW 11 P3, 21 F2
Tuggeranong ACT 25 B9, 26 G3, 28 E5
Tulendeena Tas. 131 O7
Tulkara Vic. 43 K11
Tullah Tas. 130 F10
Tullamarine Vic. 32 H3
Tullamore NSW 12 B3, 19 R1
Tullibigeal NSW 19 P4
Tulloh Vic. 36 B12
Tully Qld 115 N9
Tully Heads Qld 115 N9
Tumbarumba NSW 20 B7
Tumbi Umbi NSW 11 P3, 21 G3
Tumblong NSW 12 D12, 20 B5
Tumbulgum NSW 15 Q1, 111 Q11
Tumby Bay SA 60 E7
Tummaville Qld 108 B10
Tumorrama NSW 12 E12, 20 C5, 26 B1
Tumoulin Qld 115 M8
Tumut NSW 12 D12, 20 C5, 26 A2
Tunart Vic. 18 B8, 44 C5
Tunbridge Tas. 129 M4, 131 M13
Tuncurry NSW 13 P2
Tungamah Vic. 19 N13, 47 K4
Tungamull Qld 113 O10
Tungkillo SA 58 G8, 61 M9, 70 D1
Tunnack Tas. 129 M6
Tunnel Tas. 131 M7
Tunnel Creek National Park WA 87 L8
Tura Beach NSW 20 G11, 49 Q7
Turallin Qld 111 M10
Turill NSW 12 I2
Turkey Creek Roadhouse WA 87 Q7
Turlinjah NSW 27 M9
Turner ACT 24 G8
Turners Beach Tas. 130 H6
Turners Marsh Tas. 131 L7
Turondale NSW 10 B1, 12 H5

Tuross Head NSW 20 H8, 27 N10
Turramurra NSW 4 I1, 6 G11
Turrawan NSW 14 G8
Turrella NSW 9 L4
Turriff Vic. 18 E11, 42 I1, 44 I11
Turriff East Vic. 42 I1, 44 I11
Turriff West Vic. 42 H1, 44 H11
Turtons Creek Vic. 37 R13
Tusmore SA 55 L7
Tutunup WA 79 F7, 80 C9
Tutye Vic. 44 D10
Tweed Heads NSW 15 Q1, 111 Q11
Twelve Mile NSW 12 G3
Two Mile Flat NSW 12 G3
Two Rocks WA 80 C2
Two Wells SA 58 A5, 61 K8
Tyaak Vic. 37 K1, 46 G11
Tyabb Vic. 37 L10, 38 E7
Tyagarah NSW 15 Q2, 111 Q12
Tyagong NSW 12 E8, 20 C1
Tyalgum NSW 15 P1, 111 Q11
Tyalla Vic. 44 D10
Tycannah NSW 14 G6
Tyenna Tas. 126 B3, 129 J7
Tyers Vic. 39 K6
Tyers Junction Vic. 39 J5
Tylden Vic. 36 G2, 38 A1, 41 R2, 43 R13, 46 D12
Tyndale NSW 15 P5
Tynong Vic. 37 N9, 38 G6
Tyntynder Central Vic. 45 N10
Tyntynder South Vic. 45 N10
Typo Vic. 47 N9, 48 A7
Tyrendarra Vic. 40 E8
Tyrendarra East Vic. 40 F8
Tyringham NSW 15 N8
Tyrrell Downs Vic. 45 K11

Uarbry NSW 12 H1
Ubobo Qld 111 M1, 113 P13
Ucolta SA 61 M2, 63 L12
Uki NSW 15 Q1, 111 Q11
Ulamambri NSW 14 F11
Ulan NSW 12 H2
Ulinda NSW 14 F12
Ulladulla NSW 13 J13, 20 I6, 27 P4
Ullina Vic. 36 D2, 41 O1, 43 O13, 46 A11
Ullswater Vic. 42 C11
Ulmarra NSW 15 P6
Ulong NSW 15 P8
Ulooloo SA 61 L3
Ultima Vic. 18 I11, 43 L1, 45 M12
Ultimo NSW 2 B13, 5 M11, 9 O1
Ulupna Vic. 19 M13, 46 I3
Uluru NT 98 E12
Uluru-Kata Tjuta National Park NT 98 E12
Ulva WA 80 I2
Ulverstone Tas. 130 H6
Umbakumba NT 95 P9
Umbiram Qld 108 D8
Umina NSW 11 P5, 21 F9
Undalya SA 61 L6
Undara Volcanic National Park Qld 115 K10
Undera Vic. 46 H5
Undera North Vic. 46 H5
Underbool Vic. 18 C10, 44 E10
Undercliffe NSW 9 L4
Underdale SA 54 F5
Underwood Qld 107 L8
Underwood Tas. 131 M7
Ungarie NSW 12 A7, 19 Q5
Ungarra SA 60 E6
Unley SA 52 E13, 54 I8
Unley Park SA 55 J9
Upper Beaconsfield Vic. 37 M8, 38 F5
Upper Bingara NSW 14 I7
Upper Blessington Tas. 131 N9
Upper Bowman NSW 13 M1, 15 L13
Upper Castra Tas. 130 H7
Upper Cedar Creek Qld 109 L6
Upper Colo NSW 11 K4
Upper Coomera Qld 109 N11
Upper Esk Tas. 131 N9
Upper Ferntree Gully Vic. 34 F13, 50 A12
Upper Freestone Qld 108 G13
Upper Gellibrand Vic. 36 B13
Upper Horton NSW 14 I7
Upper Kedron Qld 104 B10
Upper Kinchela NSW 15 P10
Upper Koondah Qld 108 C2

Upper Laceys Creek Qld 109 K5
Upper McDonald NSW 11 L2
Upper Mangrove NSW 11 N2
Upper Mangrove Creek NSW 11 N2
Upper Manilla NSW 14 I9
Upper Mount Hicks Tas. 130 F6
Upper Myall NSW 13 O2
Upper Natone Tas. 130 G7
Upper Pappinbarra NSW 15 N11
Upper Plenty Vic. 37 K3, 38 D1, 46 G12
Upper Scamander Tas. 131 Q9
Upper Sturt SA 55 N13
Upper Swan WA 77 P1, 78 C3
Upper Tenthill Qld 108 G9
Upper Widgee Qld 111 O5
Upper Woodstock Tas. 126 F9
Upper Yarra Dam Vic. 37 P5
Upper Yarraman Qld 108 F2
Upwey Vic. 34 E13, 37 L7
Uraidla SA 55 Q8, 58 C10, 59 H1
Uralla NSW 15 L9
Urana NSW 19 O11
Urandangi Qld 99 R4, 118 B6
Urangeline East NSW 19 P11
Urania SA 60 I8
Uranno SA 60 D7
Uranquinty NSW 12 B12, 19 Q10
Urbenville NSW 15 O2, 111 O11
Urrbrae SA 55 L9
Urunga NSW 15 P9
Uxbridge Tas. 126 D4, 129 J8

Vacy NSW 13 M3
Vale Park SA 55 K3
Vale View Qld 108 E8
Valencia Creek Vic. 39 M4, 48 C13
Valla Beach NSW 15 P9
Valley Heights NSW 11 J7
Valley View SA 57 M10
Varley WA 82 G9
Vasey Vic. 40 F2
Vasse WA 79 D7, 80 B9
Vaucluse NSW 5 P9
Vaughan Vic. 36 E1, 41 Q1, 43 Q12, 46 C11
Vectis Vic. 42 G9
Veitch SA 61 Q8
Venman Bushland National Park Qld 107 P8
Ventnor Vic. 37 L12, 38 E9
Venus Bay SA 60 A3, 69 Q13
Venus Bay Vic. 38 H10
Verdun SA 58 D11, 59 H1
Veresdale Qld 109 L11
Vermont Vic. 33 R10, 34 A10
Verona Sands Tas. 126 F12, 129 K11
Verran SA 60 E5
Victor Harbor SA 59 G8, 61 L11, 70 B4
Victoria Hill Qld 108 D11
Victoria Park WA 75 J5
Victoria Point Qld 109 O9, 111 Q9
Victoria Point Vic. 40 G4
Victoria River Wayside Inn NT 94 E12, 96 E2
Victoria Valley Tas. 129 J5
Victoria Valley Vic. 40 H4
View Bank Vic. 33 O5
Villawood NSW 4 B11, 8 D1
Villeneuve Qld 109 K3
Vimy Qld 113 N12
Vincentia NSW 13 K12, 20 I5, 27 R1
Vineyard NSW 11 L6
Vinifera Vic. 18 G10, 45 M10
Violet Town Vic. 47 J8
Virginia Qld 104 H6, 108 G5
Virginia SA 58 B6, 61 K8
Vista SA 57 R10
Vite Vite Vic. 41 L6
Vite Vite North Vic. 41 L5
Viveash WA 77 P9
Vivonne Bay SA 60 H13

W Tree Vic. 20 B12, 48 H10
Waaia Vic. 19 L13, 46 H4
Waarre Vic. 41 K10
Wacol Qld 106 D8
Wadbilliga National Park NSW 20 F9, 27 J11, 49 P3
Waddamana Tas. 129 J3, 131 J13
Waddi NSW 19 N8
Waddikee SA 60 E3
Wadeye Community NT 94 B9

Waeel WA 80 F2
Wagaman NT 91 H4
Wagant Vic. 44 I9
Wagerup WA 78 C13, 79 H1
Wagga Wagga NSW 12 B12, 19 R10
Wagin WA 82 E10
Wagonga NSW 20 G8, 27 M11
Wagstaffe NSW 11 P5, 21 G9
Wahgunyah Vic. 19 O13, 47 N3
Wahring Vic. 46 H8
Wahroonga NSW 6 G10
Waikerie SA 61 O6
Waikiki WA 78 B8, 80 C5
Wail Vic. 42 G8
Wairewa Vic. 48 I12
Waitara NSW 6 F10
Waitchie Vic. 18 G11, 45 L11
Waitpinga SA 59 F9
Wakerley Qld 105 M11
Wakool NSW 19 J11, 43 R1, 45 R12
Wal Wal Vic. 42 I10
Walang NSW 10 D4
Walbundrie NSW 19 P12, 47 O1
Walcha NSW 15 L10
Walcha Road NSW 15 L10
Walgett NSW 14 C7
Walgoolan WA 82 F7
Walhalla Vic. 39 K5
Walkamin Qld 115 M7
Walkaway WA 82 B4
Walker Flat SA 61 N9, 70 E1
Walkers Creek Qld 108 B1
Walkerston Qld 113 K5
Walkerville SA 55 J3
Walkerville Vic. 38 I11
Walkerville South Vic. 38 I11
Walla Walla NSW 19 Q12, 47 P2
Wallabadah NSW 15 J12
Wallabrook SA 70 H8
Wallace Vic. 36 E4, 41 P3, 46 B13
Wallace Rockhole Aboriginal Community NT 98 I9
Wallacedale Vic. 40 E6
Wallacetown NSW 12 B11, 19 R9
Wallacia NSW 11 K8, 13 K8
Wallaga Lake National Park NSW 20 H9, 27 M13, 49 R4
Wallaloo Vic. 43 K9
Wallaloo East Vic. 43 K10
Wallaman Falls National Park see Lumholtz National Park
Wallan Vic. 37 J3, 38 D1, 46 F12
Wallangarra Qld 15 M3, 111 N12
Wallangra NSW 15 J4, 111 L13
Wallaroo Qld 113 L11
Wallaroo SA 60 I6
Wallaville Qld 111 N3
Wallendbeen NSW 12 D10, 20 B3
Wallerawang NSW 10 F4, 12 I6
Walli NSW 12 F7
Wallingford Qld 108 C8
Wallington Vic. 36 G10
Walloon Qld 109 J9
Walloway SA 61 K2, 63 K12
Walls of Jerusalem National Park Tas. 128 H2, 130 H11
Wallumbilla Qld 110 H6
Wallup Vic. 42 G7
Walmer NSW 12 F4
Walpa Vic. 39 P4, 48 E13
Walpeup Vic. 18 D10, 44 F9
Walpole WA 80 F13, 82 D12
Walpole-Nornalup National Park WA 80 E13, 82 D12
Walsh Qld 114 I6
Waltowa SA 61 N11, 70 E4
Walwa Vic. 20 A8, 48 G1
Walyunga National Park WA 78 D2
Wamberal NSW 11 Q4, 21 H5
Wambidgee NSW 12 D11, 20 B4
Wamboyne NSW 12 B7, 19 Q5
Waminda NSW 14 C7
Wammon NSW 19 O8
Wampoony SA 70 H7
Wamuran Qld 109 L4, 111 P8
Wamuran Basin Qld 109 L4
Wanaaring NSW 16 I4
Wanalta Vic. 46 F7
Wanbi SA 61 P9, 70 G1
Wandandian NSW 13 J12, 27 Q2

Wandearah SA 61 J4
Wandearah West SA 61 J4
Wandella NSW 20 G9, 27 K12, 49 Q3
Wandering WA 78 H11, 80 E6
Wandiligong Vic. 47 P8, 48 C6
Wandilo SA 70 H11
Wandin North Vic. 34 H7, 37 M6, 38 F4, 50 C9
Wandin Yallock Vic. 34 I8, 37 M6, 50 C9
Wando Bridge Vic. 40 C3
Wando Vale Vic. 40 C3
Wandoan Qld 111 J5
Wandong Vic. 37 K2, 38 D1, 46 G12
Wandsworth NSW 15 L7
Wang Wauk NSW 13 O2
Wangara WA 76 G2
Wangarabell Vic. 20 F13, 49 O10
Wangaratta Vic. 47 M6
Wangary SA 60 C8
Wangenella NSW 19 K10
Wangi Wangi NSW 13 M5
Wangoom Vic. 40 I9
Wanguri NT 91 H3
Wanilla SA 60 D8
Wanneroo WA 78 B3, 82 B8
Wanniassa ACT 25 D8
Wannon Vic. 40 E5
Wanora Qld 109 J8
Wantabadgery NSW 12 C12, 20 A5
Wantirna Vic. 34 B11
Wanwin Vic. 40 B7, 70 I12
Wapengo NSW 20 G10, 49 Q5
Wappinguy NSW 13 J2
Warakurna Community WA 85 Q9
Warakurna Roadhouse WA 85 Q9
Waramanga ACT 25 B5
Warana Qld 109 N1
Waranga Vic. 46 G7
Waratah Tas. 130 E8
Waratah Bay Vic. 38 I11
Waratah North Vic. 38 I10
Warawarrup WA 79 H2, 80 D7
Warburton Vic. 37 O6, 38 G3, 50 H9
Warburton Aboriginal Community WA 85 N11
Warburton Roadhouse WA 85 N11
Wardell NSW 15 Q3, 111 Q13
Wards River NSW 13 N2
Wareemba NSW 5 J9
Warge Rock NSW 12 C3
Wargela NSW 12 F10, 20 D3
Warialda NSW 14 I5
Warialda Rail NSW 14 I5
Warkton NSW 14 F12
Warkworth NSW 13 L3
Warmga Qld 108 C2
Warmun Community WA 87 Q7
Warmur Vic. 43 J5
Warncoort Vic. 36 B11, 41 N9
Warne Vic. 43 L3, 45 L13
Warneet Vic. 38 E7
Warner Qld 104 B4
Warnertown SA 61 J3, 63 J13
Warooka SA 60 H9
Waroona WA 78 C12, 80 C6, 82 C9
Warra Qld 111 L7
Warrabah National Park NSW 15 J8
Warrabrook Vic. 40 F6
Warracknabeal Vic. 42 H6
Warradale SA 54 E12
Warraderry NSW 12 D7
Warragamba NSW 11 J9, 13 J8, 20 I1
Warragamba Vic. 43 R7, 46 D6
Warragul Vic. 37 P10, 38 H6
Warrah Creek NSW 15 J13
Warrak Vic. 41 L2, 43 L13
Warralakin WA 82 F6
Warrall NSW 15 J11
Warrambine Vic. 36 C7, 41 O6
Warramboo SA 60 C3, 62 C13
Warrandyte Vic. 34 B5
Warrane Tas. 125 K6
Warranook Vic. 43 J9
Warrawee NSW 6 G10
Warrayure Vic. 40 G5
Warrego NT 97 J10
Warrell Creek NSW 15 P9
Warren NSW 14 B13
Warren Qld 113 N11
Warren National Park WA 80 C11
Warrenbayne Vic. 47 K8

Warrenmang Vic. 43 M11
Warrentinna Tas. 131 O6
Warriewood NSW 7 P8
Warrill View Qld 109 J10
Warrimoo NSW 11 J7
Warringa Tas. 130 H7
Warrion Vic. 36 B10, 41 N8
Warrnambool Vic. 40 I9
Warrong Vic. 40 H8
Warrow SA 60 C7
Warrumbungle National Park NSW 14 E11
Warruwi NT 94 I3
Warup WA 80 F8
Warwick Qld 15 M1, 108 F13, 111 N11
Warwick WA 76 E6
Warwick Farm NSW 8 B3
Washpool National Park NSW 15 N5, 111 O13
Wasleys SA 58 C4
Watarrka National Park NT 98 F9
Watchem Vic. 43 J5
Watchman SA 61 K6
Watchupga Vic. 43 J3
Waterfall NSW 11 M11, 13 L9
Waterfall Gully SA 55 N9
Waterford Qld 107 O12, 109 M10
Waterford Vic. 39 N2, 47 Q13, 48 D11
Waterford WA 75 J8
Waterford Park Vic. 37 K2
Waterhouse Tas. 131 O5
Waterloo SA 61 L6
Waterloo Tas. 126 E10, 129 K10
Waterloo WA 79 G4, 80 C8
Waterloo Corner SA 56 H2, 58 B7
Waterman WA 76 B7
Watervale SA 61 L6
Waterview Heights NSW 15 P6
Wathe Vic. 42 H2, 44 H12
Watheroo WA 82 C6
Watheroo National Park WA 82 C5
Watson ACT 24 I6
Watson SA 68 H4
Watsonia Vic. 33 O4, 37 K5
Watsons Bay NSW 5 Q8, 11 O8
Watsons Creek NSW 15 J9
Watsons Creek Vic. 34 C2, 37 L5
Watsonville Qld 115 M8
Wattamolla NSW 11 N11
Wattamondara NSW 12 E8, 20 D1
Wattle Flat NSW 10 C1, 12 H5
Wattle Glen Vic. 33 R1, 34 A2, 37 L5
Wattle Grove NSW 8 B6
Wattle Grove Tas. 126 E10
Wattle Grove WA 75 Q7
Wattle Hill Tas. 127 L4, 129 N8
Wattle Park SA 55 N6
Wattle Range SA 70 H10
Wattle Valley Vic. 46 G9
Wattleup WA 78 B6
Waubra Vic. 36 B2, 41 N2, 43 N13
Wauchope NSW 15 O12
Wauchope NT 97 K13, 99 K2
Wauraltee SA 60 I8
Waurn Ponds Vic. 36 F10, 41 Q8
Wave Hill NSW 17 O6
Wavell Heights Qld 104 G7
Waverley NSW 5 P12, 9 R2
Waverton NSW 5 M8
Wayatinah Tas. 128 I5
Waygara Vic. 48 I12
Wayville SA 52 C13, 54 I7
Webbs NSW 12 D2
Webbs Creek NSW 11 M3
Wedderburn NSW 11 L11
Wedderburn Vic. 43 N7
Wedderburn Junction Vic. 43 O7
Weddin Mountains National Park NSW 12 D8, 20 B1
Wee Elwah NSW 19 L3
Wee Jasper NSW 12 F12, 20 D5, 26 E1
Wee Waa NSW 14 F8
Wee-Wee-Rup Vic. 43 R4, 46 C2
Weeaproinah Vic. 41 N11
Weemelah NSW 14 F3, 110 I13
Weeragua Vic. 20 E13, 49 N10
Weetah Tas. 131 J8
Weetaliba NSW 14 G12
Weetangera ACT 24 C7
Weethalle NSW 19 P6
Weetulta SA 60 I7

Wehla Vic. 43 N9
Weimby NSW 18 G8, 45 M6
Weipa Qld 116 B7
Weismantels NSW 13 N2
Weja NSW 12 A7, 19 Q4
Welaregang NSW 20 B8, 48 H1
Weldborough Tas. 131 P7
Welford National Park Qld 121 M3
Wellcamp Qld 108 E8
Wellesley Islands Qld 117 E6
Wellingrove NSW 15 L6
Wellington NSW 12 F3
Wellington SA 61 N10, 70 E3
Wellington Point Qld 105 Q11, 109 N8
Wellsford Vic. 43 R9, 46 D7
Welshmans Reef Vic. 43 P11, 46 B10
Welshpool Vic. 39 K10
Welshpool WA 75 L6
Wembley WA 74 E2, 76 E13
Wembley Downs WA 76 C11
Wemen Vic. 18 E9, 44 I7
Wendouree Vic. 36 C4
Wengenville Qld 108 D1
Wentworth NSW 18 C6, 44 F2
Wentworth Falls NSW 10 I7
Wentworthville NSW 4 B6
Wepowie SA 61 K2, 63 J12
Wereboldera NSW 26 A3
Werneth Vic. 36 B7, 41 N6
Werombi NSW 11 J10
Werona Vic. 36 D1
Werrap Vic. 42 F4
Werribee Vic. 32 A12, 36 H7, 38 B4
Werrikimbe National Park NSW 15 N11
Werrimull Vic. 18 C8, 44 D4
Werris Creek NSW 14 I11
Wesburn Vic. 37 N6, 50 G9
Wesley Vale Tas. 130 I7
West Beach SA 54 D7
West Cape Howe National Park WA 80 H13
West Croydon SA 54 G3
West End Qld 104 F13, 106 F1
West Frankford Tas. 131 K7
West Haldon Qld 108 F10
West Hill National Park Qld 113 L7
West Hobart Tas. 124 F8
West Lakes SA 54 C2, 56 C13, 58 A9
West Lakes Shore SA 54 B1, 56 B12
West MacDonnell National Park NT 98 H8
West Montagu Tas. 130 B4
West Moonah Tas. 124 D4
West Pennant Hills NSW 4 D2, 6 C12
West Perth WA 72 A1, 74 G3
West Pine Tas. 130 G6
West Pymble NSW 4 I3, 6 G13
West Ridgley Tas. 130 F6
West Ryde NSW 4 G6
West Scottsdale Tas. 131 N7
West Swan WA 77 O6
West Takone Tas. 130 E6
West Wyalong NSW 12 B8, 19 Q6
Westbourne Park SA 54 I9
Westbrook Qld 108 E8
Westbury Tas. 131 K9
Westbury Vic. 37 R10, 39 J6
Westby Vic. 43 P2, 45 P13, 46 A1
Westdale NSW 15 J11
Westdale WA 78 H8, 80 E5
Western Creek Tas. 130 I10
Western District, The Vic. 40 C5
Western Flat SA 70 H7
Western Junction Tas. 131 M9
Western River SA 60 G12
Westerway Tas. 126 E2, 129 J7
Westlake Qld 106 B6
Westleigh NSW 6 D10
Westmar Qld 111 J10
Westmead NSW 4 B6
Westmeadows Vic. 32 I1
Westmere Vic. 41 K5
Weston ACT 24 D13, 25 B4
Weston NSW 13 M4
Weston Creek ACT 24 A13, 26 G3, 28 D4
Westonia WA 82 F7
Westons Flat SA 61 O6
Westwood Qld 113 N11
Westwood Tas. 131 L9
Weymouth Tas. 131 M6
Whale Beach NSW 7 R3, 11 P6, 21 H11

Wharminda SA 60 E6
Wharparilla Vic. 46 E4
Wharparilla North Vic. 46 E4
Wheatsheaf Vic. 36 F2
Wheeler Heights NSW 5 P1, 7 N10
Wheelers Hill Vic. 33 R13, 34 A13, 35 G1
Wheeo NSW 12 G10, 20 F3
Whichello Qld 108 F5
Whim Creek WA 81 H1, 84 B2
Whiporie NSW 15 P4, 111 P13
Whirily Vic. 43 K4
White Beach Tas. 127 L10, 129 N10
White Cliffs NSW 16 F8
White Flat SA 60 D8
White Gum Valley WA 74 C11
White Hills Tas. 131 M9
White Mountains National Park Qld 112 B3, 119 Q3
White Patch Qld 109 N4
White Rock NSW 10 C4
Whitefoord Tas. 129 M6
Whiteheads Creek Vic. 46 H10
Whiteman WA 77 M4, 78 C3
Whitemark Tas. 128 A12
Whitemore Tas. 131 K9
Whitewood Qld 119 N6
Whitfield Vic. 47 N8
Whitsunday Island Qld 113 K2
Whitsunday Islands National Park Qld 113 K3
Whittlesea Vic. 37 K4, 38 D2, 46 G13
Whitton NSW 19 O8
Whitwarta SA 61 K6
Whoorel Vic. 36 C11
Whoroully South Vic. 48 A5
Whorouly Vic. 47 N7, 48 A4
Whorouly South Vic. 47 N7
Whroo Vic. 46 G8
Whyalla SA 60 I2, 62 H13
Whyte Yarcowie SA 61 L3, 63 L13
Wialki WA 82 F6
Wiangaree NSW 15 P2, 111 P12
Wickepin WA 80 G6, 82 E9
Wickham WA 81 G1
Wickliffe Vic. 41 J5
Widgiemooltha WA 82 I7
Widgiewa NSW 19 O10
Wilberforce NSW 11 L5, 13 K7
Wilburville Tas. 129 K3, 131 K12
Wilby Vic. 19 N13, 47 L4
Wilcannia NSW 16 G10
Wild Horse Plains SA 61 K7
Wiley Park NSW 8 I4
Wilga WA 80 D9
Wilgul Vic. 36 A7, 41 N6
Wilkawatt SA 61 P11, 70 G3
Wilkur Vic. 43 J5
Willa Vic. 42 G1, 44 G11
Willagee WA 74 E10
Willalooka SA 70 G7
Willamulka SA 60 I5
Willandra National Park NSW 19 L3
Willare Bridge Roadhouse WA 87 J8
Willatook Vic. 40 G8
Willaura Vic. 41 J4
Willawarrin NSW 15 O10
Willawong Qld 106 G5
Willbriggle NSW 19 N8
Willenabrina Vic. 42 G5
Willetton WA 75 J10
William Bay National Park WA 80 G13
William Creek SA 64 E11
Williams WA 80 F7, 82 D9
Williamsdale NSW 26 G5, 28 F8
Williamsford Tas. 128 E1, 130 E10
Williamstown SA 58 E6, 61 L8, 70 C1
Williamstown Vic. 33 J11, 37 J7
Williamtown NSW 13 N4
Willigulli WA 82 A3
Willina NSW 13 O2
Willoughby NSW 5 N5
Willow Grove Vic. 37 R9, 38 I6
Willow Tree NSW 15 J12
Willowie SA 61 K1, 63 J11
Willowmavin Vic. 37 J1, 46 F11
Willows Qld 112 H11
Willows Gemfields Qld 112 H11
Willowvale Qld 108 F12
Willowvale Vic. 36 A6, 41 M5
Willson River SA 61 J12

Willung Vic. 39 M7
Willung South Vic. 39 L8
Willunga SA 58 B13, 59 F4, 61 K10, 70 B3
Wilmington SA 61 J1, 62 I11
Wilmot Tas. 130 H8
Wilora NT 99 J4
Wilpena SA 63 K7
Wilroy WA 82 C3
Wilson WA 75 K8
Wilsons Downfall NSW 15 M3
Wilsons Promontory National Park Vic. 39 J11
Wilston Qld 104 F10
Wilton NSW 11 K12
Wiltshire Junction Tas. 130 D4
Wiluna WA 84 E11
Wimba Vic. 36 B13, 41 N11
Wimmera, The Vic. 42 D4
Winchelsea Vic. 36 D10, 41 P8
Windarra WA 83 J3
Windellama NSW 12 I11, 20 G4
Windermere Tas. 131 L8
Windermere Vic. 36 C3
Windeyer NSW 12 H4
Windjana Gorge National Park WA 87 L8
Windomal NSW 18 G9, 45 M7
Windorah Qld 121 L4
Windowie NSW 26 A2
Windsor NSW 11 L6, 13 K7
Windsor Qld 104 G10
Windsor SA 61 K7
Windsor Gardens SA 55 L1, 57 L12
Windurong NSW 14 D12
Windy Corner WA 85 L6
Windy Harbour WA 80 D12
Wingala NSW 5 Q3, 7 O13
Wingamin SA 61 O10, 70 F2
Wingeel Vic. 36 C9, 41 O7
Wingello NSW 12 I10, 20 H3
Wingen NSW 13 K1, 15 J13
Wingfield SA 56 G11
Wingham NSW 13 O1, 15 N13
Winiam Vic. 42 D7
Winiam East Vic. 42 E7
Winjallok Vic. 43 L10
Winkie SA 61 Q7
Winkleigh Tas. 131 K7
Winmalee NSW 11 J7
Winnaleah Tas. 131 O6
Winnambool Vic. 45 J8
Winnap Vic. 40 C6
Winnellie NT 90 I6, 91 G13, 92 C2
Winnindoo Vic. 39 L6
Winninowie SA 61 J1, 62 I11
Winnunga NSW 12 A7, 19 Q5
Winslow Vic. 40 I8
Winston Hills NSW 4 B4
Winthrop WA 74 F10
Winton Qld 119 M8
Winton Vic. 47 L7
Winulta SA 60 I7
Winwill Qld 108 G8
Winya Qld 109 K3
Wirha SA 61 Q10, 70 H2
Wirlinga NSW 19 Q13, 47 Q3, 48 C1
Wirrabara SA 61 K2, 63 J13
Wirrega SA 70 H6
Wirrega North SA 61 Q13, 70 H5
Wirrida SA 67 Q13
Wirrimah NSW 12 E9, 20 C1
Wirrinya NSW 12 C7
Wirrinya West NSW 12 C7
Wirrulla SA 69 Q10
Wisanger SA 60 H11
Wiseleigh Vic. 39 Q4, 48 G12
Wisemans Creek NSW 10 C6, 12 H7
Wisemans Ferry NSW 11 M3, 13 L6
Wishart Qld 107 K5
Wishbone WA 80 H7
Wistow SA 58 E12, 59 I3
Witchcliffe WA 79 C10
Withcott Qld 108 F8
Witheren Qld 109 M13
Withersfield Qld 112 H11
Witjira National Park SA 64 B2, 99 M13
Witta Qld 109 L1, 111 P7
Wittenbra NSW 14 E10
Wittenoom WA 81 I4, 84 B4
Wittitrin NSW 15 O11
Wivenhoe Tas. 130 G6

Wivenhoe Pocket Qld 109 J7
Woden ACT 24 E13, 25 C4, 26 G3, 28 E4
Wodonga Vic. 19 P13, 47 P4, 48 B2
Wokalup WA 79 H2, 80 C7
Woko National Park NSW 15 L12
Wokurna SA 61 J5
Wolfdene Qld 109 N10
Wollar NSW 12 I2
Wollemi National Park NSW 10 I2, 13 J3
Wollert Vic. 37 K4, 38 D2, 46 G13
Wollogorang Roadhouse NT 97 R5, 117 A7
Wollombi NSW 13 L4
Wollomombi NSW 15 M8
Wollongbar NSW 15 Q3
Wollongong NSW 11 M13, 13 K10
Wollstonecraft NSW 5 L7
Wollun NSW 15 K10
Wolseley SA 42 A7, 70 I7
Wolumla NSW 20 G11, 49 Q7
Womalilla Qld 110 E6
Wombarra NSW 11 M12
Wombat NSW 12 D10, 20 C2
Wombelano Vic. 42 D11
Wombeyan Caves NSW 10 F13
Womboota NSW 19 K13, 46 E3
Won Wron Vic. 39 L9
Wonboyn Lake NSW 20 G12, 49 Q9
Wondai Qld 111 N6
Wondalga NSW 12 D13, 20 B6
Wonga Qld 115 M5
Wonga Park Vic. 34 C5
Wongan Hills WA 82 D6
Wongarbon NSW 12 F2
Wonglepong Qld 109 M12
Wongulla SA 61 N8, 70 E1
Wonnerup WA 79 E7, 80 B8
Wonthaggi Vic. 38 G10
Wonwondah East Vic. 42 G10
Wonwondah North Vic. 42 G10
Wonyip Vic. 39 K9
Wood Wood Vic. 18 G10, 45 M9
Woodanilling WA 80 G8
Woodbridge Tas. 126 G10, 129 L10
Woodburn NSW 15 Q4, 111 Q13
Woodburne Vic. 36 D6, 41 P5
Woodbury Tas. 129 M4, 131 M13
Woodchester SA 58 F13, 61 L10, 70 C2
Woodenbong NSW 15 O1, 111 P11
Woodend Vic. 36 G2, 38 A1, 41 R2, 46 D12
Woodfield Vic. 47 K10
Woodford NSW 10 I7
Woodford Qld 109 L3, 111 P7
Woodforde SA 55 N4
Woodgate Qld 111 P3
Woodglen Vic. 39 O4, 48 E13
Woodhill Qld 109 L11
Woodhouselee NSW 12 H10, 20 F3
Woodlands Qld 108 H8
Woodlands WA 76 D11
Woodlawn Qld 108 C2
Woodleigh Vic. 37 O12
Woodleighton Qld 108 D3
Woodridge Qld 107 L9, 109 M9
Woods Point SA 61 N10, 70 E2
Woods Point Vic. 37 R4, 39 J2, 47 M13
Woods Reef NSW 15 J8
Woods Well SA 61 N13, 70 E5
Woodsdale Tas. 129 N6
Woodside SA 58 E10, 59 I1, 61 L9, 70 C2
Woodside Vic. 39 M9
Woodside Beach Vic. 39 M9
Woodstock NSW 12 F7
Woodstock Qld 112 F1, 115 P13
Woodstock Tas. 126 F9, 129 K10
Woodstock Vic. 37 K4, 38 D2, 46 G13
Woodstock Vic. 43 P10, 46 B9
Woodvale Vic. 43 Q9, 46 C8
Woodvale WA 76 D3
Woodville NSW 13 M3
Woodville SA 54 E2, 56 E13
Woodville Gardens SA 54 F1, 56 F13
Woodville North SA 54 F1, 56 F13
Woodville West SA 54 D3
Woohlpooer Vic. 40 G2, 42 G13
Wool Bay SA 60 I9
Wool Wool Vic. 36 A10, 41 M8
Woolamai Vic. 37 N13, 38 F9
Woolbrook NSW 15 K10
Woolgoolga NSW 15 P7

Wooli NSW 15 Q6
Woollahra NSW 5 O11, 9 Q1
Woolloongabba Qld 101 H13, 104 G13, 106 H1, 109 M8
Woolomin NSW 15 K11
Woolooga Qld 111 O5
Woolooware NSW 9 L11
Wooloowin Qld 104 G9
Woolshed Vic. 47 O5, 48 A3
Woolsthorpe Vic. 40 H8
Woolwich NSW 5 K8
Woomargama NSW 19 Q12, 47 R2
Woombye Qld 109 M1
Woomelang Vic. 18 F12, 43 J2, 45 J13
Woomera SA 62 F6
Woongoolba Qld 109 O10
Woorabinda Aboriginal Community Qld 113 L12
Wooragee Vic. 47 O5, 48 B3
Wooragee North Vic. 47 O4, 48 B2
Woorak Vic. 42 E6
Woorak West Vic. 42 E6
Wooramel Roadhouse WA 81 C10
Woorarra Vic. 39 K9
Wooreen Vic. 37 P12, 38 H8
Woori Yallock Vic. 37 N6, 38 F4, 50 D9
Woorim Qld 109 N5
Woorinen Vic. 18 H11, 45 M10
Woorinen North Vic. 45 M10
Woornack Vic. 44 I10
Woorndoo Vic. 41 J6
Wooroolin Qld 111 N6
Wooroonook Vic. 43 L6
Wooroonooran National Park Qld 115 N7
Woosang Vic. 43 M7
Wootha Qld 109 L2
Wootong Vale Vic. 40 E4
Wootton NSW 13 O2
Worongary Qld 109 N13
Woronora NSW 8 G10
Woronora Heights NSW 8 G10
Worsley WA 79 I4
Wowan Qld 113 N12
Woy Woy NSW 11 P4, 13 L6, 21 F8
Wrattonbully SA 40 A1, 42 A12, 70 I9
Wrightley Vic. 47 L9
Wroxham Vic. 20 F12, 49 O10
Wubin WA 82 D5
Wudinna SA 60 C3, 62 B13
Wujal Wujal Qld 115 M4
Wuk Wuk Vic. 39 P4, 48 E13
Wulagi NT 91 I5
Wulgulmerang Vic. 20 B11, 48 I8
Wundowie WA 78 F3, 80 E3
Wunghnu Vic. 19 M13, 46 I4
Wunkar SA 61 P8
Wurdiboluc Vic. 36 E11
Wurruk Vic. 39 N6
Wurtulla Qld 109 N2
Wutul Qld 108 E3, 111 N8
Wy Yung Vic. 39 P4, 48 F13
Wyalkatchem WA 80 G1, 82 E7
Wyalong NSW 12 B8, 19 R6
Wyan NSW 15 O4, 111 P13
Wyandra Qld 110 B8
Wyanga NSW 12 D3
Wyangala Dam NSW 12 F8, 20 E1
Wybong NSW 13 K2
Wycarbah Qld 113 N11
Wycheproof Vic. 18 G13, 43 L5
Wychitella Vic. 43 N6
Wycliffe Well Roadhouse NT 97 K13, 99 K2
Wye River Vic. 41 O11
Wyee NSW 11 Q1, 13 M5
Wyeebo Vic. 48 E3
Wyena Tas. 131 M7
Wyening WA 80 E1
Wylie Creek NSW 15 N2
Wymah NSW 19 R13, 47 R3, 48 D1
Wymlet Vic. 44 G8
Wynarka SA 61 O10, 70 F2
Wynbring SA 69 N4
Wyndham NSW 20 F11, 49 P7
Wyndham WA 87 P4
Wynn Vale SA 57 O7
Wynnum Qld 105 N9, 109 N7
Wynnum West Qld 105 M10
Wynyard Tas. 130 F5
Wyomi SA 70 F8
Wyoming NSW 21 F5

Wyong NSW 11 P2, 13 M6, 21 F1
Wyong Creek NSW 11 P2, 21 D2
Wyperfeld National Park Vic. 18 C11, 42 D2, 44 E12
Wyreema Qld 108 E8
Wyrra NSW 12 B8, 19 R5
Wyrrabalong National Park NSW 11 Q4, 21 H4
Wyuna Vic. 46 G5
Wyurta Downs NSW 17 P6

Yaamba Qld 113 N10
Yaapeet Vic. 18 D12, 42 G3
Yabba Vic. 47 R5, 48 D3
Yabba North Vic. 47 J5
Yabba South Vic. 47 J5
Yabmana SA 60 F5
Yacka SA 61 K4
Yackandandah Vic. 47 P5, 48 B3
Yagoona NSW 4 D12, 8 G2
Yahl SA 40 A6, 70 H12
Yalangur Qld 108 E6
Yalata SA 68 I7
Yalata Roadhouse SA 68 I7
Yalboroo Qld 113 J4
Yalbraith NSW 10 D13, 12 H9, 20 G2
Yalca Vic. 46 H3
Yalca North Vic. 46 H3
Yalgogrin North NSW 12 A8, 19 Q6
Yalgogrin South NSW 12 A9, 19 P7
Yalgoo WA 82 D3
Yalgorup National Park WA 78 A11, 79 G1, 80 B6, 82 B9
Yalla Y Poora Vic. 41 K3
Yallakool NSW 19 J11
Yallambie Vic. 33 O4, 41 K3
Yallaroi NSW 14 I4, 111 K13
Yalleroi Qld 112 D12, 119 R12
Yallingup WA 79 B7, 80 A9, 82 B10
Yallourn North Vic. 39 J7
Yallunda Flat SA 60 D7
Yaloak Vale Vic. 36 F5
Yalwal NSW 13 J11, 20 I4
Yamala Qld 113 J11
Yamba NSW 15 Q5
Yamba Roadhouse SA 18 A7, 61 R7
Yambacoona Tas. 128 A8
Yambuk Vic. 40 G9
Yambuna Vic. 46 G4
Yamsion Qld 108 C3
Yan Yean Vic. 37 K4, 38 D2, 46 G13
Yanac Vic. 42 C5
Yanac South Vic. 42 C6
Yanakie Vic. 39 J11
Yanchep WA 78 A1, 80 C2, 82 C7
Yanchep National Park WA 78 A1, 80 C2, 82 B7
Yanco NSW 19 O8
Yandaran Qld 111 O2
Yanderra NSW 11 J13, 13 J9, 20 I2
Yandilla Qld 108 A10
Yando Vic. 18 I13, 43 O5, 46 A4
Yandoit Vic. 36 E1, 41 P1, 43 P12, 46 B11
Yangan Qld 15 N1, 108 G13, 111 O11
Yaninee SA 60 B2, 62 B12
Yanipy Vic. 42 C7
Yankalilla SA 59 D7, 61 K11, 70 B3
Yantabulla NSW 17 L3
Yantanabie SA 60 A1, 69 Q11
Yaouk NSW 26 E7, 28 B12
Yapeen Vic. 36 E1, 41 Q1, 43 Q12, 46 C11
Yaraka Qld 121 O2
Yarck Vic. 37 N1, 47 J10
Yarding WA 80 I3
Yarloop WA 78 C13, 79 H1, 80 C7
Yaroona SA 58 C12, 59 G3
Yarra NSW 12 H11, 20 F4
Yarra Bend Vic. 33 M8
Yarra Creek Tas. 128 B9
Yarra Glen Vic. 34 F2, 37 M5, 38 E3, 50 B6
Yarra Junction Vic. 37 N6, 38 G4, 50 F9
Yarra Ranges National Park Vic. 37 O4, 38 G2, 47 J13, 50 F6
Yarra Valley Vic. 50
Yarrabandai NSW 12 C5
Yarrabin NSW 12 G3
Yarraby Vic. 45 M9
Yarragee NSW 27 M8
Yarragon Vic. 37 Q10, 38 I7
Yarralin NT 96 D3

165

Yarralumla ACT 23 B10, 24 F11, 25 D1
Yarram Vic. 39 L9
Yarramalong NSW 11 O2, 21 B1
Yarraman NSW 14 H12
Yarraman Qld 108 F2, 111 N7
Yarramony WA 80 E2
Yarrangobilly NSW 20 C6, 26 C5
Yarranlea Qld 108 B9
Yarrara Vic. 18 B8, 44 C5
Yarras NSW 15 N12
Yarraville Vic. 32 I9
Yarrawalla South Vic. 43 P6, 46 B4
Yarrawarrah NSW 8 G12
Yarrawonga Vic. 19 N13, 47 L3
Yarrie Lake NSW 14 F8
Yarrock Vic. 42 B6
Yarroweyah Vic. 19 M13, 46 I3
Yarrowitch NSW 15 M11
Yarrowyck NSW 15 K8
Yarto Vic. 42 G1, 44 H12
Yarwun Qld 113 P12
Yass NSW 12 F11, 20 D4
Yatala Qld 109 N10
Yatala Vale SA 57 Q6
Yatchaw Vic. 40 F5
Yatina SA 61 L2, 63 K12
Yatpool Vic. 18 D7, 44 G4
Yatte Yattah NSW 13 J12, 20 I5, 27 P3
Yea Vic. 37 M1, 46 I11
Yealering WA 80 H5, 82 E9
Yearinan NSW 14 F11
Yearinga Vic. 42 B7
Yednia Qld 109 J1
Yeelanna SA 60 D6
Yeerip Vic. 47 L5
Yeerongpilly Qld 106 F4

Yelarbon Qld 15 J2, 111 L12
Yellangip Vic. 42 H5
Yellingbo Vic. 37 N6, 50 D10
Yellowdine WA 82 G7
Yelta Vic. 44 F3
Yelta SA 60 I6
Yelverton WA 79 C8
Yenda NSW 19 O7
Yendon Vic. 36 D5, 41 P4
Yengo National Park NSW 11 L1, 13 K5
Yennora NSW 4 B10
Yeo Yeo NSW 12 D10, 20 B3
Yeodene Vic. 36 B12, 41 N9
Yeoval NSW 12 E4
Yeppoon Qld 113 O10
Yering Vic. 34 G3
Yerong Creek NSW 12 A13, 19 Q11
Yeronga Qld 106 G3
Yerranderie NSW 10 G11
Yerrinbool NSW 11 J13, 13 J9, 20 I2
Yetholme NSW 10 D4, 12 H6
Yetman NSW 15 J3, 111 L12
Yeungroon Vic. 43 M7
Yilliminning WA 80 G6
Yimbun Qld 108 I3
Yinkanie SA 61 P7
Yinnar Vic. 39 J8
Yirrkala NT 95 P5
Yokine WA 76 G10
Yolla Tas. 130 F6
Yongala SA 61 L2, 63 K13
Yoogali NSW 19 N7
Yoongarillup WA 79 E8
York WA 78 I4, 80 F3, 82 D8
York Plains Tas. 129 M5
Yorke Peninsula SA 60 H8

Yorke Valley SA 60 I7
Yorketown SA 60 I9
Yornaning WA 80 F6
Yoting WA 80 H3
Youanmite Vic. 19 M13, 47 J4
Youarang Vic. 47 J4
Youndegin WA 80 G3
Young NSW 12 E9, 20 C2
Younghusband SA 61 N9, 70 E1
Yowah Qld 121 P10
Yowie Bay NSW 9 J11
Yowrie NSW 27 K12
Yuelamu NT 98 G5
Yuendumu NT 98 F5
Yugar Qld 109 L6
Yulara NT 98 E11
Yuleba Qld 110 I7
Yulecart Vic. 40 F5
Yumali SA 61 O11, 70 F3
Yuna WA 82 B3
Yundi SA 59 G5
Yundool Vic. 47 K5
Yungaburra Qld 115 M7
Yungera Vic. 45 L7
Yunta SA 61 N1, 63 M11
Yuraygir National Park NSW 15 Q5
Yurgo SA 61 O10, 70 F2
Yuroke Vic. 37 I4, 38 C2, 46 F13
Yuulong Vic. 41 L11

Zanthus WA 83 L6
Zeehan Tas. 128 D1, 130 D11
Zeerust Vic. 46 H5
Zetland NSW 5 M12, 9 O2
Zillmere Qld 104 G6
Zumsteins Vic. 40 H1, 42 H12

ACCIDENT ACTION

Simple first aid can save a life.

When you approach the scene of an accident, remember to follow the DRABC action plan:

D DANGER
R RESPONSE
A AIRWAY
B BREATHING
C CIRCULATION

1. Check for DANGER –
to yourself and others.

- Do not touch occupants or vehicle if live wires are in contact with car.

- Turn off ignition of crashed car.

- If power lines are causing sparks nearby but not touching car, remove people quickly in case spilt petrol is set alight.

- Ensure no one is smoking.

- Station people to warn oncoming cars and people of the danger ahead.

- At night, light up area and use flashing indicators on vehicles as additional warning.

- Where possible, people, vehicles and debris should be cleared from roadway.

- Only move victim when unconscious or in danger (e.g. from fire, traffic or burns from hot roadway) or when victim's position makes it impossible to carry out essential treatment (such as stopping bleeding).

- If you do have to move victim, get three or four people to help if possible. Avoid bending or twisting neck or back – keep them straight. Support any injured limbs.

REMEMBER: Most casualties will be suffering some degree of shock. One of the best ways of treating this is by reassuring them – but never give alcohol. Keep casualties calm and protect them from uncomfortable weather conditions, particularly hot sun.

2. Check for RESPONSE –
see if the casualty is conscious.

- Gently shake and ask 'Can you hear me?'.

- If conscious, check for bleeding (see Stopping Bleeding on opposite page).

3. Check and clear AIRWAY –
if unconscious, ensure airway is not blocked.

- Remove any obstructions, such as blood, vomit, loose teeth or broken dentures and teeth.

- Lie victim on side and tilt head back to clear airway.

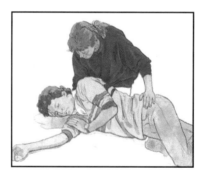

- Quickly clear mouth, using fingers if necessary. If breathing, leave on side.

- If victim is trapped in car, tilt head back and support jaw to clear airway.

4. Check BREATHING –
see if casualty is breathing.

- Look, listen and feel for breathing.

- If breathing, leave on side and check for other injuries.

- If not breathing, turn on to back and commence Expired Air Resuscitation (see opposite page).

5. Check CIRCULATION –
check for pulse.

- Feel for pulse by placing end of your finger in groove behind the Adam's apple, on either side of neck.

- If no pulse, perform cardiopulmonary resuscitation, if you have been taught this procedure (15 compressions to 2 breaths in 15 seconds).

LEARN BASIC FIRST AID

There are several organisations including St John Ambulance Australia that teach cardiopulmonary resuscitation and how to handle emergencies.